W9-AGI-427

American Democracy

A DOCUMENTARY RECORD

VOLUME II: 1865–1961

American Democracy

A DOCUMENTARY RECORD

Volume II: 1865–1961

Edited by

J. ROGERS HOLLINGSWORTH University of Illinois

BELL I. WILEY Emory University

THOMAS Y. CROWELL COMPANY

New York, Established 1834

TO OUR RESPECTIVE PARENTS

Copyright © 1962 by Thomas Y. Crowell Company

All Rights Reserved

No part of this book may be reproduced in any form, by mimeograph or any other means, without permission in writing from the publisher, except by a reviewer, who may quote brief passages in a review to be published in a magazine or newspaper.

Library of Congress Catalog Card Number: 61–16899

First Printing, January, 1962
Second Printing, September, 1963

Designed by Laurel Wagner
Cover design by Herbert Stoltz

Manufactured in the United States of America

Preface

This compilation of documents is intended primarily as a supplement to a textbook in American history. It is designed especially for college survey courses, but the compilers hope that it will serve as a convenient reference for anyone who delves into American history, whether for information, diversion, or some other purpose.

Our fundamental aim is to introduce the reader to the basic and most important documents in American political history. But in making the selections we have interpreted political history broadly and have included some sources which are primarily social or economic in character but which nevertheless have important bearing on political episodes or trends.

With a view to making their use as convenient and simple as possible, we have arranged the documents chronologically. Since we assumed that the compilation would usually supplement a textbook, we have refrained from writing elaborate introductions. For the same reason we have not grouped the sources into major sections or tried to tie them together in a continuous narrative.

A distinctive feature of the book is the inclusion of comments illustrating reaction to the documents. In most instances the comments are contemporary with the sources to which they pertain, but in a few cases, and particularly where enduring significance is involved, the re-

action of a prominent historian or some other outstanding authority of a later period is given. For many documents more than one comment is given, and in instances of some of the more controversial items, reactions reflect opposing points of view. The purpose of the comments is to make the documents more meaningful to the reader, and the furtherance of this aim was the guiding rule in making the selections. In no sense are the comments to be construed as representing the views of the compilers or the publisher.

As a general rule, documents were reproduced *in toto*. In some cases our needs were best served by extracting the pertinent portion of a source treating of a number of subjects. In other cases excisions were made in the interest of brevity or in order to eliminate trivial or extraneous material. In the cutting, every effort was made to avoid changing the essential character of the document.

Many people have generously aided us in the preparation of this book. We are especially indebted to Professor Daniel J. Boorstin of the University of Chicago for counsel and encouragement and to Mr. John T. Hawes and his associates of the Thomas Y. Crowell Company for moral support and expert editorial assistance. We particularly wish to thank Alice Kay and Ruth Necheles for their assistance on all stages of the manuscript, and Mrs. Florence Bauer for her assistance in typing the manuscript. Leonard Bates, James Chase, Richard Harwell, David Hebert, Walter Johnson, Donald Meiklejohn, Marvin Meyers, Paul Roley, Alan Simpson, and many other friends and colleagues did much to facilitate and encourage our work. Finally, we express our thanks to Ellen Jane Hollingsworth who was a source of inestimable help and encouragement at all times.

J. ROGERS HOLLINGSWORTH
University of Illinois

BELL I. WILEY
Emory University

Contents

1. MARCH 4, 1865

President Lincoln's Second Inaugural Address

On the rainy March day of Lincoln's second inauguration, General William T. Sherman's jubilant soldiers were completing their destructive march through the deep South, and General U. S. Grant's large and well-equipped forces were preparing to overwhelm the ragged and hungry remnant of Lee's army near Richmond. The President knew that victory was near and he chose to make his address brief. It proved to be the shortest inaugural address ever delivered by an American president. After a brief review of the causes of the war, with emphasis on slavery, Lincoln made a moving and eloquent appeal for forbearance toward the vanquished, generosity for the needy and sorrowing, and "a just and lasting peace among ourselves and with all nations." His concluding paragraph is regarded as one of the sublimest passages in the literature of American statesmanship.

FELLOW-COUNTRYMEN: At this second appearing to take the oath of the Presidential office there is less occasion for an extended address than there was at the first. Then a statement somewhat in detail of a course to be pursued seemed fitting and proper. Now, at the expiration of four years, during which public declarations have been constantly called forth on every point and phase of the great contest which still absorbs the atten-

JAMES D. RICHARDSON, ed., *Messages and Papers of the Presidents* (Washington, D.C., 1897), VI, 276–77.

tion and engrosses the energies of the nation, little that is new could be presented. The progress of our arms, upon which all else chiefly depends, is as well known to the public as to myself, and is, I trust, reasonably satisfactory and encouraging to all. With high hope for the future, no prediction in regard to it is ventured.

On the occasion corresponding to this four years ago all thoughts were anxiously directed to an impending civil war. All dreaded it, all sought to avert it. While the inaugural address was being delivered from this place, devoted altogether to *saving* the Union without war, insurgent agents were in the city seeking to *destroy* it without war—seeking to dissolve the Union and divide effects by negotiation. Both parties deprecated war, but one of them would *make* war rather than let the nation survive, and the other would *accept* war rather than let it perish, and the war came.

One-eighth of the whole population were colored slaves, not distributed generally over the Union, but localized in the southern part of it. These slaves constituted a peculiar and powerful interest. All knew that this interest was somehow the cause of the war. To strengthen, perpetuate, and extend this interest was the object for which the insurgents would rend the Union even by war while the Government claimed no right to do more than to restrict the territorial enlargement of it. Neither party expected for the war the magnitude or the duration which it has already attained. Neither anticipated that the *cause* of the conflict might cease with or even before the conflict itself should cease. Each looked for an easier triumph, and a result less fundamental and astounding. Both read the same Bible and pray to the same God, and each invokes His aid against the other. It may seem strange that any men should dare to ask a just God's assistance in wringing their bread from the sweat of other men's faces, but let us judge not, that we be not judged. The prayers of both could not be answered. That of neither has been answered fully. The Almighty has His own purposes "Woe unto the world because of offenses: for it must needs be that offenses come, but woe to that man by whom the offense cometh." If we shall suppose that American slavery is one of those offenses which, in the providence of God, must needs come, but which, having continued through His appointed time, He now wills to remove, and that He gives to both North and South this terrible war as the woe due to those by whom the offense came, shall we discern therein any departure from those divine attributes which the believers in a living God always ascribe to Him? Fondly do we hope, fervently do we pray, that this mighty scourge of war may speedily pass away. Yet, if God wills that it continue until all the wealth piled by the bondsman's two hundred and fifty years of unrequited toil shall be sunk, and until every drop of blood drawn with the lash shall be paid by another drawn with the sword, as was said three thousand years ago, so still it must be said "the judgments of the Lord are true and righteous altogether."

With malice toward none, with charity for all, with firmness in the right as God gives us to see the right, let us strive on to finish the work we are in, to bind up the nation's wounds, to care for him who shall have borne the battle and for his widow and his orphans, to do all which may achieve and cherish a just and lasting peace among ourselves and with all nations.

COMMENT

This inaugural strikes me in its grand simplicity and directness as being for all times the historical keynote of this war; in it a people seemed to speak in . . . sublimely simple utterance. . . . Not a prince or minister in all Europe could have risen to such an equality with the occasion.

> Letter of Colonel Charles F. Adams, Jr., Union Army of the Potomac, to his father, U.S. ambassador to England, March 7, 1865. In W. C. Ford, ed., *A Cycle of Adams Letters* (Boston: Houghton Mifflin Company, 1920), II, 257–58.

It was a noble speech, just and true and solemn.

> Letter of Duke of Argyle to Senator Charles Sumner of Massachusetts, in *Massachusetts Historical Society Proceedings*, XLVI, 87. Quoted in J. G. Randall and Richard Current, *Lincoln the President: The Last Full Measure* (New York: Dodd, Mead & Company, 1955), IV, 343.

Lincoln's inaugural, while the sentiments are noble, is one of the most awkwardly expressed documents I ever read. . . . Why under the heavens did he not make it a little more creditable to American *scholarship?*

> Letter of A. B. Bradford of Pennsylvania to ex-Secretary of War Simon Cameron, March 8, 1865. Cameron MSS., Library of Congress.

2. APRIL 10, 1865

General Robert E. Lee's Farewell to His Troops

As General Robert E. Lee withdrew toward Lynchburg after the Federals broke his line at Five Forks, his situation became increasingly critical. Hunger fatigue, and fighting reduced his command from 33,000 men on April 1 to an effective strength estimated by Lee to be "not over 15,000 muskets," on April 8. Hemmed in by General U. S. Grant's vastly superior forces, and convinced that continuing resistance could only mean the futile sacrifice of many brave men, Lee surrendered the Army of Northern Virginia on April 9 at Appomattox. The next morning he directed his aide, Colonel Charles Marshall, to draft a farewell message to the army. When this was finished, Lee crossed out one paragraph on the ground that it might perpetuate hatred and made one or two minor changes. In its revised form the farewell was signed by Lee and promulgated as General Order Number Nine, the last to be issued from the headquarters of the gallant army that he had commanded since June 1, 1862.

HEADQUARTERS, ARMY OF
NORTHERN VIRGINIA

April 10, 1865

After four years of arduous service, marked by unsurpassed courage and for-titude, the Army of Northern Virginia has been compelled to yield to overwhelming numbers and resources. I need not tell the brave survivors of so many hard-fought battles, who have remained steadfast to the last, that I have consented to the result from no distrust of them. But, feeling that valor and devotion could accomplish nothing that could compensate for the loss that may have attended the continuance of the contest, I determined to avoid the useless sacrifice of those whose past services have endeared them to their countrymen. By the terms of the agreement officers and men can return to their homes and remain until exchanged. You will take with you the satisfaction that proceeds from the consciousness of duty faithfully performed; and I earnestly pray that a merciful God will extend to you his blessing and protection. With an unceasing admiration of your constancy and devotion to your country, and a grateful remembrance of your kind and generous considerations for myself, I bid you all an affectionate farewell.

R. E. LEE, *General.*

Official Records, series 1, XLVI (Washington, D.C., 1894), pt. 3, p. 744.

COMMENT

When the proud and sensitive sons of Dixie came to a full realization that . . . their leader had been compelled to surrender his once invincible army, they could no longer control their emotions, and tears ran like water down their shrunken faces.

General John B. Gordon, Army of Northern Virginia, *Reminiscences of the Civil War* (New York: Charles Scribner's Sons, 1903), p. 444.

The Union men were held steady in their lines. . . . There was though, a twitching of the muscles of their faces and . . . their battle-bronzed cheeks were not altogether dry. Our men felt the import of the occasion, and realized fully how they would have been affected if defeat and surrender had been their lot.

> Article by General Joshua L. Chamberlain, Union Army of the Potomac, in New York *Times*, May 4, 1901. Quoted in John B. Gordon, *Reminiscences of the Civil War* (New York; Charles Scribner's Sons, 1905), p. 445.

---

3. MAY 29, 1865

President Andrew Johnson's Amnesty Proclamation

The formal surrender of the Trans-Mississippi forces of General Kirby Smith on May 26, 1865, terminated hostilities between North and South. Three days later, President Andrew Johnson, following the example set by Lincoln on December 8, 1863, issued a proclamation granting amnesty and pardon to southerners who would take an oath of allegiance to the United States. Both Lincoln and Johnson withheld general pardon from certain specified groups including high officials of the Confederacy's civil and military establishments as well as United States congressmen and officers of the Federal army and navy who had left their positions to support the southern cause. Johnson's proclamation added several classes to the excepted list, including persons who had engaged in privateering, former Confederate governors, Confederate officers who had been educated at West Point or Annapolis, residents of loyal areas who had left their homes to espouse the Confederate cause,

JAMES D. RICHARDSON, ed., *Messages and Papers of the Presidents* (Washington, D.C., 1897), VI, 310–312.

and all ex-Confederates whose taxable property was worth $20,000. Persons belonging to the excepted classes were allowed to apply for presidential pardon.

Whereas the President of the United States, on the 8th day of December, A.D., 1863, and on the 26th day of March, 1864, did, with the object to suppress the existing rebellion, to induce all persons to return to their loyalty, and to restore the authority of the United States, issue proclamations offering amnesty and pardon to certain persons who had directly, or by implication, participated in the said rebellion; and

Whereas many persons who had so engaged in said rebellion have, since the issuance of said proclamations, failed or neglected to take the benefits offered thereby; and

Whereas many persons who have been justly deprived of all claim to amnesty and pardon thereunder by reason of their participation, directly or by implication, in said rebellion, and continued hostility to the Government of the United States since the date of said proclamations, now desire to apply for and obtain amnesty and pardon.

To the end, therefore, that the authority of the Government of the United States may be restored, and that peace, order, and freedom may be established, I, Andrew Johnson, President of the United States, do proclaim and declare that I hereby grant to all persons who have, directly or indirectly, participated in the existing rebellion, except as hereinafter excepted, amnesty and pardon, with restoration of all rights of property, except as to slaves and except in cases where legal proceedings, under the laws of the United States providing for the confiscation of property of persons engaged in rebellion, have been instituted; but upon the condition, nevertheless, that every such person shall take and subscribe the following oath (or affirmation), and thenceforward keep and maintain said oath inviolate; and which oath shall be registered for permanent preservation, and shall be of the tenor and effect following, to wit:

I, ———— ————, do solemnly swear (or affirm), in presence of Almighty God, that I will henceforth faithfully support, protect, and defend the Constitution of the United States, and the Union of the States thereunder; and that I will, in like manner, abide by and faithfully support all laws and proclamations which have been made during the existing rebellion, with reference to the emancipation of slaves. So help me God.

The following classes of persons are excepted from the benefits of this proclamation:

First. All who are or shall have been pretended civil or diplomatic officers or otherwise domestic or foreign agents of the pretended Confederate government.

Second. All who left judicial stations under the United States to aid the rebellion.

Third. All who shall have been military or naval officers of said pretended Confederate government above the rank of colonel in the army or lieutenant in the navy.

Fourth. All who left seats in the Congress of the United States to aid the rebellion.

Fifth. All who resigned or tendered resignations of their commissions in the army or navy of the United States to evade duty in resisting the rebellion.

Sixth. All who have engaged in any way in treating otherwise than lawfully as prisoners of war persons found in the United States service as officers, soldiers, seamen, or in other capacities.

Seventh. All persons who have been or are absentees from the United States for the purpose of aiding in the rebellion.

Eighth. All military and naval officers in the rebel service who were educated by the Government in the Military Academy at West Point or the United States Naval Academy.

Ninth. All persons who held the pretended offices of governors of States in insurrection against the United States.

Tenth. All persons who left their homes within the jurisdiction and protection of the United States and passed beyond the Federal military lines into the pretended Confederate States for the purpose of aiding the rebellion.

Eleventh. All persons who have been engaged in the destruction of the commerce of the United States upon the high seas and all persons who have made raids into the United States from Canada or been engaged in destroying the commerce of the United States upon the lakes and rivers that separate the British Provinces from the United States.

Twelfth. All persons who, at the time when they seek to obtain the benefits hereof by taking the oath herein prescribed, are in military, naval, or civil confinement or custody, or under bonds of the civil, military, or naval authorities or agents of the United States as prisoners of war, or persons detained for offenses of any kind, either before or after conviction.

Thirteenth. All persons who have voluntarily participated in said rebellion, and the estimated value of whose taxable property is over $20,000.

Fourteenth. All persons who have taken the oath of amnesty prescribed in the President's proclamation of December 8, A.D. 1863, or an oath of allegiance to the Government of the United States since the date of said proclamation, and who have not thenceforward kept and maintained the same inviolate.

Provided, That special application may be made to the President for pardon by any person belonging to the excepted classes, and such clemency will be liberally extended as may be consistent with the facts of the case and the peace and dignity of the United States. . . .

COMMENT

I accept in good faith continued union and the abolition of slavery as irreversible results of the late struggle. . . . [I approve] your plan of reorganizing the Southern states, commending it as a great benefaction to the Southern people when compared to other plans.

> Letter of Benjamin H. Hill, ex-Confederate senator from Georgia, to President Andrew Johnson, July 4, 1865. Benjamin H. Hill, Jr., ed., *Senator Benjamin H. Hill of Georgia: His Life, Speeches and Writings* (Atlanta, Ga., 1893), p. 47.

Among all the Union men of the North with whom I have intercourse I do not find one who approves your policy. . . . Can you not hold your hand and wait the action of Congress and in the meantime govern them by military rulers? Profuse pardoning also will greatly embarrass Congress if they should wish to make the enemy pay the expense of the war or a part of it.

> Letter of Thaddeus Stevens, congressman from Pennsylvania, to President Andrew Johnson, July 6, 1865. Johnson Papers, MSS in Library of Congress. Quoted by Fawn M. Brodie, *Thaddeus Stevens* (New York: W. W. Norton & Co., Inc., 1959), pp. 226–27.

4. *NOVEMBER 22–25, 1865*

Black Code Laws of Mississippi

Emancipation and the widespread tendency among the Negroes to "test their freedom" by leaving their former masters, at least temporarily, caused southern legislatures to draw up laws defining the status of the freedmen and regulating

Laws of the State of Mississippi, Passed at a Regular Session of the Mississippi Legislature, . . . October, November and December, 1865 (Jackson, Miss., 1865), pp. 82–93.

their activities. These laws, commonly known as black codes, accorded certain basic rights to the freedmen, such as suing in the courts, making contracts, and holding property. But they also subjected the Negroes to many restrictions not applicable to whites. The total effect of these laws was to make of the blacks a distinct and subordinate class in society. The first state to enact the discriminating legisla-

tion was Mississippi, whose black code was spelled out in a series of laws enacted in late November 1865. One of these laws provided for the apprenticing, preferably to former owners, of all Negroes under eighteen who were orphans or whose parents failed to provide for their support. Another declared unemployed or unlawfully assembled Negroes to be vagrants, subjected them to heavy fine and ordered that those unable to pay the fine should be hired out, preferably to former owners, until they had earned the amount of the penalty. The third and most comprehensive of the series was entitled "An Act to Confer Civil Rights on Freedmen," but it withheld more than it gave. It forbade negroes to rent or lease lands or dwellings except in towns, required them to have written contracts or licenses showing that they were employed, and prescribed stringent regulations for the enforcement of labor agreements. These laws were regarded as extreme by many Mississippians and they were widely denounced in the North as an effort to thwart the freedom won by Union arms.

An act to regulate the relation of master and apprentice, as relates to freedmen, free negroes, and mulattoes.

SECTION 1. . . . It shall be the duty of all sheriffs, justices of the peace, and other civil officers of the several counties in this State, to report to the probate courts of their respective counties semi-annually, at the January and July terms of said courts, all freedmen, free negroes, and mulattoes, under the age of eighteen, in their respective counties, beats, or districts, who are orphans, or whose parent or parents have not the means or who refuse to provide for and support said minors; and thereupon it shall be the duty of said probate court to order the clerk of said court to apprentice said minors to some competent and suitable person on such terms as the court may direct, having a particular care to the interest of said minor: Provided, that the former owner of said minors shall have the preference when, in the opinion of the court, he or she shall be a suitable person for that purpose.

SEC. 2. . . . The said court shall be fully satisfied that the person or persons to whom said minor shall be apprenticed shall be a suitable person to have the charge and care of said minor, and fully to protect the interest of said minor. The said court shall require the said master or mistress to execute bond and security, payable to the State of Mississippi, conditioned that he or she shall furnish said minor with sufficient food and clothing; to treat said minor humanely; furnish medical attention in case of sickness; teach, or cause to be taught, him or her to read and write, if under fifteen years old, and will conform to any law that may be hereafter passed for the regulation of the duties and relation of master and apprentice: Provided, that said apprentice shall be bound by indenture, in case of males, until they are twenty-one years old, and in case of females until they are eighteen years old.

SEC. 3. . . . In the management and control of said apprentices, said master or mistress shall have the power to inflict such moderate corporeal chastisement as a father or guardian is allowed to inflict on his or her child or ward at common law: Provided, that in no case shall cruel or inhuman punishment be inflicted.

SEC. 4. . . . If any apprentice shall leave the employment of his or her master or mistress, without his or her consent, said master or mistress may pursue and recapture said apprentice, and bring him or her before any justice of the peace of the county, whose duty it shall be to remand said apprentice to the service of his or her master or mistress; and in the event of a refusal on the part of said apprentice so to return, then said justice shall commit said apprentice to the jail of said county, on failure to give bond, to the next term of the county court; and it shall be the duty of said court at the first term thereafter to investigate said case, and if the court shall be of opinion that said apprentice left the employment of his or her master or mistress without good cause, to order him or her to be punished, as provided for the punishment of hired freedmen, as may be from time to time provided for by law for desertion, until he or she shall agree to return to the service of his or her master or mistress: Provided, that the court may grant continuances as in other cases: And provided further, that if the court shall believe that said apprentice had good cause to quit his said master or mistress, the court shall discharge said apprentice from said indenture, and also enter a judgment against the master or mistress for not more than one hundred dollars, for the use and benefit of said apprentice, to be collected on execution as in other cases.

SEC. 5. . . . If any person entice away any apprentice from his or her master or mistress, or shall knowingly employ an apprentice, or furnish him or her food or clothing without the written consent of his or her master or mistress, or shall sell or give said apprentice ardent spirits without such consent, said person so offending shall be guilty of a misdemeanor, and shall, upon conviction thereof before the county court, be punished as provided for the punishment of persons enticing from their employer hired freedmen, free negroes or mulattoes.

SEC. 6. . . . It shall be the duty of all civil officers of their respective counties to report any minors within their respective counties to said probate court who are subject to be apprenticed under the provisions of this act, from time to time as the facts may come to their knowledge, and it shall be the duty of said court from time to time as said minors shall be reported to them, or otherwise come to their knowledge, to apprentice said minors as hereinbefore provided.

SEC. 9. . . . It shall be lawful for any freedman, free negro, or mulatto, having a minor child or children, to apprentice the said minor child or children, as provided for by this act.

SEC. 10. . . . In all cases where the age of the freedman, free negro, or mulatto cannot be ascertained by record testimony, the judge of the county court shall fix the age. . . .

An act to amend the vagrant laws of the State.

SEC. 1. . . . All rogues and vagabonds, idle and dissipated persons, beggars, jugglers, or persons practicing unlawful games or plays, runaways, common drunkards, common night-walkers, pilferers, lewd, wanton, or lascivious persons, in speech or behavior, common railers and brawlers, persons who neglect their calling or employment, misspend what they earn, or do not provide for the support of themselves or their families, or dependents, and all other idle and disorderly persons, including all who neglect all lawful business, habitually misspend their time by frequenting houses of ill-fame, gaming-houses, or tippling shops, shall be deemed and considered vagrants, under the provisions of this act, and upon conviction thereof shall be fined not exceeding one hundred dollars, with all accruing costs, and be imprisoned, at the discretion of the court, not exceeding ten days.

SEC. 2. . . . All freedmen, free negroes and mulattoes in this State, over the age of eighteen years, found on the second Monday in January, 1866, or thereafter, with no lawful employment or business, or found unlawfully assembling themselves together, either in the day or night time, and all white persons assembling themselves with freedmen, free negroes or mulattoes, or usually associating with freedmen, free negroes or mulattoes, on terms of equality, or living in adultery or fornication with a freed woman, freed negro or mulatto, shall be deemed vagrants, and on conviction thereof shall be fined in a sum not exceeding, in the case of a freedman, free negro or mulatto, fifty dollars, and a white man two hundred dollars, and imprisonment at the discretion of the court, the free negro not exceeding ten days, and the white man not exceeding six months.

SEC. 3. . . . All justices of the peace, mayors, and aldermen of incorporated towns, counties, and cities of the several counties in this State shall have jurisdiction to try all questions of vagrancy in their respective towns, counties, and cities, and it is hereby made their duty, whenever they shall ascertain that any person or persons in their respective towns, counties and cities are violating any of the provisions of this act, to have said party or parties arrested, and brought before them, and immediately investigate said charge, and, on conviction, punish said party or parties, as provided for herein. And it is hereby made the duty of all sheriffs, constables, town constables, and all such like officers, and city marshals, to report to some officer having jurisdiction all violations of any of the provisions of this act, and in case any officer shall fail or neglect any duty herein it shall be the duty of the county court to fine said officer, upon conviction, not exceeding one hundred dollars, to be paid into the county treasury for county purposes.

SEC. 4. . . . Keepers of gaming-houses, houses of prostitution, prostitutes, public or private, and all persons who derive their chief support in the employments that militate against good morals, or against law, shall be deemed and held to be vagrants.

SEC. 5. . . . All fines and forfeitures collected under the provisions of this act shall be paid into the county treasury for general county purposes, and in case of any freedman, free negro or mulatto shall fail for five days after the imposition of any fine or forfeiture upon him or her for violation of any of the provisions of this act to pay the same, that it shall be, and is hereby, made the duty of the sheriff of the proper county to hire out said freedman, free negro or mulatto, to any person who will, for the shortest period of service, pay said fine and forfeiture and all costs: Provided, a preference shall be given to the employer, if there be one, in which case the employer shall be entitled to deduct and retain the amount so paid from the wages of such freedman, free negro or mulatto, then due or to become due; and in case said freedman, free negro or mulatto cannot hire out, he or she may be dealt with as a pauper.

SEC. 6. . . . The same duties and liabilities existing among white persons of this State shall attach to freedmen, free negroes or mulattoes, to support their indigent families and all colored paupers; and that in order to secure a support for such indigent freedmen, free negroes, or mulattoes, it shall be lawful, and is hereby made the duty of the county police of each county in this State, to levy a poll or capitation tax on each and every freedman, free negro, or mulatto, between the ages of eighteen and sixty years, not to exceed the sum of one dollar annually to each person so taxed, which tax, when collected, shall be paid into the county treasurer's hands, and constitute a fund to be called the Freedman's Pauper Fund, which shall be applied by the commissioners of the poor for the maintenance of the poor of the freedmen, free negroes and mulattoes of this State, under such regulations as may be established by the boards of county police in the respective counties of this State.

SEC. 7. . . . If any freedman, free negro, or mulatto shall fail or refuse to pay any tax levied according to the provisions of the sixth section of this act, it shall be *prima facie* evidence of vagrancy, and it shall be the duty of the sheriff to arrest such freedman, free negro, or mulatto, or such person refusing or neglecting to pay such tax, and proceed at once to hire for the shortest time such delinquent taxpayer to any one who will pay the said tax, with accruing costs, giving preference to the employer, if there be one.

SEC. 8. . . . Any person feeling himself or herself aggrieved by judgment of any justice of the peace, mayor, or alderman in cases arising under this act, may within five days appeal to the next term of the county court of the proper county, upon giving bond and security in a sum not less than twenty-five dollars nor more than one hundred and fifty dollars, conditioned to appear and prosecute said appeal, and abide by the judgment of the county court; and said appeal shall be tried *de novo* in the county court, and the decision of the said court shall be final. . . .

An act to confer civil rights on freedmen, and for other purposes.

SECTION 1. . . . All freedmen, free negroes and mulattoes may sue and be sued, implead and be impleaded, in all the courts of law and equity of this State, and may acquire personal property, and choses in action, by descent or purchase, and may dispose of the same in the same manner and to the same extent that white persons may: Provided, That the provisions of this section shall not be so construed as to allow any freedman, free negro or mulatto to rent or lease any lands or tenements except in incorporated cities or towns, in which places the corporate authorities shall control the same.

SEC. 2. . . . All freedmen, free negroes and mulattoes may intermarry with each other, in the same manner and under the same regulations that are provided by law for white persons: Provided, that the clerk of probate shall keep separate records of the same.

SEC. 3. . . . All freedmen, free negroes or mulattoes who do now and have herebefore lived and cohabited together as husband and wife shall be taken and held in law as legally married, and the issue shall be taken and held as legitimate for all purposes; and it shall not be lawful for any freedman, free negro or mulatto to intermarry with any white person; nor for any white person to intermarry with any freedman, free negro or mulatto; and any person who shall so intermarry shall be deemed guilty of felony, and on conviction thereof shall be confined in the State penitentiary for life; and those shall be deemed freedmen, free negroes and mulattoes who are of pure negro blood, and those descended from a negro to the third generation, inclusive, though one ancestor in each generation may have been a white person.

SEC. 4. . . . In addition to cases in which freedmen, free negroes and mulattoes are now by law competent witnesses, freedmen, free negroes or mulattoes shall be competent in civil cases, when a party or parties to the suit, either plaintiff or plaintiffs, defendant or defendants; also in cases where freedmen, free negroes and mulattoes is or are either plaintiff or plaintiffs, defendant or defendants. They shall also be competent witnesses in all criminal prosecutions where the crime charged is alleged to have been committed by a white person upon or against the person or property of a freedman, free negro or mulatto: Provided, that in all cases said witnesses shall be examined in open court, on the stand; except, however, they may be examined before the grand jury, and shall in all cases be subject to the rules and tests of the common law as to competency and credibility.

SEC. 5. . . . Every freedman, free negro and mulatto shall, on the second Monday of January, one thousand eight hundred and sixty-six, and annually thereafter, have a lawful home or employment, and shall have written evidence thereof as follows, towit: if living in any incorporated city, town, or village, a license from the mayor thereof; and if living outside of an incorporated city, town, or village, from the member of the board of police of his beat, authorizing him or her to do irregular and job work; or a written contract, as provided in Section 6 in this act; which license may be revoked for cause at any time by the authority granting the same.

SEC. 6. . . . All contracts for labor made with freedmen, free negroes and mulattoes for a longer period than one month shall be in writing, and a duplicate, attested and read to said freedman, free negro or mulatto by a beat, city or county officer, or two disinterested white persons of the county in which the labor is to be performed, of which each party shall have one: and said contracts shall be taken and held as entire contracts, and if the laborer shall quit the service of the employer before the expiration of his term of service, without good cause, he shall forfeit his wages for that year up to the time of quitting.

SEC. 7. . . . Every civil officer shall, and every person may, arrest and carry back to his or her legal employer any freedman, free negro, or mulatto who shall have quit the service of his or her employer before the expiration of his or her term of service without good cause; and said officer and person shall be entitled to receive for arresting and carrying back every deserting employe aforesaid the sum of five dollars, and ten cents per mile from the place of arrest to the place of delivery; and the same shall be paid by the employer, and held as a set off for so much against the wages of said deserting employe: Provided, that said arrested party, after being so returned, may appeal to the justice of the peace or member of the board of police of the county, who, on notice to the alleged employer, shall try summarily whether said appellant is legally employed by the alleged employer, and has good cause to quit said employer. Either party shall have the right of appeal to the county court, pending which the alleged deserter shall be remanded to the alleged employer or otherwise disposed of, as shall be right

and just; and the decision of the county court shall be final.

SEC. 8. . . . Upon affidavit made by the employer of any freedman. free negro or mulatto, or other credible person, before any justice of the peace or member of the board of police, that any freedman, free negro or mulatto legally employed by said employer has illegally deserted said employment, such justice of the peace or member of the board of police shall issue his warrant or warrants, returnable before himself or other such officer, to any sheriff, constable or special deputy, commanding him to arrest said deserter, and return him or her to said employer, and the like proceedings shall be had as provided in the preceding section; and it shall be lawful for any officer to whom such warrant shall be directed to execute said warrant in any county in this State; and that said warrant may be transmitted without endorsement to any like officer of another county, to be executed and returned as aforesaid; and the said employer shall pay the costs of said warrants and arrest and return, which shall be set off for so much against the wages of said deserter.

SEC. 9. . . . If any person shall persuade or attempt to persuade, entice, or cause any freedman, free negro or mulatto to desert from the legal employment of any person before the expiration of his or her term of service, or shall knowingly employ any such deserting freedman, free negro or mulatto, or shall knowingly give or sell to any such deserting freedman, free negro or mulatto, any food, raiment, or other thing, he or she shall be guilty of a misdemeanor, and, upon conviction, shall be fined not less than twenty-five dollars and not more than two hundred dollars and costs; and if the said fine and costs shall not be immediately paid, the court shall sentence said convict to not exceeding two months' imprisonment in the county jail, and he or she shall moreover be liable to the party injured in damages: Provided, if any person shall, or shall attempt to, persuade, entice, or cause any freedman, free negro or mulatto to desert from any legal employment of any person, with the view to employ said freedman, free negro or mulatto without the limits of this State, such person, on conviction, shall be fined not less than fifty dollars, and not more than five hundred dollars and costs; and if said fine and costs shall not be immediately paid, the court shall sentence said convict to not exceeding six month's imprisonment in the county jail.

SEC. 10. . . . It shall be lawful for any freedman, free negro, or mulatto, to charge any white person, freedman, free negro or mulatto by affidavit, with any criminal offense against his or her person or property, and upon such affidavit the proper process shall be issued and executed as if said affidavit was made by a white person, and it shall be lawful for any freedman, free negro, or mulatto, in any action, suit or controversy pending, or about to be instituted in any court of law equity in this State, to make all needful and lawful affidavits as shall be necessary for the institution, prosecution or defense of such suit or controversy.

SEC. 11. . . . The penal laws of this State, in all cases not otherwise specially provided for, shall apply and extend to all freedmen, free negroes and mulattoes. . . .

COMMENT

Several hundred thousand of the negro race, unfitted for political equality with the white race, have been turned loose upon society; and in the guardianship she may assume over this race, she must deal justly with them. . . . But they cannot be admitted to political or social equality with the white race. . . . Ours is and ever shall be a government of white men. . . . Caste must be maintained. . . . To work is the law of God. . . . The negro is peculiarly adapted to the cultivation of the great staples of the South. He should be encouraged to engage at once in their production. . . . The planter cannot venture upon their cultivation unless the laborer is compelled to comply with his contract.

> Message of Governor B. G. Humphrey to Mississippi Legislature, October 16, 1865. Quoted in J. S. McNeily, "From Organization to Overthrow of Mississippi's Provisional Government, 1865–1868," Mississippi Historical Society *Publications*, Centenary Series, I (Jackson, Miss., 1916), 16.

We tell the white men of Mississippi that the men of the North will convert the state of Mississippi into a frog pond before they will ever allow any such laws to disgrace one foot of soil in which the bones of our soldiers sleep and over which the flag of freedom waves.

> Editorial in Chicago *Tribune*, December 1, 1865. Quoted in J. W. Garner, *Reconstruction in Mississippi* (New York: The Macmillan Company, 1901), p. 115.

5. *DECEMBER 4, 1865*

President Andrew Johnson's First Annual Message to Congress

When Andrew Johnson first succeeded to the presidency he made some statements, such as "treason is a crime and must be punished," which left the impression that he intended to deal harshly with the defeated South. But his basic ideas— that the Union was inviolable, that the southern states in attempting a secession had simply suspended their normal functions, and that the restoration of these states was primarily a presidential responsibility—were identical with Lincoln's, and the plan of reconstruction which he soon adopted was practically the same as that initiated by his predecessor. When Congress met in December, 1865, reconstruction governments, fashioned in accordance with conditions specified in presidential proclamations, had been completed in all of the seceded states except Texas. Johnson's message to congress of December 4, a paper notable for its dignity and persuasiveness, outlined his theories of reconstruction and told what had been done toward putting them into effect. Many years later it was discovered that the message had been written by the historian George Bancroft. But Johnson provided basic materials and the ideas were his rather than Bancroft's.

Without States one great branch of the legislative government would be wanting. And if we look beyond the letter of the Constitution to the character of our

JAMES D. RICHARDSON, ed., *Messages and Papers of the Presidents* (Washington, D.C., 1897), VI, 356–62.

country, its capacity for comprehending within its jurisdiction a vast continental empire is due to the system of States. The best security for the perpetual existence of the States is the "supreme authority" of the Constitution of the United States. The perpetuity of the Constitution brings with it the perpetuity of the States; their mutual relation makes us what we are, and in our political system their connection is indissoluble. The whole can not exist without the parts, nor the parts without the whole. So long as the Constitution of the United States endures, the States will endure. The destruction of the one is the destruction of the other: the preservation of the one is the preservation of the other.

I have thus explained my views of the mutual relations of the Constitution and the States, because they unfold the principles on which I have sought to solve the momentous questions and overcome the appalling difficulties that met me at the very commencement of my Administration. It has been my steadfast object to escape from the sway of monetary passions and to derive a healing policy from the fundamental and unchanging principles of the Constitution.

I found the States suffering from the effects of a civil war. Resistance to the General Government appeared to have exhausted itself. The United States had recovered possession of their forts and arsenals, and their armies were in the occupation of every State which had attempted to secede. Whether the territory within the limits of those States should be held as conquered territory, under military authority emanating from the President as the head of the Army, was the first question that presented itself for decision.

Now military governments, established for an indefinite period, would have offered no security for the early suppression of discontent, would have divided the people into the vanquishers and the vanquished, and would have envenomed hatred rather than have restored affection. Once established, no precise limit to their continuance was conceivable. They would have occasioned an incalculable and exhausting expense. Peaceful emigration to and from that portion of the country is one of the best means that can be thought of for the restoration of harmony, and that emigration would have been prevented; for what emigrant from abroad, what industrious citizen at home, would place himself willingly under military rule? The chief persons who would have followed in the train of the Army would have been dependents on the General Government or men who expected profit from the miseries of their erring fellow-citizens. The powers of patronage and rule which would have been exercised, under the President, over a vast and populous and naturally wealthy region are greater than, unless under extreme necessity, I should be willing to intrust to any one man. They are such as, for myself, I could never, unless on occasions of great emergency, consent to exercise. The willful use of such powers, if continued through a period of years, would have endangered the purity of the general administration and the liberties of the States which remained loyal.

Besides, the policy of military rule over a conquered territory would have implied that the States whose inhabitants may have taken in the rebellion had by the act of those inhabitants ceased to exist. But the true theory is that all pretended acts of secession were from the beginning null and void. The States can not commit treason nor screen the individual citizens who may have committed treason any more than they can make valid treaties or engage in lawful commerce with any foreign power. The States attempting to secede placed themselves in a condition where their vitality was impaired, but not extinguished; their functions suspended, but not destroyed.

But if any State neglects or refuses to perform its offices there is the more need that the General Government should maintain all its authority and as soon as practicable resume the exercise of all its functions. On this principle I have acted, and have gradually and quietly, and by almost imperceptible steps, sought to restore the rightful energy of the General Government and of the States. To that end provisional governors have been appointed, conventions called, governors elected, legislatures assembled, and Senators and Representatives chosen to the Congress of the United States. At the same time the courts of the United States, as far as could be done, have been reopened, so that the laws of the United States may be enforced through their agency. The blockade has been removed and the custom-houses reestablished in ports of entry so that the revenue of the United States may be collected. The Post-Office Department renews its ceaseless activity, and the General Government is thereby enabled to communicate promptly with its officers and agents. The courts bring security to persons and property; the opening of the ports invites the restoration of industry and commerce; the post-office renews the facilities of social intercourse and of business. And is it not happy for us all that the restoration of each one of these functions of the General Government brings with it a blessing to the States over which they are extended? It is not a sure promise of harmony and renewed attachment to the Union that after all that has happened the return of the General Government is known only as a beneficence?

I know very well that this policy is attended with some risk; that for its success it requires at least the acquiescence of the States which it concerns; that it implies an invitation to those States, by renewing their allegiance to the United States, to resume their functions as States of the Union. But it is a risk that must be taken. In the choice of difficulties it is the smallest risk: and to diminish and if possible to remove all danger. I have felt it incumbent on me to assert one other power of the General Government—the power of pardon. As no State can throw a defense over the crime of treason, the power of pardon is exclusively vested in the executive government of the United States. In exercising that power I have taken every precaution to connect it with the clearest recognition of the binding force of the laws of the United States and an unqualified acknowledgment of the great social change of condition in regard to slavery which has grown out of the war.

The next step which I have taken to restore the constitutional relations of the States has been an invitation to them to participate in the high office of amending the Constitution. Every patriot wish for a general amnesty at the earliest epoch consistent with public safety. For this great end there is need of a concurrence of all opinions and the spirit of mutual conciliation. All parties in the late terrible conflict must work together in harmony. It is not too much to ask, in the name of the whole people, that on the one side the plan of restoration shall proceed in conformity with a willingness to cast the disorders of the past into oblivion, and that on the other the evidence of sincerity in the future maintenance of the Union shall be put beyond any doubt by the ratification of the proposed amendment to the Constitution, which provides for the abolition of slavery forever within the limits of our country. So long as the adoption

of this amendment is delayed, so long will doubt and jealousy and uncertainty prevail. This is the measure which will efface the sad memory of the past; this is the measure which will most certainly call population and capital and security to those parts of the Union that need them most. Indeed, it is not too much to ask of the States which are now resuming their places in the family of the Union to give this pledge of perpetual loyalty and peace. Until it is done the past, however much we may desire it, will not be forgotten. The adoption of the amendment reunites us beyond all power of disruption; it heals the wound that is still imperfectly closed; it removes slavery, the element which has so long perplexed and divided the country; it makes of us once more a united people, renewed and strengthened, bound more than ever to mutual affection and support.

The amendment to the Constitution being adopted, it would remain for the States whose powers have been so long in abeyance to resume their places in the two branches of the National Legislature, and thereby complete the work of restoration. Here it is for you, fellow-citizens of the Senate, and for you, fellow-citizens of the House of Representatives, to judge, each of you for yourselves, of the elections, returns, and qualifications of your own members.

The full assertion of the powers of the General Government requires the holding of circuit courts of the United States within the districts where their authority has been interrupted. In the present posture of our public affairs strong objections have been urged to holding those courts in any of the States where the rebellion has existed; and it was ascertained by inquiry that the circuit court of the United States would not be held within the district of Virginia during the autumn or early winter, nor until Congress should have "an opportunity to consider and act on the whole subject." To your deliberations the restoration of this branch of the civil authority of the United States is therefore necessarily referred. with the hope that early provision will be made for the resumption of all its functions. It is manifest that treason, most flagrant in character, has been committed. Persons who are charged with its commission should have fair and impartial trials in the highest civil tribunals of the country, in order that the Constitution and the laws may be fully vindicated, the truth clearly established and affirmed that treason is a crime, that traitors should be punished and the offense made infamous, and, at the same time, that the question may be judicially settled, finally and forever, that no State of its own will has the right to renounce its place in the Union.

The relations of the General Government toward the 4,000,000 inhabitants whom the war has called into freedom have engaged my most serious consideration. On the propriety of attempting to make the freedmen electors by the proclamation of the Executive I took for my counsel the Constitution itself, the interpretations of that instrument by its authors and their contemporaries, and recent legislation by Congress. When, at the first movement toward independence, the Congress of the United States instructed the several States to institute governments of their own, they left each State to decide for itself the conditions for the enjoyment of the elective franchise. During the period of the Confederacy there continued to exist a very great diversity in the qualifications of electors in the several States, and even within a State a distinction of qualifications prevailed with regard to the officers who were to be chosen. The Constitution of the United States recognizes these diversities when it enjoins that in the choice of members of the House of Representatives of the United States "the electors in each State shall have the qualifications requisite for electors of the most numerous branch of the State legislature." After the formation of the Constitution it remained, as before, the uniform usage for each State to enlarge the body of its electors according to its own judgment, and under this system one State after another has proceeded to increase the number of its electors, until now universal suffrage, or something very near it, is the general rule. So fixed was this reservation of power in the habits of the people and so unquestioned has been the interpretation of the Constitution that during the civil war the late President never harbored the purpose—certainly never avowed the purpose—of disregarding it; and in the acts of Congress during that period nothing can be found which, during the continuance of hositilities, much less after their close, would have sanctioned any departure by the Executive from a policy which has so uniformly obtained. Moreover, a concession of the elective franchise to the freedom by act of the President of the United States must have been extended to all colored men, wherever found, and so must have established a change of suffrage in the Northern, Middle, and Western States, not less than in the Southern and Southwestern. Such an act would have created a new class of voters, and would have been an assumption of power by the President which nothing in the Constitution or laws of the United States would have warranted.

On the other hand, every danger of conflict is avoided when the settlement of the question is referred to the several States. They can, each for itself, decide on the measure, and whether it is to be adopted at once and absolutely or introduced gradually and with conditions. In my judgment the freedmen, if they show patience and manly virtues, will sooner obtain a participation in the elective franchise through the States than through the General Government, even if it had power to intervene. When the tumult of emotions that have been raised by the suddenness of the social change shall have subsided, it may prove that they will receive the kindest usage from some of those on whom they have heretofore most closely depended.

But while I have no doubt that now, after the close of the war, it is not competent for the General Government to extend the elective franchise in the several States, it is equally clear that good faith requires the security of the freedmen in their liberty and their property, their right to labor, and their right to claim the just return of their labor. I can not too strongly urge a dispassionate treatment of this subject, which should be carefully kept aloof from all party strife. We must equally avoid hasty assumptions of any natural impossibility for the two races to live side by side in a state of mutual benefit and good will. The experiment involves us in no inconsistency; let us, then, go on and make that experiment in good faith, and not be too easily disheartened. The country is in need of labor, and the freedmen are in need of employment, culture, and protection. While their right of voluntary migration and expatriation is not to be questioned, I would not advise their forced removal and colonization. Let us rather encourage them to honorable and useful industry, where it may be beneficial to themselves and to the country; and, instead of hasty anticipations of the certainty of failure, let there be nothing wanting to the fair trial of the experiment. The change in their condition is the substitution of labor by contract for the status of slavery. The freedman can not fairly be accused of unwillingness to work so long as a doubt remains about his freedom of choice in his pursuits and the certainty of his recovering his stipulated wages. In this the interests of the employer and the employed coincide. The employer desires in his workmen spirit and alacrity, and these can be permanently secured in no other way. And if the one ought to be able to enforce the contract, so ought the other. The public interest will be best promoted if the several States

will provide adequate protection and remedies for the freedmen. Until this is in some way accomplished there is no chance for the advantageous use of their labor, and the blame of ill success will not rest on them.

I know that sincere philanthropy is earnest for the immediate realization of its remotest aim; but time is always an element in reform. It is one of the greatest acts on record to have brought 4,000,000 people into freedom. The career of free industry must be fairly opened to them, and then their future prosperity and condition must, after all, rest mainly on themselves. If they fail, and so perish away, let us be careful that the failure shall not be attributable to any denial of justice. In all that relates to the destiny of the freedmen we need not be too anxious to read the future; many incidents which, from a speculative point of view, might raise alarm will quietly settle themselves. Now that slavery is at an end, or near its end, the greatness of its evil in the point of view of public economy becomes more and more apparent. Slavery was essentially a monopoly of labor, and as such locked the States where it prevailed against the incoming of free industry. Where labor was the property of the capitalist, the white man was excluded from employment, or had but the second best chance of finding it; and the foreign emigrant turned away from the region where his condition would be so precarious. With the destruction of the monopoly free labor will hasten from all parts of the civilized world to assist in developing various and immeasurable resources which have hitherto lain dormant. The eight or nine States nearest the Gulf of Mexico have a soil of exuberant fertility, a climate friendly to long life, and can sustain a denser population than is found as yet in any part of our country. And the future influx of population to them will be mainly from the North or from the most cultivated nations in

Europe. From the sufferings that have attended them during our late struggle let us look away to the future, which is sure to be laden for them with greater prosperity than has ever before been known. The removal of the monopoly of slave labor is a pledge that those regions will be peopled by a numerous and enterprising population, which will vie with any in the Union in compactness, inventive genius, wealth, and industry.

Our Government springs from and was made for the people—not the people for the Government. To them it owes allegiance; from them it must derive its courage, strength, and wisdom. But while the Government is thus bound to defer to the people, from whom it derives its existence, it should, from the very consideration of its origin, be strong in its power of resistance to the establishment of inequalities. Monopolies, perpetuities, and class legislation are contrary to the genius of free government, and ought not to be allowed. Here there is no room for favored classes or monopolies; the principle of our Government is that of equal laws and freedom of industry. Wherever monopoly attains a foothold, it is sure to be a source of danger, discord, and trouble. We shall but fulfill our duties as legislators by according "equal and exact justice to all men," special privileges to none. The Government is subordinate to the people; but, as the agent and representative of the people, it must be held superior to monopolies, which in themselves ought never to be granted, and which, where they exist, must be subordinate and yield to the Government.

COMMENT

Probably no Executive document was ever awaited with greater interest than the Message transmitted to Congress yesterday. It is safe to say that none ever gave greater satisfaction when received. Its views, on the most momentous subjects, domestic and foreign, that ever concerned the nation, are full of wisdom, and are conveyed with great force and dignity.

Editorial in New York *Times*, December 6, 1865.

Sumner called. . . . He assumes . . . that Congress has plenary powers, the Executive none, on reestablishing the Union. He denounced the policy of the President on the question of organizing the Rebel States as the greatest and most criminal error ever committed by any government.

Diary entry, dated December 8, 1865, of Gideon Welles, Lincoln's secretary of navy. John T. Morse, Jr., ed., *Diary of Gideon Welles* (New York: Houghton Mifflin Company, 1911), II, 393.

6. DECEMBER 18, 1865

Congressman Thaddeus Stevens' Speech on the South as a Conquered Province

The reconstruction policies of Lincoln and Johnson, based on the principle that the Confederate states had never been out of the Union but only out of proper relationship with it, and proposing their restoration to normal functions when ten per cent of the voting population of 1860 had pledged loyalty to the United States, was strongly opposed from the beginning by certain Republican leaders. The opposition relied in part on a conviction that the Lincoln–Johnson program was too lenient. Radicals like Senator Benjamin F. Wade, of Ohio, Senator Zachariah Chandler of Michigan, and Representative Thaddeus Stevens of Pennsylvania regarded secessionists as traitors and thought that the road to reunion should be made hard for them. Another and a more fundamental cause of their objection was a desire to make reconstruction a congressional rather than a presidential function. One way of accomplishing this was to treat the seceded states as territories, for regulation of territories was recognized as a congressional prerogative. With Congress in charge, reconstruction could be managed in such a way as to Republicanize the seceded states and keep the Republican party in control of the national government. This was the aim of brilliant but bitter Thaddeus Stevens who became the principal architect and the dominant leader of the radical program. Stevens regarded the vanquished states as "conquered prov-

Congressional Globe, 39th Cong., 1st Sess., 1865–1866, XXXVI pp. 72–74.

inces," and advocated requiring of them an indefinite apprenticeship as territories before readmitting them to the Union at the discretion of Congress under conditions to be specified by the legislative branch of the government.

. . . The President assumes, what no one doubts, that the late rebel States have lost their constitutional relations to the Union, and are incapable of representation in Congress, except by permission of the Government. It matters but little, with this admission, whether you call them States out of the Union, and now conquered territories, or assert that because the Constitution forbids them to do what they did do, that they are therefore only dead as to all national and political action, and will remain so until the Government shall breathe into them the breath of life anew and permit them to occupy their former position. In other words, that they are not out of the Union, but are only dead carcasses lying within the Union. In either case, it is very plain that it requires the action of Congress to enable them to form a State government and send representatives to Congress. Nobody, I believe, pretends that with their old constitutions and frames of government they can be permitted to claim their old rights under the Constitution. They have torn their constitutional States into atoms, and built on their foundations fabrics of a totally different character. Dead men cannot raise themselves. Dead

States cannot restore their existence "as it was." Whose especial duty is it to do it? In whom does the Constitution place the power? Not in the judicial branch of Government, for it only adjudicates and does not prescribe laws. Not in the Executive, for he only executes and cannot make laws. Not in the Commander-in-Chief of the armies, for he can only hold them under military rule until the sovereign legislative power of the conqueror shall give them law. . . . Unless the law of nations is a dead letter, the late war between two acknowledged belligerents severed their original compacts and broke all the ties that bound them together. The future condition of the conquered power depends on the will of the conqueror. They must come in as new States or remain as conquered provinces. Congress . . . is the only power that can act in the matter. . . .

Congress alone can do it. . . . Congress must create States and declare when they are entitled to be represented. Then each House must judge whether the members presenting themselves from a recognized State possess the requisite qualifications of age, residence, and citizenship; and whether the election and returns are according to law. . . .

It is obvious from all this that the first duty of Congress is to pass a law declaring the condition of these outside or defunct States, and providing proper civil governments for them. Since the conquest they have been governed by martial law. Military rule is necessarily despotic, and ought not to exist longer than is absolutely necessary. As there are no symptoms that the people of these provinces will be prepared to participate in constitutional government for some years, I know of no arrangement so proper for them as territorial governments. There they can learn the principles of freedom and eat the fruit of foul rebellion. Under such governments, while electing members to the territorial

Legislatures, they will necessarily mingle with those to whom Congress shall extend the right of suffrage. In Territories Congress fixes the qualifications of electors; and I know of no better place nor better occasion for the conquered rebels and the conqueror to practice justice to all men, and accustom themselves to make and obey equal laws. . . .

They ought never to be recognized as capable of acting in the Union, or of being counted as valid States, until the Constitution shall have been so amended as to make it what its framers intended; and so as to secure perpetual ascendency to the party of the Union; and so as to render our republican Government firm and stable forever. The first of those amendments is to change the basis of representation among the States from Federal numbers to actual voters. . . . With the basis unchanged the eighty-three Southern members, with the Democrats that will in the best times be elected from the North, will always give a majority in Congress and in the Electoral college. . . . I need not depict the ruin that would follow. . . .

But this is not all that we ought to do before inveterate rebels are invited to participate in our legislation. We have turned, or are about to turn, loose four million slaves without a hut to shelter them or a cent in their pockets. The internal laws of slavery have prevented them from acquiring an education, understanding the common laws of contact, or of managing the ordinary business of life. This Congress is bound to provide for them until they can take care of themselves. If we do not furnish them with homesteads, and hedge them around with protective laws; if we leave them to the legislation of their late masters, we had better have left them in bondage. . . . If we fail in this great duty now, when we have the power, we shall deserve and receive the execration of history and of all future ages.

COMMENT

I had this p.m. quite an animated talk with Senator Sumner. . . . The President, he said, was the greatest enemy of the South. . . . Congress, he says, is becoming more firm and united every day . . . and while they would commence no war upon the President he must change his course, abandon his policy. The President had violated the Constitution in appointing provisional governors, in putting Rebels in office who would not take the test oath, in reestablishing rebellion. . . . He spoke of them [southerners] as a "conquered people" subject to terms which it was our duty to impose.

> Diary entry, dated January 13, 1866, of Gideon Welles, Lincoln's secretary of navy. John T. Morse, Jr., ed., *Diary of Gideon Welles* (New York: Houghton Mifflin Company, 1911), ii, 414–16.

[The plan] to govern eleven States as conquered provinces by an exercise of power unwarranted by the Constitution . . . trusts all to force, nothing to conciliation; all to revenge, nothing to charity. It treats with equal contempt the good opinion or hatred of seven millions of American citizens. It disregards the example of Ireland where the oppression of Great Britain has produced millions of enemies, breathing vengeance from every part of the civilized world.

> Speech of William M. Stewart of Nevada in U.S. Senate, December 21, 1865. *Congressional Globe*, 39th Cong., 1st Sess., 1865–1866, pt. 1 (Washington, D.C., 1866), p. 109.

---

7. *APRIL 9, 1866*

Civil Rights Act

On the ground that southerners were determined to keep the freedmen in a suppressed condition, Reconstruction leaders pushed through Congress early in 1866 a measure entitled "An Act to Protect All Persons in the United States in their Civil Rights and Furnish the Means of their Vindication." This law, passed in April over President Johnson's veto, defined federal citizenship specifically to include freedmen, enumerated their rights, placed them under the protection of the federal courts and made detailed provision for the punishment of anyone found guilty of discriminating against them. The Presi-

U.S. Statutes at Large, xiv, 27–29.

dent was authorized to use the land and naval forces of the United States in enforcing the act. President Johnson regarded the act as an unwarranted extension of federal authority and a dangerous impingement on states' rights. Essentials of the act later were included in the Fourteenth Amendment.

Be it enacted, . . . That all persons born in the United States and not subject to any foreign power, excluding Indians not taxed, are hereby declared to be citizens of the United States; and such citizens, of every race and color, without regard to any previous condition of slavery or involuntary servitude, except as a punishment for crime whereof the party shall have been duly convicted, shall have the same right, in every State and Territory in the United States, to make and enforce contracts, to sue, be parties, and give evidence, to inherit, purchase, lease, sell, hold, and convey real and personal property, and to full and equal benefit of all laws and proceedings for the security of person and property, as is enjoyed by white citizens, and shall be subject to like punishment, pains and penalties, and to none other, any law, statute, ordinance, regulation, or custom, to the contrary notwithstanding.

SEC. 2. . . . Any person who, under color of any law, statute, ordinance, regulation, or custom, shall subject, or cause to be subjected, any inhabitant of any State or Territory to the deprivation of any right secured or protected by this act, or to different punishment, pains, or penalties on account of such person having at any time been held in a condition of slavery or involuntary servitude, except as a punishment for crime whereof the party shall have been duly convicted, or by reason of his color or race, than is prescribed for the punishment of white persons, shall be deemed guilty of a misdemeanor, and, on conviction, shall be punished by fine not exceeding one thousand dollars, or imprisonment not exceeding one year, or both, in the discretion of the court.

SEC. 3. . . . The district courts of the United States . . . shall have, exclusively of the courts of the several States, cognizance of all crimes and offences committed against the provisions of this act, and also, concurrently with the circuit courts of the United States, of all causes, civil and criminal, affecting persons who are denied or cannot enforce in the courts or judicial tribunals of the State or locality where they may be any of the rights secured to them by the first section of this act; and if any suit or prosecution, civil or criminal, has been or shall be commenced in any State court, against any such person, for any cause whatsoever, or against any officer, civil or military, or other person, for any arrest or imprisonment, trespasses, or wrongs done or committed by virtue or under color of authority derived from this act or the act establishing a Bureau for the relief of Freedmen and Refugees, and all acts amendatory thereof, or for refusing to do any act upon the ground that it would be inconsistent with this act, such defendant shall have the right to remove such cause for trial to the proper district or circuit court. . . . The jurisdiction in civil and criminal matters hereby conferred on the district and circuit courts of the United States shall be exercised and enforced in conformity with the laws of the United States, so far as such laws are suitable to carry the same into effect; but in all cases where such laws are not adapted to the object, or are deficient in the provisions necessary to furnish suitable remedies and punish offenses against law, the common law, as modified and changed by the constitution and statute of the State wherein the court having jurisdiction of the cause, civil or criminal, is held, so far as the same is not inconsistent with the Constitution and laws of the United States, shall be extended to and govern said courts in the trial and disposition of said cause, and, if of a criminal nature, in the infliction of punishment on the party found guilty.

SEC. 4. . . . The district attorneys, marshals, and deputy marshals of the United States, the commissioners appointed by the circuit and territorial courts of the United States, with powers of arresting, imprisoning or bailing offenders against the laws of the United States, the officers and agents of the Freedmen's Bureau, and every other officer who may be specially empowered by the President of the United States, shall be, and they are hereby, specially authorized and required, . . . to institute proceedings against all and every person who shall violate the provisions of this act, and cause him or them to be arrested and imprisoned, or bailed, as the case may be, for trial before such court of the United States or territorial court as by this act has cognizance of the offense. And with a view to affording reasonable protection to all persons in their constitutional rights of equality before the law, without distinction of race or color, or previous condition of slavery or involuntary servitude, except as a punishment for crime, whereof the party shall have been duly convicted, and to the prompt discharge of the duties of this act, it shall be the duty of the circuit courts of the United States, and the superior courts of the Territories of the United States, from time to time, to increase the number of commissioners, so as to afford a speedy and convenient means for the arrest and examination of persons charged with a violation of this act; and such commissioners are hereby authorized and required to exercise and discharge all the powers and duties conferred on them by this act, and the same duties with regard to offenses created by this act, as they are authorized by law to exercise with regard to other offenses against the laws of the United States.

SEC. 5. . . . It shall be the duty of all marshals and deputy marshals to obey and execute all warrants and precepts issued under the provisions of this act, when to them directed; and should any marshal or deputy marshal refuse to receive such warrant or other process when tendered, or to use all proper means diligently to execute the same, he shall, on conviction thereof, be fined in the sum of one thousand dollars, to the use of the persons upon whom the accused is alleged to have committed the offense. And the better to enable the said commissioners to execute their duties faithfully and efficiently, in conformity with the Constitution of the United States and the requirements of this act, they are hereby authorized and empowered, within their counties respectively, to appoint in writing; under their hands, any one or more suitable persons, from time to time, to execute all such warrants and other such process as may be issued by them in the lawful performance of their respective duties: and the persons so appointed to execute any warrant or process as aforesaid shall have authority to summon and call to their aid the bystanders or posse comitatus of the proper county, or such portion of the land or naval forces of the United States, or of the militia, as may be necessary to the performance of the duty with which they are charged, and to insure a faithful observance of the clause of the Constitution which prohibits slavery, in conformity with the provisions of this act; and such warrants shall run and be executed by said officers anywhere in the State or Territory within which they are issued.

SEC. 6. . . . Any person who shall knowingly and wilfully obstruct, hinder or prevent any officer, or other person charged with the execution of any warrant or process issued under the provisions of this act, or any person or persons lawfully assisting him or them, from arresting any person for whose apprehension such warrant or process may have been issued, or shall rescue or attempt to rescue such person from the custody of the officer, other person or persons, or those lawfully assisting as aforesaid, when so arrested pursuant to the authority herein given and declared, or shall aid, abet, or assist any person so arrested as aforesaid, directly or indirectly, to escape from the custody of the officer or other person legally authorized as aforesaid, or shall harbor or conceal any person for whose arrest a warrant or process shall have been issued as aforesaid, so as to prevent his discovery and arrest after notice or knowledge of the fact that a warrant has been issued for the apprehension of such person, shall for either of said offenses, be subject to a fine not exceeding one thousand dollars, and imprisonment not exceeding six months, by indictment and conviction before the district court of the United States for the district in which said offense may have been committed, or before the proper court or criminal jurisdiction, if committed within any one of the organized Territories of the United States.

. . . . .

SEC. 8. . . . Whenever the President of the United States shall have reason to believe that offenses have been or are likely to be committed against the provisions of this act within any judicial district, it shall be lawful for him, in his discretion, to direct the judge, marshal, and district attorney of such district to attend at such place within the district, and for such time as he may designate, for the purpose of the more speedy arrest and trial of persons charged with violation of this act; and it shall be the duty of every judge or other officer, when any such requisition shall be received by him, to attend at the place and for the time therein designated.

SEC. 9. . . . It shall be lawful for the President of the United States, or such person as he may empower for that purpose, to employ such part of the land or naval forces of the United States, or of the militia, as shall be necessary to prevent the violation and enforce the due execution of this act.

SEC. 10. . . . Upon all questions of law arising in any cause under the provisions of this act a final appeal may be taken to the Supreme Court of the United States.

COMMENT

I regard the bill to which the attention of the Senate is now called as the most important measure that has been under its consideration since the adoption of the Constitutional amendment abolishing slavery. That amendment declared that all persons in the United States should be free. This measure is intended to give effect to that declaration and secure to all persons within the United States practical freedom . . . [by] declaring all persons born in the United States to be citizens thereof. . . . Then, they [the Negroes] will be entitled to the rights of citizens.

Speech of Lyman Trumbull of Illinois in U.S. Senate, January 29, 1866. *Congressional Globe*, 39th Cong., 1st Sess., 1865–1866, xxxvi, 474–75.

Congress [according to this bill] may, then, go into any State and break down any State constitutions or laws which discriminate in any way against any class of persons within or without the State. It may thus defy and set aside the right of each State . . . to exclude certain persons from its boundaries or to withhold from them certain civil rights. . . . We may thus . . . become substantially *Africanized, Mexicanized* or *Coolyized,* . . . and national and personal individuality give place to anarchy and weakness. . . . The proposition is alarming. It is most dangerous.

Speech of Michael C. Kerr of Indiana in U.S. House of Representatives, March 8, 1866. *Congressional Globe*, 39th Cong., 1st Sess., 1865–1866, xxxvi, 1268.

8. *JULY 16, 1866*

Freedmen's Bureau Act

On March 3, 1865, the Bureau of Refugees, Freedmen, and Abandoned Lands —commonly known as the Freedmen's Bureau—was established in the War Department and charged with the care of Negroes and displaced whites in areas occupied by the federal forces. The law creating this organization provided that it was to continue in existence for one year after the cessation of hostilities. The bureau was headed by Major General Oliver O. Howard and under him were a group of assistant commissioners each responsible for one or more states. The bureau administered relief to both whites and Negroes, supervised freedmen's labor, conducted schools, dispensed justice, rendered medical aid and performed various services. Affairs on the lower levels were conducted by a large corps of inspectors, provost marshals, missionaries, teachers, counsellors, district superintendents, and local agents. The bureau received much criticism, some of which was undoubtedly well founded; but it served a useful purpose, accomplished much good, and in general gave a far better account of itself than its disparagers acknowledged. In July 1866, Congress passed over President Johnson's veto an act extending the life and powers of the bureau. This law transferred to bureau officials many functions previously exercised by state authorities and gave to military courts jurisdiction over cases involving the rights and immunities of freedmen. Johnson considered the act to be a dangerous and unnecessary extension of military over civil authority and an attempt to increase and perpetuate

U.S. *Statutes at Large,* XIV, 173–77.

Republican influence. Passage of the measure over his veto was an important milestone in the ascendancy of the Radical Republicans.

Be it enacted . . . That the act to establish a Bureau for the relief of Freedmen and Refugees, approved March third, eighteen hundred and sixty-five, shall continue in force for the term of two years from and after the passage of this act.

SEC. 2. . . . The supervision and care of said bureau shall extend to all loyal refugees and freedmen, so far as the same shall be necessary to enable them as speedily as practicable to become self-supporting citizens of the United States, and to aid them in making the freedom conferred by the proclamation of the Commander-in-Chief, by emancipation under the laws of the States, and by constitutional amendment, available to them and beneficial to the Republic.

SEC. 3. . . . The President shall, by and with the advice and consent of the Senate, appoint two assistant commissioners, in addition to those authorized by the act to which this is an amendment, who shall give like bonds and receive the same annual salaries provided in said act; and each of the assistant commissioners of the bureau shall have charge of one district containing such refugees or freedmen, to be assigned him by the Commissioner, with the approval of the President. And the Commissioner shall, under the direction of the President, and so far as the same shall be, in his judgment, necessary for the efficient and economical administration of the affairs of the bureau, appoint such agents, clerks and assistants as may be required for the proper conduct of the bureau. Military officers or enlisted men may be detailed for service and assigned to duty under this act; and the President may, if in his judgment safe and judicious so to do, detail from the Army all the officers and agents of this bureau; but no officer so assigned shall have increase of pay or allowances. Each agent or clerk, not heretofore authorized by law, not being a military officer, shall have an annual salary of not less than $500, nor more than $1,200, according to the service required of him. And it shall be the duty of the Commissioner, when it can be done consistently with the public interest, to appoint, as assistant commissioners, agents, and clerks, such men as have proved their loyalty by faithful service in the armies of the Union during the rebellion. And all persons appointed to service under this act and the act to which this is an amendment, shall be so far deemed in the military service of the United States as to be under the military jurisdiction and entitled to the military protection of the Government while in the discharge of the duties of their office.

SEC. 4. . . . The officers of the Veteran Reserve Corps or of the volunteer service, now on duty in the Freedmen's Bureau as assistant commissioners, agents, medical officers, or in other capacities, whose regiments or corps have been or may hereafter be mustered out of service, may be retained upon such duty as officers of said bureau, with the same compensation as is now provided by law for their respective grades; and the Secretary of War shall have power to fill vacancies until other officers can be detailed in their places without detriment to the public service.

SEC. 5. . . . The second section of the act to which this is an amendment shall be deemed to authorize the Secretary of War to issue such medical stores or other supplies and transportation and afford such medical or other aid as here may be needful for the purposes named in said section: *Provided.* that no person shall be deemed "destitute," "suffering," or "dependent upon the Government for support," within the meaning of this act, who is able to find employment, and could, by proper industry or exertion, avoid such destitution, suffering, or dependence.

SEC. 6. . . . Whereas, by the provisions of [an act of February, 6, 1863] certain lands in the parishes of St. Helena and St. Luke, South Carolina, were bid in by the United States at public tax sales, and by limitation of said act the time of redemption of said lands has expired; and whereas, in accordance with instructions issued by President Lincoln on [September 16, 1863] to the United States direct tax commissioners of South Carolina, certain land bids in by the United States in the parish of St. Helena, in said State were in part sold by the said tax commissioners to "heads of families of the African race," in parcels of not more than twenty acres to each purchaser; and whereas, under the said instructions, the said tax commissioners did also set apart as "school farms" certain parcels of land in said parish, numbered on their plats from one to thirty-three inclusive, making an aggregate of six thousand acres, more or less: *Therefore, be it further enacted,* That the sales made to "heads of families of the African race," under the instructions of President Lincoln to the United States direct tax commissioners for South Carolina . . . are hereby confirmed and established; and all leases which have been made to such "heads of families" by said direct tax commissioners, shall be changed into certificates of sale in all cases wherein the lease provides for such substitution; and all the lands now remaining unsold, which come within the same designation, being eight thousand acres, more or less, shall be disposed of according to said instructions.

SEC. 7. . . . All other lands bid in by the United States at tax sales, being thirty-eight thousand acres, more or less, and now in the hands of the said tax commissioners as the property of the United States, in the parishes of St, Helena and St. Luke, excepting the "school farms," as specified in the preceding section, and so much as may be necessary for military and naval purposes at Hilton Head, Bay Point, and Land's End, and excepting also the city of Port Royal on St. Helena island, and the town of Beaufort, shall be disposed of in parcels of twenty acres, at one dollar and fifty cents per acre, to such persons, and to such only, as have acquired and are now occupying lands under and agreeably to the provisions of General Sherman's special field order, dated at Savannah, Georgia, [January 16, 1865] and the remaining lands, if any, shall be disposed of in like manner to such persons as had acquired lands agreeably to the said order of General Sherman but who have been dispossessed by the restoration of the same to former owners: Provided, That the lands sold in compliance with the provisions of this and the preceding section shall not be alienated by their purchasers within six years from and after the passage of this act.

SEC. 8. . . . The "school farms" . . . shall be sold . . . and the proceeds of said sales . . . shall be invested in United States bonds, the interest of which shall be appropriated, under the direction of the Commissioner, to the support of schools, without distinction of color or race, on the islands in the parishes of St. Helena and St. Luke.

SEC. 9. . . . The assistant commissioners for South Carolina and Georgia are hereby authorized to examine all claims to lands in their respective States which are claimed under the provisions of General Sherman's special field order, and to give each person having a valid claim a warrant upon the direct tax commissioners for South Carolina for twenty acres of land; and the said direct tax commissioners shall issue to every person, or to his or her heirs, but in no case to any assigns, presenting such warrant, a lease of twenty acres of land, as provided for in section seven, for the term of six years; but at any time thereafter, upon the payment of a sum not exceeding one dollar and fifty cents per acre, the person holding such lease shall be entitled to a certificate of sale of said tract of twenty acres from the direct tax commissioner or such officer as may be authorized to issue the same; but no warrant shall be held valid longer than two years after the issue of the same.

SEC. 10. . . . The tax commissioners for South Carolina are hereby authorized and required, at the earliest day practicable, to survey the lands designated in section seven into lots of twenty acres each, with proper metes and bounds distinctly marked, so that the several tracts shall be convenient in form, and as near as practicable have an average of fertility and woodland. . . .

SEC. 11. . . . Restoration of lands occupied by freedmen under General Sherman's field order dated at Savannah, Georgia, [January 16, 1865] shall not be made until after the crops of the present year shall have been gathered by the occupants of said lands, nor until a fair compensation shall have been made to them by the former owners of such lands, or their legal representatives, for all improvements or betterments erected or constructed thereon, and after due notice of the same being done shall have been given by the assistant commissioner.

SEC. 12. . . . The Commissioner shall have power to seize, hold, use, lease, or sell all buildings, and tenements, and any lands appertaining to the same, or otherwise, formerly held under color of title by the late so-called Confederate States, and not heretofore disposed of by the United States, and any building or lands held in trust for the same by any person or persons, and to use the same or appropriate the proceeds derived therefrom to the education of the freed people; and whenever the bureau shall cease to exist, such of said so-called Confederate States as shall have made provision for the education of their citizens without distinction of color shall receive the sum remaining unexpended of such sales or rentals, which shall be distributed among said States for educational purposes in proportion to their population.

SEC. 13.... The Commissioner of this bureau shall at all times co-operate with private benevolent associations of citizens in aid of freedmen, and with agents and teachers, duly accredited and appointed by them, and shall hire or provide by lease, buildings for purposes of education whenever such associations shall, without cost to the Government, provide suitable teachers and means of instruction; and he shall furnish such protection as may be required for the safe conduct of such schools.

SEC. 14.... In every State or district when the ordinary course of judicial proceedings has been interrupted by the rebellion, and until the same shall be fully restored, and in every State or district whose constitutional relations to the Government have been practically discontinued by the rebellion, and until such State shall have been restored in such relations, and shall be duly represented in the Congress of the United States, the right to make and enforce contracts, to sue, be parties, and give evidence, to inherit, purchase, lease, sell, hold, and convey real and personal property and to have full and equal benefit of all laws and proceedings concerning personal liberty, personal security, and the acquisition, enjoyment, and disposition of estate, real and personal, including the constitutional right to bear arms, shall be secured to

and enjoyed by all the citizens of such State or district without respect to race or color, or previous condition of slavery. And whenever in either of said States or districts the ordinary course of judicial proceedings has been interrupted by the rebellion, and until the same shall be fully restored, and until such State shall have been restored in its constitutional relations to the Government, and shall be duly represented in the Congress of the United States, the President shall, through the Commissioner and the officers of the bureau, and under such rules and regulations as the President, through the Secretary of War, shall prescribe, extend military protection and have military jurisdiction over all cases and questions concerning the free enjoyment of such immunities and rights; and no penalty or punishment for any violation of law shall be imposed or permitted because of race or color, or previous condition of slavery, other or greater than the penalty or punishment to which the white persons may be liable by law for the like offense. But the jurisdiction conferred by this section upon the officers of the bureau shall not exist in any State where the ordinary course of judicial proceedings has not been interrupted by the rebellion, and shall cease in every State when the courts of the State and the United States are not disturbed in the peaceable course of justice, and after such State shall be fully restored in its constitutional relations to the Government, and shall be duly represented in the Congress of the United States.

SEC. 15.... That all officers, agents, and employees of this bureau, before entering upon the duties of their office, shall take the oath prescribed in the first section of the act to which this is an amendment [i.e., the "ironclad" test oath] ...

COMMENT

Mr. Johnson [in vetoing the Freedmen's Bill] has made a grave mistake. ... Hereafter whatever wrongs may be inflicted upon or indignities suffered by the

Southern blacks, will be charged to the President, who has left them naked to their enemies.

Editorial in New York *Tribune*, February 20, 1866. Quoted in Ralph Korngold, *Thaddeus Stevens* (New York: Harcourt, Brace & Company, 1955), p. 314.

Breathes there the man with soul so dead,
Who never to himself hath said,
G-d d-n the Freedmen's Bureau.

Lines regularly carried on the masthead of the Panola (Miss.) *Star*, December, 1867. Quoted in John W. Kyle, "Reconstruction in Panola County," Mississippi Historical Society, *Publications*, xiii (Jackson, Miss., 1913), 49.

---

9. *JUNE 20, 1867*

Treaty between the United States and Russia over Alaska

While President Johnson and Congress fought bitterly over Reconstruction, Secretary of State William H. Seward quietly accomplished one of the most important acts of his public career. In 1859 Baron Stoeckl, Russian ambassador in Washington, discussed the possibility of selling Alaska to the United States. The price proposed by the United States was considered inadequate and the matter was dropped. Pressure of residents of the Pacific Coast area, interested in acquiring fishing and fur trading privileges, caused a resumption of negotiations concerning Alaska in 1866. Russia had for a long time been concerned about her remote and unprofitable possession in North America. To develop it seemed prohibitively expensive; to neglect it meant to risk having it seized by some unfriendly power. In February 1867, the Russian emperor authorized Stoeckl to treat for cession of Alaska to the United States. Stoeckl proposed a price of $10,000,000 dollars; Seward made a counter-offer of $5,000,000. A compromise figure of $7,200,000 was agreed

U.S. Statutes at Large, xv, 539–44.

to on the evening of March 29, 1867, and a treaty was quickly signed. The Senate, after considerable debate, ratified the treaty with only two dissenting votes. The House was slow to make the necessary appropriation but finally authorized it by a vote of 113 to 43. Alaska proved a tremendous bargain. In January 1959, it came into the Union as the forty-ninth and biggest state.

Whereas a treaty between the United States of America and his Majesty the Emperor of all the Russias was concluded and signed by their respective plenipotentiaries at the city of Washington, on the thirtieth day of March, last, which treaty . . . is, word for word, as follows:

The United States of America and His Majesty the Emperor of all the Russias, being desirous of strengthening, if possible, the good understanding which exists between them, have, for that purpose, appointed as their Plenipotentiaries: the President of the United States, William H. Seward, Secretary of State; and His Majesty the Emperor of all the Russias, the Privy Councillor Edward de

Stoeckl, his Envoy Extraordinary and Minister Plenipotentiary to the United States.

And the said Plenipotentiaries, having exchanged their full powers, which were found to be in due form, have agreed upon and signed the following articles:

ARTICLE I

His Majesty the Emperor of all the Russias agrees to cede to the United States, by this convention, immediately upon the exchange of the ratifications thereof, all the territory and dominion now possessed by his said Majesty on the continent of America and in the adjacent islands, the same being contained within the geographical limits herein set forth, to wit: The eastern limit is the line of demarcation between the Russian and the British possessions in North America, as established by the convention between Russia and Great Britain, of February 28–16, 1825, and described in Articles III and IV of said convention, in the following terms:

"Commencing from the southernmost point of the island called Prince of Wales Island, which point lies in the parallel of 54 degrees 40 minutes north latitude, and between the 131st and the 133d degree of west longitude, (meridian of Greenwich.) the said line shall ascend to the north along the channel called Portland channel, as far as the point of the continent where it strikes the 56th degree of north latitude; from this last-mentioned point, the line of demarcation shall follow the summit of the mountains situated parallel to the coast as far as the point of intersection of the 141st degree of west longitude, (of the same meridian;) and finally, from the said point of intersection, the said meridian line of the 141st degree, in its prolongation as far as the Frozen ocean.

"IV. With reference to the line of demarcation laid down in the preceding article, it is understood—

"1st. That the island called Prince of Wales Island shall belong wholly to Russia," (now, by this cession to the United States.)

"2d. That whenever the summit of the mountains which extend in a direction parallel to the coast from the 56th degree of north latitude to the point of intersection of the 141st degree of west longitude shall prove to be at the distance of more than ten marine leagues from the ocean, the limit between the British possessions and the line of coast which is to belong to Russia as above mentioned (that is to say, the limit to the possessions ceded by this convention) shall be formed by a line parallel to the winding of the coast, and which shall never exceed the distance of ten marine leagues therefrom."

The western limit within which the territories and dominion conveyed, are contained, passes through a point in Behring's straits on the parallel of sixty-five degrees thirty minutes north latitude, at its intersection by the meridian which passes midway between the islands of Krusenstern, or Ignalook, and the island of Ratmanoff, or Noonarbook, and proceeds due north, without limitation, into the same Frozen ocean. The same western limit, beginning at the same initial point, proceeds thence in a course nearly southwest through Behring's straits and Behring's sea, so as to pass midway between the northwest point of the island of St. Lawrence and the southeast point of Cape Choukotski, to the meridian of one hundred and seventy-two west longitude; thence, from the intersection of that meridian, in a southwesterly direction, so as to pass midway between the island of Atiou and the Copper island of the Kormandorski couplet or group in the North Pacific ocean, to the meridian of one hundred and ninety-three degrees west longitude, so as to include in the territory conveyed the whole of the Aleutian islands east of that meridian.

ARTICLE II

In the cession of territory and dominion made by the preceding article are included the right of property in all public lots and squares, vacant lands, and all public buildings, fortifications, barracks, and other edifices which are not private individual property. It is, however, understood and agreed, that the churches which have been built in the ceded territory by the Russian government, shall remain the property of such members of the Greek Oriental Church resident in the territory, as may choose to worship therein. Any government archives, papers, and documents relative to the territory and dominion aforesaid, which may be now existing there, will be left in the possession of the agent of the United States; but an authenticated copy of such of them as may be required, will be, at all times, given by the United States to the Russian government, or to such Russian officers or subjects as they may apply for.

ARTICLE III

The inhabitants of the ceded territory, according to their choice, reserving their natural allegiance, may return to Russia within three years; but if they should prefer to remain in the ceded territory, they, with the exception of uncivilized native tribes, shall be admitted to the enjoyment of all the rights, advantages, and immunities of citizens of the United States, and shall be maintained and protected in the free enjoyment of their liberty, property, and religion. The uncivilized tribes will be subject to such laws and regulations as the United States may, from time to time, adopt in regard to aboriginal tribes of that country.

ARTICLE IV

His Majesty the Emperor of all the Russias shall appoint, with convenient despatch, an agent or agents for the purpose of formally delivering to a similar agent or agents appointed on behalf of the United States, the territory, dominion, property, dependencies and appurtenances which are ceded as above, and for doing any other act which may be necessary in regard thereto. But the cession, with the right of immediate possession, is nevertheless to be deemed complete and absolute on the exchange of ratifications, without waiting for such formal delivery.

ARTICLE V

Immediately after the exchange of the ratifications of this convention, any fortifications or military posts which may be in the ceded territory shall be delivered to the agent of the United States, and any Russian troops which may be in the territory shall be withdrawn as soon as may be reasonably and conveniently practicable.

ARTICLE VI

In consideration of the cession aforesaid, the United States agree to pay at the treasury in Washington, within ten months after the exchange of the ratifications of this convention, to the diplomatic representative or other agent of his Majesty the Emperor of all the Russias, duly authorized to receive the same, seven million two hundred thousand dollars in gold. The cession of territory and dominion herein made is hereby declared to be free and unencumbered by any reservations, privileges, franchises, grants, or possessions, by any associated companies, whether corporate or incorporate, Russian or any other, or by any parties, except merely private individual property holders; and the cession hereby made, conveys all the rights, franchises, and privileges now belonging to Russia in the said territory or dominion, and appurtenances thereto.

ARTICLE VII

When this convention shall have been duly ratified by the President of the United States, by and with the advice and consent of the Senate, on the one part, and on the other by his Majesty the Emperor of all the Russias, the ratifications shall be exchanged at Washington within three months from the date hereof, or sooner, if possible.

In faith whereof, the respective plenipotentiaries have signed this convention, and thereto affixed the seals of their arms.

Done at Washington, the thirtieth day of March, in the year of our Lord one thousand eight hundred and sixty-seven.

[L. S.] WILLIAM H. SEWARD
[L. S.] EDOUARD DE STOECKL

And whereas the said Treaty has been duly ratified on both parts, and the respective ratifications of the same were exchanged at Washington on this twentieth day of June, by William H. Seward, Secretary of State of the United States, and the Privy Counsellor Edward de Stoeckl, the Envoy Extraordinary of His Majesty the Emperor of all the Russias, on the part of their respective governments.

Now, therefore, be it known that I, ANDREW JOHNSON, President of the United States of America, have caused the said Treaty to be made public, to the end that the same and every clause and article thereof may be observed and fulfilled with good faith by the United States and the citizens thereof.

COMMENT

Why wait till tomorrow, Mr. Stoeckl? Let us make the treaty tonight.

Frederic Bancroft, *The Life of William H. Seward* (New York: Harper & Brothers, 1900), II, 477.

Notwithstanding all the sneers that have been cast on Alaska, if it could be sold again, individuals would take it off our hands and pay us two or three millions for the bargain.

Speech of Rufus P. Spalding of Ohio in U.S. House of Representatives, July 1, 1868. Quoted in James G. Blaine, *Twenty Years of Congress* (Norwich, Conn., 1884), II, 335–36.

Many Republicans [in the House of Representatives] felt, on the eve, or rather in the midst, of a Presidential canvass, that it was a hazardous political step (deeply in debt as the Government was, and with its paper still at heavy discount) to embark in the speculation of acquiring a vast area of "rocks and ice" as Alaska was termed in the popular and derisive description of Mr. Seward's purchase.

James G. Blaine, *Twenty Years of Congress* (Norwich, Conn., 1884), II, 334.

If we are to pay this price as usury on the friendship of Russia, we are paying for it very dear indeed. If we are to pay for her friendship, I desire to give her the seven million two hundred thousand dollars in cash, and let her keep Alaska, because I think it may be a small sum to give for the friendship if we could only get rid of the land, or rather the ice, which we are to get by paying for it.

Speech of Benjamin F. Butler of Massachusetts in the U.S. House of Representatives, July 1, 1868. Quoted in James G. Blaine, *Twenty Years of Congress* (Norwich, Conn., 1884), II, 335.

10. MARCH 2–3, 1868

Articles of Impeachment against Andrew Johnson

The conflict between President Johnson and Congress grew more intense with the passing of time. Radical Republicans, stung by Johnson's earnest and not always tactful opposition, and hoping to obtain a chief executive who would subscribe to their views, decided to remove him from office. On January 7, 1867, the House adopted a resolution accusing Johnson of high crimes and misdemeanors and instructing the judiciary committee to investigate his conduct. The committee, after listening to fantastic testimony of questionable witnesses, resolved to impeach the President, but the House on December 7, 1867, rejected the recommendation. In the meantime Congress passed the Tenure of Office Act requiring the Senate's consent for dismissal of cabinet officers and declaring violation of the act a "high misdemeanor." When Johnson ordered Secretary of War Edwin Stanton to vacate his office in February, 1868, after the Senate had refused to concur in his removal, the House quickly brought forward a second resolution of impeachment which passed by a vote of 126 to 47. Resolving to impeach without prior investigation and preparation of charges was a reversal of normal procedure but this was only one of a number of irregularities resorted to by the Radicals. On March 2–3, the House adopted eleven wordy articles of impeachment, and these were used as a basis for Johnson's trial in May before the Senate. Despite tremendous pressure

Trial of Andrew Johnson . . . before the Senate of the U.S. . . . (Washington, D.C., 1868), I, 6–10.

by anti-Johnson leaders, the Senate, voting first on the eleventh article and then the second and third, failed to muster the two-thirds majority required for conviction; so the President was acquitted. Since the three ballots for conviction each fell only one vote short of the necessary two-thirds, the President's exoneration appeared very close. But Professor Howard K. Beale in The Critical Year *has shown that some Republicans who voted for conviction (to escape proscription) stood ready to vote for acquittal if the occasion demanded.*

ARTICLE I

That said Andrew Johnson, President of the United States, on [February 21, 1868], at Washington, in the District of Columbia, unmindful of the high duties of his office, of his oath of office, and of the requirement of the Constitution that he should take care that the laws be faithfully executed, did unlawfully, and in violation of the Constitution and laws of the United States issue an order in writing for the removal of Edwin M. Stanton from the office of Secretary for the Department of War, said Edwin M. Stanton having been theretofore duly appointed and commissioned by and with the advice and consent of the Senate of the United States, as such Secretary, and said Andrew Johnson, President of the United States, on [August 12, 1867], and during the recess of said Senate, having suspended by his order Edwin M. Stanton from said office, and within twenty days after the first day of the next-meeting of said Senate, that is to say, on the twelfth day of December in the year last aforesaid having reported to said Senate such suspension with the evidence and reasons for his action in the case and the name of the person designated to perform the duties of such office temporarily until the next meeting of the Senate, and said Senate thereafterwards, on [January 13, 1868], having duly considered the evidence and reasons reported by said Andrew Johnson for said suspension, and having refused to concur in said suspension, whereby and by force of the provisions of [the Tenure of Office Act, March 2, 1867] . . . said Edwin M. Stanton did forthwith resume the functions of his office, whereof the said Andrew Johnson had then and there due notice, and said Edwin M. Stanton, by reason of the premises, on said twenty-first day of February, being lawfully entitled to hold said office of Secretary for the Department of War, which said order for the removal of said Edwin M. Stanton is in substance as follows, that is to say:

"EXECUTIVE MANSION,
"*Washington, D. C.,*
February 21, 1868
"SIR: By virtue of the power and authority vested in me as President by the Constitution and laws of the United States you are hereby removed from office as Secretary for the Department of War, and your functions as such will terminate upon the receipt of this communication.

"You will transfer to Brevet Major General Lorenzo Thomas, Adjutant General of the Army, who has this day been authorized and empowered to act as Secretary of War *ad interim,* all records, books, papers, and other public property now in your custody and charge.
"Respectfully yours,
"ANDREW JOHNSON
"To the Hon. EDWIN M. STANTON,
"Washington, D. C."

Which order was unlawfully issued with intent then and there to violate the act entitled "An act regulating the tenure of certain civil offices," passed March second, eighteen hundred and sixty-seven, and with the further intent, contrary to the provisions of said act, in violation thereof, and contrary to the provisions of the Constitution of the United States, and without the advice and consent of the Senate of the United States, the said Senate then and there being in session, to remove Edwin M. Stanton from the office of Secretary for the Department of War, the said Edwin M. Stanton being then and there Secretary for the Department of War, and being then and there in the due and lawful execution and discharge of the duties of said office, whereby said Andrew Johnson, President of the United States, did then and there commit and was guilty of a high misdemeanor in office.

ARTICLE II

That on [February 21, 1868], at Washington, in the District of Columbia, said Andrew Johnson, President of the United States, unmindful of the duties of his office, of his oath of office, and in violation of the Constitution of the United States, and contrary to the provisions of [the Tenure of Office Act], without the advice and consent of the Senate of the United States, said Senate then and there being in session, and without authority of the law, did, with intent to violate the Constitution of the United States, and the act aforesaid, issue and deliver to one Lorenzo Thomas a letter of authority in substance as follows, that is to say:

EXECUTIVE MANSION,
"*Washington, D. C.,*
February 21, 1868
"SIR: The Hon. Edwin M. Stanton having been this day removed from office as Secretary for the Department of War, you are hereby authorized and empowered to act as Secretary of War *ad*

interim, and will immediately enter upon the discharge of the duties pertaining to that office.

"Mr. Stanton has been instructed to transfer to you all the records books, papers, and other public property now in his custody and charge.

        "Respectfully yours,
        "ANDREW JOHNSON

"To Brevet Major General LORENZO THOMAS, "Adjutant General U.S. Army, Washington, D. C."

Then and there being no vacancy in said office of Secretary for the Department of War, whereby said Andrew Johnson . . . did then and there commit and was guilty of a high misdemeanor in office.

ARTICLE III

That said Andrew Johnson . . . on [February 21, 1868], at Washington, in the District of Columbia, did commit and was guilty of a high misdemeanor in office in this, that, without authority of law, while the Senate of the United States was then and there in session, he did appoint one Lorenzo Thomas to be Secretary for the Department of War *ad interim,* without the advice and consent of the Senate, and with intent to violate the Constitution of the United States, no vacancy having happened in said office of Secretary for the Department of War during the recess of the Senate, and no vacancy existing in said office at the time, and which said appointment, so made by said Andrew Johnson, of said Lorenzo Thomas, is in substance as follows, that is to say: [Here is given the same note that is reproduced in Article II.]

ARTICLE IV

That said Andrew Johnson . . . [on February 21, 1868], at Washington, in the District of Columbia, did unlawfully conspire with one Lorenzo Thomas, and with other persons to the House of Representatives unknown, with intent, by intimidation and threats, unlawfully to hinder and prevent Edwin M. Stanton, then and there the Secretary for the Department of War, duly appointed under the laws of the United States, from holding said office of Secretary for the Department of War, contrary to and in violation of the Constitution of the United States, and of the provisions of an act entitled "An act to define and punish certain conspiracies," approved July thirty-first, eighteen hundred and sixty-one, whereby said Andrew Johnson, President of the United States, did then and there commit and was guilty of a high crime in office.

ARTICLE V

That said Andrew Johnson . . . [on February 21, 1868] and on divers other days and times in said year, before [March 2, 1868], at Washington, in the District of Columbia, did unlawfully conspire with one Lorenzo Thomas, and with other persons to the House of Representatives unknown, to prevent and hinder the execution of [the Tenure of Office Act] . . . and in pursuance of said conspiracy, did unlawfully attempt to prevent Edwin M. Stanton, then and there being Secretary for the Department of War, duly appointed and commissioned under the laws of the United States, from holding said office, whereby the said Andrew Johnson, President of the United States, did then and there commit and was guilty of a high misdemeanor in office.

ARTICLE VI

That said Andrew Johnson, . . . [on February 21, 1868], at Washington, in the District of Columbia, did unlawfully conspire with one Lorenzo Thomas by force to seize, take, and possess the property of the United States in the Department of War, and then and there in the custody and charge of Edwin M. Stanton, Secretary for said department, contrary to the provisions of [the Conspiracy Act, July 31, 1861] . . . and with intent to violate and disregard [the Tenure of Office Act] . . . whereby said Andrew

Johnson, President of the United States, did then and there commit a high crime in office.

ARTICLE VII

That said Andrew Johnson . . . [on February 21, 1868], at Washington, in the District of Columbia, did unlawfully conspire with one Lorenzo Thomas with intent unlawfully to seize, take, and possess the property of the United States, in the Department of War, in the custody and charge of Edwin M. Stanton, Secretary for said department, with intent to violate and disregard [the Tenure of Office Act] . . . whereby said Andrew Johnson, President of the United States, did then and there commit a high misdemeanor in office.

ARTICLE VIII

That said Andrew Johnson, . . . with intent unlawfully to control the disbursements of the moneys appropriated for the military service and for the Department of War, on [February 21, 1868] . . . at Washington, in the District of Columbia, did unlawfully and contrary to the provisions of [the Tenure of Office Act] . . . and in violation of the Constitution of the United States, and without the advice and consent of the Senate of the United States, and while the Senate was then and there in session, there being no vacancy in the office of Secretary for the Department of War, and with intent to violate and disregard the act aforesaid, then and there issue and deliver to one Lorenzo Thomas a letter of authority in writing, in substance as follows, that is to say: [Here is given the same note that is reproduced in Article II]. . . .

Whereby said Andrew Johnson, President of the United States, did then and there commit and was guilty of a high misdemeanor in office.

ARTICLE IX

That said Andrew Johnson . . . [on February 22, 1868] . . . at Washington,

in the District of Columbia, in disregard of the Constitution and the laws of the United States duly enacted, as commander-in-chief of the army of the United States, did bring before himself then and there William H. Emory, a major general by brevet in the army of the United States, actually in command of the department of Washington and the military forces thereof, and did then and there as such commander-in-chief, declare to and instruct said Emory that part of a law of the United States, passed March second, eighteen hundred and sixty-seven, entitled "An act making appropriations for the support of the army for the year ending June thirtieth, eighteen hundred and sixty-eight, and for other purposes," especially the second section thereof, which provides, among other things, that "all orders and instructions relating to military operations, issued by the President or Secretary of War, shall be issued through the General of the army, and in case of his inability, through the next in rank," was unconstitutional, and in contravention of the commission of said Emory, and which said provision of law had been therefore duly and legally promulgated by General Orders for the government and direction of the army of the United States, as the said Andrew Johnson then and there well knew, with intent thereby to induce said Emory, in his official capacity as commander of the department of Washington, to violate the provisions of said act, and to take and receive, act upon, and obey such orders as he, the said Andrew Johnson, might make and give, and which should not be issued through the General of the army of the United States, according to the provisions of said act, and with the further intent thereby to enable him, the said Andrew Johnson, to prevent the execution of the [Tenure of Office Act] . . . and to unlawfully prevent Edwin M. Stanton, then being Secretary for the Department of War, from holding said office and discharging the duties thereof, whereby said Andrew Johnson, President of the United States, did then and there commit and was guilty of a high misdemeanor in office.

And the house of Representatives, by protestation, saving to themselves the liberty of exhibiting at any time hereafter any further articles, or other accusation or impeachment against the said Andrew Johnson, President of the United States, and also of replying to his answers which he shall make unto the articles herein preferred against him, and of offering proof to the same, and every part thereof, and to every other article, accusation, or impeachment which shall be exhibited by them, as the case shall require, DO DEMAND that the said Andrew Johnson may be put to answer the high crimes and misdemeanors in office herein charged against him, and that such proceedings, examinations, trials, and judgments may be thereupon had and given as may be agreeable to law and justice.

ARTICLE X

That said Andrew Johnson, President of the United States, unmindful of the high duties of his office, and the dignity and proprieties thereof, and of the harmony and courtesies which ought to exist and be maintained between the executive and legislative branches of the government of the United States, designing and intending to set aside the rightful authority and powers of Congress, did attempt to bring into disgrace, ridicule, hatred, contempt, and reproach the Congress of the United States, and the several branches thereof, to impair and destroy the regard and respect of all the good people of the United States for the Congress and legislative powers thereof, (which all officers of the government ought inviolably to preserve and maintain,) and to excite the odium and resentment of all the good people of the United States against Congress and the laws by it duly and constitutionally enacted; and in pursuance of his said de-

sign and intent, openly and publicly, and before divers assemblages of the citizens of the United States, convened in divers parts thereof to meet and receive said Andrew Johnson as the Chief Magistrate of the United States, did, on [August 18, 1866] . . . and on divers other days and times as well before as afterward, make and deliver, with a loud voice, certain intemperate, inflammatory, and scandalous harangues, and did therein utter loud threats and bitter menaces, as well as against Congress as the laws of the United States duly enacted thereby, amid the cries, jeers, and laughter of the multitudes then assembled and in hearing, which are set forth in the several specifications hereinafter written, in substance and effect, that is to say:

Specification first. In this, that at Washington, in the District of Columbia, in the Executive Mansion, to a committee of citizens who called upon the President of the United States, speaking of and concerning the Congress of the United States, said Andrew Johnson, President of the United States, heretofore, to wit, on . . . [August 18, 1866] . . . did, in a loud voice, declare, in substance and effect, among other things, that is to say:

"So far as the executive department of the government is concerned, the effort has been made to restore the Union, to heal the breach, to pour oil into the wounds which were consequent upon the struggle, and (to speak in common phrase) to prepare, as the learned and wise physician would, a plaster healing in character and co-extensive with the wound. We thought, and we think, that we had partially succeeded; but, as the work progresses, as reconstruction seemed to be taking place, and the country was becoming reunited, we found a disturbing and marring element opposing us. In alluding to that element I shall go no further than your convention, and the distinguished gentleman who has delivered to me the report of its proceedings. I shall make no reference to it that

I do not believe the time and occasion justify.

"We have witnessed in one department of the government every endeavor to prevent the restoration of peace, harmony and union. We have seen hanging upon the verge of the government, as it were, a body called, or which assumed to be, the Congress of the United States, while, in fact, it is a Congress of only a part of the States. We have seen the Congress pretend to be for the Union, when its every step and act tended to perpetuate disunion and make a disruption of the States inevitable. . . . We have seen Congress gradually encroach, step by step, upon constitutional rights, and violate, day after day and month after month, fundamental principles of the government. We have seen a Congress that seemed to forget that there was a limit to the sphere and scope of legislation. We have seen a Congress in a minority assume to exercise power which, allowed to be consummated, would result in despotism or monarchy itself."

Specification second. In this, that at Cleveland in the State of Ohio, heretofore, to-wit, on . . . [September 3, 1866] . . . before a public assemblage of citizens and others, said Andrew Johnson, President of the United States, speaking of and concerning the Congress of the United States, did, in a loud voice, declare, in substance and effect, among other things, that is to say:

"I will tell you what I did do. I called upon your Congress that is trying to break up the government. . . .

"In conclusion, beside that, Congress had taken much pains to poison their constituents against him. But what had Congress done? Have they done anything to restore the union of these States? No; on the contrary, they have done everything to prevent it; and because he stood now where he did when the rebellion commenced, he had been denounced as a traitor. Who had run greater risks or made greater sacrifices than himself? But

Congress, factious and domineering, had undertaken to poison the minds of the American people."

Specification third. In this, that at St. Louis, in the State of Missouri, heretofore, to wit, on . . . [September 8, 1866] . . . before a public assemblage of citizens and others, said Andrew Johnson, President of the United States, speaking of and concerning the Congress of the United States, did, in a loud voice, declare in substance and effect, among other things, that is to say:

"Go on. Perhaps if you had a word or two on the subject of New Orleans you might understand more about it than you do. And if you will go back—if you will go back and ascertain the cause of the riot at New Orleans, perhaps you will not be so prompt in calling out 'New Orleans.' If you will take up the riot at New Orleans, and trace it back to its source or its immediate cause, you will find out who is responsible for the blood that was shed there. If you will take up the riot at New Orleans and trace it back to the radical Congress, you will find that the riot at New Orleans was substantially planned. If you will take up the proceedings in their caucuses you will understand that they there knew that a convention was to be called which was extinct by its power having expired; that it was said that the intention was that a new government was to be organized, and on the organization of that government the intention was to enfranchise one portion of the population, called the colored population, who had just been emancipated, and at the same time disfranchise white men. When you design to talk about New Orleans you ought to understand what you are talking about. When you read the speeches that were made, and take up the facts on the Friday and Saturday before the convention sat, you will there find that speeches were made incendiary in their character, exciting that portion of the population, the black population, to arm themselves and prepare for the shedding of blood. You will also find that the convention did assemble in violation of law, and the intention of that convention was to supersede the reorganized authorities in the State government of Louisiana, which had been recognized by the government of the United States; and every man engaged in that rebellion in that convention, with the intent of superseding and upturning the civil government which had been recognized by the government of the United States, I say that he was a traitor to the Constitution of the United States, and hence you find that another rebellion was commenced, *having its origin in the radical Congress. . . .*

"So much for the New Orleans riot. And there was the cause and the origin of the blood that was shed, and every drop of blood that was shed is upon their skirts, and they are responsible for it. I could test this thing a little closer, but will not do it here tonight. But when you talk about the causes and consequences that resulted from proceedings of that kind, perhaps, as I have been introduced here, and you have provoked questions of this kind, though it does not provoke me, I will tell you a few wholesome things that have been done by this radical Congress in connection with New Orleans and the extension of the elective franchise.

"I know that I have been traduced and abused. I know it has come in advance of me here as elsewhere, that I have attempted to exercise an arbitrary power in resisting laws that were intended to be forced upon the government; that I had exercised that power; that I had abandoned the party that elected me, and that I was a traitor, because I exercised the veto power in attempting, and did arrest for a time, a bill that was called a 'Freedman's Bureau' bill; yes, that I was a traitor. And I have been traduced, I have been slandered, I have been maligned, I have been called Judas Iscariot, and all

that. Now, my countrymen, here to-night, it is very easy to indulge in epithets; it is easy to call a man Judas and cry out traitor; but when he is called upon to give arguments and facts he is very often found wanting. Judas Iscariot—Judas. There was a Judas, and he was one of the twelve apostles. Oh! yes, the twelve apostles had a Christ. The twelve apostles had a Christ, and he never could have had a Judas unless he had had twelve apostles. If I have played the Judas, who has been my Christ that I have played the Judas with? Was it Thad. Stevens? Was it Wendell Phillips? Was it Charles Sumner? These are the men that stop and compare themselves with the Saviour; and everybody that differs with them in opinion, and to try to stay and arrest their diabolical and nefarious policy, is to be denounced as a Judas. . . .

"Well, let me say to you, if you will stand by me in this action, if you will stand by me in trying to give the people a fair chance—soldiers and citizens—to participate in these offices, God being willing, I will kick them out. I will kick them out just as fast as I can.

"Let me say to you, in concluding, that what I have said I intended to say. I was not provoked into this, and I care not for their menaces, the taunts, and the jeers. I care not for threats. I do not intend to be bullied by my enemies nor overawed by my friends. But, God willing with your help, I will veto their measures when any of them come to me."

Which said utterances, declarations, threats, and harangues, highly censurable in any, are peculiarly indecent and unbecoming in the Chief Magistrate of the United States, by means whereof said Andrew Johnson has brought the high office of the President of the United States into contempt, ridicule, and disgrace, to the great scandal of all good citizens, whereby said Andrew Johnson, President of the United States, did commit, and was then and there guilty of a high misdemeanor in office.

ARTICLE XI

That said Andrew Johnson, President of the United States, unmindful of the high duties of his office, and of his oath of office, and in disregard of the Constitution and laws of the United States, did heretofore, to-wit, on the eighteenth day of August, A.D. eighteen hundred and sixty-six, at the city of Washington, in the District of Columbia, by public speech, declare and affirm, in substance, that the thirty-ninth Congress of the United States was not a Congress of the United States authorized by the Constitution to exercise legislative power under the same, but on the contrary, was a Congress of only a part of the United States, thereby denying, and intending to deny . . . , the power of the said thirty-ninth Congress to propose amendments to the Constitution of the United States; and in pursuance of said declaration, the said Andrew Johnson, President of the United States, afterwards, to wit, on [February 21, 1868] . . . at the city of Washington, in the District of Columbia, did unlawfully, and in disregard of the requirements of the Constitution, that he should take care that the laws be faithfully executed, attempt to prevent the execution of [the Tenure of Office Act] . . . by unlawfully devising and contriving, and attempting to devise and contrive means by which he should prevent Edwin M. Stanton from forthwith resuming the functions of the office of Secretary for the Department of War, notwithstanding the refusal of the Senate to concur in the suspension [of] . . . said Edwin M. Stanton from said office . . . ; and, also, by further unlawfully devising and contriving, and attempting to devise and contrive means, then and there, to prevent the execution of . . . [the Army Appropriation Act and the Reconstruction Act, both of March 2, 1867] . . . whereby the said Andrew Johnson, President of the United States, did, then, to-wit, on . . . [February 21, 1868] . . . at the city of Washington, commit, and was guilty of, a high misdemeanor in office.

COMMENT

Never again if Andrew Johnson go quit and free this day, can the people of this or any other country by constitutional checks or guards stay the usurpations of executive power.

> Argument of Congressman Benjamin F. Butler of Massachusetts at Andrew Johnson's trial before the U.S. Senate, March 30, 1868. *Trial of Andrew Johnson* (Washington, D.C., 1868), I, 122.

What are these high crimes and misdemeanors? Has he committed treason or bribery? Has he been guilty of peculation or oppression in office? Has he appropriated the public funds or the public property unlawfully to his own use? Has he committed any crime of violence against any person, public officer, or private individual? . . . Nothing of the sort. These alleged high crimes and misdemeanors are all founded upon mere forms of executive administration.

> Argument of Henry Stanbery, former U.S. Attorney General, chief counsel for the President at Andrew Johnson's trial before the U.S. Senate, May 2, 1868. *Trial of Andrew Johnson* (Washington, D.C., 1868), II, 364.

11. 1867–1868

Reconstruction Acts

Encouraged by their success in overriding presidential vetoes of the Civil Rights and Freedmen's Bureau Acts and by victories of their candidates in the congressional elections of 1866, Radical Republican leaders, working through the Joint Committee on Reconstruction, proceeded in 1867–1868 to consummate their Reconstruction program. On March 2, 1867, they obtained enactment, over Johnson's veto, of what is generally known as the First Reconstruction Act. Based on the assumption that the seceded states were without lawful government and that their restoration was a congressional function, this act placed the South under military rule and required the states to form new governments enfranchising Negroes and disqualifying Confederate leaders. It also made ratification of the Fourteenth Amendment a condition of restoration. When it became apparent that southern authorities were not going to call conventions to draw up new constitutions, Congress on March 23, 1867 passed the Second Reconstruction Act directing commanders of the southern military districts to take the necessary steps for assembling the conventions. On July 19, 1867 Congress passed the Third Reconstruction Act, purportedly to clarify the intent and meaning of the two prior laws, but actually to enhance the power of the military commanders charged with executing the Radical program. The Fourth Reconstruction Act, March 11, 1868, changing the required vote for ratification of new state constitutions from a majority of all

U.S. *Statutes at Large,* XIV, 428–29; XV, 2–4, 14–16, 41.

registered voters to a majority of the votes cast, was passed after conservatives in Alabama blocked adoption of a Radical constitution by staying away from the polls in such numbers that the votes cast in its favor did not comprise a majority of the names appearing on the registration books.

FIRST RECONSTRUCTION ACT
March 2, 1867

Whereas no legal State governments or adequate protection for life or property now exists in the rebel States of Virginia, North Carolina, South Carolina, Georgia, Mississippi, Alabama, Louisiana, Florida, Texas, and Arkansas; and whereas it is necessary that peace and good order should be enforced in said States until loyal and republican State governments can be legally established: Therefore

Be it enacted . . . That said rebel States shall be divided into military districts and made subject to the military authority of the United States, as hereinafter prescribed, and for that purpose Virginia shall constitute the first district; North Carolina and South Carolina the second district; Georgia, Alabama and Florida, the third district; Mississippi and Arkansas the fourth district; and Louisiana and Texas the fifth district.

SEC. 2. . . . It shall be the duty of the President to assign to the command of each of said districts an officer of the army, not below the rank of brigadier general, and to detail a sufficient military force to enable such officer to perform his duties and enforce his authority within the district to which he is assigned.

SEC. 3. . . . It shall be the duty of each officer assigned as aforesaid to protect all persons in their rights of person and property, to suppress insurrection, disorder, and violence, and to punish, or cause to be punished, all disturbers of the public peace and criminals, and to this end he may allow local civil tribunals to take jurisdiction of and to try offenders, or, when in his judgment it may be necessary for the trial of offenders, he shall have power to organize military commissions or tribunals for that purpose; and all interference under color of State authority with the exercise of military authority under this act shall be null and void.

SEC. 4. . . . All persons put under military arrest by virtue of this act shall be tried without unnecessary delay, and no cruel or unusual punishment shall be inflicted; and no sentence of any military commission or tribunal hereby authorized, affecting the life or liberty of any person, shall be executed until it is approved by the officer in command of the district, and the laws and regulations for the government of the army shall not be affected by this act, except in so far as they conflict with its provisions. . . .

SEC. 5. . . . When the people of any one of said rebel States shall have formed a constitution of government in conformity with the Constitution of the United States in all respects, framed by a convention of delegates elected by the male citizens of said State twenty-one years old and upward, of whatever race, color, or previous condition, who have been resident in said State for one year previous to the day of such election, except such as may be disfranchised for participation in the rebellion, or for felony at common law, and when such constitution shall provide that the elective franchise shall be enjoyed by all such persons as have the qualifications herein stated for electors of delegates, and when such constitution shall be rati-

fied by a majority of the persons voting on the question of ratification who are qualified as electors for delegates, and when such constitution shall have been submitted to Congress for examination and approval, and Congress shall have approved the same, and when said State, by a vote of its legislature elected under said constitution, shall have adopted the amendment to the Constitution of the United States, proposed by the thirty-ninth Congress, and known as article fourteen, and when said article shall have become a part of the Constitution of the United States, said State shall be declared entitled to representation in Congress, and senators and representatives shall be admitted therefrom on their taking oaths prescribed by law, and then and thereafter the preceding sections of this act shall be inoperative in said State: *Provided,* That no person excluded from the privilege of holding office by said proposed amendment to the Constitution of the United States shall be eligible to election as a member of the convention to frame a constitution for any of said rebel States, nor shall any such person vote for members of such convention.

SEC. 6. . . . Until the people of said rebel States shall be by law admitted to representation in the Congress of the United States, any civil governments which may exist therein shall be deemed provisional only, and in all respects subject to the paramount authority of the United States at any time to abolish, modify or control, or supersede the same; and in all elections to any office under such provisional governments all persons shall be entitled to vote, and none others, who are entitled to vote under the provisions of the fifth section of this act; and no person shall be eligible to any office under any such provisional governments who would be disqualified from holding office under the provisions of the third article of said constitutional amendment.

SECOND RECONSTRUCTION ACT
March 23, 1867

Be it enacted . . . That before the first day of September, eighteen hundred and sixty-seven, the commanding general in each district defined by an act entitled "An act to provide for the more efficient government of the rebel States," passed March second, eighteen hundred and sixty-seven, shall cause a registration to be made of the male citizens of the United States, twenty-one years of age and upwards, resident in each county or parish in the State or States included in his district, which registration shall include only those persons who are qualified to vote for delegates by the act as aforesaid, and who shall have taken and subscribed the following oath or affirmation: "I, ———, do solemnly swear (or affirm,) in the presence of Almighty God, that I am a citizen of the State of ———; that I have resided in said State for ——— months next preceding this day, and now reside in the county of ———, or the parish of ———, in said State (as the case may be;) That I am twenty-one years old; that I have not been disfranchised for participation in any rebellion or civil war against the United States, nor for felony committed against the laws of any State or of the United States; that I have never been a member of any State legislature, nor held any executive or judicial office in any State and afterwards engaged in insurrection or rebellion against the United States, or given aid or comfort to the enemies thereof; and I have never taken an oath as a member of Congress of the United States, or as an officer of the United States, or as a member of any State legislature, or as an executive or judicial officer of any State, to support the Constitution of the United States, and afterwards engaged in insurrection or rebellion against the United States, or given aid or comfort to the enemies thereof; that I will faithfully support the Constitution and obey the laws of the United States, and will, to the best of my ability, encourage others so to do, so help me God;" which oath or affirmation may be administered by any registering officer.

SEC. 2. . . . After the completion of the registration hereby provided for in any State, at such time and places therein as the commanding general shall appoint and direct, of which at least thirty days' public notice shall be given, an election shall be held of delegates to a convention for the purpose of establishing a constitution and civil government for such State loyal to the Union, said convention in each State, except Virginia, to consist of the same number of members as the most numerous branch of the State legislature of such State in the year eighteen hundred and sixty, to be apportioned among the several districts, counties, or parishes of such State by the commanding general, giving to each representation in the ratio of voters registered as aforesaid, as nearly as may be. The convention in Virginia shall consist of the same number of members as represented the territory now constituting Virginia in the most numerous branch of the legislature of said State in the year eighteen hundred and sixty, to be apportioned as aforesaid.

SEC. 3. . . . At said election the registered voters of each State shall vote for or against a convention to form a constitution therefor under this act. Those voting in favor of such a constitution shall have written or printed on the ballots by which they vote for delegates, as aforesaid, the words "For a convention," and those voting against such a convention shall have written or printed on such ballots the words "Against a convention." The person appointed to superintend said election, and to make return of the votes given thereat, as herein provided, shall count and make return of the votes given for and against a convention; and the commanding general to whom the same shall have been returned shall ascertain and declare the total vote in each State for and against a convention. If a majority of the votes given on that question shall be for a convention, then such convention shall be held as hereinafter provided; but if a majority of said votes shall be against a convention, then no such convention shall be held under this act: *Provided,* That such convention shall not be held unless a majority of all such registered voters shall have voted on the question of holding such convention.

SEC. 4. . . . The commanding general of each district shall appoint as many boards of registration as may be necessary, consisting of three loyal officers or persons, to make and complete the registration, superintend the election, and make return to him of the votes, lists of voters, and of the persons elected as delegates by a plurality of the votes cast at said election; and upon receiving said returns he shall open the same, ascertain the persons elected as delegates according to the returns of the officers who conducted said election, and make proclamation thereof; and if a majority of the votes given on the question shall be for a convention, the commanding general, within sixty days from the date of election, shall notify the delegates to assemble in convention, at a time and place to be mentioned in the notification, and said convention, when organized, shall proceed to frame a constitution and civil government according to the provisions of this act and the act to which it is supplementary; and when the same shall have been so framed, said constitution shall be submitted by the convention for ratification to the persons registered under the provisions of this act at an election to be conducted by the officers or persons appointed or to be appointed by the commanding general, as hereinbefore provided, and to be held after the expiration of thirty days from the date of notice thereof, to be given by said convention; and the returns thereof shall be made to the commanding general of the district.

SEC. 5. . . . If, according to said returns, the constitution shall be ratified by a majority of the votes of the registered electors qualified as herein specified, cast at said election, at least one half of all the registered voters voting upon the question of such ratification, the president of the convention shall transmit a copy of the same, duly certified, to the President of the United States, who shall forthwith transmit the same to Congress, if then in session, and if not in session, then immediately upon its next assembling; and if it shall, moreover, appear to Congress that the election was one at which all the registered and qualified electors in the State had an opportunity to vote freely and without restraint, fear, or the influence of fraud, and if the Congress shall be satisfied that such constitution meets the approval of a majority of all the qualified electors in the State, and if the said constitution shall be declared by Congress to be in conformity with the provisions of the act to which this is supplementary, and the other provisions of said act shall have been complied with, and the said constitution shall be approved by Congress, the State shall be declared entitled to representation, and senators and representatives shall be admitted therefrom as therein provided.

SEC. 6. . . . All elections in the States mentioned in the said "Act to provide for the more efficient government of the rebel States," shall, during the operation of said act, be by ballot; and all officers making the said registration of voters and conducting said elections shall, before entering upon the discharge of their duties, take and subscribe the oath prescribed by the act approved July second, eighteen hundred and sixty-two, entitled "An act to prescribe an oath of office:" *Provided,* That if any person shall knowingly and falsely take and subscribe any oath in this act prescribed, such person so offending and being thereof duly convicted, shall be subject to the pains, penalties, and disabilities which by law are provided for the punishment of the crime of wilful and corrupt perjury.

SEC. 7. . . . All expenses incurred by the several commanding generals, or by virtue of any orders issued, or appointments made, by them, under or by virtue of this act, shall be paid out of any moneys in the treasury not otherwise appropriated.

SEC. 8. . . . The convention for each State shall prescribe the fees, salary, and compensation to be paid to all delegates and other officers and agents herein authorized or necessary to carry into effect the purposes of this act not herein otherwise provided for, and shall provide for the levy and collection of such taxes on the property in such State as may be necessary to pay the same.

SEC. 9. . . . The word "article," in the sixth section of the act to which this is supplementary, shall be construed to mean "section."

THIRD RECONSTRUCTION ACT
July 19, 1867

Be it enacted . . . That it is hereby declared to have been the true intent and meaning of the [acts of March 2, March 23, 1867] that the governments then existing in the rebel States of Virginia, North Carolina, South Carolina, Georgia, Mississippi, Alabama, Louisiana, Florida, Texas, and Arkansas, were not legal State governments; and that thereafter said governments, if continued, were to be continued subject in all respects to the military commanders of the respective districts, and to the paramount authority of Congress.

SEC. 2. . . . The commander of any district named in said act shall have power, subject to the disapproval of the General of the army of the United States, and to have effect till disapproved, whenever in the opinion of such commander the proper administration of said act shall require it, to suspend or remove from office, or from the performance of official duties and exercise of official powers, any officer or person holding or exercising, or professing to hold or exercise, any civil or military office or duty in such district under any power, election, appointment, or authority derived from, or granted by, or claimed under, any so-called State or the government thereof, or any municipal or other division thereof; and upon such suspension or removal such commander, subject to the disapproval of the General as aforesaid, shall have power to provide from time to time for the performance of the said duties of such officer or person so suspended or removed, by the detail of some competent officer or soldier of the army, or by the appointment of some other person to perform the same, and to fill vacancies occasioned by death, resignation, or otherwise.

SEC. 3. . . . The General of the army of the United States shall be invested with all the powers of suspension, removal, appointment, and detail granted in the preceding section to district commanders.

SEC. 4. . . . The acts of the officers of the army already done in removing in said districts persons exercising the functions of civil officers, and appointing others in their stead, are hereby confirmed: *Provided,* That any person heretofore or hereafter appointed by any district commander to exercise the functions of any civil office, may be removed, either by the military officer in command of the district, or by the General of the army. And it shall be the duty of such commander to remove from office as aforesaid all persons who are disloyal to the government of the United States, or who use their official influence in any manner to hinder, delay, prevent, or obstruct the due and proper administration of this act and the acts to which it is supplementary.

SEC. 5. . . . The boards of registration provided for in the act entitled "An act supplementary to an act . . . passed March 23, 1867, shall have power, and it shall be their duty before allowing the registration of any person, to ascertain, upon such facts or information as they can obtain, whether such person is entitled to be registered under said act, and the oath required by said act shall not be conclusive on such question, and no person shall be registered unless such board shall decide that he is entitled thereto; and such board shall also have power to examine under oath, (to be administered by any member of such board,) any one touching the qualification of any person claiming registration; but in every case of refusal by the board to register an applicant, and in every case of striking his name from the list as hereinafter provided, the board shall make a note or memorandum, which shall be returned with the registration list to the commanding general of the district, setting forth the grounds of such refusal or such striking from the list: *Provided,* That no person shall be disqualified as member of any board of registration by reason of race or color.

SEC. 6. . . . The true intent and meaning of the oath prescribed in said supplementary act is, (among other things,) that no person who has been a member of the legislature of any State, or who has held any executive or judicial office in any State, whether he has taken an oath to support the Constitution of the United States or not, and whether he was holding such office at the commencement of the rebellion, or had held it before, and who has afterwards engaged in insurrection or rebellion against the United States, or given aid or comfort to the enemies thereof, is entitled to be registered or to vote; and the words "executive or judicial office in any State" in said oath mentioned shall be construed to include all civil offices created by law for the administration of any general law of a State, or for the administration of justice.

SEC 7. . . . The time for completing the original registration provided for in said act may, in the discretion of the commander of any district, be extended to the 1st day of October, 1867; and the boards of registration shall have power, and it shall be their duty, commencing fourteen days prior to any election under said act, and upon reasonable public notice of the time and place thereof, to revise, for a period of five days, the registration lists, and upon being satisfied that any person not entitled thereto has been registered, to strike the name of such person from the list, and such person shall not be allowed to vote. And such board shall also, during the same period, add to such registry the names of all persons who at that time possess the qualifications required by said act who have not been already registered; and no person shall, at any time, be entitled to be registered or to vote, by reason of any executive pardon or amnesty, for any act or thing which, without such pardon or amnesty, would disqualify him for registration or voting.

SEC. 8. . . . Section four of said last-named act shall be construed to authorize the commanding general named therein, whenever he shall deem it needful, to remove any member of a board of registration and to appoint another in his stead, and to fill any vacancy in such board.

SEC. 9. . . . All members of said boards of registration and all persons hereafter elected or appointed to office in said military districts, under any so-called State or municipal authority, or by detail or appointment of the district commanders, shall be required to take and subscribe the ["iron clad" oath].

SEC. 10. . . . No district commander or member of the board of registration, or any of the officers or appointees acting under them, shall be bound in his action by any opinion of any civil officer of the United States.

SEC. 11. . . . All the provisions of this act and of the acts to which this is supplementary shall be construed liberally, to the end that all the intents thereof may be fully and perfectly carried out.

FOURTH RECONSTRUCTION ACT
March 11, 1868

Be it enacted . . . That hereafter any election authorized by the act passed March 23, 1867 . . . shall be decided by a majority of votes actually cast; and at the election in which the question of the adoption or rejection of any constitution is submitted, any person duly registered in the State may vote in the election district where he offers to vote when he has resided therein for ten days next preceding such election, upon pre-

sentation of his certificate of registration, his affidavit, or other satisfactory evidence, under such regulations as the district commanders may prescribe.

SEC. 2. . . . The constitutional convention of any of the States mentioned in the acts to which this is amendatory may provide that at the time of voting upon the ratification of the constitution the registered voters may vote also for members of the House of Representatives of the United States, and for all elective officers provided for by the said constitution; and the same election officers who shall make the return of the votes cast on the ratification or rejection of the constitution, shall enumerate and certify the votes cast for members of Congress.

COMMENT

The conqueror has a right to extend his own laws over those conquered States. . . . Now, . . . it has become the duty of Congress to assert its right and do its duty in establishing some kind of government for this people. For two years they have been in a state of anarchy. . . . Persecution, exile, murder, have been the order of the day within all these Territories so far as loyal men were concerned, whether white or black, and more especially if they happened to be black.

Speech of Thaddeus Stevens of Pennsylvania in U.S. House of Representatives, February 7, 1867, *Congressional Globe*, 39th Cong., 2d Sess., 1866–1867, xxxvii, 1076.

The legislation you propose . . . is a blow at the very principles of civil liberty. It is striking down the right of trial by jury; it is establishing military tribunals to try cases in contravention of the provisions of the Constitution of the United States. . . . The provisions of this bill strike down every important provision in your Constitution.

Speech of Francis C. LeBlond of Ohio in U.S. House of Representatives, February 7, 1867. *Congressional Globe*, 39th Cong., 2d Sess., 1866–1867, xxxvii, 1078.

12. *JULY 20, 1868*

Fourteenth Amendment

One of the most important items in the Radical program of Reconstruction was

U.S. Statutes at Large, xiv, 358–59.

the Fourteenth Amendment. This amendment was drawn up early in 1866 by the Joint Committee on Reconstruction, ap-

proved, after some modification, by Congress in June, and sent to the states for ratification. Congress, fearing that ratification would not be valid unless achieved by a vote of three-fourths of all thirty-nine states, inconsistently submitted the amendment to the eleven southern states which it regarded as "conquered provinces" outside the Union. Tennessee was the only ex-Confederate state promptly to ratify. The other ten, against the advice of some of their most distinguished leaders, withheld approval and thus helped pave the way for military rule and the setting up of governments amenable to congressional control. On July 20, 1868, Secretary Seward announced that the amendment had been ratified by twenty-nine states, including Arkansas, Florida, North Carolina, Louisiana, South Carolina, and Alabama, and hence was "valid to all intents and purposes as a part of the Constitution." The first section of the amendment defined national citizenship in accordance with the Civil Rights Act of April 9, 1866, and prohibited states from depriving any person of life, liberty, or property without due process of law. The protection accorded persons by this section was later used by corporations to shield them from state regulation. Succeeding sections provided for reduction of representation of states denying suffrage to Negroes, disqualified from officeholding persons who had aided the Confederacy after having sworn to support the federal Constitution, validated the federal debt, and declared illegal and void all Confederate obligations and all claims for loss of slaves.

SEC. 1. All persons born or naturalized in the United States, and subject to the jurisdiction thereof, are citizens of the United States and of the State wherein they reside. No State shall make or enforce any law which shall abridge the privileges or immunities of citizens of the United States; nor shall any State deprive any person of life, liberty or property,

without due process of law, nor deny to any person within its jurisdiction the equal protection of the laws.

SEC. 2. Representatives shall be apportioned among the several States according to their respective numbers, counting the whole number of persons in each State, excluding Indians not taxed. But when the right to vote at any election for the choice of electors for President and Vice President of the United States, representatives in Congress, the executive and judicial officers of a State, or the members of the legislature thereof, is denied to any of the male inhabitants of such State, being twenty-one years of age, and citizens of the United States, or in any way abridged, except for participation in rebellion or other crime, the basis of representation therein shall be reduced in the proportion which the number of such male citizens shall bear to the whole number of male citizens twenty-one years of age in such State.

SEC. 3. No person shall be a senator or representative in Congress, or elector of President and Vice-President, or hold any office, civil or military, under the United States, or under any State, who, having previously taken an oath as a member of Congress, or as an officer of the United States, or as a member of any State Legislature, or as an executive or judicial officer of any State, to support the Constitution of the United States, shall have engaged in insurrection or rebellion against the same, or given aid or comfort to the enemies thereof. But Congress may, by a vote of two-thirds of each House, remove such disability.

SEC. 4. The validity of the public debt of the United States, authorized by law, including debts incurred for payment of pensions and bounties for services in suppressing insurrection or rebellion, shall not be questioned. But neither the United States nor any State shall assume or pay any debt or obligation incurred in aid of insurrection or rebellion against the United States, or any claim for the loss or emancipation of any slave; but all such debts, obligations, and claims shall be held illegal and void.

SEC. 5. The Congress shall have power to enforce, by appropriate legislation, the provisions of this article.

COMMENT

It falls far short of my wishes, but it fulfills my hopes. . . . The third section is . . . the mildest of all punishments ever inflicted on traitors.

> Speech of Thaddeus Stevens of Pennsylvania in U.S. House of Representatives, May 8, 1866. *Congressional Globe*, 39th Congress, 1st Sess., 1865–1866, xxxvi, pt. 2, 2460.

Give us the third section or give us nothing. . . . Every rebel who shed the blood of loyal men should be prevented from exercising any power in this government. . . . They have not yet confessed their sins. . . . I shall not agree they shall come back except as supplicants in sackcloth and ashes.

> Speech of Thaddeus Stevens of Pennsylvania in U.S. House of Representatives, May 10, 1866. *Congressional Globe*, 39th Cong., 1st Sess., 1865–1866, pt. 3, 2544.

We cannot reorganize political society with any security . . . unless we give those who are by their intelligence and character the natural leaders of the people . . . an opportunity to lead them now."

> Speech of Governor John A. Andrew to Massachusetts Legislature, January 4, 1866. Quoted by J. F. Rhodes, *History of the United States* (New York: The Macmillan Company, 1904), v, 607.

13. APRIL 20, 1871

Ku Klux Klan Act

In 1865 a small group of ex-Confederates in Pulaski, Tennessee, organized a Ku Klux Klan. Soon other communities followed their example, and by early 1867 the Klan had spread over most of the South, drawn up a mystic ritual, and adopted a constitution providing for an elaborate organization headed by a Grand Wizard and extending down to local Dens presided over by Grand Cyclops. Klansmen at first confined themselves largely to social activity and pranks. But with the enfranchisement of Negroes, the ascendancy of carpetbaggers and the forma-

U.S. Statutes at Large, xvii, 13–15.

tion of Union Leagues to perpetuate Republican control, the Klan became primarily concerned with combating Radical influence and maintaining white supremacy. It did not hesitate to employ intimidation and violence to accomplish its purposes, and some of its members utilized the cloak of secrecy to avenge personal grievances and conceal crime. After a while the more respectable element began to withdraw, and in 1869 General Nathan B. Forrest, the Grand Wizard, ordered dissolution of the Klan. Local units continued to function, but the organization had lost most of its in-

fluence when Republicans in 1871, alarmed by the shrinking of their majority in Congress, pushed through the Ku Klux Klan Act. This act, which was one of a series of "force bills," aimed at compelling southern acquiescence in Negro suffrage and Republican government, declared intimidation of voters to be a high crime, and authorized the President to suspend the privilege of habeas corpus for the suppression of "armed combinations." Enforcement of the act exterminated the Klan but it failed to end intimidation and violence.

Be it enacted . . . That any person who, under color of any law, statute, ordinance, regulation, custom, or usage of any State, shall subject, or cause to be subjected, any person within the jurisdiction of the United States to the deprivation of any rights, privileges, or immunities secured by the Constitution of the United States, shall, any such law, statute, ordinance, regulation, custom, or usage of the State to the contrary notwithstanding, be liable to the party injured in any action at law, suit in equity, or other proper proceeding for redress; such proceeding to be prosecuted in the several district or circuit courts of the United States, with and subject to the same rights of appeal, review upon error, and other remedies provided in like cases in such courts, under the provisions of the [Civil Rights Act of April 9, 1866] . . . and the other remedial laws of the United States which are in their nature applicable in such cases.

SEC. 2. That if two or more persons within any State or Territory of the United States shall conspire together to overthrow, or to put down, or to destroy by force the government of the United States, or to levy war against the United States or to oppose by force the authority of the government of the United States, or by force, intimidation, or threat to prevent, hinder, or delay the execution of any law of the United States, or by force

to seize, take, or possess any property of the United States contrary to the authority thereof, or by force, intimidation, or threat to prevent any person from accepting or holding any office or trust or place of confidence under the United States, or from discharging the duties thereof, or by force, intimidation, or threat to induce any officer of the United States to leave any State, district, or place where his duties as such officer might lawfully be performed, or to injure him in his person or property on account of his lawful discharge of the duties of his office, or to injure his person while engaged in the lawful discharge of the duties of his office, or to injure his property so as to molest, interrupt, hinder, or impede him in the discharge of his official duty, or by force, intimidation, or threat to deter any party or witness in any court of the United States from attending such court, or from testifying in any matter pending in such court fully, freely, and truthfully, or to injure any such party or witness in his person or property on account of his having so attended or testified, or by force, intimidation, or threat to influence the verdict, presentment, or indictment, of any juror or grand juror in any court of the United States, or to injure such juror in his person or property on account of any verdict, presentment, or indictment lawfully assented to by him, or on account of his being or having been such juror, or shall conspire together, or go in disguise upon the public highway or upon the premises of another for the purpose, either directly or indirectly, of depriving any person or any class of persons of the equal protection of the laws, or of equal privileges or immunities under the laws, or for the purpose of preventing or hindering the constituted authorities of any State from giving or securing to all persons within such State the equal protection of the laws, or shall conspire together for the purpose of in any manner impeding, hindering, obstructing, or defeating the due course of justice in any State or Territory, with the intent to deny to any citizen of the United States the due and equal protection of the laws, or to injure any person in his person or in his property for lawfully enforcing the right of any person or class of persons to the equal protection of the laws, or by force, intimidation, or threat to prevent any citizen of the United States lawfully entitled to vote from giving his support or advocacy in a lawful manner towards or in favor of the election of any lawfully qualified person as an elector of President or Vice-President of the United States, or as a member of the Congress of the United States, or to injure any such citizen in his person or property on account of such support or advocacy, each and every person so offending shall be deemed guilty of a high crime, and, upon conviction thereof in any district or circuit court of the United States or district or supreme court of any Territory of the United States having jurisdiction of similar offenses shall be punished by a fine not less than five hundred nor more than five thousand dollars, or by imprisonment, with or without hard labor, as the court may determine, for a period of not less than six months nor more than six years, as the court may determine, or by both such fine and imprisonment as the court shall determine. And if any one or more persons engaged in any such conspiracy shall do, or cause to be done, any act in furtherance of the object of such conspiracy, whereby any person shall be injured in his person or property, or deprived of having and exercising any right or privilege of a citizen of the United States, the person so injured or deprived of such rights and privileges may have and maintain an action for the recovery of damages occasioned by such injury or deprivation of rights and privileges against any one or more of the persons engaged in such conspiracy, such action to be prosecuted

in the proper district or circuit court of the United States, with and subject to the same rights of appeal, review upon error, and other remedies provided in like cases in such courts under the provisions of the [Civil Rights Act]. . .

SEC. 3. That in all cases where insurrection, domestic violence, unlawful combinations, or conspiracies in any State shall so obstruct or hinder the execution of the laws thereof, and of the United States, as to deprive any portion or class of the people of such State of any of the rights, privileges, or immunities, or protection, named in the Constitution and secured by this act, and the constituted authorities of such State shall either be unable to protect, or shall from any cause fail in or refuse protection of the people in such rights, such facts will be deemed a denial by such State of the equal protection of the laws to which they are entitled under the Constitution of the United States; and in all such cases, or whenever any such insurrection, violence, unlawful combination, or conspiracy shall oppose or obstruct the laws of the United States or the due execution thereof, or impede or obstruct the due course of justice under the same, it shall be lawful for the President, and it shall be his duty to take such measures, by the employment of the militia or the land and naval forces of the United States, or of either, or by other means, as he may deem necessary for the suppression of such insurrection, domestic violence, or combinations; and any person who shall be arrested under the provisions of this and the preceding section shall be delivered to the marshal of the proper district, to be dealt with according to law.

SEC. 4. That whenever in any State or part of a State the unlawful combinations named in the preceding section of this act shall be organized and armed, and so numerous and powerful as to be able, by violence, to either overthrow or set at defiance the constituted authorities of such State, and of the United States within such State, or when the constituted authorities are in complicity with, or shall connive at the unlawful purposes of, such powerful and armed combinations; and whenever, by reason of either or all of the causes aforesaid, the conviction of such offender and the preservation of the public safety shall become in such district impracticable, in every such case such combinations shall be deemed a rebellion, against the government of the United States, and during the continuation of such rebellion, and within the limits of the district which shall be so under the sway thereof, such limits to be prescribed by proclamation, it shall be lawful for the President of the United States, when in his judgment the public safety shall require it, to suspend the privileges of the writ of habeas corpus, to the end that such rebellion may be overthrown: *Provided,* That all the provisions of the second section of an act entitled "An act relating to habeas corpus . . . [of March 3, 1863] which relate to the discharge of prisoners other than prisoners of war, and to the penalty for refusing to obey the order of the court, shall be in full force so far as the same are applicable to the provisions of this section. *Provided further,* That the President shall first have made proclamation, as now provided by law, commanding such insurgents to disperse: *And provided also,* That the provisions of this section shall not be in force after the end of the next regular session of Congress.

SEC. 5. That no person shall be a grand or petit juror in any court of the United States upon any inquiry, hearing, or trial of any suit, proceeding or prosecution based upon or arising under the provisions of this act who shall, in the judgment of the court, be in complicity with any such combination or conspiracy; and every such juror shall, before entering upon any such inquiry, hearing, or trial, take and subscribe an oath in open court that he has never, directly or indirectly, counselled, advised, or voluntarily aided any such combination or conspiracy; and each and every person who shall take this oath, and shall therein swear falsely, shall be guilty of perjury, and shall be subject to the pains and penalties declared against that crime, and the first section of the act [of June 17, 1862, relating to jurors in United States courts] . . . be, and the same is hereby, repealed.

SEC. 6. That any person, or persons, having knowledge that any of the wrongs conspired to be done and mentioned in the second section of this act are about to be committed, and having power to prevent or aid in preventing the same, shall neglect or refuse so to do, and such wrongful act shall be committed, such person or persons shall be liable to the person injured, or his legal representatives, for all damages caused by any such wrongful act which such first-named person or persons by reasonable diligence could have prevented; and such damages may be recovered in an action on the case in the proper circuit court of the United States, and any number of persons guilty of such wrongful neglect or refusal may be joined as defendants in such action: *Provided,* That such action shall be commenced within one year after such cause of action shall have accrued; and if the death of any person shall be caused by any such wrongful act and neglect, the legal representatives of such deceased person shall have such action therefor, and may recover not exceeding five thousand dollars damages therein, for the benefit of the widow of such deceased person, if any there be, or if there be no widow, for the benefit of the next of kin of such deceased person.

SEC. 7. That nothing herein contained shall be construed to supersede or repeal any former act or law except so far as the same may be repugnant thereto; and any offenses heretofore committed against the tenor of any former act shall be prosecuted, and any proceeding already commenced for the prosecution thereof shall be continued and completed, the same as if this act had not been passed, except so far as the provisions of this act may go to sustain and validate such proceedings.

COMMENT

We want to . . . put down the Ku Klux organizations which are the legitimate descendants of the old legalized patrol system that once existed in the South, carried on now without law. Crimes are committed under it that are shocking and appalling.

> Speech of Henry Wilson of Massachusetts in U.S. Senate, January 18, 1871. *Congressional Globe*, 41st Cong., 3d Sess., 1870–1871, xliii, 570.

There are many social disorders which it is very difficult to cure by laws, just as there are many diseases which it is impossible to cure by medicines. . . . Several provisions of this bill [are] an encroachment of the national authority upon the legitimate sphere of local self government, not warranted by the Constitution of this Republic.

> Speech of Carl Schurz of Missouri in U.S. Senate, April 14, 1871. *Congressional Globe*, 42d Cong., 1st Sess., 1871, xliii, 687.

14. MARCH 1, 1875

The Civil Rights Act

The Civil Rights Act, last of the major measures making up the Radical program of Reconstruction, originated with Charles Sumner, able and honest but sometimes unreasonable and tactless senator from Massachusetts. During the last four years of his life, Sumner tried repeatedly, but without success, to get Congress to pass a law guaranteeing to Negroes equal rights in hotels, theaters, railways, steamboats, schools, churches, and cemeteries. Just before his death in 1874, Sumner obtained the promise of Congressman E. R. Hoar to see that his civil rights project was not forgotten. Despite warnings from the floor that it

U.S. *Statutes at Large*, xviii, pt. 3, pp. 335–37.

was unconstitutional, a civil rights bill passed both houses early in 1875 and was approved by President U. S. Grant on March 1. The act fell short of Sumner's desires in that it did not prohibit discrimination in schools, cemeteries, and churches. In 1883, the Supreme Court declared the first two sections of the act unconstitutional on the ground that "the rights which they endeavored to guarantee were not strictly civil rights at all but rather social rights and that in either case the Federal government had nothing to do with them."

Whereas, it is essential to just government we recognize the equality of all men before the law, and hold that it is the duty of government in its dealings with the people to mete out equal and exact justice to all, of whatever nativity, race, color, or persuasion, religious or political; and it being the appropriate object of legislation to enact great fundamental principles into law: Therefore,

Be it enacted, . . . That all persons within the jurisdiction of the United States shall be entitled to the full and equal enjoyment of the accommodations, advantages, facilities, and privileges of inns, public conveyances on land or water, theatres, and other places of public amusement; subject only to the conditions and limitations established by law, and applicable alike to citizens of every race and color, regardless of any previous conditions of servitude.

SEC. 2. That any person who shall violate the foregoing section by denying to any citizen, except for reasons by law applicable to citizens of every race and color, and regardless of any previous condition of servitude, the full enjoyment of any of the accommodations, advantages, facilities, or privileges in said section enumerated, or by aiding or inciting such denial, shall, for every such offense, forefeit and pay the sum of five hundred dollars to the person aggrieved thereby, to be recovered in an action of debt with full costs; and shall also, for every such offense, be deemed guilty of a misdemeanor, and, upon conviction thereof, shall be fined not less than five hundred nor more than one thousand dollars, or shall be imprisoned not less than thirty days nor more than one year: *Provided*, That all persons may elect to sue for the penalty aforesaid or to proceed under their rights at common law and by State statutes; and having so elected to proceed in the one mode or the other, their right to proceed in the other jurisdiction shall be barred. But this proviso shall not apply to criminal proceedings, either under this act or the criminal law of any State: *And provided further*, That a judgment for the penalty

in favor of the party aggrieved, or a judgment upon an indictment, shall be a bar to either prosecution respectively.

SEC. 3. That the district and circuit courts of the United States shall have, exclusively of the courts of the several States, cognizance of all crimes and offenses against, and violations of, the provisions of this act; and actions for the penalty given by the preceding section may be prosecuted in the territorial, district, or circuit courts of the United States wherever the defendant may be found, without regard to the other party; and the district attorneys, marshals, and deputy marshals of the United States, and commissioners appointed by the circuit and territorial courts of the United States, with powers of arresting and imprisoning or bailing offenders against the laws of the United States, are hereby specially authorized and required to institute proceedings against every person who shall violate the provisions of this act, and cause him to be arrested and imprisoned or bailed, as the case may be, for trial before such court of the United States, or territorial court, as by law has cognizance of the offense, except in respect of the right of action accruing to the person aggrieved; and such district attorney shall cause such proceedings to be prosecuted to their termination as in other cases: *Provided*, That nothing contained in this section shall be construed to deny or defeat any right of civil action accruing to any person, whether by reason of this act or otherwise; and any district attorney who shall wilfully fail to institute and prosecute the proceedings herein required, shall, for every such offense forefeit and pay the sum of five hundred dollars to the person aggrieved thereby, to be recovered by an action of debt, with full costs, and shall, on conviction thereof, be deemed guilty of a misdemeanor, and be fined not less than one thousand nor more than five thousand dollars: *And provided further*, That a judgment for the penalty in favor of the party aggrieved against any such district attorney, or a judgment upon an indictment against any such district attorney, shall be a bar to either prosecution respectively.

Sec. 4. That no citizen possessing all other qualifications which are or may be prescribed by law shall be disqualified for service as grand or petit juror in any court of the United States, or of any State, on account of race, color, or previous condition of servitude; and any officer or other persons charged with any duty in the selection or summoning of jurors who shall exclude or fail to summon any citizen for the cause aforesaid shall, on conviction thereof, be deemed guilty of a misdemeanor, and be fined not more than five thousand dollars.

Sec. 5. That all cases arising under the provisions of this act in the courts of the United States shall be reviewable by the Supreme Court of the United States, without regard to the sum in controversy, under the same provisions and regulations as are now provided by law for the review of other causes in said court.

COMMENT

Social equality we have nothing to do with. . . . When once it is understood that the people of the United States have finally determined that men and citizens are all entitled to equality of privileges under the law, in regard to any subject which the law regulates and determines, we shall have peace, and social equality and personal tastes will take care of themselves.

Speech of E. R. Hoar of Massachusetts in the U.S. House of Representatives, February 4, 1875. *Congressional Globe,* 43d Cong., 2d Sess., xxxvii, 979.

Give us this bill . . . which has for its object the protection of human rights. . . . Then we can all truthfully say that this beautiful land of ours, over which the Star Spangled Banner so triumphantly waves, is in truth and in fact, "the land of the free and the home of the brave."

Speech of John R. Lynch, Negro Congressman from Mississippi, in the U.S. House of Representatives, February 3, 1875. *Congressional Globe,* 43d Cong., 2d Sess., xxxvii, 947.

You talk about giving these people (the negroes) the right to go to the theater when there is not one of them in a hundred who knows what they are. You talk about allowing them to go into churches when they have established churches of their own and have refused to worship with the whites. You talk about granting them the right to travel with the white people in the cars, when there is not one of them in five hundred who travels once a year in a train. You talk about giving them the right to go to hotels when there is not one of them in a thousand who desires the privilege.

Speech of James H. Blount of Georgia in the U.S. House of Representatives. February 4, 1875. *Congressional Globe,* 43d Cong., 2d Sess., 1875, xxxvii, 978.

The bill . . . is an offense and menace to the dominant race. . . . It will . . . breed mischief, prejudice and cruelty to the weaker race. . . . We will not permit all white men to come into our hotels, theaters and churches.

Speech of Simeon B. Chittenden of New York in the U.S. House of Representatives, February 4, 1875. *Congressional Globe,* 43d Cong., 2d Sess., 1875, xxxvii, 982.

15. SEPTEMBER 16, 1876

Wade Hampton's Speech to the Negroes, Abbeville, South Carolina

Wade Hampton—handsome, courageous, personable, and wealthy—was one of the most highly respected leaders in the post-bellum South. His prestige was due in part to his distinguished career as a Confederate general. But his appeal to the masses was attributable in no small measure to his unpretending ways and his simple, straightforward approach to public issues. Though he had owned many slaves, he was one of the first southern leaders to advocate enfranchisement of freedmen. When South Carolina Democrats nominated him to run for governor in 1876 against the Republican incumbent D. H. Chamberlain, Hampton set to work to woo Negroes from the Republican fold. Typical of his appeal to the blacks throughout the campaign was the speech which he delivered at Abbeville on September 16. He won many Negro votes, but these probably would have been of no avail had it not been for the effectiveness of the Democratic "rifle clubs" and the planters' economic pressure in keeping Republican Negroes away from the polls on the day that he won the election.

I feel assured that if the colored people of the State would come out, and see and hear for themselves, there will be thousands and tens of thousands, like the colored men of Abbeville, that will join the democratic party in this State. I give them the word of a man, who neither

House Miscellaneous Documents, 44th Cong., 1st Sess., No. 31, pt. 1 (Washington, D.C., 1877), pp. 307–308.

friend nor foe can say ever broke that word, that if I am elected governor of South Carolina, *I shall be the governor of the whole State; I shall render to the whole people of this State equal and impartial justice.*

The platform adopted by the democratic party in Columbia is one upon which all can stand. Talk about putting the colored men back into slavery or qualifying their suffrages. . . . It is against our interest to do either of these things, if we could. In the first place, the labor of the colored man is more valuable to us as he is than if he was slave, because they were perishable property, and, as soon as they passed away, it was so much loss to the general wealth of the country. As to qualifying your suffrages, why that is the very thing your President Grant wants to do. We want your votes; we don't want you to be deprived of them, and I can tell you, if the colored people continue to join the democratic ranks as they have been doing thus early in the campaign, we will be the last people in the world to curtail their suffrages. The northern republicans thought it was all right so long as you voted the republican ticket, but just so soon as the colored people of the South began to go democratic, they were the first to introduce a bill to qualify their suffrages. Why? Because they don't want the South to have a chance to turn the election for the President. I am not in the big fight, however. I am in this little fight to save South Carolina, and I tell you upon my honor that if you allow the white people of South Carolina to go down this time, you will go down so deep that no plummet can ever reach you. If . . . the white people of South Carolina, were to leave you the State, and give you everything, lands, houses, churches, banks, you could not live without them. *The only way to bring about prosperity in this State is to bring the two races in friendly relation together.* The Democratic party in South Carolina . . . has promised that every citizen of this State is to be the equal of all; he is to have every right given him by the Constitution of the United States and of this State. This democratic party in South Carolina pledges itself to support and accept the thirteenth, fourteenth and fifteenth amendments . . . and I pledge my faith, and I pledge it for those gentlemen who are in the ticket with me, that if we are elected, as far as in us lies, *we will observe, protect, and defend the rights of the colored man as quickly as any man in South Carolina.* (A voice, "That's right; tell them that over again.") If there is a white man in this assembly, because he is a democrat, or because he is a white man, believes that when I am elected governor . . . that I will stand between him and the law, or grant to him any privileges or immunities that shall not be granted to the colored man, he is mistaken, and I tell him so now, that if that is his reason for voting for me not to vote at all.

COMMENT

It is due not only to ourselves but to the colored people of the State that wise, just and liberal measures should prevail in our legislation. We owe much of our late success to these colored voters who were brave enough to rise above the prejudice of race and honest enough to throw off the shackles of party in their determination to save the State.

> Inaugural address of Governor Wade Hampton, December 14, 1876. Quoted in John S. Reynolds, *Reconstruction in South Carolina, 1865–1877* (Columbia, S.C.: State Co., 1905), p. 429.

Knowing you were always a good and kind man to me when your slave and knowing you are a good and kind man who will do what he promises . . . I will vote for you and will get all the black men I can to do the same.

> Reverend Francis Davie to Wade Hampton during campaign of 1876. Quoted in A. B. Williams, *Hampton and His Red Shirts: South Carolina's Deliverance in 1876.* (Charleston, S.C.: Walker, Evans & Cogswell Co., 1935), p. 201.

After 1877 there was no disposition to keep Hampton's promise that he would protect the political rights of the Negroes.

> Francis B. Simkins and Robert H. Woody, *South Carolina during Reconstruction* (Chapel Hill, N.C.: University of North Carolina Press, 1932), p. 547.

16. *1877*

Munn v. Illinois

In 1873, the Grange-controlled legisla-ture of Illinois passed an act which fixed the rates for grain storage in warehouses in cities of 100, 000 people or more. Al-most immediately, the operators of grain elevators in Chicago challenged the con-stitutionality of the law on the grounds that it infringed upon Congress' power to regulate interstate commerce and that it violated the Fourteenth Amendment. Writing for the majority of the Supreme Court, Chief Justice Morrison R. Waite upheld the law by declaring that when private property is clothed with a public interest, it is subject to public regulation. Despite its insistence upon the validity of public regulation, between 1877 and 1898, the Court slowly retreated from the dictum of Munn v. Illinois. During these twenty years, the Court gradually granted more recognition to the substantive con-cept of due process of law as related to the doctrine of vested rights. By 1898, the Supreme Court had broadened the con-cept of vested rights to such an extent that it was willing to strike down state regulatory statutes as being unconstitu-tional on the grounds that the rates they established were confiscatory and de-prived corporations of their property without due process of law.

When one becomes a member of so-ciety, he necessarily parts with some rights or privileges which, as an indi-vidual not affected by his relations to others, he might retain. "A body politic," as aptly defined in the preamble of the Constitution of Massachusetts, "is a social compact by which the whole people cov-

94 U.S. 113 (1877).

enants with each citizen, and each citizen with the whole people, that all shall be governed by certain laws for the common good." This does not confer power upon the whole people to control rights which are purely and exclusively private ... but it does authorize the establishment of laws requiring each citizen to so conduct himself, and so use his own property, as not unnecessarily to injure another. . . . From this source come the police powers.

. . . Under these powers the government regulates the conduct of its citizens one towards another, and the manner in which each shall use his own property, when such regulation becomes necessary for the public good. In their exercise it has been customary in England from time im-memorial, and in this country from its first colonization, to regulate ferries, com-mon carriers, hackmen, bakers, millers, wharfingers, innkeepers, etc., and in so doing to fix a maximum of charge to be made for services rendered, accommoda-tions furnished, and articles sold. To this day, statutes are to be found in many of the States upon some or all these subjects; and we think it has never yet been suc-cessfully contended that such legislation came within any of the constitutional pro-hibitions against interference with private property. With the Fifth Amendment in force, Congress, in 1820, conferred power upon the city of Washington "to regulate . . . the rates of wharfage at private wharves, . . . the sweeping of chimneys, and to fix the rates of fees therefor, . . . and the weight and quality of bread," . . .

From this it is apparent that, down to the time of the adoption of the Fourteenth

Amendment, it was not supposed that statutes regulating the use, or even the price of the use, of private property necessarily deprived an owner of his property without due process of law. Under some circumstances they may, but not under all. The amendment does not change the law in this particular: it simply prevents the States from doing that which will operate as such a deprivation.

This brings us to inquire as to the principles upon which this power of regulation rests, in order that we may determine what is within and what without its operative effect. . . . Property does become clothed with a public interest when used in a manner to make it of public consequence, and affect the community at large. When, therefore, one devotes his property to a use in which the public has an interest, he, in effect, grants to the public an interest in that use, and must submit to be controlled by the public for the common good, to the extent of the interest he has thus created. He may withdraw his grant by discontinuing the use; but, so long as he maintains the use, he must submit to the control. . . .

Under such circumstances it is difficult to see why, if the common carrier, or the miller, or the ferryman, or the innkeeper, or the wharfinger, or the baker, or the cartman, or the hackney-coachman, pursues a public employment and exercises "a sort of public office," these plaintiffs in error do not. They stand, to use again the language of their counsel, in the very "gateway of commerce," and take toll from all who pass. . . .

It is insisted, however, that the owner of property is entitled to a reasonable compensation for its use, even though it be clothed with a public interest, and that what is reasonable is a judicial and not a legislative question.

As has already been shown, the practice has been otherwise. In countries where the common law prevails, it has been customary from time immemorial for the legislature to declare what shall be a reasonable compensation under such circumstances, or, perhaps more properly speaking, to fix a maximum beyond which any charge made would be unreasonable. Undoubtedly, in mere private contracts, relating to matters in which the public has no interest, what is reasonable must be ascertained judicially. But this is because the legislature has no control over such a contract. . . .

. . . To limit the rate of charge for services rendered in a public employment, or for the use of property in which the public has an interest, is only changing a regulation which existed before. It establishes no new principle in the law, but only gives a new effect to an old one.

We know that this is a power which may be abused; but that is no argument against its existence. For protection against abuses by legislatures the people must resort to the polls, not to the courts. . . .

COMMENT

The same liberal construction which is required for the protection of life and liberty, in all particulars in which life and liberty are of any value, should be applied to the protection of private property. If the legislature of a State, under pretence of providing for the public good, or for any other reason, can determine, against the consent of the owner, the uses to which private property shall be devoted, or the prices which the owner shall receive for its uses, it can deprive him of the property as completely as by a special act for its confiscation or destruction. If, for instance, the owner is prohibited from using his building for the purpose for which it was designed, it is of little consequence that he is permitted to retain the title and possession; or, if he is compelled to take as compensation for its use less than the expenses to which he is subjected by its ownership, he is, for all practical purposes, deprived of the property, as effectually as if the legislature had ordered his forcible dispossession.

Justice Field dissenting in Munn v. Illinois, 944 U.S. 142.

17. MAY 6, 1882

Chinese Exclusion Act

After the admission of California to the Union, the influx of Chinese laborers into California caused serious racial, economic, and political problems. Hostility toward the Chinese stemmed from the belief that they were a servile class which constituted a threat to free labor. It was also believed that the customs and habits of the Chinese were a social menace and that they were unassimilable. Though there were mob violence and discrimination during the 1850's and 1860's, agitation reached new heights after 1877 with the formation of the California Workingmen's Party. This group quickly became the leader in directing violence against the Chinese and in demanding a federal exclusion law. Soon, there was support for such an act from every section of California. The result was a treaty with China in 1880 permitting the United States to regulate the entry of Chinese laborers. Two years later, in a departure from the traditional policy of its unrestricted admission to those who sought American shores, Congress passed this act which excluded Chinese laborers for a period of ten years. The Californians were successful in achieving support for their program because both national parties were competing for western votes and because of the absence of opposition

U.S. Statutes at Large, XXII, 58–61.

to the measure. Since 1882, Congress has put forth many criteria for exclusion and selection.

Whereas, in the opinion of the Government of the United States the coming of Chinese laborers to this country endangers the good order of certain localities within the territory: Therefore,

Be it enacted by the Senate and House of Representatives of the United States of America in Congress assembled, That from and after the expiration of ninety days next after the passage of this act, and until the expiration of ten years next after the passage of this act, the coming of Chinese laborers to the United States be, and the same is hereby, suspended; and during such suspension it shall not be lawful for any Chinese laborer to come, or, having so come after the expiration of said ninety days, to remain within the United States.

SEC. 2. That the master of any vessel who shall knowingly bring within the United States on such vessel, and land or permit to be landed, any Chinese laborer, from any foreign port or place, shall be deemed guilty of a misdemeanor, and on conviction thereof shall be punished by a fine of not more than five hundred dollars for each and every such Chinese laborer so brought, and may be also imprisoned for a term not exceeding one year.

SEC. 3. That the two foregoing sections shall not apply to Chinese laborers who were in the United States on the seventeenth day of November, eighteen hundred and eighty, or who shall have come into the same before the expiration of ninety days next after the passage of this act, and who shall produce to such master before going on board such vessel, and shall produce to the collector of the port in the United States at which such vessel shall arrive, the evidence hereinafter in this act required of his being one of the laborers in this section mentioned; nor shall the two foregoing sections apply to the case of any master whose vessel, being bound to a port not within the United States, shall come within the Jurisdiction of the United States by reason of being in distress or in stress of weather, or touching at any port of the United States on its voyage to any foreign port or place: *Provided,* That all Chinese laborers brought on such vessel shall depart with the vessel on leaving port.

. . . . .

SEC. 6. That in order to the faithful execution of articles one and two of the treaty in this act before mentioned, every Chinese person other than a laborer who may be entitled by said treaty and this act to come within the United States, and who shall be about to come to the United States, shall be identified as so entitled by the Chinese Government in each case, such identity to be evidenced by a certificate issued under the authority of said government, which certificate shall be in the English language or (if not in the English language) accompanied by a translation into English, stating such right to come, and which certificate shall state the name, title, or official rank, if any, the age, height, and all physical peculiarities, former and present occupation or profession, and place of residence in China of the person to whom the certificate is issued and that such person is entitled conformably to the treaty in this act mentioned to come within the United States. Such certificate shall be prima-facie evidence of the fact set forth therein, and shall be produced to the collector of customs, or his deputy, of the port in the district in the United States at which the person named therein shall arrive.

SEC. 7. That any person who shall knowingly and falsely alter or substitute any name for the name written in such certificate or forge any such certificate, or knowingly utter any forged or fraudulent certificate, or falsely personate any person named in any such certificate, shall be deemed guilty of a misdemeanor; and upon conviction thereof shall be fined in a sum not exceeding one thousand dollars, and imprisoned in a penitentiary for a term of not more than five years.

. . . . .

SEC. 10. That every vessel whose master shall knowingly violate any of the provisions of this act shall be deemed forfeited to the United States, and shall be liable to seizure and condemnation in any district of the United States into which such vessel may enter or in which she may be found.

SEC. 11. That any person who shall knowingly bring into or cause to be brought into the United States by land, or who shall knowingly aid or abet the landing in the United States from any vessel of any Chinese person not lawfully entitled to enter the United States, shall be deemed guilty of a misdemeanor, and shall, on conviction thereof, be fined in a sum not exceeding one thousand dollars, and imprisoned for a term not exceeding one year.

SEC. 12. That no Chinese person shall be permitted to enter the United States by land without producing to the proper officer of customs the certificate in this act required of Chinese persons seeking to land from a vessel. And any Chinese person found unlawfully within the United States shall be caused to be removed therefrom to the country from whence he came, by direction of the President of the United States, and at the cost of the United States, after being brought before some justice, judge, or commissioner of a court of the United States and found to be one not lawfully entitled to be or remain in the United States.

. . . . .

SEC. 14. That hereafter no State court or court of the United States shall admit Chinese to citizenship; and all laws in conflict with this act are hereby repealed.

SEC. 15. That the words "Chinese laborers," wherever used in this act, shall be construed to mean both skilled and unskilled laborers and Chinese employed in mining.

COMMENT

Throughout this year and a half of financial depression, stagnation and social agitation, much had been threatened and done against the Chinese; yet it may be doubted whether Chinese immigration was, after all, the storm center of the disturbance. Rather, it appears that a mushroom prosperity and great extremes of fortune, arising from speculation and chance rather than legitimate industry, and the gathering of heterogeneous idlers under the leadership of demagogues, had brought to the surface all the elements of jealousy, envy and lawlessness which, inherent in human nature, now surged and frothed about the more stable elements of society.

> Mary R. Coolidge, sociologist, in *Chinese Immigration* (New York: Henry Holt & Co., 1909), p. 116.

Let a colony of these Asiatic brethren, with souls to save, camp down beside Boston Common, with their filthy habits, their criminal practices, and their nasty vices, and how long would it be before Beacon Hill would sniff the polluted atmosphere, and all the overgodly of New England would send up their prayers for relief.

> Editorial in the San Francisco (Calif.) *Argonaut*, January 19, 1878.

18. 1883

The Civil Rights Cases

In 1875, the Radical Republicans made one last effort to establish civil equality for Negroes by having Congress pass the Civil Rights Act (see pp. 53–55). This
109 U.S. 3 (1883).

law provided that all persons, regardless of race, were entitled to "the full and equal enjoyment of the accommodations, advantages, facilities and privileges of inns, public conveyances on land or water, theaters, and other places of pub-lic amusement." A violation of these pro-visions was a misdemeanor.

In 1883, the Supreme Court in the Civil Rights Cases declared the Civil Rights Act void when it ruled that the Fourteenth Amendment did not protect the rights of individuals except when those rights were violated by state action. By ruling that an individual's violation of another's rights was not a subject for federal action, the Supreme Court served notice that the federal government could not protect Negroes against the invasion of civil rights by individuals unaided by state authority. Once these views were pronounced, the way was clear for the triumph of the southern social order of "white supremacy." In the 1960's when southern Negroes were seeking equal rights in privately owned business estab-lishments, this decision was to assume new importance.

The first section of the Fourteenth Amendment (which is the one relied on), after declaring who shall be citizens of the United States, and of the several states, is prohibitory in its character, and prohibitory upon the states. It de-clares that: "No state shall make or en-force any law which shall abridge the privileges or immunities of citizens of the United States; nor shall any state de-prive any person of life, liberty, or prop-erty without due process of law; nor deny to any person within its jurisdic-tion the equal protection of the laws."

It is state action of a particular char-acter that is prohibited. Individual inva-sion of individual rights is not the sub-ject matter of the amendment. It has a deeper and broader scope. It nullifies and makes void all state legislation, and state action of every kind, which impairs the privileges and immunities of citizens of the United States, or which injures them in life, liberty, or property with-out due process of law, or which denies to any of them the equal protection of the laws. It not only does this, but, in order that the national will, thus de-clared, may not be a mere *brutum ful-men,* the last section of the amendment invests Congress with power to enforce it by appropriate legislation. To enforce what? To enforce the prohibition. To adopt appropriate legislation for cor-recting the effects of such prohibited state laws and state acts, and thus to render them effectually null, void, and innocuous. This is the legislative power conferred upon Congress, and this is the whole of it. It does not invest Congress with power to legislate upon subjects which are within the domain of state legislation; but to provide modes of re-lief against state legislation, or state ac-tion, of the kind referred to. It does not authorize Congress to create a code of municipal law for the regulation of pri-vate rights; but to provide modes of redress against the operation of state laws, and the action of state officers, executive or judicial, when these are subversive of the fundamental rights specified in the amendment. Positive rights and privileges are undoubtedly se-cured by the Fourteenth Amendment; but they are secured by way of prohibi-tion against state laws and state proceed-ings affecting those rights and privileges, and by power given to Congress to legis-late for the purpose of carrying such prohibition into effect; and such legisla-tion must necessarily be predicated upon such supposed state laws or state pro-ceedings and be directed to the correc-tion of their operation and effect. . . .

If this legislation is appropriate for enforcing the prohibitions of the amend-ment, it is difficult to see where it is to stop. Why may not Congress with equal show of authority enact a code of laws for the enforcement and vindication of all rights of life, liberty, and property? If it is supposable that the states may de-prive persons of life, liberty, and prop-erty without due process of law (and the amendment itself does suppose this), why should not Congress proceed at once to prescribe due process of law for the protection of every one of these fundamental rights, in every possible case, as well as to prescribe equal privileges in inns, public conveyances, and theaters? The truth is that the implication of a power to legislate in this manner is based upon the assumption that if the states are forbidden to legislate or act in a particular way on a particular subject, and power is conferred upon Congress to enforce the prohibition, this gives Congress power to legislate generally upon that subject and not merely power to provide modes of redress against such state legislation or action. The assumption is certainly unsound. It is repugnant to the Tenth Amendment of the Constitution, which declares that powers not delegated to the United States by the Constitution, nor prohibited by it to the states, are reserved to the states respectively or to the people. . . .

In this connection it is proper to state that civil rights, such as are guaranteed by the Constitution against state aggression, cannot be impaired by the wrongful acts of individuals, unsupported by state authority in the shape of laws, customs, or judicial or executive proceedings. The wrongful act of an individual, unsupported by any such authority, is simply a private wrong, or a crime of that individual; an invasion of the rights of the injured party, it is true, whether they affect his person, his property, or his reputation; but if not sanctioned in some way by the state, or not done under state authority, his rights remain in full force and may presumably be vindicated by resort to the laws of the state for redress. An individual cannot deprive a man of his right to vote, to hold property, to buy and sell, to sue in the courts, or to be a witness or a juror; he may, by force or fraud, interfere with the enjoyment of the right in a particular case; he may commit an assault against the person, or commit murder,

or use ruffian violence at the polls, or slander the good name of a fellow-citizen; but, unless protected in these wrongful acts by some shield of state law or state authority, he cannot destroy or injure the right; he will only render himself amenable to satisfaction or punishment; and amenable therefore to the laws of the state where the wrongful acts are committed. Hence, in all those cases where the Constitution seeks to protect the rights of the citizen against discriminative and unjust laws of the state by prohibiting such laws, it is not individual offenses, but abrogation and denial of rights, which it denounces, and for which it clothes the Congress with power to provide a remedy. This abrogation and denial of rights, for which the states alone were or could be responsible, was the great seminal and fundamental wrong which was intended to be remedied. And the remedy to be provided must necessarily be predicated upon that wrong. It must assume that in the cases provided for, the evil or wrong actually committed rests upon some state law or state authority for its excuse and perpetration. . . .

But the power of Congress to adopt direct and primary, as distinguished from corrective, legislation, on the subject in hand, is sought, in the second place, from the Thirteenth Amendment, which abolishes slavery. This amendment declares that "neither slavery, nor involuntary servitude, except as a punishment for crime, whereof the party shall have been duly convicted, shall exist within the United States, or any place subject to their jurisdiction"; and it gives Congress power to enforce the amendment by appropriate legislation. . . .

It may be that by the Black Code . . . in the times when slavery prevailed, the proprietors of inns and public conveyances were forbidden to receive persons of the African race, because it might assist slaves to escape from the control of their masters. This was merely a means of preventing such escapes and was no part of the servitude itself. A law of that kind could not have any such object now, however justly it might be deemed an invasion of the party's legal right as a citizen, and amenable to the prohibitions of the Fourteenth Amendment.

The long existence of African slavery in this country gave us very distinct notions of what it was, and what were its necessary incidents. Compulsory service of the slave for the benefit of the master, restraint of his movements except by the master's will, disability to hold property, to make contracts, to have a standing in court, to be a witness against a white person, and such like burdens and incapacities were the inseparable incidents of the institution. Severer punishments for crimes were imposed on the slave than on free persons guilty of the same offenses. Congress, . . . by the Civil Rights Bill of 1866, passed in view of the Thirteenth Amendment, before the Fourteenth was adopted, undertook to wipe out these burdens and disabilities, the necessary incidents of slavery, constituting its substance and visible form; and to secure to all citizens of every race and color, and without regard to previous servitude, those fundamental rights which are the essence of civil freedom, namely, the same right to make and enforce contracts, to sue, be parties, give evidence, and to inherit, purchase, lease, sell, and convey property, as is enjoyed by white citizens. Whether this legislation was fully authorized by the Thirteenth Amendment alone, without the support which it afterward received from the Fourteenth Amendment, after the adoption of which it was re-enacted with some additions, it is not necessary to inquire. It is referred to for the purpose of showing that at that time (in 1866) Congress did not assume, under the authority given by the Thirteenth Amendment, to adjust what may be called the social rights of men and races in the community; but only to

declare and vindicate those fundamental rights which appertain to the essence of citizenship, and the enjoyment or deprivation of which constitutes the essential distinction between freedom and slavery. . . .

When a man has emerged from slavery, . . . there must be some stage in the progress of his elevation when he takes the rank of a mere citizen and ceases to be the special favorite of the laws, and when his rights as a citizen, or a man, are to be protected in the ordinary modes by which other men's rights are protected. There were thousands of free colored people in this country before the abolition of slavery, enjoying all the essential rights of life, liberty, and property the same as white citizens; yet no one at that time, thought that it was any invasion of his personal status as a freeman because he was not admitted to all the privileges enjoyed by white citizens, or because he was subjected to discriminations in the enjoyment of accommodations in inns, public conveyances, and places of amusement. Mere discriminations on account of race or color were not regarded as badges of slavery. If, since that time, the enjoyment of equal rights in all these respects has become established by constitutional enactment, it is not by force of the Thirteenth Amendment (which merely abolishes slavery), but by force of the Fourteenth and Fifteenth amendments.

On the whole we are of opinion that no countenance of authority for the passage of the law in question can be found in either the Thirteenth or Fourteenth Amendment of the Constitution; and, no other ground of authority for its passage being suggested, it must necessarily be declared void, at least so far as its operation in the several states is concerned. . . .

MR. JUSTICE HARLAN DISSENTING

The opinion in these cases proceeds, it seems to me, upon grounds entirely too narrow and artificial. I cannot resist the conclusion that the substance and spirit of the recent amendments of the Constitution have been sacrificed by a subtle and ingenious verbal criticism. "It is not the words of the law but the internal sense of it makes the law: the letter of the law is the body; the sense and reason of the law is the soul." Constitutional provisions, adopted in the interest of liberty, and for the purpose of securing, through national legislation, if need be, rights inhering in a state of freedom, and belonging to American citizenship, have been so construed as to defeat the ends the people desired to accomplish, which they attempted to accomplish, and which they supposed they had accomplished by changes in their fundamental law. By this I do not mean that the determination of these cases should have been materially controlled by considerations of mere expediency or policy. I mean only, in this form, to express an earnest conviction that the Court has departed from the familiar rule requiring, in the interpretation of constitutional provisions, that full effect be given to the intent with which they were adopted.

The purpose of the first section of the act of Congress of March 1, 1875, was to prevent *race* discrimination in respect of the accommodations and facilities of inns, public conveyances, and places of public amusement. . . .

That there are burdens and disabilities which constitute badges of slavery and servitude, and that the power to enforce by appropriate legislation the Thirteenth Amendment may be exerted by legislation of a direct and primary character, for the eradication, not simply of the institution, but of its badges and incidents, are propositions which ought to be deemed indisputable. . . .

Congress has not, in these matters, entered the domain of state control and supervision. It does not, as I have said, assume to prescribe the general conditions and limitations under which inns, public conveyances, and places of public amusement shall be conducted or managed. It simply declares, in effect, that since the nation has established universal freedom in this country, for all time, there shall be no discrimination, based merely upon race or color, in respect of the accommodations and advantages of public conveyances, inns, and places of public amusement.

I am of the opinion that such discrimination practiced by corporations and individuals in the exercise of their public or quasi-public functions is a badge of servitude the imposition of which Congress may prevent under its power, by appropriate legislation, to enforce the Thirteenth Amendment; and, consequently, without reference to its enlarged power under the Fourteenth Amendment, the act of March 1, 1875, is not, in my judgment, repugnant to the Constitution.

It remains now to consider these cases with reference to the power Congress has possessed since the adoption of the Fourteenth Amendment. Much that has been said as to the power of Congress under the Thirteenth Amendment is applicable to this branch of the discussion and will not be repeated.

Before the adoption of the recent amendments, it had become, as we have seen, the established doctrine of this Court that Negroes, whose ancestors had been imported and sold as slaves, could not become citizens of a state, or even of the United States, with the rights and privileges guaranteed to citizens by the national Constitution; further, that one might have all the rights and privileges of a citizen of a state without being a citizen in the sense in which that word was used in the national Constitution, and without being entitled to the privileges and immunities of citizens of the several states. Still, further, between the adoption of the Thirteenth Amendment and the proposal by Congress of the Fourteenth Amendment, on June 16, 1866, the statute books of several of the states, as we have seen, had become loaded down with enactments which, under the guise of apprentice, vagrant, and contract regulations, sought to keep the colored race in a condition, practically, of servitude. It was openly announced that whatever might be the rights which persons of that race had, as freemen, under the guarantees of the national Constitution, they could not become citizens of a state, with the privileges belonging to citizens, except by the consent of such state; consequently, that their civil rights, as citizens of the state, depended entirely upon state legislation. To meet this new peril to the black race, that the purposes of the nation might not be doubted or defeated, and by way of further enlargement of the power of Congress, the Fourteenth Amendment was proposed for adoption. . . .

But what was secured to colored citizens of the United States—as between them and their respective states—by the national grant to them of state citizenship? With what rights, privileges, or immunities did this grant invest them? There is one, if there be no other—exemption from race discrimination in respect of any civil right belonging to citizens of the whole race in the same state. That, surely, is their constitutional privilege when within the jurisdiction of other states. And such must be their constitutional right, in their own state, unless the recent amendments be splendid baubles, thrown out to delude those who deserved fair and generous treatment at the hands of the nation. Citizenship in this country necessarily imports at least equality of civil rights among citizens of every race in the same state. It is fundamental in American citizenship that, in respect of such rights, there shall be no discrimination by the state, or its officers, or by individuals or corporations exercising public functions or authority, against any citizen because of his race or previous condition of servitude. . . .

. . . . .

In every material sense applicable to the practical enforcement of the Fourteenth Amendment, railroad corporations, keepers of inns, and managers of places of public amusement are agents or instrumentalities of the state, because they are charged with duties to the public, and are amenable, in respect of their duties and functions, to governmental regulation. . . .

My brethren say that when a man has emerged from slavery, and by the aid of beneficent legislation has shaken off the inseparable concomitants of that state, there must be some stage in the progress of his elevation when he takes the rank of a mere citizen and ceases to be the special favorite of the laws, and when his rights as a citizen, or a man, are to be protected in the ordinary modes by which other men's rights are protected. It is, I submit, scarcely just to say that the colored race has been the special favorite of the laws. The statute of 1875, now adjudged to be unconstitutional is for the benefit of ctizens of every race and color. What the nation, through Congress, has sought to accomplish in reference to that race is—what had already been done in every state of the Union for the white race—to secure and protect rights belonging to them as freemen and citizens; nothing more. It was not deemed enough "to help the feeble up, but to support him after." The one underlying purpose of congressional legislation has been to enable the black race to take the rank of mere citizens. The difficulty has been to compel a recognition of the legal right of the black race to take the rank of citizens, and to secure the enjoyment of privileges belonging, under the law, to them as a component part of the people for whose welfare and happiness government is ordained. At every step, in this direction, the nation has been confronted with class tyranny, ...

Today, it is the colored race which is denied, by corporations and individuals wielding public authority, rights fundamental in their freedom and citizenship. At some future time, it may be that some other race will fall under the ban of race discrimination. If the constitutional amendments be enforced, according to the intent with which, as I conceive, they were adopted, there cannot be, in this republic, any class of human beings in practical subjection to another class, with power in the latter to dole out to the former just such privileges as they may choose to grant. The supreme law of the land has decreed that no authority shall be exercised in this country upon the basis of discrimination, in respect of civil rights, against freemen and citizens because of their race, color, or previous condition of servitude. To that decree—for the due enforcement of which, by appropriate legislation, Congress has been invested with express power—everyone must bow, whatever may have been, or whatever now are, his individual views as to the wisdom or policy, either of the recent changes in the fundamental law, or of the legislation which has been enacted to give them effect.

For the reasons stated I feel constrained to withhold my assent to the opinion of the Court.

19. *1883*

William Graham Sumner on Social Classes

During the last three decades of the nineteenth century, the writings of Charles Darwin had a profound impact on American thought. The first to grasp the Darwinian concepts were the laissez-faire conservatives who were anxious to defend the political status quo. Such Darwinian terms as the "struggle for existence" and the "survival of the fittest" were used to suggest that competition was a law of nature and that the best competitors would succeed in society.

The most influential social Darwinist in America was William Graham Sumner, a sociologist at Yale University. To Sumner, life was a grim experience. Viewing competition as a law of life, he denounced the efforts of socialists to legislate social equality. To restrict competition and to promote equality would merely favor the

WILLIAM GRAHAM SUMNER, *What Social Classes Owe to Each Other* (New York: Harper and Brothers, 1883), pp. 12–24, 95–98, 116–20.

survival of the unfittest and penalize the hard-working and the thrifty. The result would be social chaos.

Unlike many proponents of laissez-faire, Sumner was true to his convictions and opposed all forms of government interference in the economy. Moreover, he disagreed with those social democrats who cited Darwin to justify imperialism and "Jim Crow" laws.

I now propose to try to find out whether there is any class in society which lies under the duty and burden of fighting the battles of life for any other class, or of solving social problems for the satisfaction of any other class; also, whether there is any class which has the right to formulate demands on "society" —that is, on other classes; also, whether there is anything but a fallacy and a superstition in the notion that "the State" owes anything to anybody except peace, order and the guarantees of rights.

. . . . .

Certain ills belong to the hardships of human life. They are natural. They are part of the struggle with Nature for existence. We cannot blame our fellow-men for our share of these. . . .

. . . . .

The humanitarians, philanthropists, and reformers, looking at the facts of life as they present themselves, find enough which is sad and unpromising in the condition of many members of society. They see wealth and poverty side by side. They note great inequality of social position and social chances. They eagerly set about the attempt to account for what they see, and to devise schemes for remedying what they do not like. In their eagerness to recommend the less fortunate classes to pity and consideration they forget all about the rights of other classes; they gloss over all the faults of the classes in question, and they exaggerate their misfortunes and their virtues. They invent new theories of property, distorting rights and perpetuating injustice, as anyone is sure to do who sets about the readjustment of social relations with the interests of one group distinctly before his mind, and the interests of all other groups thrown into the background. . . . In all these schemes and projects the organized intervention of society through the State is either planned or hoped for, and the State is thus made to become the protector and guardian of certain classes. The agents who are to direct the State action are, of course, the reformers and philanthropists. Their schemes, therefore, may always be reduced to this type—that A and B decide what C shall do for D. It will be interesting to inquire, at a later period of our discussion, who C is, and what the effect is upon him of all these arrangements. In all the discussions attention is concentrated on A and B, the noble social reformers, and on D, the

"poor man." I call C the Forgotten Man, because I have never seen that any notice was taken of him in any of the discussions. When we have disposed of A, B, and D we can better appreciate the case of C, and I think that we shall find that he deserves our attention, for the worth of his character and the magnitude of his unmerited burdens. Here it may suffice to observe that, on the theories of the social philosophers to whom I have referred, we should get a new maxim of judicious living: Poverty is the best policy. If you get wealth, you will have to support other people; if you do not get wealth, it will be the duty of other people to support you.

. . . . .

I have said that trades-unions are right and useful, and, perhaps, necessary; but trades-unions are, in fact, in this country, an exotic and imported institution, and a great many of their rules and modes of procedure, having been developed in England to meet English circumstances, are out of place here. The institution itself does not flourish as it would if it were in a thoroughly congenial environment. It needs to be supported by special exertion and care. Two things here work against it. First, the mobility of our population. A trades-union, to be strong, needs to be composed of men who have grown up together, who have close personal acquaintance and mutual confidence, who have been trained to the same code, and who expect to live on together in the same circumstances and interests. In this country, where workmen move about frequently and with facility, the unions suffer in their harmony and stability. It was a significant fact that the unions declined during the hard times. It was only when the men were prosperous that they could afford to keep up the unions, as a kind of social luxury. When the time came to use the union it ceased to be. Secondly, the American workman really has such personal independence, and such an independent and strong position in the labor market, that he does not need the union. He is farther on the road toward the point where personal liberty supplants the associative principle than any other workman. Hence, the association is likely to be a clog to him, especially if he is a good laborer, rather than an assistance. If it were not for the notion brought from England, that trades-unions are, in some mysterious way, beneficial to the workmen—which notion has now become an article of faith—it is very doubtful whether American workmen would find that the unions were of any use, unless they were converted into organizations for accomplishing the purposes enumerated in the last paragraph.

The fashion of the time is to run to Government boards, commissions, and inspectors to set right everything which is wrong. No experience seems to damp the faith of our public in these instrumentalities. The English Liberals in the middle of this century seemed to have full grasp of the principle of liberty, and to be fixed and established in favor of non-interference. Since they have come to power, however, they have adopted the old instrumentalities, and have greatly multiplied them since they have had a great number of reforms to carry out. They seem to think that interference is good if only they interfere. In this country the party which is "in" always interferes, and the party which is "out" favors non-interference. The system of interference is a complete failure of the ends it aims at, and sooner or later it will fall of its own expense and be swept away. The two notions—one to regulate things by a committee of control, and the other to let things regulate themselves by the conflict of interests between free men— are diametrically opposed; and the former is corrupting to free institutions, because men who are taught to expect Government inspectors to come and take

care of them lose all true education in liberty. If we have been all wrong for the last three hundred years in aiming at a fuller realization of individual liberty, as a condition of general and widely-diffused happiness, then we must turn back to paternalism, disipline, and authority; but to have a combination of liberty and dependence is impossible.

. . . . .

The amateur social doctors are like the amateur physicians—they always begin with the question of *remedies,* and they go at this without any diagnosis or any knowledge of the anatomy or physiology of society. They never have any doubt of the efficacy of their remedies. They never take account of any ulterior effects which may be apprehended from the remedy itself. It generally troubles them not a whit that their remedy implies a complete reconstruction of society, or even a reconstitution of human nature. Against all such social quackery the obvious injunction to the quacks is, to mind their own business.

. . . . .

. . . But we have inherited a vast number of social ills which never came from Nature. They are the complicated products of all the tinkering, muddling, and blundering of social doctors in the past. These products of social quackery are now buttressed by habit, fashion, prejudice, platitudinarian thinking, and new quackery in political economy and social science. . . .

. . . . .

Society, therefore, does not need any care or supervision. If we can acquire a science of society, based on observation of phenomena and study of forces, we may hope to gain some ground slowly toward the elimination of old errors and the reestablishment of a sound and natural social order. Whatever we gain that way will be by growth, never in the world by any reconstruction of society on the plan of some enthusiastic social architect. The latter is only repeating the old error over again, and postponing all our chances of real improvement. Society needs first of all to be freed from these meddlers—that is, to be let alone. Here we are, then, once more back at the old doctrine—*Laissez faire*. Let us translate it into blunt English, and it will read, Mind your own business. . . .

COMMENT

Our industry . . . is a fight of every man for himself. The prize we give the fittest is monopoly of the necessaries of life, and we leave these winners of the powers of life and death to wield them over us by the same "self-interest" with which they took them from us. . . . "There is no hope for any of us, but the weakest must go first," is the golden rule of business. There is no other field of human associations in which any such rule of action is allowed. The man who should apply in his family or in his citizenship this "survival of the fittest" theory as it is practically professed and operated in business would be a monster, and would be speedily made extinct.

Social reformer Henry D. Lloyd in *Wealth Against Commonwealth* (New York, 1894), pp. 494–95.

We civilised men . . . do our utmost to check the process of elimination; we build asylums for the imbecile, the maimed, and the sick; we institute poor-laws; and our medical men exert their utmost skill to save the life of every one to the last moment. . . . Thus the weak members of civilised society propagate their kind. No one who has attended to the breeding of domestic animals will doubt that this must be highly injurious to the race of man.

Naturalist Charles Darwin in *The Descent of Man* (New York, 1874), pp. 151–52.

The growth of a large business is merely a survival of the fittest. . . . This is not an evil tendency in business. It is merely the working-out of a law of nature and a law of God.

Oil magnate John D. Rockefeller. Quoted from William J. Ghent, *Our Benevolent Feudalism* (New York: The Macmillan Company, 1902), p. 29.

20. FEBRUARY 4, 1887

Interstate Commerce Act

By the end of the nineteenth century, state regulation of railroads had proven to be ineffective because of the interposition of the judiciary and because each railroad was too closely tied up with a network ex-

U.S. *Statutes at Large*, XXIV, 379–87.

tending into other states. But some type of regulation was necessary, as abuses by the railroads were rapidly becoming a national scandal. Rate fixing and pools were ruining certain roads. Eventually, not only the public, but many railroad executives began to demand some type of government regulation which would end the throat-cutting competition. Congress responded by passing the Interstate Commerce Act. The act marked a turning point in American constitutional history by creating the Interstate Commerce Commission, the first permanent administrative board with a quasi-judicial, quasi-legislative, and quasi-executive character. Though the Commission was in theory a part of the executive branch of the government, it was to conduct itself as a court in holding hearings, taking evidence, and handing down decisions. Since its administrative orders had the effect of law, the Commission also assumed certain legislative functions.

The federal courts later restricted the powers of the Commission by denying its power to fix rates and impairing its authority as a fact-finding body. As a result, the Commission did not become an effective regulatory agency until after the passage of the Hepburn Act in 1906.

Be it enacted by the Senate and House of Representatives of the United States of America in Congress assembled, That the provisions of this act shall apply to any common carrier or carriers engaged in the transportation of passengers or property wholly by railroad, or partly by railroad and partly by water when both are used, under a common control, management, or arrangement, for a continuous carriage or shipment, from one State or Territory of the United States, or the District of Columbia, to any other State or Territory of the United States, or the District of Columbia, or from any place in the United States to an adjacent foreign country, or from any place in the United States through a foreign country to any other place in the United States, and also to the transportation in like manner of property shipped from any place in the United States to a foreign country and carried from such place to a port of transshipment, or shipped from a foreign country to any place in the United States and carried to such place from a port of entry either in the United States or an adjacent foreign country: *Provided, however,* That the provisions of this act shall not apply to the transportation of passengers or property, or to the receiving, delivering, storage, or handling of property, wholly within one State, and not shipped to or from a foreign country from or to any State or Territory as aforesaid.

The term "railroad" as used in this act shall include all bridges and ferries used or operated in connection with any railroad, and also all the road in use by any corporation operating a railroad, whether owned or operated under a contract, agreement, or lease; and the term "transportation" shall include all instrumentalities of shipment or carriage.

All charges made for any service rendered or to be rendered in the transportation of passengers or property as aforesaid, or in connection therewith, or for the receiving, delivering, storage, or handling of such property, shall be reasonable and just; and every unjust and unreasonable charge for such service is prohibited and delivered to be unlawful.

SEC. 2. That if any common carrier subject to the provisions of this act shall, directly or indirectly, by any special rate, rebate, drawback, or other device, charge, demand, collect, or receive from any person or persons a greater or less compensation for any service rendered, or to be rendered in the transportation of passengers or property, subject to the provisions of this act, than it charges, demands, collects, or receives from any other person or persons for doing for him or them a like and contemporaneous service in the transportation of a like kind of traffic under substantially similar circumstances and conditions, such common carrier shall be deemed guilty of unjust discrimination, which is hereby prohibited and declared to be unlawful.

. . . . .

Sec. 4. That it shall be unlawful for any common carrier subject to the provisions of this act to charge or receive any greater compensation in the aggregate for the transportation of passengers or of like kind of property, under substantially similar circumstances and conditions, for a shorter than for a longer distance over the same line, in the same direction, the shorter being included within the longer distance; but this shall not be construed as authorizing any common carrier within the terms of this act to charge and receive as great compensation for a shorter as for a longer distance: *Provided, however,* That upon application to the Commission appointed under the provisions of this act, such common carrier may, in special cases, after investigation by the Commission, be authorized to charge less for longer than for shorter distances for the transportation of passengers or property; and the Commission may from time to time prescribe the extent to which such designated common carrier may be relieved from the operation of this section of this act.

Sec. 5. That it shall be unlawful for any common carrier subject to the provisions of this act to enter into any contract, agreement, or combination with any other common carrier or carriers for the pooling of freights of different and competing railroads, or to divide between them the aggregate or net proceeds of the earnings of such railroads, or any portion thereof; and in any case of an agreement for the pooling of freights as aforesaid, each day of its continuance shall be deemed a separate offense.

Sec. 6. That every common carrier subject to the provisions of this act shall print and keep for public inspection schedules showing the rates and fares and charges for the transportation of passengers and property which any such

common carrier has established and which are in force at the time upon its railroad, as defined by the first section of this act. The schedules printed as aforesaid by any such common carrier shall plainly state the places upon its railroad between which property and passengers will be carried, and shall contain the classification of freight in force upon such railroad, and shall also state separately the terminal charges and any rules or regulations which in any wise change, affect, or determine any part or the aggregate of such aforesaid rates and charges. Such schedules shall be plainly printed in large type, of at least the size of ordinary pica, and copies for the use of the public shall be kept in every depot or station upon any such railroad, in such places and in such form that they can be conveniently inspected.

Any common carrier subject to the provisions of this act receiving freight in the United States to be carried through a foreign country to any place in the United States shall also in like manner print and keep for public inspection, at every depot where such freight is received for shipment, schedules showing the through rates established and charged by such common carrier to all points in the United States beyond the foreign country to which it accepts freight for shipment; and any freight shipped from the United States through a foreign country into the United States, the through rate on which shall not have been made public as required by this act, shall, before it is admitted into the United States from said foreign country, be subject to customs duties as if said freight were of foreign production; and any law in conflict with this section is hereby repealed.

No advance shall be made in the rates, fares, and charges which have been established and published as aforesaid by any common carrier in compliance with the requirements of this section, except after ten days' public notice, which shall plainly state the changes proposed to be made in the schedule then in force, and the time when the increased rates, fares, or charges will go into effect; . . . .

And when any such common carrier shall have established and published its rates, fares, and charges in compliance with the provisions of this section, it shall be unlawful for such common carrier to charge, demand, collect, or receive from any person or persons a greater or less compensation for the transportation of passengers or property, or for any services in connection therewith, than is specified in such published schedule of rates, fares, and charges as may at the time be in force.

Every common carrier subject to the provisions of this act shall file with the Commission hereinafter provided for copies of its schedules of rates, fares, and charges which have been established and published in compliance with the requirements of this section, and shall promptly notify said Commission of all changes made in the same. Every such common carrier shall also file with said Commission copies of all contracts, agreements, or arrangements with other common carriers in relation to any traffic affected by the provisions of this act to which it may be a party. . . .

. . . . .

SEC. 10. That any common carrier subject to the provisions of this act, or, whenever such common carrier is a corporation, any director or officer thereof, or any receiver, trustee, lessee, agent, or person acting for or employed by such corporation, who, alone or with any other corporation, company, person, or party, shall willfully do or cause to be done, or shall willingly suffer or permit to be done, any act, matter, or thing in this act prohibited or declared to be unlawful, or who shall aid or abet therein, or shall willfully omit or fail to do any act, matter, or thing in this act required to be done, or shall cause or willingly suffer or permit any act, matter, or thing so directed

or required by this act to be done not to be so done, or shall aid or abet any such omission or failure, or shall be guilty of any infraction of this act, or shall aid or abet therein, shall be deemed guilty of a misdemeanor, and shall, upon conviction thereof in any district court of the United States within the jurisdiction of which such offense was committed, be subject to a fine of not to exceed five thousand dollars for each offense.

SEC. 11. That a Commission is hereby created and established to be known as the Inter-State Commerce Commission, which shall be composed of five Commissioners, who shall be appointed by the President, by and with the advice and consent of the Senate. The Commissioners first appointed under this act shall continue in office for the term of two, three, four, five, and six years, respectively, from the first day of January, anno Domini eighteen hundred and eighty-seven, the term of each to be designated by the President; but their successors shall be appointed for terms of six years, except that any person chosen to fill a vacancy shall be appointed only for the unexpired term of the Commissioner whom he shall succeed. Any Commissioner may be removed by the President for inefficiency, neglect of duty, or malfeasance in office. Not more than three of the Commissioners shall be appointed from the same political party. No person in the employ of or holding any official relation to any common carrier subject to the provisions of this act, or owning stock or bonds thereof, or who is in any manner pecuniarily interested therein, shall enter upon the duties of or hold such office. Said Commissioners shall not engage in any other business, vocation, or employment. No vacancy in the Commission shall impair the right of the remaining Commissioners to exercise all the powers of the Commission.

SEC. 12. That the Commission hereby created shall have authority to inquire into the management of the business of all common carriers subject to the provisions of this act, and shall keep itself informed as to the manner and method in which the same is conducted, and shall have the right to obtain from said common carriers full and complete information necessary to enable the Commission to perform the duties and carry out the objects for which it was created; and for the purposes of this act the Commission shall have power to require the attendance and testimony of witnesses and the production of all books, papers, tariffs, contracts, agreements, and documents relating to any matter under investigation, and to that end may invoke the aid of any court of the United States in requiring the attendance and testimony of witnesses and the production of books, papers, and documents under the provisions of this section.

. . . . .

SEC. 13. That any person, firm, corporation, or association, any mercantile, agricultural, or manufacturing society, or any body politic or municipal organization complaining of anything done or omitted to be done by any common carrier subject to the provisions of this act in contravention of the provisions thereof, may apply to said Commission by petition, which shall briefly state the facts; whereupon a statement of the charges thus made shall be forwarded by the Commission to such common carrier, who shall be called upon to satisfy the complaint or to answer the same in writing within a reasonable time, to be specified by the Commission. If such common carrier, within the time specified, shall make reparation for the injury alleged to have been done, said carrier shall be relieved of liability to the complainant only for the particular violation of law thus complained of. If such carrier shall not satisfy the complaint within the time specified, or there shall appear to be any reasonable ground for investigating said complaint, it shall be the duty of the Commission to investigate the matters complained of in such manner and by such means as it shall deem proper.

Said Commission shall in like manner investigate any complaint forwarded by the railroad commissioner or railroad commission of any State or Territory at the request of such commissioner or commission, and may institute any inquiry on its own motion in the same manner and to the same effect as though complaint had been made.

No complaint shall at any time be dismissed because of the absence of direct damage to the complainant.

. . . . .

SEC. 16. That whenever any common carrier, as defined in and subject to the provisions of this act, shall violate or refuse or neglect to obey any lawful order or requirement of the Commission in this act named, it shall be the duty of the Commission, and lawful for any company or person interested in such order or requirement, to apply, in a summary way, by petition, to the circuit court of the United States sitting in equity in the judicial district in which the common carrier complained of has its principal office, or in which the violation or disobedience of such order or requirement shall happen, alleging such violation or disobedience, as the case may be; and the said court shall have power to hear and determine the matter, on such short notice to the common carrier complained of as the court shall deem reasonable; . . .

. . . . .

COMMENT

The railroads . . . are not run for the benefit of the *dear public*. That cry is all nonsense! They are built for men who invest their money and expect to get a fair percentage on the same.

Financier William H. Vanderbilt speaking to a newspaper reporter. New York *Times*, April 3, 1882.

The Inter-State Commerce Law . . . is supported because it is a law, because it is the presumed wisdom, or compromised wisdom, of Congress upon the subject, and it has a special body of officers, selected with great care by the President, whose duty it is to see that it is enforced. The main feature of its passage was that the country wanted something upon the subject, that it was not best even to leave it over until another Congress, and, in the conflicting ideas, there was a general consensus to let something go through upon the subject, not very special reference being had as to what that something might be.

Social critic John C. Welch in "The Inter-State Railway Solvent," *North American Review*, CXLV (July, 1887), 87.

21. DECEMBER 6, 1887

Grover Cleveland Advocates Tariff Revision

During the 1880's, the Democratic party drifted in the direction of a low tariff policy, due largely to the urging of President Cleveland. To lower the government's surplus revenue, Cleveland had more than one alternative. He could have demanded a cut in taxes on domestic whiskey and tobacco and a lowering of tariffs on luxuries such as silk and wine, while leaving intact the duties which protected American industry. However, the President did just the opposite. He was unwilling to disturb internal taxes and luxury tariffs. In his annual speech of December 6, 1887, he demanded a cut in tariffs on the necessities of life and on the raw materials used in the manufacture of necessities.

The speech alienated the protectionists within the president's party. Moreover, the professional politicians thought that Cleveland had already reached his

JAMES D. RICHARDSON, ed., *Messages and Papers of the Presidents* (Washington, D.C., 1897), VII, 580–91.

maximum strength as president and that his tariff program would lose more support than it would gain for him. Subsequent events were to prove that they were correct. When the voters were given an opportunity to pass judgment on the tariff issue in 1888, it was obvious that Cleveland had pushed the party to higher ground than it was capable of maintaining. Had he delivered his message a year earlier, he might have been able to win sufficient support for his program.

Despite the defeat which he suffered at the polls in 1888, Cleveland had committed the Democratic party to a policy of tariff reform. Some twenty-six years later, another Democratic president, Woodrow Wilson, had some success in achieving tariff reform. But there was no lasting tariff reform until Franklin Roosevelt temporarily deprived Congress of the power to set rates.

TO THE CONGRESS OF THE UNITED STATES: You are confronted at the threshold of your legislative duties with a condition of the national finances which imperatively demands immediate and careful consideration.

The amount of money annually exacted, through the operation of present laws, from the industries and necessities of the people largely exceeds the sum necessary to meet the expenses of the Government.

When we consider that the theory of our institutions guarantees to every citizen the full enjoyment of all the fruits of his industry and enterprise, with only such deduction as may be his share toward the careful and economical maintenance of the Government which protects him, it is plain that the exaction of more than this is indefensible extortion and a culpable betrayal of American fairness and justice. This wrong inflicted upon those who bear the burden of national taxation, like other wrongs, multiplies a brood of evil consequences. The public Treasury, which should only exist as a conduit conveying the people's tribute to its legitimate objects of expenditure, becomes a hoarding place for money needlessly withdrawn from trade and the people's use, thus crippling our national energies, suspending our country's development, preventing investment in productive enterprise, threatening financial disturbance, and inviting schemes of public plunder.

This condition of our Treasury is not altogether new, and it has more than once of late been submitted to the people's representatives in the Congress, who alone can apply a remedy. And yet the situation still continues, with aggravated incidents, more than ever presaging financial convulsion and widespread disaster.

It will not do to neglect this situation because its dangers are not now palpably imminent and apparent. They exist none the less certainly, and await the unforeseen and unexpected occasion when suddenly they will be precipitated upon us.

On the 30th day of June, 1885, the excess of revenues over public expenditures, after complying with the annual requirement of the sinking-fund act, was $17,859,735.84; during the year ended June 30, 1886, such excess amounted to $49,405,545.20, and during the year ended June 30, 1887, it reached the sum of $55,567,849.54.

. . . . .

Our scheme of taxation, by means of which this needless surplus is taken from the people and put into the public Treasury, consists of a tariff or duty levied upon importations from abroad and internal-revenue taxes levied upon the consumption of tobacco and spirituous and malt liquors. It must be conceded that none of the things subjected to internal-revenue taxation are, strictly speaking, necessaries. There appears to be no just complaint of this taxation by the consumers of these articles, and there seems to be nothing so well able to bear the burden without hardship to any portion of the people.

But our present tariff laws, the vicious, inequitable, and illogical source of unnecessary taxation, ought to be at once revised and amended. These laws, as their primary and plain effect, raise the price to consumers of all articles imported and subject to duty by precisely the sum paid for such duties. Thus the amount of the duty measures the tax paid by those who purchase for use these imported articles. Many of these things, however, are raised or manufactured in our own country, and the duties now levied upon foreign goods and products are called protection to these home manufactures, because they render it possible for those of our people who are manufacturers to make these taxed articles and sell them for a price equal to that demanded for the imported goods that have paid customs duty. So it happens that while comparatively a few use the imported articles, millions of our people, who never used and never saw any of the foreign products, purchase and use things of the same kind made in this country, and pay therefor nearly or quite the same enhanced price which the duty adds to the imported articles. Those who buy imports pay the duty charged thereon into the public Treasury, but the great majority of our citizens, who buy domestic articles of the same class, pay a sum at least approximately equal to this duty to the home manufacturer. This reference to the operation of our tariff laws is not made by way of instruction, but in order that we may be constantly reminded of the manner in which they impose a burden upon those who consume domestic products as well as those who consume imported articles, and thus create a tax upon all our people.

It is not proposed to entirely relieve the country of this taxation. It must be extensively continued as the source of the Government's income; and in a readjustment of our tariff the interests of American labor engaged in manufacture should be carefully considered, as well as the preservation of our manufacturers. It may be called protection or by any other name, but relief from the hardships and dangers of our present tariff laws should be devised with especial precaution against imperiling the existence of our manufacturing interests. But this existence should not mean a condition which, without regard to the public welfare or a national exigency, must always insure the realization of immense profits instead of moderately profitable returns. As the volume and diversity of our national activities increase, new recruits are added to those who desire a continuation of the advantages which they conceive the present system of tariff directly affords them. So stubbornly have all efforts to reform the present condition been resisted by those of our fellow-citizens thus engaged that they can hardly complain of the suspicion, entertained to a certain extent, that there exists an or-ganized combination all along the line to maintain their advantage.

We are in the midst of centennial celebrations, and with becoming pride we rejoice in American skill and ingenuity, in American energy and enterprise, and in the wonderful natural advantages and resources developed by a century's national growth. Yet when an attempt is made to justify a scheme which permits a tax to be laid upon every consumer in the land for the benefit of our manufacturers, quite beyond a reasonable demand for governmental regard, it suits the purposes of advocacy to call our manufactures infant industries still needing the highest and greatest degree of favor and fostering care that can be wrung from Federal legislation.

It is also said that the increase in the price of domestic manufactures resulting from the present tariff is necessary in order that higher wages may be paid to our workingmen employed in manufactories than are paid for what is called the pauper labor of Europe. All will acknowledge the force of an argument which involves the welfare and liberal compensation of our laboring people. Our labor is honorable in the eyes of every American citizen; and as it lies at the foundation of our development and progress, it is entitled, without affectation or hypocrisy, to the utmost regard. The standard of our laborers' life should not be measured by that of any other country less favored, and they are entitled to their full share of all our advantages.

By the last census it is made to appear that of the 17,392,099 of our population engaged in all kinds of industries 7,670,493 are employed in agriculture, 4,074,238 in professional and personal service (2,934,876 of whom are domestic servants and laborers), while 1,810,256 are employed in trade and transportation and 3,837,112 are classed as employed in manufacturing and mining.

For present purposes, however, the last number given should be considerably

reduced. Without attempting to enumerate all, it will be conceded that there
should be deducted from those which it
includes 375,143 carpenters and joiners,
285,401 milliners, dressmakers, and
seamstresses, 172,726 blacksmiths, 133,
756 tailors and tailoresses, 102,473
masons, 76,241 butchers, 41,309 bakers,
22,083 plasterers, and 4,891 engaged in
manufacturing agricultural implements,
amounting in the aggregate to 1,214,023,
leaving 2,623,089 persons employed in
such manufacturing industries as are
claimed to be benefited by a high tariff.

To these the appeal is made to save
their employment and maintain their
wages by resisting a change. There should
be no disposition to answer such suggestions by the allegation that they are in a
minority among those who labor, and
therefore should forego an advantage in
the interest of low prices for the majority.
Their compensation, as it may be affected
by the operation of tariff laws, should at
all times be scrupulously kept in view;
and yet with slight reflection they will not
overlook the fact that they are consumers
with the rest; that they too have their
own wants and those of their families to
supply from their earnings, and that the
price of the necessaries of life, as well as
the amount of their wages, will regulate
the measure of their welfare and comfort.

But the reduction of taxation demanded should be so measured as not to
necessitate or justify either the loss of
employment by the workingman or the
lessening of his wages; and the profits
still remaining to the manufacturer after
a necessary readjustment should furnish
no excuse for the sacrifice of the interests
of his employees, either in their opportunity to work or in the diminution of
their compensation. Nor can the worker
in manufactures fail to understand that
while a high tariff is claimed to be necessary to allow the payment of remunerative wages, it certainly results in a very
large increase in the price of nearly all
sorts of manufactures, which, in almost

countless forms, he needs for the use of
himself and his family. He receives at
the desk of his employer his wages, and
perhaps before he reaches his home is
obliged, in a purchase for family use of
an article which embraces his own labor,
to return in the payment of the increase
in price which the tariff permits the hard-
earned compensation of many days of
toil.

The farmer and the agriculturist, who
manufacture nothing, but who pay the
increased price which the tariff imposes
upon every agricultural implement, upon
all he wears, and upon all he uses and
owns, except the increase of his flocks and
herds and such things as his husbandry
produces from the soil, is invited to aid
in maintaining the present situation; and
he is told that a high duty on imported
wool is necessary for the benefit of those
who have sheep to sheer, in order that the
price of their wool may be increased.
They, of course, are not reminded that
the farmer who has no sheep is by this
scheme obliged, in his purchases of clothing and woolen goods, to pay a tribute to
his fellow-farmer as well as to the manufacturer and merchant; nor is any mention made of the fact that the sheep owners themselves and their households must
wear clothing and use other articles
manufactured from the wool they sell at
tariff prices, and thus as consumers must
return their share of this increased price
to the tradesman.

. . . . .

The question thus imperatively presented for solution should be approached
in a spirit higher than partisanship and
considered in the light of that regard for
patriotic duty, which should characterize the action of those intrusted with the
weal of a confiding people. But the obligation to declared party policy and principle is not wanting to urge prompt and
effective action. Both of the great political parties now represented in the Government have by repeated and authorita-

tive declarations condemned the condition of our laws which permit the collection from the people of unnecessary revenue, and have in the most solemn manner promised its correction; and neither as citizens nor partisans are our countrymen in a mood to condone the deliberate violation of these pledges.

Our progress toward a wise conclusion will not be improved by dwelling upon the theories of protection and free trade. This savors too much of bandying epithets. It is a *condition* which confronts us, not a theory. Relief from this condition may involve a slight reduction of the advantages which we award our home productions, but the entire withdrawal of such advantages should not be contemplated. The question of free trade is absolutely irrelevant, and the persistent claim made in certain quarters that all the efforts to relieve the people from unjust and unnecessary taxation are schemes of so-called free traders is mischievous and far removed from any consideration for the public good.

The simple and plain duty which we owe the people is to reduce taxation to the necessary expenses of an economical operation of the Government and to restore to the business of the country the money which we hold in the Treasury through the perversion of governmental powers. These things can and should be done with safety to all our industries, without danger to the opportunity for remunerative labor which our workingmen need, and with benefit to them and all our people by cheapening their means of subsistence and increasing the measure of their comforts.

. . . . .

COMMENT

The President's plan is a cruel one, and if carried out by Congress will strike a blow at the poorest paid of our laborers. . . . His utterances are as those of a free-trader, his arguments are in the same line, and to put his proposals into execution would destroy American industry, turn our home market over to foreigners, and reduce the compensation of those who labor for a living.

Editorial in the New York *Press*, December 7, 1887.

Mr. Cleveland has done an act of statesmanship in the best sense. Recognizing a great duty, he has performed it with courage, with firmness, and at the right time.

Editorial in the New York *Times*, December 7, 1887.

The reasoning of the President is precisely that of the Bright and Cobden school. Happily the world has discarded the doctrine as unsound. Every strong government of modern times, except England, protects its home labor from foreign competition.

Editorial in the Mobile *Register*, December 11, 1887.

22.

Limitation of Negro Suffrage in the Mississippi Constitution of 1890

The last decade of the nineteenth century witnessed a movement throughout the South to restrict the suffrage. Some of those who sponsored this movement were interested primarily in eliminating the Negro vote; others were concerned mainly with disfranchising poor whites who leaned to Populism and imperiled conservative control. Those whose objective was disfranchisement of Negroes were often influenced by factors other than race. Conservatives and their opponents each resented use of colored votes by the other; and up-country sections disliked the manipulation of low-country Negro votes in the interest of the planter class. There was also a real fear in the 1890's that Republicans would capitalize on their victory in the presidential campaign of 1888 to renew and extend their power in the South. Mississippi set the pattern for legalizing Negro disfranchisement and strengthening white conservatism by writing into the Constitution of 1890 a poll tax, designed to deter poor voters of both races, and by requiring that all voters be able to understand and interpret the Constitution, which permitted denial of suffrage to all Negroes without disfranchising the most ignorant whites. This provision was upheld by the Supreme Court in 1898 in the case of Williams v. Mississippi.

SEC. 241. Every male inhabitant of this State, except idiots, insane persons and Indians not taxed, who is a citizen of the United States, twenty-one years old

Constitution of the State of Mississippi Adopted Nov. 1, 1890 (Jackson, Miss., 1891), pp. 54–62.

and upwards, who has resided in this State two years, and one year in the election district, or in the incorporated city or town in which he offers to vote, and who is duly registered as provided in this article, and who has never been convicted of bribery, burglary, theft, arson, obtaining money or goods under false pretenses, perjury, forgery, embezzlement or bigamy, and who has paid, on or before the first day of February of the year in which he shall offer to vote, all taxes which may have been legally required of him, and which he has had an opportunity of paying according to law for the two preceding years . . . and who shall produce to the officers holding the election satisfactory evidence that he has paid said taxes, is declared to be a qualified elector. . . .

SEC. 242. The Legislature shall provide by law for the registration of all persons entitled to vote at any election. . . .

SEC. 243. A uniform poll tax of two dollars to be used in aid of the common schools . . . is hereby imposed on every male inhabitant of this State between the ages of twenty-one and sixty years. . . . No criminal proceedings shall be allowed to enforce the collection of the poll tax.

SEC. 244. On and after the first day of January, A.D. 1892 . . . every elector . . . shall be able to read any section of the constitution of this State; or he shall be able to understand the same when read to him, or give a reasonable interpretation thereof. . . .

SEC. 264. No person shall be a grand or petit juror unless a qualified elector and able to read and write.

COMMENT

Literacy (in its legal sense) is no test of fitness to vote. . . . If every negro in Mississippi was a graduate of Harvard, and had been selected as class orator . . . he still would not be as well fitted to exercise the right of suffrage as the Anglo-Saxon farm laborer . . . of the South and West.

Editorial in Jackson (Miss.) *Clarion-Ledger*, August 14, 1890.

Every state suffers more or less from corrupt practices at elections, but it was reserved for the State of Mississippi to make its very Constitution the instrument and shield of fraud.

Editorial in Port Gibson (Miss.) *Reveille.* Quoted in Jackson (Miss.) *Clarion-Ledger*, October 9, 1890.

23. *JULY 2, 1890*

Sherman Anti-trust Act

At the end of the nineteenth century, a number of monopolies and trusts emerged in the nation with the power to fix prices without the benefit of competition. After much public pressure, fourteen states in their constitutions forbade trusts and monopolies, while thirteen others prohibited them by statute. State action, however, was not enough. Most of the monopolies operated across state lines and could be controlled only by federal action. In 1888, both major political parties called for government action against monopolies. In December, 1889, Senator John Sherman of Ohio introduced into Congress a bill which prohibited combinations in restraint of trade. After a lengthy debate, Congress somewhat reluctantly passed the Sherman Anti-trust Act. The provisions of the act were purposely phrased in indefinite terms, leaving the courts the task of interpreting them. Meantime, Presidents Harrison, Cleveland, and McKinley demon-

U.S. Statutes at Large, XXVI, 209–10.

strated very little interest in enforcing the statute. Until 1901, the government instituted only eighteen suits under the act. In one case, the United States v. Knight (1895), the Supreme Court interpreted the act so narrowly that it became almost meaningless as applied to trusts and monopolies. By drawing a distinction between commerce and manufacturing, the Court ruled that the statute could be used to regulate concerns engaged in interstate commerce, but that it could not be used to regulate a trust which attempted to monopolize the manufacturing of a commodity.

Be it enacted by the Senate and House of Representatives of the United States of America in Congress assembled,

SEC. 1. Every contract, combination in the form of trust or otherwise, or conspiracy, in restraint of trade or commerce among the several States, or with foreign nations, is hereby declared to be illegal. Every person who shall make any such contract or engage in any such combination or conspiracy, shall be deemed guilty of a misdemeanor, and, on conviction thereof, shall be punished by fine not exceeding five thousand dollars, or by imprisonment not exceeding one year, or by both said punishments, in the discretion of the court.

SEC. 2. Every person who shall monopolize, or attempt to monopolize, or combine or conspire with any other person or persons, to monopolize any part of the trade or commerce among the several States, or with foreign nations, shall be deemed guilty of a misdemeanor, and, on conviction thereof, shall be punished by fine not exceeding five-thousand dollars, or by imprisonment not exceeding one year, or both said punishments, in the discretion of the court.

SEC. 3. Every contract, combination in form of trust or otherwise, or conspiracy, in restraint of trade or commerce in any Territory of the United States or of the District of Columbia, or in restraint of trade or commerce between any such Territory and another, or between any such Territory or Territories and any State or States or the District of Columbia, or with foreign nations, or between the District of Columbia and any State or States or foreign nations, is hereby declared illegal. Every person who will make any such contract or engage in any such combination or conspiracy, shall be deemed guilty of a misdemeanor, and, on conviction thereof, shall be punished by fine not exceeding five thousand dollars, or by imprisonment not exceeding one year, or by both said punishments, in the discretion of the court.

SEC. 4. The several circuit courts of the United States are hereby invested with jurisdiction to prevent and restrain violations of this act; and it shall be the duty of the several district attorneys of the United States, in their respective districts, under the direction of the Attorney-General, to institute proceedings in equity to prevent and restrain such violations. Such proceedings may be by way of petition setting forth the case and praying that such violation shall be enjoined or otherwise prohibited. When the parties complained of shall have been duly notified of such petition the court shall proceed, as soon as may be, to the hearing and determination of the case; and pending such petition and before final decree, the court may at any time make such temporary restraining order or prohibition as shall be deemed just in the premises.

SEC. 5. Whenever it shall appear to the court before which any proceeding under section four of this act may be pending, that the ends of justice require that other parties should be brought before the court, the court may cause them to be summoned, whether they reside in the district in which the court is held or not; and subpoenas to that end may be served in any district by the marshal thereof.

SEC. 6. Any property owned under any contract or by any combination, or pursuant to any conspiracy (and being the subject thereof) mentioned in section one of this act, and being in the course of transportation from one State to another, or to a foreign country, shall be forfeited to the United States, and may be seized and condemned by like proceedings as those provided by law for the forfeiture, seizure, and condemnation of property imported into the United States contrary to law.

SEC. 7. Any person who shall be injured in his business or property by any other person or corporation by reason of anything forbidden or declared to be unlawful by this act, may sue therefore in any circuit court of the United States in the district in which the defendant resides or is found, without respect to the amount in controversy, and shall recover threefold the damages by him sustained, and the costs of suit, including a reasonable attorney's fee.

SEC. 8. That the word "person," or "persons," wherever used in this act shall be deemed to include corporations and associations existing under or authorized by the laws of either the United States, the laws of any of the Territories, the laws of any State, or the laws of any foreign country.

COMMENT

. . . trusts . . . are largely private affairs with which neither President nor any private citizen has any particular right to interfere.

> Republican presidential candidate James G. Blaine in a speech delivered in Portland, Maine, on August 15, 1888. Cincinnati (O.) *Commercial Gazette*, August 19, 1888.

We declare our opposition to all combinations of capital organized in trusts or otherwise to control arbitrarily the conditions of trade among our citizens, and we commend to Congress and the State legislatures, in their respective jurisdictions, such legislation as will prevent the execution of all schemes to oppress the people by undue charges on their supplies, or by unjust rates for the transportation of their products to market.

> Portion of the Republican Party Platform as adopted at the Republican National Convention in Chicago on June 21, 1888. St. Louis (Mo.) *Globe Democrat*, August 20, 1888.

Free competition could be let run only in a community where everyone had learned to say and act "I am the state." We have had an era of material inventions. We now need a renaissance of moral inventions, contrivances to tap the vast currents of moral magnetism flowing uncaught over the face of society. Morals and values rise and fall together. If our combinations have no morals, they can have no values. If the tendency to combination is irresistible, control of it is imperative.

> H. D. Lloyd, one of the keenest social observers of late nineteenth-century America, in "Lords of Industry," *North American Review*, CXXXVIII (June, 1884), 552.

24. JANUARY, 1891

Henry Cabot Lodge on Immigration

Following Congress' limitation of Chinese immigration, organized nativism began to spread throughout the nation. Its origins lay primarily in the social tensions of the period. Economic depressions and industrial strife created an awareness of the hardening of class lines and of the inequality which had resulted from

HENRY CABOT LODGE, "The Restriction of Immigration," *The North American Review*, CLII (January, 1891), 27–36.

the emergence of an urban, industrial society. As millions of immigrants arrived on the shores of America during the late nineteenth and early twentieth centuries, many Americans feared that the new population would lower wages and corrupt the "American way of life." Americans were losing faith in the process of assimilation. Shortly after the Haymarket bomb affair of 1886, a number of secret anti-Catholic societies came into exist-

ence, the largest being the American Protective Association.

Anti-foreignism arose not only from popular antipathies but also from the theorizing of a number of race-conscious New Englanders. Among many old New England families, there was disillusionment and skepticism as their grip on the nation's political and economic institutions loosened. The new immigration was beginning to replace the old stock. To combat this movement, a group of New England intellectuals established the Immigration Restriction League in 1894. Below, Henry Cabot Lodge, a member of the House of Representatives from Massachusetts, reflects alarm over the increasing number of eastern and southern European immigrants who were arriving on American shores. It was not until 1921, however, that Congress passed legislation which effectively limited European immigration.

The immigration into the United States from 1874 to 1889, inclusive,—a period of sixteen years,—has amounted to 6,418,633 persons, without counting since 1884 the overland immigration from Canada or Mexico. To put it in another form, the immigration into the United States during the last sixteen years is equal to one-tenth of the entire population of the country at the present time, and has furnished probably every four years enough voters to decide a Presidential election, if rightly distributed. During those sixteen years immigration has fluctuated with the business prosperity of the country, the highest point being reached in 1881 and 1882, 720,645 persons arriving in the former year and 730,349 in the latter, while the average annual immigration has been 401,164. If we divide these sixteen years into two periods of eight years each, one of the two heaviest years coming in the first and one in the second half, we find that for the eight years from 1874 to 1881, inclusive, the average annual rate of immigration was 307,185, and for the eight years from 1882 to 1889, inclusive, it was 482,643—a gain of 57.1 per cent. During the last eight years the exclusion of the Chinese since 1882 has caused the immigration from Asia to decline from over thirty thousand to a few hundreds annually, and in addition to this real loss no attempt has been made since 1883 to compute the very heavy overland immigration from Canada, which, of course, makes a still further apparent decrease. Yet, despite these important deductions, there has been the large gain of 175,458 persons in the average annual immigration of the last eight years as compared with the eight years next preceding. As it is thus apparent that immigration is increasing in quantity, the next point is to determine its quality.

In the consular reports on "Emigration and Immigration," published by the State Department in 1887, when Mr. Bayard was Secretary, a table is given which classifies the immigration into the United States from 1873 to 1886, inclusive, as follows:

Professional	31,803
Skilled	587,349
Miscellaneous	2,052,294
Occupation not stated	128,782
Without occupation	2,596,188

Taking the table as it stands, and throwing out those immigrants "with occupations not stated," it appears that of all the vast immigration during those fourteen years 48.1 per cent., or nearly one-half, are persons avowedly without occupation or training, or, in other words, unskilled labor of the lowest kind, while professional and skilled labor amounts to only 11.49 per cent. of the whole. "Miscellaneous," which is neither skilled nor professional labor, amounts to 38 per cent. It may be assumed that the same proportions hold good for the three years from 1886 to 1889, and it must be noted also that the detailed tables indicate that the number of persons without occupations increases in a slightly larger ratio than the rate of increase of the total immigration.

These figures give an idea of the general character of the foreign immigration into the United States during a long period of fourteen years. It is more important, however, to determine whether the immigration of this general character improves or deteriorates as it increases. This can be ascertained best by examining the rate of increase in the immigration from the different countries from which it chiefly comes during the two periods of eight years each from 1874 to 1881 and from 1882 to 1889, respectively:

	Annual Average		Percentage of Difference
	1874–81	1882–89	
France	6,064	4,885	19.4
Norway	10,767	16,862	59.5
Great Britain and Ireland	86,649	145,461	67.8
Germany	76,416	135,052	76.7
Switzerland	4,159	7,831	88.3
Netherlands	2,535	4,847	91.2
Sweden	18,224	37,730	107.
Denmark	4,042	8,663	114.3
Austria	9,272	21,926	136.5
Belgium	847	2,023	138.8
Poland	1,691	4,498	166.
Italy	7,893	30,474	286.
Russia	5,430	21,567	297.
Hungary	2,273	13,101	476.4

These percentages of increase are interesting and deeply significant. The nations of Europe which chiefly contributed to . . . the upbuilding of the original thirteen colonies were the English, the Scotch-Irish, so called, the Dutch, the Germans, and the Huguenot French. With the exception of the last they were practically all people of the same stock. During this century and until very recent years these same nations, with the addition of Ireland and the Scandinavian countries, have continued to furnish the chief component parts of the immigration which has helped to populate so rapidly the territory of the United States. Among all these people, with few exceptions, community of race or language, or both, has facilitated the work of assimilation. In the last ten years, however, as appears from the figures just given, new and wholly different elements have been introduced into our immigration, and—what is more important still—the rate of immigration of these new elements has risen with much greater rapidity than that of those which previously had furnished the bulk of the population of the country. The mass of immigration, absolutely speaking, continues, of course, to come from the United Kingdom and from Germany, but relatively the immigration from these two sources is declining rapidly in comparison with the immigration from Italy and from the Slavic countries of Russia, Poland, Hungary, and Bohemia, the last of which appears under the head of Austria. Of the generally good character of the immigration from the United Kingdom, Germany, and the Scandinavian countries it is hardly necessary to speak; but I will quote a single sentence from the State Department report already referred to, in regard to the immigration from the United Kingdom and Germany:

The diagrams show the remarkable predominance of the United Kingdom and

Germany in supplying the United States with skilled labor, and also the fact that the Germans represent those industries that depend upon hand labor for the requirements of everyday life, while the English supply the mechanical element. While Germany sends blacksmiths, butchers carpenters, coopers, saddlers, shoemakers, and tailors, the United Kingdom supplies miners, engineers, iron- and steel-workers, mechanics and artisans, weavers and spinners. This distinction is clearly marked and is certainly important.

Now as to the immigration from the other countries, which has been increasing so much faster than that to which we have been accustomed, and which we know from experience to be in the main valuable. Consul-General Jüssen says in his report (1886) in regard to the Austrian immigration:

The young men who want to escape military service, the ultra-socialist, the anarchist, the men who have lost all social and business footing here, the bankrupt, embezzler, and swindler, stop not to obtain permission of the government, and naturally the authorities have no sort of record here either as to the number or the place of destination of this class of emigrants. . . The government would, as a matter of course, prohibit, if it could do so, the emigration of all young men subject to military duty, but it is quite natural that it feels no regret to get rid of the ultra-socialists and anarchists, and that it is quite willing the bankrupt and swindler should depart for foreign countries and that the paupers should find support away from home. . . .

In regard to Hungarian emigration, Mr. Sterne, consul at Budapest, speaks (1886) as follows:

I am of the opinion that with the present condition of the labor market in the United States there is no room there at present for this class of people. I even believe that under more favorable conditions in the United States these Slovacks are not a desirable acquisition for us to make, since they appear to have so many items in common with the Chinese. Like these, they are extremely frugal, the love of whiskey of the former being balanced by the opium habit of the latter. Their ambition lacks both in quality and quantity. Thus they will work similarly cheap as the Chinese, and will interfere with a civilized laborer's earning a "white" laborer's wages.

The emigration from Italy comes largely from the southern provinces—from Naples and Sicily; a smaller proportion being drawn from the finer population of northern Italy. In regard to this Italian emigration, Mr. Alden, consul-general at Rome, says (1886):

As to the habits and morals of the emigrants to the United States from the northern and central portions of Italy, both men and women are sober and industrious, and as a rule trustworthy and moral. They are generally strong, powerful workers, and capable of enduring great fatigue. A less favorable view may be taken of the emigrants from the southern districts and Sicily. These are the most illiterate parts of Italy, and in these districts brigandage was for many years extremely prevalent.

In regard to the emigration from Russia, Mr. Young, the consul-general, says (1886):

The government of Russia does not encourage emigration. On the contrary, it prohibits all Russian subjects from leaving the empire of Russia except Poles and Jews. . . . The Mennonites have emigrated perhaps more extensively than any other class of Russian subjects. . . . The lowest classes generally form the greater part of emigration.

Thus it is proved, first, that immigration to this country is increasing, and, second, that it is making its greatest relative increase from races most alien to the body of the American people and from the lowest and most illiterate classes among those races. In other words, it is apparent that, while our immigration is increasing, it is showing at the same time a marked tendency to deteriorate in character.

It has been the policy of the United

States until very recent years to encourage immigration in all possible ways, which was, under the circumstances, a wise and abvious course to pursue. The natural growth of the people established in the thirteen colonies was not sufficient to occupy or develop the vast territory and valuable resources of the Union. We therefore opened our arms to the people of every land and invited them to come in, and when all the region beyond the Alleghanies, or even beyond the Mississippi, was still a wilderness, the general wisdom of this policy could not be gainsaid. To the practical advantages to be gained from the rapid filling-up of the country we also joined the sentimental and generous reason that this free country was to be a haven of refuge for the unfortunate of every land.

This liberality toward immigration, combined with the normal growth of the population, in the course of the present century rapidly filled the country, and the conditions under which, at the outset we had opened our doors and asked every one to come in changed radically. The first sign or an awakening to this altered state of things was in the movement against the Chinese. When that great reservoir of cheap labor was opened and when its streams began to pour into the United States, the American people, first on the western coast and then elsewhere, suddenly were roused to the fact that they were threatened with a flood of low-class labor which would absolutely destroy good rates of wages among American workingmen by a competition which could not be met, and which at the same time threatened to lower the quality of American citizenship. The result was the Chinese-Exclusion Act, much contested in its inception, but the wisdom of which everybody now admits. The next awakening came upon the discovery that employers of labor were engaged in making contracts with large bodies of working people in other countries, and importing them into the United States to work for

a remuneration far below that which American workmen were accustomed to receive. This resulted in the passage of the Alien Contract-Labor Law, intended to stop the importation of this low-priced labor. No one doubts to-day that the general principle of that law is sound, although its details are defective and its enforcement so imperfect that it has little practical effect.

Such have been the actual departures thus far from the former policy of the United States in regard to immigration. That they were needed is certain. That they are insufficient appears to be equally so. . . .

. . . We have now a large population, the natural increase of which is quite sufficient to take up our unoccupied lands and develop our resources with due rapidity. In many parts of the country the struggle for existence in large cities has become as fierce as in the old world. Our labor market, if we may judge from the statistics of the unemployed, is overstocked in many places, and that means a tendency toward a decline in wages. This tendency is perilous both socially and politically. In a country where every man has a vote, and where the government is of and by the people, it is as essential as it is right everywhere that the rate of wages should be high and the average standard of living good. If it comes to be otherwise, our whole system is in serious danger.

That this is not a fanciful anxiety is only too readily proved. Any one who is desirous of knowing in practical detail the degrading effect of this constant importation of the lowest forms of labor can find a vivid picture of its results in the very interesting book just published by Mr. Riis; entitled "How the Other Half Lives." The story which he tells of the condition of a large mass of the laboring population in the city of New York is enough to alarm every thinking man; and this dreadful condition of things is intensified every day by the steady inflow of immigration, which is constantly pulling down the wages of the working people of New York and affecting in a similar way the entire labor market of the United States.

In a word, the continued introduction into the labor market of four hundred thousand persons annually, half of whom have no occupation and most of whom represent the rudest form of labor, has a very great effect in reducing the rates of wages and disturbing the labor market. This, of course, is too obvious to need comment, and this tendency to constantly lower wages by the competition of an increasing and deteriorating immigration is a danger to the people of the United States the gravity of which can hardly be overestimated. Moreover, the shifting of the sources of the immigration is unfavorable, and is bringing to the country people whom it is very difficult to assimilate and who do not promise well for the standard of civilization in the United States—a matter as serious as the effect on the labor market.

The question, therefore, arises,—and there is no more important question before the American people,—What shall be done to protect our labor against this undue competition, and to guard our citizenship against an infusion which seems to threaten deterioration? We have the power, of course, to prohibit all immigration, or to limit the number of persons to be admitted to the country annually, or —which would have the same effect—to impose upon immigrants a heavy capitation tax. Such rough and stringent measures are certainly neither necessary nor desirable if we can overcome the difficulties and dangers of the situation by more moderate legislation. These methods, moreover, are indiscriminate; and what is to be desired, if possible, is restriction which shall at the same time discriminate. We demand now that immigrants shall not be paupers or diseased or criminals, but these and all other existing requirements are vague, and the methods provided for their enforcement are still more indefinite and are perfectly ineffective. Any law, to be of use, must require, in the first place, that immigrants shall bring from their native country, from the United States consul or other diplomatic representative, an effective certificate that they are not obnoxious to any of the existing laws of the United States. We ought, in addition, to make our test still more definite by requiring a medical certificate in order to exclude unsound and diseased persons. . . .

We ought also to insist that the consular certificate be given only after careful inquiry and due proof, and we must make a further definite test which will discriminate against illiteracy if we desire any intelligent restriction or sifting of the total mass of immigration. It is a truism to say that one of the greatest dangers to our free government is ignorance. Every one knows this to be the case, and that the danger can be overcome only by constant effort and vigilance. We spend millions annually in educating our children that they may be fit to be citizens and rulers of the republic. We are ready to educate also the children who come to us from other countries; but it is not right to ask us to take annually a large body of persons who are totally illiterate and who are for the most part beyond the age at which education can be imparted. We have the right to exclude illiterate persons from our immigration, and this test, combined with the others of a more general character, would in all probability shut out a large part of the undesirable portion of the present immigration. It would reduce in a discriminating manner the total number of immigrants, and would thereby greatly benefit the labor market and help to maintain the rate of American wages. At the same time it would sift the immigrants who come to this country and would shut out in a very large measure those elements which tend to lower the quality of

American citizenship, and which now in many cases gather in dangerous masses in the slums of our great cities.

The measure proposed would benefit every honest immigrant who really desired to come to the United States and become an American citizen, and would stop none. It would exclude many, if not all, of those persons whose presence no one desires, and whose exclusion is demanded by our duty to our own citizens and to American institutions. Above all, it would be a protection and a help to our workingmen, who are more directly interested in this great question than any one else can possibly be.

COMMENT

There is . . . no specific "immigration problem." There is a general labor problem, which comprises many special problems, such as organization of labor, reduction of hours of labor, child labor, unemployment, prevention of work-accidents, etc. None of these problems being affected by immigration, their solution can not be advanced by restriction or even by complete prohibition of immigration.

> Russian born statistician, lawyer, author, and lecturer, Issac A. Hourwich in his *Immigration and Labor*, 2d ed. (New York: Viking Press, Inc., 1922), p. 35.

. . . the immigration of the present time . . . is tending to bring to us no longer the more alert and enterprising members of our respective communities, but rather the unlucky, the thriftless, the worthless. . . .

> Francis A. Walker, president of Massachusetts Institute of Technology, in "Immigration and Degradation," *Forum*, xi (August, 1891), 643–44.

Freedom of migration from one country to another appears to be one of the elements in nineteenth-century liberalism that is fated to disappear. The responsibility of the state for the welfare of its individual members is progressively increasing. The democracy of today . . . cannot permit . . . social ills to be aggravated by excessive immigration.

> Editorial in the *New Republic*, vi (April 8, 1916), 254.

25. *JULY, 1892*

Populist Party Platform

In 1890, the political problems of the western farmer were closely related to falling agricultural prices and to monopolistic agreements among warehouses, railroads, and the owners of grain ele-

KIRK H. PORTER, ed., *National Party Platforms* (New York: The Macmillan Company, 1924), pp. 166–69.

vators. The scene was set for political revolt, and with unusual promptness the Populist party emerged. Most of the original party members were recruited from the Farmers' Alliances, Greenbackers, Knights of Labor, and free silverites. Finance, land, transportation—these were the three fields which the Populist believed he must control if he were to survive. His weapon was the ballot, and he fought for free silver, stay laws, and government ownership of all monopolies which affected the public interest. The history of the Populist party should be viewed as the history of the discontented struggling to save themselves by political means from the penalties imposed because of their inability to adjust to their economic conditions.

Holding their first national convention at Omaha, Nebraska in July, 1892, the Populists wrote a platform (printed below) which reflected the agrarian grievances of the times and foreshadowed much federal legislation enacted from the Administration of Theodore Roosevelt to that of his cousin, Franklin D. Roosevelt. Except for free silver and nationalization of the nation's communications system, the Populist programs have been accepted by the nation. The function of the Populist party, like most third parties, was to bring forth new ideas and to disseminate them throughout the country until one of the two major parties adopted most of their program.

Assembled upon the 116th anniversary of the Declaration of Independence, the People's Party of America, in their first national convention, invoking upon their action the blessing of Almighty God, put forth in the name and on behalf of the people of this country, the following preamble and declaration of principles:

PREAMBLE

The conditions which surround us best justify our co-operation; we meet in the midst of a nation brought to the verge of moral, political, and material ruin. Corruption dominates the ballot-box, the Legislatures, the Congress, and touches even the ermine of the bench. The people are demoralized; most of the States have been compelled to isolate the voters at the polling places to prevent universal intimidation and bribery. The newspapers are largely subsidized or muzzled, public opinion silenced, business prostrated, homes covered with mortgages, labor impoverished, and the land concentrating in the hands of capitalists. The urban workmen are denied the right to organize for self-protection, imported pauperized labor beats down their wages, a hireling standing army, unrecognized by our laws, is established to shoot them down, and they are rapidly degenerating into European conditions. The fruits of the toil of millions are boldly stolen to build up colossal fortunes for a few, unprecedented in the history of mankind; and the possessors of these, in turn, despise the Republic and endanger liberty. From the same prolific womb of governmental injustice we breed the two great classes—tramps and millionaires.

The national power to create money is appropriated to enrich bond-holders; a vast public debt payable in legal-tender currency has been funded into gold-bearing bonds, thereby adding millions to the burdens of the people.

Silver, which has been accepted as coin since the dawn of history, has been demonetized to add to the purchasing power of gold by decreasing the value of all forms of property as well as human labor, and the supply of currency is purposely abridged to fatten usurers, bankrupt enterprise, and enslave industry. A vast conspiracy against mankind has been organized on two continents, and it is rapidly taking possession of the world. If not met and overthrown at once it forebodes terrible social convulsions, the destruction of civilization, or the establishment of an absolute despotism.

We have witnessed for more than a quarter of a century the struggles of the two great political parties for power and plunder, while grievous wrongs have been inflicted upon the suffering people. We charge that the controlling influences dominating both these parties have permitted the existing dreadful conditions to develop without serious effort to prevent or restrain them. Neither do they now promise us any substantial reform. They have agreed together to ignore, in the coming campaign, every issue but one. They propose to drown the outcries of a plundered people with the uproar of a sham battle over the tariff, so that capitalists, corporations, national banks, rings, trusts, watered stock, the demonetization of silver and the oppressions of the usurers may all be lost sight of. They propose to sacrifice our homes, lives, and children on the altar of mammon; to destroy the multitude in order to secure corruption funds from the millionaires.

Assembled on the anniversary of the birthday of the nation, and filled with the spirit of the grand general and chief who established our independence, we seek to restore the government of the Republic to the hands of the "plain people," with which class it originated. We assert our purposes to be identical with the purposes of the National Constitution; to form a more perfect union and establish justice, insure domestic tranquillity, provide for the common defence, promote the general welfare, and secure the blessings of liberty for ourselves and our posterity.

We declare that this Republic can only endure as a free government while built upon the love of the people for each other and for the nation; that it cannot be pinned together by bayonets; that the Civil War is over, and that every passion and resentment which grew out of it must die with it, and that we must be in fact, as we are in name, one united brotherhood of free men.

Our country finds itself confronted by conditions for which there is no precedent in the history of the world; our annual agricultral productions amount to billions of dollars in value, which must, within a few weeks or months, be exchanged for billions of dollars' worth of commodities consumed in their production; the existing currency supply is wholly inadequate to make this exchange; the results are falling prices, the formation of combines and rings, the impoverishment of the producing class. We pledge ourselves that if given power we will labor to correct these evils by wise and reasonable legislation, in accordance with the terms of our platform.

We believe that the power of government—in other words, of the people—should be expanded (as in the case of the postal service) as rapidly and as far as the good sense of an intelligent people and the teachings of experience shall justify, to the end that oppression, injustice, and poverty shall eventually cease in the land.

While our sympathies as a party of reform are naturally upon the side of every proposition which will tend to make men intelligent, virtuous, and temperate, we nevertheless regard these questions, important as they are, as secondary to the great issues now pressing for solution, and upon which not only our individual prosperity but the very existence of free institutions depend; and we ask all men to first help us to determine whether we are to have a republic to administer before we differ as to the conditions upon which it is to be administered, believing that the forces of reform this day organized will never cease to move forward until every wrong is righted and equal rights and equal privileges securely established for all the men and women of this country.

PLATFORM

We declare, therefore—

First—That the union of the labor forces of the United States this day consummated shall be permanent and perpetual; may its spirit enter into all hearts for the salvation of the Republic and the uplifting of mankind.

Second. Wealth belongs to him who creates it, and every dollar taken from industry without an equivalent is robbery. "If any will not work, neither shall he eat." The interests of rural and civil labor are the same; their enemies are identical.

Third. We believe that the time has come when the railroad corporations will either own the people or the people must own the railroads; and should the government enter upon the work of owning and managing all railroads, we should favor an amendment to the constitution by which all persons engaged in the government service shall be placed under a civil-service regulation of the most rigid character, so as to prevent the increase of the power of the national administration by the use of such additional government employees.

FINANCE. We demand a national currency, safe, sound, and flexible issued by the general government only, a full legal tender for all debts, public and private, and that without the use of banking corporations; a just, equitable and efficient means of distribution direct to the people, at a tax not to exceed 2 per cent, per annum, to be provided as set forth in the sub-treasury plan of the Farmer's Alliance, or a better system; also by payments in discharge of its obligations for public improvements.

1. We demand free and unlimited coinage of silver and gold at the present legal ratio of 16 to 1.

2. We demand that the amount of circulating medium be speedily increased to not less than $50 per capita.

3. We demand a graduated income tax.

4. We believe that the money of the country should be kept as much as possible in the hands of the people, and hence we demand that all State and national revenues shall be limited to the necessary expenses of the government, economically and honestly administered.

5. We demand that postal savings banks be established by the government for the safe deposit of the earnings of the people and to facilitate exchange.

TRANSPORTATION. Transportation being a means of exchange and a public necessity, the government should own and operate the railroads in the interest of the people. The telegraph and telephone, like the post-office system, being a necessity for the transmission of news, should be owned and operated by the government in the interest of the people.

LAND. The land, including all the natural sources of wealth, is the heritage of the people, and should not be monopolized for speculative purposes, and alien ownership of land should be prohibited. All land now held by railroads and other corporations in excess of their actual needs, and all lands now owned by aliens should be reclaimed by the government and held for actual settlers only.

EXPRESSION OF SENTIMENTS

Your Committee on Platform and Resolutions beg leave unanimously to report the following:

Whereas, Other questions have been presented for our consideration, we hereby submit the following, not as a part of the Platform of the People's Party, but as resolutions expressive of the sentiment of this Convention.

1. *Resolved,* That we demand a free ballot and a fair count in all elections, and pledge ourselves to secure it to every legal voter without Federal intervention, through the adoption by the States of the unperverted Australian or secret ballot system.

2. *Resolved,* That the revenue derived from a graduated income tax should be applied to the reduction of the burden of taxation now levied upon the domestic industries of this country.

3. *Resolved,* That we pledge our support to fair and liberal pensions to ex-Union soldiers and sailors.

4. *Resolved,* That we condemn the fallacy of protecting American labor under the present system, which opens our ports to the pauper and criminal

classes of the world and crowds out our wage-earners; and we denounce the present ineffective laws against contract labor, and demand the further restriction of undesirable emigration.

5. *Resolved*, That we cordially sympathize with the efforts of organized workingmen to shorten the hours of labor, and demand a rigid enforcement of the existing eight-hour law on Government work, and ask that a penalty clause be added to the said law.

6. *Resolved*, That we regard the maintenance of a large standing army of mercenaries, known as the Pinkerton system, as a menace to our liberties, and we demand its abolition; and we condemn the recent invasion of the Territory of Wyoming by the hired assassins of plutocracy, assisted by Federal officers.

7. *Resolved*, That we commend to the favorable consideration of the people and the reform press the legislative system known as the initiative and referendum.

8. *Resolved*, That we favor a constitutional provision limiting the office of President and Vice-President to one term, and providing for the election of Senators of the United States by a direct vote of the people.

9. *Resolved*, That we oppose any subsidy or national aid to any private corporation for any purpose.

10. *Resolved*, That this convention sympathizes with the Knights of Labor and their righteous contest with the tyrannical combine of clothing manufacturers of Rochester, and declare it to be a duty of all who hate tyranny and oppression to refuse to purchase the goods made by the said manufacturers, or to patronize any merchants who sell such goods.

COMMENT

The rank and file of People's Party supporters . . . had to possess both moral and political courage, as well as physical courage, to withstand the fierce onslaught of the opposition. Many and varied were the methods of political repression, sometimes persecution, engaged in by the opposition. Credit was denied, farm supplies withheld, and mortgages were foreclosed. . . . Multitudinous were the continuous and repeated petty annoyances and flings of the Democratic Party influences. Whoever made the assertion that it was preferable to be kicked to death by an elephant than stung to death by mosquitos could have fully appreciated how undesirable it was to be the subject of the smallness of Democratic Party attack in the South to which Populists were often subjected.

> Joseph Columbus Manning, historian, in *The Fadeout of Populism* (New York: T. A. Hebbons, 1928), p. 34.

Wall Street owns the country. It is no longer a government of the people, by the people and for the people, but a government of Wall Street, by Wall Street and for Wall Street. The great common people of this country are slaves, and monopoly is the master. The West and South are bound and prostrate before the manufacturing East.

> Mary Ellen Lease, Populist leader from Kansas. Cited in John D. Hicks, *The Populist Revolt* (Minneapolis: University of Minnesota Press, 1931), p. 160.

26.

Frederick Jackson Turner
on the Frontier

Prior to 1890, most American historians stressed the continuity between European and American social institutions. Having grown up in the rapid changing order of the Midwest, Frederick Jackson Turner, a historian at the University of Wisconsin, reacted against such an eastern interpretation of American history. At the annual meeting of the American Historical Association in 1893, Turner focused his attention on forces which most historians had neglected by arguing that the frontier had been the most important factor in determining the development of American civilization. For the rest of his career, Turner continued to study this theme and to publish essays which further demonstrated his thesis.

To understand Turner and the impact that he had on his society, one must remember that the following essay appeared at the time the Populists and William Jennings Bryan were urging the nation to recognize the interests of the West and to reaffirm its faith in the ideal of equality of opportunity. Turner was disturbed because the "days of free land" had passed. With the frontier gone, he questioned the extent to which the nation could afford to continue the ruthless competition which the frontier had bred. Was not class conflict rapidly replacing geographical sectionalism? If the frontier had been responsible for America's democratic institutions and if the frontier was

From Frederick Jackson Turner, *The Frontier in American History*, copyright © 1920, 1947. Holt, Rinehart and Winston, Inc. By permission.

now closed, did it not stand to reason that some readjustment was necessary if democracy was to survive? It was these implications of Turner's essay which made a tremendous impact on many reformers who were urging the federal government to play a more active role in the nation's affairs.

In a recent bulletin of the Superintendent of the Census for 1890 appear these significant words: "Up to and including 1880 the country had a frontier of settlement, but at present the unsettled area has been so broken into by isolated bodies of settlement that there can hardly be said to be a frontier line. In the discussion of its extent, its westward movement, etc., it can not, therefore any longer have a place in the census reports." This brief official statement marks the closing of a great historic movement. Up to our own day American history has been in a large degree the history of the colonization of the Great West. The existence of an area of free land, its continuous recession, and the advance of American settlement westward, explain American development.

Behind institutions, behind constitutional forms and modifications, lie the vital forces that call these organs into life and shape them to meet changing conditions. The peculiarity of American institutions is, the fact that they have been compelled to adopt themselves to the changes of an expanding people—to the changes involved in crossing a continent, in winning a wilderness, and in developing at each area of this progress out of the primitive economic and political conditions of the frontier into the complexity of city life. . . . Limiting our attention to the Atlantic coast, we have the familiar phenomenon of the evolution of institutions in a limited area, such as the rise of representative government; the differentiation of simple colonial governments into complex organs; the progress from primitive industrial society, without division of labor, up to manufacturing civilization. But we have in addition to this a recurrence of the process of evolution in each western area reached in the process of expansion. Thus American development has exhibited not merely advance along a single line, but a return to primitive conditions on a continually advancing frontier line, and a new development for that area. American social development has been continually beginning over again on the frontier. This perennial rebirth, this fluidity of American life, this expansion westward with its new opportunities, its continuous touch with the simplicity of primitive society, furnish the forces dominating American character. The true point of view in the history of this nation is not the Atlantic coast, it is the Great West. Even the slavery struggle . . . occupies its important place in American history because of its relation to westward expansion.

In this advance, the frontier is the outer edge of the wave—the meeting point between savagery and civilization. Much has been written about the frontier from the point of view of border warfare and the chase, but as a field for the serious study of the economist and the historian it has been neglected.

·   ·   ·   ·   ·

In the settlement of America we have to observe how European life entered the continent, and how America modified and developed that life and reacted on Europe. Our early history is the study of European germs developing in an Ameri-

can environment. Too exclusive attention has been paid by institutional students to the Germanic origins, too little to the American factors. The frontier is the line of most rapid and effective Americanization. The wilderness masters the colonist. . . . He must accept the conditions which it furnishes, or perish, and so he fits himself into the Indian clearings and follows the Indian trails. Little by little he transforms the wilderness, but the outcome is not the old Europe, not simply the development of Germanic germs. . . . The fact is, that here is a new product that is American. At first, the frontier was the Atlantic coast. It was the frontier of Europe in a very real sense. Moving westward, the frontier became more and more American. As successive terminal moraines result from successive glaciations, so each frontier leaves its traces behind it, and when it becomes a settled area the region still partakes of the frontier characteristics. Thus the advance of the frontier has meant a steady movement away from the influence of Europe, a steady growth of independence on American lines. And to study this advance, the men who grew up under these conditions, and the political, economic, and social results of it, is to study the really American part of our history.

·   ·   ·   ·   ·

In these successive frontiers we find natural boundary lines which have served to mark and to affect the characteristics of the frontiers, namely: the "fall line;" the Alleghany Mountains; the Mississippi; the Missouri where its direction approximates north and south; the line of the arid lands, approximately the ninety-ninth meridian; and the Rocky Mountains. The fall line marked the frontier of the seventeenth century; the Alleghanies that of the eighteenth; the Mississippi that of the first quarter of the nineteenth; the Missouri that of the middle of this century (omitting the California movement); and the belt of the

Rocky Mountains and the arid tract, the present frontier. Each was won by a series of Indian wars.

At the Atlantic frontier one can study the germs of processes repeated at each successive frontier. We have the complex European life sharply precipitated by the wilderness into the simplicity of primitive conditions. The first frontier had to meet its Indian question, its question of the disposition of the public domain, of the means of intercourse with older settlements, of the extension of political organization, of religious and educational activity. And the settlement of these and similar questions for one frontier served as a guide for the next. The American student needs not to go to the "prim little townships of Sleswick" for illustrations of the law of continuity and development. For example, he may study the origin of our land policies in the colonial land policy; he may see how the system grew by adapting the statutes to the customs of the successive frontiers. He may see how the mining experience in the lead regions of Wisconsin, Illinois, and Iowa was applied to the mining laws of the Sierras, and how our Indian policy has been a series of experimentations on successive frontiers. Each tier of new States has found in the older ones material for its constitutions. Each frontier has made similar contributions to American character, ...

But with all these similarities there are essential differences, due to the place element and the time element. . . . It would be a work worth the historian's labors to mark these various frontiers and in detail compare one with another. Not only would there result a more adequate conception of American development and characteristics, but invaluable additions would be made to the history of society.

Loria, the Italian economist, has urged the study of colonial life as an aid in understanding the stages of European development, affirming that colonial settlement is for economic science what the mountain is for geology, bringing to light primitive stratifications. "America," he says, "has the key to the historical enigma which Europe has sought for centuries in vain, and the land which has no history reveals luminously the course of universal history." There is much truth in this. The United States lies like a huge page in the history of society. Line by line as we read this continental page from West to East we find the record of social evolution. It begins with the Indian and the hunter; it goes on to tell of the disintegration of savagery by the entrance of the trader, the pathfinder of civilization; we read the annals of the pastoral stage in ranch life; the exploitation of the soil by the raising of unrotated crops of corn and wheat in sparsely settled farming communities; the intensive culture of the denser farm settlement; and finally the manufacturing organization with city and factory system. This page is familiar to the student of census statistics, but how little of it has been used by our historians. Particularly in eastern States this page is a palimpsest. What is now a manufacturing State was in an earlier decade an area of intensive farming. Earlier yet it had been a wheat area, and still earlier the "range" had attracted the cattleherder. Thus Wisconsin, now developing manufacture, is a State with varied agricultural interests. But earlier it was given over to almost exclusive grain-raising, like North Dakota at the present time.

. . . . .

. . . we may next inquire what were the influences on the East and on the Old World. . . . The frontier promoted the formation of a composite nationality for the American people. The coast was preponderantly English, but the later tides of continental immigration flowed across to the free lands. This was the case from the early colonial days. The Scotch Irish and the Palatine Germans, or "Pennsylvania Dutch," furnished the dom-

inant element in the stock of the colonial
frontier. With these peoples were also the
freed indented servants, or redemption-
ers, who at the expiration of their time
of service passed to the frontier.

. . . Very generally these redemp-
tioners were of non-English stock. In the
crucible of the frontier the immigrants
were Americanized, liberated, and fused
into a mixed race, English in neither nationality nor characteristics. The process
has gone on from the early days to our
own. Burke and other writers in the
middle of the eighteenth century believed
that Pennsylvania was "threatened with
the danger of being wholly foreign in
language, manners, and perhaps even in-
clinations." The German and Scotch-Irish
elements in the frontier of the South were
only less great. In the middle of the present century the German element in Wisconsin was already so considerable that
leading publicists looked to the creation
of a German state out of the commonwealth by concentrating their colonization. Such examples teach us to beware
of misinterpreting the fact that there is
a common English speech in America
into a belief that the stock is also English.

In another way the advance of the
frontier decreased our dependence on
England. The coast, particularly of the
South, lacked diversified industries, and
was dependent on England for the bulk
of its supplies. In the South there was even
a dependence on the Northern colonies
for articles of food. . . . Before long the
frontier created a demand for merchants.
As it retreated from the coast it became
less and less possible for England to bring
her supplies directly to the consumer's
wharfs, and carry away staple crops, and
staple crops began to give way to diversified agriculture for a time. The effect of
this phase of the frontier action upon the
northern section is perceived when we
realize how the advance of the frontier
aroused seaboard cities like Boston, New
York, and Baltimore, to engage in rivalry

for what Washington called "the extensive and valuable trade of a rising empire."

The legislation which most developed
the powers of the national government,
and played the largest part in its activity,
was conditioned on the frontier. Writers
have discussed the subjects of tariff, land,
and internal improvement, as subsidiary
to the slavery question. . . .

This is a wrong perspective. The pioneer needed the goods of the coast, and
so the grand series of internal improvement and railroad legislation began, with
potent nationalizing effects. Over internal
improvements occurred great debates, in
which grave constitutional questions
were discussed. Sectional groupings appear in the votes, profoundly significant
for the historian. Loose construction increased as the nation marched westward.
But the West was not content with bringing the farm to the factory. Under the
lead of Clay—"Harry of the West"—
protective tariffs were passed, with the
cry of bringing the factory to the farm.
The disposition of the public lands was a
third important subject of national legislation influenced by the frontier.

.   .   .   .   .

It is safe to say that the legislation
with regard to land, tariff, and internal
improvements—the American system of
the nationalizing Whig party—was conditioned on frontier ideas and needs. But
it was not merely in legislative action that
the frontier worked against the sectionalism of the coast. The economic and social
characteristics of the frontier worked
against sectionalism. The men of the
frontier had closer resemblances to the
Middle region than to either of the other
sections. Pennsylvania had been the seed-
plot of frontier emigration, and, although
she passed on her settlers along the Great
Valley into the west of Virginia and the
Carolinas, yet the industrial society of
these Southern frontiersmen was always

more like that of the Middle region than like that of the tide-water portion of the South, which later came to spread its industrial type throughout the South.

. . . . .

But the most important effect of the frontier has been in the promotion of democracy here and in Europe. As has been indicated, the frontier is productive of individualism. Complex society is precipitated by the wilderness into a kind of primitive organization based on the family. The tendency is anti-social. It produces antipathy to control, and particularly to any direct control. The tax-gatherer is viewed as a representative of oppression . . . frontier conditions prevalent in the colonies are important factors in the explanation of the American Revolution, where individual liberty was sometimes confused with absense of all effective government. The same conditions aid in explaining the difficulty of instituting a strong government in the period of the confederacy. The frontier individualism has from the beginning promoted democracy.

The frontier States that came into the Union in the first quarter of a century of its existence came in with democratic suffrage provisions, and had reactive effects of the highest importance upon the older States whose peoples were being attracted there. An extension of the franchise became essential. It was *western* New York that forced an extension of suffrage in the constitutional convention of that States in 1821; and it was *western* Virginia that compelled the tide-water region to put a more liberal suffrage provision in the constitution framed in 1830, and to give to the frontier region a more nearly proportionate representation with the tide-water aristocracy. The rise of democracy as an effective force in the nation came in with western preponderance under Jackson and William Henry Harrison, and it meant the triumph of the frontier—with all of its good and with all of its evil elements. . . .

So long as free land exists, the opportunity for a competency exists, and economic power secures political power. But the democracy born of free land, strong in selfishness and individualism, intolerant of administrative experience and education, and pressing individual liberty beyond its proper bounds, has its dangers as well as its benefits. Individualism in America has allowed a laxity in regard to governmental affairs which has rendered possible the spoils system and all the manifest evils that follow from the lack of a highly developed civic spirit. In this connection may be noted also the influence of frontier conditions in permitting lax business honor, inflated paper currency and wild-cat banking. The colonial and revolutionary frontier was the region whence emanated many of the worst forms of an evil currency. The West in the War of 1812 repeated the phenomenon on the frontier of that day, while the speculation and wild-cat banking of the period of the crisis of 1837 occurred on the new frontier belt of the next tier of States. Thus each one of the periods of lax financial integrity coincides with periods when a new set of frontier communities had arisen, and coincides in area with these successive frontiers, for the most part. The recent Populist agitation is a case in point. Many a State that now declines any connection with the tenets of the Populists, itself adhered to such ideas in an earlier stage of the development of the State. A primitive society can hardly be expected to show the intelligent appreciation of the complexity of business interests in a developed society. The continual recurrence of these areas of paper-money agitation is another evidence that the frontier can be isolated and studied as a factor in American history of the highest importance.

. . . . .

From the conditions of frontier life came intellectual traits of profound importance. The works of travelers along each frontier from colonial days onward describe certain common traits, and these traits have, while softening down, still persisted as survivals in the place of their origin, even when a higher organization succeeded. The result is that to the frontier the American intellect owes its striking characteristics. That coarseness and strength combined with acuteness and inquisitiveness; that practical, inventive turn of mind, quick to find expedients; that masterful grasp of material things, lacking in the artistic but powerful to effect great ends; that restless, nervous energy; that dominant individualism, working for good and for evil, and withal that buoyancy and exuberance which comes with freedom—these are traits of the frontier, or traits called out elsewhere because of the existence of the frontier. Since the days when the fleet of Columbus sailed into the waters of the New World, America has been another name for opportunity, and the people of the United States have taken their tone from the incessant expansion which has not only been open but has even been forced upon them. He would be a rash prophet who should assert that the expansive character of American life has now entirely ceased. Movement has been its dominant fact, and, unless this train-

ing has no effect upon a people, the American energy will continually demand a wider field for its exercise. But never again will such gifts of free land offer themselves. For a moment, at the frontier, the bonds of custom are broken and unrestraint is triumphant. There is not *tabula rasa*. The stubborn American environment is there with its imperious summons to accept its conditions; the inherited ways of doing things are also there; and yet, in spite of environment, and in spite of custom, each frontier did indeed furnish a new field of opportunity, a gate of escape from the bondage of the past; and freshness, and confidence, and scorn of older society, impatience of its restraints and its ideas, and indifference to its lessons, have accompanied the frontier. What the Mediterranean Sea was to the Greeks, breaking the bond of custom, offering new experiences, calling out new institutions and activities, that, and more, the ever retreating frontier has been to the United States directly, and to the nations of Europe more remotely. And now, four centuries from the discovery of America, at the end of a hundred years of life under the Constitution, the frontier has gone, and with its going has closed the first period of American history.

COMMENT

Plainly the whole complex of institutions, habits and ideas that men brought to the frontier was left out of his formula, and it was these things, not bare geography, that had been decisive. Turner's analysis . . . hung too much on real estate, not enough on a state of mind.

Richard Hofstadter, historian, in *American Scholar*, xviii (Autumn, 1949), 438–39.

Only by a study of the origins and growth of American capitalism and imperialism can we obtain the insight into the nature and complexity of the problems confronting us today. And I am prepared to submit that perhaps the chief reason for the absence of this proper understanding was the futile hunt for a unique "American spirit" which Frederick Jackson Turner began forty years ago and in which he involved most of America's historical scholars from that time until now.

Louis M. Hacker, historian, in *Nation*, cxxxii (July 26, 1933), 108–10.

In what it proposes, the frontier hypothesis needs painstaking revision. By what it fails to mention, the theory today disqualifies itself as an adequate guide to American development.

George Wilson Pierson, historian, in *New England Quarterly*, xv (June, 1942), 255.

27. *1896*

Plessy v. Ferguson

Extreme racism resulted in the South at the end of the nineteenth century largely because of the relaxation of northern liberal opinion. The first indication of this relaxation was the abandonment by Congress in 1877 of a policy of interference in southern internal affairs. The North had become weary of the violence which was a by-product of Radical Reconstruction. Meanwhile, southern conservatives were joining with the conservative eastern wings of the Republican and Democratic parties in a defense of the new economic order. As this occurred, the issue of Reconstruction lost importance, permitting a gradual restoration of "white supremacy" in the South. Encouraging this modification of outlook was the way in which imperialism and racism acted upon each other. If the nation could impose its will on natives in colonial areas, why could not the South do the same to Negroes in South Carolina and Mississippi? As this type of thinking became widespread, racial tension increased. For example, southern states began in 1890 to disfranchise Negroes and to pass "Jim Crow" laws. Meantime, the number of lynchings in the South reached staggering proportions.

The Supreme Court assisted the capitulation to racism by reducing the significance of the Fourteenth and Fifteenth Amendments as guarantees of Negro

163 U.S. 537 (1896).

rights. In the famous case, Plessy v. Ferguson, the Court accepted the so-called "separate but equal rule." The case involved the constitutionality of a Louisiana "Jim Crow" law which required separate railroad coaches for whites and Negroes. The Court ruled that such a statute did not deprive Negroes of their constitutional rights as long as they were furnished accommodations equal to those for the whites. Eventually, southern states used the "separate but equal" concept to segregate whites and Negroes in virtually all public accommodations. In 1954, the Supreme Court in another famous case, Brown v. Board of Education, reversed the position which the Court had taken in the Plessy case.

This case turns upon the constitutionality of an act of the General Assembly of the state of Louisiana, passed in 1890, providing for separate railway carriages for the white and colored races. . . .

The constitutionality of this act is attacked upon the ground that it conflicts both with the Thirteenth Amendment of the Constitution, abolishing slavery, and the Fourteenth Amendment, which prohibits certain restrictive legislation on the part of the states.

1. That it does not conflict with the Thirteenth Amendment, which abolished slavery and involuntary servitude, except as a punishment for crime, is too clear

for argument. Slavery implies involuntary servitude—a state of bondage; the ownership of mankind as a chattel, or at least the control of the labor and services of one man for the benefit of another, and the absence of a legal right to the disposal of his own person, property, and services. . . .

A statute which implies merely a legal distinction between the white and colored races—a distinction which is founded in the color of the two races, and which must always exist so long as white men are distinguished from the other race by color—has no tendency to destroy the legal equality of the two races, or reestablish a state of involuntary servitude. Indeed, we do not understand that the Thirteenth Amendment is strenuously relied upon by the plaintiff in error in this connection.

2. By the Fourteenth Amendment, all persons born or naturalized in the United States, and subject to the jurisdiction thereof, are made citizens of the United States and of the state wherein they reside; and the states are forbidden from making or enforcing any law which shall abridge the privileges or immunities of citizens of the United States, or shall deprive any person of life, liberty, or property without due process of law, or deny to any person within their jurisdiction the equal protection of the laws. . . .

The object of the amendment was undoubtedly to enforce the absolute equality of the two races before the law, but in the nature of things it could not have been intended to abolish distinctions based upon color, or to enforce social, as distinguished from political, equality, or a commingling of the two races upon terms unsatisfactory to either. Laws permitting, and even requiring, their separation in places where they are liable to be brought into contact do not necessarily imply the inferiority of either race to the other, and have been generally, if not universally, recognized as within the competency of the state legislatures in the exercise of their police power. The most common instance of this is connected with the establishment of separate schools for white and colored children, which has been held to be a valid exercise of the legislative power even by courts of states where the political rights of the colored race have been longest and most earnestly enforced. . . .

So far, then, as a conflict with the Fourteenth Amendment is concerned, the case reduces itself to the question whether the statute of Louisiana is a reasonable regulation, and with respect to this there must necessarily be a large discretion on the part of the legislature. In determining the question of reasonableness it is at liberty to act with reference to the established usages, customs, and traditions of the people, and with a view to the promotion of their comfort, and the preservation of the public peace and good order. Gauged by this standard, we cannot say that a law which authorizes or even requires the separation of the two races in public conveyances is unreasonable or more obnoxious to the Fourteenth Amendment than the acts of Congress requiring separate schools for colored children in the District of Columbia, the constitutionality of which does not seem to have been questioned, or the corresponding acts of state legislatures.

We consider the underlying fallacy of the plaintiff's argument to consist in the assumption that the enforced separation of the two races stamps the colored race with a badge of inferiority. If this be so, it is not by reason of anything found in the act, but solely because the colored race chooses to put that construction upon it. The argument necessarily assumes that if, as has been more than once the case, and is not unlikely to be so again, the colored race should become the dominant power in the state legislature, and should enact a law in precisely similar terms, it would thereby relegate the white race to an inferior position. We imagine that the white race, at least, would not acquiesce in this assumption. The argument also assumes that social prejudices may be overcome by legislation and that equal rights cannot be secured to the Negro except by an enforced commingling of the two races. We cannot accept this proposition. If the two races are to meet upon terms of social equality, it must be the result of natural affinities, a mutual appreciation of each other's merits, and a voluntary consent of individuals. . . . Legislation is powerless to eradicate racial instincts or to abolish distinctions based upon physical differences, and the attempt to do so can only result in accentuating the difficulties of the present situation. If the civil and political rights of both races be equal, one cannot be inferior to the other civilly or politically. If one race be inferior to the other socially, the Constitution of the United States cannot put them upon the same plane.

It is true that the question of the proportion of colored blood necessary to constitute a colored person, as distinguished from a white person, is one upon which there is a difference of opinion in the different states, some holding that any visible admixture of black blood stamps the person as belonging to the colored race . . . others that it depends upon the preponderance of blood . . . and still others that the predominance of white blood must only be in the proportion of three-fourths. . . . But these are questions to be determined under the laws of each state and are not properly put in issue in this case. Under the allegations of his petition it may undoubtedly become a question of importance whether, under the laws of Louisiana, the petitioner belongs to the white or colored race.

The judgment of the court below is, therefore, *Affirmed.*

MR. JUSTICE HARLAN DISSENTING

In respect of civil rights, common to all citizens, the Constitution of the United States does not, I think, permit any public authority to know the race of those entitled to be protected in the enjoyment of such rights. Every true man has pride of race, and under appropriate circumstances when the rights of others, his equals before the law, are not to be affected, it is his privilege to express such pride and to take such action based upon it as to him seems proper. But I deny that any legislative body or judicial tribunal may have regard to the race of citizens when the civil rights of those citizens are involved. Indeed, such legislation, as that here in question, is inconsistent not only with that equality of rights which pertains to citizenship, national and state, but with the personal liberty enjoyed by everyone within the United States.

The Thirteenth Amendment does not permit the withholding or the deprivation of any right necessarily inhering in freedom. It not only struck down the institution of slavery as previously existing in the United States, but it prevents the imposition of any burdens or disabilities that constitute badges of slavery or servitude. It decreed universal civil freedom in this country. This Court has so adjudged. But that amendment having been found inadequate to the protection of the rights of those who had been in slavery, it was followed by the Fourteenth Amendment, which added greatly to the dignity and glory of the American citizenship, and to the security of personal liberty, by declaring that "all persons born or naturalized in the United States, and subject to the jurisdiction thereof, are citizens of the United States and of the state wherein they reside," and that "no state shall make or enforce any law which shall abridge the privileges or immunities of citizens of the United States; nor shall any state deprive any person of life, liberty, or property without due process of law, nor deny to any person within its jurisdiction the equal protection of the laws." These two amendments, if enforced according to their true intent and meaning, will protect all the civil rights that pertain to freedom and citizenship. Finally, and to the end that no citizen should be denied, on account of his race, the privilege of participating in the political control of his country, it was declared by the Fifteenth Amendment that "the right of citizens of the United States to vote shall not be denied or abridged by the United States or by any state on account of race, color, or previous condition of servitude."

These notable additions to the fundamental law were welcomed by the friends of liberty throughout the world. They removed the race line from our governmental systems. . . .

It was said in argument that the statute of Louisiana does not discriminate against either race but prescribes a rule applicable alike to white and colored citizens. But this argument does not meet the difficulty. Everyone knows that the statute in question had its origin in the purpose, not so much to exclude white persons from railroad cars occupied by blacks, as to exclude colored people from coaches occupied by or assigned to white persons. Railroad corporations of Louisiana did not make discrimination among whites in the matter of accommodation for travelers. The thing to accomplish was, under the guise of giving equal accommodation for whites and blacks, to compel the latter to keep to themselves while traveling in railroad passenger coaches. No one would be so wanting in candor as to assert the contrary. The fundamental objection, therefore, to the statute is that it interferes with the personal freedom of citizens. . . . If a white man and a black man choose to occupy the same public conveyance on a public highway, it is their right to do so, and no government, proceeding alone on

grounds of race, can prevent it without infringing the personal liberty of each.

It is one thing for railroad carriers to furnish, or to be required by law to furnish, equal accommodations for all whom they are under a legal duty to carry. It is quite another thing for government to forbid citizens of the white and black races from traveling in the same public conveyance, and to punish officers of railroad companies for permitting persons of the two races to occupy the same passenger coach. If a state can prescribe, as a rule of civil conduct, that whites and blacks shall not travel as passengers in the same railroad coach, why may it not so regulate the use of the streets of its cities and towns as to compel white citizens to keep on one side of a street and black citizens to keep on the other? Why may it not, upon like grounds, punish whites and blacks who ride together in streetcars or in open vehicles on a public road or street? Why may it not require sheriffs to assign whites to one side of a courtroom and blacks to the other? And why may it not also prohibit the commingling of the two races in the galleries of legislative halls or in public assemblages convened for the consideration of the political questions of the day? Further, if this statute of Louisiana is consistent with the personal liberty of citizens, why may not the state require the separation in railroad coaches of native and naturalized citizens of the United States, or of Protestants and Roman Catholics?

The answer given at the argument to these questions was that regulations of the kind they suggest would be unreasonable and could not, therefore, stand before the law. Is it meant that the determination of questions of legislative power depends upon the inquiry whether the statute whose validity is questioned is, in the judgment of the courts, a reasonable one, taking all the circumstances into consideration? A statute may be unreasonable merely because a sound public policy forbade its enactment. But I do not understand that the courts have anything to do with the policy or expediency of legislation. . . .

The white race deems itself to be the dominant race in this country. And so it is, in prestige, in achievements, in education, in wealth, and in power. So, I doubt not, it will continue to be for all time, if it remains true to its great heritage and holds fast to the principles of constitutional liberty. But in view of the Constitution, in the eye of the law, there is in this country no superior, dominant, ruling class of citizens. There is no caste here. Our Constitution is color-blind and neither knows nor tolerates classes among citizens. In respect of civil rights, all citizens are equal before the law. The humblest is the peer of the most powerful. The law regards man as man and takes no account of his surroundings or of his color when his civil rights as guaranteed by the supreme law of the land are involved. It is, therefore, to be regretted that this high tribunal, the final expositor of the fundamental law of the land, has reached the conclusion that it is competent for a state to regulate the enjoyment by citizens of their civil rights solely upon the basis of race. . . .

The sure guarantee of the peace and security of each race is the clear, distinct, unconditional recognition by our governments, national and state, of every right that inheres in civil freedom, and of the equality before the law of all citizens of the United States without regard to race. State enactments, regulating the enjoyment of civil rights, upon the basis of race, and cunningly devised to defeat legitimate results of the war, under the pretense of recognizing equality of rights, can have no other result than to render permanent peace impossible, and to keep alive a conflict of races, the continuance of which must do harm to all concerned. . . .

The arbitrary separation of citizens, on the basis of race, while they are on a public highway, is a badge of servitude wholly inconsistent with the civil freedom and the equality before the law established by the Constitution. It cannot be justified upon any legal grounds.

If evils will result from the commingling of the two races upon public highways established for the benefit of all, they will be infinitely less than those that will surely come from state legislation regulating the enjoyment of civil rights upon the basis of race. We boast of the freedom enjoyed by our people above all other peoples. But it is difficult to reconcile that boast with a state of the law which, practically, puts the brand of servitude and degradation upon a large class of our fellow-citizens, our equals before the law. The thin disguise of "equal" accommodations for passengers in railroad coaches will not mislead anyone, nor atone for the wrong this day done. . . .

I am of opinion that the statute of Louisiana is inconsistent with the personal liberty of citizens, white and black, in that state, and hostile to both the spirit and letter of the Constitution of the United States. If laws of like character should be enacted in the several states of the Union, the effect would be in the highest degree mischievous. Slavery, as an institution tolerated by law, would, it is true, have disappeared from our country, but there would remain a power in the states, by sinister legislation, to interfere with the full enjoyment of the blessings of freedom; to regulate civil rights, common to all citizens, upon the basis of race, and to place in a condition of legal inferiority a large body of American citizens, now constituting a part of the political community called the People of the United States, for whom, and by whom through representatives, our government is administered. Such a system is inconsistent with the guarantee given by the Constitution to each state of a republican form of government, and may be stricken down by congressional action, or by the courts in the discharge of their solemn duty to maintain the supreme law of the land, anything in the constitution or laws of any state to the contrary notwithstanding.

For the reasons stated, I am constrained to withhold my assent from the opinion and judgment of the majority. . . .

28. *JULY 8, 1896*

William Jennings Bryan's Cross of Gold Speech

In July, 1896, when the Democrats gathered in Chicago for their national convention, a party split on the issues of gold and silver was in the making. Not since 1860 had there been a comparable Democratic party gathering for intensity of feeling, concentration of purpose, party prejudices, and genuine fervor in behalf of specific proposals touching public policy. Nebraska delegate William Jennings Bryan delivered the speech below during the debate on the platform which endorsed free silver and bitterly attacked Cleveland policies. In contrast to the previous speakers, Bryan's clear, far-carrying musical voice caught the multitude, causing the noise to subside. He had carefully prepared the speech, rehearsing parts of it throughout the South and the Middle West. But to the convention audience, it was woven with ideas and phrases which had a novel charm.

Bryan spoke from the heart, inspired by the belief that his role was to be a crusader for humanity. For him, free silver was the answer to the needs of his time. He spoke in terms of ideological principles, but he was not concerned with a socialistic ideology, as his enemies were later to assert. The limitations of his protest were well defined. But unlike the radi-

WILLIAM JENNINGS BRYAN, *The First Battle* (Chicago, 1896), pp. 199–206.

cals of his day, he had nothing to say about government ownership and regulation of the nation's industrial and communications systems. His principles were designed to draw a line of cleavage between the small bourgeoise capitalist and the great financial capitalists of Wall Street. One of the most notable speeches in American history, it was a crucial factor in bringing Bryan the Democratic nomination in 1896. Without it, he stood little chance of success.

I would be presumptuous, indeed, to present myself against the distinguished gentlemen to whom you have listened if this were a mere measuring of abilities; but this is not a contest between persons. The humblest citizen in all the land, when clad in the armor of a righteous cause, is stronger than all the hosts of error. I come to speak to you in defense of a cause as holy as the cause of liberty—the cause of humanity.

When this debate is concluded, a motion will be made to lay upon the table the resolution offered in commendation of the administration, and also the resolution offered in condemnation of the administration. We object to bringing this question down to the level of persons. The individual is but an atom; he is born, he acts, he dies; but principles are eternal; and this has been a contest over a principle.

Never before in the history of this country has there been witnessed such a contest as that through which we have just passed. Never before in the history of American politics has a great issue been fought out as this issue has been, by the voters of a great party. On the fourth of March, 1895, a few Democrats, most of them members of Congress, issued an address to the Democrats of the nation, asserting that the money question was the paramount issue of the hour; declaring that a majority of the Democratic party had the right to control the action of the party on this paramount issue; and concluding with the request that the believers in the free coinage of silver in the Democratic party should organize, take charge of, and control the policy of the Democratic party. Three months later, at Memphis, an organization was perfected, and the silver Democrats went forth openly and courageously proclaiming their belief, and declaring that, if successful, they would crystallize into a platform the declaration which they had made. Then began the conflict. With a zeal approaching the zeal which inspired the crusaders who followed Peter the Hermit, our silver Democrats went forth from victory unto victory until they are now assembled, not to discuss, not to debate, but to enter up the judgment already rendered by the plain people of this country. In this contest brother has been arrayed against brother, father against son. The warmest ties of love, acquaintance and association have been disregarded; old leaders have been cast aside when they have refused to give expression to the sentiments of those whom they would lead, and new leaders have sprung up to give direction to this cause of truth. Thus has the contest been waged, and we have assembled here under as binding and solemn instructions as were ever imposed upon representatives of the people.

We do not come as individuals. As individuals we might have been glad to compliment the gentleman from New York (Senator Hill), but we know that the people for whom we speak would never be willing to put him in a position where he could thwart the will of the Democratic party. I say it was not a question of persons; it was a question of principle, and it is not with gladness, my friends, that we find ourselves brought into conflict with those who are now arrayed on the other side.

The gentleman who preceded me (ex-Governor Russell) spoke of the State of Massachusetts; let me assure him that not one present in all this convention entertains the least hostility to the people of the State of Massachusetts, but we stand here representing people who are the equals, before the law, of the greatest citizens in the State of Massachusetts. When you (turning to the gold delegates) come before us and tell us that we are about to disturb your business interests, we reply that you have disturbed our business interests by your course.

We say to you that you have made the definition of a business man too limited in its application. The man who is employed for wages is as much a business man as his employer; the attorney in a country town is as much a business man as the corporation counsel in a great metropolis; the merchant at the crossroads store is as much a business man as the merchant of New York; the farmer who goes forth in the morning and toils all day—who begins in the spring and toils all summer—and who by the application of brain and muscle to the natural resources of the country creates wealth, is as much a business man as the man who goes upon the board of trade and bets upon the price of grain; the miners who go down a thousand feet into the earth, or climb two thousand feet upon the cliffs, and bring forth from their hiding places the precious metals to be poured into the channels of trade are as much business men as the few financial magnates who, in a back room, corner the money of the world. We come to speak for this broader class of business men.

Ah, my friends, we say not one word against those who live upon the Atlantic coast, but the hardy pioneers who have braved all the dangers of the wilderness, who have made the desert to blossom as the rose—the pioneers away out there (pointing to the West), who rear their children near to Nature's heart, where they can mingle their voices with the voices of the birds—out there where they have erected schoolhouses for the education of their young. churches where they praise their Creator, and cemeteries where rest the ashes of their dead—these people, we say, are as deserving of the consideration of our party as any people in this country. It is for these that we speak. We do not come as aggressors. Our war is not a war of conquest; we are fighting in the defense of our homes, our families, and posterity. We have petitioned, and our petitions have been scorned; we have entreated, and our entreaties have been disregarded; we have begged, and they have mocked when our calamity came. We beg no longer; we entreat no more; we petition no more. We defy them.

The gentleman from Wisconsin has said that he fears a Robespierre. My friends, in this land of the free you need not fear that a tyrant will spring up from among the people. What we need is an Andrew Jackson to stand, as Jackson stood, against the encroachments of organized wealth.

They tell us that this platform was made to catch votes. We reply to them that changing conditions make new issues; that the principles upon which Democracy rests are as everlasting as the hills, but that they must be applied to new conditions as they arise. Conditions have arisen, and we are here to meet those conditions. They tell us that the income tax ought not to be brought in here; that

it is a new idea. They criticise us for our criticism of the Supreme Court of the United States. My friends, we have not criticised; we have simply called attention to what you already know. If you want criticisms, read the dissenting opinions of the court. There you will find criticisms. They say that we passed an unconstitutional law; we deny it. The income tax law was not unconstitutional when it was passed; it was not unconstitutional when it went before the Supreme Court for the first time; it did not become unconstitutional until one of the judges changed his mind, and we cannot be expected to know when a judge will change his mind. The income tax is just. It simply intends to put the burdens of government justly upon the backs of the people. I am in favor of an income tax. When I find a man who is not willing to bear his share of the burdens of the government which protects him, I find a man who is unworthy to enjoy the blessings of a government like ours.

They say that we are opposing national bank currency; it is true. If you will read what Thomas Benton said, you will find he said that, in searching history, he could find but one parallel to Andrew Jackson; that was Cicero, who destroyed the conspiracy of Cataline and saved Rome. Benton said that Cicero only did for Rome what Jackson did for us when he destroyed the bank conspiracy and saved America. We say in our platform that we believe that the right to coin and issue money is a function of government. We believe it. We believe that it is a part of sovereignty, and can no more with safety be delegated to private individuals than we could afford to delegate to private individuals the power to make penal statutes or levy taxes. Mr. Jefferson, who was once regarded as a good Democratic authority, seems to have differed in opinion from the gentleman who has addressed us on the part of the minority. Those who are opposed to this proposition tell us that the issue of paper money is a function of the bank, and that the Government ought to go out of the banking business. I stand with Jefferson rather than with them, and tell them, as he did, that the issue of money is a function of government, and that the banks ought to go out of the governing business.

They complain about the plank which declares against life tenure in office. They have tried to strain it to mean that which it does not mean. What we oppose by that plank is the life tenure which is being built up in Washington, and which excludes from participation in official benefits the humbler members of society.

Let me call your attention to two or three important things. The gentleman from New York says that he will propose an amendment to the platform providing that the proposed change in our monetary system shall not affect contracts already made. Let me remind you that there is no intention of affecting those contracts which according to present laws are made payable in gold; but if he means to say that we cannot change our monetary system without protecting those who have loaned money before the change was made, I desire to ask him where, in law or in morals, he can find justification for not protecting the debtors when the act of 1873 was passed, if he now insists that we must protect the creditors.

He says he will also propose an amendment which will provide for the suspension of free coinage if we fail to maintain the parity within a year. We reply that when we advocate a policy which we believe will be successful, we are not compelled to raise a doubt as to our own sincerity by suggesting what we shall do if we fail. I ask him, if he would apply his logic to us, why he does not apply it to himself. He says he wants this country to try to secure an international agreement. Why does he not tell us what he is going to do if he fails to secure an international agreement? There is more reason for him to do that than there is for us to provide against the failure to maintain the parity. Our opponents have tried for twenty years to secure an international agreement, and those are waiting for it most patiently who do not want it at all.

And now, my friends, let me come to the paramount issue. If they ask us why it is that we say more on the money question than we say upon the tariff question, I reply that, if protection has slain its thousands, the gold standard has slain its tens of thousands. If they ask us why we do not embody in our platform all the things that we believe in, we reply that when we have restored the money of the Constitution all other necessary reforms will be possible; but that until this is done there is no other reform that can be accomplished.

Why is it that within three months such a change has come over the country? Three months ago, when it was confidently asserted that those who believe in the gold standard would frame our platform and nominate our candidates, even the advocates of the gold standard did not think that we could elect a president. And they had good reason for their doubt, because there is scarcely a State here today asking for the gold standard which is not in the absolute control of the Republican Party. But note the change. Mr. McKinley was nominated at St. Louis upon a platform which declared for the maintenance of the gold standard until it can be changed into bimetallism by international agreement. Mr. McKinley was the most popular man among the Republicans, and three months ago everybody in the Republican party prophesied his election. How is it today? Why, the man who was once pleased to think that he looked like Napoleon—that man shudders today when he remembers that he was nominated on the anniversary of the battle of Waterloo. Not only that, but as he listens he can hear with ever-increasing distinctness the sound of the waves as they beat upon the lonely shores of St. Helena.

Why this change? Ah, my friends, is not the reason for the change evident to any one who will look at the matter? No private character, however pure, no personal popularity, however great, can protect from the avenging wrath of an indignant people a man who will declare that he is in favor of fastening the gold standard upon this country, or who is willing to surrender the right of self-government and place the legislative control of our affairs in the hands of foreign potentates and powers.

We go forth confident that we shall win. Why? Because upon the paramount issue of this campaign there is not a spot of ground upon which the enemy will dare to challenge battle. If they tell us that the gold standard is a good thing, we shall point to their platform and tell them that their platform pledges the party to get rid of the gold standard and substitute bimetallism. If the gold standard is a good thing, why try to get rid of it? I call your attention to the fact that some of the very people who are in this convention today and who tell us that we ought to declare in favor of international bimetallism—thereby declaring that the gold standard is wrong and that the principle of bimetallism is better—these very people four months ago were open and avowed advocates of the gold standard, and were then telling us that we could not legislate two metals together, even with the aid of all the world. If the gold standard is a good thing, we ought to declare in favor of its retention and not in favor of abandoning it; and if the gold standard is a bad thing why should we wait until other nations are willing to help us to let go? Here is the line of battle, and we care not upon which issue they force the fight; we are prepared to meet them on either issue or on both. If they tell us that the gold standard is the standard of civilization, we reply to them that this, the most enlightened of all the nations of the earth, has never declared for a gold standard and that both the great

parties this year are declaring against it. If the gold standard is the standard of civilization, why, my friends, should we not have it? If they come to meet us on that issue we can present the history of our nation. More than that; we can tell them that they will search the pages of history in vain to find a single instance where the common people of any land have ever declared themselves in favor of the gold standard. They can find where the holders of fixed investments have declared for a gold standard, but not where the masses have.

Mr. Carlisle said in 1878 that this was a struggle between "the idle holders of idle capital" and "the struggling masses, who produce the wealth and pay the taxes of the country"; and, my friends, the question we are to decide is: Upon which side will the Democratic party fight; upon the side of "the idle holders of idle capital" or upon the side of "the struggling masses?" That is the question which the party must answer first, and then it must be answered by each individual hereafter. The sympathies of the Democratic party, as shown by the platform, are on the side of the struggling masses who have ever been the foundation of the Democratic party. There are two ideas of government. There are those who believe that, if you will only legislate to make the well-to-do prosperous, their prosperity will leak through on those below. The Democratic idea, however, has been that if you legislate to make the masses prosperous, their prosperity will find its way up through every class which rests upon them.

You come to us and tell us that the great cities are in favor of the gold standard; we reply that the great cities rest upon our broad and fertile prairies. Burn down your cities and leave our farms, and your cities will spring up again as if by magic; but destroy our farms and the grass will grow in the streets of every city in the country.

My friends, we declare that this nation is able to legislate for its own people on every question, without waiting for the aid or consent of any other nation on earth; and upon that issue we expect to carry every State in the Union. I shall not slander the inhabitants of the fair State of Massachusetts nor the inhabitants of the State of New York by saying that, when they are confronted with the proposition, they will declare that this nation is not able to attend to its own business. It is the issue of 1776 over again. Our ancestors, when but three millions in number, had the courage to declare their political independence of every other nation; shall we, their descendants, when we have grown to seventy millions, declare that we are less independent than our forefathers? No, my friends, that will never be the verdict of our people. Therefore, we care not upon what lines the battle is fought. If they say bimetallism is good, but that we cannot have it until other nations help us, we reply that, instead of having a gold standard because England has, we will restore bimetallism, and then let England have bimetallism because the United States has it. If they dare to come out in the open field and defend the gold standard as a good thing, we will fight them to the uttermost. Having behind us the producing masses of this nation and the world, supported by the commercial interests, the laboring interests, and the toilers everywhere, we will answer their demand for a gold standard by saying to them: You shall not press down upon the brow of labor this crown of thorns, you shall not crucify mankind upon a cross of gold.

. . . . .

COMMENT

I have been thinking over Bryan's speech. What did he say anyway?

> Governor John Peter Altgeld of Illinois. Quoted from William Jennings Bryan, *The First Battle* (Chicago, 1896), p. 464.

A paid agent of and spokesman for the silver combine, he has not since his retirement from Congress had any other visible means of support. The richest men in the world, the proprietors of the Big Bonanzas, hire orators like Bryan exactly as other men hire fiddlers and value them highly.

> Editorial in the Chicago (Ill.) *Chronicle*, July 11, 1896.

We of the South have burned our bridges behind us so far as the Eastern Democrats are concerned. . . . We denounce the Administration of President Cleveland as undemocratic and tyrannical. . . . A plutocratic despotism is sought to be established.

> Senator Ben Tillman of South Carolina speaking to the Democratic National Convention, July 9, 1896. Quoted from the *Official Proceedings of the Democratic National Convention* (New York, 1896), pp. 207–209.

---

29. *AUGUST 11, 1896*

"What's the Matter with Kansas?"

When the Populist party supported the Democratic nominee, William Jennings Bryan, for the presidency in 1896, the Republicans responded by accusing the Democrats and the Populists of being identical. They were portrayed as cranks who advocated proposals which were un-American. But the extent to which "Populism" infested the Democratic party is debatable. There had been only a few men with real Populist sympathies at the Democratic National Convention in Chicago. Free silver had dominated the convention, but free silver and Populism were by no means synonymous. The Republicans failed to observe that there were many conservative Democrats who supported Bryan and the silver platform as a means of destroying Populism. Bryan and most of his followers could and did flirt with the Populists on the subject of silver without sharing their major premises. For Bryan, the unlimited coinage of silver at the ratio of sixteen to one was desirable because it would bring the nation out of depression and would restore a society favorable to the common man. But he was far from being the dangerous revolutionary whom his antagonists pictured. Unlike the Populists, he did not call for a serious modification of the nation's economic structure by governmental action as the Populists did. Instead, most of his demands called for a "hands off policy."

Typical of the Republican outlook on the campaign was this editorial which appeared in the Emporia (Kan.) Gazette on August 11, 1896, and which was re-

RUSSEL H. FITZGIBBON, *Forty Years on Main Street* (New York: Farrar & Rinehart, Inc., 1937), pp. 296–99.

printed and distributed throughout the nation. The author was the paper's young editor, William Allen White, who became one of the leading newspapermen in American politics during the next half century. •

Today the Kansas department of agriculture sent out a statement which indicates that Kansas has gained less than two thousand people in the past year. There are about two hundred and twenty-five thousand families in the state, and there were about ten thousand babies born in Kansas, and yet so many people have left the state that the natural increase is cut down to less than two thousand net.

This has been going on for eight years.

If there had been a high brick wall around the state eight years ago, and not a soul had been admitted or permitted to leave, Kansas would be a half million souls better off than she is today. And yet the nation has increased in population. In five years ten million people have been added to the national population, yet instead of gaining a share of this—say, half a million—Kansas has apparently been a plague spot, and in the very garden of the world, has lost populations by ten thousands every year.

Not only has she lost population, but she has lost money. Every moneyed man in the state who could get out without loss has gone. Every month in every community sees some one who has a little money pack up and leave the state. This has been going on for eight years. Money has been drained out all the time. In towns where ten years ago there were three or four or half a dozen money lending concerns stimulating industry by furnishing capital, there is now none, or one or two that are looking after the interests and principal already outstanding.

No one brings any money into Kansas any more. What community knows over one or two men who have moved in with more than $5,000 in the past three years? And what community cannot count half a score of men in that time who have left, taking all the money they could scrape together?

Yet the nation has grown rich, other states have increased in population and wealth—other neighboring states. Missouri has gained over two million, while Kansas has been losing half a million. Nebraska has gained in wealth and population while Kansas has gone down hill. Colorado has gained every way, while Kansas has lost every way since 1888.

What's the matter with Kansas?

There is no substantial city in the state. Every big town save one has lost in population. Yet Kansas City, Omaha, Lincoln, St. Louis, Denver, Colorado Springs, Sedalia, the cities of the Dakotas, St. Paul and Minneapolis and Des Moines —all cities and towns in the West have steadily grown.

Take up the government blue book and you will see that Kansas is virtually off the map. Two or three little scrubby consular places in yellow-fever-stricken communities that do not aggregate ten thousand dollars a year is all the recognition that Kansas has. Nebraska draws about one hundred thousand dollars; little old North Dakota draws about fifty thousand dollars; Oklahoma doubles Kansas; Missouri leaves her a thousand miles behind; Colorado is almost seven times greater than Kansas—the whole West is ahead of Kansas.

Take it by any standard you please, Kansas is not in it.

Go east and you hear them laugh at Kansas, go west and they sneer at her,

go south and they "cuss" her, go north and they have forgotten her. Go into any crowd of intelligent people gathered anywhere on the globe, and you will find the Kansas man on the defensive. The newspaper columns and magazines once devoted to praise of her, to boastful facts and startling figures concerning her resources, are now filled with cartoons, jibes and Pefferian speeches. Kansas just naturally isn't in it. She has traded places with Arkansas and Timbuctoo.

What's the matter with Kansas?

We all know; yet here we are at it again. We have an old moss-back Jacksonian who snorts and howls because there is a bathtub in the statehouse; we are running that old jay for governor. We have another shabby, wild-eyed, rattle brained fanatic who has said openly in a dozen speeches that "the rights of the user are paramount to the rights of the owner"; we are running him for chief justice, so that capital will come tumbling over itself to get into the state. We have raked the old ash heap of failure in the state and found an old human hoop skirt who has failed as a business man, who has failed as an editor, who has failed as a preacher, and we are going to run him for congressman-at-large. He will help the looks of the Kansas delegation at Washington. Then we have discovered a kid without a law practice and have decided to run him for attorney-general. Then for fear some hint that the state had become respectable might percolate through the civilized portions of the nation, we have decided to send three or four harpies out lecturing, telling the people that Kansas is raising hell and letting the corn go to weeds.

Oh, this is a state to be proud of! We are a people who can hold up our heads! What we need is not more money, but less capital, fewer white shirts and brains, fewer men with business judgment, and more of those fellows who boast that they are "just ordinary clodhoppers, but they know more in a minute about finance than John Sherman"; we need more men who are "posted," who can bellow about the crime of 73, who hate prosperity, and who think because a man believes in national honor, he is a tool of Wall Street. We have had a few of them—some hundred fifty thousand, but we need more.

We need several thousand gibbering idiots to scream about the "Great Red Dragon" of Lombard Street. We don't need population, we don't need wealth, we don't need well-dressed men on the streets, we don't need cities on the fertile prairies; you bet we don't! What we are after is the money power. Because we have become poorer and ornier and meaner than a spavined, distempered mule, we the people of Kansas, propose to kick; we don't care to build up, we wish to tear down.

"There are two ideas of government," said our noble Bryan at Chicago. "There are those who believe that if you just legislate to make the well-to-do prosperous, this prosperity will leak through on those below. The Democratic idea has been that if you legislate to make the masses prosperous their prosperity will find its way up and through every class and rest upon us."

That's the stuff! Give the prosperous man the dickens! Legislate the thriftless man into ease, whack the stuffing out of the creditors and tell the debtors who borrowed the money five years ago when money "per capita" was greater than it is now that the contraction of the currency gives him a right to repudiate.

Whoop it up for the ragged trousers; put the lazy, greasy fizzle who can't pay his debts on the altar, and bow down and worship him. Let the state ideal be high. What we need is not the respect of our fellow men, but the chance to get something for nothing.

Oh, yes, Kansas is a great state. Here are people fleeing from it by the score every day, capital going out of the state by the hundreds of dollars; and every industry but farming paralyzed, and that crippled, because its products have to go across the ocean before they can find a laboring man at work who can afford to buy them. Let's don't stop this year. Let's drive all the decent, self-respecting men out of the state. Let's keep the old clodhoppers who know it all. Let's encourage the man who is "posted." He can talk, and what we need is not mill hands to eat our meat, nor factory hands to eat our wheat, nor cities to oppress the farmer by consuming his butter and eggs and chickens and produce. What Kansas needs is men who can talk, who have large leisure to argue the currency question while their wives wait at home for that nickel's worth of bluing.

What's the matter with Kansas?

Nothing under the shining sun. She is losing wealth, population, and standing. She has got her statesmen, and the money power is afraid of her. Kansas is all right. She has started in to raise hell, as Mrs. Lease advised, and she seems to have an overproduction. But that doesn't matter. Kansas never did believe in diversified crops. Kansas is all right. There is absolutely nothing wrong with Kansas. "Every prospect pleases and only man is vile."

COMMENT

This is one of the most bitterly ironical arraignments of the shiftless spirit that has handicapped that rich state. . . . It is couched in language so bold yet picturesque as to seem the utterance of a wit in whom the bitterness of reality cannot wholly suppress mirth over the imbecility that has caused it.

Editorial in the Chicago (Ill.) *Times-Herald*, August 18, 1896.

30. APRIL 11, 1898

William McKinley's War Message

Under pressure from many Democrats, a large proportion of his own party, the House and the Senate, the press and the public, President McKinley finally reversed his earlier antiwar policy and sent this message to a warlike Congress. Despite the fact that Spain had made last minute concessions and assurances, McKinley requested the use of military and naval forces of the United States in order "to secure a full and final termination of hostilities between the government of Spain and the people of Cuba." Perhaps a more aggressive president would have denounced intervention, condemned the warmakers, and broken with Congress. When Spain finally yielded to his demands, perhaps a more determined president would have announced that Spain had finally declared an armistice and that his diplomatic negotiations had been successful. Such a statement might have had little effect. The consequences of such conduct could have strengthened his opposition and divided his party, leaving the nation rudderless in a time of crisis. On the other hand, such action might have prevented an unnecessary war.

Despite McKinley's capitulation, the Democrats were dissatisfied, for they regarded the war message as weak and indefinite. There was nothing in it concerning Cuban independence nor was there any approval of Cuban belligerancy. Instead, the cardinal principle of McKinley's plan was neutral intervention without regard to Cuban independence. The Democrats took this to mean that he was intent upon forcing some type of

House Documents (3743), 55th Cong., 3d Sess., pp. 750–60.

compromise solution upon the Spanish and insurgents alike. They insisted that the resolution responding to the President's message should contain not only a recognition of the independence of the Cuban people but also a recognition of the revolutionary government of Cuba. Despite the efforts of the Democrats and a few Republicans, the Administration had its way and the question of recognition was dropped. Against the Administration's wishes but at the insistence of the Democrats, Congress did pass a resolution declaring that the people of Cuba not only "of right ought to be" but "are" free and independent.

Obedient to that precept of the Constitution which commands the President to give from time to time to the Congress information of the state of the Union and to recommend to their consideration such measures as he shall judge necessary and expedient, it becomes my duty now to address your body with regard to the grave crisis that has arisen in the relations of the United States to Spain by reason of the warfare that for more than three years has raged in the neighboring island of Cuba.

· · · · ·

The present revolution is but the successor of other similar insurrections which have occurred in Cuba against the dominion of Spain, extending over a period of nearly half a century, each of which, during its progress, has subjected the United States to great effort and expense in enforcing its neutrality laws, caused enormous losses to American trade and commerce, caused irritation, annoyance, and disturbance among our citizens, and by the exercise of cruel, barbarous, and uncivilized practices of warfare, shocked the sensibilities and offended the humane sympathies of our people.

. . . . .

Our people have beheld a once prosperous community reduced to comparative want, its lucrative commerce virtually paralyzed, its exceptional productiveness diminished, its fields laid waste, its mills in ruins, and people perishing by tens of thousands from hunger and destitution. We have found ourselves constrained, in the observance of that strict neutrality which our laws enjoin, and which the law of nations commands, to police our own waters and watch our own seaports in prevention of any unlawful act in aid of the Cubans.

Our trade has suffered; the capital invested by our citizens in Cuba has been largely lost, and the temper and forbearance of our people have been so sorely tried as to beget a perilous unrest among our own citizens which has inevitably found its expression from time to time in the National Legislature, so that issues wholly external to our own body politic engross attention and stand in the way of that close devotion to domestic advancement that becomes a self-contained commonwealth whose primal maxim has been the avoidance of all foreign entanglements. All this must needs awaken, and has, indeed, aroused the utmost concern on the part of this Government, as well during my predecessor's term as in my own.

In April, 1896, the evils from which our country suffered through the Cuban war became so onerous that my predecessor made an effort to bring about a peace through the mediation of this Government in any way that might tend to an honorable adjustment of the contest between Spain and her revolted colony, on the basis of some effective scheme of self-government for Cuba under the flag and sovereignty of Spain. It failed

through the refusal of the Spanish Government then in power to consider any form of mediation or, indeed, any plan of settlement which did not begin with the actual submission of the insurgents to the mother country, and then only on such terms as Spain herself might see fit to grant. The war continued unabated. The resistance of the insurgents was in no wise diminished.

The efforts of Spain were increased, both by the dispatch of fresh levies to Cuba and by the addition to the horrors of the strife of a new and inhuman phase happily unprecedented in the modern history of civilized Christian peoples. The policy of devastation and concentration, inaugurated by the Captain-General's bando of October 21, 1896 in the Province of Pinar del Rio was thence extended to embrace all of the island to which the power of the Spanish arms was able to reach by occupation or by military operations. The peasantry, including all dwelling in the open agricultural interior, were driven into the garrison towns or isolated places held by the troops.

The raising and movement of provisions of all kinds were interdicted. The fields were laid waste, dwellings unroofed and fired, mills destroyed, and, in short, everything that could desolate the land and render it unfit for human habitation or support was commanded by one or the other of the contending parties and executed by all the powers at their disposal.

By the time the present administration took office a year ago, reconcentration—so called—had been made effective over the better part of the four central and western provinces, Santa Clara, Matanzas, Habana, and Pinar del Rio.

The agricultural population to the estimated number of 300,000 or more was herded within the towns and their immediate vicinage, deprived of the means of support, rendered destitute of shelter, left poorly clad, and exposed to the most unsanitary conditions. As the scarcity of food increased with the devastation of the depopulated areas of production, destitution and want became misery and starvation. Month by month the death rate increased in an alarming ratio. By March 1897, according to conservative estimates from official Spanish sources, the mortality among the reconcentrados from starvation and the diseases thereto incident exceeded 50 per centum of their total number.

No practical relief was accorded to the destitute. The overburdened towns, already suffering from the general dearth, could give no aid. So called "zones of cultivation" established within the immediate areas of effective military control about the cities and fortified camps proved illusory as a remedy for the suffering. The unfortunates, being for the most part women and children, with aged and helpless men, enfeebled by disease and hunger, could not have tilled the soil without tools, seed, or shelter for their own support or for the supply of the cities. Reconcentration adopted avowedly as a war measure in order to cut off the resources of the insurgents, worked its predestined result. As I said in my message of last December, it was not civilized warfare; it was extermination. The only peace it could beget was that of the wilderness and the grave.

Meanwhile the military situation in the island had undergone a noticeable change. The extraordinary activity that characterized the second year of the war, when the insurgents invaded even the thitherto unharmed fields of Pinar del Rio and carried havoc and destruction up to the walls of the city of Havana itself, had relapsed into a dogged struggle in the central and eastern provinces. The Spanish arms regained a measure of control in Pinar del Rio and part of Havana, but under the existing conditions of the rural country without immediate improvement of their productive situation. Even thus partially restricted, the revolutionists held their own, and their conquest and submission, put forward by Spain as the essential and sole basis of peace, seemed as far distant as at the outset.

In this state of affairs my Administration found itself confronted with the grave problem of its duty. My message of last December reviewed the situation and narrated the steps taken with a view to relieving its acuteness and opening the way to some form of honorable settlement. The assassination of the prime minister, Canovas, led to a change of government in Spain. The former administration, pledged to subjugation without concession, gave place to that of a more liberal party, committed long in advance to a policy of reform, involving the wider principle of home rule for Cuba and Puerto Rico.

The overtures of this Government, made through its new envoy, General Woodford, and looking to an immediate and effective amelioration of the condition of the island, although not accepted to the extent of admitted mediation in any shape, were met by assurances that home rule, in advanced phase, would be forthwith offered to Cuba, without waiting for the war to end, and that more humane methods should thenceforth prevail in the conduct of hostilities. Coincidentally with these declarations, the new Government of Spain continued and completed the policy already begun by its predecessor, of testifying friendly regard for this nation by releasing American citizens held under one charge or another connected with the insurrection, so that by the end of November not a single person entitled in any way to our national protection remained in a Spanish prison.

While these negotiations were in progress the increasing destitution of the unfortunate reconcentrados and the alarming mortality among them claimed earnest attention. The success which had attended the limited measure of relief extended to the suffering American citizens among them by the judicious expenditure through the consular agencies of the money appropriated expressly for their succor by the joint resolution approved May 24, 1897, prompted the humane extension of a similar scheme of aid to the great body of sufferers. A suggestion to this end was acquiesced in by the Spanish authorities. On the 24th of December last I caused to be issued an appeal to the American people, inviting contributions in money or in kind for the succor of the starving sufferers in Cuba, following this on the 8th of January by a similar public announcement of the formation of a central Cuban relief committee, with headquarters in New York City, composed of three members representing the American National Red Cross and the religious and business elements of the community.

The efforts of that committee have been untiring and have accomplished much. Arrangements for free transportation to Cuba have greatly aided the charitable work. The president of the American Red Cross and representatives of other contributory organizations have generously visited Cuba and cooperated with the consul-general and the local authorities to make effective distribution of the relief collected through the efforts of the central committee. Nearly $200,000 in money and supplies has already reached the sufferers and more is forthcoming. The supplies are admitted duty free, and transportation to the interior has been arranged so that the relief, at first necessarily confined to Havana and the larger cities, is now extended through most if not all of the towns where suffering exists.

Thousands of lives have already been saved. The necessity for a change in the condition of the reconcentrados is recognized by the Spanish Government. Within a few days past the orders of General Weyler have been revoked; the reconcentradoes, it is said, are to be permitted to return to their homes and aided to resume the self-supporting pursuits of peace. Public works have been ordered to give them employment, and a sum of $600,000 has been appropriated for their relief.

The war in Cuba is of such a nature that short of subjugation or extermination a final military victory for either side seems impracticable. The alternative lies in the physical exhaustion of the one or the other party, or perhaps of both—a condition which in effect ended the ten years war by the truce of Zanjon. The prospect of such a protraction and conclusion of the present strife is a contingency hardly to be contemplated with equanimity by the civilized world, and least of all by the United States, affected and injured as we are, deeply and intimately, by its very existence.

Realizing this, it appeared to be my duty, in a spirit of true friendliness, no less to Spain than to the Cubans who have so much to lose by the prolongation of the struggle, to seek to bring about an immediate termination of the war. To this end I submitted, on the 27th ultimo, as a result of much representation and correspondence, through the United States minister at Madrid, propositions to the Spanish Government looking to an armistice until October 1 for the negotiation of peace with the good offices of the President.

In addition, I asked the immediate revocation of the order of reconcentration, as to permit the people to return to their farms and the needy to be relieved with provisions and supplies from the United States, cooperating with the Spanish authorities, so as to afford full relief.

The reply of the Spanish cabinet was received on the night of the 31st ultimo. It offered, as the means to bring about peace in Cuba, to confide the preparation thereof to the insular parliament, inasmuch as the concurrence of that body would be necessary to reach a final result, it being, however, understood that the powers reserved by the constitution to the central Government are not lessened or diminished. As the Cuban parliament does not meet until the 4th of May next, the Spanish Government would not object, for its part, to accept at once a suspension of hostilities if asked for by the insurgents from the general in chief, to whom it would pertain, in such case, to determine the duration and conditions of the armistice.

The propositions submitted by General Woodford and the reply of the Spanish Government were both in the form of brief memoranda, the texts of which are before me, and are substantially in the language above given. The function of the Cuban parliament in the matter of "preparing" peace and the manner of its doing so are not expessed in the Spanish memorandum; but from General Woodford's explanatory reports of preliminary discussions preceding the final conference it is understood that the Spanish Government stands ready to give the insular congress full powers to settle the terms of peace with the insurgents— whether by direct negotiation or indirectly by means of legislation does not appear.

With this last overture in the direction of immediate peace, and its disappointing reception by Spain, the Executive is brought to the end of his effort.

In my annual message of December last I said:

Of the untried measures there remained only: Recognition of the insurgents as belligerents; recognition of the independence of Cuba; neutral intervention to end the war by imposing a rational compromise between the contestants, and intervention in favor of one or the other party. I speak not of forcible annexation, for that can not be thought of. That, by our code of morality, would be criminal aggression.

Thereupon I reviewed these alternatives, in the light of President Grant's measured words, uttered in 1875, when after seven years of sanguinary, destructive, and cruel hostilities in Cuba he reached the conclusion that the recognition of the independence of Cuba was impracticable and indefensible, and that the recognition of belligerence was not warranted by the facts according to the tests of public law. I commented especially upon the latter aspect of the question, pointing out the inconveniences and positive dangers of a recognition of belligerence which, while adding to the already onerous burdens of neutrality within our own jurisdiction, could not in any way extend our influence or effective offices in the territory of hostilities.

Nothing has since occurred to change my view in this regard, and I recognize as fully now as then that the issuance of a proclamation of neutrality, by which process the so-called recognition of belligerents is published, could, of itself and unattended by other action, accomplish nothing toward the one end for which we labor—the instant pacification of Cuba and the cessation of the misery that afflicts the island.

Turning to the question of recognizing at this time the independence of the present insurgent government in Cuba, we find safe precedents in our history from an early day. They are well summed up in President Jackson's message to Congress, December 21, 1836, on the subject of the recognition of the independence of Texas.

.   .   .   .   .

I said in my message of December last, "It is to be seriously considered whether the Cuban insurrection possesses beyond dispute the attributes of statehood which alone can demand the recognition of belligerency in its favor." The same requirement must certainly be no less seriously considered when the graver issue of recognizing independence is in question, for no less positive test can be applied to the greater act than to the lesser; while on the other hand, the influences and consequences of the struggle upon the internal policy of the recognizing State, which form important factors when the recognition of belligerency is concerned, are secondary, if not rightly eliminable, factors when the real question is whether the community claiming recognition is or is not independent beyond peradventure.

Nor from the standpoint of expediency do I think it would be wise or prudent for this Government to recognize at the present time the independence of the so-called Cuban Republic. Such recognition is not necessary in order to enable the United States to intervene and pacify the island. To commit this country now to the recognition of any particular government in Cuba might subject us to embarrassing conditions of international obligation toward the organization so recognized. In case of intervention our conduct would be subject to the approval or disapproval of such government. We would be required to submit to its direction and to assume to it the mere relation of a friendly ally.

When it shall appear hereafter that there is within the island a government capable of performing the duties and discharging the functions of a separate nation, and having, as a matter of fact, the proper forms and attributes of nationality, such government can be promptly and readily recognized and the relations and interests of the United States with such nation adjusted.

There remain the alternative forms of intervention to end the war, either as an impartial neutral by imposing a rational compromise between the contestants, or as the active ally of the one party or the other.

As to the first it is not to be forgotten that during the last few months the relation of the United States has virtually been one of friendly intervention in many ways, each not of itself conclusive, but all tending to the exertion of a potential influence toward an ultimate pacific result, just and honorable to all interests concerned. The spirit of all our acts hitherto has been an earnest, unselfish desire for peace and prosperity in Cuba, untarnished by differences between us

and Spain, and unstained by the blood of American citizens.

The forcible intervention of the United States as a neutral to stop the war, according to the large dictates of humanity and following many historical precedents where neighboring States have interfered to check the hopeless sacrifices of life by internecine conflicts beyond their borders, is justifiable on rational grounds. It involves, however, hostile constraint upon both the parties to the contest as well to enforce a truce as to guide the eventual settlement.

The grounds for such intervention may be briefly summarized as follows:

First. In the cause of humanity and to put an end to the barbarities, bloodshed, starvation, and horrible miseries now existing there, and which the parties to the conflict are either unable or unwilling to stop or mitigate. It is no answer to say this is all in another country, belonging to another nation, and is therefore none of our business. It is specially our duty, for it is right at our door.

Second. We owe it to our citizens in Cuba to afford them that protection and indemnity for life and property which no government there can or will afford, and to that end to terminate the conditions that deprive them of legal protection.

Third. The right to intervene may be justified by the very serious injury to the commerce, trade, and business of our people, and by the wanton destruction of property and devastation of the island.

Fourth, and which is of the utmost importance. The present condition of affairs in Cuba is a constant menace to our peace, and entails upon this Government an enormous expense. With such a conflict waged for years in an island so near us and with which our people have such trade and business relations: when the lives and liberty of our citizens are in constant danger and their property destroyed and themselves ruined; where our trading vessels are liable to seizure and are seized at our very door by war ships of a foreign nation, the expeditions of filibustering that we are powerless to prevent altogether, and the irritating questions and entanglements thus arising —all these and others that I need not mention, with the resulting strained relations, are a constant menace to our peace, and compel us to keep on a semi-war footing with a nation with which we are at peace.

These elements of danger and disorder already pointed out have been strikingly illustrated by a tragic event which has deeply and justly moved the American people. I have already transmitted to Congress the report of the naval court of inquiry on the destruction of the battle ship *Maine* in the harbor of Havana during the night of the 15th of February. The destruction of that noble vessel has filled the national heart with inexpressible horror. Two hundred and fifty-eight brave sailors and marines and two officers of our Navy, reposing in the fancied security of a friendly harbor, have been hurled to death, grief and want brought to their homes, and sorrow to the nation.

The naval court of inquiry, which, it is needless to say, commands the unqualified confidence of the Government, was unanimous in its conclusion that the destruction of the *Maine* was caused by an exterior explosion, that of a submarine mine. It did not assume to place the responsibility. That remains to be fixed.

In any event the destruction of the *Maine,* by whatever exterior cause, is a patent and impressive proof of a state of things in Cuba that is intolerable. That condition is thus shown to be such that the Spanish Government can not assure safety and security to a vessel of the American Navy in the harbor of Havana on a mission of peace, and rightfully there.

Further referring in this connection to recent diplomatic correspondence, a dispatch from our minister to Spain, of the 26th ultimo, contained the statement that the Spanish minister for foreign affairs assured him positively that Spain will do all that the highest honor and justice require in the matter of the *Maine.* The reply above referred to of the 31st ultimo also contained an expression of the readiness of Spain to submit to an arbitration all the differences which can arise in this matter, which is subsequently explained by the note of the Spanish minister at Washington of the 10th instant, as follows:

As to the question of fact which springs from the diversity of views between the reports of the American and Spanish boards, Spain proposes that the facts be ascertained by an impartial investigation by experts, whose decision Spain accepts in advance.

To this I have made no reply.

President Grant, in 1875, after discussing the phases of the contest as it then appeared, and its hopeless and apparent indefinite prolongation, said:

In such event, I am of opinion that other nations will be compelled to assume the responsibility which devolves upon them, and to seriously consider the only remaining measure possible— mediation and intervention. Owing, perhaps, to the large expanse of water separating the island from the Peninsula, . . . the contending parties appear to have within themselves no depository of common confidence, to suggest wisdom when passion and excitement have their sway, and to assume the part of peacemaker.

In this view in the earlier days of the contest the good offices of the United States as a mediator were tendered in good faith, without any selfish purpose, in the interest of humanity and in sincere friendship for both parties, but were at the time declined by Spain, with the declaration, nevertheless, that at a future time they would be indispensable. No intimation has been received that in the opinion of Spain that time has been reached. And yet the strife continues with all its dread horrors and all its injuries to the interests of the United States and of other nations.

Each party seems quite capable of working great injury and damage to the other, as well as to all the relations and interests dependent on the existence of peace in the island; but they seem incapable of reaching any adjustment, and both have thus far failed of achieving any success whereby one party shall possess and control the island to the exclusion of the other. Under these circumstances, the agency of others, either by mediation or intervention, seems to be the only alternative which must sooner or later be involved for the termination of the strife.

In the last annual message of my immediate predecessor, during the pending struggle, it was said:

When the inability of Spain to deal successfully with the insurrection has become manifest, and it is demonstrated that her sovereignty is extinct in Cuba for all purposes of its rightful existence, and when a hopeless struggle for its reestablishment has degenerated into a strife which means nothing more than the useless sacrifice of human life and the utter destruction of the very subject-matter of the conflict, a situation will be presented in which our obligations to the sovereignty of Spain will be superseded by higher obligations, which we can hardly hesitate to recognize and discharge.

In my annual message to Congress, December last, speaking to this question, I said:

The near future will demonstrate whether the indispensable condition of a righteous peace, just alike to the Cubans and to Spain, as well as equitable to all our interests so intimately involved in the welfare of Cuba, is likely to be attained. If not, the exigency of further and other action by the United States will remain to be taken. When that time comes that action will be determined in the line of indisputable right and duty. It will be faced, without misgiving or hesitancy, in the light of the obligation this Government owes to itself, to the people who have confided to it the protection of their interests and honor, and to humanity.

Sure of the right, keeping free from all offense ourselves, actuated only by upright and patriotic considerations, moved neither by passion nor selfishness, the Government will continue its watchful care over the rights and property of American citizens and will abate none of its efforts to bring about by peaceful agencies a peace which shall be honorable and enduring. If it shall hereafter appear to be a duty imposed by our obligations to ourselves, to civilization and humanity to intervene with force, it shall be without fault on our part and only because the necessity for such action will be so clear as to command the support and approval of the civilized world.

The long trial has proved that the object for which Spain has waged the war can not be attained. The fire of insurrection may flame or may smolder with varying seasons, but it has not been and it is plain that it can not be extinguished by present methods. The only hope of relief and repose from a condition which can no longer be endured is the enforced pacification of Cuba. In the name of humanity, in the name of civilization, in behalf of endangered American interests which give us the right and the duty to speak and to act, the war in Cuba must stop.

In view of these facts and of these considerations, I ask the Congress to authorize and empower the President to take measures to secure a full and final termination of hostilities between the Government of Spain and the people of Cuba, and to secure in the island the establishment of a stable government, capable of maintaining order and observing its international obligations, insuring peace and tranquillity and the security of its citizens as well as our own, and to use the military and naval forces of the United States as may be necessary for these purposes.

And in the interest of humanity and to aid in preserving the lives of the starving people of the island I recommend that the distribution of food and supplies be continued, and that an appropriation be made out of the public Treasury to supplement the charity of our citizens.

The issue is now with the Congress. It is a solemn responsibility. I have exhausted every effort to relieve the intolerable condition of affairs which is at our doors. Prepared to execute every obligation imposed upon me by the Constitution and the law, I await your action.

Yesterday, and since the preparation of the foregoing message, official information was received by me that the latest decree of the Queen Regent of Spain directs General Blanco, in order to prepare and facilitate peace, to proclaim a suspension of hostilities, the duration and details of which have not yet been communicated to me.

This fact with every other pertinent consideration will, I am sure, have your just and careful attention in the solemn deliberations upon which you are about to enter. If this measure attains a successful result, then our aspirations as a Christian, peace-loving people will be realized. If it fails, it will be only another justification for our contemplated action.

COMMENT

It is the weakest and most inconclusive speech sent out by any President.

Joe Bailey, Democratic minority leader in the U.S. House of Representatives, April 11, 1898. Quoted in Sam Hanna Acheson, *Joe Bailey, The Last Democrat* (New York: The Macmillan Company, 1932), p. 105.

We are all jingoes now; and the head jingo is the Hon. William McKinley, the trusted and honored Chief Executive of the nation's will.

Editorial in the New York *Sun*, April 20, 1898.

---

31. *JULY 7, 1898*

Annexation of Hawaii

During the early days of hostilities, the American people were convinced that the nation had entered the Spanish-American War for purely humanitarian reasons, and immediately they rallied to support the government. The country was united as it had not been since the time of Jackson. It was not long, however, before the war began to divide the American people. This became quite evident as it furnished the necessary impetus to bring about the long-delayed annexation of Hawaii. Realizing that the Democrats would block

U.S. *Statutes at Large,* xxx, 750–51.

a treaty of annexation, the Administration as early as March, 1898, decided to follow the precedent of Texas and to annex Hawaii by joint resolution.

The resolution languished in Congress until after the beginning of the war with Spain, when the Republicans in Congress caught up with President McKinley's desire for Hawaii. All the traditional arguments were cited by the congressmen who supported annexation. They stressed the nation's moral duty to the Hawaiians, the value of the islands to the United States, and the imminent danger

*of their seizure by some other power.
Besides the old arguments, the annexa-
tionists contended that Hawaii was
needed in the war against Spain. A few
Democrats concurred in these sentiments, but most of them refused to budge.
Throughout, the debate bore witness to a
bitter conflict between the majority of
Republicans who felt that the nation's expansion should know no immediate limits
and the majority of Democrats who clung
to the tradition that the American Republic should have no colonies.*

*For a brief period it appeared as
though the opponents of annexation
might carry the day as Speaker of the
House Czar Reed refused to permit the
proposition to be brought to a vote. As
the congressional oratory thundered on,
the President even threatened to annex
Hawaii by executive decree as a war
measure. Once these threats were taken
seriously, it became only a question of
how long Speaker Reed and a minority of
both houses would hold out. When Reed
finally gave his consent for the resolution
to go to the floor of the House, the path
was cleared for a vote. The resolution
then passed the House of Representatives
on June 15, the Senate on July 6, and
received the President's signature the
following day.*

Whereas the Government of the Republic of Hawaii having, in due form,
signified its consent, in the manner provided by its constitution, to cede absolutely and without reserve to the United
States of America all rights of sovereignty of whatsoever kind in and over
the Hawaiian Islands and their dependencies, and also to cede and transfer to
the United States the absolute fee and
ownership of all public, Government, or
Crown lands, public buildings or edifices, ports, harbors, military equipment, and all other public property of
every kind and description belonging to
the Government of the Hawaiian Islands
together with every right and appur-

tenance thereunto appertaining. Therefore,

*Resolved by the Senate and House
of Representatives of the United States of
America in Congress assembled.* That
said cession is accepted, ratified, and
confirmed, and that the said Hawaiian
Islands and their dependencies be, and
they are hereby, annexed as a part of the
territory of the United States and are
subject to the sovereign dominion
thereof, and that all and singular the
property and rights hereinbefore mentioned are vested in the United States of
America.

The existing laws of the United States
relative to public lands shall not apply to
such lands in the Hawaiian Islands; but
the Congress of the United States shall
enact special laws for their management
and disposition: *Provided*, That all revenue from or proceeds of the same, except
as regards such part thereof as may be
used or occupied for the civil, military, or
naval purposes of the United States, or
may be assigned for the use of the local
government, shall be used solely for the
benefit of the inhabitants of the Hawaiian
Islands for educational and other public
purposes.

Until Congress shall provide for the
government of such islands all the civil,
judicial, and military powers exercised
by the officers of the existing government
in said islands shall be vested in such person or persons and shall be exercised in
such manner as the President of the
United States shall direct; and the President shall have power to remove said officers and fill the vacancies so occasioned.

The existing treaties of the Hawaiian
Islands with foreign nations shall forthwith cease and determine, being replaced
by such treaties as may exist, or as may
be hereafter concluded, between the
United States and such foreign nations.
The municipal legislation of the Hawaiian Islands, not enacted for the fulfillment of the treaties so extinguished, and
not inconsistent with this joint resolution

nor contrary to the Constitution of the United States nor to any existing treaty of the United States, shall remain in force until the Congress of the United States shall otherwise determine.

Until legislation shall be enacted extending the United States customs laws and regulations to the Hawaiian Islands the existing customs relations of the Hawaiian Islands with the United States and other countries shall remain unchanged.

The public debt of the Republic of Hawaii, lawfully existing at the date of the passage of this joint resolution, including the amounts due to depositors in the Hawaiian Postal Savings Bank, is hereby assumed by the Government of the United States; but the liability of the United States in this regard shall in no case exceed four million dollars. So long, however, as the existing Government and the present commercial relations of the Hawaiian Islands are continued as hereinbefore provided said Government shall continue to pay the interest on said debt.

There shall be no further immigration of Chinese into the Hawaiian Islands, except upon such conditions as are now or may hereafter be allowed by the laws of the United States; and no Chinese, by reason of anything herein contained, shall be allowed to enter the United States from the Hawaiian Islands.

The President shall appoint five commissioners, at least two of whom shall be residents of the Hawaiian Islands, who shall, as soon as reasonably practicable, recommend to Congress such legislation concerning the Hawaiian Islands as they shall deem necessary or proper.

. . . . .

COMMENT

Hawaii is the central point of the North Pacific. It is in, or near, to the direct track of commerce from all Atlantic ports, whether American or European, via Nicaragua, and from all Pacific ports, whether of North or South America, to China and Japan. . . . It is the key to the whole system. . . . In the possession of the United States it will give us command to the Pacific.

> Editorial of the San Francisco (Calif.) *Bulletin*, January 30, 1893.

No candid American would ever think of making a State of this Union out of such a group of islands with such a population as it has and is likely to have.

> Former Secretary of the Interior Carl Schurz in "Manifest Destiny," *Harper's New Monthly Magazine*, LXXXVII (October, 1893), 743.

. . . the annexation . . . of Hawaii would be no mere sporadic effort . . . but a first-fruit and a token that the nation in its evolution has aroused itself to the necessity of carrying its life . . . beyond the borders which heretofore have sufficed for its activities. . . . Comparative religion teaches that creeds which reject missionary enterprise are foredoomed to decay. May it not be so with nations?

> Admiral Alfred T. Mahan in *The Interest of America in Sea Power, Present and Future* (Boston, 1897), pp. 32–35.

32. *1899*

William McKinley and
the Philippine Problem

When the United States entered the Span-
ish-American War, there were very few
demands for American acquisition of the
Philippine Islands. The average Ameri-
can had little knowledge of their exist-
ence. President McKinley and most of
his Administration had entertained no
thought of obtaining additional territory
as the fruits of the war. Far from having
designs on the Philippines, McKinley
was reported to have had only a vague
idea of their location when informed of
Admiral Dewey's victory at Manila. It
was not long, however, before the vic-
tories of American arms prepared the
way for a colonial career for the United
States. The bulk of the nation's press
began declaring for expansion on mili-
tary, religious, commercial, and humani-
tarian grounds. American businessmen
who had previously opposed the war
underwent a conversion and began to talk
of the Philippines as a gateway to the
markets of eastern Asia. The Protestant
clergy became convinced that expansion
could pay dividends in the salvation of
human souls. The servant of his party
rather than its leader, McKinley eventu-
ally became an expansionist as the tide
of imperialism made such a course safe
and practical. Below, McKinley relates
how he arrived at the decision to annex
the Philippines. It is significant that con-
siderations of national interest played
little part in his thinking. Moreover, he
appeared unconcerned with the difficulty

CHARLES S. OLCOTT, *The Life of William*
McKinley (Boston: Houghton Mifflin Company,
1916), II, 109–11.

of defending the islands. But in the long
run, the islands were to be a diplomatic
and military liability to American policies
in the Pacific. One scholar has even stated
that "the acquisition of the Philippines
was the greatest blunder of American
diplomacy."

I have been criticized a good deal
about the Philippines, but don't deserve
it. The truth is I didn't want the Philippines, and when they came to us, as a gift
from the gods, I did not know what to
do with them. When the Spanish War
broke out, Dewey was at Hongkong, and
I ordered him to go to Manila and to
capture or destroy the Spanish fleet, and
he had to; because, if defeated, he had
no place to refit on that side of the globe,
and if the Dons were victorious, they
would likely cross the Pacific and ravage
our Oregon and California coasts. And
so he had to destroy the Spanish fleet, and
did it! But that was as far as I thought
then.

When next I realized that the Philippines had dropped into our laps I confess I did not know what to do with them.
I sought counsel from all sides—Democrats as well as Republicans—but got
little help. I thought first we would take
only Manila; then Luzon; then other
islands, perhaps, also. I walked the floor
of the White House night after night until midnight; and I am not ashamed to
tell you, gentlemen, that I went down
on my knees and prayed Almighty God
for light and guidance more than one
night. And one night late it came to me

this way—I don't know how it was, but it came: (1) That we could not give them back to Spain—that would be cowardly and dishonorable; (2) that we could not turn them over to France, or Germany —our commercial rivals in the Orient— that would be bad business and discreditable; (3) that we could not leave them to themselves—they were unfit for self-government—and they would soon have anarchy and misrule over there worse than Spain's was; and (4) that there was nothing left for us to do but to take them all, and to educate the Filipinos, and uplift and civilize and Christianize them, and by God's grace do the very best we could by them, as our fellow-men for whom Christ also died. And then I went to bed, and went to sleep, and slept soundly, and the next morning I sent for the chief engineer of the War Department (our map-maker), and I told him to put the Philippines on the map of the United States [pointing to a large map on the wall of his office], and there they are, and there they will stay while I am President!

COMMENT

Thus . . . duty and interest alike, duty of the highest kind and interest of the highest and best kind, impose upon us the retention of the Philippines, the development of the islands, and the expansion of our Eastern commerce.

> Henry Cabot Lodge, Republican of Massachusetts, speaking in the U.S. Senate, March 7, 1900. *Congressional Record*, 56th Cong., 1st Sess., 1899–1900, xxxIII, 2629.

I believe that this democracy, the goverment of, by, and for the people, is not fitted for a colonial policy, which means conquest by force, or, as President McKinley called it "criminal aggression" and arbitrary rule over subject populations. I believe that, if it attempts such a policy on a large scale, its inevitable degeneracy will hurt the progress of civilization more than it can possibly further that progress by planting its flag upon foreign soil on which its fundamental principles of government cannot live.

> Former Secretary of the Interior Carl Schurz in a letter to Bijornstjerne Bjornson, September 22, 1898. Frederic Bancroft, ed., *Speeches, Correspondence, and Political Papers of Carl Schurz* (New York: G. P. Putnam's Sons, 1913), v, 514.

If the Philippines are annexed, what is to prevent the Chinese, the Negritos, and the Malays coming to our own country?

> Samuel Gompers, president of the American Federation of Labor, quoted in an anonymous pamphlet, *Expensive Expansion* (Boston, 1900), p. 9.

33. SEPTEMBER 6, 1899

John Hay's Open Door Policy

Immediately prior to the Spanish-American War, China granted spheres of influ-

Papers Relating to the Foreign Relations of the United States, 1899 (Washington, D.C., 1901), pp. 129–30.

ence to various European powers. Fearing that they would discriminate in favor of their own nations in matters of trade and other economic interests, Secretary of State John Hay dispatched identical notes to the governments of France, Great Britain, Italy, Japan, and Russia in which he urged the various powers to declare that they would not interfere with any existing treaty port and that the Chinese tariff would be collected on all merchandise entering their sphere. In a popular sense, the policy meant that all nations were to have equal commercial opportunities in China. During the following year, Hay expanded the Open Door concept to include the territorial integrity and administrative entity of China.

Most powers were somewhat reluctant to accept the restrictions put forth in Hay's notes. But Hay ignored the equivocations he received in response to his notes and announced that all powers had indicated final acceptance of the Open Door concept. Nevertheless, the partition of China was not prevented by Hay's policy. Rather, China was temporarily saved by the diplomatic stalemate in which the European powers found themselves.

Once it became this nation's policy to uphold the Open Door Policy, the United States was drawn further and further into the diplomatic entanglements of the Far East. Unfortunately, the United States did not have sufficient military power to enforce the Open Door policy should some other nation wish to violate China's independence. Unable and unwilling to fight for the Open Door policy in Asia, the United States on several occasions was forced to retreat from its declared principles.

At the time when the Government of the United States was informed by that of Germany that it had leased from His Majesty the Emperor of China the port of Kiao-chao and the adjacent territory in the province of Shantung, assurances were given to the ambassador of the United States at Berlin by the Imperial German minister for foreign affairs that the rights and privileges insured by treaties with China to citizens of the United States would not thereby suffer or be in anywise impaired within the area over which Germany had thus obtained control.

More recently, however, the British Government recognized by a formal agreement with Germany the exclusive right of the latter country to enjoy in said leased area and the contiguous "sphere of influence or interest" certain privileges, more especially those relating to railroads and mining enterprises; but as the exact nature and extent of the rights thus recognized have not been clearly defined, it is possible that serious conflicts of interest may at any time arise not only between British and German subjects within said area, but that the interests of our citizens may also be jeopardized thereby.

Earnestly desirous to remove any cause of irritation and to insure at the same time to the commerce of all nations in China the undoubted benefits which should accrue from a formal recognition by the various powers claiming "spheres of interest" that they shall enjoy perfect equality of treatment for their commerce and navigation within such "spheres," the Government of the United States would be pleased to see His German Majesty's Government give formal assurances, and lend its cooperation in securing like assurances from the other interested powers, that each, within its respective sphere of whatever influence—

First. Will in no way interfere with any treaty port or any vested interest within any so-called "sphere of interest" or leased territory it may have in China.

Second. That the Chinese treaty tariff of the time being shall apply to all merchandise landed or shipped to all such ports as are within said "sphere of interest" (unless they be "free ports"), no matter to what nationality it may belong, and that duties so leviable shall be collected by the Chinese Government.

Third. That it will levy no higher

harbor dues on vessels of another nationality frequenting any port in such "sphere" than shall be levied on vessels of its own nationality, and no higher railroad charges over lines built, controlled, or operated within its "sphere" on merchandise belonging to citizens or subjects of other nationalities transported through such "sphere" than shall be levied on similar merchandise belonging to its own nationals transported over equal distances.

The liberal policy pursued by His Imperial German Majesty in declaring Kiao-chao a free port and in aiding the Chinese Government in the establishment there of a custom-house are so clearly in line with the proposition which this Government is anxious to see recognized that it entertains the strongest hope that Germany will give its acceptance and hearty support.

The recent ukase of His Majesty the Emperor of Russia declaring the port of Ta-lien-wan open during the whole of the lease under which it is held from China to the merchant ships of all nations, coupled with the categorical assurances made to this Government by His Imperial Majesty's representative at this capital at the time and since repeated to me by the present Russian ambassador, seem to insure the support of the Emperor to the proposed measure. Our ambassador at the Court of St. Petersburg has in consequence been instructed to submit it to the Russian Government and to request their early consideration of it. A copy of my instruction on the subject to Mr. Tower is herewith inclosed for your confidential information.

The commercial interests of Great Britain and Japan will be so clearly served by the desired declaration of intentions, and the views of the Governments of these countries as to the desirability of the adoption of measures insuring the benefits of equality of treatment of all foreign trade throughout China are so similar to those entertained by the United States, that their acceptance of the propositions herein outlined and their cooperation in advocating their adoption by the other powers can be confidently expected. . . .

. . . . .

COMMENT

There was nothing new or original about these proposals; they were nothing but a re-edition of the British policy as it had been put forward for years. . . . The efforts of Hay, then, had no practical bearing on the situation as it was at the turn of the century.

William L. Langer, historian, in *The Diplomacy of Imperialism* (New York: Alfred A. Knopf, Inc., 1951), pp. 686–88.

. . . to keep the Open Door in China the Government of the United States was drawn further and further into the diplomatic entanglements of the Far East. . . . This was assuming responsibilities of policy compensated by no corresponding advantages to the United States.

Professor Samuel Flagg Bemis in *A Diplomatic History of the United States* (New York: Henry Holt & Co., Inc., 1953), p. 486.

34. *JANUARY 9, 1900*

Albert Beveridge on Expansion

The end of the Spanish-American War and the ratification of the Treaty of Paris failed to end the debate on the nation's colonial policy. In their fight against President McKinley, the anti-imperialists called attention to the Filipino insurrection against American rule. Especially helpful were the stories of the atrocities which the American troops committed against the civilian population. There were reports that the Americans had burned villages and crops, murdered innocent women and children, and killed unarmed Filipino troops rather than take prisoners.

During 1899 and 1900, the anti-imperialists carried their fight to all parts of the nation. They increased the number of conferences, pamphlets, magazine articles, and speeches devoted to their cause. Anti-imperialist societies were established throughout the country. As there was no hope of achieving success through the Republican party, the anti-imperialists brought increasing pressure on the Democrats, demanding that they make imperialism the paramount issue in the presidential campaign of 1900,

The imperialists met these arguments by pointing to the potential markets of the East, the White Man's Burden, America's tradition of expansion, and the danger of a general war if the Philippines were left open to a European scramble. The following speech by Indiana's Republican Senator Albert J. Beveridge on the Senate floor is typical of many arguments which the expansionists used in defense of their position.

Congressional Record, 56th Cong., 1st Sess., 1900, XXXIII, pt. I, 711–12.

. . . . .

Mr. President, this question is deeper than any question of party politics; deeper than any question of the isolated policy of our country even; deeper even than any question of constitutional power. It is elemental. It is racial. God has not been preparing the English-speaking and Teutonic peoples for a thousand years for nothing but vain and idle self-contemplation and self-admiration. No! He has made us the master organizers of the world to establish system where chaos reigns. He has given us the spirit of progress to overwhelm the forces of reaction throughout the earth. He has made us adepts in government that we may administer government among savage and senile peoples. Were it not for such a force as this the world would relapse into barbarism and night. And of all our race He has marked the American people as His chosen nation to finally lead in the regeneration of the world. This is the divine mission of America, and it holds for us all the profit, all the glory, all the happiness possible to man. We are trustees of the world's progress, guardians of its righteous peace. The judgment of the Master is upon us: "Ye have been faithful over a few things; I will make you ruler over many things."

What shall history say of us? Shall it say that we renounced that holy trust, left the savage to his base condition, the wilderness to the reign of waste, deserted duty, abandoned glory, forget our sordid profit even, because we feared our strength and read the charter of our powers with the doubter's eye and the quibbler's mind? Shall it say that, called by events to captain and command the proudest, ablest, purest race of history in history's noblest work, we declined that great commission? Our fathers would not have had it so. No! They founded no paralytic government, incapable of the simplest acts of administration. They planted no sluggard people, passive while the world's work calls them. They established no reactionary nation. They unfurled no retreating flag.

That flag has never paused in its onward march. Who dares halt it now— now, when history's largest events are carrying it forward; now, when we are at last one people, strong enough for any task, great enough for any glory destiny can bestow? How comes it that our first century closes with the process of consolidating the American people into a unit just accomplished, and quick upon the stroke of that great hour presses upon us our world opportunity, world duty, and world glory, which none but a people welded into an indivisible nation can achieve or perform?

Blind indeed is he who sees not the hand of God in events so vast, so harmonious, so benign. Reactionary indeed is the mind that perceives not that this vital people is the strongest of the saving forces of the world; that our place, therefore, is at the head of the constructing and redeeming nations of the earth; and that to stand aside while events march on is a surrender of our interests, a betrayal of our duty as blind as it is base. Craven indeed is the heart that fears to perform a work so golden and so noble; that dares not win a glory so immortal.

Do you tell me that it will cost us money? When did Americans ever measure duty by financial standards? Do you tell me of the tremendous toil required to overcome the vast difficulties of our task? What mighty work for the world, for humanity, even for ourselves, has ever been done with ease? Even our bread must we eat by the sweat of our faces.

Why are we charged with power such as no people ever knew, if we are not to use it in a work such as no people ever wrought? Who will dispute the divine meaning of the fable of the talents?

Do you remind me of the precious blood that must be shed, the lives that must be given, the broken hearts of loved ones for their slain? And this is indeed a heavier price than all combined. And yet as a nation every historic duty we have done, every achievement we have accomplished, has been by the sacrifice of our noblest sons. Every holy memory that glorifies the flag is of those heroes who have died that its onward march might not be stayed. It is the nation's dearest lives yielded for the flag that makes it dear to us; it is the nation's most precious blood poured out for it that makes it precious to us. That flag is woven of heroism and grief; of the bravery of men and women's tears, of righteousness and battle of sacrifice and anguish of triumph and of glory. It is these which make our flag a holy thing. Who would tear from that sacred banner the glorious legends of a single battle where it has waved on land or sea? What son of a soldier of the flag whose father fell beneath it on any field would surrender that proud record for the heraldry of a king? In the cause of civilization, in the service of the Republic anywhere on earth, Americans consider wounds the noblest decorations man can win, and count the giving of their lives a glad and precious duty.

Pray God that spirit never fails. Pray God the time may never come when Mammon and the love of ease shall so debase our blood that we will fear to shed it for the flag and its imperial destiny. Pray God the time may never come when American heroism is but a legend like the story of the Cid, American faith in our mission and our might a dream dissolved, and the glory of our mighty race departed.

And that time will never come. We

will renew our youth at the fountain of new and glorious deeds. We will exalt our reverence for the flag by carrying it to a noble future as well as by remembering its ineffable past. Its immortality will not pass, because everywhere and always we will acknowledge and discharge the solemn responsibilities our sacred flag, in its deepest meaning, puts upon us. And so, Senators, with reverent hearts, where dwells the fear of God, the American people move forward to the future of their hope and the doing of His work.

. . . . .

COMMENT

It is time to dismiss "the craven fear of being great," to recognize the place in the world which God has given us and to accept the responsibilities which it devolves upon us in behalf of Christian civilization.

> Clergyman Josiah Strong in *Expansion under New World Conditions* (New York: Doubleday, Page & Co., 1900), p. 295.

We hold that the policy known as imperialism is hostile to liberty and tends toward militarism, an evil from which it has been our glory to be free. We regret that it has become necessary in the land of Washington and Lincoln to reaffirm that all men, of whatever race or color, are entitled to life, liberty, and the pursuit of happiness. We maintain that governments derive their just powers from the consent of the governed. We insist that the subjection of any people is "criminal aggression" and open disloyalty to the distinctive principles of our government.

> Platform of the American Anti-Imperialist League, adopted at Chicago, October 18, 1899. *Library Tracts*, No. 10, p. 2.

. . . coming . . . as a Senator from . . . South Carolina, with 750,000 colored population and only 500,000 whites, I realize what you are doing, while you don't; and I would save this country from the injection into it of another race question which can only breed bloodshed and a costly war and the loss of the lives of our brave soldiers

> Ben Tillman, Democrat of South Carolina, speaking to the U.S. Senate, February 2, 1899. *Congressional Record*, 55th Cong., 3d Sess., 1899, xxxii, 1389.

We assert that no nation can long endure half republic and half empire, and we warn the American people that imperialism abroad will lead quickly and inevitably to despotism at home.

> Democratic national platform, 1900. Quoted from Kirk H. Porter, ed., *National Party Platforms* (New York: The Macmillan Company, 1924), p. 211.

35. DECEMBER 6, 1904

The Roosevelt Corollary to the Monroe Doctrine

When civil war left several Latin American nations bankrupt during the first years of the twentieth century, rumors reached the Department of State that various European nations were planning to use force in order to protect investments there. Fearing that the European powers would never leave, President Theodore Roosevelt during his annual message to Congress in December, 1904, announced a new Caribbean policy to the world, which subsequently became known as the Roosevelt Corollary to the Monroe Doctrine. In essence, Roosevelt's declaration provided the theoretical basis for the establishment by the United States of protectorates in Latin American nations. Public opinion in the United States expressed widespread approval of the speech, while the Latin American governments indicated little concern. Application of the Roosevelt Corollary during the next two decades was an important factor in securing the Western Hemisphere against violations of the Monroe Doctrine and in promoting economic and political stability in Latin America. But in the long run, the American policy of intervention in the Caribbean area caused such widespread resentment against the United States in Latin American nations, that in 1928 Under Secretary of State J. Reuben Clark officially repudiated the Roosevelt Corollary.

. . . . .

It is not true that the United States feels any land hunger or entertains any

House Documents (4780), 58th Cong., 3d Sess., pp. xli–xlii.

projects as regards the other nations of the Western Hemisphere save such as are for their welfare. All that this country desires is to see the neighboring countries stable, orderly, and prosperous. Any country whose people conduct themselves well can count upon our hearty friendship. If a nation shows that it knows how to act with reasonable efficiency and decency in social and political matters, if it keeps order and pays its obligations, it need fear no interference from the United States. Chronic wrongdoing, or an impotence which results in a general loosening of the ties of civilized society, may in America, as elsewhere, ultimately require intervention by some civilized nation, and in the Western Hemisphere the adherence of the United States to the Monroe Doctrine may force the United States, however reluctantly, in flagrant cases of such wrongdoing or impotence, to the exercise of an international police power. If every country washed by the Caribbean Sea would show the progress in stable and just civilization which with the aid of the Platt amendment Cuba has shown since our troops left the island, and which so many of the republics in both Americas are constantly and brilliantly showing, all question of interference by this Nation with their affairs would be at an end. Our interests and those of our southern neighbors are in reality identical. They have great natural riches, and if within their borders the reign of law and justice obtains, prosperity is sure to come to them. While they thus obey the primary laws of civilized society they may rest assured that they will be treated by us in a spirit of cordial and helpful sympathy. We would interfere with them only in the last resort, and then only if it became evident that their inability or unwillingness to do justice at home and abroad had violated the rights of the United States or had invited foreign aggression to the detriment of the entire body of American nations. It is a mere truism to say that every nation, whether in America or anywhere else, which desires to maintain its freedom, its independence, must ultimately realize that the right of such independence can not be separated from the responsibility of making good use of it.

In asserting the Monroe Doctrine, in taking such steps as we have taken in regard to Cuba, Venezuela, and Panama, and in endeavoring to circumscribe the theater of war in the Far East, and to secure the open door in China, we have acted in our own interest as well as in the interest of humanity at large. There are, however, cases in which, while our own interests are not greatly involved, strong appeal is made to our sympathies. Ordinarily it is very much wiser and more useful for us to concern ourselves with striving for our own moral and material betterment here at home than to concern ourselves with trying to better the condition of things in other nations. We have plenty of sins of our own to war against, and under ordinary circumstances we can do more for the general uplifting of humanity by striving with heart and soul to put a stop to civic corruption, to brutal lawlessness and violent race prejudices here at home than by passing resolutions about wrongdoing elsewhere. Nevertheless there are occa-

sional crimes committed on so vast a scale and of such peculiar horror as to make us doubt whether it is not our manifest duty to endeavor at least to show our disapproval of the deed and our sympathy with those who have suffered by it. The cases must be extreme in which such a course is justifiable. There must be no effort made to remove the mote from our brother's eye if we refuse to remove the beam from our own. But in extreme cases action may be justifiable and proper. What form the action shall take must depend upon the circumstances of the case; that is, upon the degree of the atrocity and upon our power to remedy it. The cases in which we could interfere by force of arms as we interfered to put a stop to intolerable conditions in Cuba are necessarily very few. Yet it is not to be expected that a people like ours, which in spite of certain very obvious shortcomings, nevertheless as a whole shows by its consistent practice its belief in the principles of civil and religious liberty and of orderly freedom, a people among whom even the worst crime, like the crime of lynching, is never more than sporadic, so that individuals and not classes are molested in their fundamental rights—it is inevitable that such a nation should desire eagerly to give expression to its horror on an occasion like that of the massacre of the Jews in Kishenef, or when it witnesses such systematic and long-extended cruelty and oppression as the cruelty and oppression of which the Armenians have been the victims, and which have won for them the indignant pity of the civilized world.

. . . . .

COMMENT

. . . the Monroe Doctrine is not a policy of aggression; it is a policy of self-defense. . . . the policy of the Monroe Doctrine does not infringe upon the independence and sovereignty of other American states. . . . Our interest is in having prosperous, peaceful and law-abiding neighbors with whom we can cooperate to mutual advantage. . . . it is apparent that the Monroe Doctrine does not stand

in the way of Pan American cooperation; rather it affords the necessary foundation for that cooperation in the independence and security of American states.

> Secretary of State Charles Evans Hughes in a speech to the American Bar Association
> at Minneapolis, Minnesota, August 30, 1923. C. E. Hughes, *Address before the
> Fifty-sixth Annual Meeting of the American Bar Association* (Washington, D.C.,
> 1928).

. . . so far as Latin America is concerned, the doctrine is now, and always has
been, not an instrument of violence and oppression, but an unbought, freely
bestowed, and wholly effective guaranty of their freedom, independence, and
territorial integrity against the imperialistic designs of Europe.

> Under Secretary of State J. Reuben Clark in *Memorandum on the Monroe Doctrine*
> (Washington, D.C., 1930), p. xxiv.

36. *1905*

Lochner v. New York

At the turn of the twentieth century,
leaders of the social justice movement
exerted pressure on state and federal
governments to pass legislation which
would alleviate social distress. The reformers were particularly anxious to
enact legislation which would uplift the
status of unprotected workers. In this
effort, the reform groups scored many
victories, but as most of the legislation
was restrictive in nature, the question of
the constitutionality of the statutes generally arose. Because the courts laid
down no rigid definition of due process,
each statute in question had to be examined before its constitutionality could
be determined. To be constitutional, a
statute had to be, in the opinion of the
courts, "reasonable legislation," but
what constituted reasonableness depended on the courts' set of values.

This aspect of the Supreme Court's
thinking is stated quite clearly in the decisions, Holden v. Hardy (1898) and
Lochner v. New York (1905). In Holden
v. Hardy, the Court upheld a Utah stat-

198 U.S. 45 (1905).

ute which made it unlawful for miners
to work more than an eight hour day. In
that decision, the Court announced that
a state must protect the health and morals
of its citizens, but it failed to make clear
how far a state might go in regulating
hours. How dangerous did an occupation
have to be before a state could exercise
such policy power? In the case of Lochner v. New York, the Court was asked
to pass on the constitutionality of a New
York statute which limited the number
of hours which bakers could work a
week. By a five to four majority, the
Court ruled that the baker's trade was
not a particularly unhealthy one and
therefore the act was a violation of the
Fourteenth Amendment. In other words,
a state could not restrict the freedom of
labor or management unless there were
compelling reasons for doing so.

The indictment, it will be seen,
charges that the plaintiff in error violated
the one hundred and tenth section of
article 8, chapter 415, of the Laws of
1897, known as the labor law of the

State of New York, in that he wrongfully and unlawfully required and permitted an employee working for him to work more than sixty hours in one week. There is nothing in any of the opinions delivered in this case, either in the Supreme Court or the Court of Appeals of the State, which construes the section, in using the word "required," as referring to any physical force being used to obtain the labor of an employee. It is assumed that the word means nothing more than the requirement arising from voluntary contract for such labor in excess of the number of hours specified in the statute. There is no pretense in any of the opinions that the statute was intended to meet a case of involuntary labor in any form. All the opinions assume that there is no real distinction, so far as this question is concerned, between the words "required" and "permitted." The mandate of the statute that "no employee shall be required or permitted to work," is the substantial equivalent of an enactment that "no employee shall contract or agree to work," more than ten hours per day, and as there is no provision for special emergencies the statute is mandatory in all cases. It is not an act merely fixing the number of hours which shall constitute a legal day's work, but an absolute prohibition upon the employer, permitting, under any circumstances, more than ten hours work to be done in his establishment. The employee may desire to earn the extra money, which would arise from his working more than the prescribed time, but this statute forbids the employer from permitting the employee to earn it.

The statute necessarily interferes with the right of contract between the employer and employees, concerning the number of hours in which the latter may labor in the bakery of the employer. The general right to make a contract in relation to his business is part of the liberty of the individual protected by the Fourteenth Amendment of the Federal Constitution. Under that provision no State can deprive any person of life, liberty or property without due process of law. The right to purchase or to sell labor is part of the liberty protected by this amendment, unless there are circumstances which exclude the right. There are, however, certain powers, existing in the sovereignty of each State in the Union, somewhat vaguely termed police powers, the exact description and limitation of which have not been attempted by the courts. Those powers, broadly stated and without, at present, any attempt at a more specific limitation, relate to the safety, health, morals and general welfare of the public. Both property and liberty are held on such reasonable conditions as may be imposed by the governing power of the State in the exercise of those powers, and with such conditions the Fourteenth Amendment was not designed to interfere.

The State, therefore, has power to prevent the individual from making certain kinds of contracts, and in regard to them the Federal Constitution offers no protection. If the contract be one which the State, in the legitimate exercise of its police power, has the right to prohibit, it is not prevented from prohibiting it by the Fourteenth Amendment. Contracts in violation of a statute, either of the Federal or state government, or a contract to let one's property for immoral purposes, or to do any other unlawful act, could obtain no protection from the Federal Constitution, as coming under the liberty of person or of free contract. Therefore, when the State, by its legislature, in the assumed exercise of its police powers, has passed an act which seriously limits the right to labor or the right of contract in regard to their means of livelihood between persons who are *sui juris* (both employer and employee), it becomes of great importance to determine which shall prevail—the right of the individual to labor for such time as he may choose, or the right of the State to prevent the individual from laboring or from entering into any contract to labor, beyond a certain time prescribed by the State.

This court has recognized the existence and upheld the exercise of the police powers of the States in many cases which might fairly be considered as border ones, and it has, in the course of its determination of questions regarding the asserted invalidity of such statutes, on the ground of their violation of the rights secured by the Federal Constitution, been guided by rules of a very liberal nature, the application of which has resulted, in numerous instances, in upholding the validity of state statutes thus assailed. Among the later cases where the state law has been upheld by this court is that of *Holden* v. *Hardy,* 169 U.S. 366. A provision in the act of the legislature of Utah was there under consideration, the act limiting the employment of workmen in all underground mines or workings, to eight hours per day, "except in cases of emergency, where life or property is in imminent danger." It also limited the hours of labor in smelting and other institutions for the reduction or refining of ores or metals to eight hours per day, except in like cases of emergency. The act was held to be a valid exercise of the police powers of the State. A review of many of the cases on the subject, decided by this and other courts, is given in the opinion. It was held that the kind of employment, mining, smelting, etc., and the character of the employees in such kinds of labor, were such as to make it reasonable and proper for the State to interfere to prevent the employees from being constrained by the rules laid down by the proprietors in regard to labor. The following citation from the observations of the Supreme Court of Utah in that case was made by the judge writing the opinion of this court, and approved: "The law in question is confined to the protection of that class of people engaged in labor in underground mines, and in smelt-

ers and other works, wherein ores are reduced and refined. This law applies only to the classes subjected by their employment to the peculiar conditions and effects attending underground mining and work in smelters, and other works for the reduction and refining of ores. Therefore it is not necessary to discuss or decide whether the legislature can fix the hours of labor in other employments."

It will be observed that, even with regard to that class of labor, the Utah statute provided for cases of emergency wherein the provisions of the statute would not apply. The statute now before this court has no emergency clause in it, and, if the statute is valid, there are no circumstances and no emergencies under which the slightest violation of the provisions of the act would be innocent. . . .

It must, of course, be conceded that there is a limit to the valid exercise of the police power by the State. There is no dispute concerning this general proposition. Otherwise the Fourteenth Amendment would have no efficacy and the legislatures of the States would have unbounded power, and it would be enough to say that any piece of legislation was enacted to conserve the morals, the health or the safety of the people; such legislation would be valid, no matter how absolutely without foundation the claim might be. The claim of the police power would be a mere pretext—become another and delusive name for the supreme sovereignty of the State to be exercised free from constitutional restraint. This is not contended for. In every case that comes before this court, therefore, where legislation of this character is concerned and where the protection of the Federal Constitution is sought, the question necessarily arises: Is this a fair, reasonable and appropriate exercise of the police power of the State, or is it an unreasonable, unnecessary and arbitrary interference with the right of the individual to his personal liberty or to enter into those contracts in relation to labor which may seem to him appropriate or necessary for the support of himself and his family? Of course the liberty of contract relating to labor includes both parties to it. The one has as much right to purchase as the other to sell labor.

This is not a question of substituting the judgment of the court for that of the legislature. If the act be within the power of the State it is valid, although the judgment of the court might be totally opposed to the enactment of such a law. But the question would still remain: Is it within the police power of the State? and that question must be answered by the court.

The question whether this act is valid as a labor law, pure and simple, may be dismissed in a few words. There is no reasonable ground for interfering with the liberty of person or the right of free contract, by determining the hours of labor, in the occupation of a baker. There is no contention that bakers as a class are not equal in intelligence and capacity to men in other trades or manual occupations, or that they are not able to assert their rights and care for themselves without the protecting arm of the State, interfering with their independence of judgment and of action. They are in no sense wards of the State. Viewed in the light of a purely labor law, with no reference whatever to the question of health, we think that a law like the one before us involves neither the safety, the morals nor the welfare of the public, and that the interest of the public is not in the slightest degree affected by such an act. The law must be upheld, if at all, as a law pertaining to the health of the individual engaged in the occupation of a baker. It does not affect any other portion of the public than those who are engaged in that occupation. Clean and wholesome bread does not depend upon whether the baker works but ten hours per day or only sixty hours a week. The limitation of the hours of labor does not come within the police power on that ground.

It is a question of which of two powers or rights shall prevail—the power of the State to legislate or the right of the individual to liberty of person and freedom of contract. The mere assertion that the subject relates though but in a remote degree to the public health does not necessarily render the enactment valid. The act must have a more direct relation, as a means to an end, and the end itself must be appropriate and legitimate, before an act can be held to be valid which interferes with the general right of an individual to be free in his person and in his power to contract in relation to his own labor. . . .

We think the limit of the police power has been reached and passed in this case. There is, in our judgment, no reasonable foundation for holding this to be necessary or appropriate as a health law to safeguard the public health or the health of the individuals who are following the trade of a baker. If this statute be valid, and, if, therefore, a proper case is made out in which to deny the right of an individual, *sui juris*, as employer or employee, to make contracts for the labor of the latter under the protection of the provisions of the Federal Constitution, there would seem to be no length to which legislation of this nature might not go. . . .

We think that there can be no fair doubt that the trade of a baker, in and of itself, is not an unhealthy one to that degree which would authorize the legislature to interfere with the right to labor, and with the right of free contract on the part of the individual, either as employer or employee. In looking through statistics regarding all trades and occupations, it may be true that the trade of a baker does not appear to be as healthy as some other trades, and is also vastly more healthy than still others. To the common understanding the trade of a baker has never been regarded as an unhealthy one. Very likely physicians would not recommend the exercise of that or of any other trade as a remedy for ill health. Some occupations are more healthy than others, but we think there are none which might not come under the power of the legislature to supervise and control the hours of working therein, if the mere fact that the occupation is not absolutely and perfectly healthy is to confer that right upon the legislative department of the Government. It might be safely affirmed that almost all occupations more or less affect the health. There must be more than the mere fact of the possible existence of some small amount of unhealthiness to warrant legislative interference with liberty. It is unfortunately true that labor, even in any department, may possibly carry with it the seeds of unhealthiness. But are we all, on that account, at the mercy of legislative majorities? A printer, a tinsmith, a locksmith, a carpenter, a cabinetmaker, a dry goods clerk, a bank's, a lawyer's or a physician's clerk, or a clerk in almost any kind of business, would all come under the power of the legislature, on this assumption. No trade, no occupation, no mode of earning one's living, could escape this all-pervading power, and the acts of the legislature in limiting the hours of labor in all employments would be valid, although such limitation might seriously cripple the ability of the laborer to support himself and his family. In our large cities there are many buildings into which the sun penetrates for but a short time in each day, and these buildings are occupied by people carrying on the business of bankers, brokers, lawyers, real estate, and many other kinds of business, aided by many clerks, messengers, and other employees. Upon the assumption of the validity of this act under review, it is not possible to say that an act, prohibiting lawyers' or bank clerks, or others, from contracting to labor for their employers more than eight hours a day, would be invalid. It might be said that it is unhealthy to work more than that number of hours in an apartment lighted by artificial light during the working hours of the day; that the occupation of the bank clerk, the law-

yer's clerk, the real estate clerk, or the broker's clerk in such offices is therefore unhealthy, and the legislature in its paternal wisdom must, therefore, have the right to legislate on the subject of and to limit the hours for such labor, and if it exercises that power and its validity be questioned, it is sufficient to say, it has reference to the public health; it has reference to the health of the employees condemned to labor day after day in buildings where the sun never shines; it is a health law, and therefore it is valid, and cannot be questioned by the courts.

It is also urged, pursuing the same line of argument, that it is to the interest of the State that its population should be strong and robust, and therefore any legislation which may be said to tend to make people healthy must be valid as health laws, enacted under the police power. If this be a valid argument and a justification for this kind of legislation, it follows that the protection of the Federal Constitution from undue interference with liberty of person and freedom of contract is visionary, wherever the law is sought to be justified as a valid exercise of the police power. Scarcely any law but might find shelter under such assumptions, and conduct, properly so called, as well as contract, would come under the restrictive sway of the legislature. Not only the hours of employees, but the hours of employers could be regulated, and doctors, lawyers, scientists, all professional men, as well as athletes and artisans, could be forbidden to fatigue their brains and bodies by prolonged hours of exercise, lest the fighting strength of the State be impaired. We mention these extreme cases because the contention is extreme. We do not believe in the soundness of the views which uphold this law. On the contrary, we think that such a law as this, although passed in the assumed exercise of the police power, and as relating to the public health, or the health of the employees named, is not within that power, and is invalid. The act is not, within any fair meaning of the term, a health law, but is an illegal interference with the rights of individuals, both employers and employees, to make contracts regarding labor upon such terms as they may think best, or which they may agree upon with the other parties to such contracts. Statutes of the nature of that under review, limiting the hours in which grown and intelligent men may labor to earn their living, are mere meddlesome interferences with the rights of the individual, and they are not saved from condemnation by the claim that they are passed in the exercise of the police power and upon the subject of the health of the individual whose rights are interfered with, unless there be some fair ground, reasonable in and of itself, to say that there is material danger to the public health or to the health of the employees, if the hours of labor are not curtailed. If this be not clearly the case the individuals, whose rights are thus made the subject of legislative interference, are under the protection of the Federal Constitution regarding their liberty of contract as well as of person; and the legislature of the State has no power to limit their right as proposed in this statute. All that it could properly do has been done by it with regard to the conduct of bakeries, as provided for in the other sections of the act, above set forth. These several sections provide for the inspection of the premises where the bakery is carried on, with regard to furnishing proper wash-rooms and water-closets, apart from the bakeroom, also with regard to providing proper drainage, plumbing and painting; the sections, in addition, provide for the height of the ceiling, the cementing or tiling of floors, where necessary in the opinion of the factory inspector, and for other things of that nature; alterations are also provided for and are to be made where necessary in the opinion of the inspector, in order to comply with the provisions of the statute. These various sections may be wise and valid regulations,

and they certainly go to the full extent of providing for the cleanliness and the healthiness, so far as possible, of the quarters in which bakeries are to be conducted. Adding to all these requirements, a prohibition to enter into any contract of labor in a bakery for more than a certain number of hours a week, is, in our judgment, so wholly beside the matter of a proper, reasonable and fair provision, as to run counter to that liberty of person and of free contract provided for in the Federal Constitution.

It was further urged on the argument that restricting the hours of labor in the case of bakers was valid because it tended to cleanliness on the part of the workers, as a man was more apt to be cleanly when not overworked, and if cleanly then his "output" was also more likely to be so. What has already been said applies with equal force to this contention. We do not admit the reasoning to be sufficient to justify the claimed right of such interference. The State in that case would assure the position of a supervisor, or *pater familias*, over every act of the individual, and its right of governmental interference with his hours of labor, his hours of exercise, the character thereof, and the extent to which it shall be carried would be recognized and upheld. In our judgment it is not possible in fact to discover the connection between the number of hours a baker may work in the bakery and the healthful quality of the bread made by the workman. The connection, if any exists, is too shadowy and thin to build any argument for the interference of the legislature. If the man works ten hours a day it is all right, but if ten and a half or eleven his health is in danger and his bread may be unhealthful and, therefore, he shall not be permitted to do it. This, we think, is unreasonable and entirely arbitrary. When assertions such as we have adverted to become necessary in order to give, if possible, a plausible foundation for the contention that the law is a "health law," it gives rise to at least a suspicion that there was some other motive dominating the legislature than the purpose to subserve the public health or welfare.

This interference on the part of the legislatures of the several States with the ordinary trades and occupations of the people seems to be on the increase. . . .

It is manifest to us that the limitation of the hours of labor as provided for in this section of the statute under which the indictment was found, and the plaintiff in error convicted, has no such direct relation to and no such substantial effect upon the health of the employee as to justify us in regarding the section as really a health law. It seems to us that the real object and purpose were simply to regulate the hours of labor between the master and his employees (all being men, *sui juris*), in a private business, not dangerous in any degree to morals or in any real and substantial degree, to the health of the employees. Under such circumstances the freedom of master and employee to contract with each other in relation to their employment, and in defining the same, cannot be prohibited or interfered with, without violating the Federal Constitution.

The judgment of the Court of Appeals of New York as well as that of the Supreme Court and of the County Court of Oneida County must be reversed and the case remanded to the County Court for further proceedings not inconsistent with this opinion.

Reversed

. . . . .

MR. JUSTICE HOLMES DISSENTING

I regret sincerely that I am unable to agree with the judgment in this case, and that I think it my duty to express my dissent.

This case is decided upon an economic theory which a large part of the country does not entertain. If it were a question whether I agreed with that theory, I should desire to study it further and long before making up my mind. But I do not conceive that to be my duty, because I strongly believe that my agreement or disagreement has nothing to do with the right of a majority to enbody their opinions in law. It is settled by various decisions of this court that state constitutions and state laws may regulate life in many ways which we as legislators might think as injudicious or if you like as tyrannical as this, and which equally with this interfere with the liberty to contract. Sunday laws and usury laws are ancient examples. A more modern one is the prohibition of lotteries. The liberty of the citizen to do as he likes so long as he does not interfere with the liberty of others to do the same, which has been a shibboleth for some well-known writers, is interfered with by school laws, by the Post Office, by every state or municipal institution which takes his money for purposes thought desirable, whether he likes it or not. The Fourteenth Amendment does not enact Mr. Herbert Spencer's Social Statics. The other day we sustained the Massachusetts vaccination law. United States and state statutes and decisions cutting down the liberty to contract by way of combination are familiar to this court. Two years ago we upheld the prohibition of sales of stock on margins or for future delivery in the constitution of California. The decision sustaining an eight hour law for miners is still recent. Some of these laws embody convictions or prejudices which judges are likely to share. Some may not. But a constitution is not intended to embody a particular economic theory, whether of paternalism and the organic relation of the citizen to the State or of *laissez faire*. It is made for people of fundamentally differing views, and the accident of our finding certain opinions natural and familiar or novel and even shocking ought not to conclude our judgment upon the question whether statutes embodying them conflict with the Constitution of the United States.

General propositions do not decide concrete cases. The decision will depend on a judgment or intuition more subtle than any articulate major premise. But I think that the proposition just stated if it is accepted, will carry us far toward the end. Every opinion tends to become a law. I think that the word liberty in the Fourteenth Amendment is perverted when it is held to prevent the natural outcome of a dominant opinion, unless it can be said that a rational and fair man necessarily would admit that the statute proposed would infringe fundamental principles as they have been understood by the traditions of our people and our law. It does not need research to show that no such sweeping condemnation can be passed upon the statute before us. A reasonable man might think it a proper measure on the score of health. Men whom I certainly could not pronounce unreasonable would uphold it as a first instalment of a general regulation of the hours of work. Whether in the latter aspect it would be open to the charge of inequality I think it unnecessary to discuss.

37.

Lincoln Steffens on Special Privilege

At the beginning of the twentieth century, a revolution took place in American journalism. It was led by a group of reporters called "muckrakers" who attempted to call to the attention of the American people the fact that their political institutions had become corrupt and that the American ideal of equality of economic opportunity was rapidly becoming anachronistic. By focusing on the shortcomings of their society, these reporters fired the righteous indignation of the American people and stirred them to support social, economic, and political reforms. Writing for such magazines as McClure's, Cosmopolitan, and Munsey's, the leading muckrakers were Ida Tarbell, Upton Sinclair, Lincoln Steffens, Samuel Hopkins Adams, Mark Sullivan, Ray Stannard Baker, and David Graham Phillips. The most successful "muckraker" of the Progressive period was

From The Autobiography of Lincoln Steffens, pp. 470–479, 492–494. Copyright 1931 by Harcourt, Brace & World, Inc.; renewed 1959 by PETER STEFFENS. Reprinted by permission of the publishers.

Lincoln Steffens. Dedicated to the task of convincing the public that American government was no longer representative, he investigated the forces responsible for political corruption in the nation's cities. In city after city, he found corrupt alliances between businessmen and politicians, which he described in McClure's magazine. The following selection is from one of his articles which subsequently appeared in his autobiography.

. . . Traveling back and forth between the east and the west, I had been crossing that State [Ohio] frequently. It tempted me. Ohio had succeeded Virginia as the source of presidents, cabinet men, judges, great statesmen; it was the State of Mark Hanna and his President McKinley, of the good governor Herrick, Boss Cox of Cincinnati, Golden Rule Jones of Toledo, as well as of Tom Johnson of Cleveland. Ohio was on the great broad way to Washington, but it was not an open road. It was a labyrinthine mix-up of crossroads and tunnels. I knew something of it. I had stopped off in Toledo, and Brand

Whitlock, who was my sort of reformer, took me to Sam Jones, who took me home, sat me down, and humorously, wonderingly, for hours read aloud to me Walt Whitman and the New Testament. Never a word about the State or the nation, nothing about the city, even, or politics. The poet and the prophet were his political leaders. He was practicing what they preached, literally, religiously, gleefully; and Brand Whitlock smiled, and Ned Cochran, a Scripps editor, jeered, at the confusion applied Christianity caused in the minds of a Christian community, and they wondered at the way the sinners understood and respected the Golden Rule. The churches, the chambers of commerce, the best clubs, hated Golden Rule Jones, who was repeatedly elected mayor; professional criminals visited but did not operate in Toledo. Jones's story was a good one, odd and significant, but it had nothing to do with Ohio and the U.S.A.—not then; not to me.

And Tom Johnson—I had stopped off in Cleveland, called on Fred Howe, who spoke my language; he introduced me to the rest of "the Johnson gang." They were sincere, able, thinking men, all of them, a well-chosen staff, and they were happy in their work. The Cleveland reformers were the happiest reformers I had ever met. But they followed and believed in, they almost adored, Tom Johnson. How easily misled reformers are! Not I. They took me to the mayor, and I watched him do business an hour or so before I met him. It was like seeing a captain of industry on the stage: he received his callers one by one, swiftly, without haste; he listened, all attention, till he understood; then he would smile or laugh, give a decision, and—"Next!" No asking for time to "think it over" or to "consult his colleagues," no talk of "commissions to investigate," no "come again next week." It was no or yes, genial, jolly, but final. Tom Johnson was the big business man, the very type. But I was

not to be taken in; no big business man could fool me. When my turn came I went, businesslike, straight to the heart of my business. Waving aside all politeness, all appearances, and the bunk, I asked my leading question.

"What are you up to, Mr. Mayor? What are you after?"

"That I cannot tell you," he answered just as straight. "You wouldn't understand if I did."

His contempt struck me, as Darrow's had, with a troubled wonder which carried the sense that I was missing something. I answered Tom Johnson's challenge with a threat. I would look around his town and see for myself what he was doing, and he agreed to that heartily.

"That's the way to do it," he said. "The town is open to you. We'll give you the freedom of the city. You may go where you like, ask anything you want to know, and if anybody refuses to open a door or answer your questions, you come back to me and I'll tell you. And then, when you know something, we can talk."

Fred Howe told me afterward that the mayor forbade them to try and influence me; they were to give me any information I might ask for, but otherwise I was to be let alone. Tom Johnson's orders were obeyed, I was as alone as I was in Pittsburgh, and I proceeded in Cleveland as I did there: talked to newspaper men, saw the politicians on the other side, and invited facts or even rumors from the enemy. I could not get anything against Tom Johnson and his administration except complaints so trivial that they only confirmed the impression I was suffering that there was nothing very bad about this city government; it was almost "good." I went away with a sense of defeat to carry on in Illinois and Wisconsin, for, you understand, I knew about big, bad business men; knew what a business government was; and knew that Tom Johnson, the street railway magnate, was not giving his time and his service to Cleveland for the city's sake. I would wait; he would soon be showing what he was after. He would be running for governor or the U.S. Senate, or his honest young associates would be passing innocently some franchise for his guilty uses. It was a year or more before I came back to Cleveland. I finished my [investigations in] Illinois, Wisconsin, and Rhode Island, and then, sure enough, Tom Johnson was running for governor. By that time, however, I had seen and I had grasped the nature of the compulsion which drove city reformers to the State and governors like LaFollette to the Senate at Washington. It was not necessarily ambition; it was a search for the seat of American sovereignty, and probably the bad business men and the bad politicians followed that same pursuit. They were all feeling for the throne whence they could wield power and do what they wanted to do.

. . . . .

When I arrived in Cleveland to study Ohio, Johnson told me his personal story. He was a poor boy, the son of southern parents ruined by the war. To help out the family he sold newspapers from the city in his small home town. Fat, jolly, and bright, he made friends, and one of them, the conductor on the train that brought in the papers, said to him one day: "See here, Tom, I like you and I'm going to boost your business. Hereafter I'll bring papers only for you. You'll have a monopoly and can charge what you like, twenty-five cents a piece for them."

Tom Johnson not only made some money, he learned the principle of monopoly; and when he grew older and the other boys in his gang used to talk about going to work at a trade or in the grocery or some other store, he wondered at their folly in choosing a competitive line. He meant to start in some monopoly, and he did; he went into the street railway business, and he applied the monopoly principle to it. The street railways were monopolies, each of its route, but they competed with one another for power, con-

trol, domination. He discovered an idea that would bring him control. Most street car lines in his day in all cities started from the center of the town and ran out to some city limit and back. Each got thus the heavy traffic, downtown in the morning to work, back home in the evening. If he could unite two such lines and run them clear through a town, his one consolidated road would get, in addition to the up and down business, the lighter but good midday traffic across town and so have an advantage that would enable him to beat the other companies and force them into one consolidated monopoly. He worked these principles to a triumph in several cities and was applying them in Cleveland; he had already got the Big Consolidated there and was driving out Mark Hanna, with his "Little Con," when something happened. Tom Johnson read a book.

The peanut butcher on a train one day was trying to sell him Henry George's *Social Problems* when the conductor passing down the aisle said, "That's a book you ought to read, Mr. Johnson." The street railway man had a soft spot for conductors; he took this one's advice, and after buying and reading the book, went to his attorney and said: "I want you to answer that book for me. I can't. And I must. For if that book is right I am all wrong and I'll have to get out of my business." The lawyer answered Henry George, but only as a lawyer, not to his client's satisfaction. Tom Johnson went to New York, called together a group of his rich friends, and put it up to them. They all read Henry George, met one night, and discussed it till daylight. Johnson defended the book; he didn't want to accept its doctrines; he begged his friends to upset them, and they tried; they were able men, too, but Tom Johnson had seen the light, and his friends not only failed to clear his mind of the single-tax theories; they were themselves convinced. They all saw what Henry George pointed out: that excessive riches came unearned to individuals and companies owning land, natural resources, like water, coal, oil, etc., and franchises, such as steam and street railways, which, being common wealth to start with, became more and more valuable as the growing population increased the need and the value of these natural monopolies. The increased value of them was created by the mere growth of the population, who should have it, and George proposed that government should take it back by taxing nothing but the values of land, natural resources and monopolies.

Tom Johnson returned to Cleveland, sold out his monopoly business, gradually, and went into politics as a successful business man with vision, a plan. He ran for Congress, was elected, and there, in Washington, worked and voted against his own interests for the public interest. He did it genially, jovially, with humor, but with all the force of his good mind and powerful will. He could not accomplish much. A large representative body is no place for an executive, he discovered, and the House of Representatives, filled with men nominated by the State machines, had long ago been organized into a stronghold of the system. Tom Johnson consulted with Henry George, and they decided that the thing for Johnson to do was to go to a city, run for mayor, and try for the control so that he could apply the George principles and set an example in policy and in achievement, for all cities, all States.

That, then, was what Tom Johnson was up to in Cleveland, that was what he was after, to make there what he called the City on a Hill.

The City on a Hill. Tom Johnson's ambition was big enough to account for him. To take one city and solve there the social, economic, political problems and so set an example to other super-business men of a job worth doing and to the world of a government as it should be— that was as understandable as the wish to make a million dollars. Especially since this business man already has his million plus. My petty suspicions of Tom Johnson vanished. He belonged in the class with Folk and LaFollette, Roosevelt, Seth Low, and Walter Fisher. He was on "our side," the people's; that was why the other side, the plutogogues, called him a demagogue. But I heard some of Tom Johnson's campaign speeches in the infamous tent he moved about for meetings in parts of the town where there were no halls or where opponents closed halls against him. His "circus" speeches were indeed entertaining; he encouraged questions from the floor, and he answered them with quick wit and barbed facts; but those political meetings were more like classes in economic and current (local) history than harangues. The only just complaint of his enemies was that he "had gone back on his class." This was said by men who almost in the same breath would declare that reform was not a class struggle, that there was no such thing as class consciousness, no classes, in America; and they meant it, too. The charge against Tom Johnson, Folk, LaFollette and, later Rudolph Spreckels, of treason to their class, is an expression of our unconscious class consciousness, and an example of our appalling sincerity, miscalled hypocrisy.

Tom Johnson had gone back on his class and on himself as well. He was a convert from plutocracy to democracy, and that made a great difference. He was not merely a good rich man, like Seth Low, out to "give" us good government; he was not merely able and efficient like Fisher, forceful and energetic like Roosevelt, honest and persistent like Joe Folk. Tom Johnson had not always been a good, honest man; he had been a street railway magnate in politics and had done some—not all, but all that he had found necessary to his business—of the corrupting things a street railway man typically does. . . .

Honesty is not enough; it takes intelligence, some knowledge or theory of economics, courage, strength, will power, humor, leadership—it takes intellectual integrity to solve our political problems. And these Tom Johnson had above all the politicians of my day. His courage was the laughing sort; his humor was the kind that saved him tears. He had the instinct and the habit of experimentation, and he had the training of a big, successful man of business on the other side of politics. A practical business man, he was a practical politician, too. He knew the game. He could pick and lead a team; men loved to follow him; he made it fun. Resourceful and understanding of the economics of a fight, he could make clear to others what they were up against and what they had to do about it. . . .

He cleared my head of a lot of rubbish, left there from my academic education and reform associations. I asked him one day why he had thought I would not understand him if he told me what he was up to in Cleveland.

"Oh, I could see," he said, "that you did not know what it was that corrupted politics. First you thought it was bad politicians, who turned out to be pretty good fellows. Then you blamed the bad business men who bribed the good fellows, till you discovered that not all business men bribed and that those who did were pretty good business men. The little business men didn't bribe; so you settled upon, you invented the phrase 'big business,' and that's as far as you and your kind have got: that it is big business that does all the harm. Hell! Can't you see that it's privileged business that does it? Whether it's a big steam railroad that wants a franchise or a little gambling-house that wants not to be raided, a temperance society that wants a law passed, a poor little prostitute, or a big merchant occupying an alley for storage —it's those who seek privileges who cor-

rupt, it's those who possess privileges that defend our corrupt politics. Can't you see that?"

This was more like a flash of light than a speech, and as I took it in and shed it around in my head, he added: "It is privilege that causes evil in the world, not wickedness; and not men."

And I remembered then something I heard him say one day to a group of the business men he was fighting, something neither they nor I understood at the time. To a remonstrance of theirs that I do not recall, he blurted out: "It's fun, running the business of the city of Cleveland; it's the biggest, most complicated, most difficult, and most satisfying business in Cleveland. A street railway is child's play, compared with it; a coal mine is a snap; a bank?—Bah. There's something that blinds you fellows, and I know what it is. It's what fooled me so long when I was running public service corporations. And I'll tell you something you want to know: how to beat me.

"If I could take away from you the things you have, the franchises, the privileges, that make you enemies of your city, you would see what I see and run my job yourselves, and you'd beat me for mayor and manage the city of Cleveland better than I do." . . .

. . . "Big business" was, and it still is, the current name of the devil, the root of all evil, political and economic. It is a blind phrase, useless; it leads nowhere. We can't abolish business, we cannot regulate big business, and we are finding that we cannot limit bigness in business, which must grow. The phrase does not cover what we mean. I know that; I must have known it, else Tom Johnson could not have told it me. As early as St. Louis I had seen and written that the big businesses which were active in political corruption were the railroads, public service corporations, banks, etc., which are "big," but also saloons, gambling and bawdy houses, which are small. And I had seen and written that what these big and little businesses all had in common was not size but the need of privileges: franchises and special legislation, which required legislative corruption; protective tariffs, interpretations of law in their special interest or leniency or "protection" in the enforcement of laws calling for pulls with judges, prosecutors, and the police. As Tom Johnson said, then, it was "privilege" that was the source of the evil; it was "privileged business" that was the devil, and I had been describing and meaning this all the time I had been writing "big business." Why? My old German professor of psychology had taught us to distinguish between perception and apperception, between seeing things with the eyes and reaching out with the mind to grasp them, what the new school of *Gestalt* psychology now calls "insight." Tom Johnson was tempting me to apperceive the perception that it was privilege that hurts us. Not easy, this; it was consequential: it went to the bottom of all our moral culture of right and wrong.

If it was privilege that caused what we call evil, it was privilege that had to be dealt with, not men. Not big men, not bad men, not crooks, and not capitalists —not even the capitalist class! Punishment of individuals, the class struggle and strikes, wars—all hatred, vengeance, force, were unscientific. To put in prison a man who bought government to get a street railway franchise was wrong; we should put the franchise where men can't get it. To shift our votes from one to another of two political parties, both of which are organized to serve the privilege-seekers, was folly. To throw out the rascals and put into office honest men without removing that which makes good men do bad things was as irrational as our experience had taught us it was "unpractical." The international wars of corrupted governments for trade routes, foreign markets, "empire" and the natural resources of backward countries, strikes and the class war for the conquest of economic power and advantages— these were as senseless as passing laws for reform and for peace. It's all upside down. What society does is to teach the ideal of success, set up the temptation of power and riches to men and nations—if they are brave enough to risk and able enough to escape the threats of penalties for getting caught. These warnings keep off all but the best men, biologically best. Then when these best men succeed we honor them, and if they slip we hate and punish them. What we ought to do is to let the losers of the race go, and take down the prizes we offer to the winners.

. . . . .

COMMENT

The muckrakers spoke to a public willing to recognize as corrupt an incredibly varied assortment of conventional acts. . . . These charges and counter-charges arose because the world has been altered radically, not because Americans fell in love with honesty. If we condemn what we once honored, if we brand as criminal the conventional acts of twenty years ago, it's because we have developed new necessities and new expectations.

Journalist Walter Lippmann, *Drift and Mastery* (New York: Henry Holt & Company, 1914), pp. 5, 9.

In Bunyan's "Pilgrim's Progress" you may recall the description of the Man with the Muck-rake, the man who could look no way but downward, with the muck-rake in his hand; who was offered a celestial crown for his muck-rake, but continued to rake to himself the filth of the floor. . . . Now, it is very necessary that we should not flinch from seeing what is vile and debasing. There is filth on the floor, and it must be scraped up with the muck-rake.

President Theodore Roosevelt in a speech at Washington, D.C., April 14, 1906. New York *Times*, April 15, 1906.

Everybody is talkin' these days about Tammany men growin' rich on graft, but nobody thinks of drawin' the distinction between honest graft and dishonest graft. There's all the difference in the world between the two. . . . I've made a big fortune out of the game, and I'm gettin' richer every day, but I've not gone in for dishonest graft . . . and neither has any of the men who have made big fortunes in politics. . . . Just let me explain by examples. My party's in power in the city, and it's goin' to undertake a lot of public improvements. Well, I'm tipped off, say, that they're going to lay out a new park at a certain place. I see my opportunity and I take it. I go to that place and I buy up all the land I can in the neighborhood. Then the board of this or that makes its plan public, and there is a rush to get my land, which nobody cared particular for before. Ain't it perfectly honest to charge a good price and make a profit on my investment and foresight? Of course, it is. Well, that's honest graft.

Observations of Tammany Hall sachem George Washington Plunkitt as recorded by William L. Riordon. Richard Hofstadter, ed., *Great Issues in American History* (New York: Alfred A. Knopf, Inc., 1959), II, 253–54.

---

38. *NOVEMBER 30, 1908*

Root–Takahira Agreement

Following the Russo-Japanese War, tension between the United States and Japan began to mount. The most dangerous development was the manifestation of anti-Japanese feeling in the United States, particularly in California, where Japanese children were frequently barred from attending white schools. Meanwhile, there were indications that Japan intended to expand in the Far East. For example, the Japanese established a protectorate over Korea and attempted to obtain economic and political control over Manchuria. Concerned for the safety of the Philippines, the Roosevelt Administration entered into the Root–Takahira Agreement, which was concluded by an exchange of notes between

Papers Relating to the Foreign Relations of the U.S., 1908 (Washington, D.C., 1912), pp. 510–11.

Secretary of State Elihu Root and the Japanese ambassador in Washington, Baron Takahira. By the agreement, the two governments declared themselves willing to respect each other's territorial possessions in the Pacific area. Moreover, the agreement recognized Japan's expanding interest in Manchuria. It is important to note that the agreement mentioned the "integrity of China" but that it failed to qualify it with the word "territorial." Roosevelt was granting the Japanese a free hand in Manchuria in return for Japan's promise not to interfere with the Philippines. In certain respects, the Root–Takahira Agreement represented a retreat from the Open Door policy of John Hay.

EXCELLENCY: I have the honor to acknowledge the receipt of your note of to-day setting forth the result of the exchange of views between us in our recent interviews defining the understanding of the two Governments in regard to their policy in the region of the Pacific Ocean.

It is a pleasure to inform you that this expression of mutual understanding is welcome to the Government of the United States as appropriate to the happy relations of the two countries and as the occasion for a concise mutual affirmation of that accordant policy respecting the Far East which the two Governments have so frequently declared in the past.

I am happy to be able to confirm to your excellency, on behalf of the United States, the declaration of the two Governments embodied in the following words:

1. It is the wish of the two Governments to encourage the free and peaceful development of their commerce on the Pacific Ocean.

2. The policy of both Governments, uninfluenced by any aggressive tendencies, is directed to the maintenance of the existing status quo in the region above mentioned, and to the defense of the principle of equal opportunity for commerce and industry in China.

3. They are accordingly firmly resolved reciprocally to respect the territorial possessions belonging to each other in said region.

4. They are also determined to preserve the common interests of all powers in China by supporting by all pacific means at their disposal the independence and integrity of China and the principle of equal opportunity for commerce and industry of all nations in that Empire.

5. Should any event occur threatening the status quo as above described or the principle of equal opportunity as above defined, it remains for the two Governments to communicate with each other in order to arrive at an understanding as to what measures they may consider it useful to take.

COMMENT

... it is regrettable ... in the light of subsequent events that these agreements had not been made much more detailed and specific.

> Historian Tyler Dennett in *Roosevelt and the Russo-Japanese War; A Critical Study of American Policy in Eastern Asia in 1902–5* (New York: Doubleday, Page & Company, 1925), pp. 314–15.

It is ... peculiarly our interest not to take any steps as regards Manchuria which will give the Japanese cause to feel, with or without reason, that we are hostile to them, or a menace ... to their interests. ... if the Japanese choose to follow a course of conduct to which we are adverse, we cannot stop it unless we are prepared to go to war, and a successful war about Manchuria would require a fleet as good as that of England, plus an army as good as that of Germany.

> Former President Theodore Roosevelt in a letter to President William Howard Taft, December 22, 1910. The Roosevelt MSS., Library of Congress.

Root was eager to leave office with some symbol of a restored Japanese-American cordiality. He was too realistic to assume that a mere paper agreement could restrain a Japan bent on conquest. But he trusted the existing regime in Tokyo, and he saw no harm and much good in a mutual subscription to general principles.

> Historian Richard W. Leopold in *Elihu Root and the Conservative Tradition* (Boston: Little Brown & Co., 1954), p. 62.

39. *AUGUST 31, 1910*

Theodore Roosevelt on New Nationalism

Borrowing the phrase "New National-
ism" from Herbert Croly's book The
Promise of American Life, *Theodore*
Roosevelt delivered the address printed
below on the occasion of the dedication
of the John Brown Battlefield at Osawa-
tomie, Kansas. He told the nation's Pro-
gressives that they must abandon their
historic creed of intense individualism
and that they must use the federal govern-
ment as a regulator and protector of busi-
ness, industry, and workers. The federal
government must do more than destroy
special privilege. It must assume a posi-
tive program of government intervention
and participation in economics and social
affairs. Roosevelt expounded this same
philosophy during the presidential cam-
paign of 1912, in contrast to his Demo-
cratic opponent Woodrow Wilson, who
still advocated many of the laissez-faire
concepts of the nineteenth century. By
1916, however, Wilson had adopted the
New Nationalism outlook as the Demo-
cratic party's platform. By then, Roose-
velt had become so partisan in his attacks
on Wilson that it made little difference to
him that the President and most of the
Democratic party had accepted many of
the ideas expressed in the Osawatomie
address.

We come here to-day to commemorate
one of the epoch-making events of the
long struggle for the rights of man—the
long struggle for the uplift of humanity.
Our country—this great republic—means
nothing unless it means the triumph of a

THEODORE ROOSEVELT, *The New Nationalism*
(New York: Outlook Co., 1910), pp. 3–5, 7–21,
22–33.

real democracy, the triumph of popular
government, and, in the long run, of an
economic system under which each man
shall be guaranteed the opportunity to
show the best that there is in him. That is
why the history of America is now the
central feature of the history of the
world; for the world has set its face hope-
fully toward our democracy; and, O my
fellow citizens, each one of you carries
on your shoulders not only the burden
of doing well for the sake of your own
country, but the burden of doing well and
of seeing that this nation does well for
the sake of mankind.

There have been two great crises in
our country's history: first, when it was
formed, and then, again, when it was perpetuated; and, in the second of these
great crises—in the time of stress and
strain which culminated in the Civil War,
on the outcome of which depended the
justification of what had been done earlier, you men of the Grand Army, you
men who fought through the Civil War,
not only did you justify your generation,
not only did you render life worth living
for our generation, but you justified the
wisdom of Washington and Washington's
colleagues. If this republic had been
founded by them only to be split asunder
into fragments when the strain came,
then the judgment of the world would
have been that Washington's work was
not worth doing. It was you who crowned
Washington's work, as you carried to
achievement the high purpose of Abraham Lincoln.

Now, with this second period of our
history the name of John Brown will be
forever associated; and Kansas was the

theater upon which the first act of the second of our great national life dramas was played. It was the result of the struggle in Kansas which determined that our country should be in deed as well as in name devoted to both union and freedom; that the great experiment of democratic government on a national scale should succeed and not fail. In name we had the Declaration of Independence in 1776; but we gave the lie by our acts to the words of the Declaration of Independence until 1865; and words count for nothing except in so far as they represent acts. This is true everywhere; but, O my friends, it should be truest of all in political life. A broken promise is bad enough in private life. It is worse in the field of politics. No man is worth his salt in public life who makes on the stump a pledge which he does not keep after election; and, if he makes such a pledge and does not keep it, hunt him out of public life. I care for the great deeds of the past chiefly as spurs to drive us onward in the present. I speak of the men of the past partly that they may be honored by our praise of them, but more that they may serve as examples for the future. . . .

I do not speak of this struggle of the past merely from the historic standpoint. Our interest is primarily in the application to-day of the lessons taught by the contest of half a century ago. It is of little use for us to pay lip loyalty to the mighty men of the past unless we sincerely endeavor to apply to the problems of the present precisely the qualities which in other crises enabled the men of that day to meet those crises. It is half melancholy and half amusing to see the way in which well-meaning people gather to do honor to the men who, in company with John Brown, and under the lead of Abraham Lincoln, faced and solved the great problems of the nineteenth century, while, at the same time, these same good people nervously shrink from, or frantically denounce, those who are trying to meet the problems of the twentieth century in the spirit which was accountable for the successful solution of the problems of Lincoln's time.

. . . . .

In every wise struggle for human betterment one of the main objects, and often the only object, has been to achieve in large measure equality of opportunity. In the struggle for this great end, nations rise from barbarism to civilization, and through it people press forward from one stage of enlightenment to the next. One of the chief factors in progress is the destruction of special privilege. The essence of any struggle for healthy liberty has always been, and must always be, to take from some one man or class of men the right to enjoy power, or wealth, or position, or immunity, which has not been earned by service to his or their fellows. That is what you fought for in the Civil War, and that is what we strive for now.

At many stages in the advance of humanity, this conflict between the men who possess more than they have earned and the men who have earned more than they possess is the central condition of progress. In our day it appears as the struggle of free men to gain and hold the right of self-government as against the special interests, who twist the methods of free government into machinery for defeating the popular will. At every stage, and under all circumstances, the essence of the struggle is to equalize opportunity, destroy privilege, and give to the life and citizenship of every individual the highest possible value both to himself and to the commonwealth. That is nothing new. All I ask in civil life is what you fought for in the Civil War. I ask that civil life be carried on according to the spirit in which the army was carried on. You never get perfect justice, but the effort in handling the army was to bring to the front the men who could do the job. Nobody grudged promotion to Grant, or Sherman, or Thomas, or Sheridan, because they earned it. The only complaint was when a man got promotion which he did not earn.

Practical equality of opportunity for all citizens, when we achieve it, will have two great results. First, every man will have a fair chance to make of himself all that in him lies; to reach the highest point to which his capacities, unassisted by special privilege of his own and un-hampered by the special privilege of others, can carry him, and to get for him-self and his family substantially what he has earned. Second, equality of opportu-nity means that the commonwealth will get from every citizen the highest service of which he is capable. No man who car-ries the burden of the special privileges of another can give to the commonwealth that service to which it is fairly entitled.

I stand for the square deal. But when I say that I am for the square deal, I mean not merely that I stand for fair play under the present rules of the game, but that I stand for having those rules changed so as to work for a more sub-stantial equality of opportunity and of reward for equally good service. One word of warning, which, I think, is hardly necessary in Kansas. When I say I want a square deal for the poor man, I do not mean that I want a square deal for the man who remains poor because he has not got the energy to work for himself. If a man who has had a chance will not make good, then he has got to quit. And you men of the Grand Army, you want justice for the brave man who fought, and punishment for the coward who shirked his work. Is not that so?

Now, this means that our government, national and state, must be freed from the sinister influence or control of special interests. Exactly as the special interests of cotton and slavery threatened our po-litical integrity before the Civil War, so now the great special business interests too often control and corrupt the men and methods of government for their own profit. We must drive the special in-terests out of politics. That is one of our tasks to-day. Every special interest is en titled to justice—full, fair, and complete —and, now, mind you, if there were any attempt by mob violence to plunder and work harm to the special interest, what ever it may be, that I most dislike, and the wealthy man, whomsoever he may be, for whom I have the greatest con tempt, I would fight for him, and you would if you were worth your salt. He should have justice. For every special in terest is entitled to justice, but not one is entitled to a vote in Congress, to a voice on the bench, or to representation in any public office. The Constitution guarantees protection to property, and we must make that promise good. But it does not give the right of suffrage to any corporation.

The true friend of property, the true conservative, is he who insists that prop-erty shall be the servant and not the mas-ter of the commonwealth; who insists that the creature of man's making shall be the servant and not the master of the man who made it. The citizens of the United States must effectively control the mighty commercial forces which they have them-selves called into being.

There can be no effective control of corporations while their political activity remains. To put an end to it will be neither a short nor an easy task, but it can be done.

We must have complete and effective publicity of corporate affairs, so that the people may know beyond peradventure whether the corporations obey the law and whether their management entitles them to the confidence of the public. It is necessary that laws should be passed to prohibit the use of corporate funds di-rectly or indirectly for political pur-poses; it is still more necessary that such laws should be thoroughly enforced. Cor-porate expenditures for political pur-poses, and especially such expenditures by public service corporations, have sup-plied one of the principal sources of cor-ruption in our political affairs.

It has become entirely clear that we

must have government supervision of the capitalization, not only of public service corporations, including, particularly, railways, but of all corporations doing an interstate business. I do not wish to see the nation forced into the ownership of the railways if it can possibly be avoided, and the only alternative is thoroughgoing and effective regulation, which shall be based on a full knowledge of all the facts, including a physical valuation of property. This physical valuation is not needed, or, at least, is very rarely needed, for fixing rates; but it is needed as the basis of honest capitalization.

We have come to recognize that franchises should never be granted except for a limited time, and never without proper provision for compensation to the public. It is my personal belief that the same kind and degree of control and supervision which should be exercised over public service corporations should be extended also to combinations which control necessaries of life, such as meat, oil, and coal, or which deal in them on an important scale. I have no doubt that the ordinary man who has control of them is much like ourselves. I have no doubt he would like to do well, but I want to have enough supervision to help him realize that desire to do well.

I believe that the officers, and, especially, the directors, of corporations should be held personally responsible when any corporation breaks the law.

Combinations in industry are the result of an imperative economic law which cannot be repealed by political legislation. The effort at prohibiting all combination has substantially failed. The way out lies, not in attempting to prevent such combinations, but in completely controlling them in the interest of the public welfare. For that purpose the Federal Bureau of Corporations is an agency of first importance. Its powers, and, therefore, its efficiency, as well as that of the Interstate Commerce Commission, should be largely increased. We have a right to

expect from the Bureau of Corporations and from the Interstate Commerce Commission a very high grade of public service. We should be as sure of the proper conduct of the interstate railways and the proper management of interstate business as we are now sure of the conduct and management of the national banks, and we should have as effective supervision in one case as in the other. The Hepburn Act, and the amendment to the Act in the shape in which it finally passed Congress at the last session, represent a long step in advance, and we must go yet further.

There is a widespread belief among our people that, under the methods of making tariffs which have hitherto obtained, the special interests are too influential. Probably this is true of both the big special interests and the little special interests. These methods have put a premium on selfishness, and, naturally, the selfish big interests have gotten more than their smaller, though equally selfish, brothers. The duty of Congress is to provide a method by which the interest of the whole people shall be all that receives consideration. To this end there must be an expert tariff commission, wholly removed from the possibility of political pressure or of improper business influence. Such a commission can find the real difference between cost of production, which is mainly the difference of labor cost here and abroad. As fast as its recommendations are made, I believe in revising one schedule at a time. A general revision of the tariff almost inevitably leads to log-rolling and the subordination of the general public interest to local and special interests.

No man should receive a dollar unless that dollar has been fairly earned. Every dollar received should represent a dollar's worth of service rendered—not gambling in stocks, but service rendered. The really big fortune, the swollen fortune, by the mere fact of its size acquires qualities which differentiate it in kind as well as in degree from what is possessed by men of relatively small means. Therefore, I believe in a graduated income tax on big fortunes, and in another tax which is far more easily collected and far more effective—a graduated inheritance tax on big fortunes, properly safeguarded against evasion and increasing rapidly in amount with the size of the estate.

The people of the United States suffer from periodical financial panics to a degree substantially unknown among the other nations which approach us in financial strength. There is no reason why we should suffer what they escape. It is of profound importance that our financial system should be promptly investigated, and so thoroughly and effectively revised as to make it certain that hereafter our currency will no longer fail at critical times to meet our needs.

Of conservation I shall speak more at length elsewhere. Conservation means development as much as it does protection. I recognize the right and duty of this generation to develop and use the natural resources of our land; but I do not recognize the right to waste them, or to rob, by wasteful use, the generations that come after us. I ask nothing of the nation except that it so behave as each farmer here behaves with reference to his own children. That farmer is a poor creature who skins the land and leaves it worthless to his children. The farmer is a good farmer who, having enabled the land to support himself and to provide for the education of his children, leaves it to them a little better than he found it himself. I believe the same thing of a nation.

Moreover, I believe that the natural resources must be used for the benefit of all our people, and not monopolized for the benefit of the few, and here again is another case in which I am accused of taking a revolutionary attitude. . . .

. . . And now a special word to the farmer. I want to see him make the farm as fine a farm as it can be made; and let him remember to see that the improve-ment goes on indoors as well as out; let him remember that the farmer's wife should have her share of thought and attention just as much as the farmer himself.

Nothing is more true than that excess of every kind is followed by reaction; a fact which should be pondered by reformer and reactionary alike. We are face to face with new conceptions of the relations of property to human welfare, chiefly because certain advocates of the rights of property as against the rights of men have been pushing their claims too far. The man who wrongly holds that every human right is secondary to his profit must now give way to the advocate of human welfare, who rightly maintains that every man holds his property subject to the general right of the community to regulate its use to whatever degree the public welfare may require it.

But I think we may go still further. The right to regulate the use of wealth in the public interest is universally admitted. Let us admit also the right to regulate the terms and conditions of labor, which is the chief element of wealth, directly in the interest of the common good. The fundamental thing to do for every man is to give him a chance to reach a place in which he will make the greatest possible contribution to the public welfare. Understand what I say there. Give him a chance, not push him up if he will not be pushed. Help any man who stumbles; if he lies down, it is a poor job to try to carry him; but if he is a worthy man, try your best to see that he gets a chance to show the worth that is in him. No man can be a good citizen unless he has a wage more than sufficient to cover the bare cost of living, and hours of labor short enough so that after his day's work is done he will have time and energy to bear his share in the management of the community, to help in carrying the general load. We keep countless men from being good citizens by the conditions of life with which we surround them. We need comprehensive workmen's compensation acts, both state and national laws to regulate child labor and work for women, and, especially, we need in our common schools not merely education in book learning, but also practical training for daily life and work. We need to enforce better sanitary conditions for our workers and to extend the use of safety appliances for our workers in industry and commerce, both within and between the states. Also, friends, in the interest of the workingman himself we need to set our faces like flint against mob violence just as against corporate greed; against violence and injustice and lawlessness by wage workers just as much as against lawless cunning and greed and selfish arrogance of employers. If I could ask but one thing of my fellow countrymen, my request would be that, whenever they go in for reform, they remember the two sides, and that they always exact justice from one side as much as from the other. . . . If the reactionary man, who thinks of nothing but the rights of property, could have his way, he would bring about a revolution; and one of my chief fears in connection with progress comes because I do not want to see our people, for lack of proper leadership, compelled to follow men whose intentions are excellent, but whose eyes are a little too wild to make it really safe to trust them. . . .

National efficiency has many factors. It is a necessary result of the principle of conservation widely applied. In the end it will determine our failure or success as a nation. National efficiency has to do, not only with natural resources and with men, but it is equally concerned with institutions. The state must be made efficient for the work which concerns only the people of the state; and the nation for that which concerns all the people. There must remain no neutral ground to serve as a refuge for lawbreakers, and especially for lawbreakers of great wealth, who can hire the vulpine legal cunning which will teach them how to

avoid both jurisdictions. It is a misfortune when the national legislature fails to do its duty in providing a national remedy, so that the only national activity is the purely negative activity of the judiciary in forbidding the state to exercise power in the premises.

I do not ask for overcentralization; but I do ask that we work in a spirit of broad and far-reaching nationalism when we work for what concerns our people as a whole. We are all Americans. Our common interests are as broad as the continent. I speak to you here in Kansas exactly as I would speak in New York or Georgia, for the most vital problems are those which affect us all alike. The national government belongs to the whole American people, and where the whole American people are interested, that interest can be guarded effectively only by the national government. The betterment which we seek must be accomplished, I believe, mainly through the national government.

The American people are right in demanding that New Nationalism, without which we cannot hope to deal with new problems. The New Nationalism puts the national need before sectional or personal advantage. It is impatient of the utter confusion that results from local legislatures attempting to treat national issues as local issues. It is still more impatient of the impotence which springs from overdivision of governmental powers, the impotence which makes it possible for local selfishness or for legal cunning, hired by wealthy special interests, to bring national activities to a deadlock. This New Nationalism regards the executive power as the steward of the public welfare. It demands of the judiciary that it shall be interested primarily in human welfare rather than in property, just as it demands that the representative body shall represent all the people rather than any one class or section of the people.

I believe in shaping the ends of government to protect property as well as human welfare. Normally, and in the long run, the ends are the same; but whenever the alternative must be faced, I am for men and not for property, as you were in the Civil War. I am far from underestimating the importance of dividends; but I rank dividends below human character. Again, I do not have any sympathy with the reformer who says he does not care for dividends. Of course, economic welfare is necessary, for a man must pull his own weight and be able to support his family. I know well that the reformers must not bring upon the people economic ruin, or the reforms themselves will go down in the ruin. But we must be ready to face temporary disaster, whether or not brought on by those who will war against us to the knife. Those who oppose all reform will do well to remember that ruin in its worst form is inevitable if our national life brings us nothing better than swollen fortunes for the few and the triumph in both politics and business of a sordid and selfish materialism.

If our political institutions were perfect, they would absolutely prevent the political domination of money in any part of our affairs. We need to make our political representatives more quickly and sensitively responsive to the people whose servants they are. More direct action by the people in their own affairs under proper safeguards is vitally necessary. The direct primary is a step in this direction, if it is associated with a corrupt practices act effective to prevent the advantage of the man willing recklessly and unscrupulously to spend money over his more honest competitor. It is particularly important that all moneys received or expended for campaign purposes should be publicly accounted for, not only after election, but before election as well. Political action must be made simpler, easier, and freer from confusion for every citizen. I believe that the prompt removal of unfaithful or incompetent public servants should be made easy and sure in whatever way experience shall show to be most expedient in any given class of cases.

One of the fundamental necessities in a representative government such as ours is to make certain that the men to whom the people delegate their power shall serve the people by whom they are elected, and not the special interests. I believe that every national officer, elected or appointed, should be forbidden to perform any service or receive any compensation, directly or indirectly, from interstate corporations; and a similar provision could not fail to be useful within the states.

The object of government is the welfare of the people. The material progress and prosperity of a nation are desirable chiefly so far as they lead to the moral and material welfare of all good citizens. Just in proportion as the average man and woman are honest, capable of sound judgment and high ideals, active in public affairs—but, first of all, sound in their home life, and the father and mother of healthy children whom they bring up well—just so far, and no farther, we may count our civilization a success. We must have—I believe we have already—a genuine and permanent moral awakening, without which no wisdom of legislation or administration really means anything; and, on the other hand, we must try to secure the social and economic legislation without which any improvement due to purely moral agitation is necessarily evanescent. . . . No matter how honest and decent we are in our private lives, if we do not have the right kind of law and the right kind of administration of the law, we cannot go forward as a nation. That is imperative; but it must be an addition to, and not a substitution for, the qualities that make us good citizens. In the last analysis, the most important elements in any man's career must be the sum of those qualities which, in the aggregate, we speak of as character. If he has not got it, then no law that the wit of man can devise, no administration of the law by the boldest and strongest executive, will avail to help him. We must have the right kind of character—character that makes a man, first of all, a good man in the home, a good father, a good husband—that makes a man a good neighbor. You must have that, and, then, in addition, you must have the kind of law and the kind of administration of the law which will give to those qualities in the private citizen the best possible chance for development. The prime problem of our nation is to get the right type of good citizenship, and, to get it, we must have progress, and our public men must be genuinely progressive.

COMMENT

The New Nationalism was . . . the consummation of a steady progression in the political thought of Roosevelt and a significant minority of progressive thinkers. . . . What [Roosevelt] proposed was a new nationalism, a dynamic democracy, that would recognize the inevitability of concentration in industry and bring the great corporations under complete federal control, that would protect and encourage the laboring man, that, in brief, would do many of the things usually associated with the modern concept of the welfare state.

> Professor Arthur S. Link in *Woodrow Wilson and the Progressive Era, 1910–1917* (New York: Harper & Brothers, 1954), pp. 18–19.

The Osawatomie address aroused wide interest for two reasons. The first was that the public mind was better prepared for the reception of such doctrines. The second was that one or two passages were alarmingly close to the socialism from which Roosevelt had already shrunk.

> Henry F. Pringle, historian, in *Theodore Roosevelt, A Biography* (New York: Harcourt, Brace & Company, Inc., 1931), p. 543.

40· *1911*

Standard Oil Company of New Jersey et al. v. U.S.

After a federal district court ruled that the Standard Oil Company of New Jersey was guilty of violating the Sherman Anti-trust Act and had ordered a dissolution of the company's component parts, the Supreme Court was asked to pass on the lower court's decision. By denying the appeal, the Supreme Court upheld the

221 U.S. 1 (1911).

lower court. But in considering the case, the Court attempted to clarify the meaning of the Sherman Anti-trust Act by answering the question: Did the statute forbid all restraints of trade? Writing for the majority, Chief Justice White reviewed the law of monopoly and then concluded that the Sherman Act prohibited only unreasonable restraints of trade.

Since the Court viewed the Standard Oil Company as an unreasonable restraint of trade, its dissolution was ordered in accordance with the decision of the lower court. By assuming the power to decide whether a business restraining interstate commerce was guilty of violating the Sherman Act, the Court, in effect, had changed the original meaning of the law. After this decision, it was difficult for the government to prosecute a monopoly successfully, for the trusts were able to rely on the argument that they were reasonable combinations. With the way prepared for the unprecedented era of combinations and the monopolies of the 1920's, the Sherman Anti-trust Act was rendered more meaningless than ever.

Duly appreciating the situation just stated, it is certain that only one point of concord between the parties is discernible, which is, that the controversy in every aspect is controlled by a correct conception of the meaning of the first and second sections of the Anti-trust Act. . . .

The debates show that doubt as to whether there was a common law of the United States which governed the subject in the absence of legislation was among the influences leading to the passage of the act. They conclusively show, however, that the main cause which led to the legislation was the thought that it was required by the economic condition of the times, that is, the vast accumulation of wealth in the hands of corporations and individuals, the enormous development of corporate organization, the facility for combination which such organizations afforded, the fact that the facility was being used, and that combinations known as trusts were being multiplied, and the widespread impression that their power had been and would be exerted to oppress individuals and injure the public generally. Although debates may not be used as a means for interpreting a statute that rule in the nature of things is not violated

by resorting to debates as a means of ascertaining the environment at the time of the enactment of a particular law, that is, the history of the period when it was adopted.

There can be no doubt that the sole subject with which the first section deals is restraint of trade as therein contemplated, and that the attempt to monopolize and monopolization is the subject with which the second section is concerned. It is certain that those terms, at least in their rudimentary meaning, took their origin in the common law, and were also familiar in the law of this country prior to and at the time of the adoption of the act in question.

We shall endeavor then, first to seek their meaning, not by indulging in an elaborate and learned analysis of the English law and of the law of this country, but by making a very brief reference to the elementary and indisputable conceptions of both the English and American law on the subject prior to the passage of the Antitrust Act.

a. It is certain that at a very remote period the words "contract in restraint of trade" in English came to refer to some voluntary restraint put by contract by an individual on his right to carry on his trade or calling. Originally all such contracts were considered to be illegal, because it was deemed they were injurious to the public as well as to the individuals who made them. In the interest of the freedom of individuals to contract this doctrine was modified so that it was only when a restraint by contract was so general as to be coterminous with the kingdom that it was treated as void. That is to say, if the restraint was partial in its operation and was otherwise reasonable the contract was held to be valid:

b. Monopolies were defined by Lord Coke as follows: " 'A monopoly is an institution, or allowance by the king by his grant, commission, or otherwise to any person or persons, bodies politic or corporate, of or for the sole buying, selling, making, working, or using of anything, whereby any person or persons, bodies politic or corporate, are sought to be restrained of any freedom or liberty that they had before, or hindered in their lawful trade.' "

. . . . .

The frequent granting of monopolies and the struggle which led to a denial of the power to create them, that is to say, to the establishment that they were incompatible with the English constitution is known to all and need not be reviewed. The evils which led to the public outcry against monopolies and to the final denial of the power to make them may be thus summarily stated: (1) The power which the monopoly gave to the one who enjoyed it to fix the price and thereby injure the public; (2) The power which it engendered of enabling a limitation on production; and, (3) The danger of deterioration in quality of the monopolized article which it was deemed was the inevitable resultant of the monopolistic control over its production and sale. As monopoly as thus conceived embraced only a consequence arising from an exertion of sovereign power, no express restrictions or prohibitions obtained against the creation by an individual of a monopoly as such. . . .

. . . It is remarkable that nowhere at common law can there be found a prohibition against the creation of monopoly by an individual. This would seem to manifest, either consciously or intuitively, a profound conception as to the inevitable operation of economic forces and the equipoise or balance in favor of the protection of the rights of individuals which resulted. . . .

In this country also the acts from which it was deemed there resulted a part if not all of the injurious consequences ascribed to monopoly, came to be referred to as a monopoly itself. . . .

Without going into detail and but very briefly surveying the whole field, it may be with accuracy said that the dread of enhancement of prices and of other wrongs which it was thought would flow from the undue limitation on competitive conditions caused by contracts or other acts of individuals or corporations, led, as a matter of public policy, to the prohibition or treating as illegal all contracts or acts which were unreasonably restrictive of competitive conditions, either from the nature or character of the contract or act or where the surrounding circumstances were such as to justify the conclusion that they had not been entered into or performed with the legitimate purpose of reasonably forwarding personal interest and developing trade, but on the contrary were of such a character as to give rise to the inference or presumption that they had been entered into or done with the intent to do wrong to the general public and to limit the right of individuals, thus restraining the free flow of commerce and tending to bring about the evils, such as enhancement of prices, which were considered to be against public policy. . . .

Let us consider the language of the first and second sections, guided by the principle that where words are employed in a statute which had at the time a well-known meaning at common law or in the law of this country they are presumed to have been used in that sense unless the context compels to the contrary. . . .

And as the contracts or acts embraced in the provision were not expressly defined, since the enumeration addressed itself simply to classes of acts, those classes being broad enough to embrace every conceivable contract or combination which could be made concerning trade or commerce or the subjects of such commerce, and thus caused any act done by any of the enumerated methods anywhere in the whole field of human activity to be illegal if in restraint of trade, it inevitably follows that the provision necessarily called for the exercise of judgment which required that some standard should be resorted to for the purpose of determining whether the prohibitions contained in the statute had or had not in any given case been violated. Thus not specifying but indubitably contemplating and requiring a standard, it follows that it was intended that the standard of reason which had been applied at the common law and in this country in dealing with subjects of the character embraced by the statute, was intended to be the measure used for the purpose of determining whether in a given case a particular act had not brought about the wrong against which the statute provided. . . .

And it is worthy of observation, as we have previously remarked concerning the common law, that although the statute by the comprehensiveness of the enumeration embodied in both the first and second sections makes it certain that its purpose was to prevent undue restraints of every kind or nature, nevertheless by the omission of any direct prohibition against monopoly in the concrete it indicates a consciousness that the freedom of the individual right to contract when not unduly or improperly exercised was the most efficient means for the prevention of monopoly, since the operation of the centrifugal and centripetal forces resulting from the right to freely contract was the means by which monopoly would be inevitably prevented if no extraneous or sovereign power imposed it and no right to make unlawful contracts having a monopolistic tendency were permitted. In other words that freedom to contract was the essence of freedom from undue restraint on the right to contract. . . .

Recurring to the acts done by the individuals or corporations who were mainly instrumental in bringing about the expansion of the New Jersey corporation during the period prior to the formation of the trust agreements of 1879 and 1882, including those agreements, not for the purpose of weighing the substantial merit of the numerous charges of wrongdoing made during such period, but solely as an aid for discovering intent and purpose, we think no disinterested mind can survey the period in question without being irresistibly driven to the conclusion that the very genius for commercial development and organization which it would seem was manifested from the beginning soon begot an intent and purpose to exclude others which was frequently manifested by acts and dealings wholly inconsistent with the theory that they were made with the single conception of advancing the development of business power by usual methods, but which on the contrary necessarily involved the intent to drive others from the field and to exclude them from their right to trade and thus accomplish the mastery which was the end in view. And, considering the period from the date of the trust agreements of 1879 and 1882, up to the time of the expansion of the New Jersey corporation, the gradual extension of the power over the commerce in oil which ensued, the decision of the Supreme Court of Ohio, the tardiness or reluctance in conforming to the commands of that decision, the method first adopted and that which finally culminated in the plan of the New Jersey corporation, all additionally serve to make manifest the continued existence of the intent which we have previously indicated and which among other things impelled the expansion of the New Jersey corporation. The exercise of the power which resulted from that organization fortifies the foregoing conclusions, since the development which came, the acquisition here and there which ensued of every efficient means by which competition could have been asserted, the slow but resistless methods which followed by which means of transportation were absorbed and brought under control, the system of marketing which was adopted by which the country was divided into districts and the trade in each district in oil was turned over to a designated corporation within the combination and all others were excluded, all lead the mind up to a conviction of a purpose and intent which we think is so certain as practically to cause the subject not to be within the domain of reasonable contention.

The inference that no attempt to monopolize could have been intended, and that no monopolization resulted from the acts complained of, since it is established that a very small percentage of the crude oil produced was controlled by the combination, is unwarranted. As substantial power over the crude product was the inevitable result of the absolute control which existed over the refined product, the monopolization of the one carried with it the power to control the other, and if the inferences which this situation suggests were developed, which we deem it unnecessary to do, they might well serve to add additional cogency to the presumption of intent to monopolize which we have found arises from the unquestioned proof on other subjects.

COMMENT

The court, in accordance with what it denominates the "rule of reason" . . . makes Congress say what it did not say; what, as I think, it plainly did not intend to say; and what, since the passage of the act, it has explicitly refused to say. It has steadily refused to amend the act so as to tolerate a restraint of interstate commerce even where such restraint could be said to be "reasonable" or "due." In short, the court now, by judicial legislation, in effect amends an act of Congress relating to a subject over which that department of the government has exclusive cognizance.

Justice Harlan dissenting in U.S. *v.* American Tobacco Company, 221 U.S. 192 (1911).

41. *1912*

Woodrow Wilson's New Freedom

Contrary to popular opinion, there was no unified and homogenous program of Progressivism. Rather, the Progressives generally operated on different levels of society and travelled in opposite directions. The movement for social justice was often independent of and separate from the movement for political reforms. Some Progressives worked only for local reforms, while others were interested only in national politics and policies. The Pro-

WOODROW WILSON, *The New Freedom* (New York: Doubleday Page & Co., 1913), pp. 3–32. Reprinted by permission of Mrs. Edith Bolling Wilson.

gressives were also divided as to the means they should employ to achieve their reforms. Could the promise of American life be achieved merely by destroying special privilege and applying the rule of equality to all groups, as Woodrow Wilson suggested? Or could Progressivism be fulfilled only through the positive interference and participation of the federal government in the nation's political and economic matters as Theodore Roosevelt argued?

During the presidential campaign of 1912, Woodrow Wilson coined the term "New Freedom" to distinguish his pro-

gram from Roosevelt's "New National-
ism." In his campaign addresses, Wilson
demanded the emancipation of American
business and labor from monopolistic
control. As a firm believer in nineteenth-
century laissez-faire concepts, he envis-
aged a New Freedom brought about by
the destruction of special privileges, the
restoration of competition, and progress
to be achieved by individual initiative.
Later, Wilson abandoned some of his
New Freedom concepts and advocated
special interest legislation in order to
benefit underprivileged groups.

There is one great basic fact which
underlies all the questions that are discussed on the political platform at the
present moment. That singular fact is that
nothing is done in this country as it was
done twenty years ago.

We are in the presence of a new organization of society. Our life has broken
away from the past. The life of America
is not the life that it was twenty years
ago; it is not the life that it was ten years
ago. We have changed our economic conditions, absolutely, from top to bottom;
and, with our economic society, the organization of our life. The old political
formulas do not fit the present problems;
they read now like documents taken out
of a forgotten age. The older cries sound
as if they belonged to a past age which
men have almost forgotten. Things which
used to be put into the party platforms of
ten years ago would sound antiquated if
put into a platform now. We are facing
the necessity of fitting a new social organization, as we did once fit the old
organization, to the happiness and prosperity of the great body of citizens; for
we are conscious that the new order of
society has not been made to fit and provide the convenience or prosperity of the
average man. The life of the nation has
grown infinitely varied. It does not centre
now upon questions of governmental
structure or of the distribution of governmental powers. It centres upon questions

of the very structure and operation of
society itself, of which government is
only the instrument. Our development has
run so fast and so far along the lines
sketched in the earlier day of constitutional definition, has so crossed and inter-
laced those lines, has piled upon them
such novel structures of trust and combination, has elaborated within them a
life so manifold, so full of forces which
transcend the boundaries of the country
itself and fill the eyes of the world, that a
new nation seems to have been created
which the old formulas do not fit or afford
a vital interpretation of.

We have come upon a very different
age from any that preceded us. We have
come upon an age when we do not do
business in the way in which we used to
do business—when we do not carry on
any of the operations of manufacture,
sale, transportation, or communication
as men used to carry them on. There is
a sense in which in our day the individual
has been submerged. In most parts of our
country men work, not for themselves,
not as partners in the old way in which
they used to work, but generally as employees—in a higher or lower grade—of
great corporations. There was a time
when corporations played a very minor
part in our business affairs, but now
they play the chief part, and most men
are the servants of corporations.

You know what happens when you are
the servant of a corporation. You have in
no instance access to the men who are
really determining the policy of the corporation. If the corporation is doing the
things that it ought not to do, you really
have no voice in the matter and must
obey the orders, and you have oftentimes
with deep mortification to co-operate in
the doing of things which you know are
against the public interest. Your individuality is swallowed up in the individuality and purpose of a great organization.

It is true that, while most men are
thus submerged in the corporation, a few,
a very few, are exalted to a power which

as individuals they could never have wielded. Through the great organizations of which they are the heads, a few are enabled to play a part unprecedented by anything in history in the control of the business operations of the country and in the determination of the happiness of great numbers of people.

Yesterday, and ever since history began, men were related to one another as individuals. To be sure there were the family, the Church, and the State, institutions which associated men in certain wide circles of relationship. But in the ordinary concerns of life, in the ordinary work, in the daily round, men dealt freely and directly with one another. To-day, the everyday relationships of men are largely with great impersonal concerns, with organizations, not with other individual men.

Now this is nothing short of a new social age, a new era of human relationships, a new stage-setting for the drama of life.

In this new age we find, for instance, that our laws with regard to the relations of employer and employee are in many respects wholly antiquated and impossible. They were framed for another age, which nobody now living remembers, which is, indeed, so remote from our life that it would be difficult for many of us to understand it if it were described to us. The employer is now generally a corporation or a huge company of some kind; the employee is one of hundreds or of thousands brought together, not by individual masters whom they know and with whom they have personal relations, but by agents of one sort or another. Workingmen are marshaled in great numbers for the performance of a multitude of particular tasks under a common discipline. They generally use dangerous and powerful machinery, over whose repair and renewal they have no control. New rules must be devised with regard to their obligations and their rights, their obligations to their employers and their responsibilities to one another. Rules must be devised for their protection, for their compensation when injured, for their support when disabled.

There is something very new and very big and very complex about these new relations of capital and labor. A new economic society has sprung up, and we must effect a new set of adjustments. We must not pit power against weakness. The employer is generally, in our day, as I have said, not an individual, but a powerful group; and yet the workingman when dealing with his employer is still, under our existing law, an individual.

Why is it that we have a labor question at all? It is for the simple and very sufficient reason that the laboring man and the employer are not intimate associates now as they used to be in time past. Most of our laws were formed in the age when employer and employees knew each other, knew each other's characters, were associates with each other, dealt with each other as man with man. That is no longer the case. You not only do not come into personal contact with the men who have the supreme command in those corporations, but it would be out of the question for you to do it. Our modern corporations employ thousands, and in some instances hundreds of thousands, of men. The only persons whom you see or deal with are local superintendents or local representatives of a vast organization, which is not like anything that the workingmen of the time in which our laws were framed knew anything about. A little group of workingmen, seeing their employer every day, dealing with him in a personal way, is one thing, and the modern body of labor engaged as employees of the huge enterprises that spread all over the country, dealing with men of whom they can form no personal conception, is another thing. A very different thing. You never saw a corporation, any more than you ever saw a government. Many a workingman to-day never saw the body of men who are conducting the industry in which he is employed. And they never saw him. What they know about him is written in ledgers and books and letters, in the correspondence of the office, in the reports of the superintendents. He is a long way off from them.

So what we have to discuss is, not wrongs which individuals intentionally do—I do not believe there are a great many of those—but the wrongs of a system. I want to record my protest against any discussion of this matter which would seem to indicate that there are bodies of our fellow-citizens who are trying to grind us down and do us injustice. There are some men of that sort. I don't know how they sleep o'nights, but there are men of that kind. Thank God, they are not numerous. The truth is, we are all caught in a great economic system which is heartless. The modern corporation is not engaged in business as an individual. When we deal with it, we deal with an impersonal element, an immaterial piece of society. A modern corporation is a means of co-operation in the conduct of an enterprise which is so big that no one man can conduct it, and which the resources of no one man are sufficient to finance. A company is formed; that company puts out a prospectus; the promoters expect to raise a certain fund as capital stock. Well, how are they going to raise it? They are going to raise it from the public in general, some of whom will buy their stock. The moment that begins, there is formed—what? A joint stock corporation. Men begin to pool their earnings, little piles, big piles. A certain number of men are elected by the stockholders to be directors, and these directors elect a president. This president is the head of the undertaking, and the directors are its managers.

Now, do the workingmen employed by that stock corporation deal with that president and those directors? Not at all. Does the public deal with that president and that board of directors? It does not.

Can anybody bring them to account? It is next to impossible to do so. If you undertake it you will find it a game of hide and seek, with the objects of your search taking refuge now behind the tree of their individual personality, now behind that of their corporate irresponsibility.

And do our laws take note of this curious state of things? Do they even attempt to distinguish between a man's act as a corporation director and as an individual? They do not. Our laws still deal with us on the basis of the old system. The law is still living in the dead past which we have left behind. This is evident, for instance, with regard to the matter of employers' liability for workingmen's injuries. Suppose that a superintendent wants a workman to use a certain piece of machinery which it is not safe for him to use, and that the workman is injured by that piece of machinery. Some of our courts have held that the superintendent is a fellow-servant, or, as the law states it, a fellow-employee, and that, therefore, the man cannot recover damages for his injury. The superintendent who probably engaged the man is not his employer. Who is his employer? And whose negligence could conceivably come in there? The board of directors did not tell the employee to use that piece of machinery; and the president of the corporation did not tell him to use that piece of machinery. And so forth. Don't you see by that theory that a man never can get redress for negligence on the part of the employer? When I hear judges reason upon the analogy of the relationships that used to exist between workmen and their employers a generation ago, I wonder if they have not opened their eyes to the modern world. You know, we have a right to expect that judges will have their eyes open, even though the law which they administer hasn't awakened.

Yet that is but a single small detail illustrative of the difficulties we are in because we have not adjusted the law to the facts of the new order.

Since I entered politics, I have chiefly had men's views confided to me privately. Some of the biggest men in the United States, in the field of commerce and manufacture, are afraid of somebody, are afraid of something. They know that there is a power somewhere so organized, so subtle, so watchful, so interlocked, so complete, so pervasive, that they had better not speak above their breath when they speak in condemnation of it.

They know that America is not a place of which it can be said, as it used to be, that a man may choose his own calling and pursue it just as far as his abilities enable him to pursue it; because to-day, if he enters certain fields, there are organizations which will use means against him that will prevent his building up a business which they do not want to have built up; organizations that will see to it that the ground is cut from under him and the markets shut against him. For if he begins to sell to certain retail dealers, to any retail dealers, the monopoly will refuse to sell to those dealers, and those dealers, afraid, will not buy the new man's wares.

And this is the country which has lifted to the admiration of the world its ideals of absolutely free opportunity, where no man is supposed to be under any limitation except the limitations of his character and of his mind; where there is supposed to be no distinction of class, no distinction of blood, no distinction of social status, but where men win or lose on their merits.

I lay it very close to my own conscience as a public man whether we can any longer stand at our doors and welcome all newcomers upon those terms. American industry is not free, as once it was free; American enterprise is not free; the man with only a little capital is finding it harder to get into the field, more and more impossible to compete with the big fellow. Why? Because the

laws of this country do not prevent the strong from crushing the weak. That is the reason, and because the strong have crushed the weak the strong dominate the industry and the economic life of this country. No man can deny that the lines of endeavor have more and more narrowed and stiffened; no man who knows anything about the development of industry in this country can have failed to observe that the larger kinds of credit are more and more difficult to obtain, unless you obtain them upon the terms of uniting your efforts with those who already control the industries of the country; and nobody can fail to observe that any man who tries to set himself up in competition with any process of manufacture which has been taken under the control of large combinations of capital will presently find himself either squeezed out or obliged to sell and allow himself to be absorbed.

There is a great deal that needs reconstruction in the United States. I should like to take a census of the businessmen —I mean the rank and file of the businessmen—as to whether they think that business conditions in this country, or rather whether the organization of business in this country, is satisfactory or not. I know what they would say if they dared. If they could vote secretly they would vote overwhelmingly that the present organization of business was meant for the big fellows and was not meant for the little fellows; that it was meant for those who are at the top and was meant to exclude those who are at the bottom; that it was meant to shut out beginners, to prevent new entries in the race, to prevent the building up of competitive enterprises that would interfere with the monopolies which the great trusts have built up.

What this country needs above everything else is a body of laws which will look after the men who are on the make rather than the men who are already made. Because the men who are already made are not going to live indefinitely, and they are not always kind enough to leave sons as able and as honest as they are.

The originative part of America, the part of America that makes new enterprises, the part into which the ambitious and gifted workingman makes his way up, the class that saves, that plans, that organizes, that presently spreads its enterprises until they have a national scope and character—that middle class is being more and more squeezed out by the processes which we have been taught to call processes of prosperity. Its members are sharing prosperity, no doubt; but what alarms me is that they are not *originating* prosperity. No country can afford to have its prosperity originated by a small controlling class. The treasury of America does not lie in the brains of the small body of men now in control of the great enterprises that have been concentrated under the direction of a very small number of persons. The treasury of America lies in those ambitions, those energies, that cannot be restricted to a special favored class. It depends upon the inventions of unknown men, upon the originations of unknown men, upon the ambitions of unknown men. Every country is renewed out of the ranks of the unknown, not out of the ranks of those already famous and powerful and in control.

There has come over the land that un-American set of conditions which enables a small number of men who control the government to get favors from the government; by those favors to exclude their fellows from equal business opportunity; by those favors to extend a network of control that will presently dominate every industry in the country, and so make men forget the ancient time when America lay in every hamlet, when America was to be seen in every fair valley, when America displayed her great forces on the broad prairies, ran her fine fires of enterprise up over the mountain-sides and down into the bowels of the earth, and eager men were everywhere captains of industry, not employees; not looking to a distant city to find out what they might do, but looking about among their neighbors, finding credit according to their character, not according to their connections, finding credit in proportion to what was known to be in them and behind them, not in proportion to the securities they held that were approved where they were not known. In order to start an enterprise now, you have to be authenticated, in a perfectly impersonal way, not according to yourself, but according to what you own that somebody else approves of your owning. You cannot begin such an enterprise as those that have made America until you are so authenticated, until you have succeeded in obtaining the goodwill of large allied capitalists. Is that freedom? That is dependence, not freedom.

We used to think in the old-fashioned days when life was very simple that all that government had to do was to put on a policeman's uniform, and say, "Now don't anybody hurt anybody else." We used to say that the ideal of government was for every man to be left alone and not interfered with, except when he interfered with somebody else; and that the best government was the government that did as little governing as possible. That was the idea that obtained in Jefferson's time. But we are coming now to realize that life is so complicated that we are not dealing with the old conditions, and the law has to step in and create new conditions under which we may live, the conditions which will make it tolerable for us to live.

Let me illustrate what I mean: It used to be true in our cities that every family occupied a separate house of its own, that every family had its own little premises, that every family was separated it its life from every other family. That is no longer the case in our great cities. Families live in tenements, they live in flats, they live on floors; they are piled layer upon layer in the great tenement houses of our crowded districts, and not only are they piled layer upon layer, but they are associated room by room, so that there is in every room, sometimes, in our congested districts, a separate family. In some foreign countries they have made much more progress than we in handling these things. In the city of Glasgow, for example (Glasgow is one of the model cities of the world), they have made up their minds that the entries and the hallways of great tenements are public streets. Therefore, the policeman goes up the stairway, and patrols the corridors; the lighting department of the city sees to it that the halls are abundantly lighted. The city does not deceive itself into supposing that that great building is a unit from which the police are to keep out and the civic authority to be excluded, but it says: "These are public highways, and light is needed in them, and control by the authority of the city."

I liken that to our great modern industrial enterprises. A corporation is very like a large tenement house; it isn't the premises of a single commercial family; it is just as much a public affair as a tenement house is a network of public highways.

When you offer the securities of a great corporation to anybody who wishes to purchase them, you must open that corporation to the inspection of everybody who wants to purchase. There must, to follow out the figure of the tenement house, be lights along the corridors, there must be police patrolling the openings, there must be inspection wherever it is known that men may be deceived with regard to the contents of the premises. If we believe that fraud lies in wait for us, we must have the means of determining whether our suspicions are well founded or not. Similarly, the treatment of labor by the great corporations is not what it was in Jefferson's time. Whenever bodies of men employ bodies of men, it ceases to be a private relationship. So that when courts hold that workingmen cannot

peaceably dissuade other workingmen from taking employment, as was held in a notable case in New Jersey, they simply show that their minds and understandings are lingering in an age which has passed away. This dealing of great bodies of men with other bodies of men is a matter of public scrutiny, and should be a matter of public regulation.

Similarly, it was no business of the law in the time of Jefferson to come into my house and see how I kept house. But when my house, when my so-called private property, became a great mine, and men went along dark corridors amidst every kind of danger in order to dig out of the bowels of the earth things necessary for the industries of a whole nation, and when it came about that no individual owned these mines, that they were owned by great stock companies, then all the old analogies absolutely collapsed and it became the right of the government to go down into these mines to see whether human beings were properly treated in them or not; to see whether accidents were properly safeguarded against; to see whether modern economical methods of using these inestimable riches of the earth were followed or were not followed. If somebody puts a derrick improperly secured on top of a building or overtopping the street, then the government of the city has the right to see that that derrick is so secured that you and I can walk under it and not be afraid that the heavens are going to fall on us. Likewise, in these great beehives where in every corridor swarm men of flesh and blood, it is the privilege of the government, whether of the State or of the United States, as the case may be, to see that human life is protected, that human lungs have something to breathe.

These, again, are merely illustrations of conditions. We are in a new world, struggling under old laws. As we go inspecting our lives to-day, surveying this new scene of centralized and complex society, we shall find many more things out of joint.

One of the most alarming phenomena of the time—or rather it would be alarming if the nation had not awakened to it and shown its determination to control it—one of the most significant signs of the new social era is the degree to which government has become associated with business. I speak, for the moment, of the control over the government exercised by Big Business. Behind the whole subject, of course, is the truth that, in the new order, government and business must be associated closely. But that association is at present of a nature absolutely intolerable; the precedence is wrong, the association is upside down. Our government has been for the past few years under the control of heads of great allied corporations with special interests. It has not controlled these interests and assigned them a proper place in the whole system of business; it has submitted itself to their control. As a result, there have grown up vicious systems and schemes of governmental favoritism (the most obvious being the extravagant tariff), far-reaching in effect upon the whole fabric of life, touching to his injury every inhabitant of the land, laying unfair and impossible handicaps upon competitors, imposing taxes in every direction, stifling everywhere the free spirit of American enterprise.

Now this has come about naturally; as we go on we shall see how very naturally. It is no use denouncing anybody, or anything, except human nature. Nevertheless, it is an intolerable thing that the government of the republic should have got so far out of the hands of the people; should have been captured by interests which are special and not general. In the train of this capture follow the troops of scandals, wrongs, indecencies, with which our politics swarm.

There are cities in America of whose government we are ashamed. There are cities everywhere, in every part of the land, in which we feel that, not the interests of the public, but the interests of special privileges, of selfish men, are served; where contracts take precedence over public interest. Not only in big cities is this the case. Have you not noticed the growth of socialistic sentiment in the smaller towns? Not many months ago I stopped at a little town in Nebraska, and while my train lingered I met on the platform a very engaging young fellow dressed in overalls who introduced himself to me as the mayor of the town, and added that he was a Socialist. I said, "What does that mean? Does that mean that this town is socialistic?" "No, sir," he said; "I have not deceived myself; the vote by which I was elected was about 20 per cent socialistic and 80 per cent protest." It was protest against the treachery to the people of those who led both the other parties of that town.

All over the Union people are coming to feel that they have no control over the course of affairs. I live in one of the greatest States in the union, which was at one time in slavery. Until two years ago we had witnessed with increasing concern the growth in New Jersey of a spirit of almost cynical despair. Men said: "We vote; we are offered the platform we want; we elect the men who stand on that platform, and we get absolutely nothing." So they began to ask: "What is the use of voting? We know that the machines of both parties are subsidized by the same persons, and therefore it is useless to turn in either direction."

This is not confined to some of the state governments and those of some of the towns and cities. We know that something intervenes between the people of the United States and the control of their own affairs at Washington. It is not the people who have been ruling there of late.

Why are we in the presence, why are we at the threshold, of a revolution? Because we are profoundly disturbed by the influences which we see reigning in the determination of our public life and our public policy. There was a time when America was blithe with self-confidence. She boasted that she, and she alone, knew the processes of popular government; but now she sees her sky overcast; she sees that there are at work forces which she did not dream of in her hopeful youth.

Don't you know that some man with eloquent tongue, without conscience, who did not care for the nation, could put this whole country into a flame? Don't you know that this country from one end to the other believes that something is wrong? What an opportunity it would be for some man without conscience to spring up and say: "This is the way. Follow me!"—and lead in paths of destruction!

The old order changeth—changeth under our very eyes, not quietly and equably, but swiftly and with the noise and heat and tumult of reconstruction.

I suppose that all struggle for law has been conscious, that very little of it has been blind or merely instinctive. It is the fashion to say, as if with superior knowledge of affairs and of human weakness, that every age has been an age of transition, and that no age is more full of change than another; yet in very few ages of the world can the struggle for change have been so widespread, so deliberate, or upon so great a scale as in this in which we are taking part.

The transition we are witnessing is no equable transition of growth and normal alteration; no silent, unconscious unfolding of one age into another, its natural heir and successor. Society is looking itself over, in our day, from top to bottom; is making fresh and critical analysis of its very elements; is questioning its oldest practices as freely as its newest, scrutinizing every arrangement and motive of its life; and it stands ready to attempt nothing less than a radical reconstruction, which only frank and honest counsels and the forces of generous co-operation can hold back from becoming a revolution. We are in a temper to reconstruct economic society, as we were once in a temper to reconstruct political society, and political society may itself undergo a radical modification in the process. I doubt if any age was ever more conscious of its task or more unanimously desirous of radical and extended changes in its economic and political practice.

We stand in the presence of a revolution—not a bloody revolution; America is not given to the spilling of blood—but a silent revolution, whereby America will insist upon recovering in practice those ideals which she has always professed, upon securing a government devoted to the general interest and not to special interests.

We are upon the eve of a great reconstruction. It calls for creative statesmanship as no age has done since that great age in which we set up the government under which we live, that government which was the admiration of the world until it suffered wrongs to grow up under it which have made many of our own compatriots question the freedom of our institutions and preach revolution against them. I do not fear revolution. I have unshaken faith in the power of America to keep its self-possession. Revolution will come in peaceful guise, as it came when we put aside the crude government of the Confederation and created the great Federal Union which governs individuals, not States, and which has been these hundred and thirty years our vehicle of progress. Some radical changes we must make in our law and practice. Some reconstructions we must push forward, which a new age and new circumstances impose upon us. But we can do it all in calm and sober fashion, like statesmen and patriots.

I do not speak of these things in apprehension, because all is open and aboveboard. This is not a day in which great forces rally in secret. The whole stupendous program must be publicly planned and canvassed. Good temper, the wisdom that comes of sober counsel, the energy of thoughtful and unselfish men, the habit of co-operation and of compromise which has been bred in us by long years of free government, in which reason rather than passion has been made to prevail by the sheer virtue of candid and universal debate, will enable us to win through to still another great age without violence.

COMMENT

. . . the "New Freedom" means nothing whatever but the old license translated into terms of pleasant rhetoric. The "New Freedom" is nothing whatever but the right of the strong to prey on the weak, of the big men to crush down the little men, and to shield their iniquity beneath the cry that they are exercising freedom. The "New Freedom" when practically applied turns out to be that old kind of dreadful freedom which leaves the unscrupulous and powerful free to make slaves of the feeble. There is but one way to interfere with this freedom to inflict slavery on others, and that is by invoking the supervisory, the regulatory, the controlling, and directing power of the government.

> Former President Theodore Roosevelt before the National Conference of Progressive Service in Portsmouth, Rhode Island, July 2, 1913. *The Works of Theodore Roosevelt* (New York: Charles Scribner's Sons, 1924), XIX, 519.

42. MARCH 4, 1913

Woodrow Wilson's First Inaugural Address

The campaign of 1912 offered to the nation several programs which reflected the existing division of political sentiment. The voters understood that William Howard Taft's re-election would mean a continuation of conservative leadership. They understood that Theodore Roosevelt would attempt to meet the nation's economic and social problems with a bold enlargement of the government's functions, a concept that was fundamentally Hamiltonian in nature. On the other hand, the voters viewed Wilson as a Progressive who feared the growth of governmental power and who preferred to

Senate Documents, 63d Cong., Spec. Sess., I, No. 3 (Serial No. 6507), 3–6.

see reforms achieved through state action, a program which was essentially Jeffersonian in character.

Without the Republican split, it is doubtful that Wilson would have been elected. As it was, he polled only forty-two per cent of the popular vote. Meanwhile, the disruption of the Republican party provided the Democrats with a sizeable majority in the House and a workable majority in the Senate.

Wilson's inaugural address was a reaffirmation of the philosophy of government which he had expounded during the campaign of 1912. The speech is significant in that it was one of the most notable expressions of the Progressive period and in that it revealed America's lack of concern with world affairs by making no reference to foreign policy.

MY FELLOW CITIZENS: There has been a change of government. It began two years ago, when the House of Representatives became Democratic by a decisive majority. It has now been completed. The Senate about to assemble will also be Democratic. The offices of President and Vice-President have been put into the hands of Democrats. What does the change mean? That is the question that is uppermost in our minds to-day. That is the question I am going to try to answer, in order, if I may, to interpret the occasion.

It means much more than the mere success of a party. The success of a party means little except when the Nation is using that party for a large and definite purpose. No one can mistake the purpose for which the Nation now seeks to use the Democratic Party. It seeks to use it to interpret a change in its own plans and point of view. Some old things with which we had grown familiar, and which had begun to creep into the very habit of our thought and of our lives, have altered their aspect as we have latterly looked critically upon them, with fresh, awakened eyes; have dropped their disguises and shown themselves alien and sinister. Some new things, as we look frankly upon them, willing to comprehend their real character, have come to assume the aspect of things long believed in and familiar, stuff of our own convictions. We have been refreshed by a new insight into our own life.

We see that in many things that life is very great. It is incomparably great in its material aspects, in its body of wealth, in the diversity and sweep of its energy, in the industries which have been conceived and built up by the genius of individual men and the limitless enterprise of groups of men. It is great, also, very great, in its moral force.

Nowhere else in the world have noble men and women exhibited in more striking forms the beauty and the energy of sympathy and helpfulness and counsel in their efforts to rectify wrong, alleviate suffering, and set the weak in the way of strength and hope. We have built up, moreover, a great system of government, which has stood through a long age as in many respects a model for those who seek to set liberty upon foundations that will endure against fortuitous change, against storm and accident. Our life contains every thing, and contains it in rich abundance.

But the evil has come with the good, and much fine gold has been corroded. With riches has come inexcusable waste. We have squandered a great part of what we might have used, and have not stopped to conserve the exceeding bounty of nature, without which our genius for enterprise would have been worthless and impotent, scorning to be careful, shamefully prodigal as well as admirably efficient. We have been proud of our industrial achievements, but we have not hitherto stopped thoughtfully enough to count the human cost, the cost of lives snuffed out, of energies overtaxed and broken, the fearful physical and spiritual cost to the men and women and children upon whom the dead weight and burden of it all has fallen pitilessly the years through. The groans and agony of it all had not yet reached our ears, the solemn, moving undertone of our life, coming up out of the mines and factories and out of every home where the struggle had its intimate and familiar seat. With the great Government went many deep secret things which we too long delayed to look into and scrutinize with candid, fearless eyes. The great Government we loved has too often been made use of for private and selfish purposes, and those who used it had forgotten the people.

At last a vision has been vouchsafed us of our life as a whole. We see the bad with the good, the debased and decadent with the sound and vital. With this vision we approach new affairs. Our duty is to cleanse, to reconsider, to restore, to correct the evil without impairing the good, to purify and humanize every process of our common life without weakening or sentimentalizing it. There has been something crude and heartless and unfeeling in our haste to succeed and be great. Our thought has been "Let every man look out for himself, let every generation look out for itself," while we reared giant machinery which made it impossible that any but those who stood at the levers of control should have a chance to look out for themselves. We had not forgotten our morals. We remembered well enough that we had set up a policy which was meant to serve the humblest as well as the most powerful, with an eye single to the standards of justice and fair play, and remembered it with pride. But we were very heedless and in a hurry to be great.

We have come now to the sober second thought. The scales of heedlessness have fallen from our eyes. We have made up our minds to square every process of our national life again with the standards we so proudly set up at the beginning and have always carried at our hearts. Our work is a work of restoration.

We have itemized with some degree of particularity the things that ought to be altered and here are some of the chief items: A tariff which cuts us off from our proper part in the commerce of the world, violates the just principles of taxation, and makes the Government a facile instrument in the hands of private interests; a banking and currency system based upon the necessity of the Government to sell its bonds fifty years ago and perfectly adapted to concentrating cash and restricting credits; an industrial system which, take it on all its sides, financial as well as administrative, holds capital in leading strings, restricts the liberties and limits the opportunities of labor, and exploits without renewing or conserving the natural resources of the country; a body of agricultural activities never yet given the efficiency of great business undertakings or served as it should be through the instrumentality of science taken directly to the farm, or afforded the facilities of credit best suited to its practical needs; watercourses undeveloped, waste places unreclaimed, forests untended, fast disappearing without plan or prospect of renewal, unregarded waste heaps at every mine. We have studied as perhaps no other nation has the most effective means of production, but we have not studied cost or economy as we should either as organizers of industry, as statesmen, or as individuals.

Nor have we studied and perfected the means by which government may be put at the service of humanity, in safeguarding the health of the Nation, the health of its men and its women and its children, as well as their rights in the struggle for existence. This is no sentimental duty. The firm basis of government is justice, not pity. These are matters of justice. There can be no equality or opportunity, the first essential of justice in the body politic, if men and women and children be not shielded in their lives, their very vitality, from the consequences of great industrial and social processes which they can not alter, control, or singly cope with. Society must see to it that it does not itself crush or weaken or damage its own constituent parts. The first duty of law is to keep sound the society it serves. Sanitary laws, pure food laws, and laws determining conditions of labor which individuals are powerless to determine for themselves are intimate parts of the very business of justice and legal efficiency.

These are some of the things we ought to do, and not leave the others undone, the old-fashioned, never-to-be-neglected, fundamental safeguarding of property and of individual right. This is the high enterprise of the new day: To lift everything that concerns our life as a Nation to the light that shines from the hearthfire of every man's conscience and vision of the right. It is inconceivable that we should do this as partisans; it is inconceivable we should do it in ignorance of the facts as they are or in blind haste. We shall restore, not destroy. We shall deal with our economic system as it is and as it may be modified, not as it might be if we had a clean sheet of paper to write upon; and step by step we shall make it what it should be, in the spirit of those who question their own wisdom and seek counsel and knowledge, not shallow self-satisfaction or the excitement of excursions whither they can not tell. Justice, and only justice, shall always be our motto.

And yet it will be no cool process of mere science. The Nation has been deeply stirred, stirred by a solemn passion, stirred by the knowledge of wrong, of ideals lost, of government too often debauched and made an instrument of evil. The feelings with which we face this new age of right and opportunity sweep across our heartstrings like some air out of God's own presence, where justice and mercy are reconciled and the judge and the brother are one. We know our task to be no mere task of politics but a task which shall search us through and through, whether we be able to understand our time and the need of our people, whether we be indeed their spokesmen and interpreters, whether we have the pure heart to comprehend and the rectified will to choose our high course of action.

This is not a day of triumph; it is a day of dedication. Here muster, not the forces of party, but the forces of humanity. Men's hearts wait upon us; men's lives hang in the balance; men's hopes call upon us to say what we will do. Who shall live up to the great trust? Who dares fail to try? I summon all honest men, all patriotic, all forward-looking men, to my side. God helping me, I will not fail them, if they will but counsel and sustain me!

COMMENT

Woodrow Wilson's inauguration as President marks the beginning of a political epoch. The United States has entered upon a new phase of popular government, and no man can foresee the outcome.

Journalist Frank I. Cobb, in the New York *World*, March 4, 1913.

President Wilson's inaugural is the call of a prophet to a Nation to repent of its sins and return, not to the methods but to the spirit of the Fathers. . . .

Editorial in *Outlook*, CIII (March 15, 1913), 573–74.

43. *AUGUST 19, 1914*

Woodrow Wilson's Appeal for Neutrality

When war broke out in Europe during the summer of 1914, most Americans were

Senate Documents, 63d Cong., 2d Sess., Senate Document, 566, XXIX, 3–4.

caught by surprise. President Wilson responded by offering the good offices of his government for peace and by issuing a formal proclamation of neutrality. Mean-

while, he urged his countrymen to be impartial in thought as well as in deed. Though the war seemed quite remote from American shores, to be neutral in thought and feeling ultimately proved impossible for most Americans as well as the president. Because of ties of language, race, culture, and political ideals, most Americans were pro-Ally from the beginning. Moreover, the British were much more effective than the Central Powers in their use of propaganda. As the war continued, the banking and commercial ties between American businessmen and England became more binding, especially after the British navy was able to cut off German markets.

The fact that a majority of Americans were sympathetic with the Allies does not imply that they desired war. Like Wilson, until 1917, most Americans hoped to stay at peace with Germany. But when Germany resorted to unrestricted submarine warfare in 1917, a break with the Central Powers was unavoidable.

I suppose that every thoughtful man in America has asked himself, during these last troubled weeks, what influence the European war may exert upon the United States, and I take the liberty of addressing a few words to you in order to point out that it is entirely within our own choice what its effects upon us will be and to urge very earnestly upon you the sort of speech and conduct which will best safeguard the Nation against distress and disaster.

The effect of the war upon the United States will depend upon what American citizens say and do. Every man who really loves America will act and speak in the true spirit of neutrality, which is the spirit of impartiality and fairness and friendliness to all concerned. The spirit of the Nation in this critical matter will be determined largely by what individuals and society and those gathered in public meetings do and say, upon what newspapers and magazines contain, upon what ministers utter in their pulpits, and men proclaim as their opinions on the street.

The people of the United States are drawn from many nations, and chiefly from the nations now at war. It is natural and inevitable that there should be the utmost variety of sympathy and desire among them with regard to the issues and circumstances of the conflict. Some will wish one nation, others another, to succeed in the momentous struggle. It will be easy to excite passion and difficult to allay it. Those responsible for exciting it will assume a heavy responsiblity, responsibility for no less a thing than that the people of the United States, whose love of their country and whose loyalty to its Government should unite them as Americans all, bound in honor and affection to think first of her and her interests, may be divided in camps of hostile opinion, hot against each other, involved in the war itself in impulse and opinion if not in action.

Such divisions among us would be fatal to our peace of mind and might seriously stand in the way of the proper performance of our duty as the one great nation at peace, the one people holding itself ready to play a part of impartial mediation and speak the counsels of peace and accommodation, not as a partisan, but as a friend.

I venture, therefore, my fellow countrymen, to speak a solemn word of warning to you against that deepest, most subtle, most essential breach of neutrality which may spring out of partisanship, out of passionately taking sides. The United States must be neutral in fact as well as in name during these days that are to try men's souls. We must be impartial in thought as well as in action, must put a curb upon our sentiments as well as upon every transaction that might be construed as a preference of one party to the struggle before another.

My thought is of America. I am speaking, I feel sure, the earnest wish and purpose of every thoughtful American that this great country of ours, which is, of course, the first in our thoughts and in our hearts, should show herself in this time of peculiar trial a Nation fit beyond others to exhibit the fine poise of undisturbed judgment, the dignity of self-control, the efficiency of dispassionate action; a Nation that neither sits in judgment upon others nor is disturbed in her own counsels and which keeps herself fit and free to do what is honest and disinterested and truly serviceable for the peace of the world.

Shall we not resolve to put upon ourselves the restraints which will bring to our people the happiness and the great and lasting influence for peace we covet for them?

COMMENT

Your address on neutrality is one of the finest things you have ever done, and it has met with universal approbation. Every day editorials of the Republican press speak of you as if you were of their party instead of being the idol of ours.

Colonel Edward M. House in a letter to President Woodrow Wilson, August 22, 1914. Charles Seymour, ed., *The Intimate Papers of Colonel House* (Boston: Houghton Mifflin Company, 1926), I, 284.

. . . I am not pro-Ally or pro-German; I am not in favor of those who began the war, or those who unnecessarily protract the war. I think the war is the crowning crime of history, the uttermost imbecility of which the human race is capable. I am glad that our American people have had intelligence enough and humanity enough to keep out of war.

Publisher William Randolph Hearst in a letter to W. Orten Tewson, exact date unknown but early in 1916. Great Britain, Foreign Office, *American Press Résumé*, May 25, 1916.

Those were the days when American citizens were being urged to remain neutral in action, in word, and even in thought. But our firm had never for one moment been neutral: we didn't know how to be. From the very start we did everything that we could to contribute to the cause of the Allies.

Thomas W. Lamont, New York financier, in a public statement. Quoted in Manchester *Guardian*, January 27, 1920.

44. *SEPTEMBER 26, 1914*

Federal Trade Commission Act

During Woodrow Wilson's first administration, many Progressives advocated an anti-trust program which would suppress unfair trade practices. Wilson at first demanded legislation in accord with his New Freedom doctrine of limited inter-

U.S. *Statutes at Large*, XXVIII, pt. I, 717–24.

vention. But after being subjected to much pressure, he supported the Federal Trade Commission Act which outlawed unfair trade practices in general terms and established a Federal Trade Commission with ample authority to move against corporations accused of suppressing competition. This act, along with the Clayton Anti-trust Act, was the first sign that Wilson was surrendering to the demands for bold economic and social legislation. Modeled after the Interstate Commerce Commission, the Federal Trade Commission was to be nonpartisan, with members appointed by the president for a term of seven years, and endowed with broad investigative powers. The heart of the new bill was contained in section five, which granted the commissioners the power to investigate and prevent unfair competition by the issuance of cease and desist orders which would be enforced by the federal district courts. Though the act was conservatively prepared and aroused comparatively little debate in Congress, Herbert Croly perceptively remarked in the New Republic *that it "contained the possibility of a radical reversal of many American notions about trusts, legislative power, and legal procedure." But during the 1920's, the Supreme Court limited the Commission's capacity as a fact-finding body, thus temporarily destroying much of its usefulness as an administrative body.*

Be it enacted by the Senate and House of Representatives of the United States of America in Congress assembled, That a commission is hereby created and established, to be known as the Federal Trade Commission (hereinafter referred to as the commission), which shall be composed of five commissioners, who shall be appointed by the President, by and with the advice and consent of the Senate. Not more than three of the commissioners shall be members of the same political party. The first commissioners appointed shall continue in office for terms of three, four, five, six, and seven years, respectively, from the date of the taking effect of this Act, the term of each to be designated by the President, but their successors shall be appointed for terms of seven years, except that any person chosen to fill a vacancy shall be appointed only for

the unexpired term of the commissioner whom he shall succeed. The commission shall choose a chairman from its own membership. No commissioner shall engage in any other business, vocation, or employment. Any commissioner may be removed by the President for inefficiency, neglect of duty, or malfeasance in office.

. . . . .

SEC. 4. That the words defined in this section shall have the following meaning when found in this Act, to wit:

"Commerce" means commerce among the several States or with foreign nations, or in any Territory of the United States or in the District of Columbia, or between any such Territory and another, or between any such Territory and any State or foreign nation, or between the District of Columbia and any State or Territory or foreign nation.

"Corporation" means any company or association incorporated or unincorporated, which is organized to carry on business for profit and has shares of capital or capital stock, and any company or association, incorporated or unincorporated, without shares of capital or capital stock, except partnerships, which is organized to carry on business for its own profit or that of its members.

"Documentary evidence" means all documents, papers, and correspondence in existence at and after the passage of this Act.

"Acts to regulate commerce" means the Act entitled "An Act to regulate commerce," approved February fourteenth, eighteen hundred and eighty-seven, and all Acts amendatory thereof and supplementary thereto.

"Antitrust acts" means the Act entitled "An Act to protect trade and commerce against unlawful restraints and monopolies," approved July second, eighteen hundred and ninety; also the sections seventy-three to seventy-seven, inclusive, of an Act entitled "An Act to reduce taxation, to provide revenue for the Government, and for other purposes," approved August twenty-seventh, eighteen hundred and ninety-four; and also the Act entitled "An Act to amend sections seventy-three and seventy-six of the Act of August twenty-seventh, eighteen hundred and ninety-four, entitled "An Act to reduce taxation, to provide revenue for the Government, and for other purposes," approved February twelfth, nineteen hundred and thirteen.

SEC. 5. That unfair methods of competition in commerce are hereby declared unlawful.

The commission is hereby empowered and directed to prevent persons, partnerships, or corporations, except banks, and common carriers subject to the Acts to regulate commerce, from using unfair methods of competition in commerce.

Whenever the commission shall have reason to believe that any such person, partnership, or corporation has been or is using any unfair method of competition in commerce, and if it shall appear to the commission that a proceeding by it in respect thereof would be to the interest of the public, it shall issue and serve upon such person, partnership, or corporation a complaint stating its charges in that respect, and containing a notice of a hearing upon a day and at a place therein fixed at least thirty days after the service of said complaint. The person, partnership, or corporation so complained of shall have the right to appear at the place and time so fixed and show cause why an order should not be entered by the commission requiring such person, partnership, or corporation to cease and desist from the violation of the law so charged in said complaint. Any person, partnership, or corporation may make application, and upon good cause shown may be allowed by the commission, to intervene and appear in said proceeding by counsel or in person. The testimony in any such proceeding shall be reduced to writing and filed in the office of the commission. If upon such hearing the commission shall be of the opinion that the method of competition in question is prohibited by this Act, it shall make a report in writing in which it shall state its findings as to the facts, and shall issue and cause to be served on such person, partnership, or corporation an order requiring such person, partnership, or corporation to cease and desist from using such method of competition. . . .

If such person, partnership, or corporation fails or neglects to obey such order of the commission while the same is in effect, the commission may apply to the circuit court of appeals of the United States, within any circuit where the method of competition in question was used or where such person, partnership, or corporation resides or carries on business, for the enforcement of its order, and shall certify and file with its application a transcript of the entire record in the proceeding, including all the testimony taken and the report and order of the commission. Upon such filing of the application and transcript the court shall cause notice thereof to be served upon such person, partnership, or corporation and thereupon shall have jurisdiction of the proceeding and of the question determined therein, and shall have power to make and enter upon the pleadings, testimony, and proceedings set forth in such transcript a decree affirming, modifying, or setting aside the order of the commission. The findings of the commission as to the facts, if supported by testimony, shall be conclusive. . . .

Any party required by such order of the commission to cease and desist from using such method of competition may obtain a review of such order in said circuit court of appeals by filing in the court a written petition praying that the order of the commission be set aside.

. . . . .

SEC. 6. That the commission shall also have power—

(a) To gather and compile information concerning, and to investigate from time to time the organization, business, conduct, practices, and management of any corporation engaged in commerce, excepting banks and common carriers subject to the Act to regulate commerce, and its relation to other corporations and to individuals, associations, and partnerships.

(b) To require, by general or special orders, corporations engaged in commerce, excepting banks, and common carriers subject to the Act to regulate commerce, or any class of them, or any of them, respectively, to file with the commission in such form as the commission may prescribe annual or special, or both annual and special, reports or answers in writing to specific questions, furnishing to the commission such information as it may require as to the organization, business, conduct, practices, management, and relation to other corporations, partnerships, and individuals of the respective corporations filing such reports or answers in writing. Such reports and answers shall be made under oath, or otherwise, as the commission may prescribe, and shall be filed with the commission within such reasonable period as the commission may prescribe, unless additional time be granted in any case by the commission.

(c) Whenever a final decree has been entered against any defendant corporation in any suit brought by the United States to prevent and restrain any violation of the antitrust Acts, to make investigation, upon its own initiative, of the manner in which the decree has been or is being carried out, and upon the application of the Attorney General it shall be its duty to make such investigation. It shall transmit to the Attorney General a report embodying its findings and recommendations as a result of any such investigation, and the report shall be made public in the discretion of the commission.

. . . . .

SEC. 9. That for the purposes of this Act the commission, or its duly author-

ized agent or agents, shall at all reasonable times have access to, for the purpose of examination, and the right to copy any documentary evidence of any corporation being investigated or proceeded against; and the commission shall have power to require by subpœna the attendance and testimony of witnesses and the production of all such documentary evidence relating to any matter under investigation. Any member of the commission may sign subpœnas, and members and examiners of the commission may administer oaths and affirmations, examine witnesses, and receive evidence.

Such attendance of witnesses, and the production of such documentary evidence, may be required from any place in the United States, at any designated place of hearing. And in case of disobedience to a subpœna the commission may invoke the aid of any court of the United States in requiring the attendance and testimony of witnesses and the production of documentary evidence.

Any of the district courts of the United States within the jurisdiction of which such inquiry is carried on may, in case of contumacy or refusal to obey a subpœna issued to any corporation or other person, issue an order requiring such corporation or other person to appear before the commission, or to produce documentary evidence if so ordered, or to give evidence touching the matter in question; and any failure to obey such order of the court may be punished by such court as a contempt thereof.

Upon the application of the Attorney General of the United States, at the request of the commission, the district courts of the United States shall have jurisdiction to issue writs of mandamus commanding any person or corporation to comply with the provisions of this Act or any order of the commission made in pursuance thereof.

. . . . .

SEC. 10. That any person who shall neglect or refuse to attend and testify, or to answer any lawful inquiry, or to produce documentary evidence, if in his power to do so, in obedience to the subpœna or lawful requirement of the commission, shall be guilty of an offense and upon conviction thereof by a court of competent jurisdiction shall be punished by a fine of not less than $1,000 nor more than $5,000, or by imprisonment for not more than one year, or by both such fine and imprisonment.

. . . . .

COMMENT

I predict that in the days to come the Federal Trade Commission and its enforcement of the section with regard to unfair competition . . . will be found to be the most efficient protection to the people of the United States that Congress has ever given the people by way of a regulation of commerce, and that it will rank in future years with the antitrust law. . . .

Albert B. Cummins, Republican of Iowa, speaking in the U.S. Senate, September 5, 1914. Congressional Record, 63d Cong. 2d Sess., 1914, LI, 14770.

. . . the Congress has sought, in the Trade-Commission bill . . . to make men in a small way of business as free to succeed as men in a big way, and to kill monopoly in the seed. . . . It is our purpose to destroy monopoly and maintain competition as the only effectual instrument of business liberty. . . .

President Woodrow Wilson in a letter to Oscar Underwood of Alabama, October 17, 1914. Ray Stannard Baker (ed.), The Public Papers of Woodrow Wilson (New York: Doubleday, Doran & Company, Inc., 1931), III, 187–94.

45. OCTOBER 15, 1914

Clayton Anti-trust Act

Though Woodrow Wilson promised in the presidential campaign of 1912 to destroy monopolies and to restore economic competition, it was not until November, 1913, that he gave serious thought to details. Then after many months of study, the result was the Clayton Anti-trust Act which was an effort to supplement and strengthen the Sherman Anti-trust Act. Among its chief provisions was the prohibition of holding companies, interlocking corporate directorates, exclusive selling arrangements, and practices which lessened competition by price discrimination

U.S. *Statutes at Large*, XXXIII, pt. I, 730–40.

against purchasers. Because the American Federation of Labor had demanded that labor be immune to the provisions of the Sherman Act, Congress added sections six and twenty to the Clayton Act which forbade the use of an injunction in labor disputes unless necessary to prevent irreparable injury to property. Labor responded by hailing the act as its "Magna Carta" and tried to convince the nation that labor unions were free from the inhibitions of anti-trust laws.

When the federal courts overturned much of the Progressives' legislation during the 1920's, one of the statutes which received unfriendly judicial interpreta-

tion was the Clayton Anti-trust Act. In the Duplex Printing Press Company v. Deering (1921), the Supreme Court virtually thrust aside section twenty of the Clayton Act by ruling that it did not confer upon labor unions immunity from prosecution for violating the anti-trust laws. Later, Congress undid the effect of the Duplex case by passing the Norris-La Guardia Act which restored the original intent of the Clayton Act.

"Antitrust laws," as used herein, includes the Act entitled "An Act to protect trade and commerce against unlawful restraints and monopolies," approved July second, eighteen hundred and ninety; sections seventy-three to seventy-seven, inclusive, of an Act entitled "An Act to reduce taxation, to provide revenue for the Government, and for other purposes," of August twenty-seventh, eighteen hundred and ninety-four; an Act entitled "An Act to amend sections seventy-three and seventy-six of the Act of August twenty-seventh, eighteen hundred and ninety-four, entitled 'An Act to reduce taxation, to provide revenue for the Government, and for other purposes,'" approved February twelfth, nineteen hundred and thirteen; and also this Act.

"Commerce," as used herein, means trade or commerce among the several States and with foreign nations, or between the District of Columbia or any Territory of the United States and any State, Territory, or foreign nation, or between any insular possessions or other places under the jurisdiction of the United States, or between any such possession or place and any State or Territory of the United States or the District of Columbia or any foreign nation, or within the District of Columbia or any Territory or any insular possession or other place under the jurisdiction of the United States: *Provided,* That nothing in this Act contained shall apply to the Philippine Islands.

The word "person" or persons"

wherever used in this Act shall be deemed to include corporations and associations existing under or authorized by the laws of either the United States, the laws of any of the Territories, the laws of any State, or the laws of any foreign country.

SEC. 2. That it shall be unlawful for any person engaged in commerce, in the course of such commerce, either directly or indirectly to discriminate in price between different purchasers of commodities, which commodities are sold for use, consumption, or resale within the United States or any Territory thereof or the District of Columbia or any insular possession or other place under the jurisdiction of the United States, where the effect of such discrimination may be to substantially lessen competition or tend to create a monopoly in any line of commerce: . . .

SEC. 3. That it shall be unlawful for any person engaged in commerce, in the course of such commerce, to lease or make a sale or contract for sale of goods, wares, merchandise, machinery, supplies or other commodities, whether patented or unpatented, for use, consumption or resale within the United States or any Territory thereof or the District of Columbia or any insular possession or other place under the jurisdiction of the United States, or fix a price charged therefor, or discount from, or rebate upon, such price, on the condition, agreement or understanding that the lessee or purchaser thereof shall not use or deal in the goods, wares, merchandise, machinery, supplies or other commodities of a competitor or competitors of the lessor or seller, where the effect of such lease, sale, or contract for sale or such condition, agreement or understanding may be to substantially lessen competition or tend to create a monopoly in any line or commerce.

. . . . .

SEC. 6. That the labor of a human being is not a commodity or article of commerce. Nothing contained in the antitrust laws shall be construed to forbid the existence and operation of labor, agricultural, or horticultural organizations, instituted for the purposes of mutual help, and not having capital stock or conducted for profit, or to forbid or restrain individual members of such organizations from lawfully carrying out the legitimate objects thereof; nor shall such organizations, or the members thereof, be held or construed to be illegal combinations or conspiracies in restraint of trade, under the antitrust laws.

SEC. 7. That no corporation engaged in commerce shall acquire, directly or indirectly, the whole or any part of the stock or other share capital of another corporation engaged also in commerce, where the effect of such acquisition may be to substantially lessen competition between the corporation whose stock is so acquired and the corporation making the acquisition, or to restrain such commerce in any section or community, or tend to create a monopoly of any line of commerce.

No corporation shall acquire, directly or indirectly, the whole or any part of the stock or other share capital of two or more corporations engaged in commerce where the effect of such acquisition, or the use of such stock by the voting or granting of proxies or otherwise, may be to substantially lessen competition between such corporations, or any of them, whose stock or other share capital is so acquired, or to restrain such commerce in any section of community, or tend to create a monopoly of any line of commerce.

This section shall not apply to corporations purchasing such stock solely for investment and not using the same by voting or otherwise to bring about, or in attempting to bring about, the substantial lessening of competition. Nor shall anything contained in this section prevent a corporation engaged in commerce from causing the formation of subsidiary corporations for the actual carrying on of their immediate lawful business, or the

natural and legitimate branches or extensions thereof, or from owning and holding all or a part of the stock of such subsidiary corporations, when the effect of such formation is not to substantially lessen competition.

. . . . .

SEC. 8. That from and after two years from the date of the approval of this Act no person shall at the same time be a director or other officer or employee of more than one bank, banking association or trust company, organized or operating under the laws of the United States, either of which has deposits, capital, surplus, and undivided profits aggregating more than $5,000,000; and no private banker or person who is a director in any bank or trust company, organized and operating under the laws of a State, having deposits, capital, surplus, and undivided profits aggregating more than $5,000,-000, shall be eligible to be a director in any bank or banking association organized or operating under the laws of the United States. . . .

. . . . .

That from and after two years from the date of the approval of this Act no person at the same time shall be a director in any two or more corporations, any one of which has capital, surplus, and undivided profits aggregating more than $1,000,000, engaged in whole or in part in commerce, other than banks, banking associations, trust companies and common carriers subject to the Act to regulate commerce, approved February fourth, eighteen hundred and eighty-seven, if such corporations are or shall have been theretofore, by virtue of their business and location of operation, competitors, so that the elimination of competition by agreement between them would constitute a violation of any of the provisions of any of the antitrust laws . . .

. . . . .

SEC. 10. That after two years from the approval of this Act no common carrier engaged in commerce shall have any dealings in securities, supplies or other articles of commerce, or shall make or have any contracts for construction or maintenance of any kind, to the amount of more than $50,000, in the aggregate, in any one year, with another corporation, firm, partnership or association when the said common carrier shall have upon its board of directors or as its president, manager or as its purchasing or selling officer, or agent in the particular transaction, any person who is at the same time a director, manager, or purchasing or selling officer of, or who has any substantial interest in, such other corporation, firm, partnership or association, unless and except such purchases shall be made from, or such dealings shall be with, the bidder whose bid is the most favorable to such common carrier, to be ascertained by competitive bidding under regulations to be prescribed by rule or otherwise by the Interstate Commerce Commission. . . .

. . . . .

SEC. 11. That authority to enforce compliance with sections two, three, seven and eight of this Act by the persons respectively subject thereto is hereby vested: in the Interstate Commerce Commission where applicable to common carriers, in the Federal Reserve Board where applicable to banks, banking associations and trust companies, and in the Federal Trade Commission where applicable to all other character of commerce. . . .

. . . . .

SEC. 14. That whenever a corporation shall violate any of the penal provisions of the antitrust laws, such violation shall be deemed to be also that of the individual directors, officers, or agents of such corporation who shall have authorized, ordered, or done any of the acts constituting in whole or in part such violation, and such violation shall be deemed a misdemeanor, and upon conviction therefor

of any such director, officer, or agent he shall be punished by a fine of not exceeding $5,000 or by imprisonment for not exceeding one year, or by both, in the discretion of the court.

. . . . .

SEC. 20. That no restraining order or injunction shall be granted by any court of the United States, or a judge or the judges thereof, in any case between an employer and employees, or between employers and employees, or between employees, or between persons employed and persons seeking employment, involving, or growing out of, a dispute concerning terms or conditions of employment, unless necessary to prevent irreparable injury to property, or to a property right, of the party making the application, for which injury there is no adequate remedy at law, and such property or property right must be described with particularity in the application, which must be in writing and sworn to by the applicant or by his agent or attorney.

And no such restraining order or injunction shall prohibit any person or persons, whether singly or in concert, from terminating any relation of employment, or from ceasing to perform any work or labor, or from recommending, advising, or persuading others by peaceful means so to do; or from attending at any place where any such person or persons may lawfully be, for the purpose of peacefully obtaining or communicating information, or from peacefully persuading any person to work or to abstain from working; or from ceasing to patronize or to employ any party to such dispute, or from recommending, advising, or persuading others by peaceful and lawful means so to do; or from paying or giving to, or withholding from, any person engaged in such dispute, any strike benefits or other moneys or things of value; or from peaceably assembling in a lawful manner, and for lawful purposes; or from doing any act or thing which might lawfully be done in the absence of such dispute by any party thereto; nor shall any of the acts specified in this paragraph be considered or held to be violations of any law of the United States.

. . . . .

COMMENT

. . . the original Section 7 of the Anti-trust bill . . . added nothing material, but seemed a pretty good compromise proposition.

> Congressman Edwin Y. Webb of North Carolina in a public statement. New York *Times,* June 14, 1914.

The Clayton bill makes few changes in existing laws relating to labor unions, injunctions and contempts of court, and those are of slight practical importance.

> A public statement by Daniel Davenport, general counsel of the American Anti-Boycott Association. Springfield (Mass.) *Republican,* October 11, 1914.

46. *1915*

United States v. Midwest Oil Company

At the turn of the twentieth century, a number of government officials began to fear that the nation was using its natural resources at too rapid a rate and that in the future it would be faced with shortages. But no comprehensive policy of setting aside nationally owned lands was adopted until President Theodore Roosevelt started a major forest reclamation program. Soon, the concept of conservation was widened to include not only forests, but coal and mineral lands, oil reserves, and power sites. But despite presidential leadership and extensive publicity, many people remained opposed to the conservation of natural resources.

It was not until the Supreme Court handed down its decision in United States v. Midwest Oil Company that the powers of the central government over public lands were clarified. Though the Midwest decision had a specialized meaning for federal oil lands in California and Wyo-

236 U.S. 459 (1915).

ming, it has a broader meaning in American constitutional history in that the Court explicitly upheld the right of the executive power to withdraw and protect the public lands of the United States. Thus, the Court vindicated the conservation policies of Theodore Roosevelt which had so often been attacked. Had the Court taken a contrary position in the Midwest decision, it is possible that there would have been a complete collapse of the nation's conservation programs.

Mr. Justice Lamar delivered the opinion of the court:

All public lands containing petroleum or other mineral oils, and chiefly valuable therefor, have been declared by Congress to be "free and open to occupation, exploration, and purchase by citizens of the United States . . . under regulations prescribed by law." Act of February 11, 1897.

As these regulations permitted exploration and location without the payment of any sum, and as title could be obtained for a merely nominal amount, many persons availed themselves of the provisions of the statute. Large areas in California were explored; and petroleum having been found, locations were made, not only by the discoverer, but by others on adjoining land. And, as the flow through the well on one lot might exhaust the oil under the adjacent land, the interest of each operator was to extract the oil as soon as possible, so as to share what would otherwise be taken by the owners of nearby wells.

The result was that oil was so rapidly extracted that on September 17, 1909, the Director of the Geological Survey made a report to the Secretary of the Interior which, with inclosures, called attention to the fact that, while there was a limited supply of coal on the Pacific coast, and the value of oil as a fuel had been fully demonstrated, yet, at the rate at which oil lands in California were being patented by private parties, it would "be impossible for the people of the United States to continue ownership of oil lands for more than a few months. After that the government will be obliged to repurchase the very oil that it has practically given away. . . ." "In view of the increasing use of fuel by the American Navy there would appear to be an immediate necessity for assuring the conservation of a proper supply of petroleum for the government's own use. . . ." and "pending the enactment of adequate legislation on this subject, the filing of claims to oil lands in the state of California should be suspended."

This recommendation was approved by the Secretary of the Interior. Shortly afterwards he brought the matter to the attention of the President, who, on September 27, 1909, issued the following proclamation:

TEMPORARY PETROLEUM WITHDRAWAL NO. 5

In aid of proposed legislation affecting the use and disposition of the petroleum deposits on the public domain, all public lands in the accompanying lists are hereby temporarily withdrawn from all forms of location, settlement, selection, filing, entry, or disposal under the mineral or nonmineral public-land laws. All locations or claims existing and valid on this date may proceed to entry in the usual manner after filing, investigation, and examination.

The list attached described an area aggregating 3,041,000 acres in California and Wyoming—though, of course, the order only applied to the public lands therein, the acreage of which is not shown.

On March 27, 1910, six months after the publication of the proclamation, William T. Henshaw and others entered upon a quarter section of this public land in Wyoming, so withdrawn. They made explorations, bored a well, discovered oil, and thereafter assigned their interest to the appellees, who took possession and extracted large quantities of oil. On May 4, 1910, they filed a location certificate.

As the explorations by the original claimants, and the subsequent operation of the well, were both long after the date of the President's proclamation, the government filed, in the district court of the United States for the district of Wyoming, a bill in equity against the Midwest Oil Company and the other appellees, seeking to recover the land and to obtain an accounting for 50,000 barrels of oil alleged to have been illegally extracted. The court sustained the defendant's demurrer and dismissed the bill. Thereupon the government took the case to the circuit court of appeals of the eighth circuit, which rendered no decision, but certified certain questions to this court, where an order was subsequently passed, directing the entire record to be sent up for consideration.

The case has twice been fully argued. Both parties, as well as other persons interested in oil lands similarly affected, have submitted lengthy and elaborate briefs on the single and controlling question as to the validity of the withdrawal order. On the part of the government it is urged that the President, as Commander in Chief of the Army and Navy, had power to make the order for the purpose of retaining and preserving a source of supply of fuel for the Navy, instead of allowing the oil land to be taken up for a nominal sum, the government being then obliged to purchase at a great cost what it had previously owned. It is argued that the President, charged with the care of the public domain, could, by virtue of the executive power vested in him by the Constitution, and also in conformity with the tacit consent of Congress, withdraw, in the public interest, any public land from entry or location by private parties.

The appellees, on the other hand, insist that there is no dispensing power in the Executive, and that he could not suspend a statute or withdraw from entry or location any land which Congress had affirmatively declared should be free and open to acquisition by citizens of the United States. They further insist that the withdrawal order is absolutely void, since it appears on its face to be a mere attempt to suspend a statute—supposed to be unwise—in order to allow Congress to pass another more in accordance with what the Executive thought to be in the public interest.

1. We need not consider whether, as an original question, the President could have withdrawn from private acquisition what Congress had made free and open to occupation and purchase. The case can be determined on other grounds and in the light of the legal consequences flowing from a long-continued practice to make orders like the one here involved. For the President's proclamation of September 27, 1909, is by no means the first instance in which the Executive, by a special order, has withdrawn lands which Congress, by general statute, had thrown open to acquisition by citizens. And while it is not known when the first of these

orders was made, it is certain that "the practice dates from an early period in the history of the government." Scores and hundreds of these orders have been made; and treating them as they must be, as the act of the President, an examination of official publications will show that (excluding those made by virtue of special congressional action) he has, during the past eighty years, without express statutory,—but under the claim of power so to do,—made a multitude of Executive orders which operated to withdraw public land that would otherwise have been open to private acquisition. They affected every kind of land—mineral and nonmineral. The size of the tracts varied from a few square rods to many square miles, and the amount withdrawn has aggregated millions of acres. The number of such instances cannot, of course, be accurately given, but the extent of the practice can best be appreciated by a consideration of what is believed to be a correct enumeration of such Executive orders mentioned in public documents.

They show that prior to the year 1910 there had been issued

99 Executive orders establishing or enlarging Indian reservations;
109 Executive orders establishing or enlarging military reservations and setting apart land for water, timber, fuel, hay, signal stations, target ranges, and rights of way for use in connection with military reservations;
44 Executive orders establishing bird reserves.

In the sense that these lands may have been intended for public use, they were reserved for a public purpose. But they were not reserved in pursuance of law, or by virtue of any general or special statutory authority. For it is to be specially noted that there was no act of Congress providing for bird reserves or for these Indian reservations. There was no law for the etablishment of these military reservations or defining their size or location. There was no statute empowering the President to withdraw any of these lands from settlement, or to reserve them for any of the purposes indicated.

But when it appeared that the public interest would be served by withdrawing or reserving parts of the public domain, nothing was more natural than to retain what the government already owned. And in making such orders, which were thus useful to the public, no private interest was injured. For, prior to the initiation of some right given by law, the citizen had no enforceable interest in the public statute, and no private right in land which was the property of the people. The President was in a position to know when the public interest required particular portions of the people's lands to be withdrawn from entry or location; his action inflicted no wrong upon any private citizen, and being subject to disaffirmance by Congress, could occasion no harm to the interest of the public at large. Congress did not repudiate the power claimed or the withdrawal orders made. On the contrary, it uniformly and repeatedly acquiesced in the practice, and, as shown by these records, there had been, prior to 1910, at least 252 Executive orders making reservations for useful, though nonstatutory, purposes.

This right of the President to make reservations—and thus withdraw land from private acquisition—was expressly recognized in Grisar v. McDowell, 6 Wall. 364, where it was said that "from an early period in the history of the government it has been the practice of the President to order from time to time, as the exigencies of the public service required, parcels of land belonging to the United States, to be reserved from sale and set apart for public uses."

But, notwithstanding this decision and the continuity of this practice, the absence of express statutory authority was the occasion of doubt being expressed as to the power of the President to make these orders. The matter was therefore several times referred to the law officers of the government for an opinion on the subject. One of them stated that the validity of such orders rested on "a long-established and long-recognized power in the President to withhold from sale or settlement at discretion, portions of the public domain." Another reported that "the power of the President was recognized by Congress, and that such recognition was equivalent to a grant." Again, when the claim was made that the power to withdraw did not extend to mineral land, the Attorney General gave the opinion that the power must be "regarded as extending to any lands which belong to the public domain, and capable of being exercised with respect to such lands so long as they remain unappropriated."

Similar views were expressed by officers in the Land Department. Indeed, one of the strongest assertions of the existence of the power is the frequently quoted statement of Secretary Teller, made in 1881:

"That the power resides in the Executive from an early period in the history of the country to make reservations has never been denied either legislatively or judicially, but, on the contrary, has been recognized. It constitutes in fact a part of the Land Office law, exists *ex necessitate rei*, as indispensable to the public weal, and in that light, by different laws enacted as herein indicated, has been referred to as an existing undisputed power too well settled ever to be disputed.

2. It may be argued that while these facts and rulings prove a usage, they do not establish its validity. But government is a practical affair, intended for practical men. Both officers, lawmakers, and citizens naturally adjust themselves to any long-continued action of the Executive Department, on the presumption that unauthorized acts would not have been allowed to be so often repeated as to crystallize into a regular practice. That presumption is not reasoning in a circle, but the basis of a wise and quieting rule that,

in determining the meaning of a statute or the existence of a power, weight shall be given to the usage itself,—even when the validity of the practice is the subject of investigation.

3. . . . rules or laws for the disposal of public land are necessarily general in their nature. Emergencies may occur, or conditions may so change as to require that the agent in charge should, in the public interest, withhold the land from sale; and while no such express authority has been granted, there is nothing in the nature of the power exercised which prevents Congress from granting it by implication just as could be done by any other owner of property under similar conditions. The power of the Executive, as agent in charge, to retain that property from sale, need not necessarily be expressed in writing.

. . . it must be borne in mind that Congress not only has a legislative power over the public domain, but it also exercises the powers of the proprietor therein. Congress "may deal with such lands precisely as an ordinary individual may deal with farming property. It may sell or withhold them from sale." Like any other owner it may provide when, how, and to whom its land can be sold. It can permit it to be withdrawn from sale. Like any other owner, it can waive its strict rights, as it did when the valuable privilege of grazing cattle on this public land was held to be based upon an "implied license growing out of the custom of nearly a hundred years." So, too, in the early days, the "government, by its silent acquiescence, assented to the general occupation of the public lands for mining." If private persons could acquire a privilege in public land by virtue of an implied congressional consent, then, for a much stronger reason, an implied grant of power to preserve the public interest would arise out of like congressional acquiescence.

The Executive, as agent, was in charge of the public domain; by a multitude of orders extending over a long period of time, and affecting vast bodies of land, in many states and territories, he withdrew large areas in the public interest. These orders were known to Congress, as principal, and in not a single instance was the act of the agent disapproved. Its acquiescence all the more readily operated as an implied grant of power in view of the fact that its exercise was not only useful to the public, but did not interfere with any vested right of the citizen.

4. The appellees, however, argue that the practice thus approved related to reservations,—to cases where the land had been reserved for military or other special public purposes,—and they contend that even if the President could reserve land for a public purpose or naval uses, it does not follow that he can withdraw land in aid of legislation.

When analyzed, this proposition, in effect, seeks to make a distinction between a reservation and a withdrawal,—between a reservation for a purpose not provided for by existing legislation, and a withdrawal made in aid of future legislation. It would mean that a permanent reservation for a purpose designated by the President, but not provided for by a statute, would be valid, while a merely temporary withdrawal to enable Congress to legislate in the public interest would be invalid. It is only necessary to point out that, as the greater includes the less, the power to make permanent reservations includes power to make temporary withdrawals. For there is no distinction in principle between the two. The character of the power exerted is the same in both cases. In both, the order is made to serve the public interest, and in both the effect on the intending settler or miner is the same.

But the question need not be left solely to inference, since the validity of withdrawal orders, in aid of legislation, has been expressly recognized in a series of cases involving a number of such orders, made between 1850 and 1862.

In 1846 Congress made to the territory of Iowa, a grant of land on both sides of the Des Moines, for the purpose of improving the navigation from the mouth of the river to Raccoon Fork. There was from the outset a difference of opinion as to whether the grant extended throughout the entire course of the river, or was limited to the land opposite that portion of the stream which was to be improved. In Dubuque & P. R. Co. v. Litchfield, 23 How. 66, 16 L. ed. 500, decided in 1860, it was held that the grant only included the land between the mouth of the river and Raccoon Fork. But for eleven years prior to that decision there had been various and conflicting rulings by the Land Department. It was first held that the grant included land *above* the Fork, and certificate were issued to the territory as the work progressed. That ruling was shortly followed by another, that the grant extended only *up to* the Fork.

"On April 6, 1850, Secretary Ewing, while concurring with Attorney General Crittenden in his opinion that the grant of 1846 did not extend beyond the Raccoon Fork, issued an order withholding all the lands then in controversy from market 'until the close of the then session of Congress,' which order has been continued ever since" (we italicize) *"in order to give the state the opportunity of petitioning for an extension of the grant by Congress."*

The withdrawal was made in 1851. The hoped-for legislation was not passed until several years later. Between those dates various private citizens made settlements by which, under various statutes, they initiated rights and acquired an interest in the land—if the withdrawal order was void. But by such settlements they obtained no rights if the withdrawal order was valid. A subsequent ratification could have related back to 1851, but if the withdrawal was originally void, the ratification, of course, could not cut out intervening rights of settlers.

There was litigation between settlers claiming, as here, under existing land laws, and those whose title depended upon the original validity of the *withdrawals made in aid of legislation.* In those suits, the withdrawal orders were not treated as having derived their validity from the legislation subsequently passed in aid of Iowa and its assignees, but they were treated as having been effective from their dates, regardless of the fact that the land included therein had not originally been granted to Iowa. In one of them it was said that:

"This court has decided in a number of cases, in regard to these lands, that this withdrawal operated to exclude from sale, purchase, or pre-emption all the lands in controversy."

5. Beginning in 1850 with this order of Secretary Ewing, in aid of legislation on behalf of Iowa, and its continuance even after this court had decided that no land above the Fork passed to the territory, the practice of making withdrawals continued down to 1910. The reasons for making the withdrawal orders varied, but the power exerted was the same, and was supported by the same implied consent of Congress.

For, if any distinction can be drawn between the principle decided in the Iowa cases and this; or if the power involved in making a reservation could differ from that exercised in making a withdrawal,— then the Executive practice and congressional acquiescence, which operated as a grant of an implied power to make permanent reservations, are also present to operate as a grant of an implied power to make temporary withdrawals. It may be well to refer to some of the public records showing the existence and extent of the practice.

Withdrawals in aid of legislation were made in particular cases and many others more general in their nature and much more extensive in their operation.

For example: The Land Department passed an order suspending the location and settlement of certain islands and all isolated tracts containing less than 40 acres "with a view to submitting to Congress" the question as to whether legislation on the subject was not needed.

Reports to the 56th and 57th Congresses contained a list of "temporary withdrawals" made to prevent the disposal of land pending the consideration of the question of the advisability of setting the same apart as forest reservations.

Phosphate land was "temporarily withdrawn, pending action by Congress."

There were also temporary withdrawals of oil land from agricultural entry, in aid of subsequent legislation.

In pursuance of a like practice and power, public land containing coal was withdrawn "pending the enactment of new legislation." In the message of the President to the 2d session of the 59th Congress attention was called to the withdrawal of coal lands in aid of legislation. There was no repudiation of the order or of the practice either at that session, or at any succeeding session of Congress. It was claimed in the argument that the act of 1908 was the legislation contemplated by the Executive when coal lands were temporarily withdrawn by the order of 1906; and reference has already been made to the act of 1861 concerning the Iowa lands withdrawn in 1849. There were other instances in which there was congressional action at a more or less remote period after the order of temporary withdrawal. The land for the Wind Cave Park was withdrawn in 1900 and the Park was established in 1903, bird reserves were established in 1903, and, in 1906, an act was passed making it an offense to interfere with birds on reserves established by law, proclamation, or *Executive order. . . .* In the majority of cases there was no subsequent legislation in reference to such lands, although the withdrawal orders prevented the acquisition of any private interest in such land until after the order was revoked.

Whether, in a particular case, Congress acted or not, nothing was done by it which could, in any way, be construed as a denial of the right of the Executive to make temporary withdrawals of public land in the public interest. Considering the size of the tracts affected and the length of time they remained in force, without objection, these orders by which *islands, isolated tracts, coal, phosphate, and oil lands were withdrawn in aid of legislation,* furnish, in and of themselves, ample proof of congressional recognition of the power to withdraw.

But that the existence of this power was recognized and its exercise by the Executive assented to by Congress is emphasized by the fact that the above-mentioned withdrawals were issued after the report which the Secretary of the Interior made in 1902, in response to a resolution of the Senate calling for information "as to what, if any, of the public lands, have been withdrawn from disposition under the settlement or other laws by order of the Commissioner of the General Land Office, and *what, if any, authority of law exists for such order of withdrawal.*"

The answer to this specific inquiry was returned March 3, 1902. On that date the Secretary transmitted to the Senate the elaborate and detailed report of the Commissioner of the Land Office, who, in response to the inquiry as to the authority by which withdrawals had been made, answered that:

"The power of the Executive Department of the government to make reservations of land for public use, and to temporarily withdraw lands from appropriation by individuals as exigencies might demand, to prevent fraud, to aid in proper administration, and in aid of pending legislation, is one that has been long recognized both in the acts of Congress and the decisions of the court; . . . that this power has been long exercised by the Commissioner of the General Land Office is shown by reference to the date of some of the withdrawals enumerated. . . . The attached list embraces only such lands as were withdrawn by this office, acting on its own motion, in cases where the emergencies appeared to demand such action in furtherance of public interest, and does not include lands withdrawn under express statutes so directed."

The list, which is attached, refers to withdrawal orders, about 100 in number, issued between 1870 and 1902. Many of them were in aid of the administration of the land laws: to correct boundaries; to prevent fraud; to make a classification of the land; and like good—but nonstatutory—reasons. Some were made to prevent settlements while the question was being considered as to whether the lands might not be included in a forest reservation to be thereafter established. One in 1889 was made in order to afford the state of Nebraska an opportuinty to procure legislative relief, as in the *Iowa* cases above cited.

This report refers to *withdrawals,* and not to *reservations.* It is most important in connection with the present inquiry as to whether Congress knew of the practice to make temporary withdrawals and knowingly assented thereto. It will be noted that the resolution called on the Department to state the extent of such withdrawals and the authority by which they were made. The officer of the Land Department, in his answer, shows that there have been a large number of withdrawals made for good, but for nonstatutory, reasons. He shows that these 92 orders had been made by virtue of a long-continued practice and under claim of a right to take such action in the public interest "as exigencies might demand . . ." Congress, with notice of this practice and of this claim of authority, received the report. Neither at that session nor afterwards did it ever repudiate the action taken or the power claimed. Its silence was acquiescence. Its acquiescence was equivalent to consent to continue the practice until the power was revoked by some subsequent action by Congress.

6. Nor is the position of the appellees strengthened by the act of June 25, 1910, to authorize the President to make withdrawals of public lands, and requiring a list of the same to be filed with Congress.

It was passed after the President's Proclamation of September 27, 1909, and months after the occupation and attempted location by virtue of which the appellees claim to have acquired a right to the land. This statute expressly provided that it should not "be construed as a recognition, abridgment, or enlargement of any asserted rights or claims initiated upon any oil or gas bearing lands after any withdrawal of such lands, made prior to the passage of this act."

True, as argued, the act provides that it shall not be construed as an *"abridgment"* of asserted rights initiated in oil lands after they had been withdrawn." But it likewise provides that it shall not be considered as a "recognition of such rights." There is, however, nothing said indicating the slightest intent to repudiate the withdrawals already made.

The legislative history of the statute shows that there was no such intent and no purpose to make the act retroactive, or to disaffirm what the agent in charge had already done. The proclamation of September 27, 1909, withdrawing oil lands from private acquisition, was of far-reaching consequence both to individuals and to the public. It gave rise to much discussion, and the old question as to the authority of the President to make these orders was again raised. Various bills were introduced on the subject, and the President himself sent a message to Congress, calling attention to the existence of the doubt, and suggesting the desirability of legislation to expressly grant the power and ratify what had been done. A bill passed the House, containing such ratification and authorizing future withdrawals. When the bill came to the Senate it was referred to a committee, and, as its members did not agree in their view of the law, two reports were made. The majority, after a review of the practice of the Department, the acquiescence of Congress in the practice, and the decisions of the courts, reported that the President already had a general power of withdrawal, and recommended the passage of the pending bill, inasmuch as it operated to restrict the greater power already possessed. But having regard to the fact that private persons, on withdrawn land, had raised a question as to the validity of the order, and that such question presented a matter for judicial determination, Congress was studious to avoid doing anything which would affect either the public or private rights. It therefore used language which showed not only that the statute was not intended to be retrospective, but was not to be construed either as a recognition, enlargement, or repudiation of rights like those asserted by appellees.

In other words, if, notwithstanding the withdrawal, any locator had initiated a right which, however, had not been perfected, Congress did not undertake to take away his rights. On the other hand, if the withdrawal order had been legally made under the existing power, it needed no ratification, and if a location made after the withdrawal gave the appellees no right, Congress, by this statute, did not legislate against the public and validate what was then an invalid location. The act left the rights of parties in the position of these appellees, to be determined by the state of the law when the proclamation was issued. As heretofore pointed out, the long-continued practice, the acquiescence of Congress, as well as the decisions of the courts, all show that the President had the power to make the order.

The case is therefore remanded to the District Court with directions that the decree dismissing the bill be reversed.

. . . . .

COMMENT

Conservation, above all, was a scientific movement, and its role in history arises from the implications of science and technology in modern society. Conservation leaders spring from such fields as hydrology, forestry, agrostology, geology, and anthropology. Vigorously active in professional circles in the national capital, these leaders brought the ideals and practices of their crafts into federal resource policy.

> Historian Samuel P. Hays in *Conservation and the Gospel of Efficiency* (Cambridge: Harvard University Press, 1959), p. 2.

The moral tonic which the conservation movement has given to the entire country has been more effective for the general good of the American people than any one thing in our generation. . . .

> Chicago conservationist Alfred L. Baker in a letter to Gifford Pinchot, December 27, 1910. Gifford Pinchot MSS., The Library of Congress.

. . . the conservation [movement] was an effort to implement democracy for twentieth-century America, to stop the stealing and exploitation, to inspire high standards of government, to preserve the beauty of mountain and stream, to distribute more equitably the profits of this economy.

> Historian J. Leonard Bates in "Fulfilling American Democracy: The Conservation Movement, 1907 to 1921," *Mississippi Valley Historical Review*, XLIV (June, 1957), 57.

47. *APRIL 2, 1917*

Woodrow Wilson's War Message

Even though President Wilson hoped to avoid war, he thought Germany's resort to unrestricted submarine warfare in January, 1917, left him with little alternative but to break diplomatic relations with the government of Kaiser Wilhelm. Hopeful that Germany might reconsider its policy, he proceeded cautiously in his diplomacy throughout February, 1917. But in late February, events took a turn for the worse when the British intercepted a message from German Foreign Secretary Alfred Zimmerman designed to entice Mexico to form an alliance with his government should the United States and Germany engage in war.

From that point on, events moved toward war. Anger swept the United States. German submarines began sinking American vessels without warning or regard for loss of life. The cry for war spread throughout the nation. Slowly, but surely, the position that America should defend her rights to be neutral was driving the nation to war. Wilson became convinced that Germany's disregard of American rights left him no honorable alternative but to request Congress to recognize a state of war with the Imperial German Government.

In his address to Congress, the President did not speak in terms of national interest. Rather, he sought moral justification for America's intervention: "The world must be made safe for democracy." Not knowing what the struggle was about, the American people followed Wilson's lead in believing the war was being fought to end all wars. Subsequent events

Senate Documents, 65th Cong., 1st Sess., Senate Document 5, x, 3–8.

were to demonstrate that Wilson erred by failing to inform the American people of the vital stake which they had in maintaining a balance of power in Europe. The tragedy was not that the United States went to war in 1917. Rather, it was that the nation went to war for the wrong reasons.

I have called the Congress into extraordinary session because there are serious, very serious, choices of policy to be made, and made immediately, which it was neither right nor constitutionally permissible that I should assume the responsibility of making.

On the third of February last I officially laid before you the extraordinary announcement of the Imperial German Government that on and after the first day of February it was its purpose to put aside all restraints of law or of humanity and use its submarines to sink every vessel that sought to approach either the ports of Great Britain and Ireland or the western coasts of Europe or any of the ports controlled by the enemies of Germany within the Mediterranean. That had seemed to be the object of the German submarine warfare earlier in the war, but since April of last year the Imperial Government had somewhat restrained the commanders of its undersea craft in conformity with its promise then given to us that passenger boats should not be sunk and that due warning would be given to all other vessels which its submarines might seek to destroy, when no resistance was offered or escape attempted, and care taken that their crews were given at least a fair chance to save their lives in their open boats. The precautions taken were meagre and haphazard enough, as was proved in distressing instance after instance in the progress of the cruel and unmanly business, but a certain degree of restraint was observed. The new policy has swept every restriction aside. Vessels of every kind, whatever their flag, their character, their cargo, their destination, their errand, have been ruthlessly sent to the bottom without warning and without thought of help or mercy for those on board the vessels of friendly neutrals along with those of belligerents. Even hospital ships and ships carrying relief to the sorely bereaved and stricken people of Belgium, though the latter were provided with safe conduct through the proscribed areas by the German Government itself and were distinguished by unmistakable marks of identity, have been sunk with the same reckless lack of compassion or of principle.

I was for a little while unable to believe that such things would in fact be done by any government that had hitherto subscribed to the humane practices of civilized nations. International law had its origin in the attempt to set up some law which would be respected and observed upon the seas, where no nation had right of dominion and where lay the free highways of the world. By painful stage after stage has that law been built up, with meagre enough results, indeed, after all was accomplished that could be accomplished, but always with a clear view, at least, of what the heart and conscience of mankind demanded. This minimum of right the German Government has swept aside under the plea of retaliation and necessity and because it had no weapons which it could use at sea except these which it is impossible to employ as it is employing them without throwing to the winds all scruples of humanity or of respect for the understandings that were supposed to underlie the intercourse of the world. I am not now thinking of the

loss of property involved, immense and serious as that is, but only of the wanton and wholesale destruction of the lives of non-combatants, men, women, and children, engaged in pursuits which have always, even in the darkest periods of modern history, been deemed innocent and legitimate. Property can be paid for; the lives of peaceful and innocent people cannot be. The present German submarine warfare against commerce is a warfare against mankind.

It is a war against all nations. American ships have been sunk, American lives taken, in ways which it has stirred us very deeply to learn of, but the ships and people of other neutral and friendly nations have been sunk and overwhelmed in the waters in the same way. There has been no discrimination. The challenge is to all mankind. Each nation must decide for itself how it will meet it. The choice we make for ourselves must be made with a moderation of counsel and a temperateness of judgment befitting our character and our motives as a nation. We must put excited feeling away. Our motive will not be revenge or the victorious assertion of the physical might of the nation, but only the vindication of right, of human right, of which we are only a single champion.

When I addressed the Congress on the twenty-sixth of February last I thought that it would suffice to assert our neutral rights with arms, our right to use the seas against unlawful interference, our right to keep our people safe against unlawful violence. But armed neutrality, it now appears, is impracticable. Because submarines are in effect outlaws when used as the German submarines have been used against merchant shipping, it is impossible to defend ships against their attacks as the law of nations has assumed that merchantmen would defend themselves against privateers or cruisers, visible craft giving chase upon the open sea. It is common prudence in such circumstances, grim necessity indeed, to endeavour to destroy them before they have shown their own intention. They must be dealt with upon sight, if dealt with at all. The German Government denies the right of neutrals to use arms at all within the areas of the sea which it has proscribed, even in the defense of rights which no modern publicist has ever before questioned their right to defend. The intimation is conveyed that the armed guards which we have placed on our merchant ships will be treated as beyond the pale of law and subject to be dealt with as pirates would be. Armed neutrality is ineffectual enough at best; in such circumstances and in the face of such pretensions it is worse than ineffectual: it is likely only to produce what it was meant to prevent; it is practically certain to draw us into the war without either the rights or the effectiveness of belligerents. There is one choice we cannot make, we are incapable of making: we will not choose the path of submission and suffer the most sacred rights of our nation and our people to be ignored or violated. The wrongs against which we now array ourselves are no common wrongs; they cut to the very roots of human life.

With a profound sense of the solemn and even tragical character of the step I am taking and of the grave responsibilities which it involves, but in unhesitating obedience to what I deem my constitutional duty, I advise that the Congress declare the recent course of the Imperial German Government to be in fact nothing less than war against the government and people of the United States; that it formally accept the status of belligerent which has thus been thrust upon it; and that it take immediate steps not only to put the country in a more thorough state of defense but also to exert all its power and employ all its resources to bring the Government of the German Empire to terms and end the war. What this will involve is clear. It will involve the utmost practicable cooperation in counsel and action with the governments now at war with Germany, and, as incident to that, the extension to those governments of the most liberal financial credits, in order that our resources may so far as possible be added to theirs. It will involve the organization and mobilization of all the material resources of the country to supply the materials of war and serve the incidental needs of the nation in the most abundant and yet the most economical and efficient way possible. It will involve the immediate full equipment of the navy in all respects but particularly in supplying it with the best means of dealing with the enemy's submarines. It will involve the immediate addition to the armed forces of the United States already provided for by law in case of war at least five hundred thousand men, who should, in my opinion, be chosen upon the principle of universal liability to service, and also the authorization of subsequent additional increments of equal force so soon as they may be needed and can be handled in training. It will involve also, of course, the granting of adequate credits to the Government, sustained, I hope, so far as they can equitably be sustained by the present generation, by well conceived taxation. . . .

I say sustained so far as may be equitable by taxation because it seems to me that it would be most unwise to base the credits which will now be necessary entirely on money borrowed. It is our duty, I most respectfully urge, to protect our people so far as we may against the very serious hardships and evils which would be likely to arise out of the inflation which would be produced by vast loans.

In carrying out the measures by which these things are to be accomplished we should keep constantly in mind the wisdom of interfering as little as possible in our own preparation and in the equipment of our own military forces with the duty,—for it will be a very practical duty, —of supplying the nations already at war with Germany with the materals which they can obtain only from us or by our assistance. They are in the field and we should help them in every way to be effective there.

I shall take the liberty of suggesting, through the several executive departments of the Government, for the consideration of your committees, measures for the accomplishment of the several objects I have mentioned. I hope that it will be your pleasure to deal with them as having been framed after very careful thought by the branch of the Government upon which the responsibility of conducting the war and safeguarding the nation will most directly fall.

While we do these things, these deeply momentous things, let us be very clear, and make very clear to all the world what our motives and our objects are. My own thought has not been driven from its habitual and normal course by the unhappy events of the last two months, and I do not believe that the thought of the nation has been altered or clouded by them. I have exactly the same things in mind now that I had in mind when I addressed the Senate on the twenty-second of January last; the same that I had in mind when I addressed the Congress on the third of February and on the twenty-sixth of February. Our object now, as then, is to vindicate the principles of peace and justice in the life of the world as against selfish and autocratic power and to set up amongst the really free and self-governed peoples of the world such a concert of purpose and of action as will henceforth ensure the observance of those principles. Neutrality is no longer feasible or desirable where the peace of the world is involved and the freedom of its peoples, and the menace to that peace and freedom lies in the existence of autocratic governments backed by organized force which is controlled wholly by their will, not by the will of their people. We have seen the last of neutrality in such circumstances. We are at the beginning of an age in which it will be insisted that the same standards of conduct and of responsibility for wrong done shall be observed among nations and their governments that are observed among the individual citizens of civilized states.

We have no quarrel with the German people. We have no feeling towards them but one of sympathy and friendship. It was not upon their impulse that their government acted in entering this war. It was not with their previous knowledge or approval. It was a war determined upon as wars used to be determined upon in the old, unhappy days when peoples were nowhere consulted by their rulers and wars were provoked and waged in the interest of dynasties or of little groups of ambitious men who were accustomed to use their fellow men as pawns and tools. Self-governed nations do not fill their neighbour states with spies or set the course of intrigue to bring about some critical posture of affairs which will give them an opportunity to strike and make conquest. Such designs can be successfully worked out only under cover and where no one has the right to ask questions. Cunningly contrived plans of deception or aggression, carried, it may be, from generation to generation, can be worked out and kept from the light only within the privacy of courts or behind the carefully guarded confidences of a narrow and privileged class. They are happily impossible where public opinion commands and insists upon full information concerning all the nation's affairs.

A steadfast concert for peace can never be maintained except by a partnership of democratic nations. No autocratic government could be trusted to keep faith within it or observe its covenants. It must be a league of honour, a partnership of opinion. Intrigue would eat its vitals away; the plotting of inner circles who could plan what they would and render account to no one would be a corruption seated at its very heart. Only free peoples can hold their purpose and their honour steady to a common end and prefer the interests of mankind to any narrow interest of their own.

Does not every American feel that assurance has been added to our hope for the future peace of the world by the wonderful and heartening things that have been happening within the last few weeks in Russia? Russia was known by those who knew it best to have been always in fact democratic at heart, in all the vital habits of her thought, in all the intimate relationships of her people that spoke their natural instinct, their habitual attitude towards life. The autocracy that crowned the summit of her political structure, long as it had stood and terrible as was the reality of its power, was not in fact Russian in origin, character, or purpose; and now it has been shaken off and the great, generous Russian people have been added in all their naive majesty and might to the forces that are fighting for freedom in the world, for justice, and for peace. Here is a fit partner for a League of Honour.

One of the things that has served to convince us that the Prussian autocracy was not and could never be our friend is that from the very outset of the present war it has filled our unsuspecting communities and even our offices of government with spies and set criminal intrigues everywhere afoot against our national unity of counsel, our peace within and without, our industries and our commerce. Indeed it is now evident that its spies were here even before the war began; and it is unhappily not a matter of conjecture but a fact proved in our courts of justice that the intrigues which have more than once come perilously near to disturbing the peace and dislocating the industries of the country have been carried on at the instigation, with the support, and even under the personal direction of official agents of the Imperial Government accredited to the Government of the United States. Even in checking these things and trying to extirpate them we have sought to put the most generous interpretation possible upon them because we knew that their source lay, not in any hostile feeling or purpose of the German people towards us (who were, no doubt as ignorant of them as we ourselves were), but only in the selfish designs of a Government that did what it pleased and told its people nothing. But they have played their part in serving to convince us at last that that Government entertains no real friendship for us and means to act against our peace and security at its convenience. That it means to stir up enemies against us at our very doors the intercepted note to the German Minister at Mexico City is eloquent evidence.

We are accepting this challenge of hostile purpose because we know that in such a government, following such methods, we can never have a friend; and that in the presence of its organized power, always lying in wait to accomplish we know not what purpose, there can be no assured security for the democratic governments of the world. We are now about to accept gauge of battle with this natural foe to liberty and shall, if necessary, spend the whole force of the nation to check and nullify its pretensions and its power. We are glad, now that we see the facts with no veil of false pretence about them, to fight thus for the ultimate peace of the world and for the liberation of its peoples, the German peoples included: for the rights of nations great and small and the privilege of men everywhere to choose their way of life and of obedience. The world must be made safe for democracy. Its peace must be planted upon the tested foundations of political liberty. We have no selfish ends to serve. We desire no conquest, no dominion. We seek no indemnities for ourselves, no material compensation for the sacrifices we shall freely make. We are but one of the champions of the rights of mankind. We shall be satisfied when those rights have been made as secure as the faith and the freedom of nations can make them.

Just because we fight without rancour and without selfish object, seeking nothing for ourselves but what we shall wish to share with all free peoples, we shall, I feel confident, conduct our operations as belligerents without passion and ourselves observe with proud punctilio the principles of right and of fair play we profess to be fighting for.

I have said nothing of the governments allied with the Imperial Government of Germany because they have not made war upon us or challenged us to defend our right and our honour. The Austro-Hungarian Government has, indeed, avowed its unqualified endorsement and acceptance of the reckless and lawless submarine warfare adopted now without disguise by the Imperial German Government, and it has therefore not been possible for this Government to receive Count Tarnowski, the Ambassador recently accredited to this Government by the Imperial and Royal Government of Austria-Hungary; but that Government has not actually engaged in warfare against citizens of the United States on the seas, and I take the liberty, for the present at least, of postponing a discussion of our relations with the authorities at Vienna. We enter this war only where we are clearly forced into it because there are no other means of defending our rights.

It will be all the easier for us to conduct ourselves as belligerents in a high spirit of right and fairness because we act without animus, not in enmity towards a people or with the desire to bring any injury or disadvantage upon them, but only in armed opposition to an irresponsible government which has thrown aside all considerations of humanity and of right and is running amuck. We are, let me say again, the sincere friends of the German people, and shall desire nothing so much as the early re-establishment of intimate relations of mutual advantage between us,—however hard it may be for them, for the time being, to believe that this is spoken from our hearts. We have borne with their present government through all these bitter months because of that friendship,—exercising a patience and forbearance which would otherwise have been impossible. We shall, happily, still have an opportunity to prove that friendship in our daily attitude and actions towards the millions of men and women of German birth and native sympathy who live amongst us and share our life, and we shall be proud to prove it towards all who are in fact loyal to their neighbours and to the Government in the hour of test. They are, most of them, as true and loyal Americans as if they had never known any other fealty or allegiance. They will be prompt to stand with us in rebuking and restraining the few who may be of a different mind and purpose. If there should be disloyalty, it will be dealt with with a firm hand of stern repression; but, if it lifts its head at all, it will lift it only here and there and without countenance except from a lawless and malignant few.

It is a distressing and oppressive duty, Gentlemen of the Congress, which I have performed in thus addressing you. There are, it may be, many months of fiery trial and sacrifice ahead of us. It is a fearful thing to lead this great peaceful people into war, into the most terrible and disastrous of all wars, civilization itself seeming to be in the balance. But the right is more precious than peace, and we shall fight for the things which we have always carried nearest our hearts—for democracy, for the right of those who submit to authority to have a voice in their own governments, for the rights and liberties of small nations, for a universal dominion of right by such a concert of free peoples as shall bring peace and safety to all nations and make the world itself at last free. To such a task we can dedicate our lives and our fortunes, everything that we are and everything that we have, with the pride of those who know that

the day has come when America is privileged to spend her blood and her might
for the principles that gave her birth and

happiness and the peace which she has
treasured. God helping her, she can do no
other.

COMMENT

We are now dealing with madmen, whose sole purpose is to kill, by all foul as well
as fair means. . . . We will war as civilized men should, but we will not quit
until the very last fang has been pulled from the bloody frothing jaws of the
world's mad-dog.

> Editorial in the Natchez (Miss.) *Democrat* April 10, 1917.

If it is wrong for a king to plunge his subjects into the vortex of war without
their consent, it can not be less reprehensible for the President of the United
States and the Congress to involve their constituents in a war without their consent.

> James K. Vardaman, Democrat of Mississippi, speaking in the Senate, April 4, 1917.
> *Congressional Record,* 65th Cong., 1st Sess., 1916–1917, LV, pt. 1, 209.

In my judgement, we could keep out of the war with Germany as we kept out
of war with Great Britain, by keeping our ships and our citizens out of the war
zone of Germany as we did out of the war zone of Great Britain, and we would
sacrifice no more honor, surrender no more rights in the one case than in the
other.

> Claude Kitchin, Democrat of North Carolina, speaking in the U.S. House of Repre-
> sentatives, April 5, 1917. *Congressional Record,* 65th Cong., 1st Sess., 1917, CV, pt. 1,
> 332.

---

48. *APRIL 4, 1917*

Senator George Norris Opposes War

*After President Wilson asked Congress
for a formal declaration of war, there was
a popular demand for immediate action.
Nevertheless, there were a few stubborn
opponents of war. Most of them were Progressives from the Middle and Far West
who feared that war would destroy their
domestic reform program. They flatly
denied that America's national interests
were threatened. Rather, they argued that
the real forces making for war were the*

Congressional Record, 65th Cong., 1st Sess.,
1917, LV, pt. 1, 213–14.

*munitions makers and bankers who had
invested the savings of the American people in an Allied victory which they now
expected the government to protect. Below is the speech which Senator George
Norris, Republican from Nebraska, made
in opposition to the resolution for war.
    There is no evidence, however, that
the munitions makers and bankers influenced the decision for war. In the final
analysis, it was Woodrow Wilson who
made the decision, and his thinking was
determined almost exclusively by the*

submarine issue. In spite of the staunch opposition to war by such congressional leaders as Norris, Bob LaFollette, Claude Kitchin, and Jeannette Rankin, the House and Senate quickly approved Wilson's request for war, thus beginning a new epoch in American history.

. . . We have loaned many hundreds of millions of dollars to the allies in this controversy. While such action was legal and countenanced by international law, there is no doubt in my mind but the enormous amount of money loaned to the allies in this country has been instrumental in bringing about a public sentiment in favor of our country taking a course that would make every bond worth a hundred cents on the dollar and making the payment of every debt certain and sure. Through this instrumentality and also through the instrumentality of others who have not only made millions out of the war in the manufacture of munitions, etc., and who would expect to make millions more if our country can be drawn into the catastrophe, a large number of the great newspapers and news agencies of the country have been controlled and enlisted in the greatest propaganda that the world has ever known, to manufacture sentiment in favor of war. It is now demanded that the American citizens shall be used as insurance policies to guarantee the safe delivery of munitions of war to belligerent nations. The enormous profits of munition manufacturers, stockbrokers, and bond dealers must be still further increased by our entrance into the war. This has brought us to the present moment, when Congress, urged by the President and backed by the artificial sentiment, is about to declare war and engulf our country in the greatest holocaust that the world has ever known.

. . . . .

To whom does war bring prosperity? Not to the soldier who for the munificent compensation of $16 per month shoulders his musket and goes into the trench, there to shed his blood and to die if necessary; not to the broken-hearted widow who waits for the return of the mangled body of her husband; not to the mother who weeps at the death of her brave boy; not to the little children who shiver with cold; not to the babe who suffers from hunger; nor to the millions of mothers and daughters who carry broken hearts to their graves. War brings no prosperity to the great mass of common and patriotic citizens. It increases the cost of living of those who toil and those who already must strain every effort to keep soul and body together. War brings prosperity to the stock gambler on Wall Street—to those who are already in possession of more wealth than can be realized or enjoyed. Again this writer says that if we can not get war, "it is nevertheless good opinion that the preparedness program will compensate in good measure for the loss of the stimulus of actual war." That is, if we can not get war, let us go as far in that direction as possible. If we can not get war, let us cry for additional ships, additional guns, additional munitions, and everything else that will have a tendency to bring us as near as possible to the verge of war. And if war comes do such men as these shoulder the musket and go into the trenches?

Their object in having war and in preparing for war is to make money. Human suffering and the sacrifice of human life are necessary, but Wall Street considers only the dollars and the cents. The men who do the fighting, the people who make the sacrifices, are the ones who will not be counted in the measure of this great prosperity that he depicts. The stock brokers would not, of course, go to war, because the very object they have in bringing on the war is profit, and therefore they must remain in their Wall Street offices in order to share in that great prosperity which they say war will bring. The volunteer officer, even the drafting officer, will not find them. They will be concealed in their palatial offices on Wall Street, sitting behind mahogany desks, covered up with clipped coupons—coupons soiled with the sweat of honest toil, coupons stained with mothers' tears, coupons dyed in the lifeblood of their fellow men.

We are taking a step to-day that is fraught with untold danger. We are going into war upon the command of gold. We are going to run the risk of sacrificing millions of our countrymen's lives in order that other countrymen may coin their lifeblood into money. And even if we do not cross the Atlantic and go into the trenches, we are going to pile up a debt that the toiling masses that shall come many generations after us will have

to pay. Unborn millions will bend their backs in toil in order to pay for the terrible step we are now about to take. We are about to do the bidding of wealth's terrible mandate. By our act we will make millions of our countrymen suffer, and the consequences of it may well be that millions of our brethren must shed their lifeblood, millions of broken-hearted women must weep, millions of children must suffer with cold, and millions of babes must die from hunger, and all because we want to preserve the commercial right of American citizens to deliver munitions of war to belligerent nations.

. . . . .

COMMENT

The American people did not and do not want this war. They have not been consulted about the war and have had no part in declaring war. They have been plunged into this war by the trickery and treachery of the ruling class of the country through its representatives in the national administration and National Congress, its demagogic agitators, its subsidized press ,and other servile instruments of public expression.

Excerpt from the resolutions on war adopted by Socialist party leaders on April 7, 1917. Quoted from H. C. Peterson and Gilbert C. Fite, *Opponents of War, 1917–1918* (Madison: University of Wisconsin Press, 1957), p. 9.

The Senator from Nebraska, I fear, is so obsessed with a fear of "money" and of "profits" and of "fortunes" that all that it is necessary to suggest is that some wealthy concern may have an interest, remote, contingent, or direct, in the subject matter under consideration in order to confuse his mental vision. . . . Sir, this was is not being waged over dollars. It is not being waged over commerce. It is not being waged over profits and losses. It is a war for the maintenance of the sovereign rights of the American Republic and for the preservation of American dignity in the councils of the nations of the earth.

James Reed, Democrat from Missouri, speaking in the U.S. Senate, April 4, 1917. *Congressional Record*, 65th Cong., Spec. Sess., 1917, LV, 215–18.

Once lead this people into war and they'll forget there ever was such a thing as tolerance. To fight you must be brutal and ruthless and the spirit of ruthless brutality will enter into the very fibre of our national life, infecting Congress, the courts, the policeman on the beat, the man in the street.

Statement by President Wilson to journalist Frank I. Cobb on April 2, 1917. John L. Heaton, *Cobb of "The World"* (New York: E. P. Dutton & Co., Inc., 1924), p. 270.

49. *JANUARY 8, 1918*

Woodrow Wilson's Fourteen Points

Throughout 1917, in both Europe and America, there was a growing demand for a statement of war aims. President Wilson responded with his campaign for a liberal and just peace settlement. Addressing Congress on January 8, 1918, Wilson put forth fourteen points as the only program for peace from the viewpoint of the United States. In a number of other addresses, Wilson commented further on the Fourteen Points, thus becoming a self-appointed spokesman for the Allied cause. Though the governments of the other Allied powers paid lip service to the Fourteen Points, the secret treaties that several of them had entered into made it unlikely that they would acccept the Wilsonian program.

The Fourteen Points made a powerful impact on the liberal groups in the various Allied nations, as well as in Germany. Though Wilson's program provided an excellent platform on which to wage a war, the Fourteen Points were too illusory and contradictory to provide a basis for a lasting peace. Had the people of the world understood that the Fourteen Points should not be taken literally, perhaps there would not have been so much disillusionment over the peace settlement which finally emerged. The remarkable thing about the treaties of 1919 is not that they departed so much from the Fourteen Points, but that out of the European chaos of 1918, as much of Wilson's program emerged as it did.

Gentlemen of the Congress, once more, as repeatedly before, the spokes-

Congressional Record, 65th Cong., 2d Sess., 1918, CVI, pt. 1, 680–81.

men of the Central Empires have indicated their desire to discuss the objects of the war and the possible bases of a general peace. Parleys have been in progress at Brest-Litovsk between Russian representatives and representatives of the Central Powers, to which the attention of all the belligerents has been invited for the purpose of ascertaining whether it may be possible to extend these parleys into a general conference with regard to terms of peace and settlement. The Russian representatives presented not only a perfectly definite statement of the principles upon which they would be willing to conclude peace, but also an equally definite programme of the concrete application of those principles. The representatives of the Central Powers, on their part, presented an outline of settlement which, if much less definite, seemed susceptible of liberal interpretation until their specific programme of practical terms was added. That programme proposed no concessions at all either to the sovereignty of Russia or to the preferences of the populations with whose fortunes it dealt, but meant, in a word, that the Central Empires were to keep every foot of territory their armed forces had occupied—every province, every city, every point of vantage—as a permanent addition to their territories and their power. It is a reasonable conjecture that the general principles of settlement which they at first suggested originated with the more liberal statesmen of Germany and Austria, the men who have begun to feel the force of their own peoples' thought and purpose, while the concrete terms of actual settlement came from the military leaders who have no thought but to keep what they have got. The negotiations have been broken off. The Russian representatives were sincere and in earnest. They cannot entertain such proposals of conquest and domination.

The whole incident is full of significance. It is also full of perplexity. With whom are the Russian representatives dealing? For whom are the representatives of the Central Empires speaking? Are they speaking for the majorities of their respective parliaments or for the minority parties, that military and imperialistic minority which has so far dominated their whole policy and controlled the affairs of Turkey and of the Balkan states which have felt obliged to become their associates in the war? The Russian representatives have insisted, very justly, very wisely, and in the true spirit of modern democracy, that the conferences they have been holding with the Teutonic and Turkish statesmen should be held within open, not closed, doors, and all the world has been audience, as was desired. To whom have we been listening, then? To those who speak the spirit and intention of the Resolutions of the German Reichstag of the ninth of July last, the spirit and intention of the liberal leaders and parties of Germany, or to those who resist and defy that spirit and intention and insist upon conquest and subjugation? Or are we listening, in fact, to both, unreconciled and in open and hopeless contradiction? These are very serious and pregnant questions. Upon the answer to them depends the peace of the world.

.   .   .   .   .

We entered this war because violations of right had occurred which touched us to the quick and made the life of our own people impossible unless they were corrected and the world secured once for all against their recurrence. What we demand in this war, therefore, is nothing peculiar to ourselves. It is that the world be made fit and safe to live in; and particularly that it be made safe for every peace-loving nation which, like our own, wishes to live its own life, determine its own institutions, be assured of justice and fair dealing by the other peoples of the world as against force and selfish aggression. All the peoples of the world are in effect partners in this interest, and for our own part we see very clearly that unless justice be done to others it will not be done to us. The programme of the world's peace, therefore, is our programme; and that programme, the only possible programme, as we see it, is this:

I. Open covenants of peace, openly arrived at, after which there shall be no private international understandings of any kind but diplomacy shall proceed always frankly and in the public view.

II. Absolute freedom of navigation upon the seas, outside territorial waters, alike in peace and in war, except as the seas may be closed in whole or in part by international action for the enforcement of international covenants.

III. The removal, so far as possible, of all economic barriers and the establishment of an equality of trade conditions among all the nations consenting to the peace and associating themselves for its maintenance.

IV. Adequate guarantees given and taken that national armaments will be reduced to the lowest point consistent with domestic safety.

V. A free, open-minded, and absolutely impartial adjustment of all colonial claims, based upon a strict observance of the principle that in determining all such questions of sovereignty the interests of the populations concerned must have equal weight with the equitable claims of the government whose title is to be determined.

VI. The evacuation of all Russian territory and such a settlement of all questions affecting Russia as will secure the best and freest cooperation of the other nations of the world in obtaining for her an unhampered and unembarrassed opportunity for the independent determination of her own political development and national policy and assure her of a sincere welcome into the society of free nations under institutions of her own choosing; and, more than a welcome, assistance also of every kind that she may need and may herself desire. The treatment accorded Russia by her sister nations in the months to come will be the acid test of their good will, of their comprehension of her needs as distinguished from their own interests, and of their intelligent and unselfish sympathy.

VII. Belgium, the whole world will agree, must be evacuated and restored, without any attempt to limit the sovereignty which she enjoys in common with all other free nations. No other single act will serve as this will serve to restore confidence among the nations in the laws which they have themselves set and determined for the government of their relations with one another. Without this healing act the whole structure and validity of international law is forever impaired.

VIII. All French territory should be freed and the invaded portions restored, and the wrong done to France by Prussia in 1871 in the matter of Alsace-Lorraine, which has unsettled the peace of the world for nearly fifty years, should be righted, in order that peace may once more be made secure in the interest of all.

IX. A readjustment of the frontiers of Italy should be effected along clearly recognizable lines of nationality.

X. The peoples of Austria-Hungary, whose place among the nations we wish to see safeguarded and assured, should be accorded the freest opportunity of autonomous development.

XI. Rumania, Serbia, and Montenegro should be evacuated; occupied territories restored; Serbia accorded free and secure access to the sea; and the relations of the several Balkan states to one another determined by friendly counsel along historically established lines of allegiance and nationality; and international guarantees of the political and economic independence and territorial integrity of the several Balkan states should be entered into.

XII. The Turkish portions of the present Ottoman Empire should be assured a secure sovereignty, but the other nationalities which are now under Turkish rule should be assured an undoubted security of life and an absolutely unmolested opportunity of autonomous development, and the Dardanelles should be permanently opened as a free passage to the ships and commerce of all nations under international guarantees.

XIII. An independent Polish state should be erected which should include the territories inhabited by indisputably Polish populations, which should be assured a free and secure access to the sea, and whose political and economic independence and territorial integrity should be guaranteed by international covenant.

XIV. A general association of nations must be formed under specific covenants for the purpose of affording mutual guarantees of political independence and territorial integrity to great and small states alike.

In regard to these essential rectifications of wrong and assertions of right we feel ourselves to be intimate partners of all the governments and peoples associated together against the Imperialists. We cannot be separate in interest or divided in purpose. We stand together until the end.

For such arrangements and covenants we are willing to fight and to continue to fight until they are achieved; but only because we wish the right to prevail and desire a just and stable peace such as can be secured only by removing the chief provocations to war, which this programme does remove. We have no jealousy of German greatness, and there is nothing in this programme that impairs it. We grudge her no achievement or distinction of learning or of pacific enter-prise such as have made her record very bright and very enviable. We do not wish to injure her or to block in any way her legitimate influence or power. We do not wish to fight her either with arms or with hostile arrangements of trade if she is willing to associate herself with us and the other peace-loving nations of the world in covenants of justice and law and fair dealing. We wish her only to accept a place of equality among the peoples of the world—the new world in which we now live—instead of a place of mastery.

Neither do we presume to suggest to her any alteration or modification of her institutions. But it is necessary, we must frankly say, and necessary as a preliminary to any intelligent dealings with her on our part, that we should know whom her spokesmen speak for when they speak to us, whether for the Reichstag majority or for the military party and the men whose creed is imperial domination.

We have spoken now, surely, in terms too concrete to admit of any further doubt or question. An evident principle runs through the whole programme I have outlined. It is the principle of justice to all peoples and nationalities, and their right to live on equal terms of liberty and safety with one another, whether they be strong or weak. Unless this principle be made its foundation no part of the structure of international justice can stand. The people of the United States could act upon no other principle; and to the vindication of this principle they are ready to devote their lives, their honor, and everything that they possess. The moral climax of this the culminating and final war for human liberty has come, and they are ready to put their own strength, their own highest purpose, their own integrity and devotion to the test.

COMMENT

The phrase [self-determination] is simply loaded with dynamite. It will raise hopes which can never be realized. . . . What a calamity that the phrase was ever uttered! What misery it will cause!

> Secretary of State Robert Lansing, December 30, 1918. Quoted in Thomas A. Bailey. *Woodrow Wilson and the Lost Peace* (New York: The Macmillan Company, 1944), p. 18.

Conspicuously absent from the Fourteen Points was any meaningful demand for a substantial change in international economic relations. . . . the treaty and the League Covenant were an attempt, in the language of democracy, peace, and self-determination, to retain the competitive national state system of the nineteenth century without removing the admitted [economic] source of its rivalries and animosities.

> Richard Hofstadter, historian, in *The American Political Tradition and the Men Who Made It* (New York: Alfred A. Knopf, 1948), pp. 269–70, 272.

50.   SEPTEMBER 25, 1919

President Wilson's Speech at Pueblo, Colorado

When President Wilson sent the Treaty of Versailles to the Senate for ratification in July, 1919, a majority of the American people apparently favored it. A poll of newspaper editors demonstrated that most of them supported the treaty. Thirty-two state legislatures passed resolutions endorsing it, while a majority of state governors spoke out in support of the League of Nations. The opposition to the treaty, led by Senator Henry Cabot Lodge of Massachusetts, decided to delay the Senate vote on ratification by prolonged committee hearings in order to provide time for the pro-League sentiment to cool. The opponents also hoped to add so many reservations to the treaty that even Wilson and the Democrats would reject it. To counter such tactics, Wilson took the issue to the people, traveling over 8,000 miles and delivering thirty-seven speeches. He stumped the sections that furnished the most opposition to the treaty, the Old Northwest, the Upper Mississippi Valley, and the Far West. Despite the academic quality of his speeches, Wilson appeared to be making headway. But shortly after his Pueblo speech, one of the longest and most important, he broke down and was rushed to Washington, where he suffered a stroke. Secluded from friends and advisers, Wilson was unable to provide the necessary leadership to guide the treaty through the Senate. As subsequent events demonstrated, Wilson would have been advised not to have undertaken his trip to the west.

Congressional Record, 66th Cong., 1st Sess., 1919, LVIII, pt. 7, 6424–27.

Rather, he should have remained in the White House, conserved his strength, and attempted by compromise to have the Senate ratify the treaty.

. . . . .

The chief pleasure of my trip has been that it has nothing to do with my personal fortunes, that it has nothing to do with my personal reputation, that it has nothing to do with anything except great principles uttered by Americans of all sorts and of all parties which we are now trying to realize at this crisis of the affairs of the world. But there have been unpleasant impressions as well as pleasant impressions, my fellow citizens, as I have crossed the continent. I have perceived more and more that men have been busy creating an absolutely false impression of what the treaty of peace and the covenant of the league of nations contain and mean. I find, moreover, that there is an organized propaganda against the league of nations and against the treaty proceeding from exactly the same sources that the organized propaganda proceeded from which threatened this country here and there with disloyalty, and I want to say—I can not say too often—any man who carries a hyphen about with him carries a dagger that he is ready to plunge into the vitals of this Republic whenever he gets ready. If I can catch any man with a hyphen in this great contest I will know that I have got an enemy of the Republic. My fellow citizens, it is only certain bodies of foreign sympathies, certain bodies of sympathy with foreign nations that are organized against this great document which the American representatives have brought back from Paris. Therefore, in order to clear away the mists, in order to remove the impressions, in order to check the falsehoods that have clustered around this great subject, I want to tell you a few very simple things about the treaty and the covenant.

Do not think of this treaty of peace as merely a settlement with Germany. It is that. It is a very severe settlement with Germany, but there is not anything in it that she did not earn. Indeed, she earned more than she can ever be able to pay for, and the punishment exacted of her is not a punishment greater than she can bear, and it is absolutely necessary in order that no other nation may ever plot such a thing against humanity and civilization. But the treaty is so much more than that. It is not merely a settlement with Germany; it is a readjustment of those great injustices which underlie the whole structure of European and Asiatic society. This is only the first of several treaties. They are all constructed upon the same plan. The Austrian treaty follows the same lines. The treaty with Hungary follows the same lines. The treaty with Bulgaria follows the same lines. The treaty with Turkey, when it is formulated, will follow the same lines. What are those lines? They are based upon the purpose to see that every government dealt with in this great settlement is put in the hands of the people and taken out of the hands of coteries and of sovereigns who had no right to rule over the people. It is a people's treaty, that accomplishes by a great sweep of practical justice the liberation of men who never could have liberated themselves, and the power of the most powerful nations has been devoted not to their aggrandizement but to the liberation of people whom they could have put under their control if they had chosen to do so. Not one foot of territory is demanded by the conquerors, not one single item of submission to their authority is demanded by them. The men who sat around that table in Paris knew that the time had come when the people were no longer going to consent to live under masters, but were going to live the lives that they chose themselves, to live under such governments as they chose themselves to erect. That is the fundamental principle of this great settlement.

And we did not stop with that. We added a great international charter for the rights of labor. Reject this treaty, impair it, and this is the consequence to the laboring men of the world, that there is no international tribunal which can bring the moral judgments of the world to bear upon the great labor questions of the day. What we need to do with regard to the labor questions of the day, my fellow countrymen, is to lift them into the light, is to lift them out of the haze and distraction of passion, of hostility, out into the calm spaces where men look at things without passion. The more men you get into a great discussion the more you exclude passion. Just so soon as the calm judgment of the world is directed upon the question of justice to labor, labor is going to have a forum such as it never was supplied with before, and men everywhere are going to see that the problem of labor is nothing more nor less than the problem of the elevation of humanity. We must see that all the questions which have disturbed the world, all the questions which have eaten into the confidence of men toward their governments, all the questions which have disturbed the processes of industry, shall be brought out where men of all points of view, men of all attitudes of mind, men of all kinds of experience, may contribute their part to the settlement of the great questions which we must settle and can not ignore.

At the front of this great treaty is put the covenant of the league of nations. It will also be at the front of the Austrian treaty and the Hungarian treaty and the Bulgarian treaty and the treaty with

Turkey. Every one of them will contain the covenant of the league of nations, because you can not work any of them without the covenant of the league of nations. Unless you get the united, concerted purpose and power of the great Governments of the world behind this settlement, it will fall down like a house of cards. There is only one power to put behind the liberation of mankind, and that is the power of mankind. It is the power of the united moral forces of the world, and in the covenant of the league of nations the moral forces of the world are mobilized. For what purpose? Reflect, my fellow citizens, that the membership of this great league is going to include all the great fighting nations of the world, as well as the weak ones. It is not for the present going to include Germany, but for the time being Germany is not a great fighting country. All the nations that have power that can be mobilized are going to be members of this league, including the United States. And what do they unite for? They enter into a solemn promise to one another that they will never use their power against one another for aggression; that they never will impair the territorial integrity of a neighbor; that they never will interfere with the political independence of a neighbor; that they will abide by the principle that great populations are entitled to determine their own destiny and that they will not interfere with that destiny; and that no matter what differences arise amongst them they will never resort to war without first having done one or the other of two things—either submitted the matter of controversy to arbitration, in which case they agree to abide by the result without question, or submitted it to the consideration of the council of the league of nations, laying before that council all the documents, all the facts, agreeing that the council can publish the documents and the facts to the whole world, agreeing that there shall be six months allowed for the mature consideration of those facts by the council, and agreeing that at the expiration of the six months, even if they are not then ready to accept the advice of the council with regard to the settlement of the dispute, they will still not go to war for another three months. In other words, they consent, no matter what happens, to submit every matter of difference between them to the judgment of mankind, and just so certainly as they do that, my fellow citizens, war will be in the far background, war will be pushed out of that foreground of terror in which it has kept the world for generation after generation, and men will know that there will be a calm time of deliberate counsel. The most dangerous thing for a bad cause is to expose it to the opinion of the world. The most certain way that you can prove that a man is mistaken is by letting all his neighbors know what he thinks, by letting all his neighbors discuss what he thinks, and if he is in the wrong you will notice that he will stay at home, he will not walk on the street. He will be afraid of the eyes of his neighbors. He will be afraid of their judgment of his character. He will know that his cause is lost unless he can sustain it by the arguments of right and of justice. The same law that applies to individuals applies to nations.

But, you say, "we have heard that we might be at a disadvantage in the league of nations." Well, whoever told you that either was deliberately falsifying or he had not read the covenant of the league of nations. I leave him the choice. I want to give you a very simple account of the organization of the league of nations and let you judge for yourselves. It is a very simple organization. The power of the league, or rather the activities of the league, lie in two bodies. There is the council, which consists of one representative from each of the principal allied and associated powers—that is to say, the United States, Great Britain, France, Italy, and Japan—along with four other representatives of smaller powers chosen out of the general body of the membership of the league. The council is the source of every active policy of the league, and no active policy of the league can be adopted without a unanimous vote of the council. That is explicitly stated in the covenant itself. Does it not evidently follow that the league of nations can adopt no policy whatever without the consent of the United States? The affirmative vote of the representative of the United States is necessary in every case. Now you have heard of six votes belonging to the British Empire. Those six votes are not in the council. They are in the assembly, and the interesting thing is that the assembly does not vote. I must qualify that statement a little, but essentially it is absolutely true. In every matter in which the assembly is given a voice, and there are only four or five, its vote does not count unless concurred in by the representatives of all the nations represented on the council, so that there is no validity to any vote of the assembly unless in that vote also the representative of the United States concurs. That one vote of the United States is as big as the six votes of the British Empire. I am not jealous for advantage, my fellow citizens, but I think that is a perfectly safe situation. There is no validity in a vote, either by the council or the assembly, in which we do not concur. So much for the statements about the six votes of the British Empire.

Look at it in another aspect. The assembly is the talking body. The assembly was created in order that anybody that purposed anything wrong should be subjected to the awkward circumstance that everybody could talk about it. This is the great assembly in which all the things that are likely to disturb the peace of the world or the good understanding between nations are to be exposed to the general view, and I want to ask you if you think it was unjust, unjust to the United States, that speaking parts should be assigned to the several portions of the British Empire? Do you think it unjust that there

should be some spokesman in debate for that fine little stout Republic down in the Pacific, New Zealand? Do you think it was unjust that Australia should be allowed to stand up and take part in the debate—Australia, from which we have learned some of the most useful progressive policies of modern time, a little nation only five million in a great continent, but counting for several times five in its activities and in its interest in liberal reform? Do you think it unjust that that little Republic down in South Africa, whose gallant resistance to being subjected to any outside authority at all we admired for so many months and whose fortunes we followed with such interest, should have a speaking part? Great Britain obliged South Africa to submit to her sovereignty, but she immediately after that felt that it was convenient and right to hand the whole self-government of that colony over to the very men whom she had beaten. The representatives of South Africa in Paris were two of the most distinguished generals of the Boer Army, two of the realest men I ever met, two that could talk sober counsel and wise advice, along with the best statesmen in Europe. To exclude Gen. Botha and Gen. Smuts from the right to stand up in the parliament of the world and say something concerning the affairs of mankind would be absurd. And what about Canada? Is not Canada a good neighbor? Is not Canada more likely to agree with the United States than with Great Britain? Canada has a speaking part. And then, for the first time in the history of the world, that great voiceless multitude, that throng hundreds of millions strong in India, has a voice, and I want to testify that some of the wisest and most dignified figures in the peace conference at Paris came from India, men who seemed to carry in their minds an older wisdom than the rest of us had, whose traditions ran back into so many of the unhappy fortunes of mankind that they seemed very useful counselors as to how some ray of hope and some prospect of happiness could be opened to its people. I for my part have no jealousy whatever of those five speaking parts in the assembly. Those speaking parts can not translate themselves into five votes that can in any matter override the voice and purpose of the United States.

Let us sweep aside all this language of jealousy. Let us be big enough to know the facts and to welcome the facts, because the facts are based upon the principles that America has always fought for, namely, the equality of self-governing peoples, whether they were big or little—not counting men, but counting rights, not counting representation, but counting the purpose of that representation. When you hear an opinion quoted, you do not count the number of persons who hold it; you ask, "Who said that?" You weigh opinions, you do not count them, and the beauty of all democracies is that every voice can be heard, every voice can have its effect, every voice can contribute to the general judgment that is finally arrived at. That is the object of democracy. Let us accept what America has always fought for, and accept it with pride that America showed the way and made the proposal. I do not mean that America made the proposal in this particular instance; I mean that the principle was an American principle, proposed by America.

When you come to the heart of the covenant, my fellow citizens, you will find it in article 10, and I am very much interested to know that the other things have been blown away like bubbles. There is nothing in the other contentions with regard to the league of nations, but there is something in article 10 that you ought to realize and ought to accept or reject. Article 10 is the heart of the whole matter. What is article 10? I never am certain that I can from memory give a literal repetition of its language, but I am sure that I can give an exact interpretation of its meaning. Article 10 provides that

every member of the league covenants to respect and preserve the territorial integrity and existing political independence of every other member of the league as against external aggression. Not against internal disturbance. There was not a man at that table who did not admit the sacredness of the right of self-determination, the sacredness of the right of any body of people to say that they would not continue to live under the Government they were then living under, and under article 11 of the covenant they are given a place to say whether they will live under it or not. For following article 10 is article 11, which makes it the right of any member of the league at any time to call attention to anything, anywhere, that is likely to disturb the peace of the world or the good understanding between nations upon which the peace of the world depends. I want to give you an illustration of what that would mean.

You have heard a great deal—something that was true and a great deal that was false—about that provision of the treaty which hands over to Japan the rights which Germany enjoyed in the Province of Shantung in China. In the first place, Germany did not enjoy any rights there that other nations had not already claimed. For my part, my judgment, my moral judgment, is against the whole set of concessions. They were all of them unjust to China, they ought never to have been exacted, they were all exacted by duress from a great body of thoughtful and ancient and helpless people. There never was any right in any of them. Thank God, America never asked for any, never dreamed of asking for any. But when Germany got this concession in 1898, the Government of the United States made no protest whatever. That was not because the Government of the United States was not in the hands of high-minded and conscientious men. It was. William McKinley was President and John Hay was Secretary of State —as safe hands to leave the honor of the

United States in as any that you can cite. They made no protest because the state of international law at that time was that it was none of their business unless they could show that the interests of the United States were affected, and the only thing that they could show with regard to the interests of the United States was that Germany might close the doors of Shantung Province against the trade of the United States. They, therefore, demanded and obtained promises that we could continue to sell merchandise in Shantung. Immediately following that concession to Germany there was a concession to Russia of the same sort, of Port Arthur, and Port Arthur was handed over subsequently to Japan on the very territory of the United States. Don't you remember that when Russia and Japan got into war with one another the war was brought to a conclusion by a treaty written at Portsmouth, N.H., and in that treaty, without the slightest intimation from any authoritative sources in America that the Government of the United States had any objection, Port Arthur, Chinese territory, was turned over to Japan? I want you distinctly to understand that there is no thought of criticism in my mind. I am expounding to you a state of international law. Now, read articles 10 and 11. You will see that international law is revolutionized by putting morals into it. Article 10 says that no member of the league, and that includes all these nations that have demanded these things unjustly of China, shall impair the territorial integrity or the political independence of any other member of the league. China is going to be a member of the league. Article 11 says that any member of the league can call attention to anything that is likely to disturb the peace of the world or the good understanding between nations, and China is for the first time in the history of mankind afforded a standing before the jury of the world. I, for my part, have a profound sympathy for China, and I am proud to have taken part in an arrangement which promises the protection of the world to the rights of China. The whole atmosphere of the world is changed by a thing like that, my fellow citizens. The whole international practice of the world is revolutionized.

"But you will say, 'What is the second sentence of article 10? That is what gives very disturbing thoughts.' The second sentence is that the council of the league shall advise what steps, if any, are necessary to carry out the guaranty of the first sentence, namely, that the members will respect and preserve the territorial integrity and political independence of the other members. I do not know any other meaning for the word "advise" except "advise." The council advises, and it can not advise without the vote of the United States. Why gentlemen should fear that the Congress of the United States would be advised to do something that it did not want to do I frankly can not imagine, because they can not even be advised to do anything unless their own representative has participated in the advice. It may be that that will impair somewhat the vigor of the league, but, nevertheless, the fact is so, that we are not obliged to take any advice except our own, which to any man who wants to go his own course is a very satisfactory state of affairs. Every man regards his own advice as best, and I dare say every man mixes his own advice with some thought of his own interest. Whether we use it wisely or unwisely, we can use the vote of the United States to make impossible drawing the United States into any enterprise that she does not care to be drawn into.

Yet article 10 strikes at the taproot of war. Article 10 is a statement that the very things that have always been sought in imperialistic wars are henceforth forgone by every ambitious nation in the world. I would have felt very lonely, my fellow countrymen, and I would have felt very much disturbed if, sitting at the peace table in Paris, I had supposed that

I was expounding my own ideas. Whether you believe it or not, I know the relative size of my own ideas; I know how they stand related in bulk and proportion to the moral judgments of my fellow countrymen, and I proposed nothing whatever at the peace table at Paris that I had not sufficiently certain knowledge embodied the moral judgment of the citizens of the United States. I had gone over there with, so to say, explicit instructions. Don't you remember that we laid down 14 points which should contain the principles of the settlement? They were not my points. In every one of them I was conscientiously trying to read the thought of the people of the United States, and after I uttered those points I had every assurance given me that could be given me that they did speak the moral judgment of the United States and not my single judgment. Then when it came to that critical period just a little less than a year ago, when it was evident that the war was coming to its critical end, all the nations engaged in the war accepted those 14 principles explicitly as the basis of the armistice and the basis of the peace. In those circumstances I crossed the ocean under bond to my own people and to the other governments with which I was dealing. The whole specification of the method of settlement was written down and accepted beforehand, and we were architects building on those specifications. It reassures me and fortifies my position to find how before I went over men whose judgment the United States has often trusted were of exactly the same opinion that I went abroad to express. Here is something I want to read from Theodore Roosevelt:

"The one effective move for obtaining peace is by an agreement among all the great powers in which each should pledge itself not only to abide by the decisions of a common tribunal but to back its decisions by force. The great civilized nations should combine by solemn agreement in a great world league for the peace of righteousness; a court should be established. A changed and amplified Hague court would meet the requirements, composed of representatives from each nation, whose representatives are sworn to act as judges in each case and not in a representative capacity." Now there is article 10. He goes on and says this: "The nations should agree on certain rights that should not be questioned, such as territorial integrity, their right to deal with their domestic affairs, and with such matters as whom they should admit to citizenship. All such guarantee each of their number in possession of these rights."

Now, the other specification is in the covenant. The covenant in another portion guarantees to the members the independent control of their domestic questions. There is not a leg for these gentlemen to stand on when they say that the interests of the United States are not safeguarded in the very points where we are most sensitive. You do not need to be told again that the covenant expressly says that nothing in this covenant shall be construed as affecting the validity of the Monroe doctrine, for example. You could not be more explicit than that. And every point of interest is covered, partly for one very interesting reason. This is not the first time that the Foreign Relations Committee of the Senate of the United States has read and considered this covenant. I brought it to this country in March last in a tentative, provisional form, in practically the form that it now has, with the exception of certain additions which I shall mention immediately. I asked the Foreign Relations Committees of both Houses to come to the White House and we spent a long evening in the frankest discussion of every portion that they wished to discuss. They made certain specific suggestions as to what should be contained in this document when it was to be revised. I carried those suggestions to Paris, and every one of them was adopted. What more could I have done? What more could have been obtained?

The very matters upon which these gentlemen were most concerned were, the right of withdrawal, which is now expressly stated; the safeguarding of the Monroe doctrine, which is now accomplished; the exclusion from action by the league of domestic questions, which is now accomplished. All along the line, every suggestion of the United States was adopted after the covenant had been drawn up in its first form and had been published for the criticism of the world. There is a very true sense in which I can say this is a tested American document.

I am dwelling upon these points, my fellow citizens, in spite of the fact that I dare say to most of you they are perfectly well known, because in order to meet the present situation we have got to know what we are dealing with. We are not dealing with the kind of document which this is represented by some gentlemen to be; and inasmuch as we are dealing with a document simon-pure in respect of the very principles we have professed and lived up to, we have got to do one or other of two things—we have got to adopt it or reject it. There is no middle course. You can not go in on a special-privilege basis of your own. I take it that you are too proud to ask to be exempted from responsibilities which the other members of the league will carry. We go in upon equal terms or we do not go in at all; and if we do not go in, my fellow citizens, think of the tragedy of that result—the only sufficient guaranty to the peace of the world withheld! Ourselves drawn apart with that dangerous pride which means that we shall be ready to take care of ourselves, and that means that we shall maintain great standing armies and an irresistible navy; that means we shall have the organization of a military nation; that means we shall have a general staff, with the kind of power that the general staff of Germany had, to mobilize this great manhood of the Nation when it pleases, all the energy of our young men drawn into the thought and preparation

for war. What of our pledges to the men that lie dead in France? We said that they went over there, not to prove the prowess of America or her readiness for another war but to see to it that there never was such a war again. It always seems to make it difficult for me to say anything, my fellow citizens, when I think of my clients in this case. My clients are the children; my clients are the next generation. They do not know what promises and bonds I undertook when I ordered the armies of the United States to the soil of France, but I know, and I intend to redeem my pledges to the children; they shall not be sent upon a similar errand.

Again and again, my fellow citizens, mothers who lost their sons in France have come to me and, taking my hand, have shed tears upon it not only, but they have added, 'God bless you, Mr. President!' Why, my fellow citizens, should they pray God to bless me? I advised the Congress of the United States to create the situation that led to the death of their sons. I ordered their sons oversea. I consented to their sons being put in the most difficult parts of the battle line, where death was certain, as in the impenetrable difficulties of the forest of Argonne. Why should they weep upon my hand and call down the blessings of God upon me? Because they believe that their boys died for something that vastly transcends any of the immediate and palpable objects of the war. They believe, and they rightly believe, that their sons saved the liberty of the world. They believe that wrapped up with the liberty of the world is the continuous protection of that liberty by the concerted powers of all civilized people. They believe that this sacrifice was made in order that other sons should not be called upon for a similar gift—the gift of life, the gift of all that died—and if we did not see this thing through, if we fulfilled the dearest present wish of Germany and now dissociated ourselves from those alongside whom we fought in the war, would not something of the halo go away from the gun over the mantelpiece, or the sword? Would not the old uniform lose something of its significance? These men were crusaders. They were not going forth to prove the might of the United States. They were going forth to prove the might of justice and right, and all the world accepted them as crusaders, and their transcendent achievement has made all the world believe in America as it believes in no other nation organized in the modern world. There seems to me to stand between us and the rejection or qualification of this treaty the serried ranks of those boys in khaki, not only these boys who came home, but those dear ghosts that still deploy upon the fields of France.

My friends, on last Decoration Day I went to a beautiful hillside near Paris, where was located the cemetery of Suresnes, a cemetery given over to the burial of the American dead. Behind me on the slopes was rank upon rank of living American soldiers, and lying before me upon the levels of the plain was rank upon rank of departed American soldiers. Right by the side of the stand where I spoke there was a little group of French women who had adopted those graves, had made themselves mothers of those dear ghosts by putting flowers every day upon those graves, taking them as their own sons, their own beloved, because they had died in the same cause—France was free and the world was free because America had come! I wish some men in public life who are now opposing the settlement for which these men died could visit such a spot as that. I wish that the thought that comes out of those graves could penetrate their consciousness. I wish that they could feel the moral obligation that rests upon us not to go back on those boys, but to see the thing through, to see it through to the end and make good their redemption of the world. For nothing less depends upon this decision, nothing less than the liberation and salvation of the world.

You will say, "Is the league an abso-

lute guaranty against war?" No; I do not know any absolute guaranty against the errors of human judgment or the violence of human passion, but I tell you this: With a cooling space of nine months for human passion, not much of it will keep hot. I had a couple of friends who were in the habit of losing their tempers, and when they lost their tempers they were in the habit of using very unparliamentary language. Some of their friends induced them to make a promise that they never would swear inside the town limits. When the impulse next came upon them, they took a street car to go out of town to swear, and by the time they got out of town they did not want to swear. They came back convinced that they were just what they were, a couple of unspeakable fools, and the habit of getting angry and of swearing suffered great inroads upon it by that experience. Now, illustrating the great by the small, that is true of the passions of nations. It is true of the passions of men however you combine them. Give them space to cool off. I ask you this: If it is not an absolute insurance against war, do you want no insurance at all? Do you want nothing? Do you want not only no probability that war will not recur, but the probability that it will recur? The arrangements of justice do not stand of themselves, my fellow citizens. The arrangements of this treaty are just, but they need the support of the combined power of the great nations of the world. And they will have that support. Now that the mists of this great question have cleared away, I believe that men will see the truth, eye to eye and face to face. There is one thing that the American people always rise to and extend their hand to, and that is the truth of justice and of liberty and of peace. We have accepted that truth and we are going to be led by it, and it is going to lead us, and through us the world, out into pastures of quietness and peace such as the world never dreamed of before.

COMMENT

The record clearly shows that on every major question but that of Reparation, the Treaty of Versailles would have been a worse treaty had Wilson remained in Washington. With all his mistakes, he emerges as the only man of real stature at Paris.

> Paul Birdsall, historian, in *Versailles Twenty Years After* (New York: Reynal & Hitchcock, 1941), p. 295.

The collapse of President Wilson at the Paris Peace Conference is one of the major tragedies of modern history. To a very large extent that collapse can be attributed to the defects of his own intelligence and character.

> Harold Nicolson, historian, in *Peacemaking, 1919* (New York: Houghton Mifflin Company, 1933), p. 195.

The Treaty of Versailles contained some of the most severe terms that one civilized nation has ever imposed on another, while elsewhere it soared heavenward in the lofty idealism of the Covenant of the League of Nations. It was harsh enough to humiliate and anger the Germans but not drastic enough permanently to enchain them—assuming that this could ever be done. It was idealistic enough to create the illusion of workable peace machinery, but selfish enough to make that machinery unworkable in a real crisis.

> Thomas A. Bailey, historian, in *Woodrow Wilson and the Lost Peace* (New York: The Macmillan Company, 1944) pp. 313–14.

51. *NOVEMBER 19, 1919*

Senator William S. Borah Fights the Treaty of Versailles

The Senate opposition to the Treaty of Versailles was divided into moderates led by Senator Henry Cabot Lodge of Massachusetts who favored ratification with reservations and irreconcilables led by Senator William S. Borah of Idaho who favored complete rejection of the treaty. After the Senate added fourteen "Lodge reservations," President Wilson urged his Democratic following to vote against the treaty. The crucial vote took place on November 19, 1919, when the treaty, with

Congressional Record, 66th Cong., 1st Sess., 1919, LXIII, pt. 9, 8982–84.

the Lodge reservations, was defeated by the vote of forty-two Democrats and thirteen "irreconcilable" Republicans. The speech by Senator Borah which follows was delivered to the Senate on the same day the vote was taken.

Since Democratic votes defeated the treaty, there is some truth to the view that Wilson helped to keep the nation out of the League of Nations. Nevertheless, there were Democrats and Republicans who refused to accept the vote as final. In February, 1920, the Senate decided to resume debate on the treaty. Hoping that the voters in the presidential election of 1920 would demand the nation's acceptance of the League, Wilson again urged the Democrats to vote against the treaty with reservations. Had Wilson not been ill and cut off from public affairs, perhaps he could have accepted the reservations as the only possible means of America's acceptance of the League. As it was, America's tradition of isolation, partisan hatred of Wilson, and ignorance of the treaty triumphed.

. . . . .

We have said, Mr. President, that we would not send our troops abroad without the consent of Congress. Pass by now for a moment the legal proposition. If we create executive functions, the Executive will perform those functions without the authority of Congress. Pass that question by and go to the other question. Our members of the council are there. Our members of the assembly are there. Article 11 is complete, and it authorizes the league, a member of which is our representative, to deal with matters of peace and war, and the league through its council and its assembly deals with the matter, and our accredited representative joins with the others in deciding upon a certain course, which involves a question of sending troops. What will the Congress of the United States do? What right will it have left, except the bare technical right to refuse, which as a moral proposition it will not dare to exercise? Have we not been told day by day for the last nine months that the Senate of the United States, a coordinate part of the treaty-making power, should accept this league as it was written because the wise men sitting at Versailles had so written it, and has not every possible influence and every source of power in public opinion been organized and directed against the Senate to compel it to do that thing? How much stronger will be the moral compulsion upon the Congress of the United States when we ourselves have indorsed the

proposition of sending our accredited representatives there to vote for us?

Ah, but you say that there must be unanimous consent, and that there is vast protection in unanimous consent.

I do not wish to speak disparagingly; but has not every division and dismemberment of every nation which has suffered dismemberment taken place by unanimous consent for the last 300 years? Did not Prussia and Austria and Russia by unanimous consent divide Poland? Did not the United States and Great Britain and Japan and Italy and France divide China and give Shantung to Japan? Was that not a unanimous decision? Close the doors upon the diplomats of Europe, let them sit in secret, give them the material to trade on, and there always will be unanimous consent.

How did Japan get unanimous consent? I want to say here, in my parting words upon this proposition, that I have no doubt the outrage upon China was quite as distasteful to the President of the United States as it is to me. But Japan said: "I will not sign your treaty unless you turn over to me Shantung, to be turned back at my discretion," and you know how Japan's discretion operates with reference to such things. And so, when we are in the league, and our accredited representatives are sitting at Geneva, and a question of great moment arises, Japan, or Russia, or Germany, or Great Britain will say, "Unless this matter is adjusted in this way I will depart from your league." It is the same thing, operating in the same way, only under a different date and under a little different circumstances.

Mr. President, if you have enough territory, if you have enough material, if you have enough subject peoples to trade upon and divide, there will be no difficulty about unanimous consent.

Do our Democratic friends ever expect any man to sit as a member of the council or as a member of the assembly equal in intellectual power and in standing before the world with that of our representative at Versailles? Do you expect a man to sit in the council who will have made more pledges, and I shall assume made them in sincerity, for self-determination and for the rights of small peoples, than had been made by our accredited representative? And yet, what became of it? The unanimous consent was obtained nevertheless.

But take another view of it. We are sending to the council one man. That one man represents 110,000,000 people.

Here, sitting in the Senate, we have two from every State in the Union, and over in the other House we have Representatives in accordance with population, and the responsibility is spread out in accordance with our obligations to our constituency. But now we are transferring to one man the stupendous power of representing the sentiment and convictions of 110,000,000 people in tremendous questions which may involve the peace or may involve the war of the world.

However you view the question of unanimous consent, it does not protect us.

What is the result of all this? We are in the midst of all of the affairs of Europe. We have entangled ourselves with all European concerns. We have joined in alliance with all the European nations which have thus far joined the league, and all nations which may be admitted to the league. We are sitting there dabbling in their affairs and intermeddling in their concerns. In other words, Mr. President —and this comes to the question which is fundamental with me—we have forfeited and surrendered, once and for all, the great policy of "no entangling alliances" upon which the strength of this Republic has been founded for 150 years.

My friends of reservations, tell me where is the reservation in these articles which protects us against entangling alliances with Europe?

Those who are differing over reservations, tell me what one of them protects the doctrine laid down by the Father of his Country. That fundamental proposition is surrendered, and we are a part of the European turmoils and conflicts from the time we enter this league.

Let us not underestimate that. There has never been an hour since the Venezuelan difficulty that there has not been operating in this country, fed by domestic and foreign sources, a powerful propaganda for the destruction of the doctrine of no entangling alliances.

Lloyd George is reported to have said just a few days before the conference met at Versailles that Great Britain could give up much, and would be willing to sacrifice much, to have America withdraw from that policy. That was one of the great objects of the entire conference at Versailles, so far as the foreign representatives were concerned. Clemenceau and Lloyd George and others like them were willing to make any reasonable sacrifice which would draw America away from her isolation and into the internal affairs and concerns of Europe. This league of nations, with or without reservations, whatever else it does or does not do, does surrender and sacrifice that policy; and once having surrendered and become a part of the European concerns, where, my friends, are you going to stop?

You have put in here a reservation upon the Monroe doctrine. I think that, in so far as language could protect the Monroe doctrine, it has been protected. But as a practical proposition, as a working proposition, tell me candidly, as men familiar with the history of your country and of other countries, do you think that you can intermeddle in European affairs. . . .

When Mr. Monroe wrote to Jefferson, he asked him his view upon the Monroe doctrine, and Mr. Jefferson said, in substance, our first and primary obligation should be never to interfere in European affairs; and, secondly, never to permit Europe to interfere in our affairs.

He understood, as every wise and

practical man understands, that if we intermeddle in her affairs, if we help to adjust her conditions, inevitably and remorselessly Europe then will be carried into our affairs, in spite of anything you can write upon paper.

We can not protect the Monroe doctrine unless we protect the basic principle upon which it rests, and that is the Washington policy. I do not care how earnestly you may endeavor to do so, as a practical working proposition your league will come to the United States. . . .

. . . . .

If the league includes the affairs of the world, does it not include the affairs of all the world? Is there any limitation of the jurisdiction of the council or of the assembly upon the question of peace or war? Does it not have now, under the reservations, the same as it had before, the power to deal with all matters of peace or war throughout the entire world? How shall you keep from meddling in the affairs of Europe or keep Europe from meddling in the affairs of America?

Mr. President, there is another and even a more commanding reason why I shall record my vote against this treaty. It imperils what I conceive to be the underlying, the very first principles of this Republic. It is in conflict with the right of our people to govern themselves free from all restraint, legal or moral, of foreign powers. It challenges every tenet of my political faith. If this faith were one of my own contriving, if I stood here to assert principles of government of my own evolving, I might well be charged with intolerable presumption, for we all recognize the ability of those who urge a different course. But I offer in justification of my course nothing of my own save the deep and abiding reverence I have for those whose policies I humbly but most ardently support. I claim no merit save fidelity to American principles and devotion to American ideals as they were wrought out from time to time by those who built the Republic and as

they have been extended and maintained throughout these years. In opposing the treaty I do nothing more than decline to renounce and tear out of my life the sacred traditions which throughout 50 years have been translated into my whole intellectual and moral being. I will not, I can not, give up my belief that America must, not alone for the happiness of her own people, but for the moral guidance and greater contentment of the world, be permitted to live her own life. Next to the tie which binds a man to his God is the tie which binds a man to his country, and all schemes, all plans, however ambitious and fascinating they seem in their proposal, but which would embarrass or entangle and impede or shackle her sovereign will, which would compromise her freedom of action, I unhesitatingly put behind me.

Sir, since the debate opened months ago those of us who have stood against this proposition have been taunted many times with being little Americans. Leave us the word American, keep that in your presumptuous impeachment, and no taunt can disturb us, no gibe discompose our purposes. Call us little Americans if you will, but leave us the consolation and the pride which the term American, however modified, still imparts. Take away that term and though you should coin in telling phrase your highest eulogy we would hurl it back as common slander. We have been ridiculed before, forsooth, of our limited vision. Possibly that charge may be true. Who is there here that can read the future? Time, and time alone, unerring and remorseless, will give us each our proper place in the affections of our countrymen and in the esteem and commendation of those who are to come after us. We neither fear nor court her favor. But if our vision has been circumscribed it has at all times within its compass been clear and steady. We have sought nothing save the tranquillity of our own people and the honor and independence of our own Republic. No foreign flattery, no possible world glory and power have disturbed our poise or come between us and our devotion to the traditions which have made us a people or the policies which have made us a Nation, unselfish and commanding. If we have erred we have erred out of too much love for those things which from childhood you and we together have been taught to revere—yes, to defend even at the cost of limb and life. If we have erred it is because we have placed too high an estimate upon the wisdom of Washington and Jefferson, too exalted an opinion upon the patriotism of the sainted Lincoln. And blame us not therefore if we have, in our limited vision, seemed sometimes bitter and at all times uncompromising, for the things for which we have spoken, feebly spoken, the things which we have endeavored to defend, have been the things for which your fathers and our fathers were willing to die.

Senators, even in an hour so big with expectancy we should not close our eyes to the fact that democracy is something more, vastly more, than a mere form of government by which society is restrained into free and orderly life. It is a moral entity, a spiritual force, as well. And these are things which live only and lone in the atmosphere of liberty. The foundation upon which democracy rests is faith in the moral instincts of the people. Its ballot boxes, the franchise, its laws, and constitutions are but the outward manifestations of the deeper and more essential thing—a continuing trust in the moral purposes of the average man and woman. When this is lost or forfeited your outward forms, however democratic in terms, are a mockery. Force may find expression through institutions democratic in structure equal with the simple and more direct processes of a single supreme ruler. These distinguishing virtues of a real republic you can not commingle with the discordant and destructive forces of the Old World and still preserve them.

You cannot yoke a government whose fundamental maxim is that of liberty to a government whose first law is that of force and hope to preserve the former. These things are in eternal war, and one must ultimately destroy the other. You may still keep for a time the outward form, you may still delude yourself, as others have done in the past, with appearances and symbols, but when you shall have committed this Republic to a scheme of world control based upon force, upon the combined military force of the four great nations of the world, you will have soon destroyed the atmosphere of freedom, of confidence in the self-governing capacity of the masses, in which alone a democracy may thrive. We may become one of the four dictators of the world, but we shall no longer be master of our own spirit. And what shall it profit us as a Nation if we shall go forth to the dominion of the earth and share with others the glory of world control and lose that fine sense of confidence in the people, the soul of democracy?

Look upon the scene as it is now presented. Behold the task we are to assume, and then contemplate the method by which we are to deal with this task. Is the method such as to address itself to a Government "conceived in liberty and dedicated to the proposition that all men are created equal"? When this league, this combination, is formed four great powers representing the dominant people will rule one-half of the inhabitants of the globe as subject peoples—rule by force, and we shall be a party to the rule of force. There is no other way by which you can keep people in subjection. You must either give them independence, recognize their rights as nations to live their own life and to set up their own form of government, or you must deny them these things by force. That is the scheme, the method proposed by the league. It proposes no other. We will in time become inured to its inhuman precepts and its soulless methods, strange as this doctrine now seems to a free people. If we stay with our contract, we will come in time to declare with our associates that force —force, the creed of the Prussian military oligarchy—is after all the true foundation upon which must rest all stable governments. Korea, despoiled and bleeding at every pore; India, sweltering in ignorance and burdened with inhuman taxes after more than a hundred years of dominant rule; Egypt, trapped and robbed of her birthright; Ireland, with 700 years of sacrifice for independence —this is the task, this the atmosphere, and this is the creed in and under which we are to keep alive our belief in the moral purposes and self-governing capacity of the people, a belief without which the Republic must disintegrate and die. The maxim of liberty will soon give way to the rule of blood and iron. We have been pleading here for our Constitution. Conform this league, it has been said, to the technical terms of our charter, and all will be well. But I declare to you that we must go further and conform to those sentiments and passions for justice and freedom which are essential to the existence of democracy. You must respect not territorial boundaries, not territorial integrity, but you must respect and preserve the sentiments and passions for justice and for freedom which God in His infinite wisdom has planted so deep in the human heart that no form of tyranny however brutal, no persecution however prolonged, can wholly uproot and kill. Respect nationality, respect justice, respect freedom, and you may have some hope of peace, but not so if you make your standard the standard of tyrants and despots, the protection of real estate regardless of how it is obtained.

Sir, we are told that this treaty means peace. Even so, I would not pay the price. Would you purchase peace at the cost of any part of our independence? We could have had peace in 1776—the price was high, but we could have had it. James Otis, Sam Adams, Hancock, and Warren were surrounded by those who urged peace and British rule. All through that long and trying struggle, particularly when the clouds of adversity lowered upon the cause, there was a cry of peace —let us have peace. We could have had peace in 1860; Lincoln was counseled by men of great influence and accredited wisdom to let our brothers—and, thank Heaven, they are brothers—depart in peace. But the tender, loving Lincoln, bending under the fearful weight of impending civil war, an apostle of peace, refused to pay the price, and a reunited country will praise his name forevermore—bless it because he refused peace at the price of national honor and national integrity. Peace upon any other basis than national independence, peace purchased at the cost of any part of our national integrity, is fit only for slaves, and even when purchased at such a price it is a delusion, for it can not last.

But your treaty does not mean peace —far, very far, from it. If we are to judge the future by the past it means war. Is there any guaranty of peace other than the guaranty which comes of the control of the war-making power by the people? Yet what great rule of democracy does the treaty leave unassailed? The people in whose keeping alone you can safely lodge the power of peace or war nowhere, at no time and in no place, have any voice in this scheme for world peace. Autocracy which has bathed the world in blood for centuries reigns supreme. Democracy is everywhere excluded. This, you say, means peace.

Can you hope for peace when love of country is disregarded in your scheme, when the spirit of nationality is rejected, even scoffed at? Yet what law of that moving and mysterious force does your treaty not deny? With a ruthlessness unparalleled your treaty in a dozen instances runs counter to the divine law of nationality. Peoples who speak the same language, kneel at the same ancestral tombs, moved by the same traditions, animated by a common hope, are torn asunder, broken in pieces, divided, and parceled out to antagonistic nations. And this you call justice. This, you cry, means peace. Peoples who have dreamed of independence, struggled and been patient, sacrificed and been hopeful, peoples who were told that through this peace conference they should realize the aspirations of centuries, have again had their hopes dashed to earth. One of the most striking and commanding figures in this war, soldier and statesman, turned away from the peace table at Versailles declaring to the world, "The promise of the new life, the victory of the great humane ideals for which the peoples have shed their blood and their treasure without stint, the fulfillment of their aspirations toward a new international order and a fairer and better world, are not written into the treaty." No; your treaty means injustice. It means slavery. It means war. And to all this you ask this Republic to become a party. You ask it to abandon the creed under which it has grown to power and accept the creed of autocracy, the creed of repression and force.

Mr. President, I turn from this scheme based upon force to another scheme, planned 143 years ago in old Independence Hall, in the city of Philadelphia, based upon liberty. I like it better. I have become so accustomed to believe in it that it is difficult for me to reject it out of hand. I have difficulty in subscribing to the new creed of oppression, the creed of dominant and subject peoples. I feel a reluctance to give up the belief that all men are created equal—the eternal principle in government that all governments derive their just powers from the consent of the governed. I can not get my consent to exchange the doctrine of George Washington for the doctrine of Frederick the Great translated into mendacious phrases of peace. I go back to that serene and masterful soul who pointed the way to power and glory for the new and then weak Republic, and

whose teachings and admonitions even in our majesty and dominance we dare not disregard.

I know well the answer to my contention. It has been piped about of late from a thousand sources—venal sources, disloyal sources, sinister sources—that Washington's wisdom was of his day only and that his teachings are out of fashion —things long since sent to the scrap heap of history—that while he was great in character and noble in soul he was untrained in the arts of statecraft and unlearned in the science of government. The puny demagogue, the barren editor, the sterile professor now vie with each other in apologizing for the temporary and commonplace expedients which the Father of his Country felt constrained to adopt in building a republic!

What is the test of statesmanship? Is it the formation of theories, the utterance of abstract and incontrovertible truths, or is it the capacity and the power to give to a people that concrete thing called liberty, that vital and indispensable thing in human happiness called free institutions, and to establish over all and above all the blessed and eternal reign of order and law? If this be the test, where shall we find another whose name is entitled to be written beside the name of Washington? His judgment and poise in the hour of turmoil and peril, his courage and vision in times of adversity, his firm grasp of fundamental principles, his almost inspired power to penetrate the future and read there the result, the effect of policies, have never been excelled, if equalled, by any of the world's commonwealth builders. Peter the Great, William the Silent, and Cromwell the Protector, these and these alone perhaps are to be associated with his name as the builders of States and the founders of governments. But in exaltation of moral purpose, in the unselfish character of his work, in the durability of his policies, in the permanency of the institutions which he more than anyone else called into effect, his service to mankind stands out separate and apart in a class by itself. The works of these other great builders, where are they now? But the work of Washington is still the most potent influence for the advancement of civilization and the freedom of the race.

Reflect for a moment over his achievements. He led the Revolutionary Army to victory. He was the very first to suggest a union instead of a confederacy. He presided over and counseled with great wisdom the convention which framed the Constitution. He guided the Government through its first perilous years. He gave dignity and stability and honor to that which was looked upon by the world as a passing experiment, and finally, my friends, as his own peculiar and particular contribution to the happiness of his countrymen and to the cause of the Republic, he gave us his great foreign policy under which we have lived and prospered and strengthened for nearly a century and a half. This policy is the most sublime confirmation of his genius as a statesman. It was then, and it now is, an indispensable part of our whole scheme of government. It is to-day a vital, indispensable element in our entire plan, purpose, and mission as a nation. To abandon it is nothing less than a betrayal of the American people. I say betrayal deliberately, in view of the suffering and the sacrifice which will follow in the wake of such a course.

But under the stress and strain of these extraordinary days, when strong men are being swept down by the onrushing force of disorder and change, when the most sacred things of life, the most cherished hopes of a Christian world seem to yield to the mad forces of discontent—just such days as Washington passed through when the mobs of Paris, wild with new liberty and drunk with power, challenged the established institutions of all the world, but his steadfast soul was unshaken—under these conditions come again we are about to abandon this policy so essential to our happiness and tranquillity as a people and our stability as a Government. No leader with his commanding influence and his unquailing courage stands forth to stem the current. But what no leader can or will do experience, bitter experience, and the people of this country in whose keeping, after all, thank God, is the Republic, will ultimately do. If we abandon his leadership and teachings, we will go back. We will return to this policy. Americanism shall not, can not, die. We may go back in sackcloth and ashes, but we will return to the faith of the fathers. America will live her own life. The independence of this Republic will have its defenders. Thousands have suffered and died for it, and their sons and daughters are not of the breed who will be bertayed into the hands of foreigners. The noble face of the Father of his Country, so familiar to every boy and girl, looking out from the walls of the Capitol in stern reproach, will call those who come here for public service to a reckoning. The people of our beloved country will finally speak, and we will return to the policy which we now abandon. America disenthralled and free in spite of all these things will continue her mission in the cause of peace, of freedom, and of civilization.

. . . . .

COMMENT

Americans would be fools if they permitted themselves to be embroiled in a system of European alliances. America promised to underwrite a stable peace. Mr. Wilson has failed. The peace cannot last. America should withdraw from all commitments which would impair her freedom of action.

Statement which appeared on the cover of *New Republic*, XIX (May 24, 1919).

I shall always believe ratification would have been possible if Wilson's health had not given way; when that tragedy occurred, not even his best friends could exercise any considerable influence on him.

Senator Gilbert Hitchcock, Democrat from Nebraska, December 7, 1922. Quoted in Thomas A. Bailey, *Woodrow Wilson and the Great Betrayal* (New York: The Macmillan Company, 1945), p. 243.

52. *1919*

Schenck v. United States

Like all wars in which the United States has been a participant, the First World War brought into the open the conflict between military necessity and the Bill of Rights. Shortly after the United States entered the war, Congress passed the Espionage Act on June 15, 1917, which made it illegal to cause insubordination in the armed forces or to obstruct recruiting. Moreover, the act authorized the Postmaster General to bar from the mails any letter, book, pamphlet, or newspaper which violated any provision of the act or which advocated treason, insurrection, or resistance to any laws of the United States. To enforce the provisions of the law, the Department of Justice took vigorous action. Even such publications as the New York Times and the Saturday Evening Post were temporarily barred from the mails. During the war, approximately two thousand cases dealing with the Espionage Act appeared in the lower courts, but it was not until 1919 that the Supreme Court first passed on the military provisions of the act.

On August 28, 1917, Charles T. Schenck and several other Socialists were arrested in Philadelphia for violating the Espionage Act on the grounds that they had circulated material in an attempt to cause insubordination in the military

249 U.S. 47 (1919).

forces and had obstructed recruitment and enlistment for service. Speaking for a unanimous court in the case of Schenck v. United States, Justice Oliver Wendell Holmes upheld the constitutionality of the Espionage Act by putting forth a new constitutional doctrine. He stated that in peacetime the defendant, Schenck, might urge resistance to a military draft. But in wartime, Congress had the right to prevent actions that constituted a "clear and present" danger to society. In the future, "the clear and present" danger concept was to become an important guide rule for the Court in dealing with cases involving the First Amendment.

. . . . .

This is an indictment in three counts. The first charges a conspiracy to violate the Espionage Act of June 15, 1917, by causing and attempting to cause insubordination, etc., in the military and naval forces of the United States, and to obstruct the recruiting and enlistment service of the United States, when the United States was at war with the German Empire; to wit, that the defendant wilfully conspired to have printed and circulated to men who had been called and accepted for military service under the Act of May 18, 1917, a document set forth and alleged to be calculated to cause such insubordination and obstruction. The count alleges overt acts in pursuance of the conspiracy, ending in the distribution of the document set forth. The second count alleges a conspiracy to commit an offense against the United States; to wit, to use the mails for the transmission of matter declared to be nonmailable by . . . the Act of June 15, 1917, to wit, the above mentioned document, with an averment of the same overt acts. The third count charges an unlawful use of the mails for the transmission of the same matter and otherwise as above. The defendants were found guilty on all the counts. They set up the 1st Amendment to the Constitution, forbidding Congress to make any law abridging the freedom of speech or of the press, and, bringing the case here on that ground, have argued some other points also of which we must dispose.

It is argued that the evidence, if admissible, was not sufficient to prove that the defendant Schenck was concerned in sending the documents. According to the testimony Schenck said he was general secretary of the Socialist party and had charge of the Socialist headquarters from which the documents were sent. He identified a book found there as the minutes of the executive committee of the party. The book showed a resolution of August 13, 1917, that 15,000 leaflets should be printed on the other side of one of them in use, to be mailed to men who had passed exemption boards, and for distribution. Schenck personally attended to the printing. On August 20 the general secretary's report said, "Obtained new leaflets from the printer and started work addressing envelopes," etc.; and there was a resolve that Comrade Schenck be allowed $125 for sending leaflets through the mail. He said that he had about fifteen or sixteen thousand printed. There were files of the circular in question in the inner office which he said were printed on the other side of the one-sided circular and were there for distribution. Other copies were proved to have been sent through the mails to drafted men. Without going into confirmatory details that were proved, no reasonable man could doubt that the defendant Schenck was largely instrumental in sending the circulars about. As to the defendant Baer, there was evidence that she was a member of the executive board and that the minutes of its transactions were hers. The argument as to the sufficiency of the evidence that the defendants conspired to send the documents only impairs the seriousness of the real defense.

It is objected that the documentary evidence was not admissible, because obtained upon a search warrant, valid, so far as appears. The contrary is established. The search warrant did not issue against the defendant, but against the Socialist headquarters at 1326 Arch street, and it would seem that the documents technically were not even in the defendant's possession. Notwithstanding some protest in argument, the notion that evidence even directly proceeding from the defendant in a criminal proceeding is excluded in all cases by the 5th Amendment is plainly unsound.

The document in question, upon its first printed side, recited the 1st section of the 13th Amendment, said that the idea embodied in it was violated by the Conscription Act, and that a conscript is little better than a convict. In impassioned language it intimated that conscription was despotism in its worst form and a monstrous wrong against humanity, in the interest of Wall Street's chosen few. It said: "Do not submit to intimidation;" but in form at least confined itself to peaceful measures, such as a petition for the repeal of the act. The other and later printed side of the sheet was headed, "Assert Your Rights." It stated reasons for alleging that anyone violated the Constitution when he refused to recognize "your right to assert your opposition to the draft," and went on: "If you do not assert and support your rights, you are helping to deny or disparage rights which it is the solemn duty of all citizens and residents of the United States to retain." It described the arguments on the other side as coming from cunning politicians and a mercenary capitalist press, and even silent consent to the Conscription Law as helping to support an infamous conspiracy. It denied the power to send our citizens away to foreign shores to shoot up the people of other lands, and added that words could not express the condemnation such cold-blooded ruthlessness deserves, etc., etc., winding up, "You must do your share to maintain, support, and uphold the rights of the people of this country." Of course the document would not have been sent unless it had been intended to have some effect, and we do not see what effect it could be expected to have upon persons subject to the draft except to influence them to obstruct the carrying of it out. The defendants do not deny that the jury might find against them on this point.

But it is said, suppose that that was the tendency of this circular, it is protected by the 1st Amendment to the Constitution. Two of the strongest expressions are said to be quoted respectively from well-known public men. It well may be that the prohibition of laws abridging the freedom of speech is not confined to previous restraints, although to prevent them may have been the main purpose. . . . We admit that in many places and in ordinary times the defendants, in saying all that was said in the circular, would have been within their constitutional rights. But the character of every act depends upon the circumstances in which it is done. The most stringent protection of free speech would not protect a man in falsely shouting fire in a theater, and causing a panic. It does not even protect a man from an injunction against uttering words that may have all the effect of force. The question in every case is whether the words used are used in such circumstances and are of such a nature as to create a clear and present danger that they will bring about the substantive evils that Congress has a right to prevent. It is a question of proximity and degree. When a nation is at war many things that might be said in time of peace are such a hindrance to its effort that their utterance will not be endured so long as men fight, and that no court could regard them as protected by any constitutional right. It seems to be admitted that if an actual obstruction of the recruiting service were proved, liability for words that produced that effect might be enforced. The Statute of 1917, in § 4, punishes conspiracies to obstruct as well as actual obstruction. If the act (speaking, or circulating a paper), its tendency and the intent with which it is done, are the same, we perceive no ground for saying that success alone warrants making the act a crime. Indeed, that case might be said to dispose of the present contention if the precedent covers all media concludendi. But as the right to free speech was not referred to specially, we have thought fit to add a few words.

It was not argued that a conspiracy to obstruct the draft was not within the words of the Act of 1917. The words are, 'obstruct the recruiting or enlistment service;' and it might be suggested that they refer only to making it hard to get volunteers. Recruiting heretofore usually having been accomplished by getting volunteers, the word is apt to call up that method only in our minds. But recruiting is gaining fresh supplies for the forces, as well by draft as otherwise. It is put as an alternative to enlistment or voluntary enrolment in this act. The fact that the Act of 1917 was enlarged by the amending Act of May 16, 1918, of course, does not affect the present indictment, and would not, even if the former had been repealed.

Judgments affirmed.

COMMENT

My heartsickness in politics comes not from the crook and the rogue, but from the honest and well-intentioned who blindly stab and destroy with their good intentions.

> Hiram Johnson to Former President Theodore Roosevelt, August 20, 1914, Theodore Roosevelt MSS., Library of Congress.

In war time military necessity has everywhere the right of way. Its censorship must be thorough and unquestioned.

> Editorial in the Louisville (Ky.) *Courier-Journal*, April 25, 1917.

It is safe to say that never in its history has this country been so thoroughly policed.

> U.S. Attorney General Thomas Watt Gregory in a letter to Gilbert A. Currie, April 12, 1918, in Committee on Public Information, *The Official Bulletin*, II, No. 285, 2.

53. *1923*

Adkins v. Children's Hospital

In 1920, the nation appeared physically tired by efforts at reform, the bitterness of the war, the lengthy debate on the League of Nations, the Red Scare, and postwar inflation. In a speech in May, 1920, Senator Warren G. Harding of Ohio caught the spirit of the times by stating that what the country needed was a "return to normalcy." As the Progressives' pleas for social reform were forgotten, the nation seemed to subscribe to the notion that prosperity rested with business leadership.

Meanwhile, organized labor suffered a decline. Business launched a determined campaign to break the power of labor unions, while the Supreme Court handed down a series of decisions which greatly weakened labor organizations. In 1918, the Court ruled that the Child Labor Act of 1916 was unconstitutional

261 U.S. 525 (1923).

on the grounds that Congress could not use its commerce power to regulate labor conditions. The *Adkins* v. *Children's Hospital* case is typical of the decisions handed down by the Supreme Court, making it virtually impossible to enact the most rudimentary forms of legislation which would regulate the conditions under which labor worked. The *Adkins* case involved the constitutionality of a District of Columbia minimum wage statute for women. The defense presented an excellent brief on social and economic data which demonstrated the connection between the number of hours women worked and their health and morals. But Justice George Sutherland, speaking for the majority of the Court, brushed these considerations aside as being irrelevant and argued that the statute was unconstitutional on the grounds that it violated the freedom of women to make a labor contract.

The question presented for determination by these appeals is the constitutionality of the Act of September 19, 1918, providing for the fixing of minimum wages for women and children in the District of Columbia . . .

It is declared that the purposes of the act are "to protect the women and minors of the District from conditions detrimental to their health and morals, resulting from wages which are inadequate to maintain decent standards of living; and the act in each of its provisions and in its entirety, shall be interpreted to effectuate these purposes." . . .

The statute now under consideration is attacked upon the ground that it authorizes an unconstitutional interference with the freedom of contract included within the guaranties of the due process clause of the 5th Amendment. That the right to contract about one's affairs is a part of the liberty of the individual protected by this clause is settled by the decisions of this Court and is no longer open to question. Within this liberty are contracts of employment of labor. In making such contracts, generally speaking, the parties have an equal right to obtain from each other the best terms they can as the result of private bargaining. . . .

There is, of course, no such thing as absolute freedom of contract. It is subject to a great variety of restraints. But freedom of contract is, nevertheless, the general rule and restraint the exception; and the exercise of legislative authority to abridge it can be justified only by the existence of exceptional circumstances.

If now, in the light furnished by the foregoing exceptions to the general rule forbidding legislative interference with freedom of contract, we examine and analyze the statute in question, we shall see that it differs from them in every material respect. It is not a law dealing with any business charged with a public interest, or with public work, or to meet and tide over a temporary emergency. It has nothing to do with the character, methods or periods of wage payments. It does not prescribe hours of labor or conditions under which labor is to be done. It is not for the protection of persons under legal disability or for the prevention of fraud. It is simply and exclusively a price-fixing law, confined to adult women (for we are not now considering the provisions relating to minors), who are legally as capable of contracting for themselves as men. It forbids two parties having lawful capacity—under penalties as to the employer—to freely contract with one another in respect to the price for which one shall render service to the other in a purely private employment where both are willing, perhaps anxious, to agree, even though the consequence may be to oblige one to surrender a desirable engagement and the other to dispense with the services of a desirable employee. The price fixed by the board need have no relation to the capacity or earning power of the employee, the number of hours which may happen to constitute the day's work, the character of the place where the work is to be done, or the circumstances or surroundings of the employment; and, while it has no other basis to support its validity than the assumed necessities of the employee, it takes no account of any independent resources she may have. It is based wholly on the opinions of the members of the board and their advisers—perhaps an average of their opinions, if they do not precisely agree—as to what will be necessary to provide a living for a woman, keep her in health and preserve her morals. It applies to any and every occupation in the District, without regard to its nature or the character of the work.

The standard furnished by the statute for the guidance of the board is so vague as to be impossible of practical application with any reasonable degree of accuracy. What is sufficient to supply the necessary cost of living for a woman worker and maintain her in good health and protect her morals is obviously not a precise or unvarying sum—not even approximately so. The amount will depend upon a variety of circumstances: the individual temperament, habits of thrift, care, ability to buy necessaries intelligently, and whether the woman live alone or with her family. To those who practice economy, a given sum will afford comfort, while to those of a contrary habit the same sum will be wholly inadequate. The coöperative economies of the family group are not taken into account though they constitute an important consideration in estimating the cost of living for it is obvious that the individual expense will be less in the case of a member of a family than in the case of one living alone. The relation between earnings and morals is not capable of standardization. It cannot be shown that well paid women safeguard their morals more carefully than those who are poorly paid. Morality rests upon other considerations than wages; and there is, certainly, no such prevalent connection between the two as to justify a broad attempt to adjust the latter with reference to the former. As a means of safeguarding morals the attempted classification in our opinion, is without reasonable basis. No distinction can be made between women who work for others and those who do not; nor is there ground for distinction between women and men, for, certainly, if women require a minimum wage to preserve their morals men require it to preserve their honesty. For these reasons, and others which might be stated, the inquiry in respect of the necessary cost of living and of the income necessary to preserve health and morals, presents an individual and not a composite question, and must be answered for each individual considered by herself and not by a general formula prescribed by a statutory bureau. . . .

The law takes account of the necessities of only one party to the contract. It ignores the necessities of the employer by compelling him to pay not less than a certain sum, not only whether the employee is capable of earning it, but irrespective of the ability of his business to sustain the burden, generously leaving him, of course, the privilege of abandoning his business as an alternative for going on at a loss. Within the limits of the minimum sum, he is precluded, under penalty of fine and imprisonment, from adjusting compensation to the differing merits of his employees. It compels him to pay at least the sum fixed in any event, because the employee needs it, but requires no service of equivalent value from the employee. It therefore undertakes to solve but one-half of the problem. The other half is the establishment of a corresponding standard of efficiency, and this forms no part of the policy of the legislation, although in practice the former half without the latter must lead to ultimate failure, in accordance with the inexorable law that no one can continue indefinitely to take out more than he puts in without ultimately exhausting the supply. The law . . . takes no account of periods of stress and business depression, of crippling losses, which may leave the employer himself without adequate means of livelihood. To the extent that the sum fixed exceeds the fair value of the services rendered, it amounts to a compulsory exaction from the employer for the support of a partially indigent person, for whose condition there rests upon him no peculiar responsibility, and therefore, in effect, arbitrarily shifts to his shoulders a burden which, if it belongs to anybody, belongs to society as a whole.

The feature of this statute which perhaps more than any other, puts upon it the stamp of invalidity is that it exacts from the employer an arbitrary payment for a purpose and upon a basis having no causal connection with his business, or the contract or the work the employee engages to do. The declared basis as already pointed out, is not the value of the service rendered but the extraneous circumstances that the employee needs to get a prescribed sum of money to insure her subsistence, health and morals. The ethical right of every worker, man or woman, to a living wage, may be conceded. One of the declared and important purposes of trade organizations is to secure it. And with that principle and with every legitimate effort to realize it in fact, no one can quarrel; but the fallacy of the proposed method of attaining it is that it assumes that every employer is bound at all events to furnish it. . . .

It is said that great benefits have resulted from the operation of such statutes, not alone in the District of Columbia but in the several States, where they have been in force. A mass of reports, opinions of special observers and students of the subject, and the like, has been brought before us in support of this statement, all of which we have found interesting, but only mildly persuasive. . . .

Finally, it may be said that if, in the interest of the public welfare, the police power may be invoked to justify the fixing of a minimum wage, it may, when the public welfare is thought to require it, be invoked to justify a maximum wage. The power to fix high wages connotes, by like reasoning, the power to fix low wages. If, in the face of the guaranties of the 5th Amendment, this form of legislation shall be legally justified, the field for the operation of the police power will have been widened to a great and dangerous degree. If, for example, in the opinion of future lawmakers, wages in the building trades shall become so high as to preclude people of ordinary means from building and owning homes, an authority which sustains the minimum wage will be invoked to support a maximum wage for building laborers and artisans, and the same argument which has been here urged to strip the employer of his constitutional liberty of contract in one direction will be utilized to strip the employee of his constitutional liberty of contract in the opposite direction. A wrong decision does not end with itself; it is a precedent, and, with the swing of sentiment, its bad influence may run from one extremity of the arc to the other.

.   .   .   .   .

It follows from what has been said that the act in question passes the limit prescribed by the Constitution, and, accordingly, the decrees of the court below are

Affirmed

COMMENT

The right of the legislature under the 5th and 14th Amendment to limit the hours of employment on the score of the health of the employee . . . has been firmly established. . . . I do not feel, therefore, that, either on the basis of reason, experience, or authority, the boundary of the police power should be drawn to include maximum hours and exclude a minimum wage.

Justice William Howard Taft dissenting in Adkins *v.* Children's Hospital, 261 U.S. 563 (1923).

I confess that I do not understand the principle on which the power to fix a minimum for the wages of women can be denied by those who admit the power to fix a maximum for their hours of work. . . . This statute does not compel anybody to pay anything. It simply forbids employment at rates below those fixed as the minimum requirement of health and right living. . . . the law is . . . like hundreds of so-called police laws that have been upheld.

Justice Oliver Wendell Holmes dissenting in Adkins *v.* Children's Hospital, 261 U.S. 563 (1923).

54. MAY 26, 1924

Immigration Act

During the First World War, there was a widespread demand for the American-ization of immigrants. In their anxiety to promote national unity, zealous patriots pressured immigrants to learn English and to develop a respect for American ideals and institutions. Following the armistice, the anti-foreign and anti-German hatreds of the war were trans-ferred to a fear of revolutionaries and radicals, and it was not long before this type of sentiment flowed into a fear of all immigrants. As organized nativism un-derwent a revival, there were demands that Congress restrict immigration. Na-tivist groups found allies among the leaders of organized labor who believed that large scale immigration depressed the domestic labor market and impeded the progress of unionization. Moreover, a number of social workers and sociol-ogists called attention to the vast social problems created by the immigration of eastern and southern Europeans.

To these views, Congress responded in 1921 by passing a bill which limited the number of immigrants to 3 per cent of the various foreign born elements in the United States in 1910. But the re-strictionists, unsatisfied, contended that the quotas assigned to southern and east-ern Europe were too large. Subjected to mounting pressure, Congress in 1924 passed a new and more comprehensive immigration statute which limited the number of European immigrants to 2 per cent of the foreign born elements accord-ing to the census of 1890. One of the obvious purposes of the act was to dis-criminate in favor of immigrants from

U.S. Statutes at Large, XLIII, pt. 1, 153–69.

Great Britain, Ireland, and Germany. The effects of the act were immediate and widespread. No longer did workers have to fear competition from cheap im-migrant labor. On the other hand a quota system which virtually excluded oriental immigrants caused a strain in American-Japanese relations.

SEC. 2. (a) A consular officer upon the application of any immigrant (as defined in section 3) may (under the conditions hereinafter prescribed and subject to the limitations prescribed in this Act or regulations made thereunder as to the number of immigration visas which may be issued by such officer) is-sue to such immigrant an immigration visa which shall consist of one copy of the application provided for in section 7, visaed by such consular officer. Such visa shall specify (1) the nationality of the immigrant; (2) whether he is a quota immigrant (as defined in section 5) or a non-quota immigrant (as defined in section 4); (3) the date on which the validity of the immigration visa shall expire; and (4) such additional infor-mation necessary to the proper enforce-ment of the immigration laws and the naturalization laws as may be by regula-tions prescribed.

. . . . .

SEC. 3. When used in this Act the term "immigrant" means any alien de-parting from any place outside the United States, except (1) a government official, his family, attendants, servants, and em-ployees, (2) an alien visiting the United States temporarily as a tourist or tem-porarily for business or pleasure, (3) an alien in continuous transit through the United States, (4) an alien lawfully admitted to the United States who later goes in transit from one part of the United States to another through foreign contiguous territory, (5) a bona fide alien seaman serving as such on a vessel arriving at a port of the United States and seeking to enter temporarily the United States solely in the pursuit of his calling as a seaman, and (6) an alien entitled to enter the United States solely to carry on trade under and in pursuance of the provisions of a present existing treaty of commerce and navigation.

SEC. 4. When used in this Act the term "non-quota immigrant" means—

(a) An immigrant who is the unmarried child under 18 years of age, or the wife, of a citizen of the United States who resides therein at the time of the filing of a petition under section 9;

(b) An immigrant previously lawfully admitted to the United States, who is returning from a temporary visit abroad;

(c) An immigrant who was born in the Dominion of Canada, Newfoundland, the Republic of Mexico, the Republic of Cuba, the Republic of Haiti, the Dominican Republic, the Canal Zone, or an independent country of Central or South America, and his wife and his unmarried children under 18 years of age, if accompanying or following to join him;

(d) An immigrant who continuously for at least two years immediately preceeding the time of his application for admission to the United States has been, and who seeks to enter the United States solely for the purpose of, carrying on the vocation of minister of any religious denomination, or professor of a college, academy, seminary, or university; and his wife, and his unmarried children under 18 years of age, if accompanying or following to join him; or

(e) An immigrant who is a bona fide student at least 15 years of age and who seeks to enter the United States solely for the purpose of study at an accredited school, college, academy, seminary, or university, particularly designated by him and approved by the Secretary of Labor, which shall have agreed to report to the Secretary of Labor the termination of attendance of each immigrant student, and if any such institution of learning fails to make such reports promptly the approval shall be withdrawn.

SEC. 5. When used in this Act the term "quota immigrant" means any immigrant who is not a non-quota immigrant. An alien who is not particularly specified in this Act as a non-quota immigrant or a non-immigrant shall not be admitted as a non-quota immigrant or a non-immigrant by reason of relationship to any individual who is so specified or by reason of being excepted from the operation of any other law regulating or forbidding immigration.

SEC. 6. (a) In the issuance of immigration visas to quota immigrants preference shall be given—

(1) To a quota immigrant who is the unmarried child under 21 years of age, the father, the mother, the husband, or the wife, of a citizen of the United States who is 21 years of age or over; and

(2) To a quota immigrant who is skilled in agriculture, and his wife, and his dependent children under the age of 16 years, if accompanying or following to join him. The preference provided in this paragraph shall not apply to immigrants of any nationality the annual quota for which is less than 300.

·　·　·　·　·

SEC. 11. (a) The annual quota of nationality shall be 2 per cent of the number of foreign-born individuals of such nationality resident in the continental United States as determined by the United States Census of 1890, but the minimum quota of any nationality shall be 100.

·　·　·　·　·

(f) There shall be issued to quota immigrants of any nationality (1) no more immigration visas in any fiscal year than the quota for such nationality, and (2) in any calendar month of any fiscal year no more immigration visas than 10 per centum of the quota for such nationality, except that if such quota is less than 300 the number to be issued in any calendar month shall be prescribed by the Commissioner General, with the approval of the Secretary of Labor, but the total number to be issued during the fiscal year shall not be in excess of the quota for such nationality.

(g) Nothing in this Act shall prevent the issuance (without increasing the total number of immigration visas which may be issued) of an immigration visa to an immigrant as a quota immigrant even though he is a non-quota immigrant.

SEC. 12. (a) For the purposes of this Act nationality shall be determined by country of birth, treating as separate countries the colonies, dependencies, or self-governing dominions, for which separate enumeration was made in the United States census of 1890; except that (1) the nationality of a child under twenty-one years of age not born in the United States, accompanied by its alien parent not born in the United States, shall be determined by the country of birth of such parent if such parent is entitled to an immigration visa, and the nationality of a child under twenty-one years of age not born in the United States, accompanied by both alien parents not born in the United States, shall be determined by the country of birth of the father if the father is entitled to an immigration visa; and (2) if a wife is of a different nationality from her alien husband and the entire number of immigration visas which may be issued to quota immigrants of her nationality for the calendar month has already been issued, her nationality may be determined by the country of birth of her husband if she is accompanying him and he is entitled to an immigra-

tion visa, unless the total number of immigration visas which may be issued to quota immigrants of the nationality of the husband for the calendar month has already been issued. An immigrant born in the United States who has lost his United States citizenship shall be considered as having been born in the country of which he is a citizen or subject, or if he is not a citizen or subject of any country, then in the country from which he comes.

(b) The Secretary of State, the Secretary of Commerce, and the Secretary of Labor, jointly, shall, as soon as feasible after the enactment of this Act, prepare a statement showing the number of individuals of the various nationalities resident in continental United States as determined by the United States census of 1890, which statement shall be the population basis for the purposes of subdivision (a) of section 11. In the case of a country recognized by the United States, but for which a separate enumeration was not made in the census of 1890, the number of individuals born in such country and resident in continental United States in 1890, as estimated by such officials jointly, shall be considered for the purposes of subdivision (a) of section 11 as having been determined by the United States census of 1890. In the case of a colony or dependency existing before 1890, but for which a separate enumeration was not made in the census of 1890 and which was not included in the enumeration for the country to which such colony or dependency belonged, or in the case of territory administered under a protectorate, the number of individuals born in such colony, dependency, or territory, and resident in continental United States in 1890, as estimated by such officials jointly, shall be considered for the purposes of subdivision (a) of section 11 as having been determined by the United States census of 1890 to have been born in the country to which such colony or dependency belonged or which administers such protectorate.

(c) In case of changes in political boundaries in foreign countries occurring subsequent to 1890 and resulting in the creation of new countries, the Governments of which are recognized by the United States, or in the establishment of self-governing dominions, or in the transfer of territory from one country to another, such transfer being recognized by the United States, or in the surrender by one country of territory, the transfer of which to another country has not been recognized by the United States, or in the administration of territories under mandates, (1) such officials, jointly, shall estimate the number of individuals resident in continental United States in 1890 who were born within the area included in such new countries or self-governing dominions or in such territory so transferred or surrendered or administered under a mandate, and revise (for the purposes of subdivision (a) of section 11) the population basis as to each country involved in such change of political boundary, and (2) if such

changes in political boundaries occur after the determination provided for in subdivision (c) of section 11 has been proclaimed, such officials, jointly, shall revise such determination, but only so far as necessary to allot the quotas among the countries involved in such change of political boundary. For the purpose of such revision and for the purpose of determining the nationality of an immigrant, (A) aliens born in the area included in any such new country or self-governing dominion shall be considered as having been born in such country or dominion, and aliens born in any territory so transferred shall be considered as having been born in the country to which such territory was transferred, and (B) territory so surrendered or administered under a mandate shall be treated as a separate country. Such treatment of territory administered under a mandate shall not constitute consent by the United States to the proposed mandate where the United States has not consented in a treaty to the administration of the territory by a mandatory power.

.   .   .   .   .

COMMENT

New arrivals should be limited to our capacity to absorb them into the ranks of good citizenship. America must be kept American. For this purpose, it is necessary to continue a policy of restricted immigration. . . .

> President Calvin Coolidge in his State of the Union message, December 6, 1923. *Congressional Record*, 68th Cong., 1st Sess., 1923–1924, LV, pt. 1, 99.

. . . conditions in this country do not require a further departure at this time from the immigration quota declared in 1921 in the midst of a most serious economic depression. We went the limit at that time by reversing our time-honored policy. . . . "Keep America American." Yes, but do not keep out of America through discriminatory immigration laws any lover of liberty, whatever his accident of birth may be. . . .

> Democratic Senator David I. Walsh of Massachusetts, speaking to the Senate, April 15, 1924. *Congressional Record*, 68th Cong., 1st Sess., 1924, LXV, pt. 7, 6355–57.

. . . the Nordic American today is a stranger in large parts of the land his fathers gave him. Moreover, he is a most unwelcome stranger, one much spit upon, and one to whom even the right to have his own opinions and to work for his own interests is now denied with jeers and revilings. "We must Americanize the Americans," a distinguished immigrant said recently. Can anything more clearly show the state to which the real American has fallen in this country which was once his own?

Hiram W. Evans, Imperial Wizard of the Ku Klux Klan, in "The Klan's Fight for Americanism," *North American Review*, ccxxiii (March, 1926), 38.

55. AUGUST 27, 1928

Kellogg Peace Pact

During the 1920's, the American people were filled with a passion for peace in international affairs. Manifestations of the search for peace were the campaign for American membership in the World Court and American participation in several disarmament conferences.

Very much aware of the American quest for peace, French Foreign Minister Aristide Briand attempted to draw the United States and France together by proposing that the two countries join in a pact forever outlawing war between them. At first, American Secretary of State Frank B. Kellogg, was not very sympathetic to the proposal. But in May, 1927, the flight of Charles A. Lindbergh from New York to Paris stimulated such a clamor for an expression of Franco-American friendship that Kellogg gave in. He was opposed, however, to a bilateral treaty between the United States and France which could be interpreted as a military alliance. To avoid such an eventuality, Kellogg proposed that the United States and France invite other powers to join in a treaty renouncing war as an instrument of national power.

The result was the Pact of Paris which was eventually approved by most nations. Idealists throughout the world proclaimed the pact as an instrument of peace. Kellogg, however, announced that the pact did not preclude a war of self-

U.S. Statutes at Large, xlvi, 2343–47.

defense. Moreover, the Senate Foreign Relations Committee reported that "the United States regards the Monroe Doctrine as a part of its national security and self defense." Despite these reservations, the United States by ratifying the treaty had assumed a moral obligation to cooperate with the League of Nations should some nation violate the pact. Though the significance of this event should not be exaggerated, it did represent a departure in American peacetime diplomacy.

The President of the German Reich, the President of the United States of America, His Majesty the King of the Belgians, the President of the French Republic, His Majesty the King of Great Britain, Ireland and the British Dominions beyond the Seas, Emperor of India, His Majesty the King of Italy, His Majesty the Emperor of Japan, the President of the Republic of Poland, the President of the Czechoslovak Republic,

Deeply sensible of their solemn duty to promote the welfare of mankind;

Persuaded that the time has come when a frank renunciation of war as an instrument of national policy should be made to the end that the peaceful and friendly relations now existing between their peoples may be perpetuated;

Convinced that all changes in their relations with one another should be sought only by pacific means and be the result of a peaceful and orderly process, and that any signatory Power which shall hereafter seek to promote its national interests by resort to war should be denied the benefits furnished by this Treaty;

Hopeful that, encouraged by their example, all the other nations of the world will join in this humane endeavor and by adhering to the present Treaty as soon as it comes into force bring their peoples within the scope of its beneficent provisions, thus uniting the civilized nations of the world in a common renunciation of war as an instrument of their national policy;

Have decided to conclude a Treaty and for that purpose have appointed . . . their respective Plenipotentiaries . . . who, having communicated to one another their full powers found in good and due form have agreed upon the following articles:

ARTICLE I

The High Contracting Parties solemnly declare in the names of their respective peoples that they condemn recourse to war for the solution of international controversies, and renounce it as an instrument of national policy in their relations with one another.

ARTICLE II

The High Contracting Parties agree that the settlement or solution of all disputes or conflicts of whatever nature or of whatever origin they may be, which may arise among them, shall never be sought except by pacific means.

ARTICLE III

The present Treaty shall be ratified by the High Contracting Parties named in the Preamble in accordance with their constitutional requirements, and shall take effect as between them as soon as all their several instruments of ratification shall have been deposited at Washington.

This Treaty shall, when it has come into effect as prescribed in the preceding paragraph, remain open as long as may be necessary for adherence by all the other Powers of the world. Every instrument evidencing the adherence of a Power shall be deposited at Washington and the Treaty shall immediately upon such deposit become effective as between the Power thus adhering and the other Powers parties hereto.

It shall be the duty of the Government of the United States to furnish each Government named in the Preamble and every Government subsequently adhering to this Treaty with a certified copy of the Treaty and of every instrument of ratification or adherence. It shall also be the duty of the Government of the United States telegraphically to notify such Governments immediately upon the deposit with it of each instrument of ratification or adherence.

IN FAITH WHEREOF the respective Plenipotentiaries have signed this Treaty in the French and English languages both texts having equal force, and hereunto affix their seals.

DONE at Paris, the twenty-seventh day of August in the year one thousand nine hundred and twenty-eight.

. . . . .

COMMENT

Secretary Kellogg's plan, even if approved by the leading nations, still fails in two points. It leads to a false belief in America that we have taken a great step forward. It does not contribute in any way to settling matters of international controversy.

Democratic candidate for governor of New York, Franklin D. Roosevelt, in "Our Foreign Policy—A Democratic View," *Foreign Affairs*, VI (July, 1928), 585.

. . . this anemic peace pact of our able and amiable Secretary of State, Mr. Kellogg, . . . is about as effective to keep down war as a carpet would be to smother an earthquake, but which, nevertheless, has worked up all the unsophisticated humanitarians of both sexes to a high state of excitement.

W. Cabell Bruce, Democrat from Maryland, speaking in the U.S. Senate, December 15, 1928. *Congressional Record*, 70th Cong., 2d Sess., 1928, LXX, pt. 1, 678–81.

Had an agreement of this kind been in existence in 1914, there is every reason to suppose that it would have saved the situation and delivered the world from all the misery which was inflicted by the great war. . . . It holds a greater hope for peaceful relations than was ever before given to the world.

President Calvin Coolidge speaking in Wausau, Wisconsin, on August 15, 1928. New York *Times*, August 16, 1928.

---

56. *OCTOBER 23, 1928*

Herbert Hoover's Rugged Individualism Speech

In the postwar decade, the leaders of the Republican party were men who sympathized with big business, men who championed individualism and private enterprise. The epitome of American capitalism was Herbert Hoover, the Republican candidate for the presidency in 1928. Rooted in an earlier historical era in which men regulated their labors by the sun and rain, Hoover for years had spoken out against such Progressive proposals as public power projects, special interest legislation for labor, and farm price supports. For him, nature was the chief regulator of the economy, and government interference was viewed as unnecessary.

Hoover ended his campaign for the presidency on October 23, 1928 in Madison Square Garden with the following speech. Besides revealing the thinking of Hoover, the speech is significant because it reflected the attitudes which many Americans held concerning the proper relationship between the government and the economy. Suspicious of the Democratic nominee Al Smith who openly boasted that he was a wet, a Catholic, and a product of Tammany Hall, the American people elected Hoover by a resounding plurality. Besides winning his opponent's home state of New York, Hoover even carried sections of the solid South which had been loyal to the Democratic party since Reconstruction. Though the conservatives appeared completely victorious, the worst depression in the nation's history was soon to restore Progressivism to all its old strength.

New York *Times*, October 24, 1928.

• • • • •

In my acceptance speech I endeavored to outline the spirit and ideals by which I would be guided in carrying that platform into administration. Tonight, I will not deal with the multitude of issues which have been already well canvassed. I intend rather to discuss some of those more fundamental principles and ideals upon which I believe the Government of the United States should be conducted. . . . .

But in addition to this great record of contributions of the Republican Party to progress, there has been a further fundamental contribution—a contribution underlying and sustaining all the others—and that is the resistance of the Republican Party to every attempt to inject the Government into business in competition with its citizens.

After the war, when the Republican Party assumed administration of the country, we were faced with the problem of determination of the very nature of our national life. During 150 years we have builded up a form of self-government and a social system which is peculiarly our own. It differs essentially from all others in the world. It is the American system. It is just as definite and positive a political and social system as has ever been developed on earth. It is founded upon a particular conception of self-government in which decentralized local responsibility is the very base. Further than this, it is founded upon the conception that only through ordered liberty, freedom and equal opportunity to the individual will his initiative and enterprise spur on the march of progress. And in our insistence upon equality of opportunity has our system advanced beyond all the world.

During the war we necessarily turned to the Government to solve every difficult economic problem. The Government having absorbed every energy of our people for war, there was no other solution. For the preservation of the State the Federal Government became a centralized despotism which undertook unprecedented responsibilities, assumed autocratic powers, and took over the business of citizens. To a large degree we regimented our whole people temporarily into a socialistic state. However justified in time of war, if continued in peace time it would destroy not only our American system but with it our progress and freedom as well.

When the war closed, the most vital of all issues both in our own country and throughout the world was whether Governments should continue their wartime ownership and operation of many instrumentalities of production and distribution. We were challenged with a peace-time choice between the American system of rugged individualism and a European philosophy of diametrically opposed doctrines—doctrines of paternalism and state socialism. The acceptance of these ideas would have meant the destruction of self-government through centralization of government. It would have meant the undermining of the individual initiative and enterprise through which our people have grown to unparalleled greatness.

The Republican Party from the beginning resolutely turned its face away from these ideas and these war practices. A Republican Congress cooperated with the Democratic Administration to demobilize many of our war activities. At that time the two parties were in accord upon that point. When the Republican Party came into full power it went at once resolutely back to our fundamental conception of the State and the rights and responsibilities of the individual. Thereby it restored confidence and hope in the American people, it freed and stimulated enterprise, it restored the Government to its position as an umpire instead of a player in the economic game. For these reasons the American people have gone forward in progress while the rest of the world has halted, and some countries have even gone backward. If any one will study the causes of retarded recuperation in Europe, he will find much of it is due to the stifling of private initiative on one hand, and overloading of the Government with business on the other.

There has been revived in this campaign, however, a series of proposals which, if adopted, would be a long step toward the abandonment of our American system and a surrender to the destructive operation of governmental conduct of commercial business. Because the country is faced with difficulty and doubt over certain national problems —that is, prohibition, farm relief and electrical power—our opponents propose that we must thrust government a long way into the businesses which give rise to these problems. In effect, they abandon the tenets of their own party and turn to State socialism as a solution for the difficulties presented by all three. It is proposed that we shall change from prohibition to the State purchase and sale of liquor. If their agricultural relief program means anything, it means that the Government shall directly or indirectly buy and sell and fix prices of agricultural products. And we are to go into the hydro-electric power business. In other words, we are confronted with a huge program of government in business.

There is, therefore, submitted to the American people a question of fundamental principle. That is: shall we depart from the principles of our American political and economic system, upon which we have advanced beyond all the rest of the world, in order to adopt methods based on principles destructive of its very foundations? And I wish to emphasize the seriousness of these proposals. I wish to make my position clear; for this goes to the very roots of American life and progress.

I should like to state to you the effect that this projection of government in business would have upon our system of self-government and our economic system. That effect would reach to the daily life of every man and woman. It would impair the very basis of liberty and freedom not only for those left outside the fold of expanded bureaucracy but for those embraced within it.

Let us first see the effect upon self-government. When the Federal Government undertakes to go into commercial business it must at once set up the organization and administration of that business, and it immediately finds itself in a labyrinth, every alley of which leads to the destruction of self-government.

Commercial business requires a concentration of responsibility. Self-government requires decentralization and many checks and balances to safeguard liberty. Our government to succeed in business would need become in effect a despotism. There at once begins the destruction of self-government.

The first problem of the Government about to adventure in commercial business is to determine a method of administration. It must secure leadership and direction. Shall this leadership be chosen by political agencies or shall we make it elective? The hard practical fact is that leadership in business must come through the sheer rise in ability and character. That rise can only take place in the free atmosphere of competition. Competition is closed by bureaucracy. Political agencies are feeble channels through which to select able leaders to conduct commercial business.

Government, in order to avoid the possible incompetence, corruption and tyranny of too great authority in individuals entrusted with commercial business, inevitably turns to boards and commissions. To make sure that there are checks and balances, each member of such boards and commissions must have equal authority. Each has his separate responsibility to the public, and at once we have the conflict of ideas and the lack of decision which would ruin any commercial business. . . . .

Bureaucracy is ever desirous of spreading its influence and its power. You cannot extend the mastery of the Government over the daily working life of a people without at the same time making it the master of the people's souls and thoughts. Every expansion of Government in business means that Government in order to protect itself from the political consequences of its errors and wrongs is driven irresistibly without peace to greater and greater control of the nation's press and platform. Free speech does not live many hours after free industry and free commerce die.

It is a false liberalism that interprets itself into the Government operation of commercial business. Every step of bureaucratizing of the business of our country poisons the very roots of liberalism—that is, political equality, free speech, free assembly, free press and equality of opportunity. It is the road not to more liberty but to less liberty. Liberalism should be found not striving to spread bureaucracy but striving to set bounds to it. True liberalism seeks all legitimate freedom, first in the confident belief that without such freedom the pursuit of all other blessings and benefits is vain. That belief is the foundation of all American progress, political as well as economic.

Liberalism is a force truly of the spirit, a force proceeding from the deep realization that economic freedom cannot be sacrificed if political freedom is to be preserved. Even if governmental conduct of business could give us more efficiency instead of less efficiency, the fundamental objection to it would remain unaltered and unabated. It would destroy political equality. It would increase rather than decrease abuse and corruption. It would stifle initiative and invention. It would undermine the development of leadership. It would cramp and cripple the mental and spiritual energies of our people. It would extinguish equality and opportunity. It would dry up the spirit of liberty and progress. For these reasons primarily it must be resisted. For a hundred and fifty years liberalism has found its true spirit in the American system, not in the European systems.

I do not wish to be misunderstood in this statement. I am defining a general policy. It does not mean that our Government is to part with one iota of its national resources without complete protection to the public interest. I have already stated that where the Government is engaged in public works for purposes of flood control, of navigation, of irrigation, of scientific research or national defense, or in pioneering a new art, it will at times necessarily produce power or commodities as a by-product. But they must be a by-product of the major purpose itself.

Nor do I wish to be misinterpreted as believing that the United States is free-for-all and devil-take-the-hindmost. The very essence of equality of opportunity and of American individualism is that there shall be no domination by any group or combination in this Republic, whether it be business or political. On the contrary, it demands economic justice as well as political and social justice. It is no system of laissez-faire.

I feel deeply on this subject because during the war I had some practical experience with governmental operation and control. I have witnessed not only at home but abroad the many failures of Government in business. I have seen its tyrannies, its injustices, its destructions of self-government, its undermining of the very instincts which carry our people forward to progress. I have witnessed the lack of advance, the lowered standards of living, the depressed spirits of people working under such a system. My objection is based not upon theory or upon a failure to recognize wrong or abuse, but I know the adoption of such methods would strike at the very roots of American life and would destroy the very basis of American progress.

Our people have the right to know whether we can continue to solve our great problems without abandonment of our American system. I know we can. We have demonstrated that our system is responsive enough to meet any new and intricate development in our economic and business life. We have demonstrated that we can meet any economic problem and still maintain our democracy and master in its own house and that we can at the same time preserve equality of opportunity and individual freedom. . . .

And what have been the results of our American system? Our country has become the land of opportunity to those born without inheritance, not merely because of the wealth or its resources and industry, but because of this freedom of initiative and enterprise. . . .

By adherence to the principles of decentralized self-government, ordered liberty, equal opportunity and freedom to the individual our American experiment in human welfare has yielded a degree of well-being unparalleled in all the world. It has come nearer to the abolition of poverty, to the abolition of fear of want, than humanity has ever reached before. Progress of the past seven years is the proof of it. This alone furnishes the answer to our opponents who ask us to introduce destructive elements into the system by which this has been accomplished.

Let us see what this system has done for us in our recent years of difficult and trying reconstruction and let us then solemnly ask ourselves if we now wish to abandon it.

. . . . .

. . . Today there are almost nine automobiles for each ten families, where seven and a half years ago only enough automobiles were running to average less than four for each ten families. The slogan of progress is changing from the full dinner pail to the full garage. Our people have more to eat, better things to wear and better homes. We have even gained in elbow room, for the increase of residential floor space is over 25 per cent, with less than 10 per cent increase in our number of people. Wages have increased, the cost of living has decreased. The job to every man and woman has been made more secure. We have in this short period decreased the fear of poverty, the fear of unemployment, the fear of old age; and these are fears that are the greatest calamities of human kind. . . .

I have endeavored to present to you that the greatness of America has grown out of a political and social system and a method of control of economic forces distinctly its own—our American system—which has carried this great experiment in human welfare further than ever before in all history. We are nearer today to the ideal of the abolition of poverty and fear from the lives of men and women than ever before in any land. And I again repeat that the departure from our American system by injecting principles destructive to it which our opponents propose will jeopardize the very liberty and freedom of our people, will destroy equality of opportunity, not alone to ourselves but to our children.

COMMENT

Although Hoover could administer the machinery of government with great skill and efficiency and knew the world of business, he was unable to lead his party and Congress or to mold and guide public opinion.

Historian Walter Johnson in *1600 Pennsylvania Avenue* (Boston: Little, Brown & Co., 1960), p. 25.

For eight and a half years, first as Secretary of Commerce, then as President, Herbert Hoover had a unique opportunity to study the workings and influence the policies of the American business system. No one was better placed to anticipate catastrophe. And, unless it was to be assumed that depression was inevitable under capitalism, one must assume that the depression of 1929 could have been averted by wise national policy. But if in these eight and a half years Hoover was concerned about the lag of purchasing power, about inadequate returns to farmers and workers, about regressive tax policies, about reckless stock market practices, about the piling up of private debt, about the defects of the banking system, then his concern never impelled him to effective action. And in many fields in which he did act . . . his action accelerated the tendencies that caused the disaster.

> Professor Arthur M. Schlesinger, Jr., in *The Crisis of the Old Order* (Boston: Houghton Mifflin Company, 1957), p. 161.

Hoover was obviously no old-fashioned conservative, no social Darwinist. . . . on the contrary, he was a cautious progressive.

> Professor Arthur S. Link, *American Epoch* (New York: Alfred A. Knopf, Inc., 1955), p. 373.

---

57. *DECEMBER 4, 1928*

Calvin Coolidge on Prosperity

Between 1920 and 1929, the standard of living of the American people was higher than at any other time in the nation's history. Of all the causes of this increased standard of living, none was more important than the technological revolution which was rapidly transforming America from a semi-rural to a vast urban society. The decade was an Age of Big Business. The nation's two hundred largest corporations controlled 49 percent of all corporate wealth and received 43 per cent of the corporate income. To millions of Americans, big business appeared to be responsible for the prosperity. President Coolidge was so friendly to big business that his actions seemed to represent efforts to convert

New York *Times*, December 5, 1928.

the government to a businessman's government and the Republican party to a businessman's party.

In December, 1928, Coolidge, in his annual message to Congress, which follows, reflected the general optimism which he and the American people shared for the future. Such optimism was uncalled for, however, as the American economy was out of joint in many respects. Industry maintained wages and prices at artificially high levels. An agricultural depression was slowly having repercussions throughout the nation. Moreover, there were serious maladjustments in the international economy which were eventually to have worldwide effects when credits were no longer available.

No Congress of the United States ever assembled, on surveying the state of the Union, has met with a more pleasing prospect than that which appears at the present time. In the domestic field there is tranquillity and contentment, harmonious relations between management and wage earner, freedom from industrial strife, and the highest record of years of prosperity. In the foreign field there is peace, the good-will which comes from mutual understanding, and the knowledge that the problems which a short time ago appeared so ominous are yielding to the touch of manifest friendship.

The great wealth created by our enterprise and industry, and saved by our economy, has had the widest distribution among our own people, and has gone out in a steady stream to serve the charity and the business of the world. The requirements of existence have passed beyond the standard of necessity into the region of luxury. Enlarging production is consumed by an increasing demand at home and an expanding commerce abroad. The country can regard the present with satisfaction and anticipate the future with optimism.

The main source of these unexampled blessings lies in the integrity and character of the American people. They have had great faith, which they have supplemented with mighty works. They have been able to put trust in each other and trust in their government. Their candor in dealing with foreign governments has commanded respect and confidence. Yet these remarkable powers would have been exerted almost in vain without the constant cooperation and careful administration of the Federal Government.

We have been coming into a period which may be fairly characterized as a conservation of our national resources. Wastefulness in public business and private enterprise has been displaced by constructive economy. This has been accomplished by bringing our domestic and foreign relations more and more under a reign of law. A rule of force has been giving way to a rule of reason. We have substituted for the vicious circle of increasing expenditures, increasing tax rates and diminishing profits the charmed circle of diminishing expenditures, diminishing tax rates and increasing profits.

Four times we have made a drastic reduction of our internal revenue system, abolishing many taxes and substantially reducing almost all others. Each time the resulting stimulation to business has so increased taxable incomes and profits that a surplus has been produced. One-third of the national debt has been paid, while much of the other two-thirds has been refunded at lower rates, and these savings of interest and constant economies have enabled us to repeat the satisfying process of more tax reductions.

Under this sound and healthful encouragement the national income has increased nearly 50 per cent, until it is estimated to stand well over $90,000,-000,000. It has been a method which has performed the seeming miracle of leaving a much greater percentage of earnings in the hands of the taxpayers with scarcely any diminution of the government revenue. That is constructive economy in the highest degree. It is the cornerstone of prosperity. It should not fail to be continued. . . .

The combination of economy and good times now indicates a surplus of about $37,000,000. This is a margin of less than 1 per cent on our expenditures and makes it obvious that the Treasury is in no condition to undertake increases in expenditures to be made before June 30. It is necessary, therefore, during the present session to refrain from new appropriations for immediate outlay, or if such are absolutely required to provide for them by new revenue; otherwise, we shall reach the end of the year with the unthinkable result of an unbalanced budget. For the first time during my term of office we face that contingency. I am certain that the Congress would not pass and I should not feel warranted in approving legislation which would involve us in that financial disgrace. . . .

When we turn from our domestic affairs to our foreign relations, we likewise perceive peace and progress. . . .

One of the most important treaties ever laid before the Senate of the United States will be that which the fifteen nations recently signed at Paris, and to which forty-four other nations have declared their intention to adhere, renouncing war as a national policy and agreeing to resort only to peaceful means for the adjustment of international differences. It is the most solemn declaration against war, the most positive adherence to peace, that it is possible for sovereign nations to make.

It does not supersede our inalienable sovereign right and duty of national defense or undertake to commit us before the event to any mode of action which the Congress might decide to be wise if ever the treaty should be broken. But it is a new standard in the world around which can rally the informed and enlightened opinion of nations to prevent their governments from being forced into hostile action by the temporary outbreak of international animosities. The observance of this covenant, so simple and so straightforward, promises more for the peace of the world than any other agreement ever negotiated among the nations. . . .

It is desirable that the government continue its helpful attitude toward American business. . . .

In its economic life our country has rejected the long accepted law of a limitation of the wage fund, which led to pessimism and despair because it was the doctrine of perpetual poverty, and has substituted for it the American conception that the only limit to profits and wages is production, which is the doctrine of optimism and hope because it leads to prosperity. Here and there the councils of labor are still darkened by the theory that only by limiting individual production can there be any assurance of permanent employment for increasing numbers, but in general, management and wage earner alike have become emancipated from this doom and have entered a new era in industrial thought which has unleashed the productive capacity of the individual worker with an increasing scale of wages and profits, the end of which is not yet. The application of this theory accounts for our widening distribution of wealth. No discovery ever did more to increase the happiness and prosperity of the people.

Since 1922 increasing population has increased wages in general 12.9 per cent, while in certain selected trades they have run as high as 34.9 per cent and 38 per cent. . . . As the rise in living costs in this period is negligible, these figures represent real wage increases. . . .

The country is in the midst of an era of prosperity more extensive and of peace more permanent than it has ever before experienced. But, having reached this position, we should not fail to comprehend that it can easily be lost. It needs more effort for its support than the less exalted places of the world. . . .

The end of government is to keep open the opportunity for a more abundant life. Peace and prosperity are not finalities; they are only methods. It is too easy under their influence for a nation to become selfish and degenerate. This test has come to the United States. Our country has been provided with the resources with which it can enlarge its intellectual, moral and spiritual life. The issue is in the hands of the people. Our faith in man and God is the justification for the belief in our continuing success.

COMMENT

It was Fate's colossal jest that Calvin Coolidge, the advocate of hard work, who never believed in getting something for nothing . . . should have headed the nation during that era when gambling was as natural as breathing. He worshiped thrift as a Zulu does his idol; he had never made a bet in all his life. . . . he cared nothing for the luxury that money makes possible. . . . All Coolidge's Vermont training, all of his later experiences, had been the negation of "get rich quickly." It was his misfortune as a statesman that he should, by his own personal example, have been exemplifying one type of living at a period when the trend was in another direction.

Claude M. Fuess, historian, in *Calvin Coolidge: The Man from Vermont* (Boston: Little, Brown & Company, 1940), p. 437.

Calvin Coolidge was democracy functioning at its best, which sometimes is its worst. . . . Back of him were the urgent purposes of the American democracy, the lust for prosperity, the Hamiltonian faith that "the rich" are indeed the "wise and good," the Republican creed which identifies wealth with brains. . . . It is good that this thin, dry, harsh, personality should have been dramatized. But the people took his very tenuous qualities, his curt manner, his drawling Vermont *patois* by which he was able to make three syllables out of the word cow, his lank body, his parsimony of word and deed, his obvious emotional repression, the glints of his sentimentality which they saw fleetingly at times, and piecing all these together they made a man, a little man to be sure, but one of their kind, a hero in fact.

Kansas newspaperman William Allen White in *A Puritan in Babylon* (New York: The Macmillan Company, 1938), pp. 444, 446.

58. SEPTEMBER, 1932

Effects of the Depression

Throughout the 1920's, millions of Americans were convinced that they had entered a "New Era," characterized by an ever expanding economy, full employment, and the elimination of poverty. Unfortunately, however, there was widespread ignorance concerning the poverty of farmers, coal miners, textile mill hands, and many of the nation's intel-

"*No One Has Starved*," *Fortune*, IV (September, 1932), 19–28, 80. Reprinted by courtesy of *Fortune Magazine*.

lectuals. When the crash of October, 1929, came, complacency and optimism rapidly faded. No longer was there talk about the "New Era." Within a few months, unemployment became a nationwide problem. As thousands of home owners lost their property and banks began to close at an alarming rate, bread lines formed. Farm prices dropped to disastrous levels. Though city and state governments formed emergency relief administrations, they were unable to *meet the emergency. Meanwhile, appeals for private support yielded only paltry sums. When there was no sign of recovery, there was widespread talk of social revolution. The depression eventually brought about a shift in responsibility for taking care of social distress from private and local to federal agencies and resources. But as President Hoover was strongly opposed to widespread measures which would transfer responsibility for social alleviation from cities and states to the federal government, it remained to the party of Franklin D. Roosevelt to offer a broad program of relief to the nation.*

Printed below is a description of the effects which the depression had on countless Americans.

Dull mornings last winter the sheriff of Miami, Florida, used to fill a truck with homeless men and run them up to the county line. Where the sheriff of Fort Lauderdale used to meet them and load them into a second truck and run them up to *his* county line. Where the sheriff of Saint Lucie's would meet them and load them into a third truck and run them up to *his* county line. Where the sheriff of Brevard County would *not* meet them. And whence they would trickle back down the roads to Miami. To repeat.

It was a system. And it worked. The only trouble was that it worked too well. It kept the transients transient and it even increased the transient population in the process. But it got to be pretty expensive, one way or another, if you sat down and figured it all out—trucks and gas and time and a little coffee. . . .

That was last winter.

Next winter there will be no truck. And there will be no truck, not because the transients will have disappeared from Miami: if anything, there will be more blistered Fords with North Dakota licenses and more heel-worn shoes with the Boston trade-mark rubbed out next winter than there were last. But because the sheriff of Miami, like the President of the U.S., will next winter think of transients and unemployed miners and jobless mill workers in completely different terms.

The difference will be made by the Emergency Relief Act. Or rather by the fact that the Emergency Relief Act exists. For the Act itself with its $300,-000,000 for direct relief loans to the states is neither an adequate nor an impressive piece of legislation. But the passage of the Act, like the green branch which young Mr. Ringling used to lay across the forks of the Wisconsin roads for his circus to follow, marks a turning in American political history. And the beginning of a new chapter in American unemployment relief. It constitutes an open and legible acknowledgment of governmental responsibility for the welfare of the victims of industrial unemployment. And its ultimate effect must be the substitution of an ordered, realistic, and intelligent relief program for the wasteful and uneconomic methods (of which the Miami truck is an adequate symbol) employed during the first three years of the depression.

There can be no serious question of the failure of those methods. For the methods were never seriously capable of success. They were diffuse, unrelated, and unplanned. The theory was that private charitable organizations and semi-public welfare groups, established to care for the old and the sick and the indigent, were capable of caring for the casuals of a world-wide economic disaster. And the theory in application meant that social agencies manned for the service of a few hundred families, and city shelters set up to house and feed a handful of homeless men, were compelled by the brutal necessities of hunger to care for hundreds of thousands of families and whole armies of the displaced and the jobless. And to depend for their resources upon the contributions of communities no longer able to contribute, and upon the irresolution and vacillation of state Legislatures and municipal assemblies long since in the red on their annual budgets. The result was the picture now presented in city after city and state after state—heterogeneous groups of official and semi-official and unofficial relief agencies struggling under the earnest and untrained leadership of the local men of affairs against an inertia of misery and suffering and want they are powerless to overcome.

But the psychological consequence was even worse. Since the problem was never honestly attacked as a national problem, and since the facts were never frankly faced as facts, people came to believe that American unemployment was relatively unimportant. They saw little idleness and they therefore believed there was little idleness. It is possible to drive for blocks in the usual shopping and residential districts of New York and Chicago without seeing a breadline or a food station or a hungry mob or indeed anything else much more exciting than a few casuals asleep on a park bench. And for that reason, and because their newspapers played down the subject as an additional depressant in depressing times, and because they were bored with relief measures anyway, the great American public simply ignored the whole thing. They would still ignore it today were it not that the committee hearings and the Congressional debate and the Presidential veto of relief bills this last June attracted their attention. And that the final passage of the Emergency Relief and Construction Act of 1932 has committed their government and themselves to a policy of affirmative action which compels both it and them to know definitely and precisely what the existing situation is. . . .

The following minimal statements may be accepted as true—with the certainty that they underestimate the real situation:

1. Unemployment has steadily increased in the U.S. since the beginning of the depression and the rate of increase during the first part of 1932 was more rapid than in any other depression year.

2. The number of person totally unemployed is now at least 10,000,000.

3. The number of persons totally unemployed next winter will, at the present rate of increase, be 11,000,000.

4. Eleven million unemployed means better than one man out of every four employable workers.

5. This percentage is higher than the percentage of unemployed British workers registered under the compulsory insurance laws (17.1 per cent in May, 1932, as against 17.3 per cent in April and 18.4 per cent in January) and higher than the French, the Italian, and the Canadian percentages, but lower than the German (43.9 per cent of trade unionists in April, 1932) and the Norwegian.

6. Eleven million unemployed means 27,500,000 whose regular source of livelihood has been cut off.

7. Twenty-seven and a half millions without regular income includes the families of totally unemployed workers alone. Taking account of the number of workers on part time, the total of those without adequate income becomes 34,-000,000 or better than quarter of the entire population of the country.

8. Thirty-four million persons without adequate income does not mean 34,-000,000 in present want. Many families have savings. But savings are eventually dissipated and the number in actual want tends to approximate the number without adequate income. How nearly it approximates it now or will next winter no man can say. But it is conservative to estimate that the problem of next winter's relief is a problem of caring for approximately 25,000,000 souls. . . .

But it is impossible to think or to act in units of 25,000,000 human beings.

Like the casualty lists of the British War Office during the Battle of the Somme, they mean nothing. They are at once too large and too small. A handful of men and women and children digging for their rotten food in the St. Louis dumps are more numerous, humanly speaking, than all the millions that ever found themselves in an actuary's column. The 25,000,000 only become human in their cities and their mill towns and their mining vllages. And their situation only becomes comprehensible in terms of the relief they have already received.

That is to say that the general situation can only be judged by the situation in the particular localities. But certain generalizations are possible. Of which the chief is the broad conclusion that few if any of the industrial areas have been able to maintain a minimum decency level of life for their unemployed. Budgetary standards as set up by welfare organizations, public and private, after years of experiment have been discarded. Food only, in most cases, is provided and little enough of that. Rents are seldom paid. Shoes and clothing are given in rare instances only. Money for doctors and dentists is not to be had. And free clinics are filled to overflowing. Weekly allowances per family have fallen as low as $2.39 in New York with $3 and $4 the rule in most cities and $5 a high figure. And even on these terms funds budgeted for a twelve-month period have been exhausted in three or four. While city after city has been compelled to abandon a part of its dependent population. "We are merely trying to prevent hunger and exposure," reported a St. Paul welfare head last May. And the same sentence would be echoed by workers in other cities with such additions as were reported at the same time from Pittsburgh where a cut of 50 per cent was regarded as "inevitable," from Dallas where Mexicans and Negroes were not given relief, from Alabama where

discontinuance of relief in mining and agricultural sections was foreseen, from New Orleans where no new applicants were being received and 2,500 families in need of relief were receiving none, from Omaha where two-thirds of the cases receiving relief were to be discontinued, from Colorado where the counties had suspended relief for lack of funds ... from Scranton ... from Cleveland ... from Syracuse. ... But the individual localities present their own picture:

About 1,000,000 out of New York City's 3,200,000 working population are unemployed. Last April 410,000 were estimated to be in dire want. Seven hundred and fifty thousand in 150,000 families were receiving emergency aid while 160,000 more in 32,000 families were waiting to receive aid not then available. Of these latter families—families which normally earn an average of $141.50 a month—the average income from all sources was $8.20. Of families receiving relief, the allowance has been anything from a box of groceries up to $60 a month. In general, New York relief, in the phrase of Mr. William Hodson, executive director of the New York Welfare Council, has been on "a disaster basis." And the effects have been disaster effects. It is impossible to estimate the number of deaths in the last year in which starvation was a contributing cause. But ninety-five persons suffering directly from starvation were admitted to the city hospitals in 1931, of whom twenty died; and 143 suffering from malnutrition, of whom twenty-five died. While visiting nurses and welfare workers report a general increase in malnutrition, and the clinics and medical relief agencies are so overcrowded they can give adequate relief to no one, although 75 per cent of persons applying to one relief agency had some form of illness. Housing is, of course, with the general lowering of standards and the doubling-up of families, worse even than it was during the boom. Relief expenditures for 1930 were something over $6,000,000; for 1931, more than $25,000,000; and for the first four months of 1932 over $20,000,000, or $5,000,000 per month. But large as this latter figure is it must be compared with the wage and salary loss by reason of unemployment, which is at least $100,000,000 per month. . . .

The situation in Philadelphia was described by its Community Council in July, 1932, as one of "slow starvation and progressive disintegration of family life. . . ." Of the city's 445,000 families with employable workers 210,000 had workers unemployed or on part time, about one in four had no worker employed on full time, and 12 per cent had *no* worker employed. Even the average person unemployed had been out of work for thirty-seven weeks and had had only a little over one week of casual or relief work during the period. . . . The Governor of the state estimated that 250,000 persons in Philadelphia "faced actual starvation." . . . New patients in the tuberculosis clinics had doubled. And the general death rate and disease rate had risen. . . . Fifty-five gave cause for grave concern and nineteen were listed as distressed counties in dire need. Moreover, relief allowances have steadily dropped. Last December 43,000 of the 56,000 families in Philadelphia where no one was employed were receiving relief at the rate of $4.39 per week for families averaging 4.8 persons. By May the number of families receiving relief had risen to 55,000 and the amount of relief had dropped to $4.23, of which $3.93 was for food, being two-thirds of the minimum required for health. No provision is made for rents and the result is that the landlords of Philadelphia, like the landlords of the country at large, are compelled to choose between throwing their tenants into the streets or providing from their own pockets the shelter required. . . .

Unemployed in Chicago number . . . 40 per cent of its employable workers while the number for the state at large is about one in three of the gainfully employed. . . . The minimum relief budget has been $2.40 per week for an adult and $1.50 per week for a child for food, with $22 to $23 per month to a family. But these figures have since been cut to $2.15 weekly for a man, $1.10 for a child. And persons demanding relief must be completely destitute to receive it. Rents are not paid by the relief agencies and housing is, in certain sections, unspeakably bad. While the situation of city employees is tragic. Teachers in May, 1932, had had only five months cash for the last thirteen months, 3,177 of them had lost $2,367,000 in bank failures, 2,278 of them had lost $7,800,000 in lapsed policies, 805 had borrowed $232,000 from loan sharks at rates adding up to 42 per cent a year, and 759 had lost their homes. . . .

In St. Louis 125,000 of the city's 330,000 employable persons were unemployed last December, one-eight of the population was estimated to face eviction and starvation, three-fourths of the families under care presented one or more medical problems each, and relief campaigners published full-page advertisements pointing to the number of hungry men and women rifling garbage buckets for their food. Starvation is reported as a contributory cause in several deaths. And even so the relief agencies were forced by lack of funds to drop 8,000 families on July 1 and 5,000 more on July 15. Since these cuts were made, large numbers of the destitute have been living in refuse dumps along the river where they build shacks and dig in the dump for food. The city's Board of Estimate and Apportionment has petitioned the Governor to apply for a $2,000,000 loan from the federal government but the amount will not suffice to carry the city through the winter.

. . . . .

Obviously, however, urban figures give an incomplete picture of the whole industrial situation, for they do not include such areas as the industrial area of New Jersey. In Passaic County, for example, 23,749 persons, heads of families, representing 90,699 of the county's 300,-000 population, have applied for relief. The authorities have been forced to pick 12,171 families, about half, and give them relief amounting to about $9 a month per family. And in Paterson 8,500 of the registered 12,000 unemployed are without relief of any kind. Moreover, the situation in the textile areas of the state is complicated by the fact that certain employers have taken advantage of the necessity of their employees to reestablish sweatshop conditions. Under such circumstances the employed as well as the unemployed become a burden upon the community. But elsewhere in the textile mill towns even the pretense of a living wage has been dropped. North Carolina has 100,000 unemployed textile workers with another 100,000 on the payrolls of closed plants, most of whom are begging on the roads, having long ago exhausted their savings from the low wage paid them before the depression. And those employed on part time are hardly better off since the full-time wage now averages about $6.50. In Georgia, in the Piedmont Mill Village of Egan Park, fifteen families have banded together to keep alive on a total weekly income of $10. And similar stories come from other towns in the region. While some of the small steel towns are almost as badly off. At Donora, Pennsylvania, there were in March 277 workers out of a population of 13,900 while 2,500 others performed "made work" at $3.50 per week and 2,000 others "seem to have disappeared." It is hardly necessary to add that malnutrition, undernourishment, rickets, tuberculosis, and other diseases increase under such conditions. And that relief in these areas is badly organized or nonexistent.

The story of factory unemployment is, however, only part of the story. In *agriculture* and in *mining*, particularly soft-coal mining, the depression is not in its fourth year but in its eighth or tenth or twelfth. It is estimated that there is a destitute coal-mining population of 1,200,000 souls dependent upon some 240,000 unemployed and distressed bituminous miners, most of whom live in six states in regions where coal mining is the only important enterprise, where merchants are bankrupt, banks closed, schools without funds, and once wealthy residents in actual want. And this situation is of many years' standing for even in the boom years of 1928 and 1929 the industry as a whole lost a total of $41,-000,000. The American Friends Service Committee, which has worked with children in Kentucky, West Virginia and Williamson and Franklin counties, Illinois, estimates that of the 500,000 soft-coal workers making a living in 1928 only 300,000 are now employed and on wages often as low as $8 a week. Over the entire area from 20 per cent to 99 per cent of the children are found to be underweight and the probability is that 20,000 children and 20,000 adults will shortly be in actual and pressing want.

Kentucky conditions have been well aired as a result of the Fascist policy pursued by the local authorities, particularly in Harlan County. Miners in that county who work at all work one to one and a half days a week with payment in scrip from which the company deducts an average of $11.80 monthly for rent, medical attention, powder and caps, and insurance. To pay this deduction, a man must mine forty-five tons a month, which means that he must work nine days. Most of them work a total of six days and the result is a load of debt with no balance for food. As a consequence, pellagra— a deficiency disease of the nerve centers finally causing insanity—is common. In Pineville, Kentucky, 157 children are fed one meal a day at a soup kitchen—the meal consisting of boiled potatoes, boiled beans, and cornbread, an ideal pellagra-breeding diet. Most of the miners attempt to farm but the land is poor and jars for canning are too expensive for a community in which cash is practically nonexistent. Moreover, there was last year a severe drought in this district, and a great many miner's crops were destroyed by sun and pests—a fact which must be compared with the September, 1931, statement of Executive-Director Croxton of the President's Organization on Unemployment Relief to the effect that the unemployment situation in West Virginia and Kentucky would be alleviated by the "bountiful crops."

The state of Franklin and Williamson counties in Illinois is, if anything, worse. All mines in the counties were closed by April, 1932. A cross section of twelve homes in the town of Benton showed no money, worn-out clothing, houses bare of "unnecessary" furniture, dishes made of flour, emaciated parents, undernourished children, unpaid rentals, and an average family indebtedness for groceries and doctors bills of $300. Twenty-five thousand persons in the two counties were either in want last spring or rapidly approaching it. . . .

So it goes from one city to another and out into the mill towns and the mine villages and on beyond into the farms where the hides of a carload of cattle will hardly buy a pair of shoes and alfalfa costing $12 a ton to raise sells at $2.50 and the tractors rust in the fields. The difficulty with such facts is that in mass they cease to have meaning. And the reiteration of the statement that hundreds of thousands of people have faced or are facing starvation with inadequate doles to support them merely produces skepticism. "They haven't starved yet," remarks the reader. "They get along somehow."

It is true they get along somehow. But just how they get along is another matter. There were eleven days in Philadelphia last April when private funds had run out and public funds were not yet available. During that period, the relief organizations studied ninety-one families to see just how people get along under these circumstances. They found out. One woman borrowed fifty cents, bought stale bread at three and one half cents a loaf, and the family lived on it for eleven days. Another put the last food order into soup stock and vegetables and made a soup. When a member of the family was hungry, he ate as little as he could. Another picked up spoiled vegetables along the docks and except for three foodless days, the family ate them. Another made a stew with her last food order, which she cooked over and over daily to keep it from spoiling. Another family lived on dandelions. Another on potatoes. Another had no food for two and one-half days. And one in ten of the women were pregnant and one in three of the children of nursing age. And they "got along."

Such is the problem created by three years of increasing unemployment and two years of hand-to-mouth relief: city after city attempting to feed a half or a third or a quarter of its citizens upon gifts made from the reduced earnings, or from taxes levied on the over-appraised homes of the other half or the other two-thirds or the other three-quarters; city after city maintaining the lives but not the health of its unemployed on a survival ration; city after city where the whole mechanism of relief has failed or is about to fail or has survived only by abandoning a major part of its task; and beyond the cities the mill towns and the coal mines and the cropper farms where relief is merely a name.

But the depression, along with its misery, has produced its social curiosities, not the least of which is the wandering population it has spilled upon the roads. Means of locomotion vary but the objective is always the same—somewhere else. No one has yet undertaken to estimate the number of hitch-hikers whose thumbs jerk onward along the American pike, nor the number of spavined Fords dragging destitute families from town to town in search of a solvent relative or a generous friend. But the total migratory population of the country has been put at 600,000 to 1,000,-000. . . .

The presence of these wandering groups is curious and significant. It has long been recognized that the population of the U.S. was becoming increasingly migratory in character. But it was not until the depression that the meaning of the phenomenon was made clear. When millions of people have no relation to the land and are able at the same time to find cheap transportation, the effect of an economic crisis is not to fix them in one place but to drive them elsewhere. And the consequence, as regards these groups, is a complete failure of local relief. The destitute families of the Fords and the homeless men of the flat cars are entitled to relief in no city. As the history of the Bonus Expeditionary Force after its ouster from Washington makes clear.

So far at least the phenomenon of migration is the only important social consequence of the depression, and the Communistic outbreaks foreseen by extremists in both directions have not taken place. The unemployed of Passaic County, New Jersey, may be and doubtless are in ugly temper. And the state of mind of the idle miners in Harlan County, Kentucky, may have been such as to justify, through fear, the otherwise unjustifiable repressive measures adopted by the local authorities. But by and large there has been extraordinarily little unrest. The two major manifestations of the year, the January hunger march of Father Cox's army to Washington and the later Bonus Expeditionary Force, were notoriously and avowedly anti-revolutionary, and contrasted

remarkably in number with the feeble 1,500 produced for the Communist hunger march of last December. And most of the food riots reported from various cities—or not reported—have so far been bloodless, the only fatalities having occurred in the mismanaged resistance to a job march upon the Ford factories in Dearborn in March, when four were killed and fifty wounded, the July attempt of St. Louis police to prevent a mob of 300 from rushing the City Hall where the Board of Aldermen was considering (and thereupon promptly passing) special tax bills for relief, the demonstration of 400 against the employment of non-union men on public works in Marseilles, Illinois, in the same month in which one man was killed and twenty-two wounded, and the Battle of Pennsylvania Avenue. Other and milder disturbances occurred in New York in January (a riot before the Home Relief Bureau Office), in Chicago in February (a demonstration of 20,000 said to have been led by Communists), in Boston in May (a hunger march of 500), in Philadelphia in May (a demonstration before the City Hall in which twenty people were beaten), in Charleston, West Virginia, in June (a hunger siege of 500 around the State House), in Clinton, Massachusetts, in July (a demonstration for food by 300 men, women, and crying children), in Sioux City, Iowa, in July (a demonstration of 500 unemployed against the use of a steam shovel on a post office site), in North Carolina in July (a demonstration of 5,000 textile workers against a wage cut, resulting in the forced closing of the mills of five towns), and in Olympia, Washington, in July (a concentration of jobless upon the State Capitol demanding relief). But the tension has naturally increased in the industrial communities as time has passed. Indiana has recently offered the spectacle of striking miners besieging strike breakers in violation of an anti-picketing injunction with the pur-

pose of either inviting their own arrest
so that they might be fed in jail, or starving out their enemies. And it is not
necessary to appeal, as Mayor Cermak

did last winter, to class fear in order to
point out that there is a limit beyond
which hunger and misery become violent.

COMMENT

Fifty-four men were arrested yesterday morning for sleeping or idling in the
arcade connecting with the subway through 45 West Forty-second Street, but
most of them considered their unexpected meeting with a raiding party of ten
policemen as a stroke of luck because it brought them free meals yesterday and
shelter last night. . . .

Statement in the New York *Times*, October 7, 1932.

I see nothing in the present situation that is either menacing or warrants pessimism. During the winter months there may be some slackness or unemployment,
but hardly more than at this season every year. I have every confidence that there
will be a revival of activity in the spring.

Public statement by Secretary of the Treasury Andrew Mellon, January 1, 1930.
Quoted in Clement Wood, *Herbert Clark Hoover, An American Tragedy* (New York:
M. Swain, 1932), p. 322.

Darwin's theory that man can adapt himself to almost any new environment is
being illustrated . . . by thousands of New Yorkers who have discovered new
ways to live and new ways to earn a living since their formerly placid lives
were thrown into chaos by unemployment. . . . The Hall of Jurors in the
Criminal Courts Building is jammed and packed on court days. . . . Why?
Jurors get $4 for every day they serve. . . . According to the Police Department,
there are approximately 7,000 . . . "shine boys" making a living on New
York streets at present. Three years ago they were so rare as to be almost nonexistent. . . .

Statement in the New York *Times*, June 5, 1932.

59. *JANUARY 7, 1932*

The Stimson Doctrine

During the 1930's, the forces of aggression attempted to overturn the peace
structure which the Treaty of Versailles
had established. The first occurrence in
the Far East was the Japanese occupa-

*Papers Relating to the Foreign Relations
of the U.S. and Japan: 1931–1941* (Washington, D.C., 1943), I, 76–77.

tion of Manchuria during 1931 and 1932.
The Japanese move was well timed, for
the United States and England were on
the verge of economic collapse. Secretary
of State Henry L. Stimson was very much
aware that his hands were tied, as the
American public would not condone any
action which might lead to war. He first

turned to England and France for support, only to be disappointed. He then sent identical notes to Japan and China which declared that the American government would recognize no changes in the Far East which impaired the treaty rights of the United States and the independence and administrative integrity of China. This pronouncement, though it was not a new policy, eventually became known as the "Stimson Doctrine," a restatement of the same policy which William Jennings Bryan had enunciated as secretary of state on May 11, 1915. Stimson hoped that England and France would follow his lead. Instead, they issued, a public statement professing faith that the Japanese would adhere to the Open Door Policy in China. Several months later, however, the League of Nations did adopt a resolution which incorporated the ideas of the Stimson Doctrine. The policy of refusing to acquiesce in Japan's control of China was eventually to culminate in war between the United States and Japan.

Please deliver to the Foreign Office on behalf of your Government as soon as possible the following note:

With the recent military operations about Chinchow, the last remaining administrative authority of the Government of the Chinese Republic in South Manchuria, as it existed prior to September 18th, 1931, has been destroyed. The American Government continues confident that the work of the neutral commission recently authorized by the Council of the League of Nations will facilitate an ultimate solution of the difficulties now existing between China and Japan. But in view of the present situation and of its own rights and obligations therein, the American Government deems it to be its duty to notify both the Imperial Japanese Government and the Government of the Chinese Republic that it cannot admit the legality of any situation *de facto* nor does it intend to recognize any treaty or agreement entered into between those Governments, or agents thereof, which may impair the treaty rights of the United States or its citizens in China, including those which relate to the sovereignty, the independence, or the territorial and administrative integrity of the Republic of China, or to the international policy relative to China, commonly known as the open door policy; and that it does not intend to recognize any situation, treaty or agreement which may be brought about by means contrary to the covenants and obligations of the Pact of Paris of August 27, 1928, to which Treaty both China and Japan, as well as the United States, are parties.

State that an identical note is being sent to the Chinese government.

COMMENT

Mr. Stimson has said his piece. . . . [We hope] that the State Department will let it rest with that and quit sticking pins into Japan.

Editorial in the Chicago (Ill.) *Tribune*, January 9, 1932.

. . . if we avoid participation in the conflict we can thank our lucky stars and the ministrations of a Kind Providence, for an internationally minded Mr. Hoover and his spotlight seeking Secretary of State have done their utmost to place this nation in its present predicament.

Editorial in the New York *American*, October 15, 1931.

When Frank B. Kellogg was Secretary of State he used to be known as Meddlesome Mattie. In justice to Mr. Kellogg it must now be admitted that never in his palmiest days did he equal Secretary of State Henry L. Stimson as a giver of advice.

Editorial in the New York *Daily News*, January 8, 1932.

The American people don't give a hoot in a rain barrel who controls North China.

Editorial in the Philadelphia (Pa.) *Record*, February 3, 1932.

60. SEPTEMBER 23, 1932

Franklin Delano Roosevelt's Commonwealth Club Address

In 1932, the Democratic party attempted to convince the nation that it needed a change from the rugged individualism of Herbert Hoover. Though Roosevelt was vague concerning the changes he proposed to make, the mood of the country was very receptive to his appeal. Only those who were already opposed to his candidacy seemed to be aware of his compromising language or of the difficulties of fulfilling his economic program. Roosevelt made the clearest expression of his political and economic views of the campaign before the Commonwealth Club at San Francisco on September 23, 1932. Among his close advisers, there was much division over what he should say to the Commonwealth Club. General Hugh Johnson and Louis Howe wanted him to speak out as a conservative on government economy. But Adolph Berle, Rexford Tugwell, and Felix Frankfurter drafted a memorandum affirming Roosevelt's political liberalism

SAMUEL I. ROSENMAN, ed., *The Public Papers and Addresses of Franklin D. Roosevelt* (New York: Random House, Inc., 1938), I, 742–50. Reprinted by permission of Random House, Inc.

which became the basis for the speech printed below. To achieve the goals of a liberal society, Roosevelt told his audience that the government must police irresponsible economic power. Other than to state a general philosophy, he refused to put forth specific plans for the New Deal during his campaign.

I count it a privilege to be invited to address the Commonwealth Club. It has stood in the life of this city and State, and it is perhaps accurate to add, the Nation, as a group of citizen leaders interested in fundamental problems of Government, and chiefly concerned with achievement of progress in Government through nonpartisan means. The privilege of addressing you, therefore, in the heat of a political campaign, is great. I want to respond to your courtesy in terms consistent with your policy.

... I want to speak not of politics but of Government. I want to speak not of parties, but of universal principles. They are not political, except in that larger sense in which a great American once expressed a definition of politics, that nothing in all of human life is foreign to the science of politics.

I do want to give you, however, a recollection of a long life spent for a large part in public office. Some of my conclusions and observations have been deeply accentuated in these past few weeks. I have traveled far—from Albany to the Golden Gate. I have seen many people, and heard many things, and to-day, when in a sense my journey has reached the half-way mark, I am glad of the opportunity to discuss with you what it all means to me.

Sometimes, my friends, particularly in years such as these, the hand of discouragement falls upon us. It seems that things are in a rut, fixed, settled, that the world has grown old and tired and very much out of joint. This is the mood of depression, of dire and weary depression.

But then we look around us in America, and everything tells us that we are wrong. America is new. It is in the process of change and development. It has the great potentialities of youth, and particularly is this true of the great West, and of this coast, and of California.

I would not have you feel that I regard this as in any sense a new community. I have traveled in many parts of the world, but never have I felt the arresting thought of the change and development more than here, where the old, mystic East would seem to be near to us, where the currents of life and thought and commerce of the whole world meet us. This factor alone is sufficient to cause man to stop and think of the deeper meaning of things, when he stands in this community.

But more than that, I appreciate that the membership of this club consists of men who are thinking in terms beyond the immediate present, beyond their own immediate tasks, beyond their own individual interests. I want to invite you, therefore, to consider with me in the large, some of the relationships of Gov-ernment and economic life that go deeply into our daily lives, our happiness, our future and our security.

The issue of Government has always been whether individual men and women will have to serve some system of Government or economics, or whether a system of Government and economics exists to serve individual men and women. This question has persistently dominated the discussion of Government for many generations. On questions relating to these things men have differed, and for time immemorial it is probable that honest men will continue to differ.

The final word belongs to no man; yet we can still believe in change and in progress. Democracy, as a dear old friend of mine in Indiana, Meredith Nicholson, has called it, is a quest, a never-ending seeking for better things, and in the seeking for these things and the striving for them, there are many roads to follow. But, if we map the course of these roads, we find that there are only two general directions.

When we look about us, we are likely to forget how hard people have worked to win the privilege of Government. The growth of the national Governments of Europe was a struggle for the development of a centralized force in the Nation, strong enough to impose peace upon ruling barons. In many instances the victory of the central Government, the creation of a strong central Government, was a haven of refuge to the individual. The people preferred the master far away to the exploitation and cruelty of the smaller master near at hand.

But the creators of national Government were perforce ruthless men. They were often cruel in their methods, but they did strive steadily toward something that society needed and very much wanted, a strong central State able to keep the peace, to stamp out civil war, to put the unruly nobleman in his place, and to permit the bulk of individuals to live safely. The man of ruthless force had his place in developing a pioneer country, just as he did in fixing the power of the central Government in the development of Nations. Society paid him well for his services and its development. When the development among the Nations of Europe, however, had been completed, ambition and ruthlessness, having served their term, tended to overstep their mark.

There came a growing feeling that Government was conducted for the benefit of a few who thrived unduly at the expense of all. The people sought a balancing—a limiting force. There came gradually, through town councils, trade guilds, national parliaments, by constitution and by popular participation and control, limitations on arbitrary power.

Another factor that tended to limit the power of those who ruled, was the rise of the ethical conception that a ruler bore a responsibility for the welfare of his subjects.

The American colonies were born in this struggle. The American Revolution was a turning point in it. After the Revolution the struggle continued and shaped itself in the public life of the country. There were those who because they had seen the confusion which attended the years of war for American independence surrendered to the belief that popular Government was essentially dangerous and essentially unworkable. They were honest people, my friends, and we cannot deny that their experience had warranted some measure of fear. The most brilliant, honest and able exponent of this point of view was Hamilton. He was too impatient of slow-moving methods. Fundamentally he believed that the safety of the republic lay in the autocratic strength of its Government, that the destiny of individuals was to serve that Government, and that fundamentally a great and strong group of central institutions, guided by a small group of able and public spirited citizens, could best direct all Government.

But Mr. Jefferson, in the summer of 1776, after drafting the Declaration of Independence turned his mind to the same problem and took a different view. He did not deceive himself with outward forms. Government to him was a means to an end, not an end in itself; it might be either a refuge and a help or a threat and a danger, depending on the circumstances. We find him carefully analyzing the society for which he was to organize a Government. "We have no paupers. The great mass of our population is of laborers, our rich who cannot live without labor, either manual or professional, being few and of moderate wealth. Most of the laboring class possess property, cultivate their own lands, have families and from the demand for their labor, are enabled to exact from the rich and the competent such prices as enable them to feed abundantly, clothe above mere decency, to labor moderately and raise their families."

These people, he considered, had two sets of rights, those of "personal competency" and those involved in acquiring and possessing property. By "personal competency" he meant the right of free thinking, freedom of forming and expressing opinions, and freedom of personal living, each man according to his own lights. To insure the first set of rights, a Government must so order its functions as not to interfere with the individual. But even Jefferson realized that the exercise of the property rights might so interfere with the rights of the individual that the Government, without whose assistance the property rights could not exist, must intervene, not to destroy individualism, but to protect it.

You are familiar with the great political duel which followed; and how Hamilton, and his friends, building toward a dominant centralized power were at length defeated in the great election of 1800, by Mr. Jefferson's party. Out of that duel came the two parties, Republican and Democratic, as we know them today.

So began, in American political life, the new day, the day of the individual against the system, the day in which individualism was made the great watchword of American life. The happiest of economic conditions made that day long and splendid. On the Western frontier, land was substantially free. No one, who did not shirk the task of earning a living, was entirely without opportunity to do so. Depressions could, and did, come and go; but they could not alter the fundamental fact that most of the people lived partly by selling their labor and partly by extracting their livelihood from the soil, so that starvation and dislocation were practically impossible. At the very worst there was always the possibility of climbing into a covered wagon and moving west where the untilled prairies afforded a haven for men to whom the East did not provide a place. So great were our natural resources that we could offer this relief not only to our own people, but to the distressed of all the world; we could invite immigration from Europe, and welcome it with open arms. Traditionally, when a depression came a new section of land was opened in the West; and even our temporary misfortune served our manifest destiny.

It was in the middle of the nineteenth century that a new force was released and a new dream created. The force was what is called the industrial revolution, the advance of steam and machinery and the rise of the forerunners of the modern industrial plant. The dream was the dream of an economic machine, able to raise the standard of living for everyone; to bring luxury within the reach of the humblest; to annihilate distance by steam power and later by electricity, and to release everyone from the drudgery of the heaviest manual toil. It was to be expected that this would necessarily affect Government. Heretofore, Government had merely been called upon to produce conditions within which people could live happily, labor peacefully, and rest secure. Now it was called upon to aid in the consummation of this new dream. There was, however, a shadow over the dream. To be made real, it required use of the talents of men of tremendous will and tremendous ambition, since by no other force could the problems of financing and engineering and new developments be brought to a consummation.

So manifest were the advantages of the machine age, however, that the United States fearlessly, cheerfully, and, I think, rightly, accepted the bitter with the sweet. It was thought that no price was too high to pay for the advantages which we could draw from a finished industrial system. The history of the last half century is accordingly in large measure a history of a group of financial Titans, whose methods were not scrutinized with too much care, and who were honored in proportion as they produced the results, irrespective of the means they used. The financiers who pushed the railroads to the Pacific were always ruthless, often wasteful, and frequently corrupt; but they did build railroads, and we have them today. It has been estimated that the American investor paid for the American railway system more than three times over in the process; but despite this fact the net advantage was to the United States. As long as we had free land; as long as population was growing by leaps and bounds; as long as our industrial plants were insufficient to supply our own needs, society chose to give the ambitious man free play and unlimited reward provided only that he produced the economic plant so much desired.

During this period of expansion, there was equal opportunity for all and the business of Government was not to interfere but to assist in the development of industry. This was done at the request of business men themselves. The tariff was originally imposed for the purpose of "fostering our infant industry," a phrase I think the older among you will remember as a political issue not so long ago. The railroads were subsidized, sometimes by grants of money, oftener by grants of land; some of the most valuable oil lands in the United States were granted to assist the financing of the railroad which pushed through the Southwest. A nascent merchant marine was assisted by grants of money, or by mail subsidies, so that our steam shipping might ply the seven seas. Some of my friends tell me that they do not want the Government in business. With this I agree; but I wonder whether they realize the implications of the past. For while it has been American doctrine that the Government must not go into business in competition with private enterprises, still it has been traditional, particularly in Republican administrations, for business urgently to ask the Government to put at private disposal all kinds of Government assistance. The same man who tells you that he does not want to see the Government interfere in business—and he means it, and has plenty of good reasons for saying so—is the first to go to Washington and ask the Government for a prohibitory tariff on his product. When things get just bad enough, as they did two years ago, he will go with equal speed to the United States Government and ask for a loan; and the Reconstruction Finance Corporation is the outcome of it. Each group has sought protection from the Government for its own special interests, without realizing that the function of Government must be to favor no small group at the expense of its duty to protect the rights of personal freedom and of private property of all its citizens.

In retrospect we can now see that the turn of the tide came with the turn of the century. We were reaching our last frontier; there was no more free land and our industrial combinations had become great uncontrolled and irresponsible units of power within the State. Clear-sighted men saw with fear the danger that

opportunity would no longer be equal; that the growing corporation, like the feudal baron of old, might threaten the economic freedom of individuals to earn a living. In that hour, our anti-trust laws were born. The cry was raised against the great corporations. Theodore Roosevelt, the first great Republican Progressive, fought a Presidential campaign on the issue of "trust busting" and talked freely about malefactors of great wealth. If the Government had a policy it was rather to turn the clock back, to destroy the large combinations and to return to the time when every man owned his individual small business.

This was impossible; Theodore Roosevelt, abandoning the idea of "trust busting," was forced to work out a difference between "good" trusts and "bad" trusts. The Supreme Court set forth the famous "rule of reason" by which it seems to have meant that a concentration of industrial power was permissible if the method by which it got its power, and the use it made of that power, were reasonable.

Woodrow Wilson, elected in 1912, saw the situation more clearly. Where Jefferson had feared the encroachment of political power on the lives of individuals, Wilson knew that the new power was financial. He saw, in the highly centralized economic system, the despot of the twentieth century, on whom great masses of individuals relied for their safety and their livelihood, and whose irresponsibility and greed (if they were not controlled) would reduce them to starvation and penury. The concentration of financial power had not proceeded so far in 1912 as it has today; but it had grown far enough for Mr. Wilson to realize fully its implications. It is interesting, now, to read his speeches. What is called "radical" today (and I have reason to know whereof I speak) is mild compared to the campaign of Mr. Wilson. "No man can deny," he said, "that the lines of endeavor have more and more narrowed and stiffened; no man who knows anything about the development of industry in this country can have failed to observe that the larger kinds of credit are more and more difficult to obtain unless you obtain them upon terms of uniting your efforts with those who already control the industry of the country, and nobody can fail to observe that every man who tries to set himself up in competition with any process of manufacture which has taken place under the control 'of large combinations of capital will presently find himself either squeezed out or obliged to sell and allow himself to be absorbed." Had there been no World War—had Mr. Wilson been able to devote eight years to domestic instead of to international affairs—we might have had a wholly different situation at the present time. However, the then distant roar of European cannon, growing ever louder, forced him to abandon the study of this issue. The problem he saw so clearly is left with us as a legacy; and no one of us on either side of the political controversy can deny that it is a matter of grave concern to the Government.

A glance at the situation today only too clearly indicates that equality of opportunity as we have known it no longer exists. Our industrial plant is built; the problem just now is whether under existing conditions it is not overbuilt. Our last frontier has long since been reached, and there is practically no more free land. More than half of our people do not live on the farms or on lands and cannot derive a living by cultivating their own property. There is no safety valve in the form of a Western prairie to which those throw out of work by the Eastern economic machines can go for a new start. We are not able to invite the immigration from Europe to share our endless plenty. We are now providing a drab living for our own people.

Our system of constantly rising tariffs has at last reacted against us to the point of closing our Canadian frontier on the north, our European markets on the east, many of our Latin-American markets to the south, and a goodly proportion of our Pacific markets on the west, through the retaliatory tariffs of those countries. It has forced many of our great industrial institutions which exported their surplus production to such countries, within the tariff walls. This has resulted in the reduction of the operation of their American plants, and opportunity for employment.

Just as freedom to farm has ceased, so also the opportunity in business has narrowed. It still is true that men can start small enterprises, trusting to native shrewdness and ability to keep abreast of competitors; but area after area has been preempted altogether by the great corporations, and even in the fields which still have no great concerns, the small man starts under a handicap. The unfeeling statistics of the past three decades show that the independent business man is running a losing race. Perhaps he is forced to the wall; perhaps he cannot command credit; perhaps he is "squeezed out," in Mr. Wilson's words, by highly organized corporate competitors, as your corner grocery man can tell you. Recently a careful study was made of the concentration of business in the United States. It showed that our economic life was dominated by some six hundred odd corporations who controlled two-thirds of American industry. Ten million small business men divided the other third. More striking still, it appeared that if the process of concentration goes on at the same rate, at the end of the century we shall have all American industry controlled by a dozen corporations, and run by perhaps a hundred men. Put plainly, we are steering a steady course toward economic oligarchy, if we are not there already.

Clearly, all this calls for a re-appraisal of values. A mere builder of more industrial plants, a creator of more railroad systems, an organizer of more corporations, is as likely to be a danger as a help. The day of the great promoter or the financial Titan, to whom we granted anything if only he would build, or develop, is over. Our task now is not discovery or exploitation of natural resources, or necessarily producing more goods. It is the soberer, less dramatic business of administering resources and plants already in hand, of seeking to reestablish foreign markets for our surplus production, of meeting the problem of underconsumption, of adjusting production to consumption, of distributing wealth and products more equitably, of adapting existing economic organizations to the service of the people. The day of enlightened administration has come.

Just as in older times the central Government was first a haven of refuge, and then a threat, so now in a closer economic system the central and ambitious financial unit is no longer a servant of national desire, but a danger. I would draw the parallel one step farther. We did not think because national Government had become a threat in the 18th century that therefore we should abandon the principle of national Government. Nor today should we abandon the principle of strong economic units called corporations, merely because their power is susceptible of easy abuse. In other times we dealt with the problem of an unduly ambitious central Government by modifying it gradually into a constitutional democratic Government. So today we are modifying and controlling our economic units.

As I see it, the task of Government in its relation to business is to assist the development of an economic declaration of rights, an economic constitutional order. This is the common task of statesman and business man. It is the minimum requirement of a more permanently safe order of things.

Happily, the times indicate that to create such an order not only is the proper policy of Government, but it is the only line of safety for our economic structures as well. We know, now, that these economic units cannot exist unless prosperity is uniform, that is, unless purchasing power is well distributed throughout every group in the Nation. That is why even the most selfish of corporations for its own interest would be glad to see wages restored and unemployment ended and to bring the Western farmer back to his accustomed level of prosperity and to assure a permanent safety to both groups. That is why some enlightened industries themselves endeavor to limit the freedom of action of each man and business group within the industry in the common interest of all; why business men everywhere are asking a form of organization which will bring the scheme of things into balance, even though it may in some measure qualify the freedom of action of individual units within the business.

The exposition need not further be elaborated. It is brief and incomplete, but you will be able to expand it in terms of your own business or occupation without difficulty. I think everyone who has actually entered the economic struggle—which means everyone who was not born to safe wealth—knows in his own experience and his own life that we have now to apply the earlier concepts of American Government to the conditions of today.

The Declaration of Independence discusses the problem of Government in terms of a contract. Government is a relation of give and take, a contract, perforce, if we would follow the thinking out of which it grew. Under such a contract rulers were accorded power, and the people consented to that power on consideration that they be accorded certain rights. The task of statesmanship has always been the re-definition of these rights in terms of a changing and growing social order. New conditions impose new requirements upon Government and those who conduct Government.

I held, for example, in proceedings before me as Governor, the purpose of which was the removal of the Sheriff of New York, that under modern conditions it was not enough for a public official merely to evade the legal terms of official wrongdoing. He owed a positive duty as well. I said in substance that if he had acquired large sums of money, he was when accused required to explain the sources of such wealth. To that extent this wealth was colored with a public interest. I said that in financial matters, public servants should, even beyond private citizens, be held to a stern and uncompromising rectitude.

I feel that we are coming to a view through the drift of our legislation and our public thinking in the past quarter century that private economic power is, to enlarge an old phrase, a public trust as well. I hold that continued enjoyment of that power by any individual or group must depend upon the fulfillment of that trust. The men who have reached the summit of American business life know this best; happily, many of these urge the binding quality of this greater social contract.

The terms of that contract are as old as the Republic, and as new as the new economic order.

Every man has a right to life; and this means that he has also a right to make a comfortable living. He may by sloth or crime decline to exercise that right; but it may not be denied him. We have no actual famine or dearth; our industrial and agricultural mechanism can produce enough and to spare. Our Government formal and informal, political and economic, owes to everyone an avenue to possess himself of a portion of that plenty sufficient for his needs, through his own work.

Every man has a right to his own property; which means a right to be as-

sured, to the fullest extent attainable, in the safety of his savings. By no other means can men carry the burdens of those parts of life which, in the nature of things, afford no chance of labor; childhood, sickness, old age. In all thought of property, this right is paramount; all other property rights must yield to it. If, in accord with this principle, we must restrict the operations of the speculator, the manipulator, even the financier, I believe we must accept the restriction as needful, not to hamper individualism but to protect it.

These two requirements must be satisfied, in the main, by the individuals who claim and hold control of the great industrial and financial combinations which dominate so large a part of our industrial life. They have undertaken to be, not business men, but princes of property. I am not prepared to say that the system which produces them is wrong. I am very clear that they must fearlessly and competently assume the responsibility which goes with the power. So many enlightened business men know this that the statement would be little more than a platitude, were it not for an added implication.

This implication is, briefly, that the responsible heads of finance and industry instead of acting each for himself, must work together to achieve the common end. They must, where necessary, sacrifice this or that private advantage; and in reciprocal self-denial must seek a general advantage. It is here that formal Government—political Government, if you choose—comes in. Whenever in the pursuit of this objective the lone wolf, the unethical competitor, the reckless promoter, the Ishmael or Insull whose hand is against every man's, declines to join in achieving an end recognized as being for the public welfare, and threatens to drag the industry back to a state of anarchy, the Government may properly be asked to apply restraint. Likewise, should the group ever use its collective power contrary to the public welfare, the Government must be swift to enter and protect the public interest.

The Government should assume the function of economic regulation only as a last resort, to be tried only when private initiative, inspired by high responsibility, with such assistance and balance as Government can give, has finally failed. As yet there has been no final failure, because there has been no attempt; and I decline to assume that this Nation is unable to meet the situation.

The final term of the high contract was for liberty and the pursuit of happiness. We have learned a great deal of both in the past century. We know that individual liberty and individual happiness mean nothing unless both are ordered in the sense that one man's meat is not another man's poison. We know that the old "rights of personal competency," the right to read, to think, to speak, to choose and live a mode of life, must be respected at all hazards. We know that liberty to do anything which deprives others of those elemental rights is outside the protection of any compact; and that Government in this regard is the maintenance of a balance, within which every individual may have a place if he will take it; in which every individual may find safety if he wishes it; in which every individual may attain such power as his ability permits, consistent with his assuming the accompanying responsibility.

All this is a long, slow talk. Nothing is more striking than the simple innocence of the men who insist, whenever an objective is present, on the prompt production of a patent scheme guaranteed to produce a result. Human endeavor is not so simple as that. Government includes the art of formulating a policy, and using the political technique to attain so much of that policy as will receive general support; persuading, leading, sacrificing, teaching always, because the greatest duty of a statesman is to educate. But in the matters of which I have spoken, we are learning rapidly, in a severe school. The lessons so learned must not be forgotten, even in the mental lethargy of a speculative upturn. We must build toward the time when a major depression cannot occur again; and if this means sacrificing the easy profits of inflationist booms, then let them go; and good riddance.

Faith in America, faith in our tradition of personal responsibility, faith in our institutions, faith in ourselves demand that we recognize the new terms of the old social contract. We shall fulfill them, as we fulfilled the obligation of the apparent Utopia which Jefferson imagined for us in 1776, and which Jefferson, Roosevelt and Wilson sought to bring to realization. We must do so, lest a rising tide of misery, engendered by our common failure, engulf us all. But failure is not an American habit; and in the strength of great hope we must all shoulder our common load.

COMMENT

Franklin D. Roosevelt is no crusader. He is no tribune of the people. He is no enemy of entrenched privilege. He is a pleasant man who, without any important qualifications for the office, would very much like to be President.

Journalist Walter Lippmann in New York *Herald Tribune*, January 8, 1932.

Roosevelt is not sufficiently liberal to attract and hold Bryan's following. As a rabble-rouser he is badly infested by weasel words. He has a charming sense of balance, and when he seems to be going well as a progressive or a liberal he checks himself with a string of 'althoughs,' 'buts,' 'on the other hands' and

'on the contraries' which takes the heart out of Western liberals. . . . The agrarian
West is ready for a rabble-rouser. Roosevelt does not fill the bill. . . .

Editorial in the Emporia (Kan.) *Gazette*, April 30, 1932.

All through the 1932 campaign, something was in the air far more sinister than
even the miasmic climate of depression or a political campaign. I was convinced
that Roosevelt and some members of his Brain Trust were proposing to introduce
parts of the collectivism of Europe into the United States under their oft-repeated
phrase "planned economy." That was an expression common to all collectivist
systems. Paraded as liberalism, it had all the tactics and strategies of its European
counterparts.

Former President Herbert Hoover in *Memoirs of Herbert Hoover* (New York: The
Macmillan Company, 1952), III, 329.

61. MARCH 4, 1933

Franklin Delano Roosevelt's First Inaugural Address

By 1933, the nation's economic founda-
tions appeared to be in grave danger of
collapsing. All across the nation, tired
and hungry men congregated on the
edges of cities in cardboard shacks
called "Hoovervilles." Thousands of
men roamed the country in search of
employment. Food riots were common,
while angry veterans picketed the Capi-
tol. In the Middle West, farmers beat
and threatened to hang judges who fore-
closed mortgages. Early in 1933, the
entire nation looked to the government
in Washington for some sign of hope.
Taking up the challenge, Franklin
Roosevelt's First Inaugural Address in-
spired in a desperate people more cour-
age and confidence than any other
speech of his career. Though the Ameri-
can people knew little about Roosevelt,

SAMUEL I. ROSENMAN, ed., *The Public
Papers and Addresses of Franklin D. Roosevelt,*
(New York: Random House, Inc., 1938), II,
11–16. Reprinted by permission of Radnom
House, Inc.

his address convinced them that it would
not be necessary to change their funda-
mental way of life. The people were cer-
tain that here was a man who knew and
understood what they wanted and that
he had the courage to fight for economic
and social justice.

I am certain that my fellow Americans
expect that on my induction into the
Presidency I will address them with a
candor and a decision which the present
situation of our Nation impels. This is
preeminently the time to speak the truth,
the whole truth, frankly and boldly. Nor
need we shrink from honestly facing conditions in our country today. This great
Nation will endure as it has endured,
will revive and will prosper. So, first of
all, let me assert my firm belief that the
only thing we have to fear is fear itself
—nameless, unreasoning, unjustified
terror which paralyzes needed efforts to
convert retreat into advance. In every

dark hour of our national life a leadership of frankness and vigor has met with that understanding and support of the people themselves which is essential to victory. I am convinced that you will again give that support to leadership in these critical days.

In such a spirit on my part and on yours we face our common difficulties. They concern, thank God, only material things. Values have shrunken to fantastic levels; taxes have risen; our ability to pay has fallen; government of all kinds is faced by serious curtailment of income; the means of exchange are frozen in the currents of trade; the withered leaves of industrial enterprise lie on every side; farmers find no markets for their produce; the savings of many years in thousands of families are gone.

More important, a host of unemployed citizens face the grim problem of existence, and an equally great number toil with little return. Only a foolish optimist can deny the dark realities of the moment.

Yet our distress comes from no failure of substance. We are stricken by no plague of locusts. Compared with the perils which our forefathers conquered because they believed and were not afraid, we have still much to be thankful for. Nature still offers her bounty and human efforts have multiplied it. Plenty is at our doorstep, but a generous use of it languishes in the very sight of the supply. Primarily this is because rulers of the exchange of mankind's goods have failed through their own stubbornness and their own incompetence, have admitted their failure, and have abdicated. Practices of the unscrupulous money changers stand indicted in the court of public opinion, rejected by the hearts and minds of men.

True they have tried, but their efforts have been cast in the pattern of an outworn tradition. Faced by failure of credit they have proposed only the lending of more money. Stripped of the lure of profit by which to induce our people to follow their false leadership, they have resorted to exhortations, pleading tearfully for restored confidence. They know only the rules of a generation of self-seekers. They have no vision, and when there is no vision the people perish.

The money changers have fled from their high seats in the temple of our civilization. We may now restore that temple to the ancient truths. The measure of the restoration lies in the extent to which we apply social values more noble than mere monetary profit.

Happiness lies not in the mere possession of money; it lies in the joy of achievement, in the thrill of creative effort. The joy and moral stimulation of work no longer must be forgotten in the mad chase of evanescent profits. These dark days will be worth all they cost us if they teach us that our true destiny is not to be ministered unto but to minister to ourselves and to our fellow men.

Recognition of the falsity of material wealth as the standard of success goes hand in hand with the abandonment of the false belief that public office and high political position are to be valued only by the standards of pride of place and personal profit; and there must be an end to a conduct in banking and in business which too often has given to a sacred trust the likeness of callous and selfish wrongdoing. Small wonder that confidence languishes, for it thrives only on honesty, on honor, on the sacredness of obligations, on faithful protection, on unselfish performance; without them it cannot live.

Restoration calls, however, not for changes in ethics alone. This Nation asks for action, and action now.

Our greatest primary task is to put people to work. This is no unsolvable problem if we face it wisely and courageously. It can be accomplished in part by direct recruiting by the Government itself, treating the task as we would treat the emergency of a war, but at the same time, through this employment, accomplishing greatly needed projects to stimulate and reorganize the use of our natural resources.

Hand in hand with this we must frankly recognize the overbalance of population in our industrial centers and, by engaging on a national scale in a redistribution, endeavor to provide a better use of the land for those best fitted for the land. The task can be helped by definite efforts to raise the values of agricultural products and with this the power to purchase the output of our cities. It can be helped by preventing realistically the tragedy of the growing loss through foreclosure of our small homes and our farms. It can be helped by insistence that the Federal, State, and local governments act forthwith on the demand that their cost be drastically reduced. It can be helped by the unifying of relief activities which today are often scattered, uneconomical, and unequal. It can be helped by national planning for and supervision of all forms of transportation and of communications and other utilities which have a definitely public character. There are many ways in which it can be helped, but it can never be helped merely by talking about it. We must act and act quickly.

Finally, in our progress toward a resumption of work we require two safeguards against a return of the evils of the old order: there must be a strict supervision of all banking and credits and investments, so that there will be an end to speculation with other people's money; and there must be provision for an adequate but sound currency.

These are the lines of attack. I shall presently urge upon a new Congress, in special session, detailed measures for their fulfillment, and I shall seek the immediate assistance of the several States.

Through this program of action we address ourselves to putting our own national house in order and making income balance outgo. Our international trade relations, though vastly important, are in point of time and necessity secondary to the establishment of a sound national economy. I favor as a practical policy the putting of first things first. I shall spare no effort to restore world trade by international economic readjustment, but the emergency at home cannot wait on that accomplishment.

The basic thought that guides these specific means of national recovery is not narrowly nationalistic. It is the insistence, as a first consideration, upon the interdependence of the various elements in and parts of the United States—a recognition of the old and permanently important manifestation of the American spirit of the pioneer. It is the way to recovery. It is the immediate way. It is the strongest assurance that the recovery will endure.

In the field of world policy I would dedicate this Nation to the policy of the good neighbor—the neighbor who resolutely respects himself and, because he does so, respects the rights of others—the neighbor who respects his obligations and respects the sanctity of his agreements in and with a world of neighbors.

If I read the temper of our people correctly, we now realize as we have never realized before our interdependence on each other; that we cannot merely take but we must give as well; that if we are to go forward, we must move as a trained and loyal army willing to sacrifice for the good of a common discipline, because without such discipline no progress is made, no leadership becomes effective. We are, I know, ready and willing to submit our lives and property to such discipline, because it makes possible a leadership which aims at a larger good. This I propose to offer, pledging that the larger purposes will bind upon us all as a sacred obligation with a unity of duty hitherto evoked only in time of armed strife.

With this pledge taken, I assume unhesitatingly the leadership of this great army of our people dedicated to a disciplined attack upon our common problems.

Action in this image and to this end is feasible under the form of government which we have inherited from our ancestors. Our Constitution is so simple and practical that it is possible always to meet extraordnary needs by changes in emphasis and arrangement without loss of essential form. That is why our constitutional system has proved itself the most superbly enduring political mechanism the modern world has produced. It has met every stress of vast expansion of territory, of foreign wars, of bitter internal strife, of world relations

It is to be hoped that the normal balance of Executive and legislative authority may be wholly adequate to meet the unprecedented task before us. But it may be that an unprecedented demand and need for undelayed action may call for temporary departure from that normal balance of public procedure.

I am prepared under my constitutional duty to recommend the measures that a stricken Nation in the midst of a stricken world may require. These measures, or such other measures as the Congress may build out of its experience and wisdom, I shall seek, with-

in my constitutional authority, to bring to speedy adoption.

But in the event that the Congress shall fail to take one of these two courses, and in the event that the national emergency is still critical, I shall not evade the clear course of duty that will then confront me. I shall ask the Congress for the one remaing instrument to meet the crisis—broad Executive power to wage a war against the emergency, as great as the power that would be given to me if we were in fact invaded by a foreign foe.

For the trust reposed in me I will return the courage and the devotion that befit the time. I can do no less.

We face the arduous days that lie before us in the warm courage of national unity; with the clear consciousness of seeking old and precious moral values; with the clean satisfaction that comes from the stern performance of duty by old and young alike. We aim at the assurance of a rounded and permanent national life.

We do not distrust the future of essential democracy. The people of the United States have not failed. In their need they have registered a mandate that they want direct, vigorous action. They have asked for discipline and direction under leadership. They have made me the present instrument of their wishes. In the spirit of the gift I take it.

In this dedication of a Nation we humbly ask the blessing of God. May He protect each and every one of us. May He guide me in the days to come.

COMMENT

A revolution was started by the New Deal—not a revolution in the violent, turbulent sense, but a revolution nevertheless.

Louis M. Hacker, historian, in *The Shaping of the American Tradition* (New York: Columbia University Press, 1947), p. 1125.

. . . [the New Deal] has offered us no comprehensible picture of a future in which we can believe. We cannot believe that this vague eleemosynary humanitarianism, coupled with ruthless aggrandizement by politicians, is a picture of a new heaven and a new earth.

Dorothy Thompson, journalist, in *Ladies Home Journal*, LIV (September, 1937), 13.

62.

David E. Lilienthal on the Tennessee Valley Authority

Throughout the 1920's, Progressives in Congress fought for federal construction and regulation of dams to ensure flood control and electrical power for the Tennessee Valley. Blocked by Presidents Coolidge and Hoover, the Progressives bided their time and enlarged their program. On April 10, 1933, President Roosevelt responded by asking Congress to create "a corporation clothed with the power of the Government but possessed of the flexibility and initiative of private enterprise," which would plan for the development of the resources of the Tennessee Valley.

Congress acted by establishing the Tennessee Valley Authority which was to manufacture and distribute electric power and to undertake a great variety of conservation activities, including flood control, forestation, and the prevention of soil erosion. The TVA has subsequently acted as a yardstick in guiding public utilities, as it provided at reasonable rates the construction of transmission lines for villages and farms without electricity.

Though the TVA brought about widespread improvements in the living conditions of the people of the Ten-

DAVID E. LILIENTHAL, *T.V.A.; Democracy on the March* (New York: Harper & Brothers, 1944), pp. 34–40. Reprinted by permission of Harper & Brothers.

nessee Valley, many residents of the area failed to appreciate its contributions to the general welfare of the region. The TVA has continued to expand and has played an important role in the industrial development of the Tennessee Valley. Below, David E. Lilienthal, former chairman of the TVA, discusses its impact on the Tennessee Valley.

The story thus far as I have recounted it has been chiefly one of physical changes in the Tennessee Valley. But what has been the yield to the people—to those who live in the region, and to the people of the country as a whole who advanced most of the funds?

First of all the level of income of the region's people is definitely rising. By 1940, and before the effect of war expansion, the per capita income had increased in the seven valley states 73 per cent over the level of 1933; while for the same period the increase in the country as a whole was only 56 per cent. The same trend is reflected in income payment statistics. Between 1933 and 1943 the seven valley states show an increase in per capita income payments which substantially exceeds the index for the country as a whole. The rate of increase in each of the seven valley states is above the index for the country. The same is true of total income payments: the rate of increase for all the valley states, and for each of the states, exceeds the national index of rate of increase. Bank deposits increased 76 per cent between 1933 and 1939 compared to 49 per cent in the country, and retail sales increased 81 per cent compared to 71 per cent for the country.

All the available figures—and the evidence of one's eyes—show that our income level is rising. But the Tennessee Valley is still a region of low income, about half the United States average.

What has happened to the businesses of the people? Farming is the most important private enterprise in this region; that business, as I have indicated, is moving upward as the fruitfulness and stability of the land increase. What of business in the industrial sense? That too is developing, and at a rapid rate. Even before the war the valley saw the addition or expansion of several large industries devoted to the basic materials of modern industry, such as aluminum, ferro-silicon, heavy chemicals; these included two of the largest phosphatic chemical works in the country.

The war has added mightily to the list. For reasons of security little of this expansion can now be told. But when the full story of a once industrially laggard valley's part in production for war can be revealed, it will rank as one of the miracles of American enterprise, the kind of miracle that is marvelled at when it occurs across the seas, rarely comprehended close at home.

At least as important as these heavy industries is the rise of new light industries and the expansion of plants that existed before 1933. For industries added since 1933 range from those for the processing of frozen foods and the production of cheese to the manufacture of aircraft and mattresses, bottle washers, stoves, flour, inlaid wood, barrel heads and staves, electric water heaters, furniture, hats and shoes, pencils, carbon electrodes, boats, horse collars, ground

mica, oxygen and acetylene, metal dies, ax handles, and barites. Many new small industries are the immediate result of opportunities for profit provided by the chain of lakes that make the Tennessee River a new arc of beauty through the countryside.

We have a long way yet to go in the valley. There are many factories yet to be built, in an area with such great potential wealth and with less than its economic share of the nation's industry and manufacturing. There are many new jobs to be created by the laboratories and businessmen out of the region's dormant resources. There are millions of acres yet to be restored to full productiveness. When TVA began its work in 1933, of the total of eight and a half million acres of cultivated land in the valley, erosion in varying degrees had damaged seven million acres. On more than a million acres the top soil had entirely disappeared. There are more trees to plant, houses, schools, roads, and hospitals to build. Many new skills have been learned —among farmers, industrial workers in the new factories, the ten of thousands of men and women who have added to their skills in the course of their work for the TVA—but lack of training is still a heavy handicap to be overcome. The task is barely begun—but the Tennessee Valley is on its way.

Democracy is on the march in this valley. Not only because of the physical changes or the figures of increased income and economic activity. My faith in this as a region with a great future is built most of all upon what I have come to know of the great capacities and the spirit of the people. The notion that has been expressed that the region's problem, as one commentator has put it, is one of "human salvage" completely misses the mark. The human resources of this valley are its greatest asset and advantage. The people have seized upon these modern tools of opportunity and have raised up their own leadership. They have shown an ability to hold themselves to tough assignments with a singleness of purpose and a resourcefulness in doing much with little that will be difficult to match anywhere in the country.

This advent of opportunity has brought with it the rise of a confident, sure, chesty feeling. The evidence is everywhere. It is epitomized in an editorial in the Decatur, Alabama, *Daily* for May 18, 1943. The editor, a community leader, candidly relates the doleful past and contrasts it with the optimistic and fruitful present. Seven years ago Decatur was in great trouble; today it is one of the most enterprising and promising small cities in the interior United States. "What has happened in these seven years?" he asks, and then he answers:

We can write of great dams . . . of the building of home-grown industry and of electricity at last coming to the farms of thousands of farm people in the Valley. *Yet the significant advance has been made in the thinking of a people.* They are no longer afraid. *They have caught the vision of their own powers.* They can stand now and talk out in meeting and say that if industry doesn't come into the Valley from other sections, then we'll build our own industry. This they are doing today.

These changes of a decade were not, of course, wrought by TVA alone; in point of fact, the very essence of TVA's method in the undertaking, as I shall later indicate in detail, was at every hand to minimize what it was to do directly and to encourage and stimulate the broadest possible *coalition* of all forces. Private funds and private efforts, on farms and in factories; state funds and state activities; local communities, clubs, schools, associations, co-operatives—all have had major roles. Moreover, scores of federal agencies co-operated—the Civilian Conservation Corps; the Department of Agriculture through such agencies as the Farm Security Administration, the Rural Electrification Administration, the sci-

entific research bureaus, the Agricultural Adjustment Administration, the Commodity Credit Corporation, the co-operative loan banks and the Forest Service; the Public Health Service; the Army Corps of Engineers which prior to 1933 had prepared a preliminary survey of the Tennessee River widely known as "House Document 328"; the Coast Guard; the Public Works Administration; several of the bureaus of the Interior Department, the Bureau of Reclamation which prepared designs for early Norris and Wheeler dams, the Geological Survey, the Bureau of Mines, the Bureau of Fish and Wildlife Service, the National Park Service; the Geodetic Survey and the Weather Bureau—and so on; the list, if complete, would include most national agencies.

How much of the public's money has the TVA spent in these ten years? Has it been worth that cost as measured in dividends to the people?

It is as important that a public enterprise should produce benefits and values as great as or greater than their cost as it is when the undertaking is a private one. And, to those who are studying the feasibility of developments of a comparable character, the question of cost and the balancing of investment of materials and manpower against the yield the investment produces are considerations of the first consequence.

I shall not, of course, go into all the possible technical refinements of TVA's financial affairs, since they are of little interest to the general reader. The facts are all readily available in TVA's financial statements, in its annual reports to Congress, in thousands of pages of testimony before Congressional committees, and in technical books and writings on the subject. I shall here only summarize the basic facts and the considerations that may be useful in judging the significance of those facts.

The funds used by the TVA have all been advanced from funds appropriated by Congress with two major exceptions: 65 millions of TVA bonds and about 50 millions supplied by electric rate-payers and re-invested in dams and equipment. To avoid unduly complicating the statement, however, I shall treat the funds expended as if they *all* had been advanced directly from the federal treasury; the exceptions do not affect the principles. The American people who advanced these funds are entitled to a return from them.

In judging whether they have received such a return and whether the product of TVA's investment of the people's money has been worth the outlay, it must be remembered that much of the return, to the Tennessee Valley and the nation, is in benefits which cannot be exactly measured. It is only the investment in power facilities that yields the federal taxpayers a return in dollars in addition to other benefits. For power is the only major product of the TVA investment that is sold for dollars. For the other expenditures little if any of the return is in dollars, but instead is realized in benefits to citizens and their communities and business enterprises.

The benefits of a navigable channel, for example, go to shippers, to industries using the channel, to consumers of grain, oil, gasoline, and so on. This is true, of course, not only on the Tennessee but also on the Ohio, the Illinois, the Missouri, all of the many rivers where millions of federal funds have been expended for a century and more. So it is not possible to record the same precise dollar measure of navigation benefits as it is with power. But simply because they do not appear on TVA's books as incomes does not mean, of course, that there are no benefits.

Likewise, the benefits of flood control produced by these dams extend all the way down the Mississippi River to the mouth of the Red. But since TVA is not paid for those benefits in dollars, the taxpayers' return cannot be measured in

that way. And so it is with TVA's expenditures to produce phosphate plant food, and to demonstrate its use to control soil erosion not only in the Tennessee Valley but in Minnesota, Wisconsin, New York, Iowa, and seventeen other states outside this region. So with forestry, industrial research, mapping.

The *cost* of such development work appears on *TVA's books as a net expense; but the benefits appear on the balance sheet of the region and of the nation*. And, as with public improvement expenditures generally the country over, it was anticipated that such expenditures would be repaid to the taxpayers not directly in dollars, but indirectly in benefits.

Turning now to TVA's expenditures, and first the cost of developing the river: TVA's financial balance sheet shows that to provide a 650-mile navigable channel, flood protection, and power supply, the TVA has an investment in completed plant as of June 30, 1943, totaling about $475,000,000. By the end of 1944, when several dams now (September, 1943) under construction will be completed and in use, the figure will be in the neighborhood of $700,000,000. Of this amount approximately 65 per cent, or $450,000,000, will represent the power investment. The river control works will then be substantially completed.

What dividends for the people does this investment yield? Do the expenditures yield a product that justifies this cost?

As to power the answer is a relatively easy one, since the power is sold and the revenues provide a dollar measurement, and one that is reassuring. In the fiscal year ended June 30, 1943, the sale of power yielded revenues to TVA in excess of $31,500,000. Operating expenses to produce that power, including about $2,000,000 of tax payments and about $6,000,000 (or almost 20 per cent of each dollar of revenue) in depreciation charges, left a surplus of revenue over cost of more than $13,-000,000.

Actual earnings in the first months of the current fiscal year indicate that the total net income from power since the beginning of the TVA in 1933 to June 30, 1944, will be well over $40,-000,000. This substantial surplus will have been accumulated in only five or six years, for between 1933 and 1937 the TVA was not a going power concern; the system was incomplete and operations were beset by a multiplicity of lawsuits and injunctions which prevented the normal sale of the power produced by the river. The size of this net income indicates pretty clearly that the power asset of the Tennessee River certainly is worth its cost.

These calculations take into account only dollar returns to TVA, and none of the indirect benefits. But such benefits are many. Among them are the $10,000,-000 annual savings to consumers as a result of greatly reduced rates, the effects on the region's business enterprises of large amounts of low-cost power, the benefits that have resulted to business in other regions of the country, as well as the fact that 80 per cent of the equipment and materials purchased by TVA were produced in factories located in regions outside the Tennessee Valley. Nor do they seek to measure the value to the country of the fact that it was largely because of power from this river that in 1943 America was able to build huge fleets of bombers to send over Europe and the South Pacific.

COMMENT

Nothing could do this country more good. It would enrich every farm home, restore the values of farm lands, stimulate the farmer's interest, and inspire him with renewed hope. It would start an era of rural home building such as this country has never seen and would lay the foundation of a new civilization, greater perhaps than any mankind has yet known. It would place our country in her rightful position of leadership in the great onward march of modern progress. . . .

> Congressman John Rankin of Mississippi in a radio address, February 2, 1935. *Vital Speeches*, I (February 25, 1935), 344.

Those who oppose the utility organization, whether they be holding companies or operating companies, assume an attitude of superior virtue and patriotism. They seek to paint us who represent private enterprise in the utility business as anti-social, unpatriotic and the despoilers of men. . . . All that I have observed, all that I know and all that I read teaches me that I could do nothing nobler for the future financial stability and political good of my country or the social and economic well being of my fellow citizen than to stand firm and unafraid against this foolish fad and fancy of the moment.

> Wendell Willkie, president of the Commonwealth and Southern Corporation, in a speech to a joint meeting of the Economic Club of New York and the Harvard Business School Club of New York. *Vital Speeches*, I (February 11, 1935), 299.

It has been demonstrated that the fears of the power trust that competition by the TVA would prevent it from selling its own electricity had no solid basis.

> Senator George W. Norris of Nebraska in *Fighting Liberal, the Autobiography of George W. Norris* (New York: The Macmillan Company, 1946), pp. 260–76.

63. *NOVEMBER 16, 1933*

The United States Recognizes Russia

Following the Bolshevik Revolution of 1917, the United States refused to recognize the Soviet Union, despite the fact that other governments accepted Russia as a member of the family of nations. President Wilson did not recognize the new government because of its failure to assume responsibility for American loans made to the Kerensky government, the widespread confiscation of American property in Russia, and the failure to pay interest on bonds which the Tsarist regime had sold in the United States. Moreover, Americans were shocked by the ruthless way the Bolsheviks came to power and by their threats to overthrow existing governments throughout the world.

When Franklin Roosevelt became president, the United States still had not recognized the Soviet government. Meanwhile, Japan's invasion of Manchuria created a threat to the interests of the United States and Russia, which eventually resulted in the restoration of normal relations between the two countries. Maxim Litvinov, head of the Russian delegation to the London Economic Conference of 1933, first took the initiative when he proposed to American Secretary of State Cordell Hull that the two governments should reach a settlement of their differences. When Hull informed Roosevelt of the suggestion, the President invited Litvinov to Washing-

SAMUEL I. ROSENMAN, ed., *The Public Papers and Addresses of Franklin D. Roosevelt* (New York: Random House, Inc., 1938), II, 471–75. Reprinted by permission of Random House, Inc.

ton. After several conversations, the notes printed below were exchanged between Roosevelt and Litvinov on November 16, 1933. Nevertheless, diplomatic relations between the United States and Russia were not very cordial until 1941, when both nations were threatened by the power of Nazi Germany.

MY DEAR MR. LITVINOV: I am very happy to inform you that as a result of our conversations the Government of the United States has decided to establish normal diplomatic relations with the Government of the Union of Soviet Socialist Republics and to exchange ambassadors.

I trust that the relations now established between our peoples may forever remain normal and friendly, and that our Nations henceforth may cooperate for their mutual benefit and for the preservation of the peace of the world.

I am, my dear Mr. Litvinov,

Very sincerely yours,

FRANKLIN D. ROOSEVELT

MY DEAR MR. PRESIDENT: I have the honor to inform you that coincident with the establishment of diplomatic relations between our two Governments it will be the fixed policy of the Government of the Union of Soviet Socialist Republics:

1. To respect scrupulously the indisputable right of the United States to order its own life within its own jurisdiction in its own way and to refrain from interfering in any manner in the in-

ternal affairs of the United States, its territories or possessions.

2. To refrain, and to restrain all persons in Government service and all organizations of the Government or under its direct or indirect control, including organizations in receipt of any financial assistance from it, from any act overt or covert liable in any way whatsoever to injure the tranquillity, prosperity, order, or security of the whole or any part of the United States, its territories or possessions, and, in particular, from any act tending to incite or encourage armed intervention, or any agitation or propaganda having as an aim, the violation of the territorial integrity of the United States, its territories or possessions, or the bringing about by force of a change in the political or social order of the whole or any part of the United States, its territories or possessions.

3. Not to permit the formation or residence on its territory of any organization or group—and to prevent the activity on its territory of any organization or group, or of representatives or officials of any organization or group— which makes claim to be the Government of, or makes attempt upon the territorial integrity of, the United States, its territories or possessions; not to form, subsidize, support or permit on its territory military organizations or groups having the aim of armed struggle against the United States, its territories or possessions, and to prevent any recruiting on behalf of such organizations and groups.

4. Not to permit the formation or residence on its territory of any organization or group—and to prevent the activity on its territory of any organization or group, or of representatives or officials of any organization or group—which has as an aim the overthrow or the preparation for the overthrow of, or the bringing about by force of a change in, the political or social order of the whole or any part of the United States, its territories or possessions.

I am, my dear Mr. President,

Very sincerely yours,
MAXIM LITVINOV

People's Commissar for Foreign Affairs,
Union of Soviet Socialist Republics

COMMENT

The Russian issue . . . must be faced immediately. The only two great powers which really object to Japanese expansion are the United States and the Soviet Union. . . . Now America needs Russia's aid in the Pacific. The longer it takes Mr. Roosevelt to see this fact and act upon it, the more Japan will bite off. . . .

American writer, lecturer, and authority on the Soviet Union, Louis Fischer in "Recognize Russia Now," *Nation*, cxxxv (December 28, 1932), 633.

The capitalist press knows it, Roosevelt knows it, and the capitalist class knows it. . . . They know that every attempt to claim that article 4 of the Litvinov pact applies to the Communist International will meet with defeat.

Editorial in the *Daily Worker*, November 20, 1933.

One of the placards which the New Dealers put up to prove they were "liberals" was "Recognition of Russia." . . . The recognition agreement was well designed to pull wool over American eyes.

Former President Herbert Hoover, in *Memoirs of Herbert Hoover* (New York: The Macmillan Company, 1952), p. 360.

64. 1934

Report of the National Recovery Review Board

Though the Roosevelt Administration had no clear-cut program for economic recovery, the National Industrial Recovery Act was designed to revive the nation's industrial and business activity by ending cutthroat competition, raising prices to a profitable level, and guaranteeing a decent wage to labor. The act was based on the principle of voluntary self-restraint by industry, with the federal government possessing supervisory power. The purpose of the act was to be achieved by the adoption of codes of fair competition drawn up by the National Recovery Administration which was to represent management, labor, and the consumer. When small businessmen and consumer groups attacked the NRA for discriminating against small producers in favor of big business, President Roosevelt appointed a National Recovery Review Board, headed by Clarence Darrow, the famed criminal lawyer, to investigate the charges. Instead of impartially investigating the facts, Darrow proceeded as a prosecuting attorney. After the Darrow report was submitted (part of which is printed below), the fortunes of the NRA fell rapidly. Responding to mounting criticism, Roosevelt asked Hugh Johnson, the chairman of the NRA, for his resignation. But before the President had an opportunity to overhaul the NRA codes, the Supreme Court declared

National Recovery Review Board, *Third Report to the President of the United States*, (Washington, 1934), pp. 35–39.

the National Industrial Recovery Act unconstitutional.

Submitting thus our third report we feel constrained to emphasize certain conclusions that seem to us of grave moment.

1. In virtually all the codes we have examined, one condition has been persistent, undeniable and apparent to any impartial observation. It is this, that the code has offered an opportunity for the more powerful and more profitable Interests to seize control of an industry or to augment and extend a control already obtained.

In industry after industry, the larger units, sometimes through the agency of what is called an "Institute," sometimes by other means, have for their own advantage written the codes, and then, in effect and for their own advantage, assumed the administration of the code they have framed. Thus privilege has exerted itself to gather more privilege. Little else indeed has been considered in these operations. The interests of the nation and of the consuming public have been utterly ignored in all too many instances. Profit making power has been multiplied for the one purpose of gathering more profits that will mean still more power for still more profits.

The nation's need, sternly revealed by the depression, was for a better distribution of wealth. In the respects we have specified in these reports, the Recovery Act has failed to meet this need.

Nor has it been merely negative in its reactions. However beneficent may have been its intents, its practice has increased an evil fraught with grave dangers to the Republic. It has not discouraged but in the ways we have pointed out it has fostered and fortified those practices and systems under which one per cent of the nation's population has been enabled to possess itself of sixty per cent of the nation's wealth. In this respect it has become not the foe but the adjunct of depression. For of what use would it be to win the hectic and delusive prosperity when close beside wait the conditions that will inevitably produce another and greater disaster?

2. This Board was created to ascertain if the codes permitted monopolistic practices and the oppression of small enterprises. Our investigations have shown that in the instances mentioned the codes do not only permit but foster monopolistic practices and the small enterprise is not only oppressed but in many cases its exit is accelerated from the field of business. We, therefore, report what we have found.

3. It is ominous and disquieting to have to note that although these evil conditions have been demonstrated and are well known to exist, nothing has been done to remove or even to restrain them. On the contrary, there seems a sinister purpose to entrench them still more securely in the processes of the act, to make still more unquestioned the monopolistic sway of the Great Interest. Thousands upon thousands of small enterprises in many lines of business have petitioned for relief. The answer has been to drive the car of suppression still more relentlessly upon them.

4. If monopolistic business combinations in this country could have everything ordered to their wish they could not order anything better for themselves than to have the anti-trust laws suspended, industry put into their unlimited mastery and the means provided to silence, supress, eliminate or ignore their complaining small competitors. And exactly this is the situation in most of the codes we have examined.

5. Further observations should be made concerning the control of industry by trade associations, known as "institutes," or by similarly constituted bodies. In many instances this has been plainly revealed as an evil having many aspects. In general it is obtained by a voting arrangement whereby the larger interests win unfairly to an autocratic sway. But the principles of democracy must apply to industry no less than to politics. So long as men are coerced by institutions or powers in which they have no share in this country at least they will resent their servitude, and the efficiency of production and distribution will fall short. We are, therefore, forced to the conclusion that the present method of setting up code authorities is sadly defective and that the cost of administration is, in many cases, expensive and sometimes heavily burdensome to the smaller interests of the industry. Our candid and unbiased belief is that every member of an industry subject to the provisions of a code should be guaranteed a voice in the selection of the governing body known as the code authority. We are concerned, further, that all administrative members of the code authority should be selected with an eye single to their fitness and qualifications for the duties to be assumed; they should be entitled to vote upon all questions; they should be paid out of government funds.

6. The basing point system of price making is a potent instrument to protect and further monopolistic practices and to increase the oppression of small enterprises. It should be eliminated from all industry.

7. While "stop loss" provisions in the codes are desirable and in harmony with the purposes of the National Recovery Act, nevertheless, the attempt to fix prices was an error and should be abandoned as soon as possible.

8. Too many codes were attempted. Most of the codes covering small industries were worse than superfluous; they were inexcusable interferences with business enterprises conducted in the main as well as is possible.

9. The codes were too drastic and attempted too much. To abolish child labor was a most worthy object; to establish labor's right to bargain collectively was most salutary. To shorten the hours of labor was well. But to deliver industry into the hands of its greatest and most ruthless units when the protection of the anti-trust laws had been withdrawn was a grave error. It may safely be said that not in many years have monopolistic tendencies in industry been so forwarded and strengthened as they have been through the perversion of an act excellently intended to restore prosperity and promote the general welfare. These are the facts, and we believe that the sooner they are frankly recognized and bravely dealt with the better for the nation and its people.

COMMENT

The NRA has accomplished a great deal in the reemployment of labor, in improving wages, hours and working conditions, in eliminating unfair competition, in protecting small enterprises, in balancing production against consumption, in establishing a better, fairer industrial system capable of greater and more sustained service to the general welfare.

> Donald Richberg, executive director of the National Emergency Council, in a network address to the National Radio Forum. *Vital Speeches,* I (March 25, 1935), 409.

There is nothing the New Deal has so far done that could not have been done better by an earthquake.

> Benjamin Stolberg, sociologist, and Warren Vinton, New Deal housing expert, in *The Economic Consequences of the New Deal* (New York: Harcourt, Brace & Company, Inc., 1935), p. 85.

It was only after I saw the wretched administration of the NRA, with whole industries being ruled by code authorities composed of men having little or no competence in the fields in which they exercised jurisdiction, that I turned against it. The NRA came to typify in my mind the incompetence of government to run business.

> Former Speaker of the House of Representatives Joe Martin of Massachusetts in *My First Fifty Years in Politics* (New York: McGraw-Hill Publishing Co., Inc., 1960), p. 74.

65. *1934*

From the Nye Committee's Report

During the two decades following the First World War, many Americans were profoundly sorry that the United States

Senate Report 944, 74th Cong., 2d Sess., v, 8–9.

had entered the war. A number of liberals were certain that the war had brought the end to the Progressive movement. Historians were only one of many groups who were busy studying the *causes of the war, as countless Americans believed that only by understanding the reasons for their participation in the war could they keep the nation out of future conflicts.*

In 1933, the House Foreign Affairs Committee conducted an investigation into the influences of arms traffic on international politics, and in the following year, the Senate approved a committee investigation into the munitions industry. After many months of taking testimony, the committee, headed by Senator Gerald P. Nye of North Dakota, issued a report which implied that armament manufacturers and bankers had been responsible for America's entry into the First World War.

In 1935, journalist Walter Millis published Road to War, *in which he expressed the same views that the Nye Committee had set forth in its report. Charles A. Beard, the nation's foremost reform historian, also lent credence to such views in his* The Devil Theory of War. *These explanations for America's entrance into the First World War strengthened isolationist sentiment and were important factors responsible for the neutrality legislation of the 1930's.*

．　．　．　．　．

The Committee wishes to point out most definitely that its study of events resulting from the then existing neutrality legislation, or lack of it, is in no way a criticism, direct or implied, of the sincere devotion of the then President, Woodrow Wilson, to the high causes of peace and democracy. Like other leaders in government, business and finance, he had watched the growth of militarism in the pre-war years. Militarism meant the alliance of the military with powerful economic groups to secure appropriations on the one hand for a constantly increasing military and naval establishment, and on the other hand, the constant threat of the use of that swollen military establishment in behalf of the economic interests at home and abroad of the industrialists supporting it. I meant the subjugation of the people of the various countries to the uniform, the self-interested identification of patriotism with commercialism, and the removal of the military from the control of civil law. After the war had begun President Wilson and a great number of leading Americans became convinced that the war was the logical outcome of militarism, and that the success of militarism anywhere was a constant threat to the democracies of the world. All the members of the Committee and its staff shared that conviction.

This belief was also shared by munitions makers, bankers, exporters and producers in this country who had enormous profits at stake in the war. In the unrestricted pursuit of these profits they became involved in a situation which made it to their interest to support the allies and to favor war against Germany. Public opinion became so powerful that it threatened the existence of the party in power and the prestige of the President of the United States. President Wilson was personally impelled by the highest motives and the most profound convictions as to the justice of the cause of our country and was devoted to peace. He was caught up by a situation created largely by the profit-making interests in the United States, and such interests spread to nearly everybody in the country. It seemed necessary to the prosperity of our people that their markets in Europe remain unimpaired.

President Wilson, himself, stated that he realized that the economic rivalries of European nations had played their part in bringing on the war in 1914. After the war had started the great democracies, England and France, were fighting for their very lives. No reflection of any kind on them in their hour of need is intended by discussion of the terms which they ound it necessary to offer other powers in return for support. The Committee's interest in those terms revolved around their function in a war which we entered for purposes of establishing our neutral rights by force of arms and which finally failed to secure acknowledgement throughout the world of those neutral rights, even after the war had been successfully concluded.

While the Committee's function is to discuss the adequacy of existing legislation in the light of the most immediate experience available, which in this case has been the World War, the Committee wishes to go out of its way to pay tribute to those soldiers, dead, wounded, or otherwise suffering from the results of that war, who accepted the ideal of making the world safe for democracy, and of regretting to them that there has not been the will or power or confidence or effective cooperation between the nations of the world to have accomplished that ideal.

. . . . .

COMMENT

I know who makes wars. The International Jewish bankers arrange them so they can make money out of them. I know it's true because a Jew on the peace ship told me.

Industrialist Henry Ford, in a public interview. New York *Times*, December 5, 1921.

Having broken down the ban on credits and then on loans, bankers made the most of their opportunity. Loan after loan was floated to pay Americans for American goods. As the days and weeks passed the fate of American bankers, manufacturers, farmers, merchants, workers, and white-collar servants became more deeply entangled in the fate of the Allies on the battlefield—in the war.

Charles A. Beard, historian, in *The Devil Theory of War* (New York: Vanguard Press, Inc., 1936), p. 89.

66. *1935*

Schechter Poultry Corporation
v. United States

After the National Recovery Review Board issued its devastating report in 1934, the fortunes of the National Recovery Administration fell hard and fast. Before President Roosevelt could take the proper measures to overhaul the codes of fair competition, the Supreme Court unanimously invalidated the National Industrial Recovery act in the case of Schechter v. United States. The defendants in the Schechter case were slaughter house operators who were charged primarily with violating the NRA code's hour and wage provisions. The constitutional questions which concerned the Court were (1) Was the law justified "in the light of the grave na-

295 U.S. 495 (1935).

tional crisis with which Congress was confronted? (2) Did the law illegally delegate legislative power to the executive? (3) Did the law go beyond the interstate commerce power of Congress?

Answering the first question negatively and the other two affirmatively, Chief Justice Hughes made it plain that the Court viewed the act with extreme distaste. The government could hardly have chosen a worse case on which to test the constitutionality of the NIRA. The government would have made a better public showing had it chosen steel or coal codes, or some other industry which obviously affected the public welfare. Instead, the government was somewhat embarrassed when this case became known as the "sick chicken" case, as the defendants, among other counts, had been charged with selling an "unfit chicken." Even the liberal Justices Cardoza and Brandeis could not tolerate the extreme delegation of authority and minute regulation so obviously involved in this case.

Petitioners were convicted in the District Court of the United States for the Eastern District of New York on eighteen counts of an indictment charging violations of what is known as the "Live Poultry Code," and on an additional counts for conspiracy to commit such violations. By demurrer to the indictment and appropriate motions on the trial, the defendants contended (1) that the Code had been adopted pursuant to an unconstitutional delegation by Congress of legislative power; (2) that it attempted to regulate intrastate transactions which lay outside the authority of Congress; and (3) that in certain provisions it was repugnant to the due process clause of the Fifth Amendment. . . .

The defendants are slaughterhouse operators of the latter class. A.L.A. Schechter Poultry Corporation and Schechter Live Poultry Market are cor-

porations conducting wholesale poultry slaughterhouse markets in Brooklyn New York City. Joseph Schechter operated the latter corporation and also guaranteed the credits of the former corporation which was operated by Martin Alex and Aaron Schechter. Defendants ordinarily purchase their live poultry from commission men at the West Washington Market in New York City or at the railroad terminals serving the City, but occasionally they purchased from commission men in Philadelphia. They buy the poultry for slaughter and resale. After the poultry is trucked to their slaughterhouse markets in Brooklyn, it is there sold, usually within twenty-four hours, to retail poultry dealers and butchers who sell directly to consumers. The poultry purchased from the defendants is immediately slaughtered, prior to delivery, by shochtim in defendants' employ. Defendants do not sell poultry in interstate commerce.

The "Live Poultry Code" was promulgated under §3 of the National Industrial Recovery Act. That section—the pertinent provisions of which are set forth in the margin—authorizes the President to approve "codes of fair competition." Such a code may be approved for a trade or industry, upon application by one or more trade or industrial associations or groups, if the President finds (1) that such associations or groups "impose no inequitable restrictions on admission to membership therein and are truly representative," and (2) that such codes are not designed "to promote monopolies or to eliminate or oppress small enterprises and will not operate to discriminate against them, and will tend to effectuate the policy" of Title I of the Act. Such codes "shall not permit monopolies or monopolistic practices." As a condition of his approval, the President may "impose such conditions (including requirements for the making of reports and the keeping of accounts) for the protection of consumers, competitors, employees, and others, in furtherance of the public interest, and may provide such exceptions to and exemptions from the provisions of such codes as the President in his discretion deems necessary to effectuate the policy herein declared." Where such a code has not been approved, the President may prescribe one, either on his own motion or on complaint. Violation of any provision of a code (so approved or prescribed) "in any transaction in or affecting interstate or foreign commerce" is made a misdemeanor punishable by a fine of not more than $500 for each offense, and each day the violation continues is to be deemed a separate offense.

The "Live Poultry Code" was approved by the President on April 13, 1934. Its divisions indicate its nature and scope. The Code has eight articles entitled (1) purposes, (2) definition, (3) hours, (4) wages, (5) general labor provisions, (6) administration, (7) trade practice provisions, and (8) general.

The declared purpose is "To effect the policies of title I of the National Industrial Recovery Act." The Code is established as "a code of fair competition for the live poultry industry of the metropolitan area in and about the City of New York." That area is described as embracing the five boroughs of New York City, the counties of Rockland, Westchester, Nassau and Suffolk in the State of New York, the counties of Hudson and Bergen in the State of New Jersey, and the county of Fairfield in the State of Connecticut.

The "industry" is defined as including "every person engaged in the business of selling, purchasing for resale, transporting or handling and/or slaughtering live poultry, from the time such poultry comes into the New York metropolitan area to the time it is first sold in slaughtered form," and such "related branches" as may from time to time be included by amendment. Employers are styled "members of the industry," and the term employee is defined to embrace "any and all persons engaged in the industry, however compensated," except "members."

The Code fixes the number of hours for work-days. It provides that no employee, with certain exceptions, shall be permitted to work in excess of forty (40) hours in any one week, and that no employee, save as stated, "shall be paid in any pay period less than at the rate of fifty (50) cents per hour." The article containing "general labor provisions" prohibits the employment of any person under sixteen years of age, and declares that employees shall have the right of "collective bargaining," and freedom of choice with respect to labor organizations, in the terms of §7(a) of the Act. The minimum number of employees, who shall be employed by slaughterhouse operators, is fixed, the number being graduated according to the average volume of weekly sales.

Provision is made for administration through an "industry advisory committee," to be selected by trade associations and members of the industry, and a "code supervisor" to be appointed, with the approval of the committee, by agreement between the Secretary of Agriculture and the Administrator for Industrial Recovery. The expenses of administration are to be borne by the members of the industry proportionately upon the basis of volume of business, or such other factors as the advisory committee many deem equitable, "subject to the disapproval of the Secretary and/or Administrator."

The seventh article, containing "trade practice provisions," prohibits various practices which are said to constitute "unfair methods of competition." The final article provides for verified reports, such as the Secretary or Administrator may require, "(1) for the protection of consumers, competitors, employees, and others, and in furtherance of the public interest, and (2) for the determination by the Secretary or Administrator of the extent to which the declared policy of the act is being effectuated by this code." The members of the industry are also required to keep books and records which "will clearly reflect all financial transactions of their respective businesses and the financial condition thereof," and "to submit weekly reports showing the range of daily prices and volume of sales" for each kind of produce. . . .

Of the eighteen counts of the indictment upon which the defendants were convicted, aside from the count for conspiracy, two counts charged violation of the minimum wage and maximum hour provisions of the Code, and ten counts were for violation of the requirement (found in the "trade practice provisions") of "straight killing." This requirement was really one of "straight" selling. The term "straight killing" was defined in the Code as "the practice of requiring persons purchasing poultry for resale to accept the run of any half coop, coop, or coops, as purchased by slaughterhouse operators, except for culls." The charges in the ten counts, respectively, were that the defendants in selling to retail dealers and butchers had permitted "selections of individual chickens taken from particular coops and half coops."

Of the other six counts, one charged the sale to a butcher of an unfit chicken; two counts charged the making of sales without having the poultry inspected or approved in accordance with regulations or ordinances of the City of New York; two counts charged the making of false reports or the failure to make reports relating to the range of daily prices and volume of sales for certain periods; and the remaining count was for sales to slaughterers or dealers who were without licenses required by the ordinances and regulations of the city of New York.

First. Two preliminary points are stressed by the Government with respect to the appropriate approach to the important questions presented. We are told that the provision of the statute authorizing the adoption of codes must be viewed in the light of the grave national crisis with which Congress was confronted. Undoubtedly, the conditions to which power is addressed are always to be considered when the exercise of power is challenged. Extraordinary conditions may call for extraordinary remedies. But the argument necessarily stops short of an attempt to justify action which lies outside the sphere of constitutional authority. Extraordinary conditions do not create or enlarge constitutional power. The Constitution established a national government with powers deemed to be adequate, as they have proved to be both in war and peace, but these powers of the national government are limited by the constitutional grants. Those who act under these grants are not at liberty to transcend the imposed limits because they believe that more or different power is necessary. Such assertions of extra-constitutional authority were anticipated and precluded by the explicit terms of the Tenth Amendment—"The powers not delegated to the United States by the Constitution, nor prohibited by it to the States, are reserved to the States respectively, or to the people."

The further point is urged that the national crisis demanded a broad and intensive cooperative effort by those engaged in trade and industry, and that this necessary cooperation was sought to be fostered by permitting them to initiate the adoption of codes. But the statutory plan is not simply one for voluntary effort. It does not seek merely to endow voluntary trade or industrial associations or groups with privileges or immunities. It involves the coercive exercise of the law-making power. The codes of fair competition which that statute attempts to authorize are codes of laws. If valid, they place all persons within their reach under the obligation of positive law, binding equally those who assent and those who do not assent. Violations of the provisions of the codes are punishable as crimes.

Second. The question of the delegation of legislative power. . . . For a statement of the authorized objectives and the content of the "codes of fair competition" we are referred repeatedly to the "Declaration of Policy" in section one of Title I of the Recovery Act. Thus, the approval of a code by the President is conditioned on his finding that it "will tend to effectuate the policy of this title." §3(a). The President is authorized to impose such conditions "for the protection of consumers, competitors, employees, and others, and in furtherance of the public interest, and may provide such exceptions to and exemptions from the provisions of such codes as the President in his discretion deems necessary to effectuate the policy herein declared." *Id.* The "policy herein declared" is manifestly that set forth in section one. That declaration embraces a broad range of objectives. Among them we find the elimination of "unfair competitive practices." . . .

. . . We think the conclusion is inescapable that the authority sought to be conferred by §3 was not merely to deal with "unfair competitive practices" which offend against existing law, and could be the subject of judicial condemnation without further legislation, or to create administrative machinery for the application of established principles of law to particular instances of violation. Rather, the purpose is clearly disclosed to authorize new and controlling prohibitions through codes of laws which would embrace what the formulators would propose, and what the President would approve, or prescribe, as wise and beneficient measures for the government of trades and industries in order to bring about their rehabilitation, cor-

rection and development, according to the general declaration of policy in section one. Codes of laws of this sort are styled "codes of fair competition."

We find no real controversy upon this point and we must determine the validity of the Code in question in this aspect. . . .

The question, then, turns upon the authority which §3 of the Recovery Act vests in the President to approve or prescribe. If the codes have standing as penal statutes, this must be due to the effect of the executive action. But Congress cannot delegate legislative power to the President to exercise an unfettered discretion to make whatever laws he thinks may be needed or advisable for the rehabilitation and expansion of trade or industry. . . .

Accordingly we turn to the Recovery Act to ascertain what limits have been set to the exercise of the President's discretion. First, the President, as a condition of approval, is required to find that the trade or industrial associations or groups which propose a code, "impose no inequitable restrictions on admission to membership" and are "truly representative." That condition, however, relates only to the status of the initiators of the new laws and not to the permissible scope of such laws. Second, the President is required to find that the code is not "designed to promote monopolies or to eliminate or oppress small enterprises and will not operate to discriminate against them." And, to this is added a proviso that the code "shall not permit monopolies or monopolistic practices." But these restrictions leave virtually untouched the field of policy envisaged by section one, and, in that wide field of legislative possibilities, the proponents of a code, refraining from monopolistic design, may roam at will and the President may approve or disapprove their proposals as he may see fit. . . .

Nor is the breadth of the President's discretion left to the necessary implications of this limited requirement as to his findings. As already noted, the President in approving a code may impose his own conditions, adding to or taking from what is proposed, as "in his discretion" he thinks necessary "to effectuate the policy" declared by the Act. Of course, he has no less liberty when he prescribes a code on his own motion or on complaint, and he is free to prescribe one if a code has not been approved. The Act provides for the creation by the President of administrative agencies to assist him, but the action or reports of such agencies, or of his other assistants —their recommendations and findings in relation to the making of codes—have no sanction beyond the will of the President, who may accept, modify or reject them as he pleases. Such recommendations or findings in no way limit the authority which §3 undertakes to vest in the President with no other conditions than those there specified. And this authority relates to a host of different trades and industries, thus extending the President's discretion to all the varieties of laws which he may deem to be beneficial in dealing with the vast array of commercial and industrial activities throughout the country.

Such a sweeping delegation of legislative power finds no support in the decisions upon which the Government especially relies. . . .

To summarize and conclude upon this point: Section 3 of the Recovery Act is without precedent. It supplies no standard for any trade, industry or activity. It does not undertake to prescribe rules of conduct to be applied to particular states of fact determined by appropriate administrative procedure. Instead of prescribing rules of conduct, it authorizes the making of codes to prescribe them. For that legislative undertaking, § 3 sets up no standards, aside from the statement of the general aims of rehabilitation, correction and expansion described in section one. In view

of the scope of that broad declaration, and of the nature of the few restrictions that are imposed, the discretion of the President in approving or prescribing codes, and thus enacting laws for the government of trade and industry throughout the country, is virtually unfettered. We think that the code-making authority thus conferred is an unconstitutional delegation of legislative power.

Third. The question of the application of the provisions of the Live Poultry Code to intrastate transactions. Although the validity of the codes (apart from the question of delegation) rests upon the commerce clause of the Constitution, §3(a) is not in terms limited to interstate and foreign commerce. From the generality of its terms, and from the argument of the Government at the bar, it would appear that §3(a) was designed to authorize codes without that limitation. But under §3(f) penalties are confined to violations of a code provision "in any transaction in or affecting interstate or foreign commerce." This aspect of the case presents the question whether the particular provisions of the Live Poultry Code, which the defendants were convicted for violating and for having conspired to violate, were within the regulating power of Congress.

These provisions relate to the hours and wages of those employed by defendants in their slaughterhouses in Brooklyn and to the sales there made to retail dealers and butchers.

(1) Were these transactions *"in"* interstate commerce? Much is made of the fact that almost all the poultry coming to New York is sent there from other States. But the code provisions, as here applied, do not concern the transportation of the poultry from other States to New York, or the transactions of the commission men or others to whom it is consigned, or the sales made by such consignees to defendants. When defendants had made their purchase, whether

at the West Washington Market in New York City or at the railroad terminals serving the City, or elsewhere, the poultry was trucked to their slaughterhouses in Brooklyn for local disposition. The interstate transactions in relation to that poultry then ended. Defendants held the poultry at their slaughterhouse markets for slaughter and local sale to retail dealers and butchers who in turn sold directly to consumers. Neither the slaughtering nor the sales by defendants were transactions in interstate commerce. . . .

The undisputed facts thus afford no warrant for the argument that the poultry handled by defendants at their slaughterhouse markets was in a *"current"* or *"flow"* of interstate commerce and was thus subject to congressional regulation. The mere fact that there may be a constant flow of commodities into a State does not mean that the flow continues after the property has arrived and has become commingled with the mass of property within the State and is there held solely for local disposition and use. So far as the poultry here in question is concerned, the flow in interstate commerce had ceased. The poultry had come to a permanent rest within the State. It was not held, used, or sold by defendants in relation to any further transactions in interstate commerce and was not destined for transportation to other States. Hence, decisions which deal with a stream of interstate commerce—where goods come to rest within a State temporarily and are later to go forward in interstate commerce—and with regulations of transactions involved in that practical continuity of movement, are not applicable here. . . .

(2) Did the defendants' transactions directly *"affect"* interstate commerce so as to be subject to federal regulation? The power of Congress extends not only to the regulation of transactions which are part of interstate commerce, but to the protection of that commerce from injury. . . .

In determining how far the federal government may go in controlling intrastate transactions upon the grounds that they "affect" interstate commerce, there is a necessary and well-established distinction between direct and indirect effects. The precise line can be drawn only as individual cases arise, but the distinction is clear in principle. Direct effects are illustrated by the railroad cases we have cited, as *e.g.*, the effect of failure to use prescribed safety appliances on railroads which are the highways of both interstate and intrastate commerce, injury to an employee engaged in interstate transportation by the negligence of an employee engaged in an intrastate movement, the fixing of rates for intrastate transportation which unjustly discriminates against interstate commerce. But where the effect of intrastate transactions upon interstate commerce is merely indirect, such transactions remain within the domain of state power. If the commerce clause were construed to reach all enterprises and transactions which could be said to have an indirect effect upon interstate commerce, the federal authority would embrace practically all the activities of the people and the authority of the State over its domestic concerns would exist only by sufferance of the federal government. Indeed, on such a theory, even the development of the State's commercial facilities would be subject to federal control. . . .

The distinction between direct and indirect effects has been clearly recognized in the application of the Anti-Trust Act. Where a combination or conspiracy is formed, with the intent to restrain interstate commerce or to monopolize any part of it, the violation of the statute is clear. . . . But where that intent is absent, and the objectives are limited to intrastate activities, the fact that there may be an indirect effect upon interstate commerce does not subject the parties to the federal statute, notwithstanding its broad provisions. . . .

While these decisions related to the application of the federal statute, and not to its constitutional validity, the distinction between direct and indirect effects of intrastate transactions upon interstate commerce must be recognized as a fundamental one, essential to the maintenance of our constitutional system. Otherwise, as we have said, there would be virtually no limit to the federal power and for all practical purposes we should have a completely centralized government. We must consider the provisions here in question of the light of this distinction.

The question of chief importance relates to the provisions of the Code as to the hours and wages of those employed in defendants' slaughterhouse markets. It is plain that these requirements are imposed in order to govern the details of defendants' management of their local business. The persons employed in slaughtering and selling in local trade are not employed in interstate commerce. Their hours and wages have no direct relation to interstate commerce. The question of how many hours these employees should work and what they should be paid differs in no essential respect from similar questions in other local businesses which handle commodities brought into a State and there dealt in as a part of its internal commerce. This appears from an examination of the considerations urged by the Government with respect to conditions in the poultry trade. Thus, the Government argues that hours and wages affect prices; that slaughterhouse men sell at a small margin above operating costs; that labor represents 50 to 60 per cent of these costs; that a slaughterhouse operator paying lower wages or reducing his cost by exacting long hours of work, translates his saving into lower prices; that this results in demands for a cheaper grade of goods; and that the cutting of

prices brings about a demoralization of the price structure. Similar conditions may be adduced in relation to other businesses. The argument of the Government proves too much. If the federal government may determine the wages and hours of employees in the internal commerce of a State, because of their relation to cost and prices and their indirect effect upon interstate commerce, it would seem that a similar control might be exerted over other elements of cost, also affecting prices, such as the number of employees, rents, advertising, methods of doing business, etc. All the processes of production and distribution that enter into cost could likewise be controlled. If the cost of doing an intrastate business is in itself the permitted object of federal control, the extent of the regulation of cost would be a question of discretion and not of power.

The Government also makes the point that efforts to enact state legislation establishing high labor standards have been impeded by the belief that unless similar action is taken generally, commerce will be diverted from the States adopting such standards, and that this fear of diversion has led to demands for federal legislation on the subject of wages and hours. The apparent implication is that the federal authority under the commerce clause should be deemed to extend to the establishment of rules to govern wages and hours in intrastate trade and industry generally throughout the country, thus overriding the authority of the States to deal with domestic problems arising from labor conditions in their internal commerce.

It is not the province of the Court to consider the economic advantages or disadvantages of such a centralized system. It is sufficient to say that the Federal Constitution does not provide for it. Our growth and development have called for wide use of the commerce power of the federal government in its control over the expanded activities of interstate commerce, and in protecting that commerce from burdens, interferences, and conspiracies to restrain and monopolize it. But the authority of the federal government may not be pushed to such an extreme as to destroy the distinction, which the commerce clause itself establishes, between commerce "among the several States" and the internal concerns of a State. The same answer must be made to the contention that is based upon the serious economic situation which led to the passage of the Recovery Act—the fall in prices, the decline in wages and employment, and the curtailment of the market for commodities. Stress is laid upon the great importance of maintaining wage distributions which would provide the necessary stimulus in starting "the cumulative forces making for expanding commercial activity." Without in any way disparaging this motive, it is enough to say that the recuperative efforts of the federal government must be made in a manner consistent with the authority granted by the Constitution.

We are of the opinion that the attempt through the provisions of the Code to fix the hours and wages of employees of defendants in their intrastate business was not a valid exercise of federal power. . . .

On both the grounds we have discussed, the attempted delegation of legislative power, and the attempted regulation of intrastate transactions which affect interstate commerce only indirectly, we hold the code provisions here in question to be invalid and that the judgment of conviction must be reversed.

COMMENT

You and I know human nature. Fundamentally it comes down to this. In the long run can voluntary processes on the part of business bring about the same practical results that were attained under N.R.A?

> President Franklin D. Roosevelt in a press conference on May 31, 1935. Samuel I. Rosenman, ed., *The Public Papers and Addresses of Franklin D. Roosevelt* (New York: Random House, Inc.), IV, 217–18.

The delegated power of legislation which has found expression in this code is not canalized within banks that keep it from overflowing. It is unconfined and vagrant.

> Justice Benjamin N. Cardoza concurring in majority decision in Schechter Poultry Corporation *v.* U.S. 295 U.S. 552 (1935).

67. *SEPTEMBER 2, 1935*

Frances Perkins on the Social Security Act

Prior to the New Deal, most Americans were slow to develop an appreciation for the necessity of social security. Saving for old age, they felt, should be an individual problem and responsibility. But the depression caused many to change their thinking about the hazards of the modern industrial age. Local clubs throughout the country began to agitate for Dr. Francis A. Townsend's pension plan whereby each individual over sixty years of age would receive $200 each month. Upton Sinclair put forth a plan which would pay $50 a month to the needy of sixty years of age and over. Senator Huey Long of Louisiana advocated a share-the-wealth plan whereby each individual would be guaranteed $5,000 annually.

To study the problem of social security, President Roosevelt appointed a Committee on Economic Security in June, 1934. In the following January, Roosevelt submitted the committee's recommendations to Congress. The result was the nation's first Social Security Act. Despite widespread support for the act, it was criticized in many quarters. While the American Federation of Labor objected because it required contributions from workers, the president of the National Association of Manufacturers protested because it levied a payroll tax on employers. A number of liberals were disturbed because it excluded agricultural laborers, domestic

Vital Speeches, I (September 2, 1935), 792–94.

servants, farm workers, and many others. Despite its shortcomings, the act has provided economic assistance to millions of Americans and has done much to provide a more healthy economy for the nation.

People who work for a living in the United States of America can join with all other good citizens on this forty-eighth anniversary of Labor Day in satisfaction that the Congress has passed the Social Security Act. This act establishes unemployment insurance as a substitute for haphazard methods of assistance in periods when men and women willing and able to work are without jobs. It provides for old age pensions which mark great progress over the measures upon which we have hitherto depended in caring for those who have been unable to provide for the years when they no longer can work. It also provides security for dependent and crippled children, mothers, the indigent disabled and the blind.

Old people who are in need, unemployables, children, mothers and the sightless, will find systematic regular provisions for needs. The Act limits the Federal aid to not more than $15 per month for the individual, provided the State in which he resides appropriates a like amount. There is nothing to prevent a State from contributing more than $15 per month in special cases and there is no requirement to allow as much as $15 from either State or Federal funds when a particular case has some personal provision and needs less than the total allowed.

Following essentially the same procedure, the Act as passed provides for Federal assistance to the States in caring for the blind, a contribution by the State of up to $15 a month to be matched in turn by a like contribution by the Federal Government. The Act also contains provision for assistance to the States in providing payments to dependent children under sixteen years of age. There also is provision in the Act for cooperation with medical and health organizations charged with rehabilitation of physically handicapped children. The necessity for adequate service in the fields of public and maternal health and child welfare calls for the extension of these services to meet individual community needs.

Consider for a moment those portions of the Act which, while they will not be effective this present year, yet will exert a profound and far-reaching effect upon millions of citizens. I refer to the provision for a system of old-age benefits supported by the contributions of employer and employees, and to the section which sets up the initial machinery for unemployment insurance.

Old-age benefits in the form of monthly payments are to be paid to individuals who have worked and contributed to the insurance fund in direct proportion to the total wages earned by such individuals in the course of their employment subsequent to 1936. The minimum monthy payment is to be $10, the maximum $85. These payments will begin in the year 1942 and will be to those who have worked and contributed.

. . . . .

In conjunction with the system of old-age benefits, the Act recognizes that unemployment insurance is an integral part of any plan for the economic security of millions of gainfully employed workers. It provides for a plan of cooperative Fed-

eral-State action by which a State may enact an insurance system, compatible with Federal requirements and best suited to its individual needs.

. . . . .

Federal legislation was framed in the thought that the attack upon the problems of insecurity should be a cooperative venture participated in by both the Federal and State Governments, preserving the benefits of local administration and national leadership. It was thought unwise to have the Federal Government decide all questions of policy and dictate completely what the States should do. only very necessary minimum standards are included in the Federal measure leaving wide latitude to the States.

. . . . .

The social security measure looks primarily to the future and is only a part of the administration's plan to promote sound and stable economic life. We cannot think of it as disassociated from the Government's program to save the homes, the farms, the businesses and banks of the Nation, and especially must we consider it a companion measure to the Works Relief Act which does undertake to provide immediate increase in employment and corresponding stimulation to private industry by purchase of supplies.

While it is not anticipated as a complete remedy for the abnormal conditions confronting us at the present time, it is designed to afford protection for the individual against future major economic vicissitudes. It is a sound and reasonable plan and framed with due regard for the present state of economic recovery. It does not represent a complete solution of the problems of economic security, but it does represent a substantial, necessary beginning. It has been developed after careful and intelligent consideration of all the facts and all of the programs that have been suggested or applied anywhere.

. . . . .

This is truly legislation in the interest of the national welfare. We must recognize that if we are to maintain a healthy economy and thriving production, we need to maintain the standard of living of the lower income groups of our population who constitute ninety per cent of our purchasing power. The President's Committee on Economic Security, of which I had the honor to be chairman, in drawing up the plan, was convinced that its enactment into law would not only carry us a long way toward the goal of economic security for the individual, but also a long way toward the promotion and stabilization of mass purchasing power without which the present economic system cannot endure.

．　．　．　．　．

Our social security program will be a vital force working against the recurrence of severe depressions in the future. We can, as the principle of sustained purchasing power in hard times makes itself felt in every shop, store and mill, grow old without being haunted by the spectre of a poverty-ridden old age or of being a burden on our children.

The costs of unemployment compensation and old-age insurance are not actually additional costs. In some degree they have long been borne by the people, but irregularly, the burden falling much more heavily on some than on others, and none of such provisions offering an orderly or systematic assurance to those in need. The years of depression have brought home to all of us that unemployment entails huge costs to government, industry and the public alike.

Unemployment insurance will within a short time considerably lighten the public burden of caring for those unemployed. It will materially reduce relief costs in future years. In essence, it is a method by which reserves are built up during periods of employment from which compensation is paid to the unemployed when work is lacking.

The passage of this act with so few dissenting votes and with so much intelligent public support is deeply significant of the progress which the American people have made in thought in the social field and awareness of methods of using cooperation through government to overcome social hazards against which the individual alone is inadequate.

．　．　．　．　．

COMMENT

We do not think of the Social Security Act as being a law which will instantly transport us to some economic Utopia. We recognize that the law may be changed as experience dictates. But to condemn the Social Security Act because it is *not* perfect, is to be both unfair and unjust.

> Vincent Miles, member of the National Social Security Board, speaking over radio station WOR, New York, November 24, 1936. *Vital Speeches,* iii (December 15, 1936), 151.

... it is becoming more and more clear that the national government is the only agency whose jurisdiction is wide enough and whose powers are great enough to deal with certain fundamental problems of unemployment prevention ... and unemployment relief.

> Professor E. P. Hohman in a speech before the Retail Merchant's Committee of Chicago, January 7, 1935. *Vital Speeches,* i (January 28, 1935), 270.

68. *M A Y 4 , 1 9 3 6*

Henry Wallace on Agricultural Problems

In 1933, the nation's farmers were on the verge of despair. Everywhere, the chief concerns were low prices and the threat of foreclosure. To meet the problem, the Roosevelt Administration consolidated all federal agricultural credit agencies into the Farm Credit Administration. As part of a long-range program for agricultural recovery, Congress passed the Agricultural Adjustment Act on May 10, 1933. Its stated objective, to restore the purchasing power of the farmers, was to be achieved by limiting the production of certain basic commodities, the curtailment of which was expected to influence the prices of other commodities and lead the way to recovery. Funds were to be obtained by levying a tax on the processing of agricultural commodities. Passage of the AAA committed the government to practices in which it had never previously been engaged. Instead of encouraging the farmers to become more efficient producers and furnishing them with adequate credit to achieve these goals, the government assumed responsibility for raising the purchasing power of the farmers to levels which they had enjoyed from August, 1909, to July, 1914.

For a short while, the AAA was highly successful. But in January, 1936, the Supreme Court ruled that the act was unconstitutional on the grounds that the processing tax had been levied not for the general welfare but for the purpose of regulating agricultural production. To meet this new situation, Con-

Vital Speeches, II (May 18, 1936), 511–18.

gress passed a new Agricultural Adjustment Act of February 16, 1938.

To understand the New Deal's farm policies, it is important to remember that they were part of a much broader program aimed to help the entire economy. The New Dealers were of the opinion that special measures must be adopted to rescue agriculture from the disadvantageous position into which it had fallen and elevate it to a position of equality with other segments of the American economy. Below, Secretary of Agriculture Henry Wallace in an address to a group of midwestern farmers at the University of Nebraska stresses the importance of production control.

The United States has long been proud of its home market, as the broadest and wealthiest single market for goods in the world. The achievement of this great, undivided market was not an accident. Since 1787, no idea has been more precious to the American people than the idea of a nation undivided in its economic and political life. . . .

· · · · ·

Sectional and selfish interests from time to time have tried to break down or whittle away this idea of economic unity and interdependence. Industrial sections have tried to increase their advantage at the expense of agricultural sections, and vice versa. One class has tried to stir up jealousies of other classes and to put across the idea that prosperity for itself could be advanced if other classes had fewer benefits. Some sections or classes have benefitted for a time at the expense of other sections or classes, but never for long. During the 1920's, some industrial leaders began to think that industry could remain prosperous in spite of, or perhaps even because of, low prices and income to farmers, but this idea was exploded with the general depression of the 1930's. Since 1932, the nation has returned with greater conviction than ever to the idea of balanced and interdependent welfare of all sections and classes.

There has been one difficulty, however, in working out equably the idea of the pre-eminence of our home market. While industry looked almost entirely to the domestic market, agriculture has had to look in considerable part to the foreign market. Industry has asked and obtained high protection for its goods in the home market, while agriculture, even if it wanted and got such protection on paper, could get very little benefit from it except temporarily following a year of unusually bad weather. Industry, too, succeeded in obtaining great advantage from the corporate form of organization as a means of exploiting its markets more efficiently, while agriculture in its very nature could make little use of this mighty instrument.

Agriculture, I insist, has a right to some equivalent to the tariff and the corporate form of organization as used by industry, and I believe that to give agriculture such an equivalent is in the best interests of the nation. Let me assure you that I shall not cease to work for such an equivalent to be made available to agriculture.

We know what we are talking about when we demand equality for agriculture with respect to the tariff. Since 1920, farmers' troubles have largely been the result of difficulties growing out of their unprotected export position. The collapse of the War market, coupled with a high industrial tariff policy and great foreign indebtedness to the United States, and coincident with a shift on the farms from animal to tractor power, left farmers with some 50 million excess acres under cultivation. The products of these acres

could no longer be sold profitably abroad and piling up at home, they smashed prices for the home market as well. No adequate effort was made to meet this situation prior to 1933. Since 1933, the Government has grappled with the task of helping farmers to make the needed adjustment. The aim has been to adjust exportable surpluses to demand, and thus to keep those surpluses from weakening the home market as well as the foreign market. Surely no resonable person, believing in the American ideal of a high standard of living, could deny the right of agriculture to a program which would put it on a level with industry in being able to participate in the benefits of the home market. And in the face of declining foreign markets, this could be done only by adjusting exportable surplus to actual export opportunities.

Difficulties with the farm export situation have continued. Many nations have felt it necessary to adopt nationalistic policies, setting up quotas, embargoes, domestic subsidies and the like, on farm products. Through its high tariff policy, the United States has been guilty with other nations of making international trade difficult. In our case there has been little excuse for this policy, since we are now not a debtor nation, but a creditor nation, and we need to enable foreign nations to send us goods to pay their debts and pay for our exports. Recently, a beginning has been made through reciprocal trade agreements toward increased foreign trade, and I should like to say right here that farmers more than any other group have the most to gain through this policy if wisely carried out. The progress, however, has necessarily been slow. In view of continuing difficulties in international trade, many Americans have lost faith in expansion of the foreign market as a way to renewed prosperity. They believe we should concentrate on the home market instead. Many of them are suggesting that agriculture as well as industry take the nationalistic view, that the time has come for the United States to become self-sufficient in every way possible.

. . . . .

A number of answers are being suggested at this time. I will mention them briefly first, and then discuss each one at more length. Some people, observing the increase in farm imports during the last two years, are saying that the thing to do is cut out all imports of farm products that can possibly be grown in this country. Give the American farmer exclusive right to his home market, they suggest, even if it means an embargo on all conpetitive imports. Nationalism for the farmer, they say, is the way to farm prosperity.

Another suggestion is that we set up a two-price system with no production control and sell the export part of our crops at low prices abroad, and the domestic part at a higher price at home, with the Government or the farmers themselves absorbing the difference.

Other people have another suggestion. They point to the traditional ingenuity of American industry in developing new industrial products and methods, and they say, encourage new industrial uses for American farm products, and we won't have to worry about foreign markets or domestic surpluses. They present maps and charts showing the acreage that would be needed to produce for these new industries providing that they can be successfuly launched.

. . . . .

. . . some are suggesting that we discard all checks upon production and adopt a two-price system, or export bounty, which would be a straight subsidy of production. This, they believe, would enable farmers to send surpluses abroad at lower prices, while selling the domestic part of the crop at home at higher prices.

I believe this plan can work for a given commodity when certain foreign conditions are favorable, and for a short time. In 1933, we were able to promote the sale of a quantity of wheat in this manner. However, as a long-time policy applied on a large scale, the dual-price or export-subsidy system would be certain to bring more grief than benefit to farmers and to the nation, particularly if the system were used in place of some sort of control over production. If the export market should be underwritten in this manner, it would surely bring into production an increasing acreage of the commodity affected. Increasing production would mean increased export surpluses which in turn would require higher and higher subsidies to maintain price. Finally it would result in the economic insanity of virtually giving away to foreign nations a large part of our wealth and soil fertility—very much as we gave away our crops and our soil fertility during the 1920's by lending to foreign countries money which they could not repay. I don't think we want to return to that kind of insanity. The pain of heavy surpluses and low price when the thing finally crashes is too great.

Besides, it is extremely probable that we could not get rid of huge surpluses in this manner, no matter how big the subsidy, especially if at the same time we refused to accept imports. And in passing, let me call your attention to the fact that many of those who argue for an export bounty are also vociferous advocates of embargoing imports. Other countries do not want to accept our products if we will not accept some of theirs. They are able to put up trade barriers overnight to keep out any of our products that they do not want to accept. Let us face the fact that the use of export subsidies by the nations of the world is really international price-cutting. It is a form of cut-throat competition which ruins everybody if it is carried far enough. The only kind of international trade which is worth anything, on a large scale and in the long run, is the kind which trades goods and services for goods and services.

. . . . .

As you know, efforts are being made by the State Department to work out better foreign trade conditions through the reciprocal trade agreement policy. I have been interested to see just how this new approach might compare with the old approach of Congressional tariff making. My conclusion, on the basis of what has been done to date, is that it is a much fairer approach, from the standpoint of agriculture at least, than the old log-rolling methods. . . .

I believe that agriculture has obtained real benefits through the reciprocal trade agreement policy. Though temporary adjustments may need to be made by certain producers, I believe that farmers as a whole have very much to gain from the policy. However, I can assure you that wherever it seems to me that farmers as a whole are not getting a square deal in proposed trade agreements, I hope to be the first to point that out and seek for a remedy.

Among other suggestions for bettering the market of farm products is that of encouraging greater industrial use of farm products. This is a program which any friend of the farmer wants to encourage in every way possible. Industry, of course, is a big customer of the farmer even now. It buys more than 40% of its raw materials from the farmer today. It buys cotton for making clothes, it buys tobacco, it buys some of our corn for starch, for syrup, and other products; it buys a certain amount of soy bean oil for paints, varnishes, and other industrial uses. The Department of Agriculture has long been experimenting in new industrial uses for farm products and has made important discoveries in this field. . . .

. . . . .

In the present Agricultural Conservation program of the AAA, farmers are making another approach to the supply problem, although from a long-time as well as an immediate point of view. Farmers know that the reasons for ruthless exploitation of the soil have often been economic—that under pressure of extreme supply and price fluctuation they have been alternately forced by ruinously low returns and induced by boom conditions to mine and sell soil fertility, or to expand the farm plant by turning under millions of acres of grass lands which should have remained in sod. I believe that farmers understand the public and private importance of stabilizing production, stabilizing prices, and of maintaining the productivity of farm land for years to come.

I think they also appreciate that, while the AAA conservation program will be of immediate help in stabilizing supplies, still the program is not a direct production control measure. It is well fitted to present needs, because the drought helped to dissipate surpluses. But farmers know that normal weather would bring surplus problems again, and will look forward to utilizing the method which the Supreme Court left open to them. The year 1938 is sure to see an interesting experimental effort by farmers to meet their supply problem through cooperation of the States. The Supreme Court did not abolish the farm surplus problem, nor did agriculture's interest in a balanced supply situation evaporate with the Hoosac Mills decision. But farmers were forced to look forward to using the method of cooperating through the States that the Court has left open to them. Agriculture will fight against recurrence of the surplus condition that ruined farmers in 1932.

. . . . .

I wonder if the farmers have an adequate appreciation of the size of the market which could be opened to them in this country if the ten or eleven millions of our people who are now unemployed were working, had incomes, and could become buyers of the goods of farm and factory. Besides the jobless, vast numbers of others have incomes so low or so uncertain that they can buy only meagerly.

The great problem of an industrial nation is to find methods which will assure distribution of the fruits of industry back to the masses of workers. Mass producing industries can function steadily and successfully only on a basis of mass consumption. Otherwise goods pile up, purchasing power becomes concentrated in a few hands, and civilization is shaken by recurrent plagues of unemployment and depression.

Our people have not yet solved this crucial problem of distribution. They are not expecting that a Utopian solution will materialize from nowhere overnight. But the terrifying experiences of 1932 convinced them that the time has come to make serious and constructive efforts in that direction. In 1933, our Government undertook to cope with the problem before it was too late.

. . . . .

During the first three months of 1936, farm income from the sale of products was over a billion and a half dollars, an increase of 20 percent over the income for January, February and March of 1935, not including benefit payments. The recession in farm income and rural retail business that followed the Hoosac Mills decision has been succeeded by new gains as farm confidence has been restored, as benefit payments have been resumed, and the price situation has been strengthened. This increase in farm income came about not through increased prices, but through the ability of consumers to absorb a larger amount of farm products at a seasonable price through increased purchasing power. Even so, the improvement in farm income was about twice as great as the improvement in consumers' income. This was due in part to the fact that farmers receive approximately half of the consumers' dollar spent for food, so that when a consumer benefits from 10 percent

more income, the increased expenditure on food, if it all goes to the producer means a 20 percent increase in the receipts of farmers.

. . . . .

Now, I think we can all see where the real hope of attaining and maintaining a great home market for American agriculture actually lies. It lies in keeping a healthy farm supply situation; in opening and keeping open the channels of international trade, so that surpluses of our great basic commodities will not back up on the farm; it lies in conservation of soil resources by sound production of sufficient supplies, not in the waste of those resources by reckless production of price-breaking surpluses.

On the demand side, agriculture's interests are served by building up the home market. Agriculture benefits from increased industrial activity and from measures designed to put purchasing power in the hands of the large numbers of people who still have almost none. This is agriculture's great stake in the national welfare.

What agriculture wants is customers with money to buy the products of the farm. For we all know that farmers with large quantities of stuff which they can't sell for want of customers with money, may be nearly as poor as people who need that stuff badly but who can't buy it. . . .

Of course there are some rich and powerful interests in this country which reject and obstruct every Government undertaking, whether it falls in the first or the second group of measures I have named.

These people fought the Agricultural Adjustment programs first in Congress and then in the courts. They have created subsidized organizations pretending to speak for the farmers in opposition to the farmers' adjustment and conservation programs, and to talk up regimentation, imports, chemical salvation or anything else that happened to come in handy in their efforts to arouse the farmers, or persuade the country that the farmers were aroused against measures which, for reasons of their own, these interests disliked.

The attacks on agriculture's programs have been accompanied by assaults directed against every effort of the Government to provide relief, create employment, and spread buying power among more people. The technique already familiar to farmers has been used in creating and subsidizing organizations to speak, in the name of liberty, or Constitution, or independence or Republic, but always to speak for those interests which are fighting the Government's reemployment, relief and recovery efforts.

The welfare of American agriculture is inseparably linked with the national welfare. The long depression that beset agriculture in the decade of the 20's was an important factor in the national depression of the 30's.

. . . . .

COMMENT

What is behind all of this policy of curtailment, restriction, scarcity and money manipulation? I say to you advisedly that there is but one idea back of it and that is to regiment the American farmer into a form of control just as absolute as that asserted over the Russian farmer today; to limit the amount of crops which he can raise; to select his markets for him; and, in fact, to take all profit out of his business.

> Lawyer Elisha Hanson, speaking at a dinner in honor of New York State Agriculture, August 28, 1935. *Vital Speeches*, I (September 23, 1935), 810.

The AAA was introduced to this country as a temporary, emergency measure. It is being continued as apparently permanent Socialistic control and regimentation of agriculture.

> Agricultural expert and author Dr. Charles W. Burkett. Quoted in Earl Reeves, *Truth About the New Deal* (New York: Longmans, Green & Company, 1936), p. 99.

The farmers of Russia supported the Bolsheviki against the newborn democracy on the promise of the land. Today they have the choice of Siberia or the collectivist farms. I have seen freedom, the most priceless heritage, torn from children that this generation might escape its responsibilities. I wish to say to you unhesitatingly that our country has been following step by step the road through which these millions of people in foreign countries lost their liberties. Our farmers have had the blessing of individual liberty in greater fullness in their lives than any other part of even our own people. It was the farmers who fired the first shot at Lexington. It must be the farmers of America who defend that heritage. I ask you to stop, look and listen.

> Former President Herbert Hoover speaking in Lincoln, Nebraska on January 16, 1936. *Vital Speeches*, II (January 27, 1936), 275.

The crocodile tears shed by the professional mourners of an old and obsolete order over the slaughter of little pigs and other measures to reduce surplus agricultural inventories deceive very few thinking people, and least of all the farmers themselves.

> President Franklin D. Roosevelt's "Address to Farmers" made in Washington, D.C., May 14, 1935. *Vital Speeches*, I (May 20, 1935), 523.

69. SEPTEMBER 15, 1936

Cordell Hull on American Foreign Policy

When Secretary of State Cordell Hull delivered this speech in New York on September 15, 1936, aggressive forces in Europe and the Far East were making the peace structure of the Versailles Conference and the 1920's appear ridiculous. Japan had occupied Manchuria, Hitler was re-arming Germany, Italy had invaded Ethiopia, and Spain was in the midst of a Civil War in which fascists and communists from all over the world joined battle.

Congress had passed neutrality legislation which required President Roosevelt to place an embargo on the shipment of war materials to all nations at war. Roosevelt very much feared that in the long run the neutrality legislation would drag the nation into war rather than keep it out. Though he was in a better position to judge the international situation than Congress, Roosevelt realized that he could not move without public support. He found himself in a dilemma, for many of the leaders of the isolationist bloc in Congress were key supporters of his domestic program. Nevertheless, the President and his Secretary of State made many efforts between 1936 and 1940 to change public opinion toward support of collective security. In the speech below Hull outlined the main features of American foreign policy during these troubled times. Largely due to the efforts of Hull and Roosevelt, the country eventually made the difficult adjustment to the re-

Peace and War: United States Foreign Policy, 1931–1941 (Washington, D.C., 1943), pp. 333–39.

sponsibilities of a great power in world affairs.

Our foreign relations are largely shaped by the physical geography of our country, the characteristics of our people, and our historical experience. Those who are in charge of the conduct of foreign policy must suit their actions to these underlying facts with due regard to the shifting circumstances of the times. This is particularly true in a democracy, where even in the short run the policies of the government must rest upon the support of the people.

We inhabit a large country which provides the basis for satisfactory and improving conditions of life. We do not seek or threaten the territory or great possessions of others. Great oceans lie between us and the powers of Asia and Europe. Though these are now crossed much more quickly and easily than they used to be, they still enable us to feel somewhat protected against physical impacts from abroad. We are a numerous, strong, active people. We have lived and developed in deep traditions of tolerance, of neighborly friendliness, of personal freedom, and of self-government. We have had long training in the settlement of differences of opinion and interest among ourselves by discussion and compromise. The winds of doctrines that are blowing so violently in many other lands are moderated here in our democratic atmosphere and tradition.

Our contribution must be in the spirit of our own situation and conceptions. It lies in the willingness to be friends but not allies. We wish extensive and mutually beneficial trade relations. We have the impulse to multiply our personal contacts, as shown by the constant American travel abroad. We would share and exchange the gifts which art, the stage, the classroom, and the scientists' and thinkers' study contribute to heighten life and understanding; we have led the world in promoting this sort of interchange among students, teachers, and artists. Our wish that natural human contacts be deeply and fully realized is shown by the great number of international conferences in which we participate, both private and intergovernmental. In such ways we would have our relations grow.

In deciding upon the character of our political relations with the outside world we naturally take into account the conditions prevailing there. These, today, are not tranquil or secure, but on the contrary in many countries are excited and haunted by mutual dread. In less than 20 years events have occurred that have taken away from international agreements their force and reliability as a basis of relations between nations. There appears to have been a great failure of the spirit, and out of this has come a many-sided combat of national ambitions, dogmas, and fears. In many lands the whole national energy has been organized to support absolute aims, far reaching in character but vaguely defined. These flare like a distant fire in the hills, and no one can be sure as to what they mean. There is an increasing acceptance of the idea that the end justifies all means. Under these conditions the individual who questions either means or end is frightened or crushed. For he encounters two controlling rules—compulsory subordination to autocratic will and the ruthless pressure of might. The result is dread and growing confusion.

Behind this lies the knowledge that laboratories and shops are producing instruments which can blow away human beings as though they were mites in a thunder storm, and these instruments have been placed in the hands of an increasing number of young men whom their leaders dedicate to the horrors of war. When Foreign Offices engage in discussion with each other today, they have an inescapable vision of men living in concrete chambers below the earth and concrete and steel forts and tanks upon the earth and operating destructive machines above the earth. They have strained and striven in many negotiations since the war to dispel that vision, but it appears to grow clearer and clearer.

The world waits. You may be sure that in most human hearts there is the steady murmur of prayer that life need not be yielded up in battle and that there may be peace, at least in our time.

It is in these circumstances we must shape our foreign relations. It is also these circumstances that present to us the problem of seeking to achieve a change in the dominant trend that is so full of menace.

I find as I review the line of foreign policy we have followed that we come close to Thomas Jefferson's expression—"peace, commerce, and honest friendship with all nations, entangling alliances with none." It is dangerous to take liberties with the great words of a great man, but I would add—settlement of disputes by peaceful means, renunciation of war as an instrument of national policy.

I think that the term "good neighbor" is an apt description of that policy. We have tried to give full meaning to that term. The good neighbor in any community minds his own essential business and does not willfully disturb the business of others. He mends his fences but does not put up spite fences. He firmly expects that others will not seek to disturb his affairs or dictate to him. He is tolerant, but his toleration does not include those who would introduce discord from elsewhere. He observes his agreements to the utmost of his ability; he adjusts by friendly methods any troubles that arise; he mingles freely in the give and take of life and concerns himself with the community welfare. All of this is in contrast with the hermit who isolates himself, who ignores the community, and, in his resistance to change, decays in a mean and bitter isolation. But the role of the good neighbor is a positive and active one which calls upon the energies, the friendliness, and the self-restraint of man or nation.

In affairs between nations the neighborliness obviously is less direct than between individuals in the local community. Its expression takes the form of just and fair dealings, without encroachment upon the rights of others, or oppression of the weak, or envy of the more fortunate. It contemplates liberal economic relations on the basis of mutual benefit, observance of law, and respect for agreements, and reliance upon peaceful processes when controversies arise.

In the everyday work of the Department of State dealing with critical issues, we have resolutely pursued this course.

We have tried to bring together American opinion and opinion in other countries in a common determination against the use of force for the settlement of disputes or for other national purposes. In that connection we have sought to maintain the vitality of the international agreement to renounce war which was signed by virtually all countries of the world when Mr. Kellogg was Secretary of State. But strong nations have chosen to proceed in disregard of that agreement, and this basis for international trust has thus been greatly impaired. We have tried to soften quarrels between other countries when they have arisen.

At times there has been criticism because we would not depart from our traditional policy and join with other governments in collective arrangements carrying the obligation of employing force, if necessary, in case disputes between

other countries brought them into war. That responsibility, carrying direct participation in the political relations of the whole of the world outside, we cannot accept, eager as we are to support means for the prevention of war. For current experience indicates how uncertain is the possibility that we, by our action, could vitally influence the policies or activities of other countries from which war might come. It is for the statesmen to continue their effort to effect security by new agreements which will prove more durable than those that have been broken. This Government would welcome that achievement. It would be like full light overcoming dense darkness. It is difficult to see how responsible governments can refrain from pushing compromise to its utmost limits to accomplish that result.

Of late we have increased our defense forces substantially. This has appeared essential in the face of the universal increase of armaments elsewhere and the disturbed conditions to which I have alluded. We would not serve the cause of peace by living in the world today without adequate powers of self-defense. We must be sure that in our desire for peace, we will not appear to any other country weak and unable to resist the imposition of force or to protect our just rights. At the same time I would make clear with the utmost emphasis that we stand ready to participate in all attempts to limit armaments by mutual accord and await the day when this may be realized.

I need say little of our relations with our great neighbor Canada. The American people and the Canadian people have lived in unbroken friendship. A new index of that friendship is the trade agreement signed last year. I have had to reckon with a number of attacks on this or that schedule of the agreement. In virtually every instance I have found, and I do not wish to be partisan in this remark, that the criticism represents misjudgment or distortion of the facts. I have watched the malicious attempts of some to juggle a few minor figures in the trade returns in such a way as to prejudice the minds of particular groups against an agreement which was the first step taken within the past half century to enable the American and Canadian peoples to obtain greater mutual benefit from their work and trade.

We have confirmed our good-neighbor policy by our actions in dealing with the American republics to the south of us. This Administration has made it clear that it would not intervene in any of those republics. It has endorsed this principle by signing at the Montevideo Conference the inter-American convention on the rights and duties of states; it has abrogated the Platt Amendment contained in our treaty with Cuba; it has withdrawn the American occupying forces from Haiti; it has negotiated new treaties with Panama, which, while fully safeguarding our rights to protect and operate the Canal, eliminate the rights we previously possessed to interfere in that republic. In all this we have shown that we have no wish to dictate to other countries, that we recognize equality of nations, and that we believe in the possibility of full cooperation between nations. Later this year there will be held in Argentina a conference between the American republics, which has been warmly welcomed, and there is general confidence that further ways can be found to assure the maintenance of peace on this continent.

Certainly the economic troubles that have pressed so hard on the world during these past few years are one of the main causes of the disturbance of spirit and upset of relations that have taken place. This Government has taken the lead in trying to bring about changes in the international trade situation which would improve conditions everywhere. The needs of our own domestic situation have coincided completely with this undertaking. By 1933 a serious emergency had arisen in our trade relationships with other countries. We had repeatedly increased the barriers to the entry of foreign products into this country, and the sale of American goods abroad was being subjected to increasingly drastic retaliation and restriction on the part of other governments. In addition, we had most substantial investments in foreign countries which our previous policy had thrown into great jeopardy. Many branches of American agriculture and industry required a revival of our trade with other countries if they were to escape continued depression, idleness of resources, and unemployment. The other countries had no smaller need.

Under the authority conferred by the Trade Agreements Act of 1934, we have entered into numerous commercial agreements whereby most carefully selected and limited reductions have been made in our own tariffs. In return, we have secured reductions of the barriers imposed against American goods by other countries and assurance of various kinds against the operation of the trade-control systems that have come into existence elsewhere. The vast decline in our foreign trade has ceased. A substantial and steady increase is being recorded. During 1935 our sales abroad exceeded those of 1932, the lowest year, by 671 millions of dollars. The trade records of 1936 to date indicate that this figure will be surpassed. This has been an extremely wholesome factor in the improvement in our own conditions and in building up the world's purchasing power. Our imports of foreign goods have similarly increased, reflecting chiefly the enlarged American demand for raw materials, arising from the improvement of productive activity in the United States and our increased purchasing power.

In the negotiation of these agreements the principle of equality has been maintained in the belief that trade conducted on this basis brings the greatest economic benefit, has the greatest possibilities of expansion, and involves the least conflict.

We are vigorously striving to secure similar equality of treatment on the part of other countries with which we have negotiated. In connection with this program we have refused to be drawn into a system of bilateral balancing between pairs of countries because this system is comparatively sterile and requires direct government management of international trade, which soon extends to management of domestic production. At the same time, we have been alert to the problem of protecting our trade interests against the incidental disadvantages that we might suffer from the practice of such a system by other countries.

The trade policy this country is pursuing fits well into our domestic economic situation and policies. I am willing to leave this judgment to the arbitration of facts. Certainly by now it should be clear, even to those engaged in industries that have been the most direct beneficiaries of excessive tariffs, that this alone will not bring them prosperity. It should also be apparent that they can thrive only when other branches of production thrive, including those that habitually dispose of a large part of their products in foreign markets.

The rebuilding of international trade offers a splendid opportunity for governments to improve the conditions of their people and to assure them the necessary means of acquiring the essentials of well-being and the raw materials for production. If this result can be achieved, one of the fertile causes of dissension and possible war would be weakened or removed. The plans and hopes of millions of individuals now appear to have no place except in military formation. An improvement of economic conditions would guarantee another place. Advancement in this direction need not await a solution of all political difficulties. Terms have been found by which advance can be made even in the face of the monetary uncertainty which still exists. A great opportunity awaits great leadership.

In trade interchange baleful elements enter particularly the trade in arms, ammunition, and implements of war. This trade is at present mainly incidental to the preparation for war. However, in some times and circumstances, it may itself be an element in stimulating or provoking war. Therefore, we have established a system requiring full disclosure regarding American trade in this field by placing those engaged in it under a license plan. Whether and to what extent it may be wise to regulate or restrict such trade between ourselves and other nations, for reasons other than the protection of military secrets, is a matter on which we are constantly weighing our current experience. Our existing legal authority is limited. But, as in the present Spanish situation, we assert our influence to the utmost to prevent arms shipped from this country from thwarting national or international efforts to maintain peace or end conflict. But action of that character cannot best be governed by inflexible rule, for, to a large extent, it must be determined in the light of the facts and circumstances of each situation. This much is certain—we are always ready to discourage to the utmost the traffic in arms when required in the interest of peace.

Up to this point I have dealt with the principles of our policies and relationships with other countries when peace prevails. Lately, after a lapse of almost 20 years, we have been called upon to consider with great seriousness the question of what these relationships should be if war were unhappily to occur again among the other great countries of the world. We must squarely face the fact that to stay clear of a widespread major war will require great vigilance, poise, and careful judgment in dealing with such interferences with our peaceful rights and activities as may take place.

Legislation recently passed provides some of the main essentials in a wise anticipatory policy. I have in mind the resolutions of Congress of 1935 and 1936 which, in addition to providing for the licensing of all imports and exports of arms, ammunition, and implements of war, prohibit their shipment to belligerent nations. Those same resolutions prohibit the flotation of loans and the establishment of credits in our market by belligerent countries, and otherwise strengthen our existing neutrality laws. On some of these matters the Congress by law has modified policies formerly pursued by this Government in times of war abroad. There are other vital aspects of this problem which will continue to receive the careful attention and study of the Department of State.

The problems arising during a period of neutrality are so great that they constantly renew in one the determination to spare no reasonable effort to play a full part in the encouragement of the maintenance of peace. We have sought to demonstrate that we are interested in peace everywhere. Surely this endeavor must continue to command our full abilities if war elsewhere can create such difficulties for us, if it can change for the worse the world in which we must live, if it can threaten the civilization with which all of us are concerned.

COMMENT

Beyond the maintenance of neighborly relations on the American continents and the opening of the channels of foreign commerce, Mr. Hull's indications of policy were negative and vague.

Editorial in the New York *Times*, September 17, 1936.

His moral indignation against wrong and the judicial quality and strength of his convictions, coupled with his mildness and patience, are about as fine an indication of our Americanism as there is left.

Former U.S. Ambassador to Russia, Joseph E. Davies in *Mission to Moscow* (New York: Simon & Schuster, Inc., 1941), p. 147.

What was needed . . . was not a further reiteration of principles that had been reiterated time and again ever since the Treaty of Versailles. What was needed, on the contrary, was some clear indication that the United States was willing to act in order to try to prevent war in Europe, and thus save those principles from oblivion. . . . Until the outbreak of the war in 1939 Hull seemed to believe that what he termed "preachments" to foreign governments, together with the series of trade agreements for which he so ably worked, would be sufficient to halt the triumphal march of the dictators and to bring the world back to paths of virtue and peace.

Former Under Secretary of State Sumner Welles in *Seven Decisions That Shaped History* (New York: Harper & Brothers, 1950), pp. 10–12.

70. MARCH 9, 1937

President Roosevelt on
Judiciary Reorganization

The Supreme Court during the early New Deal overturned several of Roosevelt's key legislative programs. To achieve his objectives, what was the President to do in order to get around these judicial obstacles? In early 1937, additional New Deal measures were on the docket of the Supreme Court. Yet, Roosevelt had no vacancies to fill on the Court. Finally, he decided to attempt a reorganization of the judiciary. In February, he submitted to Congress a proposal for (1) increasing the membership of the Supreme Court from nine to a maximum of fifteen if the judges after reaching the age of seventy refused to retire and (2) an addition of a total of not more than fifty judges to all classes of the federal courts. Though Roosevelt expected his proposals to encounter some opposition, he counted on public support to push them through Congress. Instead, his plan met widespread opposition. Town meetings denounced the proposals, bar associations protested, and mail flooded congressional offices. The President simply had not understood the country's deep reverence for the courts.

Realizing that opposition was developing among many who had supported him in 1932 and 1936, Roosevelt delivered a fireside chat to the nation on March 9, 1937, in which he reminded his listeners of the condition of the country four years earlier. Denying that his plans

SAMUEL I. ROSENMAN, ed., *The Public Papers and Addresses of Franklin D. Roosevelt*, (New York: Random House, Inc., 1941), VI, 122–33. Reprinted by permission of Random House, Inc.

were unconstitutional, he argued that the nation must save the Constitution from the Court. But Roosevelt was acting too late to repair the damage that his plan had suffered. Eventually, he was forced to back down, as the plan met increasing opposition and as the Supreme Court handed down several decisions which were more in tune with the times.

Last Thursday I described in detail certain economic problems which everyone admits now face the Nation. For the many messages which have come to me after that speech, and which it is physically impossible to answer individually, I take this means of saying "thank you."

Tonight, sitting at my desk in the White House, I make my first radio report to the people in my second term of office.

I am reminded of that evening in March, four years ago, when I made my first radio report to you. We were then in the midst of the great banking crisis.

Soon after, with the authority of the Congress, we asked the Nation to turn over all of its privately held gold, dollar for dollar, to the Government of the United States.

Today's recovery proves how right that policy was.

But when, almost two years later, it came before the Supreme Court its constitutionality was upheld only by a five-to-four vote. The change of one vote would have thrown all the affairs of this great Nation back into hopeless chaos. In effect, four Justices ruled that the right under a private contract to exact a pound of flesh was more sacred than the main objectives of the Constitution to establish an enduring Nation.

In 1933 you and I knew that we must never let our economic system get completely out of joint again—that we could not afford to take the risk of another great depression.

We also became convinced that the only way to avoid a repetition of those dark days was to have a government with power to prevent and to cure the abuses and the inequalities which had thrown that system out of joint.

We then began a program of remedying those abuses and inequalities—to give balance and stability to our economic system—to make it bomb-proof against the causes of 1929.

Today we are only part-way through that program—and recovery is speeding up to a point where the dangers of 1929 are again becoming possible, not this week or month perhaps, but within a year or two.

National laws are needed to complete that program. Individual or local or state effort alone cannot protect us in 1937 any better than ten years ago.

It will take time—and plenty of time—to work out our remedies administratively even after legislation is passed. To complete our program of protection in time, therefore, we cannot delay one moment in making certain that our National Government has power to carry through.

Four years ago action did not come until the eleventh hour. It was almost too late.

If we learned anything from the depression we will not allow ourselves to run around in new circles of futile discussion and debate, always postponing the day of decision.

The American people have learned from the depression. For in the last three national elections an overwhelming majority of them voted a mandate that the Congress and the President begin the task

of providing that protection—not after long years of debate, but now.

The Courts, however, have cast doubts on the ability of the elected Congress to protect us against catastrophe by meeting squarely our modern social and economic conditions.

We are at a crisis in our ability to proceed with that protection. It is a quiet crisis. There are no lines of depositors outside closed banks. But to the far-sighted it is far-reaching in its possibilities of injury to America.

I want to talk wth you very simply about the need for present action in this crisis—the need to meet the unanswered challenge of one-third of a Nation ill-nourished, ill-clad, ill-housed.

Last Thursday I described the American form of Government as a three horse team provided by the Constitution to the American people so that their field might be plowed. The three horses are, of course, the three branches of government—the Congress, the Executive and the Courts. Two of the horses are pulling in unison today; the third is not. Those who have intimated that the President of the United States is trying to drive that team, overlook the simple fact that the President, as Chief Executive, is himself one of the three horses.

It is the American people themselves who are in the driver's seat.

It is the American people themselves who want the furrow plowed.

It is the American people themselves who expect the third horse to pull in unison with the other two.

I hope that you have re-read the Constitution of the United States in these past few weeks. Like the Bible, it ought to be read again and again.

It is an easy document to understand when you remember that it was called into being because the Articles of Confederation under which the original thirteen States tried to operate after the Revolution showed the need of a National Government with power enough to handle national problems. In its Preamble, the Constitution states that it was intended to form a more perfect Union and promote the general welfare; and the powers given to the Congress to carry out those purposes can be best described by saying that they were all the powers needed to meet each and every problem which then had a national character and which could not be met by merely local action.

But the framers went further. Having in mind that in succeeding generations many other problems then undreamed of would become national problems, they gave to the Congress the ample broad powers "to levy taxes . . . and provide for the common defense and general welfare of the United States."

That, my friends, is what I honestly believe to have been the clear and underlying purpose of the patriots who wrote a Federal Constitution to create a National Government with national power, intended as they said, "to form a more perfect union . . . for ourselves and our posterity."

For nearly twenty years there was no conflict between the Congress and the Court. Then Congress passed a statute which, in 1803, the Court said violated an express provision of the Constitution. The Court claimed the power to declare it unconstitutional and did so declare it. But a little later the Court itself admitted that it was an extraordinary power to exercise and through Mr. Justice Washington laid down this limitation upon it: "It is but a decent respect due to the wisdom, the integrity and the patriotism of the legislative body, by which any law is passed, to presume in favor of its validity until its violation of the Constitution is proved beyond all reasonable doubt."

But since the rise of the modern movement for social and economic progress through legislation, the Court has more and more often and more and more boldly asserted a power to veto laws passed by the Congress and State Legislatures in complete disregard of this original limitation.

In the last four years the sound rule of giving statutes the benefit of all reasonable doubt has been cast aside. The Court has been acting not as a judicial body, but as a policy-making body.

When the Congress has sought to stabilize national agriculture, to improve the conditions of labor, to safeguard business against unfair competition, to protect our national resources, and in many other ways, to serve our clearly national needs, the majority of the Court has been assuming the power to pass on the wisdom of these Acts of the Congress —and to approve or disapprove the public policy written into these laws.

That is not only my accusation. It is the accusation of most distinguished Justices of the present Supreme Court. I have not the time to quote to you all the language used by dissenting Justices in many of these cases. But in the case holding the Railroad Retirement Act unconstitutional, for instance, Chief Justice Hughes said in a dissenting opinion that the majority opinion was "a departure from sound principles," and placed "an unwarranted limitation" upon the commerce clause." And three other Justices agreed with him.

In the case holding the A.A.A. unconstitutional, Justice Stone said of the majority opinion that it was a "tortured construction of the Constitution." And two other Justices agreed with him.

In the case holding the New York Minimum Wage Law unconstitutional, Justice Stone said that the majority were actually reading into the Constitution their "personal economic predilections," and that if the legislative power is not left free to choose the methods of solving the problems of poverty, subsistence and health of large numbers in the community, then "government is to be rendered impotent." And two other Justices agreed with him.

In the face of these dissenting opinions, there is no basis for the claim made by some members of the Court that something in the Constitution has compelled them regretfully to thwart the will of the people.

In the face of such dissenting opinions, it is perfectly clear, that as Chief Justice Hughes has said: "We are under a Constitution, but the Constitution is what the Judges say it is."

The Court in addition to the proper use of its judicial functions has improperly set itself up as a third House of the Congress—a super-legislature, as one of the justices has called it—reading into the Constitution words and implications which are not there, and which were never intended to be there.

We have, therefore, reached the point as a Nation where we must take action to save the Constitution from the Court and the Court from itself. We must find a way to take an appeal from the Supreme Court to the Constitution itself. We want a Supreme Court which will do justice under the Constitution—not over it. In our Courts we want a government of laws and not of men.

I want—as all Americans want—an independent judiciary as proposed by the framers of the Constitution. That means a Supreme Court that will enforce the Constitution as written—that will refuse to amend the Constitution by the arbitrary exercise of judicial power—amendment by judicial say-so. It does not mean a judiciary so independent that it can deny the existence of facts universally recognized.

How then could we proceed to perform the mandate given us? It was said in last year's Democratic platform, "If these problems cannot be effectively solved within the Constitution, we shall seek such clarifying amendment as will assume the power to enact those laws, adequately to regulate commerce, protect public health and safety, and safeguard economic security." In other words, we said we would seek an amendment only if every

other possible means by legislation were to fail.

When I commenced to review the situation with the problem squarely before me, I came by a process of elimination to the conclusion that, short of amendments, the only method which was clearly constitutional, and would at the same time carry out other much needed reforms, was to infuse new blood into all our Courts. We must have men worthy and equipped to carry out impartial justice. But, at the same time, we must have Judges who will bring to the Courts a present-day sense of the Constitution—Judges who will retain in the Courts the judicial functions of a court, and reject the legislative powers which the courts have today assumed.

In forty-five out of the forty-eight States of the Union, Judges are chosen not for life but for a period of years. In many States Judges must retire at the age of seventy. Congress has provided financial security by offering life pensions at full pay for Federal Judges on all Courts who are willing to retire at seventy. In the case of Supreme Court Justices, that pension is $20,000 a year. But all Federal Judges, once appointed, can, if they choose, hold office for life, no matter how old they may get to be.

What is my proposal? It is simply this: whenever a Judge or Justice of any Federal Court has reached the age of seventy and does not avail himself of the opportunity to retire on a pension, a new member shall be appointed by the President then in office, with the approval, as required by the Constitution, of the Senate of the United States.

That plan has two chief purposes. By bringing into the judicial system a steady and continuing stream of new and younger blood, I hope, first, to make the administration of all Federal justice speedier and, therefore, less costly; secondly, to bring to the decision of social and economic problems younger men who have had personal experience and contact with modern facts and circumstances under which average men have to live and work. This plan will save our national Constitution from hardening of the judicial arteries.

The number of Judges to be appointed would depend wholly on the decision of present Judges now over seventy, or those who would subsequently reach the age of seventy.

If, for instance, any one of the six Justices of the Supreme Court now over the age of seventy should retire as provided under the plan, no additional place would be created. Consequently, although there never can be more than fifteen, there may be only fourteen, or thirteen, or twelve. And there may be only nine.

There is nothing novel or radical about this idea. It seeks to maintain the Federal bench in full vigor. It has been discussed and approved by many persons of high authority ever since a similar proposal passed the House of Representatives in 1869.

Why was the age fixed at seventy? Because the laws of many States, the practice of the Civil Service, the regulations of the Army and Navy, and the rules of many of our Universities and of almost every great private business enterprise, commonly fix the retirement age at seventy years or less.

The statute would apply to all the courts in the Federal system. There is general approval so far as the lower Federal courts are concerned. The plan has met opposition only so far as the Supreme Court of the United States itself is concerned. If such a plan is good for the lower courts it certainly ought to be equally good for the highest Court from which there is no appeal.

Those opposing this plan have sought to arouse prejudice and fear by crying that I am seeking to "pack" the Supreme Court and that a baneful precedent will be established.

What do they mean by the words "packing the Court"?

Let me answer this question with a bluntness that will end all *honest* misunderstanding of my purposes.

If by that phrase "packing the Court" it is charged that I wish to place on the bench spineless puppets who would disregard the law and would decide specific cases as I wished them to be decided, I make this answer: that no President fit for his office would appoint, and no Senate of honorable men fit for their office would confirm, that kind of appointees to the Supreme Court.

But if by that phrase the charge is made that I would appoint and the Senate would confirm Justices worthy to sit beside present members of the Court who understand those modern conditions, that I will appoint Justices who will not undertake to override the judgment of the Congress on legislative policy, that I will appoint Justices who will act as Justices and not as legislators—if the appointment of such Justices can be called "packing the Courts," then I say that I and with me the vast majority of the American people favor doing just that thing—now.

Is it a dangerous precedent for the Congress to change the number of the Justices? The Congress had always had, and will have, that power. The number of Justices has been changed several times before, in the Administrations of John Adams and Thomas Jefferson—both signers of the Declaration of Independence—Andrew Jackson, Abraham Lincoln and Ulysses S. Grant.

I suggest only the addition of Justices to the bench in accordance with a clearly defined principle relating to a clearly defined age limit. Fundamentally, if in the future, America cannot trust the Congress it elects to refrain from abuse of our Constitutional usages, democracy will have failed far beyond the importance to it of any kind of precedent concerning the Judiciary.

We think it so much in the public interest to maintain a vigorous Judiciary that we encourage the retirement of elderly Judges by offering them a life pension at full salary. Why then should we leave the fulfillment of this public policy to chance or make it dependent upon the desire or prejudice of any individual Justice?

It is the clear intention of our public policy to provide for a constant flow of new and younger blood into the Judiciary. Normally every President appoints a large number of District and Circuit Judges and a few members of the Supreme Court. Until my first term practically every President of the United States had appointed at least one member of the Supreme Court. President Taft appointed five members and named a Chief Justice; President Wilson, three; President Harding, four, including a Chief Justice; President Coolidge, one; President Hoover, three, including a Chief Justice.

Such a succession of appointments should have provided a Court well-balanced as to age. But chance and the disinclination of individuals to leave the Supreme bench have now given us a Court in which five Justices will be over seventy-five years of age before next June and one over seventy. Thus a sound public policy has been defeated.

I now propose that we establish by law an assurance against any such ill-balanced Court in the future. I propose that hereafter, when a Judge reaches the age of seventy, a new and younger Judge shall be added to the Court automatically. In this way I propose to enforce a sound public policy by law instead of leaving the composition of our Federal Courts, including the highest, to be determined by chance or the personal decision of individuals.

If such a law as I propose is regarded as establishing a new precedent, is it not a most desirable precedent?

Like all lawyers, like all Americans, I regret the necessity of this controversy. But the welfare of the United States, and indeed of the Constitution itself, is what we all must think about first. Our difficulty with the Court today rises not from the Court as an institution but from human beings within it. But we cannot yield our constitutional destiny to the personal judgment of a few men who, being fearful of the future, would deny us the necessary means of dealing with the present.

This plan of mine is no attack on the Court; it seeks to restore the Court to its rightful and historic place in our system of Constitutional Government and to have it resume its high task of building anew on the Constitution "a system of living law." The Court itself can best undo what the Court has done.

I have thus explained to you the reasons that lie behind our efforts to secure results by legislation within the Constitution. I hope that thereby the difficult process of constitutional amendment may be rendered unnecessary. But let us examine that process.

There are many types of amendment proposed. Each one is radically different from the other. There is no substantial group within the Congress or outside it who are agreed on any single amendment.

It would take months or years to get substantial agreement upon the type and language of an amendment. It would take months and years thereafter to get a two-thirds majority in favor of that amendment in *both* Houses of the Congress.

Then would come the long course of ratification by three-fourths of all the States. No amendment which any powerful economic interests or the leaders of any powerful political party have had reason to oppose has ever been ratified within anything like a reasonable time. And thirteen States which contain only five percent of the voting population can block ratification even though the thirty-five States with ninety-five percent of the population are in favor of it.

A very large percentage of newspaper publishers, Chambers of Commerce, Bar Associations, Manufacturers' Associaions, who are trying to give the impression that they really do want a constitutional amendment would be the first to exclaim as soon as an amendment was proposed, "Oh! I was for an amendment all right, but this amendment that you have proposed is not the kind of an amendment that I was thinking about. I am, therefore, going to spend my time, my efforts and my money to block that amendment, although I would be awfully glad to help get some other kind of amendment ratified."

Two groups oppose my plan on the ground that they favor a constitutional amendment. The first includes those who fundamentally object to social and economic legislation along modern lines. This is the same group who during the campaign last Fall tried to block the mandate of the people.

Now they are making a last stand. And the strategy of that last stand is to suggest the time-consuming process of amendment in order to kill off by delay the legislation demanded by the mandate.

To them I say: I do not think you will be able long to fool the American people as to your purposes.

The other group is composed of those who honestly believe the amendment process is the best and who would be willing to support a reasonable amendment if they could agree on one.

To them I say: we cannot rely on an amendment as the immediate or only answer to our present difficulties. When the time comes for action, you will find that many of those who pretend to support you will sabotage any constructive amendment which is proposed. Look at these strange bed-fellows of yours. When before have you found them really at your side in your fights for progress?

And remember one thing more. Even if an amendment were passed, and even if in the years to come it were to be ratified, its meaning would depend upon the kind of Justices who would be sitting on the Supreme Court bench. An amend-ment, like the rest of the Constitution, is what the Justices say it is rather than what its framers or you might hope it is.

This proposal of mine will not infringe in the slightest upon the civil or religious liberties so dear to every American.

My record as Governor and as President proves my devotion to those liberties.

You who know me can have no fear that I would tolerate the destruction by any branch of government of any part of our heritage of freedom.

The present attempt by those opposed to progress to play upon the fears of danger to personal liberty brings again to mind that crude and cruel strategy tried by the same opposition to frighten the workers of America in a pay-envelope propaganda against the Social Security Law. The workers were not fooled by that propaganda then. The people of America will not be fooled by such propaganda now.

I am in favor of action through legislation:

First, because I believe that it can be passed at this session of the Congress.

Second, because it will provide a reinvigorated, liberal-minded Judiciary necessary to furnish quicker and cheaper justice from bottom to top.

Third, because it will provide a series of Federal Courts willing to enforce the Constitution as written, and unwilling to assert legislative powers by writing into it their own political and economic policies.

During the past half century the balance of power between the three great branches of the Federal Government, has been tipped out of balance by the Courts in direct contradiction of the high purposes of the framers of the Constitution. It is my purpose to restore that balance. You who know me will accept my solemn assurance that in a world in which democracy is under attack, I seek to make American democracy succeed. You and I will do our part.

COMMENT

There is a lot of talk of the President "packing" the Court. Let's not be misled by a red herring. The Court has been "packed" for years—"packed" in the interests of Economic Royalists, "packed" for the benefit of the Liberty Leaguers, "packed" in the cause of Reaction and Laissez-faire.

> Senator Robert M. LaFollette, Jr., of Wisconsin in a radio broadcast, February 13, 1937. *Vital Speeches*, III (March 1, 1937), 313.

Even if every charge brought against the so-called "reactionary" members of this Court be true, it is far better that we await orderly but inevitable change of personnel than that we impatiently overwhelm them with new members. Exhibiting this restraint, thus demonstrating our faith in the American system, we shall set an example that will protect the independent American judiciary from attack as long as this Government stands.

> Report of the Senate Judiciary Committee on Supreme Court Reform, June 7, 1937. *Senate Report* No. 711, 75th Cong., 1st Sess., p. 3.

The court can, by relying on one set of precedents rather than another, shut its eyes to fundamental economic and social trends. It can do this, but it will be at the loss of the faith of the people . . . and ultimately at the cost . . . of the court itself.

> Secretary of Agriculture Henry Wallace in *Newsweek*, VIII (July 4, 1936), 11.

71. *1937*

NLRB v. Jones and Laughlin Steel Corporation

Throughout the spring and summer of 1937, public opinion continued to turn against President Roosevelt's plan to reorganize the federal judiciary. During the debate, the Supreme Court surprised much of the nation by approving New Deal legislation which had previously been under judicial clouds. One example was the decision in the case of NLRB v. Jones and Laughlin. The issue confronting the Court in that case was the constitutionality of the National Labor Relations Act which imposed detailed controls over labor-management relations in in-

301 U.S. 1 (1937).

dustry. To Roosevelt's surprise, Justices Hughes and Roberts joined with the liberals of the Court in sustaining the constitutionality of the act. Arguing from the "stream of commerce" doctrine, Chief Justice Hughes rejected the old categorical distinction between direct and indirect effects upon commerce, and maintained instead that the extent to which Congress might regulate manufacturing depended on the degree to which the industries involved were engaged in interstate commerce. Justice McReynolds argued in a vigorous dissent that the principles laid down in Schechter Poultry

Corporation v. *U.S.* (*see pp. 277–285*) *were applicable in this case.*

Roosevelt and his advisers later contended that Hughes and Roberts joined with the liberal Justices (Cardoza, Stone, and Brandeis) in an effort to save the Court from the President's judiciary reorganization scheme. This led one observer to remark, "A switch in time saves nine." The results of the 1936 election probably had some effect on the thinking of Hughes and Roberts. On the other hand, the extent to which the Court actually reversed itself in the NLRB v. *Jones and Laughlin case from the position it took in the case of Schechter* v. *U.S. is still a matter of dispute among constitutional experts.*

In a proceeding under the National Labor Relations Act of 1935, the National Labor Relations Board found that the respondent, Jones & Laughlin Steel Corporation, had violated the Act by engaging in unfair labor practices affecting commerce. The proceeding was instituted by the Beaver Valley Lodge No. 200, affiliated with the Amalgamated Association of Iron, Steel and Tin Workers of America, a labor organization. The unfair labor practices charged were that the corporation was discriminating against members of the union with regard to hire and tenure of employment, and was coercing and intimidating its employees in order to interfere with their self-organization. The discriminatory and coercive action alleged was the discharge of certain employees.

The National Labor Relations Board, sustaining the charge, ordered the corporation to cease and desist from such discrimination and coercion, to offer reinstatement to ten of the employees named, to make good their losses in pay, and to post for thirty days notices that the corporation would not discharge or discriminate against members, or those desiring to become members, of the labor union. As the corporation failed to comply, the Board petitioned the Circuit Court of Appeals to enforce the order. The court denied the petition, holding that the order lay beyond the range of federal power. . . . We granted certiorari.

The scheme of the National Labor Relations Act . . . is too long to be quoted in full. . . . The first section sets forth findings with respect to the injury to commerce resulting from the denial by employers of the right of employees to organize and from the refusal of employers to accept the procedure of collective bargaining. There follows a declaration that it is the policy of the United States to eliminate these causes of obstruction to the free flow of commerce. The Act then defines the terms it uses, including the terms "commerce" and "affecting commerce." . . . The labor union filed with the Board its verified charge. The Board thereupon issued its complaint against the respondent alleging that its action in discharging the employees in question constituted unfair labor practices affecting commerce within the meaning of § 8, subdivisions (1) and (3), and § 2, subdivisions (6) and (7) of the Act. Respondent, appearing specially for the purpose of objecting to the jurisdiction of the Board, filed its answer. Respondent admitted the discharges, but alleged that they were made because of inefficiency or violation of rules or for other good reasons and were not ascribable to union membership or activities. As an affirmative defense respondent challenged the constitutional validity of the statute and its applicability in the instant case . . . the Board received evidence upon the merits and at its close made its findings and order.

Contesting the ruling of the Board, the respondent argues (1) that the Act is in reality a regulation of labor relations and not of interstate commerce; (2) that the Act can have no application to the respondent's relations with its production employees because they are not subject to regulation by the federal government; and (3) that the provisions of the Act violate § 2 of Article III and the Fifth and Seventh Amendments of the Constitution of the United States.

The facts as to the nature and scope of the business of the Jones & Laughlin Steel Corporation have been found by the Labor Board and, so far as they are essential to the determination of this controversy, they are not in dispute. The Labor Board has found: The corporation is organized under the laws of Pennsylvania and has its principal office at Pittsburgh. It is engaged in the business of manufacturing iron and steel in plants situated in Pittsburgh and nearby Aliquippa, Pennsylvania. It manufactures and distributes a widely diversified line of steel and pig iron, being the fourth largest producer of steel in the United States. With its subsidiaries—nineteen in number—it is a completely integrated enterprise, owning and operating ore, coal and limestone properties, lake and river transportation facilities and terminal railroads located at its manufacturing plants. It owns or controls mines in Michigan and Minnesota. It operates four ore steamships on the Great Lakes, used in the transportation of ore to its factories. It owns coal mines in Pennsylvania. It operates towboats and steam barges used in carrying coal to its factories. It owns limestone properties in various places in Pennsylvania and West Virginia. It owns the Monongahela connecting railroad which connects the plants of the Pittsburgh works and forms an interconnection with the Pennsylvania, New York Central and Baltimore and Ohio Railroad systems. It owns the Aliquippa and Southern Railroad Company which connects the Aliquippa works with the Pittsburgh and Lake Erie, part of the New York Central system. Much of its product is shipped to its warehouses in Chicago, Detroit, Cincinnati and Memphis,—to the last two places by means of its own barges and transportation equipment. In Long Island City, New York, and in New Orleans it operates structural steel fabricating shops in connection with the warehousing of semi-finished materials sent from its works. Through one of its wholly-owned subsidiaries it owns, leases and operates stores, warehouses and yards for the distribution of equipment and supplies for drilling and operating oil and gas wells and for pipe lines, refineries and pumping stations. It has sales offices in twenty cities in the United States and a wholly-owned subsidiary which is devoted exclusively to distributing its product in Canada. Approximately 75 per cent of its product is shipped out of Pennsylvania.

Summarizing these operations, the Labor Board concluded that the works in Pittsburgh and Aliquippa "might be likened to the heart of a self-contained, highly integrated body. They draw in the raw materials from Michigan, Minnesota, West Virginia, Pennsylvania in part through arteries and by means controlled by the respondent; they transform the materials and then pump them out to all parts of the nation through the vast mechanism which the respondent has elaborated.". . . .

Practically all the factual evidence in the case, except that which dealt with the nature of respondent's business, concerned its relations with the employees in the Aliquippa plant whose discharge was the subject of the complaint. These employees were active leaders in the labor union. Several were officers and others were leaders of particular groups. Two of the employees were motors inspectors; one was a tractor driver; three were crane operators; one was a washer in the coke plant; and three were laborers. Three other employees were mentioned in the complaint but it was withdrawn as to one of them and no evidence was heard on the action taken with respect to the other two.

While respondent criticises the evidence and the attitude of the Board, which is described as being hostile toward employers and particularly toward those who insisted upon their constitutional rights, respondent did not take advantage of its opportunity to present evidence to refute that which was offered to show discrimination and coercion. In this situation, the record presents no ground for setting aside the order of the Board so far as the facts pertaining to the circumstances and purpose of the discharge of the employees are concerned. Upon that point it is sufficient to say that the evidence supports the findings of the Board that respondent discharged these men "because of their union activity and for the purpose of discouraging membership in the union." We turn to the questions of law which respondent urges in contesting the validity and application of the Act.

First. *The scope of the Acts.* The Act is challenged in its entirety as an attempt to regulate all industry, thus invading the reserved powers of the States over their local concerns. It is asserted that the references in the Act to interstate and foreign commerce are colorable at best; that the Act is not a true regulation of such commerce or of matters which directly affect it but on the contrary has the fundamental object of placing under the compulsory supervision of the federal government all industrial labor relations within the nation. The argument seeks support in the broad words of the preamble (section one) and in the sweep of the provisions of the Act, and it is further insisted that its legislative history shows an essential universal purpose in the light of which its scope cannot be limited by either construction or by the application of the separability clause.

If this conception of terms, intent and consequent inseparability were sound, the Act would necessarily fall by reason of the limitation upon the federal power which inheres in the constitutional grant, as well as because of the explicit reservation of the Tenth Amendment. . . . The authority of the federal government may not be pushed to such an extreme as to

destroy the distinction, which the commerce clause itself establishes, between commerce "among the several States" and the internal concerns of a State. That distinction between what is national and what is local in the activities of commerce is vital to the maintenance of our federal system.

But we are not at liberty to deny effect to specific provisions, which Congress has constitutional power to enact, by superimposing upon them inferences from general legislative declarations of an ambiguous character, even if found in the same statute. The cardinal principle of statutory construction is to save and not to destroy. We have repeatedly held that as between two possible interpretations of a statute, by one of which it would be unconstitutional and by the other valid, our plain duty is to adopt that which will save the Act. Even to avoid a serious doubt the rule is the same. . . .

We think it clear that the National Labor Relations Act may be construed so as to operate within the sphere of constitutional authority. The jurisdiction conferred upon the Board, and invoked in this instance, is found in § 10(a), which provides:

SEC. 10(a). The Board is empowered, as hereinafter provided, to prevent any person from engaging in any unfair labor practice (listed in section 8) affecting commerce.

The critical words of this provision, prescribing the limits of the Board's authority in dealing with the labor practices, are "affecting commerce." The Act specifically defines the "commerce" to which it refers (§ 2[6]):

The term "commerce" means trade, traffic, commerce, transportation, or communication among the several States, or between the District of Columbia or any Territory of the United States and any State or other Territory, or between any foreign country and any State, Territory, or the

District of Columbia, or within the District of Columbia or any Territory, or between points in the same State but through any other State or any Territory or the District of Columbia or any foreign country.

There can be no question that the commerce thus contemplated by the Act (aside from that within a Territory or the District of Columbia) is interstate and foreign commerce in the constitutional sense. The Act also defines the term "affecting commerce" (§ 2[7]):

The term "affecting commerce" means in commerce, or burdening or obstructing commerce or the free flow of commerce, or having led or tending to lead to a labor dispute burdening or obstructing commerce or the free flow of commerce.

This definition is one of exclusion as well as inclusion. The grant of authority to the Board does not purport to extend to the relationship between all industrial employees and employers. Its terms do not impose collective bargaining upon all industry regardless of effects upon interstate or foreign commerce. It purports to reach only what may be deemed to burden or obstruct that commerce and, thus, qualified, it must be construed as contemplating the exercise of control within constitutional bounds. It is a familiar principle that acts which directly burden or obstruct interstate or foreign commerce, or its free flow, are within the reach of the congressional power. Acts having that effect are not rendered immune because they grow out of labor disputes. . . . It is the effect upon commerce, not the source of the injury, which is the criterion. . . . Whether or not particular action does affect commerce in such a close and intimate fashion as to be subject to federal control, and hence to lie within the authority conferred upon the Board, is left by the statute to be determined as individual cases arise. We are thus to inquire whether in the instant case the constitutional boundary has been passed.

Second. *The unfair labor practices in question.* The unfair labor practices found by the Board are those defined in § 8, subdivisions (1) and (3). These provide:

SEC. 8. It shall be an unfair labor practice for an employer—

(1) To interfere with, restrain, or coerce employees in the exercise of the rights guaranteed in section 7.

(3) By discrimination in regard to hire or tenure of employment or any term or condition of employment to encourage or discourage membership in any labor organization: . . .

Section 8, subdivision (1), refers to § 7, which is as follows:

SEC. 7. Employees shall have the right to self-organization, to form, join, or assist labor organizations, to bargain collectively through representatives of their own choosing, and to engage in concerted activities, for the purpose of collective bargaining or other mutual aid or protection.

Thus, in its present application, the statute goes no further than to safeguard the right of employees to self-organization and to select representatives of their own choosing for collective bargaining or other mutual protection without restraint or coercion by their employer.

That is a fundamental right. Employees have as clear a right to organize and select their representatives for lawful purposes as the respondent has to organize its business and select its own officers and agents. Discrimination and coercion to prevent the free exercise of the right of employees to self-organization and representation is a proper subject for condemnation by competent legislative authority. Long ago we stated the reason for labor organizations. We said that they were organized out of the necessities of the situation; that a single employee was helpless in dealing with an employer; that he was dependent ordinarily on his daily wage for the maintenance of himself and family; that if the employer refused to pay him the wages that he thought fair, he was nevertheless unable to leave the employ and resist arbitrary and unfair treatment; that union was essential to give laborers opportunity to deal on an equality with their employer. . . . We reiterated these views when we had under consideration the Railway Labor Act of 1926. Fully recognizing the legality of collective action on the part of employees in order to safeguard their proper interests, we said that Congress was not required to ignore this right but could safeguard it. Congress could seek to make appropriate collective action of employees an instrument of peace rather than of strife. We said that such collective action would be a mockery if representation were made futile by interference with freedom of choice. Hence the prohibition by Congress of interference with the selection of representatives for the purpose of negotiation and conference between employers and employees, "instead of being an invasion of the constitutional right of either, was based on the recognition of the rights of both." . . .

Third. *The application of the Act to employees engaged in production. The principle involved.* Respondent says that whatever may be said of employees engaged in interstate commerce, the industrial relations and activities in the manufacturing department of respondent's enterprise are not subject to federal regulation. The argument rests upon the proposition that manufacturing in itself is not commerce. . . .

The Government distinguishes these cases. The various parts of respondent's enterprise are described as interdependent and as thus involving "a great movement of iron ore, coal and limestone along well-defined paths to the steel mills, thence through them, and thence in the form of steel products into the consuming centers of the country—a definite and well-understood course of business." It is urged that these activities constitute a "stream" or "flow" of commerce, of which the Aliquippa manufacturing plant is the focal point, and that industrial

strife at that point would cripple the entire movement. Reference is made to our decision sustaining the Packers and Stockyards Act. . . . The Court found that the stockyards were but a "throat" through which the current of commerce flowed and the transactions which there occurred could not be separated from that movement. . . .

Respondent contends that the instant case presents material distinctions. Respondent says that the Aliquippa plant is extensive in size and represents a large investment in buildings, machinery and equipment. The raw materials which are brought to the plant are delayed for long periods and, after being subjected to manufacturing processes, "are changed substantially as to character, utility and value." The finished products which emerge "are to a large extent manufactured without reference to pre-existing orders and contracts and are entirely different from the raw materials which enter at the other end." Hence respondent argues that "If importation and exportation in interstate commerce do not singly transfer purely local activities into the field of congressional regulation, it should follow that their combination would not alter the local situation." . . .

We do not find it necessary to determine whether these features of defendant's business dispose of the asserted analogy to the "stream of commerce" cases. . . . The congressional authority to protect interstate commerce from burdens and obstructions is not limited to transactions which can be deemed to be an essential part of a "flow" of interstate or foreign commerce. Burdens and obstructions may be due to injurious action springing from other sources. The fundamental principle is that the power to regulate commerce is the power to enact "all appropriate legislation" for "its protection and advancement" . . . to adopt measures "to promote its growth and insure its safety" . . . "to foster, protect, control and restrain." . . . Although activities may be intrastate in character when separately considered, if they have such a close and substantial relation to interstate commerce that their control is essential or appropriate to protect that commerce from burdens and obstructions, Congress cannot be denied the power to exercise that control. . . . Undoubtedly the scope of this power must be considered in the light of our dual system of government and may not be extended so as to embrace effects upon interstate commerce so indirect and remote that to embrace them, in view of our complex society, would effectually obliterate the distinction between what is national and what is local and create a completely centralized government. Id. The question is necessarily one of degree. . . .

It is thus apparent that the fact that the employees here concerned were engaged in production is not determinative. The question remains as to the effect upon interstate commerce of the labor practice involved. . . .

Fourth. *Effects of the unfair labor practice in respondent's enterprise.* Giving full weight to respondent's contention with respect to a break in the complete continuity of the "stream of commerce" by reason of respondent's manufacturing operations, the fact remains that the stoppage of those operations by industrial strife would have a most serious effect upon interstate commerce. In view of respondent's far-flung activities, it is idle to say that the effect would be indirect or remote. It is obvious that it would be immediate and might be catastrophic. We are asked to shut our eyes to the plainest facts of our national life and to deal with the question of direct and indirect effects in an intellectual vacuum. Because there may be but indirect and remote effects upon interstate commerce in connection with a host of local enterprises throughout the country, it does not follow that other industrial activities do not have

such a close and intimate relation to interstate commerce as to make the presence of industrial strife a matter of the most urgent national concern. When industries organize themselves on a national scale, making their relation to interstate commerce the dominant factor in their activities, how can it be maintained that their industrial labor relations constitute a forbidden field into which Congress may not enter when it is necessary to protect interstate commerce from the paralyzing consequences of industrial war? We have often said that interstate commerce itself is a practical conception. It is equally true that interferences with that commerce must be appraised by a judgment that does not ignore actual experience.

Experience has abundantly demonstrated that the recognition of the right of employees to self-organization and to have representatives of their own choosing for the purpose of collective bargaining is often an essential condition of industrial peace. Refusal to confer and negotiate has been one of the most prolific causes of strife. This is such an outstanding fact in the history of labor disturbances that it is a proper subject of judicial notice and requires no citation of instances. . . . But with respect to the appropriateness of the recognition of self-organization and representation in the promotion of peace, the question is not essentially different in the case of employees in industries of such a character that interstate commerce is put in jeopardy from the case of employees of transportation companies. And of what avail is it to protect the facility of transportation, if interstate commerce is throttled with respect to the commodities to be transported!

These questions have frequently engaged the attention of Congress and have been the subject of many inquiries. The steel industry is one of the great basic industries of the United States, with ramifying activities affecting interstate commerce at every point. The Government aptly refers to the steel strike of 1919–1920 with its far-reaching consequences. The fact that there appears to have been no major disturbance in that industry in the more recent period did not dispose of the possibilities of future and like dangers to interstate commerce which Congress was entitled to foresee and to exercise its protective power to forestall. It is not necessary again to detail the facts as to respondent's enterprise. Instead of being beyond the pale, we think that it presents in a most striking way the close and intimate relation which a manufacturing industry may have to interstate commerce and we have no doubt that Congress had constitutional authority to safeguard the right of respondent's employees to self-organization and freedom in the choice of representatives for collective bargaining.

Fifth. *The means which the Act employs. Questions under the due process clause and other constitutional restrictions.* Respondent asserts its right to conduct its business in an orderly manner without being subjected to arbitrary restraints. What we have said points to the fallacy in the argument. Employees have their correlative right to organize for the purpose of securing the redress of grievances and to promote agreements with employers relating to rates of pay and conditions of work. . . . Restraint for the purpose of preventing an unjust interference with that right cannot be considered arbitrary or capricious. The provisions of § 9(a) that representatives, for the purpose of collective bargaining, of the majority of the employees in an appropriate unit shall be the exclusive representatives of all the employees in that unit, imposes upon the respondent only the duty of conferring and negotiating with the authorized representatives of its employees for the purpose of settling a labor dispute. . . .

The Act does not compel agreements between employers and employees. It does not compel any agreement whatever. It does not prevent the employer "from refusing to make a collective contract and hiring individuals on whatever terms" the employer "may by unilateral action determine." The Act expressly provides in § 9(a) that any individual employee or a group of employees shall have the right at any time to present grievances to their employer. The theory of the Act is that free opportunity for negotiation with accredited representatives of employees is likely to promote industrial peace and may bring about the adjustments and agreements which the Act in itself does not attempt to compel. . . . The Act does not interfere with the normal exercise of the right of the employer to select its employees or to discharge them. The employer may not, under cover of that right, intimidate or coerce its employees with respect to their self-organization and representation, and, on the other hand, the Board is not entitled to make its authority a pretext for interference with the right of discharge when that right is exercised for other reasons than such intimidation and coercion. The true purpose is the subject of investigation with full opportunity to show the facts. It would seem that when employers freely recognize the right of their employees to their own organizations and their unrestricted right of representation there will be much less occasion for controversy in respect to the free and appropriate exercise of the right of selection and discharge.

The Act has been criticised as onesided in its application; that it subjects the employer to supervision and restraint and leaves untouched the abuses for which employees may be responsible; that it fails to provide a more comprehensive plan,—with better assurances of fairness to both sides and with increased chances of success in bringing about, if not compelling, equitable solutions of industrial disputes affecting interstate commerce. But we are dealing with the power of Congress, not with a particular policy or with the extent to which policy should go. We have frequently said that the legislative authority, exerted within its proper field, need not embrace all the evils within its reach. The Constitution does not forbid "cautious advance, step by step," in dealing with the evils which are exhibited in activities within the range of legislative power. . . . The question in such cases is whether the legislature, in what it does prescribe, has gone beyond constitutional limits.

The procedural provisions of the Act are assailed. But these provisions, as we construe them, do not offend against the constitutional requirements governing the creation and action of administrative bodies. . . . The Act establishes standards to which the Board must conform. There must be complaint, notice and hearing. The Board must receive evidence and make findings. The findings as to the facts are to be conclusive, but only if supported by evidence. The order of the Board is subject to review by the designated court, and only when sustained by the court may the order be enforced. Upon that review all questions of the jurisdiction of the Board and the regularity of its proceedings, all questions of constitutional right or statutory authority, are open to examination by the court. We construe the procedural provisions as affording adequate opportunity to secure judicial protection against arbitrary action in accordance with the well-settled rules applicable to administrative agencies set up by Congress to aid in the enforcement of valid legislation. It is not necessary to repeat these rules which have frequently been declared. None of them appears to have been transgressed in the instant case. Respondent was notified and heard. It had opportunity to meet the charge of

unfair labor practices upon the merits, and by withdrawing from the hearing it declined to avail itself of that opportunity. The facts found by the Board support its order and the evidence supports the findings. Respondent has no just ground for complaint on this score.

The order of the Board required the reinstatement of the employees who were found to have been discharged because of their "union activity" and for the purpose of "discouraging membership in the union." The requirement was authorized by the Act. . . .

Respondent complains that the Board not only ordered reinstatemet but directed the payment of wages for the time lost by the discharge, less amounts earned by the employee during that period. This part of the order was also authorized by the Act, § 10(c). It is argued that the requirement is equivalent to a money judgment and hence contravenes the Seventh Amendment with respect to trial by jury. The Seventh Amendment provides that "In suits at common law, where the value in controversy shall exceed twenty dollars, the right of trial by jury shall be preserved." The Amendment thus preserves the right which existed under the common law when the Amendment was adopted. . . . Thus it has no application to cases where recovery of money damages is an incident to equitable relief even though damages might have been recovered in an action at law. . . . It does not apply where the proceeding is not in the nature of a suit at common law. . . .

The instant case is not a suit at common law or in the nature of such a suit. The proceeding is one unknown to the common law. It is a statutory proceeding. Reinstatement of the employee and payment for time lost are requirements imposed for violation of the statute and are remedies appropriate to its enforcement. The contention under the Seventh Amendment is without merit.

Our conclusion is that the order of

the Board was within its competency and that the Act is valid as here applied. The judgment of the Circuit Court of Appeals is reversed and the cause is remanded for further proceedings in conformity with this opinion.

COMMENT

The Circuit Courts of Appeals have held the power of Congress under the commerce clause does not extend to relations between employers and their employees engaged in manufacture. . . . therefore the Act conferred upon the National Labor Relations Board no authority in respect of matters covered by the questioned orders. . . . No decision or judicial opinion to the contrary has been cited, and we find none.

Justice McReynolds dissenting in NLRB *v.* Jones and Laughlin Steel Corporation. 301 U.S. 76 (1937).

72. *MAY 1, 1937*

Neutrality Act

Disillusioned with the results of World War I, Congress, during the 1930's, attempted to insulate the United States against future wars. During the fall of 1934, Senator Gerald P. Nye of North Dakota convinced many Americans that the United States had gone to war in 1917 in order to protect its trade and loans with the Allies. If America was to stay out of wars, Nye argued that trade and loans with future belligerents must be prohibited. Influenced by this outlook, Congress passed the Neutrality Acts of 1935 and 1936, which directed the President to prohibit the exportation of ammunition and other implements of war to belligerent nations. These acts were experimental in nature and were to expire on May 1, 1937. As a result, Congress passed a third Neutrality Act which was designed to modify the two previous acts and to give them permanent form.

Neutrality legislation received much

U.S. *Statutes at Large*, I, pt. I, 121–28.

criticism on the grounds that it served notice to armed dictators that if they attacked their democratic neighbors, the United States would not aid either nation. The weakness of the neutrality legislation was clearly exposed when Japan launched its attack on China in July, 1937. To have applied the provisions of the act would have cut the Chinese off from their major source of supply. This placed the Administration in a difficult position, for the provisions of the Neutrality Act would aid Japan. As no formal declaration of war existed between China and Japan, Roosevelt refused to invoke the act.

. . . . .

EXPORT OF ARMS, AMMUNITION, AND IMPLEMENTS OF WAR

SECTION 1. (a) Whenever the President shall find that there exists a state of war between, or among, two or more foreign states, the President shall proclaim such fact, and it shall thereafter be unlawful to export, or attempt to export, or cause to be exported, arms, ammunition, or implements of war from any place in the United States to any belligerent state named in such proclamation, or to any neutral state for transshipment to, or for the use of, any such belligerent state.

(b) The President shall, from time to time, by proclamation, extend such embargo upon the export of arms, ammunition, or implements of war to other states as and when they may become involved in such war.

(c) Whenever the President shall find that a state of civil strife exists in a foreign state and that such civil strife is of a magnitude or is being conducted under such conditions that the export of arms, ammunition, or implements of war from the United States to such foreign state would threaten or endanger the peace of the United States, the President shall proclaim such fact, and it shall thereafter be unlawful to export, or attempt to export, or cause to be exported, arms, ammunition, or implements of war from any place in the United States to such foreign state, or to any neutral state for transshipment to, or for the use of, such foreign state.

(d) The President shall, from time to time by proclamation, definitely enumerate the arms, ammunition, and implements of war, the export of which is prohibited by this section. The arms, ammunition, and implements of war so enumerated shall include those enumerated in the President's proclamation Numbered 2163, of April 10, 1936, but shall not include raw materials or any other articles or materials not of the same general character as those enumerated in the said proclamation, and in the Convention for the Supervision of the International Trade in Arms and Ammunition and in Implements of War, signed at Geneva June 17, 1925.

(e) Whoever, in violation of any of the provisions of this Act, shall export, or attempt to export, or cause to be exported, arms, ammunitions, or implements of war from the United States shall be fined not more than $10,000, or imprisoned not more than five years, or both, and the property, vessel, or vehicle containing the same shall be subject to the provisions of sections 1 to 8, inclusive, title 6, chapter 30, of the Act approved June 15, 1917. . . .

. . . . .

(g) Whenever, in the judgment of the President, the conditions which have caused him to issue any proclamation under the authority of this section have ceased to exist, he shall revoke the same, and the provisions of this section shall thereupon cease to apply with respect to the state or states named in such proclamation, except with respect to offenses committed, or forfeitures incurred, prior to such revocation.

EXPORT OF OTHER ARTICLES
AND MATERIALS

SEC. 2. (a) Whenever the President shall have issued a proclamation under the authority of section 1 of this Act and he shall thereafter find that the placing of restrictions on the shipping of certain articles or materials in addition to arms, ammunition, and implements of war from the United States to belligerent states, or to a state wherein civil strife exists, is necessary to promote the security or preserve the peace of the United States or to protect the lives of citizens of the United States, he shall so proclaim, and it shall thereafter be unlawful, except under such limitations and exceptions as the President may prescribe as to lakes, rivers, and inland waters bordering on the United States, and as to transportation on or over lands bordering on the United States, for any American vessel to carry such articles or materials to any belligerent state, or to any state wherein civil strife exists, named in such proclamation issued under the authority of section 1 of this Act, or to any neutral state for transshipment to, or for the use of, any such belligerent state or any such state wherein civil strife exists. The President shall by proclamation from time to time definitely enumerate the articles and materials which it shall be unlawful for American vessels to so transport.

(b) Whenever the President shall have issued a proclamation under the authority of section 1 of this Act and he shall thereafter find that the placing of restrictions on the export of articles or materials from the United States to belligerent states, or to a state wherein civil strife exists, is necessary to promote the security or preserve the peace of the United States or to protect the lives or commerce of citizens of the United States, he shall so proclaim, and it shall thereafter be unlawful, except under such limitations and exceptions as the President may prescribe as to lakes, rivers, and inland waters bordering on the United States, and as to transportation on or over land bordering on the United States, to export or transport, or attempt to export or transport, or cause to be exported or transported, from the United States to any belligerent state, or to any state wherein civil strife exists, named in such proclamation issued under the authority of section 1 of this Act, or to any neutral state for transshipment to, or for the use of, any such belligerent state or any such state wherein civil strife exists, any articles or materials whatever until all right, title, and interest therein shall have been transferred to some foreign government, agency, institution, association, partnership, corporation, or national. The shipper of such articles or materials shall be required to file with the collector of the port from which they are to be exported a declaration under oath that there exists in citizens of the United States no right, title, or interest in such articles or materials, and to comply with such rules and regulations as shall be promulgated from time to time by the President. Any such declaration so filed shall be a conclusive estoppel against any claim of any citizen of the United States of right, title, or interest in such articles or materials. Insurance written by underwriters on any articles or materials the export of which is prohibited by this Act, or on articles or materials carried by an American vessel in violation of subsection (a) of this section, shall not be deemed an American interest therein, and no insurance policy issued on such articles or materials and no loss incurred thereunder or by the owner of the vessel carrying the same shall be made a basis of any claim put forward by the Government of the United States.

(c) The President shall from time to time by proclamation extend such restrictions as are imposed under the authority of this section to other states as and when they may be declared to become belligerent states under proclamations issued under the authority of section 1 of this Act.

(d) The President may from time to time change, modify, or revoke in whole or in part any proclamations issued by him under the authority of this section.

. . . . .

FINANCIAL TRANSACTIONS

SEC. 3 (a) Whenever the President shall have issued a proclamation under the authority of section 1 of this Act, it shall thereafter be unlawful for any person within the United States to purchase, sell, or exchange bonds, securities, or other obligations of the government of any belligerent state or of any state wherein civil strife exists, named in such proclamation, or of any political subdivision of any state, or of any person acting for or on behalf of the government of any state, or of any faction or asserted government within any such state wherein civil strife exists, or of any person acting for or on behalf of any faction or asserted government within any such state wherein civil strife exists, issued after the date of such proclamation, or to make any loan or extend any credit to any such government, political subdivision, faction, asserted government, or person, or to solicit or receive any contribution for any such government, political subdivision, faction, asserted government, or person: *Provided,* That if the President shall find that such action will serve to protect the commercial or other interests of the United States or its citizens, he may, in his discretion, and to such extent and under such regulations as he may prescribe, except from the operation of this section ordinary commercial credits and short-time obligations in aid of legal transactions and of a character customarily used in normal peacetime commercial transactions. Nothing in this subsection shall be construed to prohibit the solicitation or collection of funds to be used for medical aid and assistance, or for food and clothing to relieve human suffering, when such solicitation or collection of funds is made on behalf of and for use by any person or organization which is not acting for or on behalf of any such government, political subdivision, faction, or asserted government, but all such solicitations and collections of funds shall be subject to the approval of the President and shall be made under such rules and regulations as he shall prescribe.

(b) The provisions of this section shall not apply to a renewal or adjustment of such indebtedness as may exist on the date of the President's proclamation.

(c) Whoever shall violate the provisions of this section or of any regulations issued hereunder shall, upon conviction thereof, be fined not more than $50,000 or imprisoned for not more than five years, or both. Should the violation be by a corporation, organization, or association, each officer or agent thereof participating in the violation may be liable to the penalty herein prescribed.

. . . . .

EXCEPTIONS—AMERICAN REPUBLICS

SEC. 4. This Act shall not apply to an American republic or republics engaged in war against a non-American state or states, provided the American republic is not cooperating with a non-American state or states in such war.

NATIONAL MUNITIONS CONTROL BOARD

SEC. 5. (a) There is hereby established a National Munitions Control Board (hereinafter referred to as the 'Board') to carry out the provisions of this Act. The Board shall consist of the Secretary of State, who shall be chairman and executive office of the Board, the Secretary of the Treasury, the Secretary of War, the Secretary of the Navy, and the Secretary of Commerce. Except as otherwise provided in this Act, or by other law, the administration of this Act is vested in the Department of State. The Secretary of State shall promulgate such rules and regulations with regard to the enforcement of this section as he may deem necessary to carry out its provisions. The Board shall be convened by the chairman and shall hold at least one meeting a year.

(b) Every person who engages in the business of manufacturing, exporting, or importing any of the arms, ammunition, or implements of war referred to in this Act, whether as an exporter, importer, manufacturer, or dealer, shall register with the Secretary of State his name, or business name, principal place of business, and places of business in the United States, and a list of the arms, ammunition, and implements of war which he manufactures, imports, or exports.

(c) Every person required to register under this section shall notify the Secretary of State of any change in the arms, ammunition, or implements of war which he exports, imports, or manufactures; and upon such notification the Secretary of States shall issue to such person an amended certificate of registration, free of charge, which shall remain valid until the date of expiration of the original certificate. Every person required to register under the provisions of this section shall pay a registration fee of $500, unless he manufactured, exported, or imported arms, ammunition, and implement of war to a total sales value of less than $50,000 during the twelve months immediately preceding his registration, in which case he shall pay a registration fee of $100. Upon receipt of the required registration fee, the Secretary of State shall issue a registration certificate valid for five years, which shall be renewable for further periods of five years upon the payment of each renewal of a fee of $500 in the case of persons who manufactured, exported, or imported arms, ammunitions, and implements of war to a total sales value of more than $50,000 during the twelve months immediately preceding the renewal, or a fee of $100 in the case of persons who manufactured, exported, or imported arms, ammunition, and implements of war to a total sales value of less than $50,000 during the twelve months immediately preceding the renewal. The Secretary of the Treasury is hereby directed to refund, out of any moneys in the Treasury not otherwise appropriated, the sum of $400

to every person who shall have paid a registration fee of $500 pursuant to this Act, who manufactured, exported, or imported arms, ammunition, and implements of war to a total sales value of less than $50,000 during the twelve months immediately preceding his registration.

(d) It shall be unlawful for any person to export, or attempt to export, from the United States to any other state, any of the arms, ammunition, or implements of war referred to in this Act, or to import, or attempt to import, to the United States from any other state, any of the arms, ammunition, or implements of war referred to in this Act, without first having obtained a license therefor.

. . . . .

(k) The President is hereby authorized to proclaim upon recommendation of the Board from time to time a list of articles which shall be considered arms, ammunition, and implements of war for the purposes of this section.

AMERICAN VESSELS PROHIBITED FROM CARRYING ARMS TO BELLIGERENT STATES

SEC. 6. (a) Whenever the President shall have issued a proclamation under the authority of section 1 of this Act, it shall thereafter be unlawful, until such proclamation is revoked, for any American vessel to carry any arms, ammunition, or implements of war to any belligerent state, or to any state wherein civil strife exists, named in such proclamation, or to any neutral state for transshipment to, or for the use of, any such belligerent state or any state wherein civil strife exists.

(b) Whoever, in violation of the provisions of this section, shall take, or attempt to take, or shall authorize, hire, or solicit another to take, any American vessel carrying such cargo out of port or from the jurisdiction of the United States shall be fined not more than $10,-000, or imprisoned not more than five years, or both; and, in addition, such vessel, and her tackle, apparel, furniture, and equipment, and the arms, ammunition, and implements of war on board, shall be forfeited to the United States.

USE OF AMERICAN PORTS AS BASE OF SUPPLY

SEC. 7. (a) Whenever, during any war in which the United States is neutral, the President, or any person thereunto authorized by him, shall have cause to believe that any vessel, domestic or foreign, whether requiring clearance or not, is about to carry out of a port of the United States, fuel, men, arms, ammunition, implements of war, or other supplies to any warship, tender, or supply ship of a belligerent state, but the evidence is not deemed sufficient to justify forbidding the departure of the vessel . . ., and if, in the President's judgment, such action will serve to maintain peace between the United States and foreign states, or to protect the commercial interests of the United States and its citizens, or to promote the security or neutrality of the United States, he shall have the power and it shall be his duty to require the owner, master, or person in command thereof, before departing from a port of the United States, to give a bond to the United States, with sufficient sureties, in such amount as he shall deem proper, conditioned that the vessel will not deliver the men, or any part of the cargo, to any warship, tender, or supply ship of a belligerent state.

(b) If the President, or any person thereunto authorized by him, shall find that a vessel, domestic or foreign, in a port of the United States, has previously cleared from a port of the United States during such war and delivered its cargo, or any part thereof to a warship, tender, or supply ship of a belligerent state, he may prohibit the departure of such vessel during the duration of the war.

SUBMARINES AND ARMED MERCHANT VESSELS

SEC. 8. Whenever, during any war in which the United States is neutral, the President shall find that special restrictions placed on the use of the ports and territorial waters of the United States by the submarines or armed merchant vessels of a foreign state, will serve to maintain peace between the United States and foreign states, or to protect the commercial interests of the United States and its citizens, or to promote the security of the United States, and shall make proclamation thereof, it shall thereafter be unlawful for any such submarine or armed merchant vessel to enter a port or the territorial waters of the United States or to depart therefrom, except under such conditions and subject to such limitations as the President may prescribe. Whenever, in his judgment, the conditions which have caused him to issue his proclamation have ceased to exist, he shall revoke his proclamation and the provisions of this section shall thereupon cease to apply.

TRAVEL ON VESSELS OF BELLIGERENT STATES

SEC. 9. Whenever the President shall have issued a proclamation under the authority of section 1 of this Act it shall thereafter be unlawful for any citizen of the United States to travel on any vessel of the state or states named in such proclamation, except in accordance with such rules and regulations as the President shall prescribe: *Provided, however,* That the provisions of this section shall not apply to a citizen of the United States traveling on a vessel whose voyage was begun in advance of the date of the President's proclamation, and who had no opportunity to discontinue his voyage after that date: *And provided further,* That they shall not apply under ninety days after the date of the President's proclamation to a citizen of the United States returning from a foreign state to the United States. Whenever, in the President's judgment, the conditions which have caused him to issue his proclamation have ceased to exist, he shall revoke his proclamation and the provisions of this section shall thereupon cease to apply with respect to the state or states named in such proclamation, except with respect to offenses committed prior to such revocation.

ARMING OF AMERICAN MERCHANT VESSELS PROHIBITED

SEC. 10. Whenever the President shall have issued a proclamation under the authority of section 1, it shall thereafter be unlawful, until such proclamation is revoked, for any American vessel engaged in commerce with any belligerent state, or any state wherein civil strife exists, named in such proclamation, to be armed or to carry any armament, arms, ammunition, or implements of war, except small arms and ammunition therefor which the President may deem necessary and shall publicly designate for the preservation of discipline aboard such vessels.

REGULATIONS

SEC. 11. The President may, from time to time, promulgate such rules and regulations, not inconsistent with law, as may be necessary and proper to carry out any of the provisions of this Act; and he may exercise any power or authority conferred on him by this Act through such officer or officers, or agency or agencies, as he shall direct.

. . . . .

COMMENT

The attempt to write a binding, cast-iron law today to fix American neutrality policy . . . is like saying . . . I have decided that my grandchild is to be a prize fighter without knowing whether your grandchild is to be a boy or a girl.

Walter Lippmann in a radio address, January 18, 1936. *Vital Speeches*, II (January 27, 1936), 262–63.

We have learned that when we deliberately try to legislate neutrality, our neutrality laws may operate unevenly and unfairly—may actually give aid to the aggressor and deny it to the victim. The instinct of self-preservation should warn us that we ought not to let that happen any more.

President Franklin D. Roosevelt in his annual message to Congress, January 4, 1939. *Roosevelt's Foreign Policy, 1933–41: Franklin D. Roosevelt's Unedited Speeches and Messages* (New York, 1942), p. 156.

73. *OCTOBER 5, 1937*

President Roosevelt's Quarantine the Aggressors Speech

In October, 1937, the United States joined with the League of Nations in labeling Japan as a treaty violator. The same month, in a speech delivered at Chicago, President Roosevelt surprised the public by appealing to the "peace-loving nations" of the world to make an effort to "quarantine" war like an epidemic disease. Though the President mentioned no nation specifically, it was clear that he was referring to Japan. Roosevelt did not spell out what he meant by "quarantine," but it was assumed that he was advocating the severance of diplomatic relations with a nation judged to be an aggressor. The speech was one of many attempts by Roosevelt to bring about a transition of public opinion toward support of collective security. Instead of being successful, the speech provoked a violent reaction among isolationists who charged that Roosevelt was trying to lead the nation into war. One poll demonstrated that a sizeable majority in Congress opposed supporting the League of Nations in any type of action against Japan. When Secretary of State Cordell Hull and other prominent Democrats failed to rally to the President's defense, Roosevelt became convinced that the public would not support him in any policy which might attempt to deter armed aggression in the world.

SAMUEL I. ROSENMAN, ed., *The Public Papers and Addresses of Franklin D. Roosevelt* (New York: Random House, Inc., 1941), VI, 406–11. Reprinted by permission of Random House, Inc.

. . . . .

The political situation in the world, which of late has been growing progressively worse, is such as to cause grave concern and anxiety to all the peoples and nations who wish to live in peace and amity with their neighbors.

Some fifteen years ago the hope of mankind for a continuing era of international peace were raised to great heights when more than sixty nations solemnly pledged themselves not to resort to arms in furtherance of their national aims and policies. The high aspirations expressed in the Briand–Kellogg Peace Pact and the hopes for peace thus raised have of late given way to a haunting fear of calamity. The present reign of terror and international lawlessness began a few years ago.

It began through unjustified interference in the internal affairs of other nations or the invasion of alien territory in violation of treaties; and has now reached a stage where the very foundations of civilization are seriously threatened. The landmarks and traditions which have marked the progress of civilization toward a condition of law, order and justice are being wiped away.

Without a declaration of war and without warning or justification of any kind, civilians, including vast numbers of women and children, are being ruthlessly murdered with bombs from the air. In times of so-called peace, ships are being attacked and sunk by submarines without cause or notice. Nations are fomenting and taking sides in civil warfare in nations that have never done them any harm. Nations claiming freedom for themselves deny it to others.

Innocent peoples, innocent nations, are being cruelly sacrificed to a greed for power and supremacy which is devoid of all sense of justice and humane considerations.

To paraphrase a recent author "perhaps we foresee a time when men, exultant in the technique of homicide, will rage so hotly over the world that every precious thing will be in danger, every book and picture and harmony, every treasure garnered through two millenniums, the small, the delicate, the defenseless—all will be lost or wrecked or utterly destroyed."

If those things come to pass in other parts of the world, let no one imagine that America will escape, that America may expect mercy, that this Western Hemisphere will not be attacked and that it will continue tranquilly and peacefully to carry on the ethics and the arts of civilization.

If those days come "there will be no safety by arms, no help from authority, no answer in science. The storm will rage till every flower of culture is trampled and all human beings are leveled in a vast chaos."

If those days are not to come to pass—if we are to have a world in which we can breathe freely and live in amity without fear—the peace-loving nations must make a concerted effort to uphold laws and principles on which alone peace can rest secure.

The peace-loving nations must make a concerted effort in opposition to those violations of treaties and those ignorings of humane instincts which today are creating a state of international anarchy and instability from which there is no escape through mere isolation or neutrality.

Those who cherish their freedom and recognize and respect the equal right of their neighbors to be free and live in peace, must work together for the triumph of law and moral principles in order that peace, justice and confidence may prevail in the world. There must be a return to a belief in the pledged word, in the value of a signed treaty. There must be recognition of the fact that national morality is as vital as private morality.

A bishop wrote me the other day: "It seems to me that something greatly needs to be said in behalf of ordinary humanity against the present practice of carrying the horrors of war to helpless civilians, especially women and children. It may be that such a protest might be regarded by many, who claim to be realists, as futile, but may it not be that the heart of mankind is so filled with horror at the present needless suffering that that force could be mobilized in sufficient volume to lessen such cruelty in the days ahead. Even though it may take twenty years, which God forbid, for civilization to make effective its corporate protest against this barbarism, surely strong voices may hasten the day."

There is a solidarity and interdependence about the modern world, both technically and morally, which makes it impossible for any nation completely to isolate itself from economic and political upheavals in the rest of the world, especially when such upheavals appear to be spreading and not declining. There can be no stability or peace either within nations or between nations except under laws and moral standards adhered to by all. International anarchy destroys every foundation for peace. It jeopardizes either the immediate or the future security of every nation, large or small. It is, therefore, a matter of vital interest and concern to the people of the United States that the sanctity of international treaties and the maintenance of international morality be restored.

The overwhelming majority of the peoples and nations of the world today want to live in peace. They seek the removal of barriers against trade. They want to exert themselves in industry, in agriculture and in business, that they may increase their wealth through the production of wealth-producing goods rather than striving to produce military planes and bombs and machine guns and cannon for the destruction of human lives and useful property.

In those nations of the world which seem to be piling armament on armament for purposes of aggression, and those other nations which fear acts of aggression against them and their security, a very high proportion of their national income is being spent directly for armaments. It runs from thirty to as high as fifty percent. We are fortunate. The proportion that we in the United States spend is far less—eleven or twelve percent.

How happy we are that the circumstances of the moment permit us to put our money into bridges and boulevards, dams and reforestation, the conservation of our soil and many other kinds of useful works rather than into huge standing armies and vast supplies of implements of war.

I am compelled and you are compelled, nevertheless, to look ahead. The peace, the freedom and the security of ninety percent of the population of the world is being jeopardized by the remaining ten percent who are threatening a breakdown of all international order and law. Surely the ninety percent who want to live in peace under law and in accordance with moral standards that have received almost universal acceptance through the centuries, can and must find some way to make their will prevail.

The situation is definitely of universal concern. The questions involved relate not merely to violations of specific provisions of particular treaties; they are questions of war and of peace, of international law and especially of principles of humanity. It is true that they involve definite violations of agreements, and especially of the Covenant of the League of Nations, the Briand–Kellogg Pact and the Nine Power Treaty. But they also involve problems of world economy, world security and world humanity.

It is true that the moral consciousness of the world must recognize the importance of removing injustices and well-founded grievances; but at the same time it must be aroused to the cardinal necessity of honoring sanctity of treaties, of respecting the rights and liberties of others and of putting an end to acts of international aggression.

It seems to be unfortunately true that the epidemic of world lawlessness is spreading.

When an epidemic of physical disease starts to spread, the community approves and joins in a quarantine of the patients in order to protect the health of the community against the spread of the disease.

It is my determination to pursue a policy of peace. It is my determination to adopt every practicable measure to avoid involvement in war. It ought to be inconceivable that in this modern era, and in the face of experience, any nation could be so foolish and ruthless as to run the risk of plunging the whole world into war by invading and violating, in contravention of solemn treaties, the territory of other nations that have done them no real harm and are too weak to protect themselves adequately. Yet the peace of the world and the welfare and security of every nation, including our own, is today being threatened by that very thing.

No nation which refuses to exercise forbearance and to respect the freedom and rights of others can long remain strong and retain the confidence and respect of other nations. No nation ever loses its dignity or its good standing by conciliating its differences, and by exercising great patience with, and consideration for, the rights of other nations.

War is a contagion, whether it be declared or undeclared. It can engulf states and peoples remote from the original scene of hostilities. We are determined to keep out of war, yet we cannot insure ourselves against the disastrous effects of war and the dangers of involvement. We are adopting such measures as will minimize our risk of involvement, but we cannot have complete protection in a world of disorder in which confidence and security have broken down.

If civilization is to survive the principles of the Prince of Peace must be restored. Trust between nations must be revived.

Most important of all, the will for peace on the part of peace-loving nations that may be tempted to violate their agreements and the rights of others will desist from such a course. There must be positive endeavors to preserve peace.

America hates war. America hopes for peace. Therefore, America actively engages in the search for peace.

COMMENT

If Mr. Roosevelt had no further thought than to give voice to moral indignation, he chose an unfortunate manner and time. The note he struck was hectoring and supercilious. . . . Surely he does not suppose that the United States can impose its own standards of political morality on other nations by the simple process of slapping them rhetorically on the wrist.

Editorial in the New York *Sun*, October 6, 1937.

Americans must not, knowingly or unknowingly, jointly or alone, embark on another costly attempt to reform the world.

Editorial in the Boston (Mass.) *Herald*, October 8, 1937.

This Chicago utterance says forcibly things which need saying and utters warnings that should be uttered.

Editorial in the Los Angeles (Calif.) *Times*, October 6, 1937.

---

74. *MAY 3, 1939*

Adolph Berle on American Policy in Latin America

Students of American foreign policy have long been in disagreement about the meaning of the term "dollar diplomacy" as applied to Latin America prior to 1930. Some have argued that the American government, while making honest efforts to forestall foreign intervention

Department of State, *Press Releases*, No. 501, Publication 1328, xx, 378.

in Latin America, urged American bankers to invest there in order to promote stability. Dollars were used to carry out the ends of American diplomacy. In areas where American capital was invested, the danger of foreign intervention decreased. Other students have contended that dollar diplomacy is but another name for economic exploitation and that American *investments in Latin America were generally devoid of strategic considerations. Diplomacy was used to advance and protect American business interests abroad. To help clarify the matter, Adolph Berle, Jr., an assistant secretary of state, made the following statement before the American Academy of Political Science on May 3, 1939.*

. . . . .

Many of our own major mistakes, indeed, in this hemisphere have been due more to the fear of European domination than to any desire to increase the area of our territory. Conspicuous among these were the interventions beginning at the time of the Panama Canal incident, the Nicaraguan occupation, and the occupations of Haiti and Santo Domingo. It has been customary, particularly among students who hold the Marxist view of history, to ascribe these to desire to protect American capital, which thus became the forerunner of imperialism. Yet as the history becomes increasingly clear, and as the documents are more completely available, the Marxian student finds that the facts do not bear him out. In many cases the intervention of American capital in Central America and in the West Indian republics was undertaken not at the instance of American capitalists seeking outlet for their funds. It was un-

dertaken at the direct instance of the American Government; and the motive appears to have been the fear lest European capital, affected with European politics, might find foothold on this side of the Atlantic. An example may be found in the occupations of Haiti and Santo Domingo. In each case American banks had purchased the control of the banks previously serving those island countries; but the documents today make it clear that the American financiers did so rather unwillingly, at the direct urging of the State Department; and that the State Department urged the American financial moves as a means of eliminating European financial moves. It may also be noted that alone among the great powers of the world, having accomplished that objective, public sentiment in the United States swiftly mobilized against the continuance of the occupations, they were withdrawn freely and without reserve, largely in consequence, first, of the continuous urging of the present Under Secretary, Mr. Sumner Welles, then a staff member of the State Department, and finally, as a part of the broad policy laid out and executed by Secretary Hull. The final result has been the firmer establishment of independent nations who owe their safety not to their military force but to the strength of the pan-American idea.

COMMENT

The diplomacy of the present administration has sought to respond to modern ideas of commercial intercourse. This policy has been characterized as substituting dollars for bullets. It is one that appeals alike to idealistic humanitarian sentiments, to the dictates of sound policy and strategy, and to legitimate commercial aims.

President William Howard Taft in his annual message to Congress, December 3, 1912. James D. Richardson, ed., *Messages and Papers of the Presidents* (New York, 1917), XVII, 7770–71.

The logic of political geography and of strategy, and now our tremendous national interest created by the Panama Canal, make the safety, the peace, and the prosperity of Central America and the zone of the Caribbean of paramount interest to the Government of the United States. Thus the malady of revolutions and financial collapse is most acute precisely in the region where it is most dangerous to us. It is here that we seek to apply a remedy.

> Secretary of State Philander C. Knox in an address before the New York State Bar Association, January 19, 1912. *Papers Relating to the Foreign Relations of the United States, 1912* (Washington, 1919), p. 1092.

75.

Wendell Willkie on
Domestic Issues of 1940

When the Republicans assembled in Philadelphia for their national convention in June, 1940, the leading candidates for their party's presidential nomination were Robert A. Taft, Arthur H. Vandenberg, and Thomas E. Dewey. But the party at the last minute surprised most of the nation by nominating a former Democrat, Wendell Willkie, president of Commonwealth and Southern Corporation. Although Willkie had fought against the Tennessee Valley Authority, he was no economic Tory. Rather, he was in basic agreement with most of Roosevelt's domestic and foreign policies. He directed his campaign against the waste and inefficiency of the New Deal. Though Willkie's campaign was poorly organized, he provided the Republican party with more dramatic leadership than it had received since the days of Theodore Roosevelt. But the urgency of the war crisis and the return of prosperity made the nation reluctant to change presidents. Thus, Franklin Roosevelt became the first and

WENDELL WILLKIE in *This Is Wendell Willkie* (New York: Dodd, Mead and Company, Inc., 1940), pp. 222–24, 230–33. Reprinted by permission of Dodd, Mead and Company, Inc. Copyright 1940 by Dodd, Mead and Company, Inc.

only president in the nation's history to be elected for more than two terms.

The great liberal movement of the early twentieth century, led by such men as Theodore Roosevelt, by the elder Robert M. La Follette and Woodrow Wilson, was the expression of an effort to make this adjustment. The last of these great leaders, Woodrow Wilson, in the program for what he called "the new freedom," thought that this adjustment had been made. Perhaps the program would have succeeded if it had been organized at a normal period in the world's history. Unfortunately, the time was not normal: the next year the world was plunged into a war. When it was over, the liberal faith, which is always one of the first casualties of war, was slow to recover. The United States was rich. People were making money. Industry was expanding so fast that there wasn't time to think about controls. A few men in business and in banking managed to concentrate in their hands an enormous amount of money and influence, and the investor, the employee and the consumer began to feel helpless before their secret manipulations.

It is clear now that the system of 1929 could not be permitted to stand.

Democracy in this third phase needed more social controls. These the New Deal supplied, in a vast network of regulation. The liberal cannot object to these reforms in principle. He realizes the national character of the great American corporations and of many business and financial operations; he realizes that an extension of Federal authority is necessary to establish adequate control over these matters. It is certainly a proper question for the defenders of the present government, therefore, to turn to him and say, "If you are opposed to this government, what powers would you take away?"

For example, the conscientious liberal would surely not rescind Securities and Exchange Commission acts and return that regulation to the states. He would not demand that the Federal government keep its hands off interstate utilities or utility holding companies. He would not challenge the wisdom of having the right of collective bargaining recognized by law. He would not say it was no concern of the Federal government whether or not the aged had pensions or the worker had unemployment allowances. In fact, the liberal would find himself in agreement with most of the objects of this new legislation, although he might want to modify many of its provisions and change many of its methods.

What attitude, then, does the liberal take toward the present government?

The answer is what it has always been. To the liberal the purpose of government is unchangeable. It is to leave men free. Whether democracy is in its first phase or its second phase or its third phase, that is the objective.

NEW CONCEPT OF GOVERNMENT

And the liberal does not see in the present Administration any will to leave men free. He sees only an attempt to increase the powers of government. For the old American principle that government is a liability to be borne by the citizens for the sake of peace, order and security, the New Deal has substituted the notion that government is an asset without which none of us can survive. The present huge Federal organization with its payroll of over a million employees, its dozens of agencies and commissions, its expenses of several billion dollars a year, represents an entirely new concept of government. It is government regarded, not as a supplementary influence, but as a dominant force in the lives of the people. Its growth becomes desirable in itself, instead of desirable only if it promotes the ease and expansion of the people's activities, the happiness and independence of their lives. Our forefathers believed that progress came from the energies of the people: the function of government was merely to prevent those energies from getting out of bounds. Today the government publicly proclaims the failure of the people's enterprises and has adopted the principle that progress comes from government itself.

This hostility toward domestic business is the more extraordinary in view of the government's friendly attitude toward foreign trade. Without entering here into technical arguments as to methods by which they are to be brought about, international trade agreements which lead to further interchange of goods between nations and the establishment of an international monetary standard are, in my opinion, indispensable to our complete recovery and future economy. America might live without international trade, but only with an economy managed either by business monopolies or government control. Likewise, despite recent pronouncements to the contrary by some opposed to the present Administration, we do have a vital interest in continuance of the English and French way of life.

. . . . .

Government has never created an invention, never founded an industry and never successfully operated a business. Our quarrel with the New Deal is on exactly the issue defined by Mr. Jackson: whether the government or the people shall manage the people's enterprises.

Well, we have given the government eight years to prove its theory and it has failed to do so. One-third of the nation is still in need. Ten million men are still unemployed. The deficit continues to increase. The people, I hope, are now ready to try again the other theory: to release the enterprises of the people from the terrific weight of bureaucracy and to rededicate the government to the purpose of leaving men free. This does not mean, as Mr. Roosevelt suggested in his speech to the Young Democrats, a return to the 1929 way of life. The country's liberals are not all in Washington.

In a time of bitter argument, it is often helpful to turn to an outside expert who has no connection with either side of the controversy and whose opinion is, therefore, unemotional and unbiased. The internationally known magazine "The Economist," of London, belongs in that category. In a recent issue "The Economist" discusses the theory that the United States "is growing old" and says that "It is difficult to take this theory seriously—or to know whether its partisans themselves take it seriously." "The Economist" raises this question:

"If the United States with its vast areas, its low debt, its inexhaustible natural resources, its rising population is a mature economy, what is Great Britain? And yet our 'decadent' economy has contrived, during the decade when America was standing still, to go ahead as fast as on the average of the great Victorian era of expansion. Ten years ago the per capita national income of the United States was one-third larger than the British. Today it is probably no larger at all. . . . The American economy

seems to have forgotten, for the moment, how to grow. But the probable explanation of this economic anemia is to be found not in any arrival at 'maturity' but rather in the existence of institutional obstructions to a free flow of capital."

For the development of any economic enterprise three human factors are fundamental. The first is the inventor, who has the idea for a new device or a new method or a new product; the second is the investor, who has sufficient confidence in the inventor's dream to give him the necessary capital to develop it; the third is the administrator or manager, who can organize the business and keep it going.

I believe that we have more men in these three categories in America today than ever before in our history. We have always been an inventive nation. We spend several hundred million dollars a year on industrial research. Last year we patented 43,000 inventions. And there are plenty of potential investors. Never before in the history of the country has there been so much money lying idle in the banks. In these two categories of invention and investment, the condition of abundance can be statistically proved. I have no statistical proof for the condition of the third factor of business management, but I have this personal conviction: that never before in American history have there been so many business executives who are not only skilled in the technique of running their jobs, but who have a new and far more enlightened attitude toward their social responsibilities.

These three types of men have constituted the triumphant triumvirate of our economic past. They are equally important to our future. Their activities, if released from government restrictions, can provide jobs enough and products enough to restore prosperity to America. But first we shall have to remove the political restrictions. The activities of the

present Administration have drained
the vitality and confidence from American industry. It is ironic that in view of
these conditions the government should
then turn upon industry and denounce
it for its failure to recover and make
wild charges concerning a "strike" of
capital. Industry is being criticized for
being unable to do what government
prevents it from doing.

COMMENT

An element in Willkie's troubles . . . was that he tended to assume that Republicans would vote for him, and he concentrated his efforts on independents and anti-
Roosevelt Democrats. In doing so he took positions on social reforms that
rankled conservative Republicans, who recoiled at the notion of trying to out-
Roosevelt Roosevelt.

> Representative Joe Martin of Massachusetts, former speaker of the House of Rep-
> resentatives, in *My First Fifty Years in Politics* (New York: McGraw-Hill Book
> Company, Inc., 1960), p. 108.

It was not a choice between leaders but a choice between the New Deal and that
vague something called Republicanism. To the man on the bench the New Deal
was something specific to him personally. It meant more money in his pocket, a
sense of security in his job, and the knowledge that people in positions of responsibility were looking after his interests. He did not know what the Republican Party meant to him and, if he had a long memory, he was not inclined to
trust it.

> Professor Irving Bernstein in "John L. Lewis and the Voting Behavior of the C.I.O.,"
> *Public Opinion Quarterly*, v (June, 1941), 248.

Frankly, as a labor man I am not interested in the virtues and qualifications of
Mr. Willkie. So far as labor is concerned, the masses of those who work for a living hope and pray that Franklin Roosevelt will be a candidate for reelection.

> Statement by Max Zaritsky, president of the United Hatters, Cap, and Millinery
> Workers, A.F. of L. New York *Times*, June 29, 1940.

In the opinion of this newspaper . . . the Republican party has chosen to put
forward the best candidate at its command, a candidate who has stood head and
shoulders above his rivals for the party's nomination. . . . He is both courageous
enough and intelligent enough to rebuke his party when he believes it to be
wrong on an important public issue. He has sufficient knowledge of business
and the productive process to know what needs to be done either for domestic
prosperity or for securing the maximum production for national defense. He is
a good liberal, a generous opponent, a defender of civil liberties.

> Editorial in the New York *Times*, June 28, 1940.

76. DECEMBER 17, 1940

President Roosevelt on Lend Lease

Following Roosevelt's third term victory, British Prime Minister Winston Church-ill informed President Roosevent that England could no longer pay for military supplies necessary to sustain its war ef-fort. Roosevelt decided to act swiftly. He began informing the American public of the necessity of providing greater assist-ance to the Allies. During his press con-ference of December 17, he suggested that America should either lease or lend supplies to Britain. In the following month, the President asked Congress to enact the Lend Lease Bill. Though the proposal encountered stiff opposition from Congress and the press, it finally became law on March 11, 1941.

At first, the lend lease program was a modest one. But, before the end of World War II, the United States provided over fifty billion dollars to its friends and allies in lend lease assistance. The pas-sage of the Lend Lease program marked the end of the policy of isolationism which the nation had pursued since the end of the First World War. The program actively committed the nation's economic resources to the defeat of Germany, thus greatly strengthening the Allied cause. Such action was based on the assumption that by providing the Allies with military assistance, the United States would gain time to strengthen its own defenses. Meanwhile, the Lend Lease Act caused tension between the United States and Germany to increase.

SAMUEL I. ROSENMAN, ed., *The Public Papers and Addresses of Franklin D. Roosevelt* (New York: Random House, Inc., 1941), IX, 604–608. Reprinted by permission of Random House, Inc.

I have read a great deal of nonsense in the last few days by people who can only think in what we may call traditional terms about finances. . . . In my memory, and your memory, and in all history, no major war has ever been won or lost through lack of money.

. . . . .

It is possible . . . for the United States to take over British orders, and, because they are essentially the same kind of munitions that we use ourselves, turn them into American orders. We have enough money to do it. And thereupon, as to such portion of them as the military events of the future determine to be right and proper for us to allow to go to the other side, either lease or sell the ma-terials, subject to mortgage, to the people on the other side. That would be on the general theory that it may still prove true that the best defense of Great Britain is the best defense of the United States, and therefore that these materials would be more useful to the defense of the United States if they were used in Great Britain, than if they were kept in storage here.

Now, what I am trying to do is to eliminate the dollar sign. That is some-thing brand new in the thoughts of prac-tically everybody in this room, I think— get rid of the silly, foolish old dollar sign.

Well, let me give you an illustration: Suppose my neighbor's home catches fire, and I have a length of garden hose four or five hundred feet away. If he can take my garden hose and connect it up with his hydrant, I may help him to put out his fire. Now, what do I do? I don't say to him before that operation, "Neighbor, my garden hose cost me $15; you have to pay me $15 for it." What is the transaction that goes on? I don't want $15—I want my garden hose back after the fire is over. All right. If it goes through the fire all right, intact, without any damage to it, he gives it back to me and thanks me very much for the use of it. But suppose it gets smashed up—holes in it—during the fire; we don't have to have too much formality about it, but I say to him, "I was glad to lend you that hose; I see I can't use it any more, it's all smashed up." He says, "How many feet of it were there?" I tell him, "There were 150 feet of it." He says, "All right, I will replace it." Now, if I get a nice garden hose back, I am in pretty good shape.

In other words, if you lend certain munitions and get the munitions back at the end of the war, if they are intact—haven't been hurt—you are all right; if they have been damaged or have deteriorated or have been lost completely, it seems to me you come out pretty well if you have them replaced by the fellow to whom you have lent them.

. . . . .

COMMENT

The lend-lease-give program is the New Deal's triple A foreign policy; it will plow under every fourth American boy. . . . Approval of this legislation means war, open and complete warfare. I, therefore, ask the American people before they supinely accept it, was the last World War worth while? . . . Considered on its merits and stripped of its emotional appeal to our sympathies, the lend-lease-give bill is both ruinous and ridiculous. . . .

Burton K. Wheeler, Democrat from Montana, speaking to the U.S. Senate, January 21, 1941. *Congressional Record*, 77th Cong., 1st Sess., 1940–1941, LXXXVII, pt. 10, A178–79.

If we go to war to save democracy in Europe we shall wind up by losing democracy at home.

Former Governor Philip La Follette of Wisconsin in a radio address delivered over a nation-wide hook-up of the National Broadcasting Company, January 6, 1941. *Vital Speeches*, VII (February 15, 1941), 265.

The American people should insistently demand that Congress put a stop to step-by-step projection of the United States into undeclared war. . . . Exceeding its expressed purpose, the Lend-Lease Bill has been followed by naval action, by military occupation of bases outside the Western Hemisphere, by promise of unauthorized aid to Russia and by other belligerent moves. . . .

We have gone as far as is consistent either with law, with sentiment or with security. . . . [the war] is not purely a world conflict between tyranny and freedom. The Anglo-Russian alliance has dissipated that illusion. . . .

Few people honestly believe that the Axis is now, or will in the future, be in a position to threaten the independence of any part of this Hemisphere if our defenses are properly prepared.

Freedom in America does not depend on the outcome of struggle for material power between other nations.

Public statement by fifteen Republicans outside Congress, including Frank Lowden, Herbert Hoover, Alf Landon, Robert M. Hutchins, John L. Lewis, and Charles G. Dawes. New York *Times*, August 6, 1941.

77. *APRIL 23, 1941*

Charles A. Lindbergh on Isolation

Even after Congress passed the Lend Lease Act in March, 1941, a number of isolationist organizations attempted to turn the public against assistance to the Allies. Among the groups which opposed aid to the Allies were the Socialists, the German-American Bund, Father Coughlin's Christian Front, William Dudley Pelley's Silver Shirts, the War Debts Defense Committee, and the Make Europe Pay War Debts Committee. Leadership against American intervention in the war came from the America First Committee, headed by a number of New Dealers and midwestern businessmen. The committee's leading spokesman eventually became the famed aviator, Charles A. Lindbergh, who opposed all American assistance to the Allies. The America First Committee refused to accept President Roosevelt's contention that a British victory was necessary for American security. Instead, the Committee argued that aid to the Allies would "involve America in war abroad." Only by maintaining military strength at home could America be safe from European wars. Throughout 1941, the committee tried to focus the debate on the issue of war or peace. Typical of the committee's strategy was the following speech which Charles A. Lindbergh delivered in New York on April 23, 1941. Roosevelt responded by working in close co-operation with the Committee to Defend America by Aiding the Allies, headed by Kansas newspaperman William Allen White. The President saw to it that the debate did not concentrate on the issue of war or peace.

New York *Times,* April 23, 1941.

Rather, Roosevelt attempted to make the issue one of aid to Britain or a loss of American security.

. . . . .

There are many viewpoints from which the issues of this war can be argued. Some are primarily idealistic. Some are primarily practical. One should, I believe, strive for a balance of both. But, since the subjects that can be covered in a single address are limited, tonight I shall discuss the war from a viewpoint which is primarily practical. It is not that I believe ideals are unimportant, even among the realities of war; but if a nation is to survive in a hostile world, its ideals must be backed by the hard logic of military practicability. If the outcome of war depended upon ideals alone, this would be a different world than it is to-day.

I know I will be severely criticized by the interventionists in America when I say we should not enter a war unless we have a reasonable chance of winning. That, they will claim, is far too materialistic a viewpoint. They will advance again the same arguments that were used to persuade France to declare war against Germany in 1939. But I do not believe that our American ideals, and our ways of life, will gain through an unsuccessful war. And I know that the United States is not prepared to wage war in Europe successfully at this time. We are no better prepared today than France was when the interventionists in Europe persuaded her to attack the Siegfried Line.

I have said before, and I will say again, that I believe it will be a tragedy to the entire world if the British Empire collapses. That is one of the main reasons why I opposed this war before it was declared, and why I have constantly advocated a negotiated peace. I did not feel that England and France had a reasonable chance of winning. France has now been defeated: and, despite the propaganda and confusion of recent months, it is now obvious that England is losing the war. I believe this is realized even by the British Government. But they have one last desperate plan remaining. They hope that they may be able to persuade us to send another American Expeditionary Force to Europe, and to share with England militarily, as well as financially, the fiasco of this war.

I do not blame England for this hope, or for asking for our assistance. But we now know that she declared a war under circumstances which led to the defeat of every nation that sided with her from Poland to Greece. We know that in the desperation of war England promised to all those nations armed assistance that she could not send. We know that she misinformed them, as she has misinformed us, concerning her state of preparation, her military strength, and the progress of the war.

In time of war, truth is always replaced by propaganda. I do not believe we should be too quick to criticize the actions of a belligerent nation. There is always the question whether we, ourselves, would do better under similar circumstances. But we in this country have a right to think of the welfare of America first, just as the people in England thought first of their own country when they encouraged the smaller nations of Europe to fight against hopeless odds. When England asks us to enter this war, she is considering her own future, and that of her empire. In making our reply, I believe we should consider the future of the United States and that of the Western Hemisphere.

It is not only our right, but it is our obligation as American citizens to look at this war objectively and to weigh our chances for success if we should enter it. I have attempted to do this, especially from the standpoint of aviation; and I have been forced to the conclusion that we cannot win this war for England, regardless of how much assistance we extend.

I ask you to look at the map of Europe today and see if you can suggest any way in which we could win this war if we entered it. Suppose we had a large army in America, trained and equipped. Where would we send it to fight? The campaigns of the war show only too clearly how difficult it is to force a landing, or to maintain an army, on a hostile coast.

Suppose we took our Navy from the Pacific, and used it to convoy British shipping. That would not win the war for England. It would, at best, permit her to exist under the constant bombing of the German air fleet. Suppose we had an air force that we could send to Europe. Where could it operate? Some of our squadrons might be based in the British Isles; but it is physically impossible to base enough aircraft in the British Isles alone to equal in strength the aircraft that can be based on the Continent of Europe.

I have asked these questions on the supposition that we had in existence an Army and an air force large enough and well enough equipped to send to Europe; and that we would dare to remove our Navy from the Pacific. Even on this basis, I do not see how we could invade the Continent of Europe successfully as long as all of that Continent and most of Asia is under Axis domination. But the fact is that none of these suppositions are correct. We have only a one-ocean Navy. Our Army is still untrained and inadequately equipped for foreign war. Our air force is deplorably lacking in modern fighting planes because most of them have already been sent to Europe.

When these facts are cited, the interventionists shout that we are defeatists, that we are undermining the principles of democracy, and that we are giving comfort to Germany by talking about our military weakness. But everything I mention here has been published in our newspapers, and in the reports of congressional hearings in Washington. Our military position is well known to the governments of Europe and Asia. Why, then, should it not be brought to the attention of our own people?

I say it is the interventionist in America, as it was in England and in France, who gives comfort to the enemy. I say it is they who are undermining the principles of democracy when they demand that we take a course to which more than 80 per cent of our citizens are opposed. I charge them with being the real defeatists, for their policy has led to the defeat of every country that followed their advice since this war began. There is no better way to give comfort to an enemy than to divide the people of a nation over the issue of foreign war. There is no shorter road to defeat than by entering a war with inadequate preparation. Every nation that has adopted the interventionist policy of depending on some one else for its own defense has met with nothing but defeat and failure.

When history is written, the responsibility for the downfall of the democracies of Europe will rest squarely upon the shoulders of the interventionists who led their nations into war uninformed and unprepared. With their shouts of defeatism, and their disdain of reality, they have already sent countless thousands of young men to death in Europe. From the campaign of Poland to that of Greece, their prophecies have been false and their policies have failed. Yet these are the people who are calling us defeatists in America today. And they have led this country, too, to the verge of war.

There are many such interventionists in America, but there are more people among us of a different type. That is why you and I are assembled here tonight. There is a policy open to this nation that leaves us free to follow our own way of life, and to develop our own civilization. It is not a new and untried idea. It was advocated by Washington. Under its guidance, the United States has become the greatest nation in the world.

It is based upon the belief that the security of a nation lies in the strength and character of its own people. It recommends the maintenance of armed forces sufficient to defend this hemisphere from attack by any combination of foreign powers. It demands faith in an independent American destiny. This is the policy of the America First Committee today. It is a policy not of isolation, but of independence; not of defeat, but of courage. It is a policy that led this nation to success during the most trying years of our history, and it is a policy that will lead us to success again.

We have weakened ourselves for many months, and still worse, we have divided our own people by this dabbling in Europe's wars. While we should have been concentrating on American defense we have been forced to argue over foreign quarrels. We must turn our eyes and our faith back to our own country before it is too late. And when we do this, a different vista opens before us. Practically every difficulty we would face in invading Europe becomes an asset to us in defending America. Our enemy, and not we, would then have the problem of transporting millions of troops across the ocean and landing them on a hostile shore. They, and not we, would have to furnish the convoys to transport guns and trucks and munitions and fuel across three thousand miles of water. Our battleships and our submarines would then be fighting close to their home bases. We would then do the bombing from the air and the torpedoing at sea. And if any part of an enemy convoy should ever pass our navy and our air force, they would still be faced with the guns of our coast artillery and behind them the divisions of our Army.

The United States is better situated from a military standpoint than any other nation in the world. Even in our present condition of unpreparedness no foreign power is in a position to invade us today. If we concentrate on our own defenses and build the strength that this nation should maintain, no foreign army will ever attempt to land on American shores.

War is not inevitable for this country. Such a claim is defeatism in the true sense. No one can make us fight abroad unless we ourselves are willing to do so. No one will attempt to fight us here if we arm ourselves as a great nation should be armed. Over a hundred million people in this nation are opposed to entering the war. If the principles of democracy mean anything at all, that is reason enough for us to stay out. If we are forced into a war against the wishes of an overwhelming majority of our people, we will have proved democracy such a failure at home that there will be little use fighting for it abroad.

The time has come when those of us who believe in an independent American destiny must band together and organize for strength. We have been led toward war by a minority of our people. This minority has power. It has influence. It has a loud voice. But it does not represent the American people. During the last several years I have traveled over this country from one end to the other. I have talked to many hundreds of men and women, and I have letters from tens of thousands more, who feel the same way as you and I.

Most of these people have no influence or power. Most of them have no means of expressing their convictions, except by their vote which has always been against this war. They are the citizens who have had to work too hard at their daily jobs to organize political meetings. Hitherto, they have relied upon their vote to express their feelings; but now they find that it is hardly remembered except in the oratory of a political campaign. These people— the majority of hardworking American citizens, are with us. They are the true strength of our country. And they are beginning to realize, as you and I, that there are times when we must sacrifice our normal interests in life in order to insure the safety and the welfare of our nation.

Such a time has come. Such a crisis is here. That is why the America First Committee has been formed—to give voice to the people who have no newspaper, or newsreel, or radio station at their command; to give voice to the people who must do the paying, and the fighting, and the dying if this country enters the war.

Whether or not we do enter the war rests upon the shoulders of you in this audience, upon us here on this platform, upon meetings of this kind that are being held by Americans in every section of the United States today. It depends upon the action we take, and the courage we show at this time. If you believe in an independent destiny for America, if you believe that this country should not enter the war in Europe, we ask you to join the America First Committee in its stand. We ask you to share our faith in the ability of this nation to defend itself, to develop its own civilization, and to contribute to the progress of mankind in a more constructive and intelligent way than has yet been found by the warring nations of Europe. We need your support, and we need it now. The time to act is here.

COMMENT

I have said this before, but I shall say it again and again and again. Your boys are not going to be sent into any foreign wars.

President Franklin D. Roosevelt in a campaign address to the nation, October 30, 1940. Samuel I. Rosenman, ed., *The Public Papers and Addresses of Franklin D. Roosevelt* (New York: Random House, Inc., 1941), IX, 391.

The two factors, then, primarily responsible for American isolation are: First, the existence of pro-German and anti-British ethnic prejudices; Second, the exploiting of these prejudices by an opposition political party.

> Samuel Lubell, journalist, in *The Future of American Politics* (New York: Harper & Brothers, 1952), p. 133.

I despise Hitler and I like England but in any international war situation I wouldn't trust our fate to either of them as far as I could throw a bull by the tail.

> General Hugh Johnson, former chairman of the NRA, in a personal interview. New York *World-Telegram*, February 5, 1940.

78. *AUGUST 14, 1941*

Atlantic Charter

Despite an increase in American assistance to the Allies, President Roosevelt thought the victories of the Axis powers during the first part of 1941 called for closer planning and co-operation among the democracies. To achieve this, President Roosevelt and British Prime Minister Winston Churchill met at sea off the coast of Argentia, Newfoundland, August 9–12, 1941. During the conference, they discussed at great length what aid was necessary for the Allied cause. Churchill tried to get Roosevelt to promise American belligerence if Japan should attack Britain's possessions in the Far East, but Roosevelt was unwilling to make any naval or military commitments. After several days of meetings, the two statesmen signed the Atlantic Charter which announced the principles on which they hoped a better world would be built following the Second World War. Similar in ideas to President Wilson's Fourteen Points, the Charter was not a treaty, but a carefully prepared press release. It was designed to give oppressed people

Department of State Bulletin, No. 112, v, 25–26.

throughout the world hope for the future. Later, the Soviet Union endorsed the principles of the Atlantic Charter. Moreover, the principles of the Charter were accepted by all the Allied governments which signed the Declaration by the United Nations on January 1, 1942. Unfortunately, the peace which ended World War II contained many violations of the Atlantic Charter.

The President of the United States and the Prime Minister, Mr. Churchill, representing His Majesty's Government in the United Kingdom, have met at sea.

They have been accompanied by officials of their two Governments, including high ranking officers of their military, naval, and air services.

The whole problem of the supply of munitions of war, as provided by the Lease-Lend Act, for the armed forces of the United States and for those countries actively engaged in resisting aggression has been further examined.

Lord Beaverbrook, the Minister of Supply of the British Government, has joined in these conferences. He is going to proceed to Washington to discuss further details with appropriate officials of the United States Government. These conferences will also cover the supply problems of the Soviet Union.

The President and the Prime Minister have had several conferences. They have considered the dangers to world civilization arising from the policies of military domination by conquest upon which the Hitlerite Government of Germany and other Governments associated therewith have embarked, and have made clear the steps which their countries are respectively taking for their safety in the face of these dangers.

They have agreed upon the following joint declaration:

The President of the United States of America and the Prime Minister, Mr. Churchill, representing His Majesty's Government in the United Kingdom, being met together, deem it right to make known certain common principles in the national policies of their respective countries on which they base their hopes for a better future for the world.

First, their countries seek no aggrandizement, territorial or other;

Second, they desire to see no territorial changes that do not accord with the freely expressed wishes of the peoples concerned;

Third, they respect the right of all peoples to choose the form of government under which they will live; and they wish to see sovereign rights and self-government restored to those who have been forcibly deprived of them;

Fourth, they will endeavor, with due respect for their existing obligations, t further the enjoyment by all states, grea or small, victor or vanquished, of access on equal terms, to the trade and to th raw materials of the world which ar needed for their economic prosperity;

Fifth, they desire to bring about th fullest collaboration between all Nation in the economic field with the object o securing, for all, improved labor stand ards, economic advancement, and socia security;

Sixth, after final destruction of th Nazi tyranny, they hope to see establishe a peace which will afford to all Nation the means of dwelling in safety withi their own boundaries, and which wil afford assurance that all men in all th lands may live out their lives in freedor from fear and want;

Seventh, such a peace should enabl all men to traverse the high seas an oceans without hindrance;

Eighth, they believe that all of the Na tions of the world, for realistic as well a spiritual reasons, must come to th abandonment of the use of force. Sinc no future peace can be maintained i land, sea, or air armaments continue t be employed by Nations which threaten or may threaten, aggression outside o their frontiers, they believe, pending th establishment of a wider and permanen system of general security, that the dis armament of such Nations is essentia They will likewise aid and encourage a other practicable measures which wil lighten for peace-loving peoples th crushing burden of armaments.

COMMENT

. . . The fact alone of the United States, still technically neutral, joining wit a belligerent Power in making such a declaration was astonishing. The inclusio in it of a reference to "the final destruction of the Nazi tyranny" . . . amounte to a challenge which in ordinary times would have implied warlike action.

Winston Churchill, historian and statesman, in *The Grand Alliance* (Boston: Hough ton Mifflin Company, 1950), p. 444.

The Atlantic Charter . . . turned out to be incalculably more powerful an instrument than the officers of the British Government intended it to be when they first proposed it. . . . its effect was cosmic and historic. . . . It was not long before the people of India, Burma, Malaya, Indonesia were beginning to ask if the Atlantic Charter extended also to the Pacific and Asia in general.

Robert E. Sherwood, playwright and historian, in *Roosevelt and Hopkins, An Intimate History* (New York: Harper and Brothers, 1948), pp. 362–63.

79. *DECEMBER 9, 1941*

President Roosevelt's Fireside Chat on Pearl Harbor

After months of unsuccessful negotiating with the United States on outstanding differences, the Japanese, without warning, attacked the Hawaiian Islands at Pearl Harbor on December 7, 1941. The goal of Japanese policy was to extend their sphere of influence into Southeast Asia and to establish an impregnable defense barrier running from the Kurile Islands through the Marshall Islands, around Indonesia, and to the borders of India. Since the Japanese militarists assumed that such an extension of their power would provoke the United States to war, they decided that they must first destroy the retaliatory power of the American fleet which was located at Pearl Harbor. But the Japanese miscalculated on several grounds. Had they attacked only Dutch and British possessions in Southeast Asia, the American Congress probably would have refused to declare war. Moreover, the Japanese underestimated the power of the United States. The American armor was only dented at Pearl Harbor. No aircraft carrier was

SAMUEL I. ROSENMAN, ed., *The Public Papers and Addresses of Franklin D. Roosevelt* New York: Random House, Inc., 1950), x, 22–31. Reprinted by permission of Random House, Inc.

sunk, and the installations and fuel tanks at Pearl Harbor were hardly damaged. As a result, the United States with its heavy carrier striking force was able to destroy the "heart" of the Japanese navy in the Battle of the Coral Sea in May, 1942.

The attack on Pearl Harbor caused the American people to experience so much shock and indignation that their partisan quarrels about foreign policy quickly vanished. Once again the nation looked to President Roosevelt to provide the necessary leadership. The following address was his response to the challenge.

The sudden criminal attacks perpetrated by the Japanese in the Pacific provide the climax of a decade in international immorality.

Powerful and resourceful gangsters have banded together to make war upon the whole human race. Their challenge has now been flung at the United States of America. The Japanese have treacherously violated the long-standing peace between us. Many American soldiers and sailors have been killed by enemy action. American ships have been sunk; American airplanes have been destroyed.

The Congress and the people of the United States have accepted that challenge.

Together with other free peoples, we are now fighting to maintain our right to live among our world neighbors in freedom and in common decency, without fear of assault.

I have prepared the full record of our past relations with Japan, and it will be submitted to the Congress. It begins with the visit of Commodore Perry to Japan 88 years ago. It ends with the visit of two Japanese emissaries to the Secretary of State last Sunday, an hour after Japanese forces had loosed their bombs and machine guns against our flag, our forces, and our citizens.

I can say with utmost confidence that no Americans, today or a thousand years hence, need feel anything but pride in our patience and in our efforts through all the years toward achieving a peace in the Pacific which would be fair and honorable to every Nation, large or small. And no honest person, today or a thousand years hence, will be able to suppress a sense of indignation and horror at the treachery committed by the military dictators of Japan, under the very shadow of the flag of peace borne by their special envoys in our midst.

The course that Japan has followed for the past ten years in Asia has paralleled the course of Hitler and Mussolini in Europe and in Africa. Today, it has become far more than a parallel. It is actual collaboration so well calculated that all the continents of the world, and all the oceans, are now considered by the Axis strategists as one gigantic battle-field.

In 1931, ten years ago, Japan invaded Manchukuo—without warning.

In 1935, Italy invaded Ethiopia—without warning.

In 1938, Hitler occupied Austria—without warning.

In 1939, Hitler invaded Czecho-slovakia—without warning.

Later in 1939, Hitler invaded Poland—without warning.

In 1940, Hitler invaded Norway, Denmark, the Netherlands, Belgium, and Luxembourg—without warning.

In 1940, Italy attacked France and later Greece—without warning.

And this year, in 1941, the Axis powers attacked Yugoslavia and Greece and they dominated the Balkans—without warning.

In 1941, also, Hitler invaded Russia—without warning.

And now Japan has attacked Malaya and Thailand—and the United States—without warning.

It is of one pattern.

We are now in this war. We are all in it—all the way. Every single man, woman, and child is a partner in the most tremendous undertaking of our American history. We must share together the bad news and the good news, the defeats and the victories—the changing fortunes of war.

So far, the news has been all bad. We have suffered a serious set-back in Hawaii. Our forces in the Philippines, which include the brave people of that Commonwealth, are taking punishment but are defending themselves vigorously. The reports from Guam and Wake and Midway islands are still confused, but we must be prepared for the announcement that all these three outposts have been seized.

The casualty lists of these first few days will undoubtedly be large. I deeply feel the anxiety of all the families of the men in our armed forces and the relatives of people in cities which have been bombed. I can only give them my solemn promise that they will get news just as quickly as possible.

This Government will put its trust in the stamina of the American people and will give the facts to the public just as soon as two conditions have been fulfilled: first, that the information has been definitely and officially confirmed and, second, that the release of the information at the time it is received will not prove valuable to the enemy directly or indirectly.

Most earnestly I urge my countrymen to reject all rumors. These ugly little hints of complete disaster fly thick and fast in wartime. They have to be examined and appraised.

As an example, I can tell you frankly that until further surveys are made, I have not sufficient information to state the exact damage which has been done to our naval vessels at Pearl Harbor. Admittedly the damage is serious. But no one can say how serious, until we know how much of this damage can be repaired and how quickly the necessary repairs can be made.

I cite as another example a statement made on Sunday night that a Japanese carrier had been located and sunk off the Canal Zone. And when you hear statements that are attributed to what they call "an authoritative source," you can be reasonably sure from now on that under these war circumstances the "authoritative source" is not any person in authority.

Many rumors and reports which we now hear originate with enemy sources. For instance, today the Japanese are claiming that as a result of their one action against Hawaii they have gained naval supremacy in the Pacific. This is an old trick of propaganda which has been used innumerable times by the Nazis. The purposes of such fantastic claims are, of course, to spread fear and confusion among us, and to goad us into revealing military information which our enemies are desperately anxious to obtain.

Our Government will not be caught in this obvious trap—and neither will the people of the United States.

It must be remembered by each and every one of us that our free and rapid communication these days must be greatly restricted in wartime. It is not possible to receive full, speedy, accurate reports from distant areas of combat. This is particularly true where naval operations are concerned. For in these days of the marvels of radio it is often impossible for the commanders of various units to report their activities by radio at all, for the very simple reason that this information would become available to the enemy, and would disclose their position and their plan of defense or attack.

Of necessity there will be delays in officially confirming or denying reports of operations but we will not hide facts from the country if we know the facts and if the enemy will not be aided by their disclosure.

To all newspapers and radio stations —all those who reach the eyes and ears of the American people—I say this: You have a most grave responsibility to the Nation now and for the duration of this war.

If you feel that your Government is not disclosing enough of the truth, you have every right to say so. But—in the absence of all the facts, as revealed by official sources—you have no right in the ethics of patriotism to deal out unconfirmed reports in such a way as to make people believe that they are gospel truth.

Every citizen, in every walk of life, shares this same responsibility. The lives of our soldiers and sailors—the whole future of this Nation—depend upon the manner in which each and every one of us fulfills his obligation to our country.

Now a word about the recent past— and the future. A year and a half has elapsed since the fall of France, when the whole world first realized the mechanized might which the Axis Nations had been building for so many years. America has used that year and a half to great advantage. Knowing that the attack might reach us in all too short a time, we immediately began greatly to increase our industrial strength and our capacity to meet the demands of modern warfare.

Precious months were gained by

sending vast quantities of our war material to the Nations of the world still able to resist Axis aggression. Our policy rested on the fundamental truth that the defense of any country resisting Hitler or Japan was in the long run the defense of our own country. That policy has been justified. It has given us time, invaluable time, to build our American assembly lines of production.

Assembly lines are now in operation. Others are being rushed to completion. A steady stream of tanks and planes, of guns and ships, and shells and equipment —that is what these eighteen months have given us.

But it is all only a beginning of what still has to be done. We must be set to face a long war against crafty and powerful bandits. The attack at Pearl Harbor can be repeated at any one of many points, points in both oceans and along both our coast lines and against all the rest of the hemisphere.

It will not only be a long war, it will be a hard war. That is the basis on which we now lay all our plans. That is the yardstick by which we measure what we shall need and demand; money, materials, doubled and quadrupled production—ever-increasing. The production must be not only for our own Army and Navy and Air Forces. It must reinforce the other armies and navies and air forces fighting the Nazis and the war lords of Japan throughout the Americas and throughout the world.

I have been working today on the subject of production. Your Government has decided on two broad policies.

The first is to speed up all existing production by working on a seven-day-week basis in every war industry, including the production of essential raw materials.

The second policy, now being put into form, is to rush additions to the capacity of production by building more new plants, by adding to old plants, and by using the many smaller plants for war needs.

Over the hard road of the past months, we have at times met obstacles and difficulties, divisions and disputes, indifference and callousness. That is now all past—and, I am sure, forgotten.

The fact is that the country now has an organization in Washington built around men and women who are recognized experts in their own fields. I think the country knows that the people who are actually responsible in each and every one of these many fields are pulling together with a teamwork that has never before been excelled.

On the road ahead there lies hard work—grueling work—day and night, every hour and every minute.

I was about to add that ahead there lies sacrifice for all of us.

But it is not correct to use that word. The United States does not consider it a sacrifice to do all one can, to give one's best to our Nation, when the Nation is fighting for its existence and its future life.

It is not a sacrifice for any man, old or young, to be in the Army or the Navy of the United States. Rather is it a privilege.

It is not a sacrifice for the industrialist or the wage earner, the farmer or the shopkeeper, the trainman or the doctor, to pay more taxes, to buy more bonds, to forgo extra profits, to work longer or harder at the task for which he is best fitted. Rather is it a privilege.

It is not a sacrifice to do without many things to which we are accustomed if the national defense calls for doing without.

A review this morning leads me to the conclusion that at present we shall not have to curtail the normal use of articles of food. There is enough food today for all of us and enough left over to send to those who are fighting on the same side with us.

But there will be a clear and definite

shortage of metals of many kinds for civilian use, for the very good reason that in our increased program we shall need for war purposes more than half of that portion of the principal metals which during the past year have gone into articles for civilian use. Yes, we shall have to give up many things entirely.

And I am sure that the people in every part of the Nation are prepared in their individual living to win this war. I am sure that they will cheerfully help to pay a large part of its financial cost while it goes on. I am sure they will cheerfully give up those material things that they are asked to give up.

And I am sure that they will retain all those great spiritual things without which we cannot win through.

I repeat that the United States can accept no result save victory, final and complete. Not only must the shame of Japanese treachery be wiped out, but the sources of international brutality, wherever they exist, mut be absolutely and finally broken.

In my message to the Congress yesterday I said that we "will make it very certain that this form of treachery shall never again endanger us." In order to achieve that certainty, we must begin the great task that is before us by abandoning once and for all the illusion that we can ever again isolate ourselves from the rest of humanity.

In these past few years—and, most violently, in the past three days—we have learned a terrible lesson.

It is our obligation to our dead—it is our sacred obligation to their children and to our children—that we must never forget what we have learned.

And what we all have learned is this:

There is no such thing as security for any Nation—or any individual—in a world ruled by the principles of gangsterism.

There is no such thing as impregnable defense against powerful aggressors who sneak up in the dark and strike without warning.

We have learned that our ocean-girt hemisphere is not immune from severe attack—that we cannot measure our safety in terms of miles on any map any more.

We may acknowledge that our enemies have performed a brilliant feat of deception, perfectly timed and executed with great skill. It was a thoroughly dishonorable deed, but we must face the fact that modern warfare as conducted in the Nazi manner is a dirty business. We don't like it—we didn't want to get in it—but we are in it and we're going to fight it with everything we've got.

I do not think any American has any doubt of our ability to administer proper punishment to the perpetrators of these crimes.

Your Government knows that for weeks Germany has been telling Japan that if Japan did not attack the United States, Japan would not share in dividing the spoils with Germany when peace came. She was promised by Germany that if she came in she would receive the complete and perpetual control of the whole of the Pacific area—and that means not only the Far East, but also all of the islands in the Pacific, and also a stranglehold on the west coast of North, Central, and South America.

We know also that Germany and Japan are conducting their military and naval operations in accordance with a joint plan. That plan considers all people and Nations which are not helping the Axis powers as common enemies of each and every one of the Axis powers.

That is their simple and obvious grand strategy. And that is why the American people must realize that it can be matched only with similar grand strategy. We must realize for example that Japanese successes against the United States in the Pacific are helpful to German operations in Libya; that any German success against the Caucasus is inevitably an assistance to Japan in her operations against the Dutch East Indies; that a German attack against Algiers or Morocco opens the way to a German attack against South America, and the Canal.

On the other side of the picture, we must learn also to know that guerrilla warfare against the Germans in, let us say, Serbia or Norway helps us; that a successful Russian offensive against the Germans helps us; and that British successes on land or sea in any part of the world strengthen our hands.

Remember always that Germany and Italy, regardless of any formal declaration of war, consider themselves at war with the United States at this moment just as much as they consider themselves at war with Britain or Russia. And Germany puts all the other Republics of the Americas into the same category of enemies. The people of our sister Republics of this hemisphere can be honored by that fact.

The true goal we seek is far above and beyond the ugly field of battle. When we resort to force, as now we must, we are determined that this force shall be directed toward ultimate good as well as against immediate evil. We Americans are not destroyers—we are builders.

We are now in the midst of a war, not for conquest, not for vengeance, but for a world in which this Nation, and all that this Nation represents, will be safe for our children. We expect to eliminate the danger from Japan, but it would serve us ill if we accomplished that and found that the rest of the world was dominated by Hitler and Mussolini.

We are going to win the war and we are going to win the peace that follows.

And in the difficut hours of this day —through dark days that may be yet to come—we will know that the vast majority of the members of the human race are on our side. Many of them are fighting with us. All of them are praying for us. For in representing our cause, we represent theirs as well—our hope and their hope for liberty under God.

COMMENT

My convictions regarding international cooperation and collective security for peace took firm hold on the afternoon of the Pearl Harbor attack. That day ended isolationism for any realist.

Statement by Senator Arthur H. Vandenberg of Michigan in Arthur H. Vandenberg, Jr., and J. A. Morris, eds., *The Private Papers of Senator Vandenberg* (Boston: Houghton Mifflin Company, 1952), p. 1.

The disaster of Pearl Harbor was the failure, with attendant increase in personnel and material losses, of the Army and the Navy to institute measures designed to detect an approaching hostile force, to effect a state of readiness commensurate with the realization that war was at hand, and to employ every facility at their command in repelling the Japanese.

U.S. Senate, "Investigation of the Pearl Harbor Attack," 79th Cong., 2d Sess., *Senate Document* No. 244 (Washington, 1946), p. 251.

80. *1943*

West Virginia Board of Education v. Barnette

During the Second World War, many states were quick to suppress action which they considered to be unpatriotic. Several states required children attending public schools to salute the flag as part of a daily exercise, conduct which was highly offensive to members of the Jehovah's Witnesses, a religious sect. When the Supreme Court was asked to pass on a West Virginia salute statute, the Court ruled that the law was unconstitutional. Speaking for the majority, Justice Jackson invoked the "clear and present danger" doctrine and ruled that the failure to salute the flag did not interfere with the rights of other individuals. Jackson also declared that the rights guaranteed by the First Amendment were among the liberties protected by the due process clause of the Fourteenth Amendment.

Three years earlier, the Supreme Court in Minersville School District v. Gobitis had upheld the action of a Pennsylvania school district for expelling two students who refused to salute the flag. Thus, the Barnette decision represented a clear reversal on the part of the Court. Nevertheless, Justice Frankfurter, who wrote the majority decision in the Gobitis case, had not changed his views on the matter, and in the Barnette case he wrote a vigorous dissent which is included with the majority decision in the following passage.

Following the decision by this Court on June 3, 1940, in *Minersville School District* v. *Gobitis,* . . . the West Virginia

319 U.S. 624 (1943).

legislature amended its statutes to require all schools therein to conduct courses of instruction in history, civics, and in the constitutions of the United States and of the State "for the purpose of teaching, fostering and perpetuating the ideals, principles and spirit of Americanism, and increasing the knowledge of the organization and machinery of the government." Appellant Board of Education was directed, with advice of the State Superintendent of Schools, to "prescribe the courses of study covering these subjects" for public schools. The Act made it the duty of private, parochial and denominational schools to prescribe courses of study "similar to those required for the public schools."

The Board of Education on January 9, 1942, adopted a resolution containing recitals taken largely from the Court's *Gobitis* opinion and ordering that the salute to the flag become "a regular part of the program of activities in the public schools," that all teachers and pupils "shall be required to participate in the salute honoring the Nation represented by the Flag; provided, however that refusal to salute the Flag be regarded as an act of insubordination, and shall be dealt with accordingly."

The resolution originally required the "commonly accepted salute to the Flag" which it defined. Objections to the salute as "being too much like Hitler's" were raised by the Parent and Teachers Association, the Boy and Girl Scouts, the Red Cross, and the Federation of Women's Clubs. Some modification appears to have been made in deference to these objections, but no concession was made to Jehovah's Witnesses. What is now required is the "stiff-arm" salute, the saluter to keep the right hand raised with palm turned up while the following is repeated: "I pledge allegiance to the Flag of the United States of America and to the Republic for which it stands; one Nation, indivisible, with liberty and justice for all."

Failure to conform is "insubordination" dealt with by expulsion. Readmission is denied by statute until compliance. Meanwhile the expelled child is "unlawfully absent" and may be proceeded against as a delinquent. His parents or guardians are liable to prosecution, and if convicted are subject to fine not exceeding $50 and jail term not exceeding thirty days.

Appellees, citizens of the United States and of West Virginia, brought suit in the United States District Court for themselves and others similarly situated asking its injunction to restrain enforcement of these laws and regulations against Jehovah's Witnesses. The Witnesses are an unincorporated body teaching that the obligation imposed by law of God is superior to that of laws enacted by temporal government. Their religious beliefs include a literal version of Exodus, Chapter 20, verses 4 and 5, which says: "Thou shalt not make unto thee any graven image, or any likeness of anything that is in heaven above, or that is in the earth beneath, or that is in the water under the earth; thou shalt not bow down thyself to them nor serve them." They consider that the flag is an "image" within this command. For this reason they refuse to salute it.

Children of this faith have been expelled from school and are threatened with exclusion for no other cause. Officials threaten to send them to reformatories maintained for criminally inclined juveniles. Parents of such children have been prosecuted and are threatened with prosecutions for causing delinquency.

The Board of Education moved to dismiss the complaint setting forth these facts and alleging that the law and regulations are an unconstitutional denial of religious freedom, and of freedom of speech, and are invalid under the "due process" and "equal protection" clauses of the Fourteenth Amendment to the Federal Constitution. The cause was submitted on the pleadings to a District Court of three judges. It restrained enforcement as to the plaintiffs and those of that class. The Board of Education brought the case here by direct appeal.

This case calls upon us to reconsider a precedent decision, as the Court throughout its history often has been required to do. Before turning to the *Gobitis* case, however, it is desirable to notice certain characteristics by which this controversy is distinguished.

The freedom asserted by these appellees does not bring them into collision with rights asserted by any other individual. It is such conflicts which most frequently require intervention of the State to determine where the rights of one end and those of another begin. But the refusal of these persons to participate in the ceremony does not interfere with or deny rights of others to do so. Nor is there any question in this case that their behavior is peaceable and orderly. The sole conflict is between authority and rights of the individual. The State asserts power to condition access to public education on making a prescribed sign and profession and at the same time to coerce attendance by punishing both parent and child. The latter stand on a right of self-determination in matters that touch individual opinion and personal attitude. . . .

There is no doubt that, in connection with the pledges, the flag salute is a form of utterance. Symbolism is a primitive but effective way of communicating ideas. The use of an emblem or flag to symbolize some system, idea, institution, or personality is a short cut from mind to mind. Causes and nations, political parties, lodges and ecclesiastical groups seek to knit the loyalty of their followings to a flag or banner, a color or design. The State announces rank, function, and authority through crowns and maces, uniforms and black robes; the church speaks through the Cross, the Crucifix, the altar and shrine, and clerical raiment. Symbols of State often convey political ideas just as religious symbols come to convey theological ones. Associated with many of these symbols are appropriate gestures of acceptance or respect: a salute, a bowed or bared head, a bended knee. A person gets from a symbol the meaning he puts into it, and what is one man's comfort and inspiration is another's jest and scorn. . . .

It is also to be noted that the compulsory flag salute and pledge requires affirmation of a belief and an attitude of mind. It is not clear whether the regulation contemplates that pupils forego any contrary convictions of their own and become unwilling converts to the prescribed ceremony or whether it will be acceptable if they simulate assent by words without belief and by a gesture barren of meaning. It is now a commonplace that censorship or suppression of expression of opinion is tolerated by our Constitution only when the expression presents a clear and present danger of action of a kind the State is empowered to prevent and punish. It would seem that involuntary affirmation could be commanded only on even more immediate and urgent grounds than silence. But here the power of compulsion is invoked without any allegation that remaining passive during a flag salute ritual creates a clear and present danger that would justify an effort even to muffle expression. To sustain the compulsory flag salute we are required to say that a Bill of Rights which guards the individual's right to speak his own mind, left it open to public

authorities to compel him to utter what is not in his mind.

Whether the First Amendment to the Constitution will permit officials to order observance of ritual of this nature does not depend upon whether as a voluntary exercise we would think it to be good, bad or merely innocuous. Any credo of nationalism is likely to include what some disapprove or to omit what others think essential, and to give off different overtones as it takes on different accents or interpretations. If official power exists to coerce acceptance of any patriotic creed, what it shall contain cannot be decided by courts, but must be largely discretionary with the ordaining authority, whose power to prescribe would no doubt include power to amend. Hence validity of the asserted power to force an American citizen publicly to profess any statement of belief or to engage in any ceremony of assent to one, presents questions of power that must be considered independently of any idea we may have as to the utility of the ceremony in question.

Nor does the issue as we see it turn on one's possession of particular religious views or the sincerity with which they are held. While religion supplies appellees' motive for enduring the discomforts of making the issue in this case, many citizens who do not share these religious views hold such a compulsory rite to infringe constitutional liberty of the individual. It is not necessary to inquire whether non-conformist beliefs will exempt from the duty to salute unless we first find power to make the salute a legal duty. . . .

The very purpose of a Bill of Rights was to withdraw certain subjects from the vicissitudes of political controversy, to place them beyond the reach of majorities and officials and to establish them as legal principles to be applied by the courts. One's right to life, liberty, and property, to free speech, a free press, freedom of worship and assembly, and other fundamental rights may not be submitted to vote; they depend on the outcome of no elections.

In weighing arguments of the parties it is important to distinguish between the due process clause of the Fourteenth Amendment as an instrument for transmitting the principles of the First Amendment and those cases in which it is applied for its own sake. The test of legislation which collides with the Fourteenth Amendment, because it also collides with the principles of the First, is much more definite than the test when only the Fourteenth is involved. Much of the vagueness of the due process clause disappears when the specific prohibitions of the First become its standard. The right of a State to regulate, for example, a public utility may well include, so far as the due process test is concerned, power to impose all of the restrictions which a legislature may have a "rational basis" for adopting. But freedoms of speech and of press, of assembly, and of worship may not be infringed on such slender grounds. They are susceptible of restriction only to prevent grave and immediate danger to interests which the State may lawfully protect. It is important to note that while it is the Fourteenth Amendment which bears directly upon the State it is the more specific limiting principles of the First Amendment that finally govern this case.

Nor does our duty to apply the Bill of Rights to assertions of official authority depend upon our possession of marked competence in the field where the invasion of rights occurs. True, the task of translating the majestic generalities of the Bill of Rights, conceived as part of the pattern of liberal government in the eighteenth century, into concrete restraints on officials dealing with the problems of the twentieth century, is one to disturb self-confidence. These principles grew in soil which also produced a philosophy that the individual was the center of society, that his liberty was attainable through mere absence of governmental restraints, and that government should be entrusted with few controls and only the mildest supervision over men's affairs. We must transplant these rights to a soil in which the *laissez-faire* concept or principle of noninterference has withered at least as to economic affairs, and social advancements are increasingly sought through closer integration of society and through expanded and strengthened governmental controls. These changed conditions often deprive precedents of reliability and cast us more than we would choose upon our own judgment. But we act in these matters not by authority of our competence but by force of our commissions. We cannot, because of modest estimates of our competence in such specialties as public education, withhold the judgment that history authenticates as the function of this Court when liberty is infringed. . . .

National unity as an end which officials may foster by persuasion and example is not in question. The problem is whether under our Constitution compulsion as here employed is a permissible means for its achievement.

Struggles to coerce uniformity of sentiment in support of some end thought essential to their time and country have been waged by many good as well as by evil men. Nationalism is a relatively recent phenomenon but at other times and places the ends have been racial or territorial security, support of a dynasty or regime, and particular plans for saving souls. As first and moderate methods to attain unity have failed, those bent on its accomplishment must resort to an ever-increasing severity. As governmental pressure toward unity becomes greater, so strife becomes more bitter as to whose unity it shall be. Probably no deeper division of our people could proceed from any provocation than from finding it necessary to choose what doctrine and whose program public education officials shall compel youth to unite in embracing. Ultimate futility of such attempts to compel coherence is the lesson of every such effort from the Roman drive to stamp out Christianity as a disturber of its pagan unity, the Inquisition, as a means to religious and dynastic unity, the Siberian exiles as a means to Russian unity, down to the fast failing efforts of our present totalitarian enemies. Those who begin coercive elimination of dissent soon find themselves exterminating dissenters. Compulsory unification of opinion achieves only the unanimity of the graveyard.

It seems trite but necessary to say that the First Amendment to our Constitution was designed to avoid these ends by avoiding these beginnings. There is no mysticism in the American concept of the State or of the nature or origin of its authority. We set up government by consent of the governed, and the Bill of Rights denies those in power any legal opportunity to coerce that consent. Authority here is to be controlled by public opinion, not public opinion by authority.

The case is made difficult not because the principles of its decision are obscure but because the flag involved is our own. Nevertheless, we apply the limitations of the Constitution with no fear that freedom to be intellectually and spiritually diverse or even contrary will disintegrate the social organization. To believe that patriotism will not flourish if patriotic ceremonies are voluntary and spontaneous instead of a compulsory routine is to make an unflattering estimate of the appeal of our institutions to free minds. We can have intellectual individualism and the rich cultural diversities that we owe to exceptional minds only at the price of occasional eccentricity and abnormal attitudes. When they are so harmless to others or to the State as those we deal with here, the price is not too great. But freedom to differ is not limited to things that do not matter much. That would be a mere shadow of freedom. The test of its substance is the right to differ as to things that touch the heart of the existing order.

If there is any fixed star in our constitutional constellation, it is that no official, high or petty, can prescribe what shall be orthodox in politics, nationalism, religion, or other matters of opinion or force citizens to confess by word or act their faith therein. If there are any circumstances which permit an exception, they do not now occur to us.

We think the action of the local authorities in compelling the flag salute and pledge transcends constitutional limitations on their power and invades the sphere of intellect and spirit which it is the purpose of the First Amendment to our Constitution to reserve from all official control.

The decision of this Court in *Minersville School District* v. *Gobitis* and the holdings of those few *per curiam* decisions which preceded and foreshadowed it are overruled, and the judgment enjoining enforcement of the West Virginia Regulation is

Affirmed

.   .   .   .   .

MR. JUSTICE FRANKFURTER DISSENTING

One who belongs to the most vilified and persecuted minority in history is not likely to be insensible to the freedoms guaranteed by our Constitution. Were my purely personal attitude relevant I should wholeheartedly associate myself with the general libertarian views in the Court's opinion, representing as they do the thought and action of a lifetime. But as judges we are neither Jew nor Gentile, neither Catholic nor agnostic. We owe equal attachment to the Constitution and are equally bound by our judicial obligations whether we derive our citizenship from the earliest or the latest immigrants to these shores. As a member of this Court I am not justified in writing my private notions of policy into the Constitution, no matter how deeply I may cherish them or how mischievous I may deem their disregard. The duty of a judge who must decide which of two claims before the Court shall prevail, that of a State to enact and enforce laws within its general competence or that of an individual to refuse obedience because of the demands of his conscience, is not that of the ordinary person. It can never be emphasized too much that one's own opinion about the wisdom or evil of a law should be excluded altogether when one is doing one's duty on the bench. The only opinion of our own even looking in that direction that is material is our opinion whether legislators could in reason have enacted such a law. In the light of all the circumstances, including the history of this question in this Court, it would require more daring than I possess to deny that reasonable legislators could have taken the action which is before us for review. Most unwillingly, therefore, I must differ from my brethren with regard to legislation like this. I cannot bring my mind to believe that the "liberty" secured by the Due Process Clause gives this Court authority to deny to the State of West Virginia the attainment of that which we all recognize as a legitimate legislative end, namely, the promotion of good citizenship, by employment of the means here chosen.

Not so long ago we were admonished that "the only check upon our own exercise of power is our own sense of self-restraint. For the removal of unwise laws from the statute books appeal lies not to the courts but to the ballot and to the processes of democratic government." We have been told that generalities do not decide concrete cases. But the intensity with which a general principle is held may determine a particular issue, and whether we put first things first may decide a specific controversy.

The admonition that judicial self-restraint alone limits arbitrary exercise of our authority is relevant every time we are asked to nullify legislation. The Constitution does not give us greater veto power when dealing with one phase of "liberty" than with another, or when

dealing with grade school regulations than with college regulations that offend conscience, as was the case in *Hamilton* v. *Regents*. . . . In neither situation is our function comparable to that of a legislature or are we free to act as though we were a super-legislature. Judicial self-restraint is equally necessary whenever an exercise of political or legislative power is challenged. There is no warrant in the constitutional basis of this Court's authority for attributing different rôles to it depending upon the nature of the challenge to the legislation. Our power does not vary according to the particular provision of the Bill of Rights which is invoked. The right not to have property taken without just compensation has, so far as the scope of judicial power is concerned, the same constitutional dignity as the right to be protected against unreasonable searches and seizures, and the latter has no less claim than freedom of the press or freedom of speech or religious freedom. In no instance is this Court the primary protector of the particular liberty that is invoked. This court has recognized, what hardly could be denied, that all the provisions of the first ten Amendments are "specific" prohibitions, *United States* v. *Carolene Products Co.* . . . But each specific Amendment, in so far as embraced within the Fourteenth Amendment, must be equally respected, and the function of this Court does not differ in passing on the constitutionality of legislation challenged under different Amendments.

When Mr. Justice Holmes, speaking for this Court, wrote that "it must be remembered that legislatures are ultimate guardians of the liberties and welfare of the people in quite as great a degree as the courts," he went to the very essence of our constitutional system and the democratic conception of our society. He did not mean that for only some phases of civil government this Court was not to supplant legislatures and sit in judgment upon the right or wrong of a challenged measure. He was stating the comprehensive judicial duty and rôle of this Court in our constitutional scheme whenever legislation is sought to be nullified on any ground, namely, that responsibility for legislation lies with legislatures, answerable as they are directly to the people, and this Court's only and very narrow function is to determine whether within the broad grant of authority vested in legislatures they have exercised a justification can be offered.

The framers of the federal Constitution might have chosen to assign an active share in the process of legislation to this Court. They had before them the well-known example of New York's Council of Revision, which had been functioning since 1777. After stating that "laws inconsistent with the spirit of this constitution, or with the public good, may be hastily and unadvisedly passed," the state constitution made the judges of New York part of the legislative process by providing that "all bills which have passed the senate and assembly shall, before they become laws," be presented to a Council of which the judges constituted a majority, "for their revisal and consideration." But the framers of the Constitution denied such legislative powers to the federal judiciary. They chose instead to insulate the judiciary from the legislative function. They did not grant to this Court supervision over legislation.

The reason why from the beginning even the narrow judicial authority to nullify legislation has been viewed with a jealous eye is that it serves to prevent the full play of the democratic process. The fact that it may be an undemocratic aspect of our scheme of government does not call for its rejection or its disuse. But it is the best of reasons, as this Court has frequently recognized, for the greatest caution in its use. . . .

Under our constitutional system the legislature is charged solely with civil concerns of society. If the avowed or intrinsic legislative purpose is either to promote or to discourage some religious community or creed, it is clearly within the constitutional restrictions imposed on legislatures and cannot stand. But it by no means follows that legislative power is wanting whenever a general nondiscriminatory civil regulation in fact touches conscientious scruples or religious beliefs of an individual or a group. Regard for such scruples or beliefs undoubtedly presents one of the most reasonable claims for the exertion of legislative accommodation. It is, of course, beyond our power to rewrite the State's requirement, by providing exemptions for those who do not wish to participate in the flag salute or by making some other accommodations to meet their scruples. That wisdom might suggest the making of such accommodations and that school administration would not find it too difficult to make them and yet maintain the ceremony for those not refusing to conform, is outside our province to suggest. Tact, respect, and generosity toward variant views will always commend themselves to those charged with the duties of legislation so as to achieve a maximum of good will and to require a minimum of unwilling submission to a general law. But the real question is, who is to make such accommodations, the courts or the legislature?

This is no dry, technical matter. It cuts deep into one's conception of the democratic process—it concerns no less the practical differences between the means for making these accommodations that are open to courts and to legislatures. A court can only strike down. It can only say "This or that law is void." It cannot modify or qualify, it cannot make exceptions to a general requirement. And it strikes down not merely for a day. At least the finding of unconstitutionality ought not to have ephemeral significance unless the Constitution is to be reduced to the fugitive importance of mere legislation. When we are dealing with the Constitution of the United States, and more particularly with the great safeguards of the Bill of Rights, we are dealing with principles of liberty and justice "so rooted in the traditions and conscience of our peoples as to be ranked as fundamental"—something without which "a fair and enlightened system of justice would be impossible." . . . If the function of this Court is to be essentially no different from that of a legislature, if the considerations governing constitutional construction are to be substantially those that underlie legislation, then indeed judges should not have life tenure and they should be made directly responsible to the electorate. There have been many but unsuccessful proposals in the last sixty years to amend the Constitution to that end. . . .

. . . [E]very Justice—thirteen in all —who has hitherto participated in judging this matter has at one or more times found no constitutional infirmity in what is now condemned. Only the two Justices sitting for the first time on this matter have not heretofore found this legislation inoffensive to the "liberty" guaranteed by the Constitution. And among the Justices who sustained this measure were outstanding judicial leaders in the zealous enforcement of constitutional safeguards of civil liberties—men like Chief Justice Hughes, Mr. Justice Brandeis, and Mr. Justice Cardozo, to mention only those no longer on the Court.

One's conception of the Constitution cannot be severed from one's conception of a judge's function in applying it. The Court has no reason for existence if it merely reflects the pressures of the day. Our system is built on the faith that men set apart for this special function, freed from the influences of immediacy and from the deflections of worldly ambition, will become able to take a view of longer range than the period of responsibility entrusted to Congress and legislatures. We are dealing with matters as to which legislators and voters have conflicting views. Are we as judges to impose our strong convictions on where wisdom lies? That which three years ago had seemed to five successive Courts to lie within permissible areas of legislation is now outlawed by the deciding shift of opinion of two Justices. What reason is there to believe that they or their successors may not have another view a few years hence? Is that which was deemed to be of so fundamental a nature as to be written into the Constitution to endure for all times to be the sport of shifting winds of doctrine? Of course, judicial opinions, even as to questions of constitutionality, are not immutable. As has been true in the past, the Court will from time to time reverse its position. But I believe that never before these Jehovah's Witnesses cases (except for minor deviations subsequently retraced) has this Court overruled decisions so as to restrict the powers of democratic government. Always heretofore, it has withdrawn narrow views of legislative authority so as to authorize what formerly it had denied.

In view of this history it must be plain that what thirteen Justices found to be within the constitutional authority of a state, legislators cannot be deemed unreasonable in enacting. Therefore, in denying to the states what heretofore has received such impressive judicial sanction, some other tests of unconstitutionality must surely be guiding the Court than the absence of a rational justification for the legislation. . . .

In the past this Court has from time to time set its views of policy against that embodied in legislation by finding laws in conflict with what was called the "spirit of the Constitution." Such undefined destructive power was not conferred on this Court by the Constitution. Before a duly enacted law can be judicially nullified, it must be forbidden by some explicit restriction upon political authority in the Constitution. Equally inadmissible is the claim to strike down legislation because to us as individuals it seems opposed to the "plan and purpose" of the Constitution. That is too tempting a basis for finding in one's personal views the purposes of the Founders.

The uncontrollable power wielded by this Court brings it very close to the most sensitive areas of public affairs. As appeal from legislation to adjudication becomes more frequent, and its consequences more far-reaching, judicial self-restraint becomes more and not less important, lest we unwarrantably enter social and political domains wholly outside our concern. I think I appreciate fully the objections to the law before us. But to deny that it presents a question upon which men might reasonably differ appears to me to be intolerance. And since men may so reasonably differ, I deem it beyond my constitutional power to assert my view of the wisdom of this law against the view of the State of West Virginia.

Jefferson's opposition to judicial review has not been accepted by history, but it still serves as an admonition against confusion between judicial and political functions. As a rule of judicial self-re-

straint, it is still as valid as Lincoln's admonition. For those who pass laws not only are under duty to pass laws. They are also under duty to observe the Constitution. And even though legislation relates to civil liberties, our duty of deference to those who have the responsibilty for making the laws is no less relevant or less exacting. And this is so especially when we consider the accidental contingencies by which one man may determine constitutionality and thereby confine the political power of the Congress of the United States and the legislatures of forty-eight states. The attitude of judicial humility which these considerations enjoin is not an abdication of the judicial function. It is a due observance of its limits. Moreover, it is to be borne in mind that in a question like this we are not passing on the proper distribution of political power as between the states and the central government. We are not discharging the basic function of this Court as the mediator of powers within the federal system. To strike down a law like this is to deny a power to all government. . . .

81. *1944*

Korematsu v. United States

During the Second World War, persons of Japanese descent on the West Coast, many of whom were American citizens, were transferred to detention camps. There, under armed guard and behind barbed wire, most of them remained for the duration of the war, deprived of their occupations, cut off from their homes, and denied their constitutional rights. There is no evidence that more than a few of the Japanese-Americans were disloyal. Meanwhile, with the ex-

323 U.S. 214 (1944).

ception of a few individuals, German-Americans and Italian-Americans retained their constitutional liberties during the war.

Responsibility for the Japanese evacuations is a matter of controversy. Two months after Pearl Harbor, the commanding general of the Western Defense Command ordered the removal of all Japanese from the Pacific Coast area on the grounds of military necessity. Meanwhile, the relocation program was sanctioned by the President and en-

dorsed by Congress. When the exclusion orders were contested in the courts, Justice Black's majority opinion upheld the detention of the Japanese on the grounds of military necessity. Justices Murphy, Roberts, and Jackson entered vigorous dissents, two of which are printed below. As a result of the Korematsu decision, it is now written into constitutional law that during wartime a citizen of the United States may be transported to a detention camp against his will and be required to remain until his loyalty has been established.

The petitioner, an American citizen of Japanese descent, was convicted in a federal district court for remaining in San Leandro, California, a "Military Area," contrary to Civilian Exclusion Order No. 34, of the Commanding General of the Western Command, U.S. Army, which directed that after May 9, 1942, all persons of Japanese ancestry should be excluded from that area. No question was raised as to petitioner's loyalty to the United States. The Circuit Court of Appeals affirmed, and the importance of the constitutional question involved caused us to grant certiorari.

It should be noted, to begin with, that all legal restrictions which curtail the civil rights of a single racial group are immediately suspect. That is not to say that all such restrictions are unconstitutional. It is to say that courts must subject them to the most rigid scrutiny. Pressing public necessity may sometimes justify the existence of such restrictions; racial antagonism never can.

In the instant case prosecution of the petitioner was begun by information charging violation of an Act of Congress, of March 21, 1942, 56 Stat. 173, which provides that:

, . . whoever shall enter, remain in, leave, or commit any act in any military area or military zone prescribed, under the authority of an Executive order of the President, by the Secretary of War, or by any

military commander designated by the Secretary of War, contrary to the restrictions applicable to any such area or zone or contrary to the order of the Secretary of if it appears that he knew or should have known of the existence and extent of the restrictions or order and that his act was in violation thereof, be guilty of a misdemeanor and upon conviction shall be liable to a fine of not to exceed $5,000 or to imprisonment for not more than one year, or both, for each offense.

Exclusion Order No. 34, which the petitioner knowingly and admittedly violated, was one of a number of military orders and proclamations, all of which were substantially based upon Executive Order No. 9066, 7 Fed. Reg. 1407. That order, issued after we were at war with Japan, declared that "the successful prosecution of the war requires every possible protection against espionage and against sabotage to national-defense material, national-defense premises, and national-defense utilities. . . ."

One of the series of orders and proclamations, a curfew order, which like the exclusion order here was promulgated pursuant to Executive Order 9066, subjected all persons of Japanese ancestry in prescribed West Coast military areas to remain in their residences from 8 P.M. to 6 A.M. As is the case with the exclusion order here, that prior curfew order was designed as a "protection against espionage and against sabotage." In *Hirabayashi* v. *United States*, 320 U.S. 81, we sustained a conviction obtained for violation of the curfew order. The Hirabayashi conviction and this one thus rest on the same 1942 Congressional Act and the same basic executive and military orders, all of which orders were aimed at the twin dangers of espionage and sabotage.

The 1942 Act was attacked in the *Hirabayashi* case as an unconstitutional delegation of power; it was contended that the curfew order and other orders on which it rested were beyond the war powers of the Congress, the military authorities and of the President, as Commander in Chief of the Army; and finally that to apply the curfew order against none but citizens of Japanese ancestry amount to a constitutionally prohibited discrimination solely on account of race. To these questions, we gave the serious consideration which their importance justified. We upheld the curfew order as an exercise of the power of the government to take steps necessary to prevent espionage and sabotage in an area threatened by Japanese attack.

In the light of the principles we announced in the *Hirabayashi* case, we are unable to conclude that it was beyond the war power of Congress and the Executive to exclude those of Japanese ancestry from the West Coast war area at the time they did. True, exclusion from the area in which one's home is located is a far greater deprivation than constant confinement to the home from 8 P.M to 6 A.M. Nothing short of apprehension by the proper military authorities of the gravest imminent danger to the public safety can constitutionally justify either. But exclusion from a threatened area, no less than curfew, has a definite and close relationship to the prevention of espionage and sabotage. The military authorities, charged with the primary responsibility of defending our shores, concluded that curfew provided inadequate protection and ordered exclusion. They did so, as pointed out in our *Hirabayashi* opinion, in accordance with Congressional authority to the military to say who should, and who should not, remain in the threatened areas.

In this case the petitioner challenges the assumptions upon which we rested our conclusions in the *Hirabayashi* case. He also urges that by May 1942, when Order No. 34 was promulgated, all danger of Japanese invasion of the West Coast had disappeared. After careful consideration of these contentions we are compelled to reject them.

Here, as in the *Hirabayashi* case, ". . . we cannot reject as unfounded the judgment of the military authorities and of Congress that there were disloyal members of that population, whose number and strength could not be precisely and quickly ascertained. We cannot say that the war-making branches of the government did not have ground for believing that in a critical hour such persons could not readily be isolated and separately dealt with, and constituted a menace to the national defense and safety, which demanded that prompt and adequate measures be taken to guard against it."

Like curfew, exclusion of those of Japanese origin was deemed necessary because of the presence of an unascertained number of disloyal members of the group, most of whom we have no doubt were loyal to this country. It was because we could not reject the finding of the military authorities that it was impossible to bring about an immediate segregation of the disloyal from the loyal that we sustained the validity of the curfew order as applying to the whole group. In the instant case, temporary exclusion of the entire group was rested by the military on the same ground. The judgment that exclusion of the whole group was for the same reason a military imperative answers the contention that the exclusion was in the nature of group punishment based on antagonism to those of Japanese origin. That there were members of the group who retained loyalties to Japan has been confirmed by investigations made subsequent to the exclusion. Approximately five thousand American citizens of Japanese ancestry refused to swear unqualified allegiance to the United States and to renounce allegiance to the Japanese Emperor, and several thousand evacuees requested repatriation to Japan.

We uphold the exclusion order as of

the time it was made and when the petitioner violated it. . . . In doing so, we are not unmindful of the hardships imposed by it upon a large group of American citizens. . . . But hardships are part of war, and war is an aggregation of hardships. All citizens alike, both in and out of uniform, feel the impact of war in greater or lesser measure. Citizenship has its responsibilities as well as its privileges, and in time of war the burden is always heavier. Compulsory exclusion of large groups of citizens from their homes, except under circumstances of direst emergency and peril, is inconsistent with our basic governmental institutions. But when under conditions of modern warfare our shores are threatened by hostile forces, the power to protect must be commensurate with the threatened danger. . . .

. . . It is now argued that the validity of the exclusion order cannot be considered apart from the orders requiring him, after departure from the area, to report and to remain in an assembly or relocation center. The contention is that we must treat these separate orders as one and inseparable; that, for this reason, if detention in the assembly or relocation center would have illegally deprived the petitioner of his liberty, the exclusion order and his conviction under it cannot stand.

We are thus being asked to pass at this time upon the whole subsequent detention program in both assembly and relocation centers, although the only issues framed at the trial related to petitioner's remaining in the prohibited area in violation of the exclusion order. Had petitioner here left the prohibited area and gone to an assembly center we cannot say either as a matter of fact or law that his presence in that center would have resulted in his detention in a relocation center. Some who did report to the assembly center were not sent to relocation centers, but were released upon condition that they remain outside the prohibited zone until the military orders were modified or lifted. This illustrates that they pose different problems and may be governed by different principles. The lawfulness of one does not necessarily determine the lawfulness of the others. This is made clear when we analyze the requirements of the separate provisions of the separate orders. These separate requirements were that those of Japanese ancestry (1) depart from the area; (2) report to and temporarily remain in an assembly center; (3) go under military control to a relocation center there to remain for an indeterminate period until released conditionally or unconditionally by the military authorities. Each of these requirements, it will be noted, imposed distinct duties in connection with the separate steps in a complete evacuation program. Had Congress directly incorporated into one Act the language of these separate orders, and provided sanctions for their violations, disobedience of any one would have constituted a separate offense. . . . There is no reason why violations of these orders, insofar as they were promulgated pursuant to Congressional enactment, should not be treated as separate offenses.

The *Endo* case . . . graphically illustrates the difference between the validity of an order to exclude and the validity of a detention order after exclusion has been effected.

Since the petitioner has not been convicted of failing to report or to remain in an assembly or relocation center, we cannot in this case determine the validity of those separate provisions of the order. It is sufficient here for us to pass upon the order which petitioner violated. To do more would be to go beyond the issues raised, and to decide momentous questions not contained within the framework of the pleadings or the evidence in this case. It will be time enough to decide the serious constitutional issues which petitioner seeks to raise when an assembly or relocation order is applied or is certain to be applied to him, and we have its terms before us.

Some of the members of the Court are of the view that evacuation and detention in an Assembly Center were inseparable. After May 3, 1942, the date of Exclusion Order No. 34, Korematsu was under compulsion to leave the area not as he would choose but via an Assembly Center. The Assembly Center was conceived as a part of the machinery for group evacuation. The power to exclude includes the power to do it by force if necessary. And any forcible measure must necessarily entail some degree of detention or restraint whatever method of removal is selected. But whichever view is taken, it results in holding that the order under which petitioner was convicted was valid.

It is said that we are dealing here with the case of imprisonment of a citizen in a concentration camp solely because of his ancestry, without evidence or inquiry concerning his loyalty and good disposition towards the United States. Our task would be simple, our duty clear, were this a case involving the imprisonment of a loyal citizen in a concentration camp because of racial prejudice. Regardless of the true nature of the assembly and relocation centers —and we deem it unjustifiable to call them concentration camps with all the ugly connotations that term implies— we are dealing specifically with nothing but an exclusion order. To cast this case into outlines of racial prejudice, without reference to the real military dangers which were presented, merely confuses the issue. Korematsu was not excluded from the Military Area because of hostility to him or his race. He *was* excluded because we are at war with the Japanese Empire, because the properly constituted military authorities feared an invasion of our West Coast and felt constrained to take proper security measures, because they decided that the military

urgency of the situation demanded that all citizens of Japanese ancestry be segregated from the West Coast temporarily and finally, because Congress, reposing its confidence in this time of war in our military leaders—as inevitably it must—determined that they should have the power to do just this. There was evidence of disloyalty on the part of some, the military authorities considered that the need for action was great and time was short. We cannot— by availing ourselves of the calm perspective of hindsight—now say that at that time these actions were unjustified.

Affirmed

. . . . .

MR. JUSTICE MURPHY DISSENTING

This exclusion of "all persons of Japanese ancestry, both alien and non-alien," from the Pacific Coast area on a plea of military necessity in the absence of martial law ought not to be approved. Such exclusion goes over "the very brink of constitutional power" and falls into the ugly abyss of racism.

In dealing with matters relating to the prosecution and progress of a war, we must accord great respect and consideration to the judgments of the military authorities who are on the scene and who have full knowledge of the military facts. The scope of their discretion must, as a matter of necessity and common sense, be wide. And their judgments ought not to be overruled lightly by those whose training and duties ill-equip them to deal intelligently with matters so vital to the physical security of the nation.

At the same time, however, it is essential that there be definite limits to military descretion, especially where martial law has not been declared. Individuals must not be left impoverished of their constitutional rights on a plea of military necessity that has neither substance nor support. Thus, like other claims conflicting with the asserted constitutional rights of the individual, the military claim must subject itself to the judicial process of having its reasonableness determined and its conflicts with other interests reconciled. . . .

The judicial test of whether the Government, on a plea of military necessity, can validly deprive an individual of any of his constitutional rights is whether the deprivation is reasonably related to a public danger that is so "immediate, imminent, and impending" as not to admit of delay and not to permit the intervention of ordinary constitutional processes to alleviate the danger. . . . Civilian Exclusion Order No. 34, banishing from a prescribed area of the Pacific Coast "all persons of Japanese ancestry, both alien and non-alien," clearly does not meet that test. Being an obvious racial discrimination, the order deprives all those within its scope of the equal protection of the laws as guaranteed by the Fifth Amendment. It further deprives these individuals of their constitutional rights to live and work where they will, to establish a home where they choose and to move about freely. In excommunicating them without benefit of hearings, this order also deprives them of all their constitutional rights to procedural due process. Yet no reasonable relation to an "immediate, imminent, and impending" public danger is evident to support this racial restriction which is one of the most sweeping and complete deprivations of constitutional rights in the history of this nation in the absence of martial law.

It must be conceded that the military and naval situation in the spring of 1942 was such as to generate a very real fear of invasion of the Pacific Coast, accompanied by fears of sabotage and espionage in that area. The military command was therefore justified in adopting all reasonable means necessary to combat these dangers. In adjudging the military action taken in light of the then apparent dangers, we must not erect too high or too meticulous standards; it is necessary only that the action have some reasonable relation to the removal of the dangers of invasion, sabotage and espionage. But the exclusion, either temporarily or permanently, of all persons with Japanese blood in their veins has no such reasonable relation. And that relation is lacking because the exclusion order necessarily must rely for its reasonableness upon the assumption that *all* persons of Japanese ancestry may have a dangerous tendency to commit sabotage and espionage and to aid our Japanese enemy in other ways. It is difficult to believe that reason, logic or experience could be marshalled in support of such an assumption.

That this forced exclusion was the result in good measure of this erroneous assumption of racial guilt rather than bona fide military necessity is evidenced by the Commanding General's Final Report on the evacuation from the Pacific Coast area. In it he refers to all individuals of Japanese descent as "subversive," as belonging to "an enemy race" whose "racial strains are undiluted," and as constituting "over 112,000 potential enemies . . . at large today" along the Pacific Coast. In support of this blanket condemnation of all persons of Japanese descent, however, no reliable evidence is cited to show that such individuals were generally disloyal, or had generally so conducted themselves in this area as to constitute a special menace to defense installations or war industries, or had otherwise by their behavior furnished reasonable ground for their exclusion as a group.

Justification for the exclusion is sought instead, mainly upon questionable racial and sociological grounds not ordinarily within the realm of expert military judgment, supplemented by certain semi-military conclusions drawn from an unwarranted use of circumstantial evidence. Individuals of Japanese ancestry are condemned because hey are said to be "a large, unassimilated, tightly knit racial group, bound to an enemy nation by strong ties of race, culture, and religion." They are claimed to be given to "emperor worshipping ceremonies" and to "dual citizenship." Japanese language schools and allegedly pro-Japanese organizations are cited as evidence of possible group disloyalty, together with facts as to certain persons being educated and residing at length in Japan. It is intimated that many of these individuals deliberately resided "adjacent to strategic points," thus enabling them "to carry into execution a tremendous program of sabotage on a mass scale should any considerable number of them have been inclined to do so." The need for protective custody is also asserted. The report refers without identity to "numerous incidents of violence" as well as to other admittedly unverified or cumulative incidents. From this, plus certain other events not shown to have been connected with the Japanese Americans, it is concluded that the "situation was fraught with danger to the Japanese population itself" and that the general public "was ready to take matters into its own hands." Finally, it is intimated, though not directly charged or proved, that persons of Japanese ancestry were responsible for three minor isolated shellings and bombings of the Pacific Coast area, as well as for unidentified radio transmissions and night signalling.

The main reasons relied upon by those responsible for the forced evacuation, therefore, do not prove a reasonable relation between the group characteristics of Japanese Americans and the dangers of invasion, sabotage and espionage. The reasons appear, instead, to be largely an accumulation of much of the misinformation, half-truths and insinuations that for years have been directed against Japanese Americans by people with racial and economic prejudices— the same people who have been among

the foremost advocates of the evacuation. A military judgment based upon such racial and sociological considerations is not entitled to the great weight ordinarily given the judgments based upon strictly military considerations Especially is this so when every charge relative to race, religion, culture, geographical location, and legal and economic status has been substantially discredited by independent studies made by experts in these matters.

The military necessity which is essential to the validity of the evacuation order thus resolves itself into a few intimations that certain individuals actively aided the enemy, from which it is inferred that the entire group of Japanese Americans could not be trusted to be or remain loyal to the United States. No one denies, of course, that there were some disloyal persons of Japanese descent on the Pacific Coast who did all in their power to aid their ancestral land. Similar disloyal activities have been engaged in by many persons of German, Italian and even more pioneer stock in our country. But to infer that examples of individual disloyalty prove group disloyalty and justify discriminatory action against the entire group is to deny that under our system of law individual guilt is the sole basis for deprivation of rights. Moreover, this inference, which is at the very heart of the evacuation orders, has been used in support of the abhorrent and despicable treatment of minority groups by the dictatorial tyrannies which this nation is now pledged to destroy. To give constitutional sanction to that inference in this case, however well-intentioned may have been the military command on the Pacific Coast, is to adopt one of the cruelest of the rationales used by our enemies to destroy the dignity of the individual and to encourage and open the door to discriminatory actions against other minority groups in the passions of tomorrow.

No adequate reason is given for the failure to treat these Japanese Americans on an individual basis by holding investigations and hearings to separate the loyal from the disloyal, as was done in the case of persons of German and Italian ancestry. . . . It is asserted merely that the loyalties of this group "were unknown and time was of the essence." Yet nearly four months elapsed after Pearl Harbor before the first exclusion order was issued; nearly eight months went by until the last order was issued; and the last of these "subversive" persons was not actually removed until almost eleven months had elapsed. Leisure and deliberation seem to have been more of the essence than speed. And the fact that conditions were not such as to warrant a declaration of martial law adds strength to the belief that the factors of time and military necessity were not as urgent as they have been represented to be.

Moreover, there was no adequate proof that the Federal Bureau of Investigation and the military and naval intelligence services did not have the espionage and sabotage situation well in hand during this long period. Nor is there any denial of the fact that not one person of Japanese ancestry was accused or convicted of espionage or sabotage after Pearl Harbor while they were still free, a fact which is some evidence of the loyalty of the vast majority of these individuals and of the effectiveness of the established methods of combatting these evils. It seems incredible that under these circumstances it would have been impossible to hold loyalty hearings for the mere 112,000 persons involved—or at least for the 70,000 American citizens —especially when a large part of this number represented children and elderly men and women. Any inconvenience that may have accompanied an attempt to conform to procedural due process cannot be said to justify violations of constitutional rights of individuals.

I dissent, therefore, from this legalization of racism. Racial discrimination in any form and in any degree has no justifiable part whatever in our democratic way of life. It is unattractive in any setting but it is utterly revolting among a free people who have embraced the principles set forth in the constitution of the United States. All residents of this nation are kin in some way by blood or culture to a foreign land. Yet they are primarily and necessarily a part of the new and distinct civilization of the United States. They must accordingly be treated at all times as the heirs of the American experiment and as entitled to all the rights and freedoms guaranteed by the Constitution.

MR. JUSTICE JACKSON DISSENTING

Korematsu . . . has been convicted of an act not commonly a crime. It consists merely of being present in the state whereof he is a citizen, near the place where he was born, and where all his life he has lived. . . .

A citizen's presence in the locality, however, was made a crime only if his parents were of Japanese birth. . . .

Now, if any fundamental assumption underlies our system, it is that guilt is personal and not inheritable. Even if all of one's antecedents had been convicted of treason, the Constitution forbids its penalties to be visited upon him, for it provides that "no attainder of treason shall work corruption of blood, or forfeiture except during the life of the person attainted." But here is an attempt to make an otherwise innocent act a crime merely because this prisoner is the son of parents as to whom he had no choice, and belongs to a race from which there is no way to resign. . . .

But the "law" which this prisoner is convicted of disregarding is not found in an act of Congress, but in a military order. Neither the Act of Congress nor the Executive Order of the President, nor both together, would afford a basis for this conviction. It rests on the orders of General De Witt. And it is said that if the military commander had reasonable military grounds for promulgating the orders, they are constitutional and become law, and the Court is required to enforce them. There are several reasons why I cannot subscribe to this doctrine.

It would be impracticable and dangerous idealism to expect or insist that each specific military command in an area of probable operations will conform to conventional tests of constitutionality. When an area is so beset that it must be put under military control at all, the paramount consideration is that its measures be successful, rather than legal. The armed services must protect a society, not merely its Constitution. The very essence of the military job is to marshal physical force, to remove every obstacle to its effectiveness, to give it every strategic advantage. Defense measures will not, and often should not, be held within the limits that bind civil authority in peace. No court can require such a commander in such circumstances to act as a reasonable man; he may be unreasonably cautious and exacting. Perhaps he should be. But a commander in temporarily focusing the life of a community on defense is carrying out a military program; he is not making law in the sense the courts know the term. He issues orders, and they may have a certain authority as military commands, although they may be very bad as constitutional law.

But if we cannot confine military expedients by the Constitution, neither would I distort the Constitution to approve all that the military may deem expedient. That is what the Court appears to be doing, whether consciously or not. I cannot say, from any evidence before me, that the orders of General De Witt were not reasonably expedient military precautions, nor could I say that they were. But even if they were permissible military procedures, I deny that it follows that they are constitutional. If, as the Court holds, it does follow, then we may as well say that any military order will be constitutional and have done with it.

The limitation under which courts always will labor in examining the necessity for a military order are illustrated by this case. How does the Court know that these orders have a reasonable basis in necessity? No evidence whatever on that subject has been taken by this or any other court. There is sharp controversy as to the credibility of the De Witt report. So the Court, having no real evidence before it, has no choice but to accept General De Witt's own unsworn, self-serving statement, untested by any cross-examination, that what he did was reasonable. And thus it will always be when courts try to look into the reasonableness of a military order.

In the very nature of things, military decisions are not susceptible of intelligent judicial appraisal. They do not pretend to rest on evidence, but are made on information that often would not be admissible and on assumptions that could not be proved. Information in support of an order could not be disclosed to courts without danger that it would reach the enemy. Neither can courts act on communications made in confidence. Hence courts can never have any real alternative to accepting the mere declaration of the authority that issued the order that it was reasonably necessary from a military viewpoint.

Much is said of the danger to liberty from the Army program for deporting and detaining these citizens of Japanese extraction. But a judicial construction of the due process clause that will sustain this order is a far more subtle blow to liberty than the promulgation of the order itself. A military order, however unconstitutional, is not apt to last longer than the military emergency. Even during that period a succeeding commander may revoke it all. But once a judicial opinion rationalizes such an order to show that it conforms to the Constitution, or rather rationalizes the Constitution to show that the Constitution sanctions such an order, the Court for all time has validated the principle of racial discrimination in criminal procedure and of transplanting American citizens. The principle then lies about like a loaded weapon ready for the hand of any authority that can bring forward a plausible claim of an urgent need. Every repetition imbeds that principle more deeply in our law and thinking and expands it to new purposes. All who observe the work of courts are familiar with what Judge Cardozo described as "the tendency of a principle to expand itself to the limit of its logic." A military commander may overstep the bounds of constitutionality, and it is an incident. But if we review and approve, that passing incident becomes the doctrine of the Constitution. There it has a generative power of its own, and all that it creates will be in its own image. Nothing better illustrates this danger than does the Court's opinion in this case. . . .

Of course the existence of a military power resting on force, so vagrant, so centralized, so necessarily heedless of the individual, is an inherent threat to liberty. But I would not lead people to rely on this Court for a review that seems to me wholly delusive. The military reasonableness of these orders can only be determined by military superiors. If the people ever let command of the war power fall into irresponsible and unscrupulous hands, the courts wield no power equal to its restraint. The chief restraint upon those who command the physical forces of the country, in the future as in the past, must be their responsibility to the political judgments of their contemporaries and to the moral judgments of history.

My duties as a justice as I see them do not require me to make a military judgment as to whether General De Witt's evacuation and detention program was a reasonable military necessity. I do not suggest that the courts should have attempted to interfere with the Army in carrying out its task. But I do not think they may be asked to execute a military expedient that has no place in law under the Constitution. I would reverse the judgment and discharge the prisoner.

82. *FEBRUARY, 1945*

Yalta Conference

As the European phase of the Second World War approached an end, President Roosevelt of the United States, Premier Stalin of Russia, and Prime Minister

Official Documents: Texts of Selected Documents on U.S. Foreign Policy, 1918–1952 (New York: Columbia University Press, 1952), pp. 10–19. Reprinted by permission of the Woodrow Wilson Foundation.

Churchill of Great Britain met at Yalta in the Crimea to establish plans for the future. The Yalta arrangements which later caused the most disagreement among the Allied powers were details concerning (1) the United Nations Organization, (2) the future of Germany, (3) the right of self-government in the countries of Eastern Europe, and (4) *the entry of Russia into the war in the Pacific.*

One can comprehend the Yalta agreements only if he is aware of the conditions under which its participants worked. Allied peoples everywhere agreed that Germany and Japan must be severely punished. President Roosevelt assumed that Russia had been so severely damaged in the war that it would take her at least a generation to recover. Nevertheless, he assumed that Russian assistance would be valuable in defeating the Japanese and that Russian aid would not be forthcoming unless certain concessions were granted to her in the Far East. Even had Roosevelt not granted concessions to Russia, it is difficult to avoid the conclusion that Stalin would have been able to fulfill his ambitions in Europe and the Far East in some other way. In view of Russia's ability to take what she wanted in 1945 without the consent of Churchill and Roosevelt, the Yalta agreements did not seem excessive to Roosevelt in February, 1945. The tragedy of Yalta was that Stalin later broke his promises.

The Crimea Conference of the Heads of the Governments of the United States of America, the United Kingdom, and the Union of Soviet Socialist Republics which took place from February 4th to 11th came to the following conclusions:

I. WORLD ORGANISATION

It was decided:

(1) that a United Nations Conference on the proposed world organisation should be summoned for Wednesday, 25th April, 1945, and should he held in the United States of America.

(2) the Nations to be invited to this Conference should be:

(a) the United Nations as they existed on the 8th February, 1945; and

(b) such of the Associated Nations as have declared war on the common enemy by 1st March, 1945. (For this purpose by the term "Associated Nations" was meant the eight Associated Nations and Turkey.) When the Conference on World Organisation is held, the delegates of the United Kingdom and United States of America will support a proposal to admit to original membership two Soviet Socialist Republics, i.e., the Ukraine and White Russia.

(3) that the United States Government on behalf of the Three Powers should consult the Government of China and the French Provisional Government in regard to decisions taken at the present Conference concerning the proposed World Organisation.

(4) that the text of the invitation to be issued to all the nations which would take part in the United Nations Conference should be as follows:

INVITATION

The Government of the United States of America, on behalf of itself and of the Governments of the United Kingdom, the Union of Soviet Socialist Republics, and the Republic of China and the Provisional Government of the French Republic, invite the Government of ——— to send representatives to a Conference of the United Nations to be held on 25th April, 1945, or soon thereafter, at San Francisco in the United States of America to prepare a Charter for a General International Organization for the maintenance of international peace and security.

The above named governments suggest that the Conference consider as affording a basis for such a Charter the Proposals for the Establishment of a General International Organisation, which were made public last October as a result of the Dumbarton Oaks Conference, and which have now been supplemented by the following provisions for Section C of Chapter VI:

"C. Voting.

"1. Each member of the Security Council should have one vote.

"2. Decisions of the Security Council

on procedural matters should be made by an affirmative vote of seven members.

"3. Decisions of the Security Council on all other matters should be made by an affirmative vote of seven members including the concurring votes of the permanent members; provided that, in decisions under Chapter VIII, Section A and under the second sentence of paragraph I of Chapter VIII, Section C, a party to a dispute should abstain from voting."

. . . . .

TERRITORIAL TRUSTEESHIP

It was agreed that the five Nations which will have permanent seats on the Security Council should consult each other prior to the United Nations Conference on the questions of territorial trusteeship.

The acceptance of this recommendation is subject to its being made clear that territorial trusteeship will only apply to (a) existing mandates of the League of Nations; (b) territories detached from the enemy as a result of the present war; (c) any other territory which might voluntarily be placed under trusteeship; and (d) no discussion of actual territories is contemplated at the forthcoming United Nations Conference or in the preliminary consultations, and it will be a matter for subsequent agreement which territories within the above categories will be placed under trusteeship.

II. DECLARATION ON LIBERATED EUROPE

The following declaration has been approved:

The Premier of the Union of Soviet Socialist Republics, the Prime Minister of the United Kingdom and the President of the United States of America have consulted with each other in the common interests of the peoples of their countries and those of liberated Europe. They jointly declare their mutual agreement to concert during the temporary period of instability in liberated Europe the policies of their three governments in assisting the peoples of the former Axis satellite states of Europe to solve by democratic means their pressing political and economic problems.

The establishment of order in Europe and the re-building of national economic life must be achieved by processes which will enable the liberated peoples to destroy the last vestiges of Nazism and Fascism and to create democratic institutions of their own choice. This is a principle of the Atlantic Charter—the right of all peoples to choose the form of government under which they will live—the restoration of sovereign rights and self-government to those peoples who have been forcibly deprived of them by the aggressor nations.

To foster the conditions in which the liberated peoples may exercise these rights, the three governments will jointly assist the people in any European liberated state or former Axis satellite state in Europe where in their judgment conditions require (a) to establish conditions of internal peace; (b) to carry out emergency measures for the relief of distressed peoples; (c) to form interim governmental authorities broadly representative of all democratic elements in the population and pledged to the earliest possible establishment through free elections of governments responsive to the will of the people; and (d) to facilitate where necessary the holding of such elections.

The three governments will consult the other United Nations and provisional authorities or other governments in Europe when matters of direct interest to them are under consideration.

When, in the opinion of the three governments, conditions in any European liberated state or any former Axis satellite state in Europe make such action necessary, they will immediately consult together on the measures necessary to discharge the joint responsibilities set forth in this declaration.

By this declaration we reaffirm our faith in the principles of the Atlantic Charter, our pledges in the Declaration by the United Nations, and our determination to build in cooperation with other peace-loving nations world order under law, dedicated to peace, security, freedom and general well-being of all mankind.

In issuing this declaration, the Three Powers express the hope that the Provisional Government of the French Republic may be associated with them in the procedure suggested.

II. DISMEMBERMENT OF GERMANY

It was agreed that Article 12 (a) of the Surrender Terms for Germany should be amended to read as follows:

The United Kingdom, the United States of America and the Union of Soviet Socialist Republics shall possess supreme authority with respect to Germany. In the exercise of such authority they will take such steps, including the complete disarmament, demilitarisation and dismemberment of Germany as they deem requisite for future peace and security.

. . . . .

IV. ZONE OF OCCUPATION FOR THE FRENCH AND CONTROL COUNCIL FOR GERMANY

It was agreed that a zone in Germany, to be occupied by the French Forces, should be allocated to France. This zone would be formed out of the British and American zones and its extent would be settled by the British and Americans in consultation with the French Provisional Government.

It was also agreed that the French provisional Government should be invited to become a member of the Allied Control Council of Germany.

V. REPARATION

The heads of the three governments agreed as follows:

1. Germany must pay in kind for the losses caused by her to the Allied nations in the course of the war. Reparations are to be received in the first instance by those countries which have borne the main burden of the war, have suffered the heaviest losses and have organised victory over the enemy.

2. Reparation in kind to be exacted from Germany in three following forms:

(a) Removals within 2 years from the surrender of Germany or the cessation of organised resistance from the national wealth of Germany located on the territory of Germany herself as well as outside her territory (equipment, machine tools, ships, rolling stock, German investments aboard, shares of industrial, transport and other enterprises in Germany etc.), these removals to be carried out chiefly for purpose of destroying the war potential of Germany.

(b) Annual deliveries of goods from current production for a period to be fixed.

(c) Use of German labour.

3. For the working out on the above principles of a detailed plan for exaction of reparation from Germany an Allied Reparation Commission will be set up in Moscow. It will consist of three representatives—one from the Union of Soviet Socialist Republics, one from the United Kingdom and one from the United States of America.

4. With regard to the fixing of the total sum of the reparation as well as the distribution of it among the countries which suffered from the German aggression the Soviet and American delegations agreed as follows:

The Moscow Reparation Commission should take in its initial studies as a basis for discussion the suggestion of the Soviet Government that the total sum of the reparation in accordance with the points (a) and (b) of the paragraph 2 should be 20 billion dollars and that 50% of it should go to the Union of Soviet Socialist Republics.

The British delegation was of the opinion that pending consideration of the reparation question by the Moscow Reparation Commission no figures of reparation should be mentioned.

. . . . .

VI. MAJOR WAR CRIMINALS

The Conference agreed that the question of the major war criminals should be the subject of enquiry by the three Foreign Secretaries for report in due course after the close of the Conference.

VII. POLAND

The following Declaration on Poland was agreed by the Conference:

A new situation has been created in Poland as a result of her complete liberation by the Red Army. This calls for the establishment of a Polish Provisional Government which can be more broadly based than was possible before the recent liberation of Western part of Poland. The Provisional Government which is now functioning in Poland should therefore be reorganised on a broader democratic basis with the inclusion of democratic leaders from Poland itself and from Poles abroad. This new Government should then be called the Polish Provisional Government of National Unity.

M. Molotov, Mr. Harriman and Sir A. Clark Kerr are authorised as a commission to consult in the first instance in Moscow with members of the present Provisional Government and with other Polish democratic leaders from within Poland and from abroad, with a view to the reorganization of the present Government along the above lines. This Polish Provisional Government of National Unity shall be pledged to the holding of free and unfettered elections as soon as possible on the basis of universal suffrage and secret ballot. In these elections all democratic and anti-Nazi parties shall have the right to take part and to put forward candidates.

When a Polish Provisional Government of National Unity has been properly formed in conformity with the above, the Government of the U.S.S.R., which now maintains diplomatic relations with the present Provisional Government of Poland, and the Government of the United Kingdom and the Government of the United States of America will establish diplomatic relations with the new Polish Provisional Government of National Unity, and will exchange Ambassadors by whose reports the respective Governments will be kept informed about the situation in Poland.

The three Heads of Government consider that the Eastern frontier of Poland should follow the Curzon line with digressions from it in some regions of five to eight kilometres in favour of Poland. They recognize that Poland must receive substantial accession of territory in the North and West. They feel that the opinion of the new Polish Provisional Government of National Unity should be sought in due course on the extent of these accessions and that the final delimitation of the Western frontier of Poland should thereafter await the Peace Conference.

VIII. YUGOSLAVIA

It was agreed to recommend to Marshal Tito and to Dr. Subasic:

(a) that the Tito-Subasic Agreement should immediately be put into effect and a new Government formed on the basis of the Agreement

(b) that as soon as the new Government has been formed it should declare:

(i) that the Anti-Fascist Assembly of National Liberation (Aunoj) will be extended to include members of the last Yugoslav Skupstina who have not compromised themselves by collaboration with the enemy, thus forming a body to be known as a temporary Parliament and

(ii) that legislative acts passed by the Anti-Fascist Assembly of National Liberation (Aunoj) will be subject to subsequent ratification by a Constituent Assembly; and that this statement should be published in the Communiqués of the Conference.

IX. ITALO-YUGOSLAV FRONTIER— ITALO-AUSTRIA FRONTIER

Notes on these subjects were put in by the British delegation and the American and Soviet delegations agreed to consider them and give their views later.

X. YUGOSLAV-BULGARIAN RELATIONS

There was an exchange of views between the Foreign Secretaries on the question of the desirability of a Yugo-slav-Bulgarian pact of alliance. The question at issue was whether a state still under an armistice régime could be allowed to enter into a treaty with another state. Mr. Eden suggested that the Bulgarian and Yugoslav Governments should be informed that this could not be approved. Mr. Stettinius suggested that the British and American Ambassadors should discuss the matter further with M. Molotov in Moscow. M. Molotov agreed with the proposal of Mr. Stettinius.

XI. SOUTHEASTERN EUROPE

The British Delegation put in notes for the consideration of their colleagues on the following subjects:

(a) the Control Commission in Bulgaria

(b) Greek claims upon Bulgaria, more particularly with reference to reparations

(c) Oil equipment in Rumania

XII. IRAN

Mr. Eden, Mr. Stettinius and M. Molotov exchanged views on the situation in Iran. It was agreed that this matter should be pursued through the diplomatic channel.

XIII. MEETINGS OF THE THREE FOREIGN SECRETARIES

The Conference agreed that permanent machinery should be set up for consultation between the three Foreign Secretaries; they should meet as often as necessary, probably about every three or four months.

These meetings will be held in rotation in the three capitals, the first meeting being held in London.

XIV. THE MONTREUX CONVENTION AND THE STRAITS

It was agreed that at the next meeting of the three Foreign Secretaries to be held in London, they should consider proposals which it was understood the Soviet Government would put forward in relation to the Montreux Convention and report to their Governments. The Turkish Government should be informed at the appropriate moment.

. . . . .

The leaders of the three Great Powers—the Soviet Union, the United States of America and Great Britain—have agreed that in two or three months after Germany has surrendered and the war in Europe has terminated the Soviet Union shall enter into the war against Japan on the side of the Allies on condition that:

1. The status quo in Outer-Mongolia (The Mongolian People's Republic) shall be preserved;

2. The former rights of Russia violated by the treacherous attack of Japan in 1904 shall be restored, viz:

(a) the southern part of Sakhalin as well as all the islands adjacent to it shall be returned to the Soviet Union,

(b) the commercial port of Dairen shall be internationalized, the preeminent interests of the Soviet Union in this port being safeguarded and the lease of Port Arthur as a naval base of the U.S.-S.R. restored,

(c) the Chinese-Eastern Railroad and the South-Manchurian Railroad which provides an outlet to Dairen shall be jointly operated by the establishment of a joint Soviet-Chinese Company, it being understood that the preeminent interests of the Soviet Union shall be safeguarded and that China shall retain full sovereignty in Manchuria;

3. The Kurile islands shall be handed over to the Soviet Union. It is understood, that the agreement concerning

Outer-Mongolia and the ports and railroads referred to above will require concurrence of Generalissimo Chiang Kai-Shek. The President will take measures in order to obtain this concurrence on advice from Marshal Stalin.

The Heads of the three Great Powers have agreed that these claims of the Soviet Union shall be unquestionably fulfilled after Japan has been defeated.

For its part the Soviet Union expresses its readiness to conclude with the National Government of China a pact of friendship and alliance between the U.S.S.R. and China in order to render assistance to China with its armed forces for the purpose of liberating China from the Japanese yoke.

COMMENT

Nothing that was done at Yalta contributed to the loss of control over China by Chiang Kai-shek. The Yalta understanding was implemented by the Sino-Soviet agreements, which had they been carried out by Stalin, might have saved the Chinese National Government.

> Former Ambassador W. Averell Harriman in testimony to the U.S. Senate Committee on Armed Services and the Committee on Foreign Relations. See *Hearings of the Committee on Armed Services and the Committee on Foreign Relations, 82nd Congress, First Session* (Washington, 1951), pt. 5, 3340.

The second conference of the Big Three held at Yalta in February 1945 represented the high point of Soviet diplomatic success and correspondingly the low point of American appeasement.

> Journalist William H. Chamberlain in *America's Second Crusade* (Chicago: Henry Regnery Co., 1950), p. 206.

The record of the conference shows clearly that the Soviet Union made greater concessions at Yalta to the United States and Great Britain than were made to the Soviets. The agreements reached among President Roosevelt, Prime Minister Churchill and Marshall Stalin were, on the whole, a diplomatic triumph for the United States and Great Britain.

> Former Secretary of State Edward R. Stettinius, Jr., in *Roosevelt and the Russians: The Yalta Conference*, ed. Walter Johnson (Garden City: Doubleday & Co., Inc., 1949), p. 295.

83. JUNE 26, 1945

Charter of the United Nations

At the end of the Second World War, the American view of the postwar era was optimistic. The new period was to be one of peace, prosperity, individual freedom, and justice. These goals were to be embodied in the United Nations. Covenants were to be open and openly arrived at so the people of the world could then exer-

Department of State Bulletin, XII (June 24, 1945), 1119-34.

ise vigilance over statesmen in the United Nations and prevent them from entering into secret bargains which might endanger peace. World public opinion operating across national boundaries would be able to hold diplomats accountable for their actions. Power politics would be abandoned. The United Nations would then represent democracy at work in an international scale. The foreign policy of the United States was to be a "diplomacy of principles," of moral disinterestedness, instead of power politics. In sum, the American people assumed that an international organization would be the solution to the maintenance of peace. Later, the postwar disillusionment with the lack of effectiveness of the United Nations stemmed from the naive wartime expectation that it could accomplish more than was possible. Unfortunately, the United Nations could not be much stronger than the determination of the great powers to work together in harmony.

We the peoples of the United Nations determined to save succeeding generations from the scourge of war, which twice in our lifetime has brought untold sorrow to mankind, and

to reaffirm faith in fundamental human rights, in the dignity and worth of the human person, in the equal rights of men and women and of nations large and small, and

to establish conditions under which justice and respect for the obligations arising from treaties and other sources of international law can be maintained, and

to promote social progress and better standards of life in larger freedom,

and for these ends to practice tolerance and live together in peace with one another as good neighbors, and

to unite our strength to maintain international peace and security, and to ensure, by the acceptance of principles and the institution of methods, that armed force shall not be used, save in the common interest, and

to employ international machinery for the promotion of the economic and social advancement of all peoples, have resolved to combine our efforts to accomplish these aims.

Accordingly, our respective Governments, through representatives assembled in the city of San Francisco, who have exhibited their full powers found to be in good and due form, have agreed to the present Charter of the United Nations and do hereby establish an international organization to be known as the United Nations.

CHAPTER I: PURPOSES AND PRINCIPLES

Article 1

The Purposes of the United Nations are:

1. To maintain international peace and security, and to that end: to take effective collective measures for the prevention and removal of threats to the peace, and for the suppression of acts of aggression or other breaches of the peace, and to bring about by peaceful means, and in conformity with the principles of justice and international law, adjustment or settlement of international disputes or situations which might lead to a breach of the peace;

2. To develop friendly relations among nations based on respect for the principle of equal rights and self-determination of peoples, and to take other appropriate measures to strengthen universal peace;

3. To achieve international cooperation in solving international problems of an economic, social, cultural, or humanitarian character, and in promoting and encouraging respect for human rights and for fundamental freedoms for all without distinction as to race, sex, language, or religion; and

4. To be a center for harmonizing the actions of nations in the attainment of these common ends.

Article 2

The Organization and its Members, in pursuit of the Purposes stated in Article 1, shall act in accordance with the following Principles.

1. The Organization is based on the principle of the sovereign equality of all its Members.

2. All Members, in order to ensure to all of them the rights and benefits resulting from membership, shall fulfill in good faith the obligations assumed by them in accordance with the present Charter.

3. All Members shall settle their international disputes by peaceful means in such a manner that international peace and security, and justice, are not endangered.

4. All Members shall refrain in their international relations from the threat or use of force against the territorial integrity or political independence of any state, or in any other manner inconsistent with the Purposes of the United Nations.

5. All Members shall give the United Nations every assistance in any action it takes in accordance with the present Charter, and shall refrain from giving assistance to any state against which the United Nations is taking preventive or enforcement action.

6. The Organization shall ensure that states which are not Members of the United Nations act in accordance with the Principles so far as may be necessary for the maintenance of international peace and security.

7. Nothing contained in the present Charter shall authorize the United Nations to intervene in matters which are essentially within the domestic jurisdiction of any state or shall require the Members to submit such matters to settlement under the present Charter; but this principle shall not prejudice the applica-

tion of enforcement measures under Chapter VII.

CHAPTER II: MEMBERSHIP

Article 3

The original Members of the United Nations shall be the states which, having participated in the United Nations Conference on International Organization at San Francisco, or having previously signed the Declaration by United Nations of January 1, 1942, sign the present Charter and ratify it in accordance with Article 110.

Article 4

1. Membership in the United Nations is open to all other peace-loving states which accept the obligations contained in the present Charter and, in the judgment of the Organization, are able and willing to carry out these obligations.

2. The admission of any such state to membership in the United Nations will be effected by a decision of the General Assembly upon the recommendation of the Security Council.

Article 5

A Member of the United Nations against which preventive or enforcement action has been taken by the Security Council may be suspended from the exercise of the rights and privileges of membership by the General Assembly upon the recommendation of the Security Council. The exercise of these rights and privileges may be restored by the Security Council.

Article 6

A Member of the United Nations which has persistently violated the Principles contained in the present Charter may be expelled from the Organization by the General Assembly upon the recommendation of the Security Council.

CHAPTER III: ORGANS

Article 7

1. There are established as the principal organs of the United Nations: a General Assembly, a Security Council, an Economic and Social Council, a Trusteeship Council, an International Court of Justice, and a Secretariat.

2. Such subsidiary organs as may be found necessary may be established in accordance with the present Charter.

Article 8

The United Nations shall place no restrictions on the eligibility of men and women to participate in any capacity and under conditions of equality in its principal and subsidiary organs.

CHAPTER IV: THE GENERAL ASSEMBLY

Article 9

COMPOSITION

1. The General Assembly shall consist of all the Members of the United Nations.

2. Each Member shall have not more than five representatives in the General Assembly.

Article 10

FUNCTIONS AND POWERS

The General Assembly may discuss any questions or any matters within the scope of the present Charter or relating to the powers and functions of any organs provided for in the present Charter, and, except as provided in Article 12, may make recommendations to the Members of the United Nations or to the Security Council or to both on any such questions or matters.

Article 11

1. The General Assembly may consider the general principles of cooperation in the maintenance of international peace and security, including the principles governing disarmament and the regulation of armaments, and may make recommendations with regard to such principles to the Members or to the Security Council or to both.

2. The General Assembly may discuss any questions relating to the maintenance of international peace and security brought before it by any Member of the United Nations, or by the Security Council, or by a state which is not a Member of the United Nations in accordance with Article 35, paragraph 2, and, except as provided in Article 12, may make recommendations with regard to any such questions to the state or states concerned or to the Security Council or to both. Any such question on which action is necessary shall be referred to the Security Council by the General Assembly either before or after discussion.

3. The General Assembly may call the attention of the Security Council to situations which are likely to endanger international peace and security.

4. The powers of the General Assembly set forth in this Article shall not limit the general scope of Article 10.

Article 12

1. While the Security Council is exercising in respect of any dispute or situation the functions assigned to it in the present Charter, the General Assembly shall not make any recommendation with regard to that dispute or situation unless the Security Council so requests.

2. The Secretary-General, with the consent of the Security Council, shall notify the General Assembly at each session of any matters relative to the maintenance of international peace and security which are being dealt with by the Security Council and shall similarly notify

the General Assembly, or the Members of the United Nations if the General Assembly is not in session, immediately the Security Council ceases to deal with such matters.

Article 13

1. The General Assembly shall initiate studies and make recommendations for the purpose of:

a. promoting international cooperation in the political field and encouraging the progressive development of international law and its codification;

b. promoting international cooperation in the economic, social, cultural, educational, and health fields, and assisting in the realization of human rights and fundamental freedoms for all without distinction as to race, sex, language, or religion.

2. The further responsibilities, functions, and powers of the General Assembly with respect to matters mentioned in paragraph 1 (b) above are set forth in Chapters IX and X.

Article 14

Subject to the provisions of Article 12, the General Assembly may recommend measures for peaceful adjustment of any situation, regardless of origin, which it deems likely to impair the general welfare or friendly relations among nations, including situations resulting from a violation of the provisions of the present Charter setting forth the Purposes and Principles of the United Nations.

Article 15

1. The General Assembly shall receive and consider annual and special reports from the Security Council; these reports shall include an account of the measures that the Security Council has

decided upon or taken to maintain international peace and security.

2. The General Assembly shall receive and consider reports from the other organs of the United Nations.

Article 16

The General Assembly shall perform such functions with respect to the international trusteeship system as are assigned to it under Chapters XII and XIII, including the approval of the trusteeship agreements for areas not designated as strategic.

Article 17

1. The General Assembly shall consider and prove the budget of the Organization.

2. The expenses of the Organization shall be borne by the Members as apportioned by the General Assembly.

3. The General Assembly shall consider and approve any financial and budgetary arrangements with specialized agencies referred to in Article 57 and shall examine the administrative budgets of such specialized agencies with a view to making recommendations to the agencies concerned.

Article 18

VOTING

1. Each member of the General Assembly shall have one vote.

2. Decisions of the General Assembly on important questions shall be made by a two-thirds majority of the members present and voting. These questions shall include: recommendations with respect to the maintenance of international peace and security, the election of the non-permanent members of the Security Council, the election of the members of the Economic and Social Council, the election of members of the Trusteeship Council in accordance

with paragraph 1 (c) of Article 86, the admission of new Members to the United Nations, the suspension of the rights and privileges of membership, the expulsion of Members, questions relating to the operation of the trusteeship system, and budgetary questions.

3. Decisions on other questions, including the determination of additional categories of questions to be decided by a two-thirds majority, shall be made by a majority of the members present and voting.

Article 19

A Member of the United Nations which is in arrears in the payment of its financial contributions to the Organization shall have no vote in the General Assembly if the amount of its arrears equals or exceeds the amount of the contributions due from it for the preceding two full years. The General Assembly may, nevertheless, permit such a Member to vote if it is satisfied that the failure to pay is due to conditions beyond the control of the Member.

Article 20
PROCEDURE

The General Assembly shall meet in regular annual sessions and in such special sessions as occasion may require. Special sessions shall be convoked by the Secretary-General at the request of the Security Council or of a majority of the Members of the United Nations.

Article 21

The General Assembly shall adopt its own rules of procedure. It shall elect its President for each session.

Article 22

The General Assembly may establish such subsidiary organs as it deems necessary for the performance of its functions.

CHAPTER V: THE SECURITY COUNCIL

Article 23
COMPOSITION

1. The Security Council shall consist of eleven Members of the United Nations. The Republic of China, France, the Union of Soviet Socialist Republics, the United Kingdom of Great Britain and Northern Ireland, and the United States of America shall be permanent members of the Security Council. The General Assembly shall elect six other Members of the United Nations to be non-permanent members of the Security Council, due regard being specially paid, in the first instance to the contribution of Members of the United Nations to the maintenance of international peace and security and to the other purposes of the Organization, and also to equitable geographical distribution.

2. The non-permanent members of the Security Council shall be elected for a term of two years. In the first election of the non-permanent members, however, three shall be chosen for a term of one year. A retiring member shall not be eligible for immediate re-election.

3. Each member of the Security Council shall have one representative.

Article 24
FUNCTIONS AND POWERS

1. In order to ensure prompt and effective action by the United Nations, its Members confer on the Security Council primary responsibility for the maintenance of international peace and security, and agree that in carrying out its duties under this responsibility the Security Council acts on their behalf.

2. In discharging these duties the Security Council shall act in accordance

with the Purposes and Principles of the United Nations. The specific powers granted to the Security Council for the discharge of these duties are laid down in Chapters VI, VII, VIII, and XII.

3. The Security Council shall submit annual and, when necessary, special reports to the General Assembly for its consideration.

Article 25

The Members of the United Nations agree to accept and carry out the decisions of the Security Council in accordance with the present Charter.

Article 26

In order to promote the establishment and maintenance of international peace and security with the least diversion for armaments of the world's human and economic resources, the Security Council shall be responsible for formulating, with the assistance of the Military Staff Committee referred to in Article 47, plans to be submitted to the Members of the United Nations for the establishment of a system for the regulation of armaments.

Article 27

VOTING

1. Each member of the Security Council shall have one vote.

2. Decisions of the Security Council on procedural matters shall be made by an affirmative vote of seven members.

3. Decisions of the Security Council on all other matters shall be made by an affirmative vote of seven members including the concurring votes of the permanent members; provided that, in decisions under Chapter VI, and under paragraph 3 of Article 52, a party to a dispute shall abstain from voting.

Article 28

PROCEDURE

1. The Security Council shall be so organized as to be able to function continuously. Each member of the Security Council shall for this purpose be represented at all times at the seat of the Organization.

2. The Security Council shall hold periodic meetings at which each of its members may, if it so desires, be represented by a member of the government or by some other specially designated representative.

3. The Security Council may hold meetings at such places other than the seat of the Organization as in its judgment will best facilitate its work.

Article 29

The Security Council may establish such subsidiary organs as it deems necessary for the performance of its functions.

Article 30

The Security Council shall adopt its own rules of procedure, including the method of selecting its President.

Article 31

Any Member of the United Nations which is not a member of the Security Council may participate, without vote, in the discussion of any question brought before the Security Council whenever the latter considers that the interests of that Member are specially affected.

Article 32

Any Member of the United Nations which is not a member of the Security Council or any state which is not a Member of the United Nations, if it is a party to a dispute under consideration by the Security Council, shall be invited to participate, without vote, in the discussion relating to the dispute. The Security Council shall lay down such conditions as it deems just for the participation of a state which is not a Member of the United Nations.

CHAPTER VI: PACIFIC SETTLEMENT
OF DISPUTES

Article 33

1. The parties to any dispute, the continuance of which is likely to endanger the maintenance of international peace and security, shall, first of all, seek a solution by negotiation, enquiry, mediation, conciliation, arbitration, judicial settlement, resort to regional agencies or arrangements, or other peaceful means of their own choice.

2. The Security Council shall, when it deems necessary, call upon the parties to settle their dispute by such means.

Article 34

The Security Council may investigate any dispute, or any situation which might lead to international friction or give rise to a dispute, in order to determine whether the continuance of the dispute or situation is likely to endanger the maintenance of international peace and security.

Article 35

1. Any Member of the United Nations may bring any dispute, or any situation of the nature referred to in Article 34, to the attention of the Security Council or of the General Assembly.

2. A state which is not a Member of the United Nations may bring to the attention of the Security Council or of the General Assembly any dispute to which

it is a party if it accepts in advance, for the purposes of the dispute, the obligations of pacific settlement provided in the present Charter.

3. The proceedings of the General Assembly in respect of matters brought to its attention under this Article will be subject to the provisions of Articles 11 and 12.

Article 36

1. The Security Council may, at any stage of a dispute of the nature referred to in Article 33 or of a situation of like nature, recommend appropriate procedures or methods of adjustment.

2. The Security Council should take into consideration any procedures for the settlement of the dispute which have already been adopted by the parties.

3. In making recommendations under this Article the Security Council should also take into consideration that legal disputes should as a general rule be referred by the parties to the International Court of Justice in accordance with the provisions of the Statute of the Court.

Article 37

1. Should the parties to a dispute of the nature referred to in Article 33 fail to settle it by the means indicated in that Article, they shall refer it to the Security Council.

2. If the Security Council deems that the continuance of the dispute is in fact likely to endanger the maintenance of international peace and security, it shall decide whether to take action under Article 36 or to recommend such terms of settlement as it may consider appropriate.

Article 38

Without prejudice to the provisions of Articles 33 to 37, the Security Council may, if all the parties to any dispute so request, make recommendations to the parties with a view to a pacific settlement of the dispute.

CHAPTER VIII: ACTION WITH RESPECT TO THREATS TO THE PEACE, BREACHES OF THE PEACE, AND ACTS OF AGGRESSION

Article 39

The Security Council shall determine the existence of any threat to the peace, breach of the peace, or act of aggression and shall make recommendations, or decide what measures shall be taken in accordance with Articles 41 and 42, to maintain or restore international peace and security.

Article 40

In order to prevent an aggravation of the situation, the Security Council may, before making the recommendations or deciding upon the measures provided for in Article 39, call upon the parties concerned to comply with such provisional measures as it deems necessary or desirable. Such provisional measures shall be without prejudice to the rights, claims, or position of the parties concerned. The Security Council shall duly take account of failure to comply with such provisional measures.

Article 41

The Security Council may decide what measures not involving the use of armed force are to be employed to give effect to its decisions, and it may call upon the Members of the United Nations to apply such measures. These may include complete or partial interruption of economic relations and of rail, sea, air, postal, telegraphic, radio, and other means of communication, and the severance of diplomatic relations.

Article 42

Should the Security Council consider that measures provided for in Article 41 would be inadequate or have proved to be inadequate, it may take such action by air, sea, or land forces as may be necessary to maintain or restore international peace and security. Such action may include demonstrations, blockade, and other operations by air, sea, or land forces of Members of the United Nations.

Article 43

1. All Members of the United Nations, in order to contribute to the maintenance of international peace and security, undertake to make available to the Security Council, on its call and in accordance with a special agreement or agreements, armed forces, assistance, and facilities, including rights of passage, necessary for the purpose of maintaining international peace and security.

2. Such agreement or agreements shall govern the numbers and types of forces, their degree of readiness and general location, and the nature of the facilities and assistance to be provided.

3. The agreement or agreements shall be negotiated as soon as possible on the initiative of the Security Council. They shall be concluded between the Security Council and Members or between the Security Council and groups of Members and shall be subject to ratification by the signatory states in accordance with their respective constitutional processes.

Article 44

When the Security Council has decided to use force it shall, before calling upon a Member not represented on it to provide armed forces in fulfillment of the obligations assumed under Article

43, invite that Member, if the Member so desires, to participate in the decisions of the Security Council concerning the employment of contingents of that Member's armed forces.

Article 45

In order to enable the United Nations to take urgent military measures, Members shall hold immediately available national air-force contingents for combined international enforcement action. The strength and degree of readiness of these contingents and plans for their combined action shall be determined, within the limits laid down in the special agreement or agreements referred to in Article 43, by the Security Council with the assistance of the Military Staff Committee.

Article 46

Plans for the application of armed force shall be made by the Security Council with the assistance of the Military Staff Committee.

Article 47

1. There shall be established a Military Staff Committee to advise and assist the Security Council on all questions relating to the Security Council's military requirements for the maintenance of international peace and security, the employment and command of forces placed at its disposal, the regulation of armaments, and possible disarmament.

2. The Military Staff Committee shall consist of the Chiefs of Staff of the permanent members of the Security Council or their representatives. Any Member of the United Nations not permanently represented on the Committee shall be invited by the Committee to be associated with it when the efficient discharge of the Committee's responsibilities requires the participation of that Member in its work.

3. The Military Staff Committee shall be responsible under the Security Council for the strategic direction of any armed forces placed at the disposal of the Security Council. Questions relating to the command of such forces shall be worked out subsequently.

4. The Military Staff Committee, with the authorization of the Security Council and after consultation with appropriate regional agencies, may establish regional subcommittees.

Article 48

1. The action required to carry out the decisions of the Security Council for the maintenance of international peace and security shall be taken by all the Members of the United Nations or by some of them, as the Security Council may determine.

2. Such decisions shall be carried out by the Members of the United Nations directly and through their action in the appropriate international agencies of which they are members.

Article 49

The Members of the United Nations shall join in affording mutual assistance in carrying out the measures decided upon by the Security Council.

Article 50

If preventive or enforcement measures against any state are taken by the Security Council, any other state, whether a Member of the United Nations or not, which finds itself confronted with special economic problems arising from the carrying out of those measures shall have the right to consult the Security Council with regard to a solution of those problems.

Article 51

Nothing in the present Charter shall impair the inherent right of individual or collective self-defense if an armed attack occurs against a Member of the United Nations, until the Security Council has taken the measures necessary to maintain international peace and security. Measures taken by Members in the exercise of this right of self-defense shall be immediately reported to the Security Council and shall not in any way affect the authority and responsibility of the Security Council under the present Charter to take at any time such action as it deems necessary in order to maintain or restore international peace and security.

CHAPTER VIII: REGIONAL ARRANGEMENTS

Article 52

1. Nothing in the present Charter precludes the existence of regional arrangements or agencies for dealing with such matters relating to the maintenance of international peace and security as are appropriate for regional action, provided that such arrangements or agencies and their activities are consistent with the Purposes and Principles of the United Nations.

2. The Members of the United Nations entering into such arrangements or constituting such agencies shall make every effort to achieve pacific settlement of local disputes through such regional arrangements or by such regional agencies before referring them to the Security Council.

3. The Security Council shall encourage the development of pacific settlement of local disputes through such regional arrangements or by such regional agencies either on the initiative of the states concerned or by reference from the Security Council.

4. This Article in no way impairs the application of Articles 34 and 35.

Article 53

1. The Security Council shall, where appropriate, utilize such regional arrangements or agencies for enforcement action under its authority. But no enforcement action shall be taken under regional arrangements or by regional agencies without the authorization of the Security Council, with the exception of measures against any enemy state, as defined in paragraph 2 of this Article, provided for pursuant to Article 107 or in regional arrangements directed against renewal of aggressive policy on the part of any such state, until such time as the Organization may, on request of the Governments concerned, be charged with the responsibility for preventing further aggression by such a state.

2. The term enemy state as used in paragraph 1 of this Article applies to any state which during the Second World War has been an enemy of any signatory of the present Charter.

Article 54

The Security Council shall at all times be kept fully informed of activities undertaken or in contemplation under regional arrangements or by regional agencies for the maintenance of international peace and security.

CHAPTER IX: INTERNATIONAL ECONOMIC AND SOCIAL COOPERATION

Article 55

With a view to the creation of conditions of stability and well-being which are necessary for peaceful and friendly relations among nations based on respect for the principle of equal rights and self-determination of peoples, the United Nations shall promote:

a. higher standards of living, full employment, and conditions of economic and social progress and development;

b. solutions of international economic, social, health, and related problems; and international cultural and educational cooperation; and

c. universal respect for, and observance of, human rights and fundamental freedoms for all without distinction as to race, sex, language, or religion.

Article 56

All Members pledge themselves to take joint and separate action in cooperation with the Organization for the achievement of the purposes set forth in Article 55.

Article 57

1. The various specialized agencies, established by intergovernmental agreement and having wide international responsibilities, as defined in their basic instruments, in economic, social, cultural, educational, health, and related fields, shall be brought into relationship with the United Nations in accordance with the provisions of Article 63.

2. Such agencies thus brought into relationship with the United Nations are hereinafter referred to as specialized agencies.

Article 58

The Organization shall make recommendations for the coordination of the policies and activities of the specialized agencies.

Article 59

The Organization shall, where appropriate, initiate negotiations among the states concerned for the creation of any new specialized agencies required for the accomplishment of the purposes set forth in Article 55.

Article 60

Responsibility for the discharge of the functions of the Organization set forth in this Chapter shall be vested in the General Assembly and, under the authority of the General Assembly, in the Economic and Social Council, which shall have for this purpose the powers set forth in Chapter X.

CHAPTER X: THE ECONOMIC AND SOCIAL COUNCIL

Article 61

COMPOSITION

1. The Economic and Social Council shall consist of eighteen Members of the United Nations elected by the General Assembly.

2. Subject to the provisions of paragraph 3, six members of the Economic and Social Council shall be elected each year for a term of three years. A retiring member shall be eligible for immediate re-election.

3. At the first election, eighteen members of the Economic and Social Council shall be chosen. The term of office of six members so chosen shall expire at the end of one year, and of six other members at the end of two years, in accordance with arrangements made by the General Assembly.

4. Each member of the Economic and Social Council shall have one representative.

Article 62

FUNCTIONS AND POWERS

1. The Economic and Social Council may make or initiate studies and reports with respect to international economic, social, cultural, educational, health, and

related matters and may make recommendations with respect to any such matters to the General Assembly, to the Members of the United Nations, and to the specialized agencies concerned.

2. It may make recommendations for the purpose of promoting respect for, and observance of, human rights and fundamental freedoms for all.

3. It may prepare draft conventions for submission to the General Assembly, with respect to matters falling within its competence.

4. It may call, in accordance with the rules prescribed by the United Nations, international conferences on matters falling within its competence.

Article 63

1. The Economic and Social Council may enter into agreements with any of the agencies referred to in Article 57, defining the terms on which the agency concerned shall be brought into relationship with the United Nations. Such agreements shall be subject to approval by the General Assembly.

2. It may coordinate the activities of the specialized agencies through consultation with and recommendations to such agencies and through recommendations to the General Assembly and to the Members of the United Nations.

Article 64

1. The Economic and Social Council may take appropriate steps to obtain regular reports from the specialized agencies. It may make arrangements with the Members of the United Nations and with the specialized agencies to obtain reports on the steps taken to give effect to its own recommendations on matters falling within its competence made by the General Assembly.

2. It may communicate its observations on these reports to the General Assembly.

Article 65

The Economic and Social Council may furnish information to the Security Council and shall assist the Security Council upon its request.

Article 66

1. The Economic and Social Council shall perform such functions as fall within its competence in connection with the carrying out of the recommendations of the General Assembly.

2. It may, with the approval of the General Assembly, perform services at the request of Members of the United Nations and at the request of specialized agencies.

3. It shall perform such other functions as are specified elsewhere in the present Charter or as may be assigned to it by the General Assembly.

Article 67

VOTING

1. Each member of the Economic and Social Council shall have one vote.

2. Decisions of the Economic and Social Council shall be made by a majority of the members present and voting.

Article 68

PROCEDURE

The Economic and Social Council shall set up commissions in economic and social fields and for the promotion of human rights, and such other commissions as may be required for the performance of its functions.

Article 69

The Economic and Social Council shall invite any Member of the United Nations to participate, without vote, in its deliberations on any matter of particular concern to that Member.

Article 70

The Economic and Social Council may make arrangements for representatives of the specialized agencies to participate, without vote, in its deliberations and in those of the commissions established by it, and for its representatives to participate in the deliberations of the specialized agencies.

Article 71

The Economic and Social Council may make suitable arrangements for consultation with non-governmental organizations which are concerned with matters within its competence. Such arrangements may be made with international organizations and, where appropriate, with national organizations after consultation with the Member of the United Nations concerned.

Article 72

1. The Economic and Social Council shall adopt its own rules of procedure, including the method of selecting its President.
2. The Economic and Social Council shall meet as required in accordance with its rules, which shall include provision for the convening of meetings on the request of a majority of its members.

CHAPTER XI: DECLARATION REGARDING NON-SELF-GOVERNING TERRITORIES

Article 73

Members of the United Nations which have or assume responsibilities for the administration of territories whose peoples have not yet attained a full measure of self-government recognize the principle that the interests of the inhabitants of these territories are paramount, and accept as a sacred trust the obligation to promote to the utmost, within the system of international peace and security established by the present Charter, the well-being of the inhabitants of these territories, and, to this end:

a. to ensure, with due respect for the culture of the peoples concerned, their political, economic, social, and educational advancement, their just treatment, and their protection against abuses;

b. to develop self-government, to take due account of the political aspirations of the peoples, and to assist them in the progressive development of their free political institutions, according to the particular circumstances of each territory and its peoples and their varying stages of advancement;

c. to further international peace and security;

d. to promote constructive measures of development, to encourage research, and to cooperate with one another and, when and where appropriate, with specialized international bodies with a view to the practical achievement of the social, economic, and scientific purposes set forth in this Article; and

e. to transmit regularly to the Secretary-General for information purposes, subject to such limitation as security and constitutional considerations may require, statistical and other information of a technical nature relating to economic, social, and educational conditions in the territories for which they are respectively responsible other than those territories to which Chapters XII and XIII apply.

Article 74

Members of the United Nations also agree that their policy in respect of the territories to which this Chapter applies, no less than in respect of their metropolitan areas, must be based on the general principle of good-neighborliness, due account being taken of the interests and well-being of the rest of the world, in social, economic, and commercial matters.

CHAPTER XII: INTERNATIONAL TRUSTEESHIP SYSTEM

Article 75

The United Nations shall establish under its authority an international trusteeship system for the administration and supervision of such territories as may be placed thereunder by subsequent individual agreements. These territories are hereinafter referred to as trust territories.

Article 76

The basic objectives of the trusteeship system, in accordance with the Purposes of the United Nations laid down in Article 1 of the present Charter, shall be:

a. to further international peace and security;

b. to promote the political, economic, social, and educational advancement of the inhabitants of the trust territories, and their progressive development towards self-government or independence as may be appropriate to the particular circumstances of each territory and its peoples and the freely expressed wishes of the peoples concerned, and as may be provided by the terms of each trusteeship agreement;

c. to encourage respect for human rights and for fundamental freedoms for all without distinction as to race, sex, language, or religion, and to encourage recognition of the interdependence of the peoples of the world; and

d. to ensure equal treatment in social, economic, and commercial matters for all Members of the United Nations and their nationals, and also equal treatment for the latter in the administration of justice, without prejudice to the attain-

ment of the foregoing objectives and subject to the provisions of Article 80.

Article 77

1. The trusteeship system shall apply to such territories in the following categories as may be placed thereunder by means of trusteeship agreements:

a. territories now held under mandate;

b. territories which may be detached from enemy states as a result of the Second World War; and

c. territories voluntarily placed under the system by states responsible for their administration.

2. It will be a matter for subsequent agreement as to which territories in the foregoing categories will be brought under the trusteeship system and upon what terms.

Article 78

The trusteeship system shall not apply to territories which have become Members of the United Nations, relationship among which shall be based on respect for the principle of sovereign equality.

Article 79

The terms of trusteeship for each territory to be placed under the trusteeship system, including any alteration or amendment, shall be agreed upon by the states directly concerned, including the mandatory power in the case of territories held under mandate by a Member of the United Nations, and shall be approved as provided for in Articles 83 and 85.

Article 80

1. Except as may be agreed upon in individual trusteeship agreement, made under Articles 77, 79, and 81, placing

each territory under trusteeship system, and until such agreements have been concluded, nothing in this Chapter shall be construed in or of itself to alter in any manner the rights whatsoever of any states or any peoples or the terms of existing international instruments to which Members of the United Nations may respectively be parties.

2. Paragraph 1 of this Article shall not be interpreted as giving grounds for delay or postponement of the negotiation and conclusion of agreements for placing mandated and other territories under the trusteeship system as provided for in Article 77.

Article 81

The trusteeship agreement shall in each case include the terms under which the trust territory will be administered and designate the authority which will exercise the administration of the trust territory. Such authority, hereinafter called the administering authority, may be one or more states or the Organization itself.

Article 82

There may be designated, in any trusteeship agreement, a strategic area or areas which may include part or all of the trust territory to which the agreement applies, without prejudice to any special agreement or agreements made under Article 43.

Article 83

1. All functions of the United Nations relating to strategic areas, including the approval of the terms of the trusteeship agreements and of their alteration or amendment, shall be exercised by the Security Council.

2. The basic objectives set forth in Article 76 shall be applicable to the people of each strategic area.

3. The Security Council shall, subject to the provisions of the trusteeship agreements and without prejudice to security considerations, avail itself of the assistance of the Trusteeship Council to perform those functions of the United Nations under the trusteeship system relating to political, economic, social, and educational matters in the strategic areas.

Article 84

It shall be the duty of the administering authority to ensure that the trust territory shall play its part in the maintenance of international peace and security. To this end the administering authority may make use of volunteer forces, facilities, and assistance from the trust territory in carrying out the obligations towards the Security Council undertaken in this regard by the administering authority, as well as for local defense and the maintenance of law and order within the trust territory.

Article 85

1. The functions of the United Nations with regard to trusteeship agreements for all areas not designated as strategic, including the approval of the terms of the trusteeship agreements and of their alteration or amendment, shall be exercised by the General Assembly.

2. The Trusteeship Council, operating under the authority of the General Assembly, shall assist the General Assembly in carrying out these functions.

CHAPTER XIII: THE TRUSTEESHIP COUNCIL

Article 86

COMPOSITION

1. The Trusteeship Council shall consist of the following Members of the United Nations:

a. those Members administering trust territories;

b. such of those Members mentioned

by name in Article 23 as are not administering trust territories; and

c. as many other Members elected for three-year terms by the General Assembly as may be necessary to ensure that the total number of members of the Trusteeship Council is equally divided between those Members of the United Nations which administer trust territories and those which do not.

2. Each member of the Trusteeship Council shall designate one specially qualified person to represent it therein.

Article 87
FUNCTIONS AND POWERS

The General Assembly and, under its authority, the Trusteeship Council, in carrying out their functions, may:

a. consider reports submitted by the administering authority;

b. accept petitions and examine them in consultation with the administering authority;

c. provide for periodic visits to the respective trust territories at times agreed upon with the administering authority; and

d. take these and other actions in conformity with the terms of the trusteeship agreements.

Article 88

The Trusteeship Council shall formulate a questionnaire on the political, economic, social, and educational advancement of the inhabitants of each trust territory, and the administering authority for each trust territory within the competence of the General Assembly shall make an annual report to the General Assembly upon the basis of such questionnaire.

Article 89
VOTING

1. Each member of the Trusteeship Council shall have one vote.

2. Decisions of the Trusteeship Council shall be made by a majority of the members present and voting.

Article 90
PROCEDURE

1. The Trusteeship Council shall adopt its own rules of procedure, including the method of selecting its President.

2. The Trusteeship Council shall meet as required in accordance with its rules, which shall include provision for the convening of meetings on the request of a majority of its members.

Article 91

The Trusteeship Council shall, when appropriate, avail itself of the assistance of the Economic and Social Council and of the specialized agencies in regard to matters with which they are respectively concerned.

CHAPTER XIV: THE INTERNATIONAL COURT OF JUSTICE

Article 92

The International Court of Justice shall be the principal judicial organ of the United Nations. It shall function in accordance with the annexed Statute, which is based upon the Statute of the Permanent Court of International Justice and forms an integral part of the present Charter.

Article 93

1. All Members of the United Nations are *ipso facto* parties to the Statute of the International Court of Justice.

2. A state which is not a Member of the United Nations may become a party to the Statute of the International Court of Justice on conditions to be determined in each case by the General Assembly

upon the recommendation of the Security Council.

Article 94

1. Each Member of the United Nations undertakes to comply with the decision of the International Court of Justice in any case to which it is a party.

2. If any party to a case fails to perform the obligations incumbent upon it under a judgment rendered by the Court, the other party may have recourse to the Security Council, which may, if it deems necessary, make recommendations or decide upon measures to be taken to give effect to the judgment.

Article 95

Nothing in the present Charter shall prevent Members of the United Nations from entrusting the solution of their differences to other tribunals by virtue of agreements already in existence or which may be concluded in the future.

Article 96

1. The General Assembly or the Security Council may request the International Court of Justice to give an advisory opinion on any legal question.

2. Other organs of the United Nations and specialized agencies, which may at any time be so authorized by the General Assembly, may also request advisory opinions of the Court on legal questions arising within the scope of their activities.

CHAPTER XV: THE SECRETARIAT

Article 97

The Secretariat shall comprise a Secretary-General and such staff as the Organization may require. The Secretary-General shall be appointed by the General Assembly upon the recommendation of the Security Council. He shall be the chief administrative officer of the Organization.

Article 98

The Secretary-General shall act in that capacity in all meetings of the General Assembly, of the Security Council, of the Economic and Social Council, and of the Trusteeship Council, and shall perform such other functions as are entrusted to him by these organs. The Secretary-General shall make an annual report to the General Assembly on the work of the Organization.

Article 99

The Secretary-General may bring to the attention of the Security Council any matter which in his opinion may threaten the maintenance of international peace and security.

Article 100

1. In the performance of their duties the Secretary-General and the staff shall not seek or receive instructions from any government or from any other authority external to the Organization. They shall refrain from any action which might reflect on their position as international officials responsible only to the Organization.

2. Each Member of the United Nations undertakes to respect the exclusively international character of the responsibilities of the Secretary-General and the staff and not to seek to influence them in the discharge of their responsibilities.

Article 101

1. The staff shall be appointed by the Secretary-General under regulations established by the General Assembly.

2. Appropriate staffs shall be perma-

nently assigned to the Economic and Social Council, the Trusteeship Council, and, as required, to other organs of the United Nations. These staffs shall form a part of the Secretariat.

3. The paramount consideration in the employment of the staff and in the determination of the conditions of service shall be the necessity of securing the highest standards of efficiency, competence, and integrity. Due regard shall be paid to the importance of recruiting the staff on as wide a geographical basis as possible.

CHAPTER XVI: MISCELLANEOUS PROVISIONS

Article 102

1. Every treaty and every international agreement entered into by any Member of the United Nations after the present Charter comes into force shall as soon as possible be registered with the Secretariat and published by it.

2. No party to any such treaty or international agreement which has not been registered in accordance with the provisions of paragraph 1 of this Article may invoke that treaty or agreement before any organ of the United Nations.

Article 103

In the event of a conflict between the obligations of the Members of the United Nations under the present Charter and their obligations under any other international agreement, their obligations under the present Charter shall prevail.

Article 104

The Organization shall enjoy in the territory of each of its Members such legal capacity as may be necessary for the exercise of its functions and the fulfillment of its purposes.

Article 105

1. The Organization shall enjoy in the territory of each of its Members such privileges and immunities as are necessary for the fulfillment of its purposes.

2. Representatives of the Members of the United Nations and officials of the Organization shall similarly enjoy such privileges and immunities as are necessary for the independent exercise of their functions in connection with the Organization.

3. The General Assembly may make recommendations with a view to determining the details of the application of paragraphs 1 and 2 of this Article or may propose conventions to the Members of the United Nations for this purpose.

CHAPTER XVII: TRANSITIONAL SECURITY ARRANGEMENTS

Article 106

Pending the coming into force of such special agreements referred to in Article 43 as in the opinion of the Security Council enable it to begin the exercise of its responsibilities under Article 42, the parties of the Four-Nation Declaration, signed at Moscow, October 30, 1943, and France, shall, in accordance with the provisions of paragraph 5 of that Declaration, consult with one another and as occasion requires with other Members of the United Nations with a view to such joint action on behalf of the Organization as may be necessary for the purpose of maintaining international peace and security.

Article 107

Nothing in the present Charter shall invalidate or preclude action, in relation to any state which during the Second

World War has been an enemy of any signatory to the present Charter, taken or authorized as a result of that war by the Governments having responsibility for such action.

CHAPTER XVIII: AMENDMENTS

Article 108

Amendments to the present Charter shall come into force for all Members of the United Nations when they have been adopted by a vote of two thirds of the members of the General Assembly and ratified in accordance with their respective constitutional processes by two thirds of the Members of the United Nations, including all the permanent members of the Security Council.

Article 109

1. A General Conference of the Members of the United Nations for the purpose of reviewing the present Charter may be held at a date and place to be fixed by a two-thirds vote of the members of the General Assembly and by a vote of any seven members of the Security Council. Each Member of the United Nations shall have one vote in the conference.

2. Any alteration of the present Charter recommended by a two-thirds vote of the conference shall take effect when ratified in accordance with their respective constitutional processes by two thirds of the Members of the United Nations including all the permanent members of the Security Council.

3. If such a conference has not been held before the tenth annual session of the General Assembly following the coming into force of the present Charter, the proposal to call such a conference shall be placed on the agenda of that session of the General Assembly, and the conference shall be held if so decided by a majority vote of the members of the General Assembly and by a vote of any seven members of the Security Council.

CHAPTER XIX: RATIFICATION AND SIGNATURE

Article 110

1. The present Charter shall be ratified by the signatory states in accordance with their respective constitutional processes.

2. The ratifications shall be deposited with the Government of the United States of America, which shall notify all the signatory states of each deposit as well as the Secretary-General of the Organization when he has been appointed.

3. The present Charter shall come into force upon the deposit of ratifications by the Republic of China, France, the Union of Soviet Socialist Republics, the United Kingdom of Great Britain and Northern Ireland, and the United States of America, and by a majority of the other signatory states. A protocol of the ratifications deposited shall thereupon be drawn up by the Government of the United States of America which shall communicate copies thereof to all the signatory states.

4. The states signatory to the present Charter which ratify it after it has come into force will become original Members of the United Nations on the date of the deposit of their respective ratifications.

Article 111

The present Charter, of which the Chinese, French, Russian, English, and Spanish texts are equally authentic, shall remain deposited in the archives of the Government of the United States of America. Duly certified copies thereof shall be transmitted by that Government to the Governments of the other signatory states.

IN FAITH WHEREOF the representatives of the Governments of the United
Nations have signed the present Charter.

DONE at the city of San Francisco the
twenty-sixth day of June, one thousand
nine hundred and forty-five.

COMMENT

The political inadequacy of the United Nations Organization is obvious. Any political order which eliminates major violence over a long period of time must depend largely on laws defining, concretely and acceptably, what conduct is admissible and what is not. . . . The achievement of such a body of laws calls for a law-making process. And to enforce them there is required, in addition to the pressure of public opinion, a judicial system and a police force which will act automatically as the law directs.

> John Foster Dulles, advisor to the United States delegation at the San Francisco Conference, in "The United Nations: A Prospectus: The General Assembly," *Foreign Affairs*, xxiv (October, 1945), 2–3.

Experience has shown that the attempt to use the United Nations for the purpose of forcing upon either of the superpowers . . . agreement only aggravates the disagreement and increases the danger of war. . . . the Charter enables the United Nations, that is, the United States and the Soviet Union acting in unison, to prevent wars among the other nations. Built upon the foundation of the United States and the Soviet Union acting as one, the United Nations is constitutionally unable to prevent a war between those two coutries. Yet it is such a war which today threatens the United States, the Soviet Union, and all mankind. For its prevention we must look elsewhere than to the United Nations.

> Political scientist Hans J. Morgenthau in *Politics among Nations* (New York: Alfred A. Knopf, Inc., 1949), p. 387.

For the American people in 1945 victory was synonymous with utopia. . . . United States membership in the United Nations Organization was the final guarantee that the search for a new world order would not fail. In the U.N. the nations had erected at least a permanent substitute for power politics, the balance of power. . . . Yet among sovereign states no international organization can ever be more than an instrument of individual national policies. . . . If the U.N. created an excellent piece of machinery to bring nations together for debate, it did not create a new international order. And nothing would destroy it more quickly than the insistence that it perform as if some new order in international society had actually been established.

> Historian Norman A. Graebner in "The Truman Administration and the Cold War," *Current History*, xxxv (October, 1958), 223.

84.   *JULY, 1947*

George F. Kennan on Russian Aggression

By 1947, many leaders in the United States and Great Britain decided that co-operation with the Soviet Union had become impossible. Acting on the assumption that the Soviet leaders desired to spread Communism over the earth, George F. Kennan, the State Department's foremost expert on Russia, helped to devise a policy of containing Soviet power. In an anonymous, but widely read article in Foreign Affairs *magazine, he wrote that the United States must adopt a long-term policy of firmness and vigilant containment of Russian expansion.*

The assumption on which Kennan based his policy was that if the United States prevented Russian expansion, certain changes would take place within the Soviet Union which would moderate its revolutionary aims. Kennan contended that within the Soviet Union, there were certain stresses and strains which could be relieved by being channeled into an aggressive foreign policy. If this external expansion were prevented, internal tensions would be increased in such a way as to cause the Soviet system to crumble or to force the Kremlin leaders to placate domestic dissatisfaction. Since relaxing international tensions would be a prerequisite for solving domestic problems, Kennan thought the Soviet leaders would have no alternative but to come to some agreement with the Western powers on certain outstanding problems.

The political personality of Soviet power as we know it today is the product

Foreign Affairs, xxv (July, 1947), 566–82. Reprinted by special permission from *Foreign Affairs*, July, 1947 (April, 1954). Copyright by Council on Foreign Relations, Inc., New York.

of ideology and circumstances: ideology inherited by the present Soviet leaders from the movement in which they had their political origin, and circumstances of the power which they now have exercised for nearly three decades in Russia. There can be few tasks of psychological analysis more difficult than to try to trace the interaction of these two forces and the relative rôle of each in the determination of official Soviet conduct. Yet the attempt must be made if that conduct is to be understood and effectively countered.

It is difficult to summarize the set of ideological concepts with which the Soviet leaders came into power. Marxian ideology, in its Russian-Communist projection, has always been in process of subtle evolution. The materials on which it bases itself are extensive and complex. But the outstanding features of Communist thought as it existed in 1916 may perhaps be summarized as follows: (a) that the central factor in the life of man, the factor which determines the character of public life and the "physiognomy of society," is the system by which material goods are produced and exchanged; (b) that the capitalist system of production is a nefarious one which inevitably leads to the exploitation of the working class by the capital-owning class and is incapable of developing adequately the economic resources of society or of distributing fairly the material goods produced by human labor; (c) that capitalism contains the seeds of its own destruction and must, in view of the inability of the capital-owning class to adjust itself to economic change, result eventually and inescapably in a revolutionary transfer of power to the working class; and (d) that imperialism, the final phase of capitalism, leads directly to war and revolution.

The rest may be outlined in Lenin's own words: "Unevenness of economic and political development is the inflexible law of capitalism. It follows from this that the victory of Socialism may come originally in a few capitalist countries or even in a single capitalist country. The victorious proletariat of that country, having expropriated the capitalists and having organized Socialist production at home, would rise against the remaining capitalist world, drawing to itself in the process the oppressed classes of other countries." It must be noted that there was no assumption that capitalism would perish without proletarian revolution. A final push was needed from a revolutionary proletariat movement in order to tip over the tottering structure. But it was regarded as inevitable that sooner or later that push be given.

．．．．．

The circumstances of the immediate post-revolution period—the existence in Russia of civil and foreign intervention, together with the obvious fact that the Communists represented only a tiny minority of the Russian people—made the establishment of dictatorial power a necessity. The experiment with "war Communism" and the abrupt attempt to eliminate private production and trade had unfortunate economic consequences and caused further bitterness against the new revolutionary régime. While the temporary relaxation of the effort to communize Russia, represented by the New Economic Policy, alleviated some of this economic distress and thereby served its purpose, it also made it evident that the "capitalistic sector of society" was still prepared to profit at once from any relaxation of governmental pressure, and would, if permitted to continue to exist, always constitute a powerful opposing element to the Soviet régime and a serious rival for influence in the country. Somewhat the same situation prevailed with respect to the individual peasant who, in his own small way, was also a private producer.

．．．．．

Now the outstanding circumstance concerning the Soviet régime is that down to the present day this process of political consolidation has never been completed and the men in the Kremlin have continued to be predominantly absorbed with the struggle to secure and make absolute the power which they seized in November 1917. They have endeavored to secure it primarily against forces at home, within Soviet society itself. But they have also endeavored to secure it against the outside world. For ideology, as we have seen, taught them that the outside world was hostile and that it was their duty eventually to overthrow the political forces beyond their borders. The powerful hands of Russian history and tradition reached up to sustain them in this feeling. Finally, their own aggressive intransigence with respect to the outside world began to find its own reaction; and they were soon forced, to use another Gibbonesque phrase, "to chastise the contumacy" which they themselves had provoked. It is an undeniable privilege of every man to prove himself right in the thesis that the world is his enemy; for if he reiterates it frequently enough and makes it the background of his conduct he is bound eventually to be right.

．．．．．

Now the maintenance of this pattern of Soviet power, namely, the pursuit of unlimited authority domestically, accompanied by the cultivation of the semi-myth of implacable foreign hostility, has gone far to shape the actual machinery of Soviet power as we know it today. Internal organs of administration which did not serve this purpose withered on the vine. Organs which did serve this purpose became vastly swollen. The security of Soviet power came to rest on the iron discipline of the Party, on the severity and ubiquity of the secret police, and on the uncompromising economic monopolism of the state. The "organs of suppression," in which the Soviet leaders had sought security from rival forces, became in large measure the masters of those whom they were designed to serve. Today the major part of the structure of Soviet power is committed to the perfection of the dictatorship and to the maintenance of the concept of Russia as in a state of seige, with the enemy lowering beyond the walls. And the millions of human beings who form that part of the structure of power must defend at all costs this concept of Russia's position, for without it they are themselves superfluous.

As things stand today, the rulers can no longer dream of parting with these organs of suppression. The quest for absolute power, pursued now for nearly three decades with a ruthlessness unparalleled (in scope at least) in modern times, has again produced internally, as it did externally, its own reaction. The excesses of the police apparatus have fanned the potential opposition to the régime into something far greater and more dangerous than it could have been before those excesses began.

But least of all can the rulers dispense with the fiction by which the maintenance of dictatorial power has been defended. For this fiction has been canonized in Soviet philosophy by the excesses already committed in its name; and it is now anchored in the Soviet structure of thought by bonds far greater than those of mere ideology.

II

So much for the historical background. What does it spell in terms of the political personality of Soviet power as we know it today?

Of the original ideology, nothing has been officially junked. Belief is maintained in the basic badness of capitalism, in the inevitablity of its destruction, in the obligation of the proletariat to assist in that destruction and to take power into its own hands. But stress has come to be laid primarily on those concepts which relate most specifically to the Soviet régime itself: to its position as the sole truly Socialist régime in a dark and misguided world, and to the relationships of power within it.

The first of these concepts is that of the innate antagonism between capitalism and Socialism. We have seen how deeply that concept has become imbedded in foundations of Soviet power. It has profound implications for Russia's conduct as a member of international society. It means that there can never be on Moscow's side any sincere assumption of a community of aims between the Soviet Union and powers which are regarded as capitalist. It must invariably be assumed in Moscow that the aims of the capitalist world are antagonistic to the Soviet régime, and therefore to the interests of the peoples it controls. If the Soviet Government occasionally sets its signature to documents which would indicate the contrary, this is to be regarded as a tactical manœuvre permissible in dealing with the enemy (who is without honor) and should be taken in the spirit of *caveat emptor*. Basically, the antagonism remains. It is postulated. And from it flow many of the phenomena which we find disturbing in the Kremlin's conduct of foreign policy: the secretiveness, the lack of frankness, the duplicity, the wary suspiciousness, and the basic unfriendliness of purpose. These phenomena are there to stay, for the foreseeable future. There can be variations of degree and of emphasis. When there is something the Russians want from us, one or the other of these features of their policy may be thrust temporarily into the background; and when that happens there will always be Americans who will leap forward with gleeful announcements that "the Russians have changed," and some who will even try to take credit for having brought about such "changes." But we should not be misled by tactical manœuvres. These characteristics of Soviet policy, like the postulate from which they flow, are basic to the internal nature of Soviet power, and will be with us, whether in the foreground or the background, until the internal nature of Soviet power is changed.

This means that we are going to continue for a long time to find the Russians difficult to deal with. It does not mean that they should be considered as embarked upon a do-or-die program to overthrow our society by a given date. The theory of the inevitability of the eventual fall of capitalism has the fortunate connotation that there is no hurry about it. The forces of progress can take their time in preparing the final *coup de grâce*. Meanwhile, what is vital is that the "Socialist fatherland"—that oasis of power which has been already won for Socialism in the person of the Soviet Union—should be cherished and defended by all good Communists at home and abroad, its fortunes promoted, its enemies badgered and confounded. The promotion of premature, "adventuristic" revolutionary projects abroad which might embarrass Soviet power in any way would be an inexcusable, even a counter-revolutionary act. The cause of Socialism is the support and promotion of Soviet power, as defined in Moscow.

This brings us to the second of the concepts important to contemporary Soviet outlook. That is the infallibility of the Kremlin. The Soviet concept of power, which permits no focal points of organization outside the Party itself, requires that the Party leadership remain in theory the sole repository of truth. For if truth were to be found elsewhere, there would be justification for its expression in organized activity. But it is precisely that which the Kremlin cannot and will not permit.

The leadership of the Communist Party is therefore always right, and has been always right ever since in 1929 Stalin formalized his personal power by announcing that decisions of the Politburo were being taken unanimously.

On the principle of infallibility there rests the iron discipline of the Communist Party. In fact, the two concepts are mutually self-supporting. Perfect discipline requires recognition of infallibility. Infallibility requires the observance of discipline. And the two together go far to determine the behaviorism of the entire Soviet apparatus of power. But their effect cannot be understood unless a third factor be taken into account: namely, the fact that the leadership is at liberty to put forward for tactical purposes any particular thesis which it finds useful to the cause at any particular moment and to require the faithful and unquestioning acceptance of that thesis by the members of the movement as a whole. . . .

. . . . .

But we have seen that the Kremlin is under no ideological compulsion to accomplish its purposes in a hurry. Like the Church, it is dealing in ideological concepts which are of long-term validity, and it can afford to be patient. It has no right to risk the existing achievements of the revolution for the sake of vain baubles of the future. The very teachings of Lenin himself require great caution and flexibility in the pursuit of Communist purposes. Again, these precepts are fortified by the lessons of Russian history: of centuries of obscure battles between nomadic forces over the stretches of a vast unfortified plain. Here caution, circumspection, flexibility and deception are the valuable qualities; and their value finds natural appreciation in the Russian or the oriental mind. Thus the Kremlin has no compunction about retreating in the face of superior force. And being under the compulsion of no timetable, it does not get panicky under the necessity for such retreat. Its political action is a fluid stream which moves constantly, whenever it is permitted to move, toward a given goal. Its main concern is to make sure that it has filled every nook and cranny available to it in the basin of world power. But if it finds unassailable barriers in its path, it accepts these philosophically and accommodates itself to them. The main thing is that there should always be pressure, increasing constant pressure, toward the desired goal. There is no trace of any feeling in Soviet psychology that that goal must be reached at any given time.

These considerations make Soviet diplomacy at once easier and more difficult to deal with than the diplomacy of individual aggressive leaders like Napoleon and Hitler. On the one hand it is more sensitive to contrary force, more ready to yield on individual sectors of the diplomatic front when that force is felt to be too strong, and thus more rational in the logic and rhetoric of power. On the other hand it cannot be easily defeated or discouraged by a single victory on the part of its opponents. And the patient persistence by which it is animated means that it can be effectively countered not by sporadic acts which represent the momentary whims of democratic opinion but only by intelligent long-range policies on the part of Russia's adversaries—policies no less steady in their purpose, and no less variegated and resourceful in their application, than those of the Soviet Union itself.

In these circumstances it is clear that the main element of any United States policy toward the Soviet Union must be that of a long-term, patient but firm and vigilant containment of Russian expansive tendencies. It is important to note, however, that such a policy has nothing to do with outward histrionics: with threats or blustering or superfluous gestures of outward "toughness." While the Kremlin is basically flexible in its reaction to political realities, it is by no means unamenable to considerations of prestige. Like almost any other government, it can be placed by tactless and threatening gestures in a position where it cannot afford to yield even though this might be dictated by its sense of realism. The Russian leaders are keen judges of human psychology, and as such they are highly conscious that loss of temper and of self-control is never a source of strength in political affairs. They are quick to exploit such evidences of weakness. For these reasons, it is a *sine qua non* of successful dealing with Russia that the foreign government in question should remain at all times cool and collected and that its demands on Russian policy should be put forward in such a manner as to leave the way open for a compliance not too detrimental to Russian prestige.

III

In the light of the above, it will be clearly seen that the Soviet pressure against the free institutions of the western world is something that can be contained by the adroit and vigilant application of counter-force at a series of constantly shifting geographical and political points, corresponding to the shifts and manœuvres of Soviet policy, but which cannot be charmed or talked out of existence. The Russians look forward to a duel of infinite duration, and they see that already they have scored great successes. It must be borne in mind that there was a time when the Communist Party represented far more of a minority in the sphere of Russian national life than Soviet power today represents in the world community.

But if ideology convinces the rulers of Russia that truth is on their side and that they can therefore afford to wait, those of us on whom that ideology has no claim are free to examine objectively the validity of that premise. The Soviet thesis not only implies complete lack of control by the west over its own economic destiny, it likewise assumes Russian unity, discipline and patience over an infinite period. Let us bring this apocalyptic vision down to earth, and suppose that the western world finds the strength and resourcefulness to contain Soviet power over a period of ten to fifteen years. What does that spell for Russia itself?

The Soviet leaders, taking advantage of the contributions of modern technique to the arts of depotism, have solved the question of obedience within the confines of their power. Few challenge their authority; and even those who do are unable to make that challenge valid as against the organs of suppression of the state.

The Kremlin has also proved able to accomplish its purpose of building up in Russia, regardless of the interests of the inhabitants, an industrial foundation of heavy metallurgy, which is, to be sure, not yet complete but which is nevertheless continuing to grow and is approaching those of the other major industrial countries All of this, however, both the maintenance of internal political security and the building of heavy industry, has been carried out at a terrible cost in human life and in human hopes and energies. It has necessitated the use of forced labor on a scale unprecedented in modern times under conditions of peace. It has involved the neglect or abuse of other phases of Soviet economic life, particularly agriculture, consumers' goods production, housing and transportation.

To all that, the war has added its tremendous toll of destruction, death and human exhaustion. In consequence of this, we have in Russia today a population which is physically and spiritually tired. The mass of the people are disillusioned, skeptical and no longer as accessible as they once were to the magical attraction which Soviet power still radiates

to its followers abroad. The avidity with which people seized upon the slight respite accorded to the Church for tactical reasons during the war was eloquent testimony to the fact that their capacity for faith and devotion found little expression in the purposes of the régime.

In these circumstances, there are limits to the physical and nervous strength of people themselves. These limits are absolute ones, and are binding even for the cruelest dictatorship, because beyond them people cannot be driven. The forced labor camps and the other agencies of constraint provide temporary means of compelling people to work longer hours than their own volition or mere economic pressure would dictate; but if people survive them at all they become old before their time and must be considered as human casualties to the demands of dictatorship. In either case their best powers are no longer available to society and can no longer be enlisted in the service of the state.

Here only the younger generation can help. The younger generation despite all vicissitudes and sufferings, is numerous and vigorous; and the Russians are a talented people. But it still remains to be seen what will be the effects on mature performance of the abnormal emotional strains of childhood which Soviet dictatorship created and which were enormously increased by the war. Such things as normal security and placidity of home environment have practically ceased to exist in the Soviet Union outside of the most remote farms and villages. And observers are not yet sure whether that is not going to leave its mark on the overall capacity of the generation now coming into maturity.

In addition to this, we have the fact that Soviet economic development, while it can list certain formidable achievements, has been precariously spotty and uneven. Russian Communists who speak of the "uneven development of capitalism" should blush at the contemplation of their own national economy. Here certain branches of economic life, such as the metallurgical and machine industries, have been pushed out of all proportion to other sectors of economy. Here is a nation striving to become in a short period one of the great industrial nations of the world while it still has no highway network worthy of the name and only a relatively primitive network of railways. Much has been done to increase efficiency of labor and to teach primitive peasants something about the operation of machines. But maintenance is still a crying deficiency of all Soviet economy. Construction is hasty and poor in quality. Depreciation must be enormous. And in vast sectors of economic life it has not yet been possible to instill into labor anything like that general culture of production and technical self-respect which characterizes the skilled worker of the west.

It is difficult to see how these deficiencies can be corrected at an early date by a tired and dispirited population working largely under the shadow of fear and compulsion. And as long as they are not overcome, Russia will remain economically a vulnerable, and in a certain sense an impotent, nation, capable of exporting its enthusiasms and of radiating the strange charm of its primitive political vitality but unable to back up those articles of export by the real evidences of material power and prosperity.

Meanwhile, a great uncertainty hangs over the political life of the Soviet Union. That is the uncertainty involved in the transfer of power from one individual or group of individuals to others.

This is, of course, outstandingly the problem of the personal position of Stalin. We must remember that his succession to Lenin's pinnacle of preëminence in the Communist movement was the only such transfer of individual authority which the Soviet Union has experienced. That transfer took 12 years to consolidate. It cost the lives of millions of people and shook the state to its foundations. The attendant tremors were felt all through the international revolutionary movement, to the disadvantage of the Kremlin itself.

It is always possible that another transfer of preëminent power may take place quietly and inconspicuously, with no repercussions anywhere. But again, it is possible that the questions involved may unleash, to use some of Lenin's words, one of those "incredibly swift transitions" from "delicate deceit" to "wild violence" which characterize Russian history, and may shake Soviet power to its foundations.

But this is not only a question of Stalin himself. There has been, since 1938, a dangerous congealment of political life in the higher circles of Soviet power. The All-Union Congress of Soviets, in theory the supreme body of the Party, is supposed to meet not less often than once in three years. It will soon be eight full years since its last meeting. During this period membership in the Party has numerically doubled. Party mortality during the war was enormous; and today well over half of the Party members are persons who have entered since the last Party congress was held. Meanwhile, the same small group of men has carried on at the top through an amazing series of national vicissitudes. Surely there is some reason why the experiences of the war brought basic political changes to every one of the great governments of the west. Surely the causes of that phenomenon are basic enough to be present somewhere in the obscurity of Soviet political life, as well. And yet no recognition has been given to those causes in Russia.

It must be surmised from this that even within so highly disciplined an organization as the Communist Party there must be a growing divergence in age, outlook and interest between the great mass of Party members, only so recently recruited into the movement, and the little self-perpetuating clique of men at the top, whom most of these Party members have never met, with whom they have never conversed, and with whom they can have no political intimacy.

Who can say whether, in these circumstances, the eventual rejuvenation of the higher spheres of authority (which can only be a matter of time) can take place smoothly and peacefully, or whether rivals in the quest for higher power will not eventually reach down into these politically immature and inexperienced masses in order to find support for their respective claims? If this were ever to happen, strange consequences could flow for the Communist Party: for the membership at large has been exercised only in the practice of iron discipline and obedience and not in the arts of compromise and accommodation. And if disunity were ever to seize and paralyze the Party, the chaos and weakness of Russian society would be revealed in forms beyond description. For we have seen that Soviet power is only a crust concealing an amorphous mass of human beings among whom no independent organizational structure is tolerated. In Russia there is not even such a thing as local government. The present generation of Russians have never known spontaneity of collective action. If consequently, anything were ever to occur to disrupt the unity and efficacy of the Party as a political instrument, Soviet Russia might be changed overnight from the strongest to one of the weakest and most pitiable of national societies.

Thus the future of Soviet power may not be by any means as secure as Russian capacity for self-delusion would make it appear to the men in the Kremlin. That they can keep power themselves, they have demonstrated. That they can quietly and easily turn it over to others remains to be proved. Meanwhile, the hardships of their rule and the vicissitudes of international life have taken a heavy toll of the strength and hopes of the great people on whom their power rests. It is curious to note that the ideological power of Soviet authority is strongest today in areas beyond the frontiers of Russia, beyond the reach of its police power. This phenomenon brings to mind a comparison used by Thomas Mann in his great novel "Buddenbrooks." Observing that human institutions often show the greatest outward brilliance at a moment when inner decay is in reality farthest advanced, he compared the Buddenbrook family, in the days of its greatest glamour, to one of those stars whose light shines most brightly on this world when in reality it has long since ceased to exist. And who can say with assurance that the strong light still cast by the Kremlin on the dissatisfied peoples of the western world is not the powerful afterglow of a constellation which is in actuality on the wane? This cannot be proved. And it cannot be disproved. But the possibility remains (and in the opinion of this writer it is a strong one) that Soviet power, like the capitalist world of its conception, bears within it the seeds of its own decay, and that the sprouting of these seeds is well advanced.

IV

It is clear that the United States cannot expect in the foreseeable future to enjoy political intimacy with the Soviet régime. It must continue to regard the Soviet Union as a rival, not a partner, in the political arena. It must continue to expect that Soviet policies will reflect no abstract love of peace and stability, no real faith in the possibility of a permanent happy coexistence of the Socialist and capitalist worlds, but rather a cautious, persistent pressure toward the disruption and weakening of all rival influence and rival power.

Balanced against this are the facts that Russia, as opposed to the western world in general, is still by far the weaker party, that Soviet policy is highly flexible, and that Soviet society may well contain deficiencies which will eventually weaken its own total potential. This would of itself warrant the United States entering with reasonable confidence upon a policy of firm containment, designed to confront the Russians with unalterable counter-force at every point where they show signs of encroaching upon the interests of a peaceful and stable world.

But in actuality the possibilities for American policy are by no means limited to holding the line and hoping for the best. It is entirely possible for the United States to influence by its actions the internal developments, both within Russia and throughout the international Communist movement, by which Russian policy is largely determined. This is not only a question of the modest measure of informational activity which this government can conduct in the Soviet Union and elsewhere, although that, too, is important. It is rather a question of the degree to which the United States can create among the peoples of the world generally the impression of a country which knows what it wants, which is coping successfully with the problems of its internal life and with the responsibilities of a World Power, and which has a spiritual vitality capable of holding its own among the major ideological currents of the time. To the extent that such an impression can be created and maintained, the aims of Russian Communism must appear sterile and quixotic, the hopes and enthusiasm of Moscow's supporters must wane, and added strain must be imposed on the Kremlin's foreign policies. For the palsied decrepitude of the capitalist world is the keystone of Communist philosophy. Even the failure of the United States to experience the early economic depression which the ravens of the Red Square have been predicting with such complacement confidence since hostilities ceased would have deep and important repercussions throughout the Communist world.

By the same token, exhibitions of in-decision, disunity and internal distintegration within this country have an exhilarating effect on the whole Communist movement. At each evidence of these tendencies, a thrill of hope and excitement goes through the Communist world; a new jauntiness can be noted in the Moscow tread; new groups of foreign supporters climb on to what they can only view as the band wagon of international politics; and Russian pressure increases all along the line in international affairs.

It would be an exaggeration to say that American behavior unassisted and alone could exercise a power of life and death over the Communist movement and bring about the early fall of Soviet power in Russia. But the United States has it in its power to increase enormously the strains under which Soviet policy must operate, to force upon the Kremlin a far greater degree of moderation and circumspection than it has had to observe in recent years, and in this way to promote tendencies which must eventually find their outlet in either the break-up or the gradual mellowing of Soviet power. For no mystical, Messianic movement—and particularly not that of the Kremlin—can fare frustration indefinitely without eventually adjusting itself in one way or another to the logic of that state of affairs.

Thus the decision will really fall in large measure in this country itself. The issue of Soviet-American relations is in essence a test of the over-all worth of the United States as a nation among nations. To avoid destruction the United States need only measure up to its own best traditions and prove itself worthy of preservation as a great nation.

Surely, there was never a fairer test of national quality than this. In the light of these circumstances, the thoughtful observer of Russian-American relations will find no cause for complaint in the Kremlin's challenge to American society. He will rather experience a certain gratitude to a Providence which, by providing the American people with this implacable challenge, has made their entire security as a nation dependent on their pulling themselves together and accepting the responsibilities of moral and political leadership that history plainly intended them to bear.

COMMENT

There are at present two great nations in the world, which started from different points, but seem to tend towards the same end. I allude to the Russians and the Americans. . . . The principal interest of the [latter] is freedom; of the [former], servitude. Their starting point is different and their courses are not the same; yet each of them seems marked by the will of Heaven to sway the destinies of half the globe.

Alexis de Tocqueville, French historian of the nineteenth century, in *Democracy in America* (New York: Alfred A. Knopf, Inc., 1945), I, 434.

85. *MARCH 12, 1947*

Truman Doctrine

Attempting to devise a policy which would contain the expansion of the Soviet Union, the American government was shocked when Great Britain announced that it could no longer meet its commitments in the Near East. Since Turkey and Greece were on the verge of political and economic collapse, the message was clear: Russian expansion into the area could be prevented only by the United States. To prevent Greece and Turkey from gravitating into the Soviet camp, President Truman appeared before a joint session of Congress and declared "it must be the policy of the United States to support free peoples who are resisting attempted subjugation by armed minorities or outside pressures." This is the "Truman Doctrine," which subsequently became the basis for American foreign policy.

The assumption on which Truman acted in this particular instance was that

Department of State Bulletin, XVI (March 23, 1947), 534–37.

if the Communists were successful in Greece, it would only be a question of time before Turkey and Iran would be subjected to Soviet control. Communist pressure would then increase on the nations to the West. Italy would face a Communist-dominated East and a large Communist party within her borders. To the Truman Administration, such a situation would endanger the security of all western Europe. In essence, Truman was arguing that American survival was at stake in Greece and Turkey.

The gravity of the situation which confronts the world today necessitates my appearance before a joint session of the Congress.

The foreign policy and the national security of this country are involved.

One aspect of the present situation, which I wish to present to you at this time for your consideration and decision, concerns Greece and Turkey.

The United States has received from

the Greek Government an urgent appeal for financial and economic assistance. Preliminary reports from the American Economic Mission now in Greece and reports from the American Ambassador in Greece corroborate the statement of the Greek Government that assistance is imperative if Greece is to survive as a free nation.

I do not believe that the American people and the Congress wish to turn a deaf ear to the appeal of the Greek Government.

Greece is not a rich country. Lack of sufficient natural resources has always forced the Greek people to work hard to make both ends meet. Since 1940 this industrious and peace-loving country has suffered invasion, four years of cruel enemy occupation, and bitter internal strife.

When forces of liberation entered Greece they found that the retreating Germans had destroyed virtually all the railways, roads, port facilities, communications, and merchant marine. More than a thousand villages had been burned. Eighty-five percent of the children were tubercular. Livestock, poultry, and draft animals had almost disappeared. Inflation had wiped out practically all savings.

As a result of these tragic conditions, a militant minority, exploiting human want and misery, was able to create political chaos which, until now, has made economic recovery impossible.

Greece is today without funds to finance the importation of those goods which are essential to bare subsistence. Under these circumstances the people of Greece cannot make progress in solving their problems of reconstruction. Greece is in desperate need of financial and economic assistance to enable it to resume purchases of food, clothing, fuel, and seeds. These are indispensable for the subsistence of its people and are obtainable only from abroad. Greece must have help to import the goods necessary to restore internal order and security so essential for economic and political recovery.

The Greek Government has also asked for the assistance of experienced American administrators, economists, and technicians to insure that the financial and other aid given to Greece shall be used effectively in creating a stable and self-sustaining economy and in improving its public administration.

The very existence of the Greek state is today threatened by the terrorist activities of several thousand armed men, led by Communists, who defy the Government's authority at a number of points, particularly along the northern boundaries. A commission appointed by the United Nations Security Council is at present investigating disturbed conditions in northern Greece and alleged border violations along the frontier between Greece on the one hand and Albania, Bulgaria, and Yugoslavia on the other.

Meanwhile, the Greek Government is unable to cope with the situation. The Greek Army is small and poorly equipped. It needs supplies and equipment if it is to restore authority to the Government throughout Greek territory.

Greece must have assistance if it is to become a self-supporting and self-respecting democracy.

The United States must supply that assistance. We have already extended to Greece certain types of relief and economic aid, but these are inadequate.

There is no other country to which democratic Greece can turn.

No other nation is willing and able to provide the necessary support for a democratic Greek Government.

The British Government, which has been helping Greece, can give no further financial or economic aid after March 31. Great Britain finds itself under the necessity of reducing or liquidating its commitments in several parts of the world, including Greece.

We have considered how the United Nations might assist in this crisis. But the situation is an urgent one requiring immediate action, and the United Nations and its related organizations are not in a position to extend help of the kind that is required.

It is important to note that the Greek Government has asked for our aid in utilizing effectively the financial and other assistance we may give to Greece, and in improving its public administration. It is of the utmost importance that we supervise the use of any funds made available to Greece, in such a manner that each dollar spent will count toward making Greece self-supporting, and will help to build an economy in which a healthy democracy can flourish.

No government is perfect. One of the chief virtues of a democracy, however, is that its defects are always visible and under democratic processes can be pointed out and corrected. The Government of Greece is not perfect. Nevertheless it represents 85 percent of the members of the Greek Parliament who were chosen in an election last year. Foreign observers, including 692 Americans, considered this election to be a fair expression of the views of the Greek people.

The Greek Government has been operating in an atmosphere of chaos and extremism. It has made mistakes. The extension of aid by this country does not mean that the United States condones everything that the Greek Government has done or will do. We have condemned in the past, and we condemn now, extremist measures of the right or the left. We have in the past advised tolerance, and we advise tolerance now.

Greece's neighbor, Turkey, also deserves our attention.

The future of Turkey as an independent and economically sound state is clearly no less important to the freedom-loving peoples of the world than the future of Greece. The circumstances in which Turkey finds itself today are considerably different from those of Greece. Turkey has been spared the disasters that have beset Greece. And during the war the United States and Great Britain furnished Turkey with material aid.

Nevertheless, Turkey now needs our support.

Since the war Turkey has sought additional financial assistance from Great Britain and the United States for the purpose of effecting that modernization necessary for the maintenance of its national integrity.

That integrity is essential to the preservation of order in the Middle East.

The British Government has informed us that, owing to its own difficulties, it can no longer extend financial or economic aid to Turkey.

As in the case of Greece, if Turkey is to have the assistance it needs, the United States must supply it. We are the only country able to provide that help.

I am fully aware of the broad implications involved if the United States extends assistance to Greece and Turkey, and I shall discuss these implications with you at this time.

One of the primary objectives of the foreign policy of the United States is the creation of conditions in which we and other nations will be able to work out a way of life free from coercion. This was a fundamental issue in the war with Germany and Japan. Our victory was won over countries which sought to impose their will, and their way of life, upon other nations.

To insure the peaceful development of nations, free from coercion, the United States has taken a leading part in establishing the United Nations. The United Nations is designed to make possible lasting freedom and independence for all its members. We shall not realize our objectives, however, unless we are willing to help free peoples to maintain their free institutions and their national integrity against aggressive movements that seek to impose upon them totalitarian regimes.

This is no more than a frank recognition that totalitarian regimes imposed upon free peoples, by direct or indirect aggression, undermine the foundations of international peace and hence the security of the United States.

The peoples of a number of countries of the world have recently had totalitarian regimes forced upon them against their will. The Government of the United States has made frequent protests against coercion and intimidation, in violation of the Yalta agreement, in Poland, Rumania, and Bulgaria. I must also state that in a number of other countries there have been similar developments.

At the present moment in world history nearly every nation must choose between alternative ways of life. The choice is too often not a free one.

One way of life is based upon the will of the majority, and is distinguished by free institutions, representative government, free elections, guaranties of individual liberty, freedom of speech and religion, and freedom from political oppression.

The second way of life is based upon the will of a minority forcibly imposed upon the majority. It relies upon terror and oppression, a controlled press and radio, fixed elections, and the suppression of personal freedoms.

I believe that it must be the policy of the United States to support free peoples who are resisting attempted subjugation by armed minorities or by outside pressures.

I believe that we must assist free peoples to work out their own destinies in their own way.

I believe that our help should be primarily through economic and financial aid which is essential to economic stability and orderly political processes.

The world is not static, and the *status quo* is not sacred. But we cannot allow changes in the *status quo* in violation of the Charter of the United Nations by such methods as coercion, or by such subterfuges as political infiltration. In helping free and independent nations to maintain their freedom, the United States will be giving effect to the principles of the Charter of the United Nations.

It is necessary only to glance at a map to realize that the survival and integrity of the Greek nation are of grave importance in a much wider situation. If Greece should fall under the control of an armed minority, the effect upon its neighbor, Turkey, would be immediate and serious. Confusion and disorder might well spread throughout the entire Middle East.

Moreover, the disappearance of Greece as an independent state would have a profound effect upon those countries in Europe whose peoples are struggling against great difficulties to maintain their freedoms and their independence while they repair the damages of war.

It would be an unspeakable tragedy if these countries, which have struggled so long against overwhelming odds, should lose that victory for which they sacrificed so much. Collapse of free institutions and loss of independence would be disastrous not only for them but for the world. Discouragement and possibly failure would quickly be the lot of neighboring peoples striving to maintain their independence.

Should we fail to aid Greece and Turkey in this fateful hour, the effect will be far-reaching to the West as well as to the East.

We must take immediate and resolute action.

I therefore ask the Congress to provide authority for assistance to Greece and Turkey in the amount of $400,000,-000 for the period ending June 30, 1948. In requesting these funds, I have taken into consideration the maximum amount of relief assistance which would be furnished to Greece out of the $350,000,000 which I recently requested that the Congress authorize for the prevention of starvation and suffering in countries devastated by the war.

In addition to funds, I ask the Congress to authorize the detail of American civilian and military personnel to Greece and Turkey, at the request of those countries, to assist in the tasks of reconstruction, and for the purpose of supervising the use of such financial and material assistance as may be furnished. I recommend that authority also be provided for the instruction and training of selected Greek and Turkish personnel.

Finally, I ask that the Congress provide authority which will permit the speediest and most effective use, in terms of needed commodities, supplies, and equipment, of such funds as may be authorized.

If further funds, or further authority, should be needed for purposes indicated in this message, I shall not hesitate to bring the situation before the Congress. On this subject the Executive and Legislative branches of the Government must work together.

This is a serious course upon which we embark.

I would not recommend it except that the alternative is much more serious.

The United States contributed $341,-000,000,000 toward winning World War II. This is an investment in world freedom and world peace.

The assistance that I am recommending for Greece and Turkey amounts to little more than one tenth of one percent of this investment. It is only common sense that we should safeguard this investment and make sure that it was not in vain.

The seeds of totalitarian regimes are nurtured by misery and want. They spread and grow in the evil soil of poverty and strife. They reach their full growth when the hope of a people for a better life has died.

We must keep that hope alive.

The free peoples of the world look to us for support in maintaining their freedoms.

If we falter in our leadership, we may endanger the peace of the world—and we shall surely endanger the welfare of our own Nation.

Great responsibilities have been placed upon us by the swift movement of events.

I am confident that the Congress will face these responsibilities squarely.

COMMENT

I intend to vote for the Greek and Turkish loans for the reason that the President's announcements have committed the United States to this policy in the eyes of the world, and to repudiate it now would destroy his prestige in the negotiations with the Russian government, on the success of which ultimate peace depends. I do not regard this as a commitment to any similar policy in any other section of the world, or to the continuation of the same policy in Greece and Turkey. . . .

Republican Senator Robert A. Taft of Ohio in a news conference, April 11, 1947. New York *Times*, April 11, 1947.

The American arguments for assisting Turkey base themselves on the existence of a threat to the integrity of Turkish territory—though no-one and nothing actually threatens Turkey's integrity. This "assistance" is evidently aimed at putting this country also under U.S. control.

Editorial in *Izvestia*, March 13, 1947.

The assertion made in the Truman doctrine that the United States claims the right to intervene wherever free governments are overthrown by totalitarian groups, because the demise of free governments anywhere *ipso facto* menaces the safety of the United States, is too sweeping in the light of past American doctrine and practice. . . . It seems ill-advised . . . to assert an unnecessarily broad right of intervention.

> Doris A. Graber, a member of the Center for the Study of American Foreign and Military Policy at the University of Chicago, in "The Truman and Eisenhower Doctrines in the Light of the Doctrine of Non-Intervention," *Political Science Quarterly*, LXXIII (September, 1958), 333.

The epoch of isolationism and occasional intervention is ended. It is being replaced by an epoch of American responsibility.

> Editorial in the New York *Times*, March 12, 1947.

---

86. *APRIL 23, 1947*

Senator Robert Taft Advocates Labor Reforms

Following the Second World War, a series of bitter strikes took place. Unfortunately for the labor unions, public opinion tended to blame the strikers for the disruption of business and for the price increases which ensued. Moreover, the public was beginning to become concerned over the sheer strength of unions. The result was a nationwide demand for legislation which would regulate the activities of labor unions. A Republican-controlled Congress attacked this problem by passing the Taft-Hartley Labor-Management Relations Bill in June, 1947, which placed many restrictions on the unions. To use the facilities of the National Labor Relations Board, unions were required to present to the Secretary of Labor copies of their constitutions, by-laws, lists of their officers, and annual financial statements. In a period of national emergency, the President was authorized to issue temporary back-to-work orders. The closed shop was declared illegal, while the union shop was permitted, but only under rigid safe-

Congressional Record, 80th Cong., 1st Sess., XCIII, pt. 3 (April 23, 1947), 3834–40.

guards. Unions could be sued by employers for breach of contract or by third parties for injuries suffered through secondary boycotts. The unions immediately condemned the act as unconstitutional and described it as a "slave-labor act." Below, Republican Senator Robert A. Taft of Ohio, in a speech to the Senate describes the bill as an effort to equalize the powers of labor and management.

Mr. President, why is a labor bill necessary? Why is it demanded today by an overwhelming proportion of public opinion? Of course, on the surface it is due to the fact that we have had a large number of strikes, inconveniencing the public, even threatening their safety and welfare. I think even more, the widespread demand for some correction of the existing labor legislation arises because of many injustices which have developed in labor relations. . . .

I myself feel that the larger employers can well look after themselves, but throughout the United States there are hundreds of thousands of smaller employers, smaller businessmen, who, under the existing statutes, have come gradually to be at the mercy of labor-union leaders, either labor-union leaders attempting to organize their employees, or labor-union leaders interfering with the conduct of their business for one reason or for another.

Mr. President, originally, before the passage of any of these laws, the employer undoubtedly had an advantage in dealing with his employees. He was one man; the employees might be thousands; and he could deal with them one at a time. In negotiations of that character he had such a superior advantage that Congress came to feel that it must legislate specifically in order to correct that situation and bring about a balance. Congress passed the Clayton Act and the Norris–LaGuardia Act in order to limit legal actions against unions. Congress passed the Wagner National Labor Relations Act in order that the employees of a single employer might act as one in dealing with the one employer, in order that they might be on a sound and an equal basis, a principle which I think no one can question, and which certainly is not questioned in the pending bill.

The difficulty with the Clayton Act and the Norris–LaGuardia Act is that they went at the situation with a meat ax. They practically eliminated all legal remedy against unions for any action taken by them. In effect they provide—as construed by the courts, at least—that any action by a union taken in order to advance its own interests is proper, and there is no legal recourse against the union. The laws referred to do not discriminate between strikes for justifiable purposes and strikes for wholly illegal and improper purposes. They do not distinguish between strikes for higher wages and hours and better working conditions, which are entirely proper and which throughout this bill are recognized as completely proper strikes, and strikes in the nature of secondary boycotts, jurisdictional strikes, and strikes of the rack-

eteering variety. The acts simply eliminated all remedy against any union, leaving the union leaders free, practically without any control even by their members, to order strikes and boycotts and various kinds of actions that interfered, I believe certainly unlawfully under common law, with the activities of many other persons who were entirely innocent.

The National Labor Relations Act was enacted for a proper purpose, but the result of the actual administration of that act has been completely one-sided. It was simply for the one purpose of equalizing, or permitting a large number of employees to act as one; in effect to compel them to act as one if the majority desired such action.

Of course, it was one-sided, and the first board that was appointed, I believe, established a method of procedure which was completely prejudiced and completely on the side of labor unions. In 1939 I sat through the hearings for nearly 6 months on the operation of the National Labor Relations Board up to that time, and I do not think I have ever heard, certainly in America, such a series of miscarriages of justice as occurred under the first National Labor Relations Board.

The members of that board were gradually dismissed by President Roosevelt, the protests being so violent against their acts. . . .

Since then they have been succeeded by others who have proved to be much more judicial and who today I think constitute a very fair board. Yet much of the personnel that was appointed under the original law remains. Many of the precedents which were established by the original board still exist, and the result is that in the administration of that law, as testified to before our committee, there were so many injustices that it seemed impossible to correct them without legislation.

The greater part of the bill which is now before the Senate is a revision and amendment of the Wagner Labor Relations Act, which is rewritten from the first section to the last, with amendments dealing with particular injustices which were called to our attention, and which we believe can be corrected by an amendment of the law. These various injustices have been frozen into the law by the fact that for 8 years since the hearings in 1939 there has been no labor bill. . . .

Mr. President, the interpretations not only of the laws themselves but of the administrative regulations and the administrative rulings, and the decisions of the Supreme Court itself—holding in effect that there was no way in which any court could revise injustices perpetrated by the National Labor Relations Act—resulted in gradually building up the power of the labor leaders, so that today, in my opinion, the weight in collective bargaining negotiations is all on the side of the labor leaders, except perhaps against the very largest companies in the United States. In particular I believe that in dealing with small business, with farmers, and even with the workers themselves, the labor-union leaders have acquired a power which today the people resent and which inevitably has been abused. Many of our labor leaders are just as judicial and as fair as anyone could wish them to be, but extreme power, unreasonable power, cannot be granted to any group of men without a large number of them being willing to exercise it to accomplish ends which are not reasonable. Polls taken today show that union members themselves resent the power of labor-union leaders. Even on the question of the closed shop, which the union leaders are most vigorously defending, the polls show that more than half their men are actually opposed to the position the leaders are taking, because apparently they feel that today they are at a great disadvantage in dealing with union leaders, and that the power given to the leaders by existing legislation is so great that the individual is unable to exercise their right to free speech, his right to work as he pleases, and their general right to live as he pleases.

. . . . .

The problem is infinitely complicated. I suppose there are at least fifty amendments to the present law in the pending bill. Wherever we found an injustice we tried to correct it; and, of course, the net result of correcting a number of injustices is incidentally to decrease some of the power of the labor-union leaders. It seems to me that our aim should be to get back to the point where, when an employer meets with his employees, they have substantially equal bargaining power, so that neither side feels that it can make an unreasonable demand and get away with it. If neither side feels that it can get away with certain demands, I do not believe that the demands will ever be made. If there is reasonable equality at the bargaining table, I believe that there is much more hope for labor peace. That is the method pursued by the bill which is now before the Senate. It is not an antilabor bill. It is not a bill inspired by a desire to wreak vengeance on anyone because of what he may have done. It simply proposes to deal with the causes of labor trouble and the injustices and inequities of the present law.

Basically, I believe that the committee feels, almost unanimously, that the solution of our labor problems must rest on a free economy and on free collective bargaining. The bill is certainly based upon that proposition. That means that we recognize freedom to strike when the question involved is the improvement of wages, hours, and working conditions, when a contract has expired and neither side is bound by a contract. We recognize that right in spite of the inconvenience, and in some cases perhaps danger, to the people of the United States which may result from the exercise of such right. In the long run, I do not believe that that right will be abused. In the past few disputes finally reached the point where there was a direct threat to and defiance of the rights of the people of the United States.

We have considered the question whether the right to strike can be modified. I think it can be modified in cases which do not involve the basic question of wages, prices, and working conditions. But if we impose compulsory arbitration, or if we give the Government power to fix wages at which men must work for another year or for two years to come, I do not see how in the end we can escape a collective economy. If we give the Government power to fix wages, I do not see how we can take from the Government the power to fix prices; and if the Government fixes wages and prices, we soon reach the point where all industry is under Government control, and finally there is a complete socialization of our economy.

I feel very strongly that so far as possible we should avoid any system which attempts to give to the Government this power finally to fix the wages of any man. Can we do so constitutionally? Can we say to all the people of the United States, "You must work at wages fixed by the Government?" I think it is a long step from freedom and a long step from a free economy to give the Government such a right.

It is suggested that we might do so in the case of public utilities; and I suppose the argument is stronger there, because we fix the rates of public utilities, and we might, I suppose, fix the wages of public-utility workers. Yet we have hesitated to embark even on that course, because if we once begin a process of the Government fixing wages, it must end in more and more wage fixing and finally Government price fixing. It may be a popular thing to do. Today people seem to think that all that it is necessary to do is to forbid strikes, fix wages, and compel men to continue working, without consideration of the human and constitu-

tional problems involved in that process.

If we begin with public utilities, it will be said that coal and steel are just as important as public utilities. I do not know where we could draw the line. So far as the bill is concerned, we have proceeded on the theory that there is a right to strike and that labor peace must be based on free collective bargaining. We have done nothing to outlaw strikes for basic wages, hours, and working conditions after proper opportunity for mediation.

On page 48 of the bill we have provided for the delay of national emergency strikes. We have provided that when a threatened or actual strike or lock-out affecting substantially an entire industry engaged in trade, commerce, transportation, transmission, or communication among the several States, if permitted to occur or to continue, would imperil the national health or safety, the Attorney General may appoint a board of inquiry to inquire into the issues and make a statement of the issues and report back to him as promptly as he may direct. He may then seek from the court an injunction against striking for a period of 60 days, during which time the Government has another opportunity, through the Mediation Board, to try to bring about an agreement between employers and employees which will prevent a Nation-wide strike.

If such mediation should fail, then at the end of 60 days it is provided that there shall be an election by the employees to determine whether or not they accept the last offer made by the employer. If they vote to accept it, of course the strike is terminated. If they vote not to accept it, the injunction is dissolved and they are free to strike. The bill provides that when that happens the Attorney General shall submit to the President a full and comprehensive report of the proceedings, and that the President shall transmit such report, together with such recommendations as he may see fit to make, to the Congress for consideration and appropriate action.

If there finally develops a complete national emergency threatening the safety and health of the people of the United States, Congress can pass an emergency law to cover the particular emergency.

We did not feel that we should put into the law, as a part of the collective-bargaining machinery, an ultimate resort to compulsory arbitration, or to seizure, or to any other action. We feel that it would interfere with the whole process of collective bargaining. If such a remedy is available as a routine remedy, there will always be pressure to resort to it by whichever party thinks it will receive better treatment through such a process than it would receive in collective bargaining, and it will back out of collective bargaining. It will not make a bona-fide attempt to settle if it thinks it will receive a better deal under the final arbitration which may be provided.

We have felt that perhaps in the case of a general strike, or in the case of other serious strikes, after the termination of every possible effort to resolve the dispute, the remedy might be an emergency act by Congress for that particular purpose.

. . . But while such a bill might be prepared, I should be unwilling to place such a law on the book until we actually face such an emergency, and Congress applies the remedy for the particular emergency only. Eighty days will provide plenty of time within which to consider the possibility of what should be done; and we believe very strongly that there should not be anything in this law which prohibits finally the right to strike.

I have dealt with this question, Mr. President, because it is one of perhaps greater interest and one which affects more the fundamental philosophy of the bill than the other provisions. It is contained in title 3 as part of the mediation procedure.

But of course the injunctive process does not deal with the main causes of labor trouble, the injustices, and the inequalities of the present law. The bill seeks to restore equality of bargaining power and imposes on the unions the responsibility to balance the power which they have acquired. The bill is not inspired by a mere theory or by any hostility to unions. It is based on specific testimony of specific wrongs.

I shall try to summarize the changes which have been made. They are important. They make a substantial step forward toward the furnishing of equal bargaining power.

The bill provides that foremen shall not be considered employees under the National Labor Relations Act. They may form unions if they please, or join unions, but they do not have the protection of the National Labor Relations Act. They are subject to discharge for union activity, and they are generally restored to the basis which they enjoyed before the passage of the Wagner Act.

It is felt very strongly by management that foremen are part of management; that it is impossible to manage a plant unless the foremen are wholly loyal to the management. . . .

. . . . .

For many years the National Labor Relations Board held that, under the existing amendment of the National Labor Relations Act, foremen were not employees. By a two-to-one vote that was changed, and it was held that they were employees and that decision as an interpretation of the existing law was upheld by the Supreme Court by a vote of 5 to 4. The legal question in the past has been whether they are included as employees under the existing law but we felt that on the questions of theory and of intention of the law, and on the considerations which I have submitted, foremen should be excluded from the operations of the National Labor Relations Act.

. . . . .

In the third place we have provided further protection for craft unions. Today the situation is that when a new plant is organized the Board ordinarily permits the craft members of that plant to vote as to whether they will have a special craft union or join a general plant union. The Board has followed the desires of the craft unit on that question. But if at the time of the first certification a craft unit is not organized, or if no action is taken, and if by default they are all included in a plant union which is certified to the Board, the Board has taken the position that after 1 year of such bargaining no craft union will be recognized or given an opportunity to be heard in connection with establishing a craft unit.

All this bill does is to provide that such a previous finding shall not have that effect, and that if a year later the craft people want to form a separate union they shall have the same consideration at that time as they would have had if they had taken that action when the plant was first organized. In effect I think it gives greater power to the craft units to organize separately. It does not go the full way of giving them an absolute right in every case; it simply provides that the Board shall have discretion and shall not bind itself by previous decision, but that the subject shall always be open for further consideration by the Board.

The provisions of the bill regarding the closed shop are found on pages 12, 13, and 14. They present a substantial change in the present law. They present, I think, so far as I have been able to study the House bill, very much the same change as has been made in the House bill. They do not abolish the union shop. They do abolish the so-called closed shop. A closed shop is a shop in which the employer binds himself not to employ anyone unless he is a member of the union at that time. A union shop is defined as a shop in which the employer binds himself not to continue anyone in employment after the first 30 days unless he joins

the union. In other words, an employer may employ anyone whom he chooses to employ, but after 30 days such employee has to join the union or else the employer can no longer employ him. . . .

In the first place, Mr. President, the bill does not abolish the closed shop. Perhaps that is best exemplified by the so-called hiring halls on the west coast, where shipowners cannot employ anyone unless the union sends him to them. . . .

Such an arrangement gives the union tremendous power over the employees; furthermore, it abolishes a free labor market. A man cannot get a job where he wants to get it. He has to go to the union first, and if the union says that he cannot get in, then he is out of that particular labor field. Under such circumstances there is no freedom of exchange in the labor market, but all labor opportunities are frozen.

As a matter of fact, most of the so-called closed shops in the United States are union shops; there are not very many closed shops. If in a few rare cases the employer wants to use the union as an employment agency, he may do so; there is nothing to prohibit his doing so. But he cannot make a contract in advance that he will only take the men recommended by the union.

There are two conditions which we have imposed even on the union shop. In the first place, the men must vote that they wish to have such a union shop provided for in the contract with the employer, and the vote must carry by a majority of all the men in the unit not just a majority of those voting, but a majority of all the men in the unit. That follows, in a somewhat reduced form, the bill introduced by the junior Senator from Indiana [Mr. Jenner]. Certainly it seems clear to me that unless a majority of the men in the unit want a union shop, they should not have to have a union shop imposed upon them by some agreement made by their leaders, thus giving the leaders increased power over their men.

In the second place, we have proposed a proviso in the case where a man is refused admittance to a union, when an employer employs a nonunion man, and during the first 30 days of his employment he goes to the union and says, "I want to join the union," but the union refuses to take him. It is provided that in such case the employer shall not be compelled to discharge the man simply because the union will not let him join the union on the same terms and conditions as any other member. In effect, we say, "if you are going to have a union shop, then you must have an open union. You cannot say to people, 'We have a closed union shop, and we are not going to let you in under any circumstances.'"

The bill further provides that if the man is admitted to the union, and subsequently is fired from the union for any reason other than nonpayment of dues, then the employer shall not be required to fire that man. In other words, what we do, in effect, is to say that no one can get a free ride in such a shop. That meets one of the arguments for the union shop. The employee has to pay the union dues. But on the other hand, if the union discriminates against him and fires him from the union, the employer shall not be required to fire him from the job. During the testimony we heard of a case in which a union member saw a shop steward hit a foreman. That union member was called to testify in court, and he testified that he saw the shop steward hit the foreman. Subsequently, the union called him before their board for discipline, and said that for him to testify as he did was unfair to the union, although he had been subpoenaed to testify in court and sworn. Thereupon he was fired from the union, and under the union agreement the employer would have to fire him. Under this bill the employer would not have to fire that man unless he did not pay his union dues.

I think the justice of such an arrangement should be clear. As I have said, either we should have an open shop or we should have an open union. I do not believe we should permit the complete exclusion from any industry of a man who wants to work in that industry, and whom the employer wants to employ, and who is perfectly competent to work there, simply because the union says, "We do not want you and we will not let you in" or "We are going to fire you from the union because we do not like the way you act."

. . . . . .

Mr. President, on page 16 the bill contains a provision guaranteeing free speech to employers. That provision in effect carries out approximately the present rule laid down by the Supreme Court of the United States. It freezes that rule into the law itself, rather than to leave employers dependent upon future decisions. . . .

We have completely revised the nature of the National Labor Relations Board. That is required for the reason that we have created a number of unfair labor practices on the part of unions. The Senate is aware that in the past there have only been unfair labor practices on the part of employers. All action taken has been against employers. The Board has been given a necessary bias because the Board's only job has been to act against employers and to take action in the case of wrongs which it has been alleged that employers have committed. This bill designates a number of unfair labor practices on the part of employees and labor unions as being unfair. I shall describe those later. The result is that it changes the nature of the Board; it gives it more work to do, and we have increased the number of the members of the Board from 3 to 7, in order that they may sit in two panels, with 3 members on each panel, and accordingly may accomplish twice as much in the way of the number of hearings held. . . .

We have attempted to deal with the obvious fault, in the early days, that the Board not only prosecuted a man or initiated the prosecution of a man, but also judged the fairness of its own prosecution, almost completely free from any review by the courts. That has offended certainly my sense of justice and it has offended every principle of Anglo-Saxon law. We have tried in various ways to assure that there shall be a separation of those functions. We have not provided for a complete separation, because the Board itself, as time has passed since 1939, has gradually separated those functions in most respects, and a good many of the really serious abuses which occurred previously could not occur today. We have abolished the Review Section, so that this Board will act more as a court; the cases will go directly to the Board, and must be heard by the Board; and each member of the Board is to be given attorneys to work for him, just as each Justice of the Supreme Court has attorneys working for him. So the policy of the Board will not be determined by some anonymous Review Section, but will be determined by the Board itself.

It is provided that when a trial examiner makes a report he shall not then enter into secret meetings with the Board in an attempt to persuade the Board that he is right, after the hearing has been held. His point of view is to be presented in open hearings, and the other side of the matter is to be heard in open hearings. Thereafter, it will not be possible for the trial examiner to have a private or secret meeting with the Board, to argue against a possible reversal of his opinion, just as it is not permissible for a United States district judge to have a private meeting with the judges of a circuit court of appeals, after a hearing has been held before that court to determine whether the district judge's opinion shall be reversed.

· · · · ·

The general attempt is to separate those functions, so that we do not have

the confusion which has existed and which has operated unfairly against those prosecuted by the Board.

I think the very fact that we specify unfair labor practices on the part of labor unions, as well as on the part of employers, will necessarily restore the Board to a more judicial attitude of mind. I think that in itself may eliminate much of the difficulty which has arisen.

What are the new unfair labor practices on the part of unions? The provision starts on page 14 of the bill. First, it is provided that—

It shall be an unfair labor practice for a labor organization or its agents—

1. To interfere with, restrain, or coerce an employer in the selection of his representatives for the purposes of collective bargaining or the adjustment of grievances.

· · · · · ·

This unfair labor practice referred to is not perhaps of tremendous importance, but employees cannot say to their employer, "We do not like Mr. X, we will not meet Mr. X. You have to send us Mr. Y." That has been done. It would prevent their saying to the employer, "You have to fire Foreman Jones. We do not like Foreman Jones, and therefore you have to fire him, or we will not go to work." This is the only section in the bill which has any relation to Nation-wide bargaining. Under this provision it would be impossible for a union to say to a company, "We will not bargain with you unless you appoint your national employers' association as your agent so that we can bargain nationally." Under the bill the employer has a right to say, "No, I will not join in national bargaining. Here is my representative, and this is the man you have to deal with." I believe the provision is a necessary one, and one which will accomplish substantially wise purposes. . . .

Secondly, it is made an unfair labor practice for a union to try to get an employer to discharge a man who has been improperly fired from the union. That is supplemental to the provisions I have dealt with relating to the closed shop.

In the third place, it is made an unfair labor practice for a union to refuse to bargain collectively with an employer. Up to this time the obligation to bargain collectively has been solely on the employer. Now it is on both the employer and the employee.

The fourth unfair labor practice is an extremely important one. It is made an unfair labor practice for any union to engage in a secondary boycott. . . .

It is made an unfair labor practice for any union to engage in an indirect organizational strike. That is to say, the teamsters cannot go to a store and say, "Unless you sign up with the clerks' union, we are going to boycott your store," unless the clerks' union has been certified as a bargaining agent by the National Labor Relations Board.

The third type of strike which is made an unfair labor practice is the strike in which one union is certified by the National Labor Relations Board and another union strikes against the decision of the National Labor Relations Board.

The fourth type of unfair labor practice is the ordinary jurisdictional strike, in which two unions compete for work on a particular job.

I think the committee all agreed that those types of strikes are in effect racketeering strikes. They are strikes which are not direct strikes to settle questions of wages or hours or better working conditions. They are strikes which are, in effect, attempts to bring indirect pressure on third parties, to get third parties to work in some way to bring about a result which may ultimately be favorable to the one initiating the pressure, which has no direct relation to the work except perhaps with regard to the question of power.

As to the secondary boycott, I shall later describe that type of strike, but I ran into one over the last week end. The plant of a manufacturer of neon signs in Connecticut, I think in Hartford, or near Hartford, had not been organized, and finally his men were organized by a CIO union. The result was that the A.F. of L. sign hangers' union refused to hang this man's signs before any store. Almost the same type of case occurred in Ohio. . . .

The man from Hartford told me he had lost $100,000 in the last three months, and that he would be bankrupt in another three days and out of business, so far as he was concerned. That is an example of the secondary boycott, the A.F. of L. sign hangers' union boycotting an employer using certain material because it was made by a CIO union. . . .

The bill provides that that type of strike is an unfair labor practice. When a strike occurs, the man who is damaged by it is to go to the National Labor Relations Board and file a charge, and they give him a hearing. If he can persuade them to do so the Board can go to court and get a temporary injunction against further operation of the strike while the National Labor Relations Board is hearing the question as to whether it is an illegal strike or not, and deciding whether it will issue a permanent injunction against that particular strike.

Mr. President, I think what is provided in the bill is a substantial step forward. The provision is a most important one. At a later time I shall state why I think there should be a more direct remedy than is given, in this type of strike. The members of the committee who favored the method set out have provided the best possible means by which to get action if it is necessary to go to the National Labor Relations Board at all. The same remedy applies to organizational strikes and one type of jurisdictional strike.

Finally, violation of a contract by a union or an employer is also made an unfair labor practice which may be enjoined by the Board.

Mr. President, one of the matters which created the greatest complaint in the early days, and still does, is conduct of elections by the National Labor Relations Board. An election under present law may be sought only by a union. In the early days the Board exercised its discretion in favor of particular unions. It would not order an election until the union told it conditions were favorable, and it might win. Many of the greatest abuses on the part of unions occurred in the use of that discretionary power by the Board in the early days.

Today an employer is faced with this situation. A man comes into his office and says, "I represent your employees. Sign this agreement, or we strike tomorrow." Such instances have occurred all over the United States. The employer has no way in which to determine whether this man really does represent his employees or does not. The bill gives him the right to go to the Board under those circumstances, and say, "I want an election. I want to know who is the bargaining agent for my employees." Certainly I do not think anyone can question the fairness of such a proposal.

We provide, further, that there may be an election asked by the men to decertify a particular union. Today if a union is once certified, it is certified forever; there is no machinery by which there can be any decertification of that particular union. An election under this bill may be sought to decertify a union and go back to a non-union status, if the men so desire.

It is provided that where there is a ballot having three proposals on it, the A.F. of L. union, the CIO union, and no union at all, the two highest shall be certified in the run-off. Under existing conditions if, we will say, the A.F. of L. has the highest number but not a majority, the no-union has next, and the CIO union, third, the Board says that since the A.F. of L. and CIO together had a majority of the total, therefore the men want a union, and they do not put on the ballot the no-union proposal which was second in number of votes cast, they simply put the A.F. of L. and the CIO on it.

This bill requires them to pursue the policy that has been pursued in every runoff election I know of—the two highest have to be certified in the run-off. The bill also provides that elections shall be held only once a year, so that there shall not be a constant stirring up of excitement by continual elections. The men choose a bargaining agent for 1 year. He remains the bargaining agent until the end of that year.

The bill provides further that in these elections, and otherwise, there shall be equal treatment of independent unions. Today the Board refuses as a rule to certify an independent union. Most of the independent unions had some cloud on their original formation.

Originally, perhaps they were a company union, or they had some aid from the company. The Board has taken the position that if those facts are once shown, they never will certify such a union, although it may have purged itself of that connection for the last ten or fifteen years. The telephone union was originally a company union. Now, nobody can question it is bona fide.

If there be an A.F. of L. or CIO affiliate union which is company dominated, but which affiliates itself with the national A.F. of L. union, then the Board will permit it to purge itself promptly and will certify it as bargaining agent.

. . . . .

The bill provides, that in elections, one shall not have the right to vote if he has no right to be reinstated in his employment. In the Redwood case, in California, the men in a particular sawmill company plant, struck, and walked out. They have been out now for eighteen months, and gradually they have been replaced, mostly by returning veterans, until there is a full force working in the plant, and the men who were formerly employed are out, working on other jobs; and yet, when an election is held, the old men still vote, still select the bargaining agent; and there is no possible way for the employer to stop the strike or stop the picketing, that still continues, because he can deal only with the union which is represented by men who are no longer there. The men who are in the plant cannot be strikebreakers, they cannot be men who are given more money than the ordinary employee; but under present decisions if the new men are standard replacements, men willing to work, and taken on for permanent work, then they take the jobs of men who are striking and the former workers are not entitled to have their jobs back. This bill provides in that case that the former employee cannot vote in the election, so that the new men can form a union and can make finally an agreement, an effective legal agreement with their employer.

Mr. President, the bill provides that unions must file financial reports on forms certified by the Secretary of Labor, and furnish the reports to all their members, and file a copy with the Secretary of Labor. Such reports are not open to the public, any more than corporation reports are open to the public; but they are open to inspection by the members, and they are also open to proper Government officials. There is no special provision, but they are not specifically provided to be open to the public.

The filing of such report is a condition of certification as bargaining agent under the law, and is also a condition of the right to file any charges under the National Labor Relations Act. One of the most important things, I think, that the public feel should be done, is to make unions responsible. This bill provides that such reports shall be made. They are

made in many unions today. Many unions favored the proposal. No man may longer conduct a union as his private concern and conceal from his members the salary he receives or the methods by which he disposes of their funds.

The bill makes a change in the provision regarding court review of National Labor Relations Board decisions. The present rule in the law is simply that any decision supported by evidence shall be final as to the facts, and the result has been that as a practical matter it is almost impossible for a court to reverse the National Labor Relations Board.

Under this proposal, it is said that the finding of the Board with respect to questions of fact, if supported by substantial evidence on the record considered as a whole, shall be conclusive.

In the first place, the evidence must be substantial; in the second place, it must still look substantial when viewed in the light of the entire record. That does not go so far as saying that a decision can be reversed on the weight of the evidence. It does not go quite so far as the power given to a circuit court of appeals to review a district-court decision, but it goes a great deal further than the present law, and gives the court greater opportunity to reverse an obviously unjust decision on the part of the National Labor Relations Board.

Mr. President, title III of the bill, on page 53, makes unions suable in the Federal courts for violation of contract. As a matter of law unions, of course, are liable in theory on their contracts today, but as a practical matter it is difficult to sue them. They are not incorporated; they have many members; in some States all the members must be served; it is difficult to know who is to be served. But the pending bill provides they can be sued as if they were corporations and if a judgment is found against the labor organization, even though it is an unincorporated association, the liability is on the labor union and the labor-union funds, and it is not on the individual members of the union, where it has fallen in some famous cases to the great financial distress of the individual members of labor unions.

Finally, Mr. President, the bill provides for a joint committee to study and report on basic problems affecting friendly labor relations and productivity. We have not had time to study a good many fundamental questions relating to labor relations. There are various subjects which were not covered by the testimony, and we felt that there should be a more fundamental study leading to better relations between employer and employee, leading to better productivity on the part of the individual workman, with his willingness and consent, because, after all, his standard of living depends ultimately on his particular productivity.

. . . . .

The committee is to study, first, a means by which permanent friendly cooperation between employers and employees and stability of labor relations may be secured throughout the United States.

Second, the means by which the individual employee may achieve a greater productivity and higher wages, including plans for guaranteed annual wages, incentive profit-sharing and bonus systems. There are many such plans proposed as solutions of the labor problem, and we believe all of them should have a hearing and that they should be studied by Congress;

Third, the labor relations policies and practices of employers and associations of employees;

Fourth, the coordination of welfare funds with the social-security system.

We have an amendment to offer later which will deal with the question of holding up the formation of wide open welfare funds until this study is made but in any event, a study should be made of the relationship between the security funds of special corporations and industries and the social-security plan, whether they can exist alongside, whether they should be coordinated, and what the relationship should be.

Finally, the methods and procedures for best carrying out the collective-bargaining processes, with special attention to the effects of industry-wide or regional bargaining upon the national economy, and such other problems as the committee sees fit to study. That committee is to be composed of seven members of the Senate Committee on Labor and Public Welfare and seven members of the House Committee on Education and Labor, a total of fourteen, which is given the usual power of joint committees.

Mr. President, I did not mention the fact that the bill proposes to revise the Federal Mediation Service. The revision, which occurs in the section dealing with the emergency injunction process, provides for a single Director of Mediation, who is not to be under the jurisdiction of the Labor Department but is made an independent agency, for the reason that it was felt that the Labor Department was formed to represent the interests of labor, and that a conciliation service should be absolutely impartial between labor and employer. . . .

I might say that in this mediation procedure we have provided greater power for the Mediation Service. We hope that the prestige which it acquires may lead to more successful mediation than there has been.

We have provided in the revision of the collective-bargaining procedure, in connection with the mediation process, that before the end of any contract, whether it contains such a provision or not, either party who wishes to open the contract may give 60 days' notice in order to afford time for free collective bargaining, and then for the intervention of the Mediation Service. If such notice is given, the bill provides for no waiting period except during the life of the contract itself. If, however, either party neglects to give such notice and waits, let us say, until 30 days before the end of the contract to give the notice, then there is a waiting period provided during which the strike is an unlawful labor practice for 60 days from that time, or to the end of the contract and 30 days beyond that time. In that case there is a so-called waiting period during which a strike is illegal, but it is only brought about by the failure of the union itself to give the notice which the bill requires shall be given. So it seems to me to be no real limitation of the rights of labor unions.

I do not think that labor can claim that any of its legitimate rights are interfered with, but if anyone can point out language which seems to be broader than the legitimate purposes shown to be necessary by the hearings we have held, certainly we shall be glad to modify such language.

I think I can say that I support wholeheartedly the bill which is here presented, and I believe it will deal with a majority of the serious problems which now exist in the relations between employers and employees; that it will impose upon unions a responsibility more equal to the power which they have acquired, and that it will tend to bring about industrial peace in the United States.

COMMENT

I am confident that unrealistic and vindictive legislation of this kind cannot long survive. Unhappily, however, its enactment and the mere attempt to enforce it will produce unnecessary industrial strife and confusion at this most crucial time in our national history.

George Meany, secretary-treasurer of American Federation of Labor, in a symposium at Manhattan College, New York. *Vital Speeches*, xiv (December 1, 1947), 122–23.

The Taft-Hartley Bill has as its sole purpose the protection of the working man, business and the public, from the abuses of the labor bosses, and gives to the worker many new rights which he did not have previously.

William J. Walker, a New York management attorney, in a symposium at Manhattan College, New York, November 14, 1947. *Vital Speeches*, xiv (December 1, 1947), 124.

All the Taft-Hartley answer boils down to is that in national emergency disputes employees shall be ordered to work for another eighty days on the employer's terms. What we need is a law that will . . . give to the President a choice of procedures when voluntary agreement proves impossible: seizure provisions geared to the circumstances; or arbitration; or a detailed hearing and a recommendation of settlement terms; or a return of the dispute to the parties.

Former Governor Adlai E. Stevenson of Illinois in a news conference, December 8, 1959. New York *Times*, December 9, 1959.

87. *JUNE 5, 1947*

Marshall Plan

The Truman Doctrine was only the first step of the new American policy of containing Soviet expansion. Meanwhile, Europe was on the verge of an economic, social, political, and moral breakdown, a situation made to order for well organized Communist parties. The only alternative seemed to be dependence on the United States, as funds and supplies needed for European reconstruction could only be obtained there. Yet, Europe's economy was in no shape to earn the dollars needed to pay for such reconstruction. Because the United States considered Europe to be vital to American security, the Truman Administration decided that the United States should administer a large scale program of economic aid which would restore and surpass Europe's prewar agricultural production, close the dollar gap, and lead to European prosperity and political stability. Secretary of State George C. Marshall first put forward such a proposal in a commencement address (printed below) at Harvard University when he announced the willingness of the United States to co-operate in a long term plan for European economic recovery.

I need not tell you gentlemen that the world situation is very serious. That must be apparent to all intelligent people. I think one difficulty is that the problem is one of such enormous complexity that the very mass of facts presented to the public by press and radio make it exceedingly difficult for the man in the

Department of State Bulletin, XVI (June 15, 1947), 1159–60.

street to reach a clear appraisement of the situation. Furthermore, the people of this country are distant from the troubled areas of the earth and it is hard for them to comprehend the plight and consequent reactions of the long-suffering peoples, and the effects of those reactions on their governments in connection with our efforts to promote peace in the world.

In considering the requirements for the rehabilitation of Europe, the physical loss of life, the visible destruction of cities, factories, mines, and railroads was correctly estimated, but it has become obvious during recent months that this visible destruction was probably less serious than the dislocation of the entire fabric of European economy. For the past 10 years conditions have been highly abnormal. The feverish preparation for war and the more feverish maintenance of the war effort engulfed all aspects of national economies. Machinery has fallen into dispair or is entirely obsolete. Under the arbitrary and destructive Nazi rule, virtually every possible enterprise was geared into the German war machine. Long-standing commercial ties, private institutions, banks, insurance companies, and shipping companies disappeared, through loss of capital, absorption through nationalization, or by simple destruction. In many countries, confidence in the local currency has been severely shaken. The breakdown of the business structure of Europe during the war was complete. Recovery has been seriously retarded by the fact that two years after the close of hostilities a peace settlement with Germany and Austria has not been agreed upon. But even given a more prompt solution of these difficult problems, the rehabilitation of the economic structure of Europe quite evidently will require a much longer time and greater effort than had been foreseen.

There is a phase of this matter which is both interesting and serious. The farmer has always produced the foodstuffs to exchange with the city dweller for the other necessities of life. This division of labor is the basis of modern civilization. At the present time it is threatened with breakdown. The town and city industries are not producing adequate goods to exchange with the food-producing farmer. Raw materials and fuel are in short supply. Machinery is lacking or worn out. The farmer or the peasant cannot find the goods for sale which he desires to purchase. So the sale of his farm produce for money which he cannot use seems to him an unprofitable transaction. He, therefore, has withdrawn many fields from crop cultivation and is using them for grazing. He feeds more grain to stock and finds for himself and his family an ample supply of food, however short he may be on clothing and the other ordinary gadgets of civilization. Meanwhile people in the cities are short of food and fuel. So the governments are forced to use their foreign money and credits to procure these necessities abroad. This process exhausts funds which are urgently needed for reconstruction. Thus a very serious situation is rapidly developing which bodes no good for the world. The modern system of the division of labor upon which the exchange of products is based is in danger of breaking down.

The truth of the matter is that Europe's requirements for the next three or four years of foreign food and other essential products—principally from America—are so much greater than her present ability to pay that she must have substantial additional help or face economic, social, and political deterioration of a very grave character.

The remedy lies in breaking the vicious circle and restoring the confidence of the European people in the economic future of their own countries and of Europe as a whole. The manufacturer and the farmer throughout wide areas must be able and willing to exchange their products for currencies the continuing value of which is not open to question.

Aside from the demoralizing effect on the world at large and the possibilities of disturbances arising as a result of the desperation of the people concerned, the consequences to the economy of the United States should be apparent to all. It is logical that the United States should do whatever it is able to do to assist in the return of normal economic health in the world, without which there can be no political stability and no assured peace. Our policy is directed not against any country or doctrine but against hunger, poverty, desperation, and chaos. Its purpose should be the revival of a working economy in the world so as to permit the emergence of political and social conditions in which free institutions can exist. Such assistance, I am convinced, must not be on a piecemeal basis as various crises develop. Any assistance that this Government may render in the future should provide a cure rather than a mere palliative. Any government that is willing to assist in the task of recovery will find full cooperation, I am sure, on the part of the United States Government. Any government which maneuvers to block the recovery of other countries cannot expect help from us. Furthermore, governments, political parties, or groups which seek to perpetuate human misery in order to profit therefrom politically or otherwise will encounter the opposition of the United States.

It is already evident that, before the United States Government can proceed much further in its efforts to alleviate the situation and help start the European world on its way to recovery, there must be some agreement among the countries of Europe as to the requirements of the situation and the part those countries themselves will take in order to give proper effect to whatever action might be undertaken by this Government. It would be neither fitting nor efficacious for this Government to undertake to draw up unilaterally a program designed to place Europe on its feet economically. This is the business of the Europeans. The initiative, I think, must come from Europe. The role of this country should consist of friendly aid in the drafting of a European program and of later support of such a program so far as it may be practical for us to do so. The program should be a joint one, agreed to by a number, if not all, European nations.

An essential part of any successful action on the part of the United States is an understanding on the part of the people of America of the character of the problem and the remedies to be applied. Political passion and prejudice should have no part. With foresight, and a willingness on the part of our people to face up to the vast responsibility which history has clearly placed upon our country, the difficulties I have outlined can and will be overcome.

COMMENT

The relationship between this program and the United Nations deserves special emphasis. . . . The success of the United Nations depends upon the independent strength of its members and their determination and ability to adhere to the ideals and principles embodied in the Charter. The purposes of the European recovery program are in complete harmony with the purposes of the Charter. . . .

President Harry S. Truman in a news conference, December 19, 1947. New York *Times*, December 20, 1947.

The greatest nation on earth either justifies or surrenders its leadership. We must choose. There are no blueprints to guarantee results. We are entirely surrounded by calculated risks. I profoundly believe that the pending program is the best of these risks. I have no quarrel with those who disagree, because we are dealing with imponderables. But I am bound to say to those who disagree that they have not escaped to safety by rejecting or subverting this plan. They have simply fled to other risks, and I fear greater ones. For myself, I can only say that I prefer my choice of responsibilities.

Arthur H. Vandenberg, Republican of Michigan, speaking to the U.S. Senate, March 1, 1948. Arthur H. Vandenberg, Jr., and J. A. Morris, eds., *The Private Papers of Senator Vandenberg* (Boston: Houghton Mifflin Company, 1952), p. 390.

88. JANUARY 5, 1949

President Truman's Fair Deal

Shortly after winning the presidential election of 1948, President Truman in his State of the Union message called for a Fair Deal for the American people which was to be a modernization of Franklin D. Roosevelt's New Deal. Both the New and Fair Deals covered a broad range of problems, including social security, federal assistance to education, housing, and natural resources. Truman, however, moved much more swiftly and positively on two subjects than had Roosevelt— civil rights and national health insurance. By preparing the public to accept a federal program of civil rights, Truman helped develop a receptive climate for the Supreme Court's subsequent decisions on segregation. But despite the wide- spread Democratic victory of 1948, a coalition of Republicans and Southern Democrats was able to block most of the President's social and economic program. In many instances, Truman proposed a program of many parts, only to meet with a complete rebuff from Congress. Thus, the President's program was more prom- ise than it was reality. Nevertheless, he was successful in keeping reforms upper- most in the public's mind during a period which was generally unreceptive to an in- crease in the government's powers.

I am happy to report to this 81st Congress that the state of the union is good. Our nation is better able than ever before to meet the needs of the American people, and to give them their fair chance in the pursuit of happiness. It is foremost among the nations of the world in the search for peace.

Newsweek, xxvi (January 14, 1949), 58–60.

During the last sixteen years, the American people have been creating a society which offers new opportunities for every man to enjoy his share of the good things of life.

In this society, we are conservative about the values and principles which we cherish; but we are forward-looking in protecting those values and principles and in extending their benefits. We have rejected the discredited theory that the fortunes of the nation should be in the hands of a privileged few. We have abandoned the "trickle down" concept of national prosperity. Instead, we believe that our economic system should rest on a democratic foundation and that wealth should be created for the benefit of all.

The recent election shows that the American people are in favor of this kind of society and want to go on improving it.

The American people have decided that poverty is just as wasteful and just as unnecessary as preventable disease. We have pledged our common resources to help one another in the hazards and struggles of individual life. We believe that no unfair prejudice or artificial distinction should bar any citizen of the United States from an education, or from good health, or from a job that he is capable of performing.

The attainment of this kind of society demands the best efforts of every citizen in every walk of life, and it imposes increasing responsibilities on the Government.

The Government must work with industry, labor and the farmers in keeping our economy running at full speed. The Government must see that every American has a chance to obtain his fair share of our increasing abundance. These responsibilities go hand in hand.

We cannot maintain prosperity unless we have a fair distribution of opportunity and a widespread consumption of the products of our factories and farms.

Our Government has undertaken to meet these responsibilities.

We have made tremendous public investments in highways, hydroelectric power projects, soil conservation and reclamation. We have established a system of social security. We have enacted laws protecting the rights and the welfare of our working people and the income of our farmers. These federal policies have paid for themselves many times over. They have strengthened the material foundations of our democratic ideals. Without them, our present prosperity would be impossible.

Reinforced by these policies, our private enterprise system has reached new heights of production. Since the boom year of 1929, while our population has increased by only 20 per cent, our agricultural production has increased by 45 per cent, and our industrial production has increased by 75 per cent. We are turning out far more goods and more wealth per worker than we have ever done before.

This progress has confounded the gloomy prophets—at home and abroad—who predicted the downfall of American capitalism. The people of the United States, going their own way, confident in their own powers, have achieved the greatest prosperity the world has ever seen.

But, great as our progress has been, we still have a long way to go.

As we look around the country, many of our shortcomings stand out in bold relief.

We are suffering from excessively high prices.

Our production is still not large enough to satisfy our demands.

Our minimum wages are far too low.

Small business is losing ground to growing monopoly.

Our farmers still face an uncertain future. And too many of them lack the benefits of our modern civilization.

Some of our natural resources are still being wasted.

We are acutely short of electric power, although the means for developing such power are abundant.

Five million families are still living in slums and firetraps. Three million families share their homes with others.

Our health is far behind the progress of medical science. Proper medical care is so expensive that it is out of reach of the great majority of our citizens.

Our schools, in many localities, are utterly inadequate.

Our democratic ideals are often thwarted by prejudice and intolerance.

Each of these shortcomings is also an opportunity—an opportunity for the Congress and the President to work for the good of the people.

Our first great opportunity is to protect our economy against the evils of "boom and bust."

This objective cannot be attained by Government alone. Indeed, the greater part of the task must be performed by individual efforts under our system of free enterprise. We can keep our present prosperity, and increase it, only if free enterprise and free government work together to that end.

We cannot afford to float along carelessly on a postwar boom until it collapses. And it is not enough merely to prepare to weather a recession if it comes. Instead, government and business must work together constantly to achieve more and more jobs and more and more production—which mean more and more prosperity for all the people.

The business cycle is man made; and men of good will, working together, can smooth it out.

So far as business is concerned, it should plan for steady, vigorous expansion—seeking always to increase its output, lower its prices, and avoid the vices of monopoly and restriction. So long as business does this, it will be contributing to continued prosperity, and it will have the help and encouragement of the Government.

The Employment Act of 1946 pledges the Government to use all its resources to promote maximum employment, production, and purchasing power. This means that the Government is firmly committed to protect business and the people against the dangers of recession and against the evils of inflation. This means that the Government must adapt its plans and policies to meet changing circumstances.

At the present time, our prosperity is threatened by inflationary pressures at a number of critical points in our economy. The Government must be in a position to take effective action at these danger spots. To that end, I recommend that the Congress enact legislation for the following purposes:

First, to continue the power to control consumer credit and enlarge the power to control bank credit.

Second, to grant authority to regulate speculation on the commodity exchanges.

Third, to continue export-control authority and to provide adequate machinery for its enforcement.

Fourth, to continue the priorities and allocation authority in the field of transportation.

Fifth, to authorize priorities and allocations for key materials in short supply.

Sixth, to extend and strengthen rent control.

Seventh, to provide stand-by authority to impose price ceilings for scarce commodities which basically effect essential industrial production or the cost of living, and to limit unjustified wage adjustments which would force a break in an established price ceiling.

Eighth, to authorize an immediate study of the adequacy of production facilities for materials in critically short supply, such as steel; and, if found necessary, to authorize Government loans for the expansion of production facilities to relieve such shortages, and furthermore to authorize the construction of such facilities directly if action by private industry fails to meet our needs.

The Economic Report, which I shall submit to the Congress shortly, will discuss in detail the economic background for these recommendations.

One of the most important factors in maintaining prosperity is the Government's fiscal policy. At this time, it is essential not only that the federal budget be balanced, but also that there be a substantial surplus to reduce inflationary pressures, and permit a sizable reduction in the national debt, which now stands at $252 billion. I recommend, therefore, that the Congress enact new tax legislation to bring in an additional $4 billion of Government revenue. This should come principally from additional corporate taxes. A portion should come from revised estate and gift taxes. Consideration should be given to raising personal income tax rates in the middle and upper brackets.

If we want to keep our economy running in high gear, we must be sure that every group has the incentive to make its full contribution to the national welfare. At present, the working men and women of the nation are unfairly discriminated against by a statute that abridges their rights, curtails their constructive efforts, and hampers our system of free collective bargaining. That statute is the Labor-Management Relations Act of 1947, sometimes called the Taft-Hartley Act.

That Act should be repealed.

The Wagner Act should be re-enacted. However, certain improvements, which I recommended to the Congress two years ago, are needed. Jurisdictional strikes and unjustifiable secondary boycotts should be prohibited. The use of economic force to decide issues arising out of the interpretation of existing contracts should be prevented. Without endangering our democratic freedoms, means should be provided for settling or preventing strikes in vital industries which affect the public interest.

The Department of Labor should be rebuilt and strengthened and those units properly belonging within that Department should be placed in it.

The health of our economy and its maintenance at high levels further require that the minimum wage fixed by law should be raised to at least 75 cents an hour.

If our free-enterprise economy is to be strong and healthy, we must reinvigorate the forces of competition. We must assure small business the freedom and opportunity to grow and prosper. To this purpose, we should strengthen our antitrust laws by closing those loopholes that permit monopolistic mergers and consolidations.

Our national farm program should be improved—not only in the interest of the farmers, but for the lasting prosperity of the whole nation. Our goals should be abundant farm production and parity of income for agriculture. Standards of living on the farm should be just as good as anywhere else in the country.

Farm price supports are an essential part of our program to achieve these ends. Price supports should be used to prevent farm price declines which are out of line with general price levels, to facilitate adjustments in production to consumer demands, and to promote good land use. Our price-support legislation must be adapted to these objectives. The authority of the Commodity Credit Corp. to provide adequate storage space for crops should be restored.

Our program for farm prosperity should also seek to expand the domestic market for agricultural products, particularly among low-income groups, and to increase and stabilize foreign markets.

We should give special attention to extending modern conveniences and services to our farms. Rural electrification should be pushed forward. And in considering legislation relating to housing, education, health and social security, special attention should be given to rural problems.

Our growing population and the expansion of our economy depend upon the wise management of our land, water, forest and mineral wealth. In our present dynamic economy, the task of conservation is not to lock up our resources but to develop and improve them. Failure, today, to make the investments which are necessary to support our progress in the future would be false economy.

We must push forward with the development of our rivers for power, irrigation, navigation and flood control. We should apply the lessons of our Tennessee Valley experience to our other great river basins.

I again recommend that action be taken by the Congress to approve the St. Lawrence Seaway and power project. This is about the fifth time I have recommended it.

We must adopt a program for the planned use of the petroleum reserves under the sea, which are—and must remain—vested in the Federal Government. We must extend our programs of soil conservation. We must place our forests on a sustained yield basis, and encourage the development of new sources of vital minerals.

In all this we must make sure that the benefits of these public undertakings are directly available to the people. Public power should be carried to consuming areas by public transmission lines where necessary to provide electricity at the lowest possible rates. Irrigation waters should serve family farms and not land speculators.

The Government has still other opportunities—to help raise the standard of living of our citizens. These opportunities lie in the fields of social security, health, education, housing and civil rights.

The present coverage of the Social Security laws is altogether inadequate, and benefit payments are too low. One third of our workers are not covered. Those who receive old-age and survivors' insurance benefits receive an average payment of only $25 a month. Many others who cannot work because they are physically disabled are left to the mercy of charity. We should expand our Social Security program, both as to size of benefits and extent of coverage, against the economic hazards due to unemployment, old age, sickness and disability.

We must spare no effort to raise the general level of health in this country. In a nation as rich as ours, it is a shocking fact that tens of millions lack adequate medical care. We are short of doctors, hospitals and nurses. We must remedy these shortages. Moreover, we need—and we must have without further delay—a system of prepaid medical insurance which will enable every American to afford good medical care.

It is equally shocking that millions of our children are not receiving a good education. Millions of them are in overcrowded, obsolete buildings. We are short of teachers, because teachers' salaries are too low to attract new teachers or to hold the ones we have. All these school problems will become much more acute as a result of the tremendous increase in the enrollment in our elementary schools in the next few years. I cannot repeat too strongly my desire for prompt federal financial aid to the States to help them operate and maintain their school systems.

The Governmental agency which now administers the programs of health, education and social security should be given full departmental status.

The housing shortage continues to be acute. As an immediate step, the Congress should enact the provisions for low-rent public housing, slum clearance, farm housing and housing research which I have repeatedly recommended. The number of low-rent public-housing units provided for in the legislation should be increased to 1,000,000 units in the next seven years. Even this number of units will not begin to meet our need for new housing.

Most of the houses we need will have to be built by private enterprise, without public subsidy. By producing too few rental units and too large a proportion of high-priced houses, the building industry is rapidly pricing itself out of the market. Building costs must be lowered.

The Government is now engaged in a campaign to induce all segments of the building industry to concentrate on the production of lower-priced housing. Additional legislation to encourage such housing will be submitted.

The authority which I have requested, to allocate materials in short supply and to impose price ceilings on such materials, could be used, if found necessary, to channel more materials into homes large enough for family life at prices which wage earners can afford.

The driving force behind our progress is our faith in our democratic institutions. That faith is embodied in the promise of equal rights and equal opportunities which the founders of our republic proclaimed to their countrymen and to the whole world.

The fulfillment of this promise is among the highest purposes of government. The civil-rights proposals I made to the 80th Congress, I now repeat to the 81st Congress. They should be enacted in order that the Federal Government may assume the leadership and discharge the obligations clearly placed upon it by the Constitution.

I stand squarely behind those proposals.

Our domestic programs are the foundation of our foreign policy. The world today looks to us for leadership because we have so largely realized, within our borders, those benefits of democracy for which most of the peoples of the world are yearning.

We are following a foreign policy which is the outward expression of the democratic faith we profess. We are doing what we can to encourage free states and free peoples throughout the world, to aid the suffering and afflicted in foreign lands, and to strengthen democratic nations against aggression.

The heart of our foreign policy is peace. We are supporting a world organization to keep peace and a world economic policy to create prosperity for mankind. Our guiding star is the principle of international co-operation. To this concept we have made a national commitment as profound as anything in history.

To it we have pledged our resources and our honor.

Until a system of world security is established upon which we can safely rely, we cannot escape the burden of creating and maintaining armed forces sufficient to deter aggression. We have made great progress in the last year in the effective organization of our armed forces, but further improvements in our national security legislation are necessary. Universal training is essential to the security of the United States.

During the course of this session I shall have occasion to ask the Congress to consider several measures in the field of foreign policy. At this time, I recommend that we restore the Reciprocal Trade Agreements Act to full effectiveness, and extend it for three years. We should also open our doors to displaced persons without unfair discrimination.

It should be clear by now to all nations that we are not seeking to freeze the status quo. We have no intention of preserving the injustices of the past. We welcome the constructive efforts being made by many nations to achieve a better life for their citizens. In the European Recovery Program, in our Good Neighbor policy and in the United Nations, we have begun to batter down those national walls which block the economic growth and the social advancement of the peoples of the world.

We believe that if we hold resolutely to this course, the principle of international co-operation will eventually command the approval even of those nations which are now seeking to weaken or subvert it.

We stand at the opening of an era which can mean either great achievement or terrible catastrophe for ourselves and all mankind.

The strength of our nation must continue to be used in the interest of all our people rather than a privileged few. It must continue to be used unselfishly in the struggle for world peace and the betterment of mankind the world over.

This is the task before us.

It is not an easy one. It has many complications, and there will be strong opposition from selfish interests.

I hope for co-operation from farmers, from labor and from business. Every segment of our population and every individual have a right to expect from our Government a fair deal.

In 1945, when I came up before the Congress for the first time April 16, I quoted to you King Solomon's prayer that he wanted wisdom and ability to govern his people as they should be governed. I explained to you at that time that the task before me was one of the greatest in the history of the world and that it was necessary to have the complete co-operation of the Congress and the people of the United States.

Well, now, we are taking a new start with the same situation. It is absolutely essential that your President have the complete co-operation of the Congress to carry out the great work that must be done to keep the peace in this world and to keep this country prosperous.

They have a right to expect that the Congress and the President will work in the closest co-operation with one objective—the welfare of the people of this nation as a whole.

In the months ahead I know that I shall be able to co-operate with this Congress.

I am confident that the Divine Power which has guided us to this time of fateful responsibility and glorious opportunity will not desert us now.

With that help from Almighty God which we have humbly acknowledged at every turning point in our national life, we shall be able to perform the great tasks which He now sets before us.

COMMENT

President Truman's legislative proposals are the same ruinous socialism that he advocated on the stump. . . . Virtually every thing he advocates will increase inflation. . . .

> Editorial in the Chicago (Ill.) *Tribune*, January 6, 1949.

It looks as though we are going the way England went, and without the restraints and caution the Britons exercised. . . .

> Representative E. E. Cox, Democrat from Georgia. New York *Times*, January 6, 1949.

I disagree with the President's contention that our domestic programs are the foundation of our foreign policy. . . . You cannot have guns and butter at the same time.

> Representative Vito Marcantonio of the American Labor Party. New York *Times*, January 6, 1949.

The President's recommendations to Congress were well to the Left of any recommendations which have ever been made to that body by any President, including Truman's predecessor. . . . The basic premise behind every word the President spoke was simply that in every field affecting the public welfare, from health and housing to the production of steel, the state must assume the ultimate responsibility.

> Columnist Stewart Alsop in *Life*, xxvi (January 17, 1949), 29.

89. MARCH 18, 1949

Dean Acheson on NATO

As the Soviet Union continued to demonstrate that it was a menace to the

St. Louis (Mo.) *Post-Dispatch*, April 1, 1949.

security of the United States, it became obvious that the Truman Doctrine and Marshall Plan were not sufficient to stop Soviet expansion. For example, the Rus-

sians imposed a blockade on Berlin in an attempt to force the Western powers from the city. Meanwhile, Czechoslovakia disappeared behind the Iron Curtain. In an effort to contain Soviet aggression, Great Britain, France, the Netherlands, Belgium, and Luxembourg signed the Brussels Pact in 1948, whereby the contracting powers agreed that if one of the parties to the treaty was attacked in Europe, the others would come to its aid. Shortly after the signing of the Pact, the United States began negotiations with various European nations to build a new pact with American participation. The result was the North Atlantic Treaty Organization, the first treaty of alliance the United States had ever concluded in peacetime. By Article 5 of the Treaty, the parties declared that an armed attack upon any of them would be considered an attack upon all. In case of such an attack, each member would aid the nation attacked "by such action as it deems necessary." Unanswered by the treaty was the question: "If an attack should come, how much action would each signatory consider 'necessary'?" In case Russia might have doubts that the United States would meet its treaty commitments, American forces in Europe were placed in such a manner that a Soviet attack would run into them. Thus, American retaliation against Russia would be assured. On the evening of March 18, 1949, Secretary of State Dean Acheson delivered the following message on radio to the American people.

I think the American people will want to know the answers to three principal questions about the pact: How did it come about and why is it necessary? What are its terms? Will it accomplish its purpose?

The paramount purposes of the pact are peace and security. If peace and security can be achieved in the North Atlantic area, we shall have gone a long way to assure peace and security in other areas as well.

The achievement of peace and security means more than that in the final outcome we shall have prevented war and brought about the settlement of international disputes by peaceful means. There must be conviction of people everywhere that war will be prevented and that disputes will be settled peacefully. In the most practical terms, true international peace and security require a firm belief by the peoples of the world that they will not be subjected to unprovoked attack, to coercion and intimidation, to interference in their own affairs. Peace and security require confidence in the future, based on the assurance that the peoples of the world will be permitted to improve their conditions of life, free from fear that the fruits of their labor may be taken from them by alien hands.

These are goals of our own foreign policy which President Truman has emphasized many times, most recently in his inaugural address when he spoke of the hope that we could help create "the conditions that will lead eventually to personal freedom and happiness for all mankind." These are the purposes of the United Nations, whose members are pledged "to maintain international peace and security" and to promote "the economic and social advancement of all peoples."

These purposes are intimately related to the origins of the United Nations. As the second World War neared its end, the peoples who bore the brunt of the fighting were sick of the horror, the brutality, the tragedy of war. Out of that revulsion came the determination to create a system that would go as far as humanly possible in insuring international peace and security.

The United Nations seeks to maintain peace and security by enjoining its members from using force to settle international disputes. Moreover, it insists that they acknowledge tolerance and cooperation as the guiding principles for the conduct of nations.

The members are expected to settle differences by the exercise of reason and adjustment, according to the principles of justice and law. This requires a spirit of tolerance and restraint on the part of all the members.

But, as in any other institution which presupposes restraint, violence or obstruction can be used to defeat the basic undertaking. This happens in personal relations, in families, communities, churches, politics, and everywhere in human life. If the system is used in ways it was not intended to be used, there is grave danger that the system will be disrupted.

That applies to the United Nations. The system is not working as effectively as we hoped because one of its members has attempted to prevent it from working. By obstructive tactics and the misuse of the veto, the Soviet Union has seriously interfered with the work of the Security Council in maintaining international peace and security.

But the United Nations is a flexible instrument. Although the actions of the Soviet Union have disturbed the work of the United Nations, it is strong enough to be an effective instrument for peace. It is the instrument by which we hope world peace will be achieved. The Charter recognizes the importance of regional arrangements consistent with the purposes and principles of the Charter. Such arrangements can greatly strengthen it.

The Atlantic pact is a collective self-defense arrangement among the countries of the North Atlantic area. It is aimed at coordinating the exercise of the right of self-defense especially recognized in Article 51 of the United Nations Charter. It is designed to fit precisely into the framework of the United Nations and to assure practical measures for maintaining peace and security in harmony with the Charter.

It is the firm intention of the parties to carry out the pact in accordance with the provisions of the United Nations Charter and in a manner which will advance its purposes and principles.

Already one such arrangement under the Charter has been established with United States participation. The twenty-one American republics in reorganizing their regional system have specifically brought it within the framework of the United Nations Charter. We are now joining in the formation of a second arrangement, pertaining to the North Atlantic area, likewise within the framework of the United Nations.

It is important to keep in mind that the really successful national and international institutions are those that recognize and express underlying realities. The North Atlantic community of nations is such a reality. It is based on the affinity and natural identity of interests of the North Atlantic powers.

The North Atlantic treaty which will formally unite them is the product of at least 350 years of history, perhaps more. There developed on our Atlantic Coast a community, which has spread across the continent, connected with Western Europe by common institutions and moral and ethical beliefs. Similarities of this kind are not superficial, but fundamental. They are the strongest kind of ties, because they are based on moral conviction, on acceptance of the same values in life.

The very basis of Western civilization, which we share with the other nations bordering the North Atlantic, and which all of us share with many other nations, is the ingrained spirit of restraint and tolerance. This is the opposite of the Communist belief that coercion by force is a proper method of hastening the inevitable. Western civilization has lived by mutual restraint and tolerance. This civilization permits and stimulates free inquiry and bold experimentation. It creates the environment of freedom, from which flows the greatest amount of ingenuity, enterprise and accomplishment.

These principles of democracy, individual liberty and the rule of law have flourished in this Atlantic community. They have universal validity. They are shared by other free nations and find expression on a universal basis in the Charter of the United Nations; they are the standards by which its members have solemnly agreed to be judged. They are the elements out of which are forged the peace and welfare of mankind.

Added to this profoundly important basis of understanding is another unifying influence—the effect of living on the sea. The sea does not separate people as much as it joins them, through trade, travel, mutual understanding and common interests.

For this second reason, as well as the first, North America and Western Europe have formed the two halves of what is in reality one community, and have maintained an abiding interest in each other.

It is clear that the North Atlantic Pact is not an improvisation. It is the statement of the facts and lessons of history. We have learned our history lesson from two world wars in less than half a century. That experience has taught us that the control of Europe by a single aggressive, unfriendly power would constitute an intolerable threat to the national security of the United States. We participated in those two great wars to preserve the integrity and independence of the European half of the Atlantic community in order to preserve the integrity and independence of the American half. It is a simple fact, proved by experience, that an outside attack on one member of this community is an attack upon all members.

We have also learned that if the free nations do not stand together, they will fall one by one. The strategem of the aggressor is to keep his intended victims divided, or better still, set them to quarrelling among themselves. Then they can be picked off one by one without arousing unified resistance. We and the free nations of Europe are determined that history shall not repeat itself in that melancholy particular.

As President Truman has said. "If we can make it sufficiently clear, in advance, that any armed attack affecting our national security would be met with overwhelming force, the armed attack might never occur."

The same thought was expressed by the Foreign Relations Committee of the Senate last year in its report recommending approval of Senate Resolution 239. "The committee is convinced," the report said, "that the horrors of another world war can be avoided with certainty only by preventing war from starting. The experience of World War I and World War II suggests that the best deterrent to aggression is the certainty that immediate and effective counter-measures will be taken against those who violate the peace." That resolution, adopted by an overwhelming vote of the Senate, expressly encourages the development of collective self-defense and regional arrangements within the United Nations framework and the participation of the United States in these arrangements.

What are the principal provisions of the North Atlantic Pact? I should like to summarize them.

First, the pact is carefully and conscientiously designed to conform in every particular with the Charter of the United Nations. This is made clear in the first article of the pact, which reiterates and reaffirms the basic principle of the Charter. The participating countries at the very outset of their association state again that they will settle all their international disputes, not only among themselves but with any nation, by peaceful means, in accordance with the provisions of the Charter. This declaration sets the whole tone and purpose of this treaty.

The second article is equally fundamental. The associated countries assert that they will preserve and strengthen their free institutions, and will see to it that the fundamental principles upon which free institutions are founded are better understood everywhere. They also agree to eliminate conflicts in their economic life and to promote economic co-operation among themselves. Here is the ethical essence of the treaty—the common resolve to preserve, strengthen and make understood the very basis of tolerance, restraint and freedom—the really vital things with which we are concerned.

This purpose is extended further in Article 3, in which the participating countries pledge themselves to self-help and mutual aid. In addition to strengthening their free institutions, they will take practical steps to maintain and develop their own capacity and that of their partners to resist aggression. They also agree to consult together when the integrity or security of any of them is threatened. The treaty sets up a council, consisting of all the members, and other machinery for consultation and for carrying out the provisions of the pact.

Successful resistance to aggression in the modern world requires modern arms and trained military forces. As a result of the recent war, the European countries joining the pact are generally deficient in both requirements. The treaty does not bind the United States to any arms program. But we all know that the United States is now the only democratic nation with the resources and the productive capacity to help the free nations of Europe to recover their military strength.

Therefore, we expect to ask the Congress to supply our European partners some of the weapons and equipment they need to be able to resist aggression. We also expect to recommend military supplies for other free nations which will co-operate with us in safeguarding peace and security.

In the compact world of today the security of the United States cannot be defined in terms of boundaries and frontiers. A serious threat to international peace and security anywhere in the world is of direct concern to this country. Therefore it is our policy to help peoples to maintain their integrity and independence, not only in Western Europe or in the Americas, but wherever the aid we are able to provide can be effective. Our actions in supporting the integrity and independence of Greece, Turkey and Iran are expressions of that determination. Our interest in the security of these countries has been made clear, and we shall continue to pursue that policy.

In providing military assistance to other countries, both inside and outside the North Atlantic Pact, we will give clear priority to the requirements for economic recovery. We will carefully balance the military assistance program with the capacity and requirements of the total economy, both at home and abroad.

But to return to the treaty, Article 5 deals with the possibility, which unhappily cannot be excluded, that the nations joining together in the pact may have to face the eventuality of an armed attack. In this article, they agree that an armed attack on any of them, in Europe or North America, will be considered an attack on all of them. In the event of such an attack, each of them will take, individually and in concert with the other parties, whatever action it deems necessary to restore and maintain the security of the North Atlantic area, including the use of armed force.

This does not mean that the United States would be automatically at war if one of the nations covered by the pact is subjected to armed attack. Under our Constitution, the Congress alone has the power to declare war. We would be bound to take promptly the action which we deemed necessary to restore and maintain the security of the North Atlantic area. That decision would be taken in accordance with our constitutional procedures. The factors which would have to be considered would be, on the one side, the gravity of the armed attack; on the other, the action which we believed necessary to restore and maintain the security of the North Atlantic area. That is the end to be achieved. We are bound to do what in our honest judgment is necessary to reach that result. If we should be confronted again with a calculated armed attack such as we have twice seen in the Twentieth Century, I should not suppose that we would decide any action other than the use of armed force effective as an exercise of the right of collective self-defense or as necessary to restore the peace and security of the North Atlantic area. That decision will rest where the Constitution has placed it.

This is not a legalistic question. It is a question we have frequently faced, the question of faith and principle in carrying out treaties. Those who decide it will have the responsibility for taking all appropriate action under the treaty. Such a responsibility requires the exercise of will—a will disciplined by the undertaking solemnly contracted to do what they decide is necessary to restore and maintain the peace and security of the North Atlantic area. That is our obligation under this Article 5. It is equally our duty and obligation to the security of our own country.

All of these provisions of the pact are subject to the overriding provisions of the United Nations Charter. Any measure for self-defense taken under the treaty will be reported to the Security Council of the United Nations. These measures will continue only until the Security Council, with its primary responsibility, takes the necessary action to restore peace and maintain security.

The treaty has no time limit, but after it has been in effect twenty years any member can withdraw on one year's notice. It also provides that after it has been in existence ten years, it will be reviewed in the circumstances prevailing at that time. Additional countries may be ad-mitted to the pact by agreement of all the parties already signatories.

These are the principal provisions of the treaty.

Will the pact accomplish its purpose?

No one can say with certainty. We can only act on our convictions. The United States Government and the Governments with which we are associated in this treaty are convinced that it is an essential measure for strengthening the United Nations, deterring aggression, and establishing the sense of security necessary for the restoration of the economic and political health of the world.

The nations joining in the pact know that war does not pay. Others may not be as deeply convinced of this as we are. The North Atlantic treaty should help convince them also that war does not pay.

It seems absurd that it should be necessary in this era of popular education and highly developed communications, to deal with allegations which have no relation to the truth and could not stand even the crudest test of measurement against realities. Nevertheless, the power and persistence with which the lie is today employed as a weapon of international policy is such that this cannot always be avoided.

I refer here to the allegations that this treaty conceals aggressive designs on the part of its authors with respect to other countries. Anyone with the most elementary knowledge of the processes of democratic government knows that democracies do not and cannot plan aggressive wars. But for those from whom such knowledge may have been withheld I must make the following categoric and unequivocal statement, for which I stand with the full measure of my responsibility in the office I hold:

This country is not planning to make war against anyone. It is not seeking war. It abhors war. It does not hold war to be inevitable. Its policies are devised with the specific aim of bridging by peaceful means the tremendous differences which beset international society at the present time.

Allegations that aggressive designs lie behind this country's signature of the Atlantic pact can rest only on a malicious misrepresentation or a fantastic misunderstanding of the nature and aims of American society. It is hard to say which of these attitudes is more irresponsible and more dangerous to the stability of international life. For misunderstanding on a question so vital to world progress and so easily susceptible of clarification could only be willful or the product of a system that imprisons the human mind and makes it impervious to facts. It is the duty of all those who seriously and realistically wish for peace to refuse to be misled by this type of falsehood and to prevent it from poisoning the atmosphere in which the quest of a happier world must be conducted.

This treaty is designed to help toward the goal envisioned by President Truman when he said: ". . . As our stability becomes manifest, as more and more nations come to know the benefits of democracy and to participate in growing abundance, I believe that those countries which now oppose us will abandon their delusions and join with the free nations of the world in a just settlement of international differences."

To bring that time to pass, we are determined, on the one hand, to make it unmistakably clear that immediate and effective counter measures will be taken against those who violate the peace, and on the other, to wage peace vigorously and relentlessly.

Too often peace has been thought of as a negative condition—the mere absence of war. We know now that we cannot achieve peace by taking a negative attitude. Peace is positive, and it has to be waged with all our thought, energy and courage, and with the conviction that war is not inevitable.

Under the leadership of President Truman the United States is waging peace with a vigor and on a scale without precedent. While the war was being fought this country took the initiative in the organization of the United Nations and related agencies for the collective and cooperative conduct of international affairs. We withdrew our military forces, except those required for occupation duties, and quickly reduced our military establishment to about one-tenth its war-time size. We contributed generously to post-war relief and rehabilitation.

When events called for firmness as well as generosity the United States waged peace by pledging its aid to free nations threatened by aggression, and took prompt and vigorous action to fulfill that pledge. We have actively sought and are actively seeking to make the United Nations an effective instrument of international cooperation. We proposed, and, with the eager cooperation of sixteen other nations, put into effect a great concerted program for the economic recovery and spiritual reinvigoration of Europe. We joined the other American republics, and we now join with Western Europe, in treaties to strengthen the United Nations and insure international peace and security.

The United States is waging peace by promoting measures for the revival and expansion of world trade on a sound and beneficial basis. Continuance of the reciprocal trade agreements program and ratification by the United States of the Charter of the International Trade Organization are essential to the success of our foreign trade policies. We are preparing to carry out an energetic program to apply modern skills and techniques to what President Truman has called the "primitive and stagnant" economies of vast areas, so that they will yield a better and richer life for their people.

The United States is waging peace by throwing its full strength and energy into the struggle, and we shall continue to do so.

We sincerely hope we can avoid strife,

but we cannot avoid striving for what is right. We devoutly hope we can have genuine peace, but we cannot be complacent about the present uneasy and troubled peace.

A secure and stable peace is not a goal we can reach all at once and for all time. It is a dynamic state, produced by effort and faith with justice and courage.

The struggle is continuous and hard. The prize is never irrevocably ours.

To have this genuine peace we must constantly work for it. But we must do even more. We must make it clear that armed attack will be met by collective defense, prompt and effective.

That is the meaning of the North Atlantic pact.

COMMENT

I believe it will promote war in the world rather than peace. . . . The Atlantic Treaty as drawn is certainly no improvement over the United Nations, nor can it by any stretch of the imagination be regarded as a perfection of or supplement to that Charter. From the point of view of an international organization, it is a step backward.

> Robert A. Taft, Republican of Ohio, speaking in the U.S. Senate, July 11, 1949. *Congressional Record*, 81st Cong., 1st Sess., 1949, xcv, pt. 7, 9205.

Western Europe is so important to our future . . . that we cannot afford to do less than our best in making sure that it does not go down the drain.

> General Dwight D. Eisenhower in an address to the members of Congress in the Library of Congress, Washington, D.C., February 1, 1951. *Vital Speeches*, xvii (March 1, 1951), 260.

My view is that this Treaty is the most sensible, powerful, practicable, and economical step the United States can now take in the realistic interest of its own security; in the effective discouragement of aggressive conquest which would touch off World War Three; in the stabilization of Western Germany. . . .

> Senator Arthur H. Vandenberg of Michigan in the U.S. Senate, July 6, 1949. Arthur H. Vandenberg, Jr., ed., *The Private Papers of Senator Vandenberg* (Boston: Houghton Mifflin Company, 1952), p. 493.

90. *1949*

Dean Acheson Reports on China Policy

Throughout the Second World War, the United States had a two-fold policy in the Far East: to defeat Japan and to create a powerful and friendly China. President Roosevelt hoped that a strong and democratic China could then play a

U.S. Relations with China. Department of State, *Publications*, No. 3573 (1949), Far Eastern Series, No. 31, pp. 13–16.

leading role in maintaining the postwar peace in Asia. Unfortunately, there were many obstacles to such a program. Aside from the Japanese occupation of large areas of China, the Chinese were deeply divided among themselves—between the Communists and the Nationalists. To create a united China, the United States attempted to heal this split, but all the efforts of the Truman Administration to achieve this goal were in vain. After several years of civil war, the Nationalists' power collapsed. Finally, the Nationalists led by Chiang-Kai-shek abandoned the mainland and established themselves on the island of Formosa, leaving virtually all of China to Communist rule. The Communists then began to wage an intensive campaign to drive Americans out of China and to end American influence in the Far East.

Immediately, there was an outcry of indignation and surprise in the United States. The public was bewildered. Were not the Americans and Chinese supposed to be traditional friends? Sharp critics of the Truman Administration charged that Communist sympathizers in the State Department were responsible for the "Red" victory. In an effort to absolve the United States for the Nationalists' defeat, Secretary of State Dean Acheson contended in the white paper below that Chiang's inept military leadership and a collapse in the morale of his followers were the main factors responsible for the Communist victory.

The reasons for the failures of the Chinese National Government appear in some detail in the attached record. They do not stem from any inadequacy of American aid. Our military observers on the spot have reported that Nationalist armies did not lose a single battle during the crucial year of 1948 through lack of arms or ammunition. The fact was that the decay which our observers had detected in Chungking early in the war had fatally sapped the powers of resistance of the Kuomintang. Its leaders had proved incapable of meeting the crisis confronting them, its troops had lost the will to fight, and its Government had lost popular support. The Communists, on the other hand, through a ruthless discipline and fanatical zeal, attempted to sell themselves as guardians and liberators of the people. The Nationalist armies did not have to be defeated; they

disintegrated. History has proved again and again that a regime without faith in itself and an army without morale cannot survive the test of battle.

The record obviously can not set forth in equal detail the inner history and development of the Chinese Communist Party during these years. The principal reason is that, while we had regular diplomatic relations with the National Government and had the benefit of voluminous reports from our representatives in their territories, our direct contact with the Communists was limited in the main to the mediation efforts of General Hurley and General Marshall.

Fully recognizing that the heads of the Chinese Communist Party were ideologically affiliated with Moscow, our Government nevertheless took the view, in the light of the existing balance of forces in China, that peace could be established only if certain conditions were met. The Kuomintang would have to set its own house in order and both sides would have to make concessions so that the Government of China might become, in fact as well as in name, the Government of all China and so that all parties might function within the constitutional system of the Government. Both internal peace and constitutional development required that the progress should be rapid from one party government with a large opposition party in armed rebellion, to the participation of all parties, including the moderate noncommunist elements, in a truly national system of government.

None of these conditions has been realized. The distrust of the leaders of both the Nationalist and Communist Parties for each other proved too deepseated to permit final agreement, notwithstanding temporary truces and apparently promising negotiations. The Nationalists, furthermore, embarked in 1946 on an over-ambitious military campaign in the face of warnings by General Marshall that it not only would fail but would plunge China into economic chaos and eventually destroy the National Government. General Marshall pointed out that though Nationalist armies could, for a period, capture Communist-held cities, they could not destroy the Communist armies. Thus every Nationalist advance would expose their communications to attack by Communist guerrillas and compel them to retreat or to surrender their armies together with the munitions which the United States has furnished them. No estimate of a military situation has ever been more completely confirmed by the resulting facts.

The historic policy of the United States of friendship and aid toward the people of China was, however, maintained in both peace and war. Since V–J Day, the United States Government has authorized aid to Nationalist China in the form of grants and credits totaling approximately 2 billion dollars, an amount equivalent in value to more than 50 percent of the monetary expenditures of the Chinese Government and of proportionately greater magnitude in relation to the budget of that Government than the United States has provided to any nation of Western Europe since the end of the war. In addition to these grants and credits, the United States Government has sold the Chinese Government large quantities of military and civilian war surplus property with a total procurement cost of over 1 billion dollars, for which the agreed realization to the United States was 232 million dollars. A large proportion of the military supplies furnished the Chinese armies by the United States since V–J Day has, however, fallen into the hands of the Chinese Communists through the military ineptitude of the Nationalist leaders, their defections and surrenders, and the absence among their forces of the will to fight.

It has been urged that relatively small amounts of additional aid—military and economic—to the National Government would have enabled it to destroy communism in China. The most trustworthy military, economic, and political information available to our Government does not bear out this view.

A realistic appraisal of conditions in China, past and present, leads to the conclusion that the only alternative open to the United States was full-scale intervention in behalf of a Government which had lost the confidence of its own troops and its own people. Such intervention would have required the expenditure of even greater sums than have been fruitlessly spent thus far, the command of Nationalist armies by American officers, and the probable participation of American armed forces—land, sea, and air— in the resulting war. Intervention of such a scope and magnitude would have been resented by the mass of the Chinese people, would have diametrically reversed our historic policy, and would have been condemned by the American people.

It must be admitted frankly that the American policy of assisting the Chinese people in resisting domination by any foreign power or powers is now confronted with the gravest difficulties. The heart of China is in Communist hands. The Communist leaders have foresworn their Chinese heritage and have publicly announced their subservience to a foreign power, Russia, which during the last 50 years, under czars and Communists alike, has been most assiduous in its efforts to extend its control in the Far East. In the recent past, attempts at foreign domination have appeared quite clearly to the Chinese people as external aggression and as such have been bitterly and in the long run successfully resisted. Our aid and encouragement have helped them to resist. In this case, however, the foreign domination has been masked behind the facade of a vast crusading movement which apparently has seemed to many Chinese to be wholly indigenous and national. Under these circumstances, our aid has been unavailing.

The unfortunate but inescapable fact is that the ominous result of the civil war in China was beyond the control of the government of the United States. Nothing that this country did or could have done within the reasonable limits of its capabilities could have changed that result; nothing that was left undone by this country has contributed to it. It was the product of internal Chinese forces, forces which this country tried to influence but could not. A decision was arrived at within China, if only a decision by default.

And now it is abundantly clear that we must face the situation as it exists in fact. We will not help the Chinese or ourselves by basing our policy on wishful thinking. We continue to believe that, however tragic may be the immediate future of China and however ruthlessly a major portion of this great people may be exploited by a party in the interest of a foreign imperialism, ultimately the profound civilization and the democratic individualism of China will reassert themselves and she will throw off the foreign yoke. I consider that we should encourage all developments in China which now and in the future work toward this end.

In the immediate future, however, the implementation of our historic policy of friendship for China must be profoundly affected by current developments. It will necessarily be influenced by the degree to which the Chinese people come to recognize that the Communist regime serves not their interests but those of Soviet Russia and the manner in which, having become aware of the facts, they react to this foreign domination. One point, however, is clear. Should the Communist regime lend itself to the aims of Soviet Russian imperialism and attempt to engage in aggression against China's neighbors, we and the other members of the United Nations would be confronted by a situation violative of the principles of the United Nations Charter and threatening international peace and security.

Meanwhile our policy will continue to be based upon our own respect for the Charter, our friendship for China, and our traditional support for the Open Door and for China's independence and administrative and territorial integrity.

COMMENT

If we want a strategy that will save Europe and save Asia at the same time . . . we must clear out the State Department from the top to bottom, starting with Dean Acheson.

Republican Minority Leader Joe Martin of Massachusetts speaking in New York on February 12, 1951. "Military Situation in the Far East," *Joint Senate Committee on Armed Services and Foreign Relations Hearings,* 82d Cong., 1st Sess. (Washington, 1951), 3176–8.

Apparently the administration would rather lose a continent than lose a little face. There is, of course, interesting factual information in this . . . report but it is also apparent that much of the material has been carefully selected to sustain a plausible defense of our betrayal of China at Yalta rather than to bring out the shameful truth.

John Davis Lodge, Republican from Massachusetts, speaking to the House of Representatives, August 8, 1949. *Congressional Record,* 81st Cong., 1st Sess., 1949, Appendix, xcv, pt. 15, A5123.

... Throughout this whole period there was a strong pro-Communist influence in the Far Eastern Division of the State Department which swallowed and supported Communist propaganda that the Chinese Communists were just agrarian reformers, and so the 400 million people of China came under the domination of Joe Stalin.

Senator Robert Taft of Ohio in a speech before the Republican Vermonters at Barre, Vermont, February 22, 1952. *Vital Speeches*, XVIII (March 15, 1952), 332.

91. *JUNE 27, 1950*

President Truman on Korea

In order to receive the surrender of Japanese troops at the end of World War II, the United States and Russia divided Korea into two zones, which eventually resulted in the establishment of two separate governments. But in 1948, the United Nations, the United States, and other noncommunist nations recognized the South Korean government as the only lawful government in Korea. The American government also extended to South Korea technical, economic, and military aid to assist it in establishing a democratic society and in resisting Communism. After the withdrawal of American and Soviet troops from Korea, the North Korean Communists launched a full scale attack on South Korea which caught the American government by surprise. The Truman Administration reacted by identifying the survival of South Korea with the security of the United States. Since the basic strategy of American foreign policy was to prevent the further spread of Communism, Truman reasoned that the failure to halt the North Korean attack would encourage Soviet aggression in the future. Acting promptly, he announced that Amer-

Department of State Bulletin, XXIII (July 3, 1950), 5.

ican naval and air forces in the Far East would assist the South Koreans. It is still unknown just what part the Russian government actually played in planning the invasion. Most likely Stalin urged the North Koreans to undertake the attack on the assumption that the United States would not fight to prevent Communist control of the entire peninsula.

In Korea, the Government forces, which were armed to prevent border raids and to preserve internal security, were attacked by invading forces from North Korea. The Security Council of the United Nations called upon the invading troops to cease hostilities and to withdraw to the 38th Parallel. This they have not done but, on the contrary, have pressed the attack. The Security Council called upon all members of the United Nations to render every assistance to the United Nations in the execution of this resolution. In these circumstances, I have ordered United States air and sea forces to give the Korean Government troops cover and support.

The attack upon Korea makes it

plain beyond all doubt that communism has passed beyond the use of subversion to conquer independent nations and will now use armed invasion and war. It has defied the orders of the Security Council of the United Nations issued to preserve international peace and security. In these circumstances, the occupation of Formosa by Communist forces would be a direct threat to the security of the Pacific area and to United States forces performing their lawful and necessary functions in that area.

Accordingly, I have ordered the Seventh Fleet to prevent any attack on Formosa. As a corollary of this action, I am calling upon the Chinese Government on Formosa to cease all air and sea operations against the mainland. The Seventh Fleet will see that this is done. The determination of the future status of Formosa must await the restoration of security in the Pacific, a peace settlement with Japan, or consideration by the United Nations.

I have also directed that United States forces in the Philippines be strengthened and that military assistance to the Philippine Government be accelerated.

I have similarly directed acceleration in the furnishing of military assistance to the forces of France and the Associated States in Indochina and the dispatch of a military mission to provide close working relations with those forces.

I know that all members of the United Nations will consider carefully the consequences of this latest aggression in Korea in defiance of the Charter of the United Nations. A return to the rule of force in international affairs would have far-reaching effects. The United States will continue to uphold the rule of law.

I have instructed Ambassador Austin, as the representative of the United States to the Security Council, to report these steps to the Council.

COMMENT

We've got a rattlesnake by the tail and the sooner we pound its damn head in, the better.

> Charles Eaton, ranking Republican on the House Foreign Affairs Committee. *Time,* LVI (July 10, 1950), 8.

It seems strangely difficult for some to realize that here in Asia is where the Communist conspirators have elected to make their play for global conquest, and that we have joined the issue thus raised on the battlefield; that here we fight Europe's war with arms while the diplomats there still fight it with words; that if we lose this war to Communism in Asia the fall of Europe is inevitable; win it and Europe most probably would avoid war and yet preserve freedom.

> General Douglas MacArthur in a letter to House Minority Leader Joe Martin, March 20, 1951. "Military Situation in the Far East," *Joint Senate Committee on Armed Services and Foreign Relations Hearings,* 82d Cong., 1st Sess. (Washington, 1951), 3182.

I believe the general principle of the policy is right.

> Republican Senator Robert A. Taft of Ohio in *A Foreign Policy for Americans* (New York: Doubleday & Co., Inc., 1951), p. 106.

92. *JUNE 25, 1952*

From President Truman's Veto of McCarran-Walter Immigration Act

In an effort to simplify the nation's im-migration laws and to replace the out-moded 1924 immigration statute (see p. 224), a congressional committee pro-duced the McCarran-Walter Immigra-tion Bill, which Congress passed in the summer of 1952. The statute repealed the unfortunate Asiatic exclusion clause, which had injured America's relations with the Far East since 1924. Moreover, it permitted the naturalization of most Asiatics living in the United States and the admission to the country of some 2,000 orientals annually on a quota basis. But the act went beyond this by employing screening measures to keep out undesirables and by empowering the attorney general of the United States to deport immigrants who belonged to communist front affiliations. A number of liberal groups argued that certain provisions of the act discriminated against foreigners on account of national origin, race, creed, and color, and that its provisions for the deportation of aliens were too harsh. President Truman re-acted by sending a ringing veto mes-sage to Congress. Focusing on the more specialized aspects of the bill, the Presi-dent argued that it was against the best interests of the United States. Neverthe-less, on June 30, 1952, Congress passed the bill over the President's veto.

. . . . .

The greatest vice of the present quota system . . . is that it discriminates, de-

Congressional Record, 82d Cong., 2d Sess., 1952, XCVIII, pt. 6, 8083.

liberately and intentionally, against many of the peoples of the world. The purpose behind it was to cut down and virtually eliminate immigration to this country from southern and eastern Europe. A theory was invented to ra-tionalize this objective. The theory was that in order to be readily assimilable, European immigrants should be admit-ted in proportion to the numbers of per-sons of their respective national stocks already here as shown by the census of 1920. Since Americans of English, Irish, and German descent were most numer-ous, immigrants of those three national-ities got the lion's share—more than two-thirds—of total quota. The re-maining third was divided up among all the other nations given quotas.

The desired effect was obtained. Im-migration from the newer sources of southern and eastern Europe was re-duced to a trickle. The quotas allotted to English and Ireland remained largely unused, as was intended. Total quota im-migration fell to a half or third—and sometimes even less—of the annual limit of 154,000. People from such countries as Greece or Spain or Latvia were vir-tually deprived of any opportunity to come here at all, simply because Greeks or Spaniards or Latvians had not come here before 1920 in any substantial numbers.

The idea behind this discriminatory policy was, to put it baldly, that Amer-icans with English or Irish names were better people and better citizens than Americans with Italian or Greek or

Polish names. It was thought that people of west European origin made better citizens than Rumanians or Yugoslavs or Ukrainians or Hungarians or Balts or Austrians. Such a concept is utterly unworthy of our traditions and our ideals. It violates the great political doctrine of the Declaration of Independence that "all men are created equal." It denies the humanitarian creed inscribed beneath the Statue of Liberty proclaiming to all nations, "Give me your tired, your poor, your huddled masses yearning to breathe free."

It repudiates our basic religious concepts, our belief in the brotherhood of man, and in the words of St. Paul "there is neither Jew nor Greek, there is neither bond nor free, for ye are all one in Christ Jesus."

The basis of this quota system was false and unworthy in 1924. It is even worse now. At the present time, this quota system keeps out the very people we want to bring in. It is incredible to me that, in this year of 1952, we should again be enacting into law such a slur on the patriotism, the capacity, and the decency of a large part of our citizenry.

Today, we have entered into an alliance, the North Atlantic Treaty, with Italy, Greece, and Turkey against one of the most terrible threats mankind has ever faced. We are asking them to join with us in protecting the peace of the world. We are helping them to build their defenses, and train their men, in the common cause. But, through this bill, we say to their people: You are less worthy to come to this country than Englishmen or Irishmen; you Italians, who need to find homes abroad in the hundreds of thousands—you shall have a quota of 5,645; you Greeks, struggling to assist the helpless victims of a Communist civil war— you shall have a quota of 308; and you Turks, you are brave defenders of the eastern flank, but you shall have a quota of only 225.

Today we are protecting ourselves, as we were in 1924, against being flooded by immigrants from eastern Europe. This is fantastic. The countries of eastern Europe have fallen under the Communist yoke; they are silenced, fenced off by barbed wire and mine fields; no one passes their borders but at the risk of his life. We do not need to be protected against immigrants from these countries; on the contrary, we want to stretch out a helping hand, to save those who have managed to flee into Western Europe, to succor those who are brave enough to escape from barbarism, to welcome and restore them against the day when their countries will, as we hope, be free again. But this we cannot do, as we would like to do, because the quota for Poland is only 6,500, as against the 138,000 exiled Poles all over Europe, who are asking to come to these shores; because the quota for the now subjugated Baltic countries is little more than 700, against the 23,000 Baltic refugees imploring us to admit them to a new life here; because the quota for Rumania is only 289, and some 30,000 Rumanians who have managed to escape the labor camps and the mass deportations of their Soviet masters, have asked our help. These are only a few examples of the absurdity, the cruelty of carrying over into this year of 1952 the isolationist limitations of our 1924 law.

In no other realm of our national life are we so hampered and stultified by the dead hand of the past as we are in this field of immigration. We do not limit our cities to their 1920 boundaries; we do not hold corporations to their 1920 capitalizations; we welcome progress and change to meet changing condition in every sphere of life except in the field of immigration.

The time to shake off this dead weight of past mistakes is now. The time to develop a decent policy of immigration—a fitting instrument for our foreign policy and a true reflection of the ideals we stand for, at home and abroad—is now. In my earlier message on immigration, I tried to explain to the Congress that the situation we face in immigration is an emergency—that it must be met promptly. I have pointed out that in the last few years we have blazed a new trail in immigration, through our displaced persons program. Through the combined efforts of the Government and private agencies, working together not to keep people out, but to bring qualified people in, we summoned our resources of good will and human feeling to meet the task. In this program, we have found better techniques to meet the immigration problems of the 1950's.

None of this fruitful experience of the last three years is reflected in this bill before me. None of the crying human need of this time of trouble is recognized in this bill. But it is not too late. The Congress can remedy these defects, and it can adopt legislation to meet the most critical problems before adjournment.

.   .   .   .   .

COMMENT

... the act has had no real defenders. . . . Only those who have ventured to affirm that the United States must become a purely white, Anglo-Saxon, Protestant country have been able conscientiously to support the McCarran-Walter Act.

> Historian Oscar Handlin, in "We Need More Immigrants," *Atlantic*, cxci (July, 1953), 29.

... the national-origins system seems to us to represent pretty well the views of the average American on how new arrivals should be distributed among the various emigrating nations. . . . there is no universal demand for upsetting the present proportion of ethnic groups in our population. There is no demand to throw away a workable slide rule like the national-origins system. . . . Nor is there any sentiment in favor of accepting the idea. . . . that immigration to this country should be determined less by the needs and capacities of this country than by the desires of other peoples to come here. . . . much as we might wish to do so for humanitarian reasons, we cannot destroy our immigration standards to take care of people who are surplus elsewhere.

> An editorial, "Before Attacking Immigration Law, Why Not Read it?", in the *Saturday Evening Post*, ccxxv (February 21, 1953), 10.

We should guard ourselves against the chronically ill and against the incompetent and the irresponsible who might become public charges. But beyond these elementary safeguards our gates should be thrown wide to the oppressed and uprooted peoples of the world who are willing to work and to sacrifice to make a home in America.

> Congressman Jacob K. Javits, Republican from New York, in "Let Us Open Again the Gates," *New York Times Magazine*, July 8, 1951.

93. SEPTEMBER 11, 1952

Governor Adlai E. Stevenson
Campaigns for the Presidency

In 1952, the Democratic party nominated Adlai E. Stevenson, Governor of Illinois, making him the first presidential candidate to be drafted since Garfield in 1880. In terms of literary excellence, Stevenson's speeches were unsurpassed in American campaign history. He fully endorsed the Fair Deal progressivism by calling for a continuation of high agricultural price supports, civil rights legislation, and the repeal of the Taft-Hartley Act. Stevenson's basic shortcoming was that he was more concerned with the literary quality of his speeches than with the projection of an image over television. Though television had been a powerful instrument of campaigning since 1948, Stevenson was unable to make a successful adaptation to the demands of the new media. His seriousness and intellectual capacities attracted most of the nation's intellectuals, but they were not enough to defeat General Eisenhower, who talked in generalities broad enough to appeal to most classes and interests. But particularly damaging to the Democrats were (1) the belief that they had been in office too long, (2) the resentment over scandals in the Truman Administration and, (3) the unpopularity of the Korean War and the stalemated peace talks. For the first time since the 1920's, the Republicans carried the most populous states in the union, the backbone of the Roosevelt coalition.

Adlai Stevenson, *Major Campaign Speeches* (New York: Random House, Inc., 1953), pp. 114–16. Reprinted by permission of Random House, Inc.

Below is a campaign speech which Stevenson delivered in Los Angeles on September 11, 1952.

. . . my friends, the foundation of any economy is its natural resources. The new technological era toward which we are moving will make ever-growing drains upon our resources. If we are to maintain our growth we must prepare for the future prosperity of our nation and we must make those preparations today while there is still time—not twenty years from now when it may be too late.

The resources problem is partly a problem of the wise use of the things we know we have and partly the problem of discovering how to use things that have never been useful before. In the last twenty years we have recognized that our land, and what lies beneath it, is a natural patrimony. It is a reserve for all of the people, to be utilized and developed in terms of our national welfare and of the strength and the security of the free world.

The relationship between industry and resources development grows closer every day. Every day we are learning how the interactions of soil, and fertilizer, and water, and power can grow more and better things that can never be permanently exhausted.

It may not be many years, for example, before you people of Los Angeles can get your drinking water from the sea. Already our scientists have made great progress in turning salt water into fresh.

And, there are further miracles in the scientific test tubes—above all the exciting possibilities of new sources of energy. The extraction of oil from shales will soon create one more new industry in the West. Government and private industry both have vital parts to play in these developments which hold for the future possibilities larger and more exciting perhaps than the invention of the steam engine itself.

And that is only one phase of the future. Another lies in our growing control of the power in the atom. As you in the West well know, whole new cities have risen since 1940—Hanford in Washington; Arco in Idaho; Los Alamos in New Mexico—in response to this atomic age, so far only at its dawn.

Should we follow the elephant's tail away from these horizons? Or should we go forward?

This new America will be a healthier America. Our children will have a vastly increased life expectancy. To attain this goal we shall need more medical research, more hospitals, more public-health agencies, more medical schools, more doctors and nurses—and some system of protection against the economic disasters of severe illness and accident, so that adequate medical care will be available for all.

I look forward to more and better housing for our people. In the past seven years more than eight million new homes have been built, and you people in Southern California can believe that huge figure because you can see so many of those new homes with your own eyes. This progress must be continued so that all Americans will have an opportunity to get decent housing—and public housing has a role to play in this problem.

I look forward to an America with improved education. We have made great progress in twenty years which we cannot stop until we have banished illiteracy and enlarged the educational opportunities of all of the boys and girls in this land.

I look forward to an America, my friends, which can take proper care of its aged and its invalids, and which can provide strong and expanding security for all of its workers. I rejoice in the Democratic Party's record in the establishment and the development of social security; and I endorse its pledge of a stronger system of unemployment insurance.

There are those who say that social security and protection against the hazards of life in our industrial society are undermining our self-reliance. And I agree that you can't bring about prosperity by discouraging thrift. But, I don't believe that our public-assistance programs have had that effect. On the contrary, they tend to stabilize our economy, reduce anxieties and lift the level of opportunity.

I look forward to an America united in its national belief in equal rights for all its citizens. We can never stop in the battle against racial and religious bigotry, discrimination and fear. We must ensure equal opportunities of employment for citizens of all colors and creeds. Given our resources, given the productivity of our economic system, given the magic of the new technology, given the undeveloped potentialities of electrical, chemical and atomic power, given the wise use of our wealth in the service of our people, we have within our grasp the possibilities of an undreamed-of future.

The American faith has been a faith in the growth of our nation and in a just distribution of the wealth among all of our citizens. And that faith stands today on the verge of its most dramatic realization. We stand on the threshold. The question is whether we have the will to cross that threshold and move into the new era ahead. The struggle between faith and fear will decide the destiny of our nation. Today we stand bewildered and tormented by many fears, some real, some imaginary. There is the fear of war; there is the fear of depression; and the fear of communism; and the fear of ourselves. I would not decry these fears. Without fear we would never act in time to save ourselves, but I would warn with all of the certainty that I possess against permitting fear to seize your mind, to cloud our brain and to paralyze our will.

The fear of war, my friends, is a real fear, but this danger can be met if we recognize that the best deterrent against totalitarian agression is our strength and our resolution.

I hold out no easy solution to the problem of peace. I reject those who tell you that we can make the Soviet danger vanish by giving one-shot solutions, whether the solution is to retreat behind our frontiers, as one of the Republican Parties suggests, or stir up insurrection in Eastern Europe, which seems to be the doctrine of the other Republican Party. But I do say that the policy of building the strength and the unity of free nations will reduce the haunting fear of war.

The fear of depression is a real fear. But this danger can be met if we have a government determined to pursue a positive policy to prevent depression and to control inflation. I have confidence in the capacity of the American people to steer an ever-expanding economy without running it over a cliff—if their leaders in government are prepared to combat inflation or depression by something more than moans, threats and incantations.

The fear of communism is a real fear. We are confronted, at home and abroad, by a vast international conspiracy. We must, at home and abroad, take measures to protect ourselves. All loyal Americans know today that communism is incompatible with American life. We have driven them out of any places of responsibility that they may have gained in our society. We will expose and identify them at every step along the way.

And then there is the fear of ourselves. I submit to you, it is not a real fear. The real fears of war, of depression, of communism, have stirred up a fantasy of fear in which those who live by the fear of others have had a field day.

Americans do not have to go about in fear and distrust of one another. At least the Democratic Party does not believe so, and I don't think that the rank and file of the Republican Party believes so either. We have, in short, faith in the American people and in the American future.

I do not wish to belittle the towering problems which loom over us at this moment. In other speeches I have described my present policies in some detail; and I propose to continue to lay out these ideas in plain language in speeches to come. We cannot move into the future until we have surmounted the present, but we cannot surmount the present until we know where we ultimately intend to go.

I could not come to the West—the region of the future—and to Los Angeles, the city of the future—without registering my ringing confidence in the capacity of our nation to cope with tomorrow. Stern and exacting moments lie immediately ahead of us. We will be still some time in a dark valley. I cannot promise easy deliverance from the perils of this anguished age.

But I do say to you soberly and sincerely that on the evidence of science, of technology, and of our own common sense, the United States at mid-century stands on the threshold of abundance for all, so great as to exceed the happiest dreams of the pioneers who opened up this vast Western country.

Unless we allow ourselves to be held back by fear, we shall in God's good time realize the golden promise of our future. Let us reject, I say, the prophets of fear and the Party of the Past. Let us

move ahead, proud and unafraid—con- lenge of today and to realize the infinite
fident of our capacity to meet the chal- possibility of tomorrow.

COMMENT

Only a Republican Administration can restore principles of common honesty
to Washington. We can pledge without qualification the establishment of a new
regime by the appointment of honest men to office, so that the public interest
alone will guide those who handle the people's money in collecting taxes, in
spending and in lending.

> Senator Robert Taft of Ohio in a speech to the Republican Vermonters at Barre,
> Vermont, February 22, 1952. *Vital Speeches*, XVIII (March 15, 1952), 331.

You're not going to vote Republican because of what little brass glitter still
shows under the tarnish of the candidate's compromises. You're not going to
vote Republican just out of sympathy for a party which has been out of office
for twenty years because it hasn't made itself fit to govern.

> President Harry S. Truman in a campaign address at Hartford, Connecticut, October
> 16, 1952. New York *Times*, October 17, 1952.

Another four years of Achesonian or Stevensonian softness toward Communism
could conceivably be disastrous to the cause of freedom. More likely it would
mean continued retreat, enlarged McCarthyism, and a general nostalgia for
the boyish certitudes of Harry Truman. . . . Ike would change the pattern. His
grasp of the Communist problem is deeper than Stevenson's, his caution towards
it is that of a strategist.

> Editorial in *Life*, XXXIII (October 27, 1952), 32.

94. *DECEMBER 8, 1953*

President Eisenhower's
Atoms for Peace Program

Fearful of the horrors which would ac- *of atomic power for peaceful purposes.*
company an atomic war, the American *Immediately, the speech was enthusiasti-*
people urged the Eisenhower Admini- *cally received throughout the nation.*
stration to conduct a policy of maintain- *When Eisenhower asked Congress to per-*
ing peace. In this address to the General *mit the Atomic Energy Commission to*
Assembly of the United Nations, Presi- *license private agencies to develop nu-*
dent Eisenhower reacted by appealing *clear energy for peaceful purposes, Con-*
for international co-operation in the use *gress responded by passing the Atomic*

Vital Speeches, XX (December 8, 1953), *Energy Act of 1954 which incorporated*
162–65. *the President's recommendations. By*

assuming the diplomatic offensive in pursuit of peace, Eisenhower greatly increased the confidence of our allies in the peaceful intentions of the United States. But unfortunately, the President did not achieve very much immediate success in his efforts to bring about international co-operation in the area of atomic power.

Later, however, Eisenhower's proposal took on new life. Speaking at Pennsylvania State University on June 11, 1955, the President offered "research reactors to people of free nations who can use them effectively for the acquisition of skills and understanding essential to peaceful atomic progress," with the United States assuming half the costs. In August, 1955, delegates from seventy-three nations, including the Soviet Union attended the International Conference on the Peaceful Uses of Atomic Energy in Geneva. In the following spring, the atoms for peace program took another important step forward when twelve nations, again including both the Soviet Union and the United States, approved a charter for an International Atomic Energy Agency and submitted it to a conference of eighty nations at the United Nations.

. . . . .

I feel impelled to speak today in a language that, in a sense, is new—one, which I, who have spent so much of my life in the military profession, would have preferred never to use.

That new language is the language of atomic warfare.

The atomic age has moved forward at such a pace that every citizen of the world should have some comprehension, at least in comparative terms, of the extent of this development, of the utmost significance to every one of us. Clearly, if the peoples of the world are to conduct an intelligent search for peace, they must be armed with the significant facts of today's existence.

My recital of atomic danger and power is necessarily stated in United States terms, for these are the only incontrovertible facts that I know. I need hardly point out to this assembly, however, that this subject is global, not merely national in character.

On July 16, 1945, the United States set off the world's first atomic test explosion. Since that date in 1945, the United States has conducted forty-two test explosions.

Atomic bombs today are more than twenty-five times as powerful as the weapons with which the atomic age dawned, while hydrogen weapons are in the ranges of millions of tons of TNT equivalent.

Today, the United States' stockpile of atomic weapons, which, of course, increases daily, exceeds by many times the explosive equivalent of the total of all bombs and all shells that came from every plane and every gun in every theatre of war through all of the years of World War II.

A single air group, whether afloat or land based, can now deliever to any reachable target a destructive cargo exceeding in power all the bombs that fell on Britain in all of World War II.

In size and variety the development of atomic weapons has been no less remarkable. This development has been such that atomic weapons have virtually achieved conventional status within our armed services. In the United States services, the Army, the Navy, the Air Force and the Marine Corps are all capable of putting this weapon to military use.

But the dread secret and the fearful engines of atomic might are not ours alone.

In the first place, the secret is possessed by our friends and Allies, Great Britain and Canada, whose scientific genius made a tremendous contribution to our original discoveries and the designs of atomic bombs.

The secret is also known by the Soviet Union.

The Soviet Union has informed us that, over recent years, it has devoted extensive resources to atomic weapons. During this period, the Soviet Union has exploded a series of atomic devices, including at least one involving thermonuclear reactions.

If at one time the United States possessed what might have been called a monopoly of atomic power, that monopoly ceased to exist several years ago. Therefore, although our earlier start has permitted us to accumulate what is today a great quantitative advantage, the atomic realities of today comprehend two facts of even greater significance.

First, the knowledge now possessed by several nations will eventually be shared by others, possibly all others.

Second, even a vast superiority in numbers of weapons, and a consequent capability of devastating retaliation, is no preventive, of itself, against the fearful material damage and toll of human lives that would be inflicted by surprise aggression.

The free world, at least dimly aware of these facts, has naturally embarked on a large program of warning and defense systems. That program will be accelerated and expanded.

But let no one think that the expenditure of vast sums for weapons and systems of defense can guarantee absolute safety for the cities and the citizens of any nation. The awful arithmetic of the atomic bomb does not permit of such an easy solution. Even against the most powerful defense, an aggressor in possession of the effective minimum number of atomic bombs for a surprise attack could probably place a sufficient number of his bombs on the chosen target to cause hideous damage.

Should such an atomic attack be launched against the United States, our reaction would be swift and resolute. But for me to say that the defense capabilities of the United States are such that they could inflict terrible losses upon an aggressor—for me to say that the retaliation capabilities of the United States are so great that such an agressor's land would be laid waste—all this, while fact, is not the true expression of the purpose and the hope of the United States.

To pause there would be to confirm the hopeless finality of a belief that two atomic colossi are doomed malevolently to eye each other indefinitely across a trembling world. To stop there would be to accept helplessly the probability of civilization destroyed—the annihilation of the irreplaceable heritage of mankind handed down to us generation from generation—and the condemnation of mankind to begin all over again the age-old struggle upward from savagery toward decency and right and justice.

Surely no sane member of the human race could discover victory in such desolation. Could anyone wish his name to be coupled by history with such human degradation and destruction?

Occasional pages of history do record the faces of the "Great Destroyers" but the whole book of history reveals mankind's never-ending quest for peace and mankind's God-given capacity to build.

It is with the book of history, and not with isolated pages, that the United States will ever wish to be identified. My country wants to be constructive, not destructive. It wants agreements, not wars, among nations. It wants, itself, to live in freedom and in the confidence that the people of every other nation enjoy equally the right of choosing their own way of life.

So my country's purpose is to help us move out of the dark chamber of horrors into the light, to find a way by which the minds of men, the hopes of men, the souls of men everywhere, can move forward toward peace and happiness and well-being.

In this quest, I know that we must not lack patience.

I know that in a world divided, such

as ours today, salvation cannot be attained by one dramatic act.

I know that many steps will have to be taken over many months before the world can look at itself one day and truly realize that a new climate of mutually peaceful confidence is abroad in the world.

But I know, above all else, that we must start to take these steps—now.

The United States and its Allies, Great Britain and France, have, over the past months, tried to take some of these steps. Let no one say that we shun the conference table.

On the record has long stood the request of the United States, Great Britain and France, to negotiate with the Soviet Union the problems of a divided Germany.

On that record has long stood the request of the same three nations to negotiate an Austrian peace treaty.

On the same record still stands the request of the United Nations to negotiate the problems of Korea.

Most recently, we have received from the Soviet Union what is in effect an expression of willingness to hold a four-power meeting. Along with our Allies, Great Britain and France, we were pleased to see that this note did not contain the unacceptable preconditions previously put forward.

As you already know . . . the United States, Great Britain and France have agreed promptly to meet with the Soviet Union.

The Government of the United States approaches this conference with hopeful sincerity. We will bend every effort of our minds to the single purpose of emerging from that conference with tangible results toward peace—the only true way of lessening international tension.

We never have, we never will, propose or suggest that the Soviet Union surrender what is rightfully theirs.

We will never say that the peoples of Russia are an enemy with whom we have no desire ever to deal or mingle in friendly and fruitful relationship.

On the contrary, we hope that this coming conference may initiate a relationship with the Soviet Union which will eventually bring about a free intermingling of the peoples of the East and of the West—the one sure, human way of developing the understanding required for confident and peaceful relations.

Instead of the discontent which is now setting upon Eastern Germany, occupied Austria and the countries of Eastern Europe, we seek a harmonious family of free European nations, with none a threat to the other, and least of all a threat to the peoples of Russia.

Beyond the turmoil and strife and misery of Asia, we seek peaceful opportunity for these peoples to develop their natural resources and to elevate their lot.

These are not idle words of shallow vision. Behind them lies a story of nations lately come to independence, not as a result of war but through free grant or peaceful negotiation. There is a record already written of assistance gladly given by nations of the West to needy peoples and to those suffering the temporary effects of famine, drought and natural disaster.

These are deeds of peace. They speak more loudly than promises or protestations of peaceful intent.

But I do not wish to rest either upon the reiteration of past proposals or the restatement of past deeds. The gravity of the time is such that every new avenue of peace, no matter how dimly discernible, should be explored.

There is at least one new avenue of peace which has not yet been well explored—an avenue now laid out by the General Assembly of the United Nations.

In its resolution of Nov. 18, 1953, this General Assembly suggested—and I quote—"that the Disarmament Commission study the desirability of establishing a subcommittee consisting of representatives of the powers principally involved, which should seek, in private, an acceptable solution—and report such a solution to the General Assembly and to the Security Council not later than 1 September, 1954."

The United States, heeding the suggestion of the General Assembly of the United Nations, is instantly prepared to meet privately with such other countries as may be "principally involved," to seek "an acceptable solution" to the atomic armaments race which overshadows not only the peace but the very life of the world.

We shall carry into these private or diplomatic talks a new conception.

The United States would seek more than the mere reduction or elimination of atomic materials for military purposes.

It is not enough to take this weapon out of the hands of the soldiers. It must be put into the hands of those who will know how to strip its military casing and adapt it to the arts of peace.

The United States knows that if the fearful trend of atomic military build-up can be reversed, this greatest of destructive forces can be developed into a great boon for the benefit of all mankind.

The United States knows that peaceful power from atomic energy is no dream of the future. That capability, already proved, is here now—today. Who can doubt, if the entire body of the world's scientists and engineers had adequate amounts of fissionable material with which to test and develop their ideas, that this capability would rapidly be transformed into universal, efficient and economic usage?

To hasten the day when fear of the atom will begin to disappear from the minds of people and the governments of the East and West there are certain steps that can be taken now.

I therefore make the following proposals:

The governments principally involved to the extent permitted by elementary prudence, to begin now and continue to make joint contributions from their stockpiles of normal uranium and fissionable materials to an international atomic energy agency. We would expect that such an agency would be set up under the aegis of the United Nations.

The ratios of contributions, the procedures and other details would properly be within the scope of the "private conversations" I have referred to earlier.

The United States is prepared to undertake these explorations in good faith. Any partner of the United States acting in the same good faith will find the United States a not unreasonable or ungenerous associate.

Undoubtedly initial and early contributions of this plan would be small in quantity. However, the proposal has the great virtue that it can be undertaken without irritations and mutual suspicions incident to any attempt to set up a completely acceptable system of world-wide inspection and control.

The Atomic Energy Agency could be made responsible for the impounding, storage and protection of the contributed fissionable and other materials. The ingenuity of our scientists will provide special, safe conditions under which such a bank of fissionable material can be made essentially immune to surprise seizure.

The more important responsibility of this atomic energy agency would be to devise methods whereby this fissionable material would be allocated to serve the peaceful pursuits of mankind. Experts would be mobilized to apply atomic energy to the needs of agriculture, medicine and other peaceful activities. A special purpose would be to provide abundant electrical energy in the power-starved areas of the world. Thus the contributing powers would be dedicating some of their strength to serve the needs rather than the fears of mankind.

The United States would be more than

willing—it would be proud—to take up with others "principally involved" the development of plans whereby such peaceful use of atomic energy would be expedited.

Of those "principally involved" the Soviet Union must, of course, be one.

I would be prepared to submit to the Congress of the United States, and with every expectation of approval, any such plan that would:

First, encourage world-wide investigation into the most effective peacetime uses of fissionable material; and with the certainty that they had all the material needed for the conduct of all experiments that were appropriate;

Second, begin to diminish the potential destructive power of the world's atomic stockpiles;

Third, allow all peoples of all nations to see that, in this enlightened age, the great powers of the earth, both of the East and of the West, are interested in human aspirations first rather than in building up the armaments of war.

Fourth, open up a new channel for peaceful discussion and initiate at least a new approach to the many difficult problems that must be solved in both private and public conversations if the world is to shake off the inertia imposed by fear and is to make positive progress toward peace.

Against the dark background of the atomic bomb, the United States does not wish merely to present strength, but also the desire and the hope for peace.

The coming months will be fraught with fateful decisions. In this Assembly, in the capitals and military headquarters of the world; in the hearts of men everywhere, be they governed or governors, may they be the decisions which will lead this world out of fear and into peace.

To the making of these fateful decisions, the United States pledges before you—and therefore before the world—its determination to help solve the fearful atomic dilemma—to devote its entire heart and mind to find the way by which the miraculous inventiveness of man shall not be dedicated to his death, but consecrated to his life.

COMMENT

... the striking thing about his speech was the utter lack of concrete proposals on how to make those general desires and wishes into reality.

> Boris Leontiev, leading Soviet radio propaganda commentator. New York *Times*, December 10, 1953.

I'm a little short on faith regarding practical plans to achieve these aims.

> Senator Edwin C. Johnson, Democrat of Colorado, in a press interview. New York *Times*, December 10, 1953.

... our "atoms for peace" program rests more on faith than on solidly established economic and technical data. Furthermore, we have the curious situation in which economic estimates, uncertain as they are, suggest stronger reasons for nuclear power development in other countries than in our own.

> Physics professor and former member of the Atomic Energy Commission Henry DeWolf Smyth in "Nuclear Power and Foreign Policy," *Foreign Affairs*, xxxv (October, 1956), 10.

95. *MARCH 29, 1954*

John Foster Dulles on
Massive Retaliation

At the end of the Korean conflict, the Eisenhower Administration adopted a new look in military power by making nuclear weapons, large and small, the mainstay of American military power. In the future, the prime emphasis was to be placed on mobility and on power that could inflict massive retaliation on the enemy. In other words, it was the determination of the Eisenhower Administration to maximize air power and minimize the role of the foot soldier. The critics of the Eisenhower Program charged that such policies would make it impossible for the nation to meet limited challenges. They argued that to meet limited aggression with massive retaliation would be tantamount to world war. Under such an eventuality, might not the government decide that areas formerly considered to be of vital interest to American security were only of secondary interest, not worth defending at the cost of a widespread nuclear war? At the moment of crisis, would it not appear better to accept a limited loss by making a denial of the value of the area surrendered? In response to this type of criticism, Secretary of State John Foster Dulles made the following statement to the Senate Foreign Relations Committee. He unequivocally declared that the United States would co-operate in meeting localized war as well as widespread aggression. But the question remained unanswered as to how the United States could meet limited aggression without the

Department of State Bulletin, xxx (March 29, 1954), 464-65.

military forces equipped to fight a limited war.

The central goal of our policy is peace with freedom and security. The menace of Soviet bloc despotism, which now holds in its grip one-third of the world's peoples, presents the most serious danger that has ever confronted us. The main aspects of this threat are apparent.

1. The Soviet rulers seem to feel secure only in a world of conformity dominated by them. Partly, no doubt, they are driven by lust for power. But to a considerable extent, I believe, they are driven by fear of freedom. To them freedom is a threat to be stamped out wherever it approaches their world.

2. The Soviet bloc possesses what is in many ways the most formidable military establishment the world has ever known. Its great strength is manpower, but also it is strong in terms of planes, submarines, and atomic capabilities. This vast empire dominates the central Eurasian land mass extending from the River Elbe in Germany to the Pacific. From within an orbit of 20,000 miles, it could strike by land at any one of approximately 20 states of Europe, the Middle East, and Asia, and by air it could strike the North American Continent.

3. Nor is the threat only military. It also commands a political apparatus which operates in every country of the world, seeking to capitalize upon all of the discontents and unsatisfied ambitions which inevitably exist in greater or less degree throughout the free world.

4. The threat is virtually unlimited so far as time is concerned. Soviet communism operates not in terms of an individual lifetime so that the threat will end with someone's death. It operates in terms of what Lenin and Stalin called "an entire historical era."

To meet that military threat requires on our side a strategy which is both well-conceived and well-implemented. This military defense must be within the capacity of the free world to sustain it for an indefinite time without such impairment of its economic and social fabric as would expose it to piecemeal seizure from within by the political apparatus of communism.

This calls for thinking and planning which is imaginative; which takes maximum possible advantage of the special resources of the free nations; and which is steadily developed and adapted to changing conditions. The fundamental aim of our national security policies is to deter aggression and thereby avert a new war. The essentials of this problem may be briefly summarized as follows:

1. The free nations can achieve security only by a collective system of defense. No single nation can develop alone adequate power to deter Soviet bloc aggression against its vital interests. By providing joint facilities and by combining their resources, the free nations can achieve a total strength and a flexibility which can surpass that of any potential enemy and can do so at bearable cost.

This collective security concept is the most highly developed in NATO. But it is also embodied in the Rio Pact of 1947 and, in more limited form, in various security arrangements in the Far East. The Turkey-Pakistan agreement marks the beginning of applying the collective security concept in the Middle East. The United Nations is moving in the same direction, as shown by its "Uniting for Peace" Resolution.

2. In organizing their collective defense, the free nations should not attempt to match the Soviet bloc man for man and gun for gun. The best way to deter aggression is to make the aggressor know in advance that he will suffer damage outweighing what he can hope to gain. Thus an aggressor must not be able to count upon a sanctuary status for those resources which he does not use in committing aggression.

3. To apply this deterrent principle the free world must maintain and be prepared to use effective means to make aggression too costly to be tempting.

It must have the mobility and flexibility to bring collective power to bear against an enemy on a selective or massive basis as conditions may require. For this purpose its arsenal must include a wide range of air, sea, and land power based on both conventional and atomic weapons. These new weapons can be used not only for strategic purposes but also for tactical purposes. The greatest deterrent to war is the ability of the free world to respond by means best suited to the particular area or circumstances. There should be a capability for massive retaliation without delay. I point out that the possession of that capacity does not impose the necessity of using it in every instance of attack. It is not our intention to turn every local war into a general war.

4. The magnitude and duration of the present danger and the need for flexibility of means to deter that danger make it vital to the United States, as never before, that it have firm allies. A firm alliance depends not merely upon documents, although these may be important. There must also be trust, understanding, and good will as between the free nations. This implies not merely military commitments, but good economic and cultural relations as well. It is not charity on the part of the United States to be concerned with the economic health of other nations which help to support the basic strategy

I describe. Neither is their good will a matter to which we can be indifferent. All of this means that foreign policy has assumed, as never before, a vital importance for the security of the United States.

In the long haul the United States has a profound interest in insuring that its allies and the uncommitted areas of the free world are able to maintain viable economic and political systems. That is why our foreign economic policy means so much to our own security.

COMMENT

. . . if we cannot afford to fight limited wars then we cannot afford to survive, for that is the only kind of war we can afford to fight.

> Lt. General James M. Gavin of the United States Army in *Life*, XLV (August 4, 1958), 76.

. . . we can only afford to fight a big war, and if there is one, that is the kind it will be.

> Secretary of Defense Charles E. Wilson quoted in *Life*, XLV (August 4, 1958), 80.

The position of Mr. John Foster Dulles . . . is essentially a prepare-for-one-type-of-war policy.

> Henry M. Jackson, Democrat from Washington, speaking in the U.S. Senate, February 16, 1954. *Congressional Record*, 83d Cong., 2d Sess., 1954, C, pt. 2, 1782.

People have been accustomed to saying that the day of limited war is over. I would submit that the truth is exactly the opposite; that the day of total wars has passed, and that from now on limited military operations are the only ones that could conceivably serve any coherent purpose.

> Former American Ambassador to the Soviet Union and Director of the State Department's Policy Planning Staff George F. Kennan in *Realities of American Foreign Policy* (Princeton: Princeton University Press, 1954), p. 80.

96. 1954

Brown v. Topeka Board of Education

Negroes and their pressure groups have long regarded segregation in public schools as a major obstacle to equality of opportunity and as a violation of their constitutional rights. Responding cautiously to such views, the Supreme Court during the 1940's, broadened the definition of equal rights. In May, 1954, the Supreme Court reversed a long standing

347 U.S. 483 (1954).

precedent supporting school segregation and unanimously ruled that segregation in public schools violated the Fourteenth Amendment. Disregarding all historical arguments concerning the intentions of the Fourteenth Amendment, Chief Justice Warren presented a sociological argument to demonstrate the impact of segregation on the status of the Negro. Immediately, southern conservatives de-

nounced the decision as an invasion of states' rights. Senator James Eastland of Mississippi and Governors Herman Talmadge of Georgia and James F. Byrnes of South Carolina urged their constituents to ignore the decision. On the other hand, the opponents of segregation pointed to the decision as an example of judicial statesmanship. Meanwhile, many Negroes were disappointed, for the Court issued no enforcement order and failed to state when southern society would have to adjust to the decision.

These cases come to us from the States of Kansas, South Carolina, Virginia, and Delaware. They are premised on different facts and different local conditions, but a common legal question justifies their consideration together in this consolidated opinion.

In each of the cases, minors of the Negro race, through their legal representatives, seek the aid of the courts in obtaining admission to the public schools of their community on a nonsegregated basis. In each instance they had been denied admission to schools attended by white children under laws requiring or permitting segregation according to race. This segregation was alleged to deprive the plaintiffs of the equal protection of the laws under the Fourteenth Amendment. In each of the cases other than the Delaware case, a three-judge federal district court denied relief to the plaintiffs on the so-called "separate but equal" doctrine announced by this Court in *Plessy* v. *Ferguson,* 163 U.S. 537 [see p. 101]. Under that doctrine, equality of treatment is accorded when the races are provided substantially equal facilities, even though these facilities be separate. In the Delaware case, the Supreme Court of Delaware adhered to that doctrine, but ordered that the plaintiffs be admitted to the white schools because of their superiority to the Negro schools.

The plaintiffs contend that segregated public schools are not "equal" and cannot be made "equal," and that hence they are deprived of the equal protection of the laws. Because of the obvious importance of the question presented, the Court took jurisdiction. Argument was heard in the 1952 Term, and reargument was heard this Term on certain questions propounded by the Court.

Reargument was largely devoted to the circumstances surrounding the adoption of the Fourteenth Amendment in 1868. It covered exhaustively consideration of the Amendment in Congress, ratification by the states, then existing practices in racial segregation, and the views of proponents and opponents of the Amendment. This discussion and our own investigation convince us that, although these sources cast some light, it is not enough to resolve the problem with which we are faced. At best, they are inconclusive. The most avid proponents of the post-War Amendments undoubtedly intended them to remove all legal distinctions among "all persons born or naturalized in the United States." Their opponents, just as certainly, were antagonistic to both the letter and the spirit of the Amendments and wished them to have the most limited effect. What others in Congress and the state legislatures had in mind cannot be determined with any degree of certainty.

An additional reason for the inconclusive nature of the Amendment's history, with respect to segregated schools, is the status of public education at that time. In the South, the movement toward free common schools, supported by general taxation, had not yet taken hold. Education of white children was largely in the hands of private groups. Education of Negroes was almost nonexistent, and practically all of the race were illiterate. In fact, any education of Negroes was forbidden by law in some states. Today, in contrast, many Negroes have achieved outstanding success in the arts and sciences as well as in the business and professional world. It is true that public school education at the time of the Amendment had advanced further in the North, but the effect of the Amendment on Northern States was generally ignored in the congressional debates. Even in the North, the conditions of public education did not approximate those existing today. The curriculum was usually rudimentary; ungraded schools were common in rural areas; the school term was but three months a year in many states; and compulsory school attendance was virtually unknown. As a consequence, it is not surprising that there should be so little in the history of the Fourteenth Amendment relating to its intended effect on public education.

In the first cases in this Court construing the Fourteenth Amendment, decided shortly after its adoption, the Court interpreted it as proscribing all state- imposed discriminations against the Negro race. The doctrine of "separate but equal" did not make its appearance in this Court until 1896 in the case of *Plessy* v. *Ferguson, supra,* involving not education but transportation. American courts have since labored with the doctrine for over half a century. In this Court, there have been six cases involving the "separate but equal" doctrine in the field of public education. In *Cumming* v. *County Board of Education,* 175 U.S. 528, and *Gong Lum* v. *Rice,* 275 U.S. 78, the validity of the doctrine itself was not challenged. In more recent cases, all on the graduate school level, inequality was found in that specific benefits enjoyed by white students were denied to Negro students of the same educational qualifications. *Missouri ex rel. Gaines* v. *Canada,* 305 U.S. 337; *Sipuel* v. *Oklahoma,* 332 U.S. 631; *Sweatt* v. *Painter,* 339 U.S. 629; *McLaurin* v. *Oklahoma State Regents,* 339 U.S. 637. In none of these cases was it necessary to re-examine the doctrine to grant relief to the Negro plaintiff. And in *Sweatt* v. *Painter, supra,* the Court expressly reserved decision on the question whether *Plessy* v. *Ferguson* should be held inapplicable to public education.

In the instant cases, that question is directly presented. Here, unlike *Sweatt* v. *Painter,* there are findings below that the Negro and white schools involved have been equalized, or are being equalized, with respect to buildings, curricula, qualifications and salaries of teachers, and other "tangible" factors. Our decision, therefore, cannot turn on merely a comparison of these tangible factors in the Negro and white schools involved in each of the cases. We must look instead to the effect of segregation itself on public education.

In approaching this problem, we cannot turn the clock back to 1868 when the Amendment was adopted, or even to 1896 when *Plessy* v. *Ferguson* was written. We must consider public education in the light of its full development and its present place in American life throughout the Nation. Only in this way can it be determined if segregation in public schools deprives these plaintiffs of the equal protection of the laws.

Today, education is perhaps the most important function of state and local governments. Compulsory school attendance laws and the great expenditures for education both demonstrate our recognition of the importance of education to our democratic society. It is required in the performance of our most basic public responsibilities, even service in the armed forces. It is the very foundation of good citizenship. Today it is a principal instrument in awakening the child to cultural values, in preparing him for later professional training, and in helping him to adjust normally to his environment. In these days, it is doubtful that any child may reasonably be expected to succeed in life if he is denied the opportunity of an education. Such an opportunity, where the state has undertaken to provide it, is a right which must be made available to all on equal terms.

We come then to the question presented: Does segregation of children in public schools solely on the basis of race, even though the physical facilities and other "tangible" factors may be equal, deprive the children of the minority group of equal educational opportunities? We believe that it does.

In *Sweatt* v. *Painter, supra,* in finding that a segregated law school for Negroes could not provide them equal educational opportunities, this Court relied in large part on "those qualities which are incapable of objective measurement but which make for greatness in a law school." In *McLaurin* v. *Oklahoma State Regents, supra,* the Court, in requiring that a Negro admitted to a white graduate school be treated like all other students, again resorted to intangible considerations: ". . . his ability to study, to engage in discussions and exchange views with other students, and, in general, to learn his profession." Such considerations apply with added force to children in grade and high schools. To separate them from others of similar age and qualifications solely because of their race generates a feeling of inferiority as to their status in the community that may affect their hearts and minds in a way unlikely ever to be undone. The effect of this separation on their educational opportunities was well stated by a finding in the Kansas case by a court which nevertheless felt compelled to rule against the Negro plaintiffs:

Segregation of white and colored children in public schools has a detrimental effect upon the colored children. The impact is greater when it has the sanction of the law; for the policy of separating the races is usually interpreted as denoting the inferiority of the negro group. A sense of inferiority affects the motivation of a child to learn. Segregation with the sanction of law, therefore, has a tendency to [retard] the educational and mental development of negro children and to deprive them of some of the benefits they would receive in a racial[ly] integrated school system.

Whatever may have been the psychological knowledge at the time of *Plessy* v. *Ferguson,* this finding is amply supported by modern authority. Any language in *Plessy* v. *Ferguson* contrary to this finding is rejected.

We conclude that in the field of public education the doctrine of "separate but equal" has no place. Separate educational facilities are inherently unequal. Therefore, we hold that the plaintiffs and others similarly situated for whom the actions have been brought are, by reason of the segregation complained of, deprived of the equal protection of the laws guaranteed by the Fourteenth Amendment. This disposition makes unnecessary any discussion whether such segregation also violates the Due Process Clause of the Fourteenth Amendment.

Because these are class actions, because of the wide applicability of this decision, and because of the great variety of local conditions, the formulation of decrees in these cases presents problems of considerable complexity. On reargument, the consideration of appropriate relief was necessarily subordinated to the primary question— the constitutionality of segregation in public education. We have now announced that such segregation is a denial of the equal protection of the laws. In order that we may have the full assistance of the parties in formulating decrees, the cases will be restored to the docket, and the parties are requested to present further argument on Questions 4 and 5 previously propounded by the Court for the reargument this Term. The Attorney General of the United States is again invited to participate. The Attorneys General of the states requiring or permitting segregation in public education will also be permitted to appear as *amici curiae* upon request to do so by September 15, 1954, and submission of briefs by October 1, 1954.

COMMENT

We regard the decision of the Supreme Court in the school cases as clear abuse of judicial power. It climaxes a trend in the Federal judiciary undertaking to legislate, in derogation of the authority of Congress, and to encroach upon the reserved rights of the states and the people. The original Constitution does not mention education. Neither does the Fourteenth Amendment nor any other amendment.

> Declaration of ninety-six southern congressmen on integration, March 11, 1956. New York *Times*, March 12, 1956.

I don't believe you can change the hearts of men on the race issue with laws or decisions.

> President Dwight D. Eisenhower in a news conference. Quoted in *New York Times Magazine*, February 14, 1960.

There has been no progress in the South that I know of except under pressure from the Federal Government—the courts or Congress or the President.

> Ralph McGill, editor of the Atlanta (Ga.) *Constitution*. Quoted in the *New York Times Magazine*, February 14,, 1960.

Since the May, 1954 decision, the extreme pro-segregationists have extended their hold on southern state governments. . . . The private resistance groups merge almost indistinguishably with public officialdom in Mississippi, South Carolina, Georgia, and Louisiana; virtually every political figure in Georgia, for example, from the governor on down, is associated with the States Rights Council. . . . Through their dominance of the State machinery, the segregationists wield enormous power. . . . they can put all the resources of their respective states into the effort to preserve segregation and to stamp out dissenting opinion.

> Harold Fleming, executive director of the Southern Regional Council, in an unpublished memorandum, January 20, 1956, p. 23.

---

97. DECEMBER 7, 1954

Senator Joseph McCarthy on Patriotism

As victory in World War II changed to a cold war, many Americans became increasingly disillusioned. Had not American power in the past always been omnipotent? Had not the nation always been able to achieve victory over its enemies?

Senate Permanent Subcommittee on Investigations of the Committee on Government Operations, *Hearings*, 83d Cong., 2d Sess., pt. 4, December 7, 1954, pp. 205–206.

What had happened to the United States' superiority and strength? The answers were not to be found on distant shores. The answers were at home: there must be treason within the American government. Many Americans became convinced that the Roosevelt and Truman Administrations had sold the Chinese and the people of eastern Europe down the river. Soon, Senator Joseph McCarthy of Wisconsin became the self-appointed leader of the movement to expose Communists within the government. He made wild charges to the effect that the government was filled with Communists and Communist sympathizers who tailored American policy to the aims of the Soviet Union. When the North Korean Communists invaded South Korea in the early 1950's, millions of Americans became engulfed with fear that Communists had infiltrated their government and other institutions. Though the hysteria began to ebb in 1953, Senator McCarthy continued his efforts to stir up popular fear of internal Communism. In late 1954, McCarthy, during a public hearing of a Senate subcommittee, even insulted President Eisenhower and apologized for having supported him in 1952.

The exposure of Communists in defense plants handling secret weapons, which may well determine whether the sons of American mothers will live or die, is in my opinion important beyond words. In view of the fact that this may be my temporary swan song as chairman of the Investigating Committee, I think that it is important to comment briefly upon certain facts.

Our committee has been held up now for approximately ten months. The President of the United States has taken it upon himself to congratulate Senators Flanders and Watkins who have been instrumental in holding up our work. There has been considerable talk about an apol-

ogy to the Senate for my fight against Communism. I feel rather that I should apologize to the American people for what was an unintentional deception upon them.

During the Eisenhower campaign, I spoke from coast to coast, promising the American people that if they would elect the Eisenhower administration that they would be assured of a vigorous forceful fight against Communists in Government. Unfortunately, in this I was mistaken. I find that the President on the one hand congratulates Senators who hold up the work of our committee, and on the other hand urges that we be patient, that we be patient with the Communist hoodlums who as of this moment are torturing and brainwashing American uniformed men in Communist dungeons.

Anyone who knows even the ABC's of the Communist war against free civilization knows that weakness and supineness will not free a single American uniformed man. If any Senator can in the future justify a vote to draft the sons of American mothers, then he must repudiate the shrinking show of weakness, and must tell those mothers that each young man who wears the American uniform carries the entire power of this nation with him when he goes to a foreign land.

Unfortunately, the President sees fit to congratulate those who hold up the exposure of the Communists in one breath, and in the next breath urges patience, tolerance and niceties to those who are torturing American uniformed men.

COMMENT

McCarthy's voting record negates the very effort that has been designed to stop the growth of world communism. He voted against the Marshall Plan, against giving aid and assistance to governmental plans for stopping communism in Europe. . . .

Herbert Steffes, Wisconsin C.I.O. executive, in a public statement, August, 1952. Quoted in *The Nation*, CLXXV (August 30, 1952), 167.

Literally hundreds of groups and organizations have either been infiltrated or organized primarily to accomplish the purposes of promoting the interests of the Soviet Union in the United States, the promotion of Soviet war and peace aims, the exploitation of Negroes in the United States, work among foreign-language groups, and to secure a favorable viewpoint toward the Communists in domestic, political, social, and economic issues.

> Testimony of J. Edgar Hoover, director, Federal Bureau of Investigation, before the Committee on Un-American Activities, House of Representatives, 80th Cong., 1st Sess., on H.R. 1884 and H.R. 2122, March 26, 1947.

[McCarthy] has injured American prestige, undoubtedly hampered diplomatic relations and otherwise played a reckless, dangerous game from behind his shield of Congressional immunity. He has embarrassed his party and confused the whole country without revealing anything of significance through his own efforts. *Collier's* thinks he deserves the critical blast of editorial comment that most of the press has given him.

> Editorial in *Collier's Magazine*, cxxvi (July 15, 1950), 74.

Senator Joseph McCarthy exposes Reds. They call him a 'liar' and a 'character assassin' and 'smear artist.' Then time passes, investigations take place, documents are dug up, and it turns out that McCarthy is right.

> Gerald L. K. Smith, head of the Christian Nationalist Party, in *The Cross and the Flag*, April, 1952.

---

98. *AUGUST 6, 1958*

Senator James W. Fulbright on American Foreign Policy

Throughout the decade of the 1950's, there were many critics of American foreign policy. Some observers thought America was slowly losing the cold war. Toward the end of the decade, the Soviet Union indeed appeared to be making significant gains. It successfully placed a rocket in orbit around the earth, improved its relations with several Latin American nations, and made friends in the Near East. In August, 1958, the Chinese Communists created a major crisis by shelling Quemoy. As it became increasingly apparent that Chiang Kai-shek was the controlling factor in American action in most of the Far East, many

Congressional Record, 85th Cong., 2d Sess., 1958, civ, pt. 13, 16317–20.

Americans became disillusioned with American foreign policy. The myth of Chiang's power and virtue had become so ingrained in American public sentiment that a realistic foreign policy became exceedingly difficult. Disturbed by these developments, the highly respected Senator James W. Fulbright, Democrat from Arkansas, delivered the following speech on the Senate floor on August 6, 1958, during which time he earnestly called for a reappraisal of American foreign policy.

Mr. President, at this moment no one knows whether the United States military forces in Lebanon will be plunged deeper into the Middle East or whether an opportunity will arise in the near future to withdraw them. Certainly, it is the expressed hope of the executive branch, and I am sure the unspoken hope of most Americans, that these forces will be able to leave the area promptly. While they are still there, they deserve our support. The decision which put them into the Middle East was not theirs to make, though they will bear the brunt of any drastic consequences which may stem from it.

The safety of the men in the Middle East is our primary concern at the moment; but if we limit our concern to considerations of the moment, we will not really solve anything. We must look at the basic causes of our troops being in Lebanon. When we do that, we find that our present trouble in the Middle East is merely symptomatic of a much more serious malady.

The truth is, Mr. President, that our foreign policy is inadequate, outmoded, and misdirected. It is based in part on a false conception of our real, long-term national interests and in part on an erroneous appraisal of the state of the world in which we live. Worse, it reflects a dangerous apathy and a quite incomprehensible unwillingness to look facts in the face.

We should put off no longer a complete reconsideration and reorientation of our foreign policy. We have already waited far too long.

Time and again we have put things off. Time and again we have drifted until circumstances reached an intolerable state, and then we have rushed to the brink. This time we have even put one foot over the brink. There we dangle, waiting and wondering what will come next. We are now looking squarely into the abyss of war, a war which we do not seek and which can only have the most catastrophic consequences for all humanity.

But the issue of peace or war is only one of our problems. Equally troublesome—and a good deal more complicated

—are the questions of what our long-term position in the world is going to be and of what specific kind of world we think would best serve our long-term interests. It is no answer to say we want to live at peace in a free, peaceful, and secure world. That is a hope which we all share, but it is only a hope: it is not a policy.

My fear, Mr. President, is that, if we continue as we have been and are, we will lose so much ground diplomatically, politically, and economically that the question of a shooting war will really become irrelevant.

Before our remaining toeholds go, it is time that we stop to look at where we are. Even more important, it is time to ask ourselves how we have gotten into this predicament. Only the blindest of optimism would interpret our international position as a secure one. The fact is that we are in trouble, very deep trouble, regardless of what happens next in the Middle East. The exposed position we now occupy in that area is only one reflection of that trouble.

A year ago we had another reflection of it, when the Soviet Union launched the first of the sputniks. That event told us what many already knew, but what this Government chose to ignore. It told us that there had grown up elsewhere in the world a capacity for scientific, intellectual, and technical achievements, which if it had not already done so would soon surpass our own. This had happened in a country and under a system which was hostile to our own and to the freedom which we cherish. It upset the basic assumption upon which our defense had rested since World War II, the assumption of our ability to maintain a substantial scientific and technical supremacy in this country. The launching of the first sputnik shocked us, Mr. President, into a momentary confrontation with reality. Some of us recognized that for years this Nation had wallowed in a kind of fool's paradise in jolly and supercilious complacency while else-where others of more serious bent of mind had worked. There was a realization that we had seriously neglected educa-tion. There was a realization that others had labored while we had loafed. The reformation was momentary. The smug and apathetic tendencies of our leader-ship soon spread to the rest of the Nation. On the one hand, there was a disposition to live with the fact that our scientific leadership was either gone or going fast; on the other hand, there was the delusion that perhaps the sputnik was not very im-portant—a bauble, I believe somebody called it. After all, we still had the Stra-tegic Air Command and intercontinental missiles and perhaps even a shot at the moon on the way. So we went back to business as usual and pleasure as usual.

Then a few weeks ago, events oc-curred in Latin America to remind us of the precariousness of our position in the world. There, in an area with which we had once enjoyed a most cordial, friendly, and intimate association; in this area regarded as safe, above all others, a symbolic explosion occurred, no less startling in its impact on the Nation than the first sputnik. A few years back, a former Vice President had been greeted with almost hysterical approval in Latin America. The present Vice President was spat upon and stoned. This, too, was a measure of how far we had fallen. This, too, gave us cause to think. What had we done? After all, this outburst of resent-ment and fury was directed at something besides Mr. Nixon as a person. Once again, for a brief time, we turned our attention to the serious business of what had gone wrong. Once again, the soul-searching began and once again it did not last long. We found an easy reassurance in the smug belief that only a relative handful of Latin Americans participated in the riots and that they were either Com-munist or Communist sympathizers. Once again, the same apathetic inertia spread from the Government to the people. Once

again, Latin America receded from the front pages of the press to the last pages.

Now it has happened again. We awaken one morning and find strange hands in control of what we believed to be the most reliable of the Middle-Eastern nations, so reliable that we had en-couraged it to join in a friendly military pact. Its King, whom we had been given to understand was a good and progressive chap, is no more. We are face to face with new rulers of Iraq, who despite the hundreds of millions we have spent on intelligence groups, are unknown factors to us. We scarcely knew whether to take them to our bosom or send them to the same mental oblivion to which we have consigned the Chinese Communists, in the naive belief that if we failed to ac-knowledge their existence, they would somehow go away. Next morning, we find that our marines have landed in Lebanon. It has taken this shock, Mr. President, to bring our errant attention once again to the highly dangerous conditions extant in the world in which we live. How long will our fleeting awareness last this time, Mr. President, before it disappears? Perhaps it would be well to ask ourselves, Where will the shock come next? One thing is certain, if we go on as we are, more shocks await us in the not too distant fu-ture and in many parts of the world. If we go on as we are, soon—in the fashion of the cat on the hot tin roof—we shall be skipping from one crisis to another all over the globe, unable to get our footing anywhere. We shall not even have time for another spell of apathy before we are face to face with unspeakable disaster. At worst, it will be the disaster of war, which, presumably, everything we have done in the past 10 years has been designed to prevent. At best, we shall be up against the disaster of an isolation of this country from reasonable and es-sential intercourse with great areas of the world. We may well be, as we already are in China and in the Soviet sphere, per-sona non grata in vast areas of Asia and

Africa and Latin America, and even perhaps in Europe.

There is an irony in this, Mr. President. For decades, we sought to isolate ourselves from the rest of the world. We have abadoned that course, only to find that now, increasingly, the rest of the world seeks isolation from us.

It is time, Mr. President, to ask ourselves some very searching questions. Think about it for a moment. This country emerged from World War II at an unprecedented pinnacle of world power and influence. Most of the world was with us. We were looked upon from one end of the earth to the other as the great hope of mankind. Even our erstwhile enemies were ostensibly not unfriendly. In deed as well as in word, we stood for peace, progress, and the international leadership of freedom. This was the wave of the future, not communism, and no power of Soviet propaganda was able to shake that almost universal conviction. I need hardly remind the Senate that a decade later this conviction had disappeared in large areas of the world, and in many others it was gravely shaken. The first question which we must ask ourselves is, why have we slipped? Is it Soviet propaganda which has been responsible for the change? Does the fault lie in the diabolical genius of the Russians for spreading lies and having them believed, or does it lie in ourselves?

An aphorism I heard the other day has some pertinence in this connection. A man may fall many times, this saying goes, but he is not really a failure until he starts blaming others. I suggest this is true of nations, too, Mr. President, and it is painfully descriptive of the United States Government at this point in history. Everything that goes wrong is laid at the door of communism. I suggest, that some of the blame belongs closer to home.

We can bewail the fact that the Russians did their homework and launched the sputnik, but we had better look to our own failure to place greater emphasis on scientific progress and intellectual achievement. We can berate the Soviet Union for attempting to enlarge its relations with Latin America, or we can look to ourselves for losing the beneficial intimacy which we once enjoyed with that part of the world. We can denounce the Soviet Union for seeking a foothold in the Middle East, or we can examine our own failure to develop policies which win the acceptance of the peoples of that region. We can decry the Soviet Union's great influence in China, or we can look to ourselves for cutting off all our contacts with the Chinese people by emulating the habits of the ostrich. We can complain of Soviet efforts to undermine NATO, or we can ask ourselves why we have failed to give affirmative leadership to the free nations of the West. We can berate the Soviet Union for posing before the world as the defender of the ordinary man's vital interest in peace, or we can look to ourselves for our failure to give an intelligent leadership to mankind's hope for peace.

Mr. President, for years now we have taken the easy way. Let something go wrong—whether it be in China or Nigeria—and we have had a ready answer. The Soviet Union was behind it. What a perfect formula for the evasion of reality and I may add, what a futile formula. If there is a single factor which more than any other explains the predicament in which we now find ourselves, it is our readiness to use the spectre of Soviet communism as a cloak for the failure of our own leadership. The Soviet Union has indeed been our greatest menace— not so much because of what it has done but because of the excuses it has provided us for our own failures. I am told that even now leaders of the administration go to bed with tracts from the Marxist litany in order better to understand their adversaries. Now, Mr. President, I am not averse to these studious pursuits. I suggest, however, that they ought not to be followed to the point of obsession. They ought not to be used, like a hot pad, as a comforting device to provide surcease from the more chilly business of examining our policies with a view to removing the weaknesses and inadequacies which the Communists are only too happy to exploit.

There was a time, perhaps, when we could afford the use of the Communist crutch to excuse us from the disagreeable task of facing up to our own inadequacies. We had a margin of power and good will throughout the world which enabled us to put off the day of reckoning. We no longer have that margin. Now, we will either look at ourselves, our policies, and our practices abroad with the closest of scrutiny, or we will face the gravest of consequences. For those who would still take comfort in the belief that all our difficulties arise from what they apparently regard as the superhuman capabilities of the Russians, I can only say, what nonsense is this. Are we to admit that we are, as men, less capable, less astute, less able than the Russians? If that is the case, we had better will the world to them without further ado—and ourselves along with it. But, if we are their equals as men, and if the ideologies for which we bear witness are superior to theirs, then in heaven's name when are we going to stop taking refuge in this excuse that they are responsible for our difficulties? I cannot believe that the Russians are any more capable than any other people. I can accept the obvious fact that they have worked harder at world domination by communism than we have for the spread of freedom. I am impelled, further, to consider the likelihood that they have been aided by the inadequacies of our own policies and even more specifically by the conduct of these policies. And I may add that I believe their job has become easier and easier as the conduct of these policies has become worse and worse.

That is why I urge the Senate to put aside now this blinder, this comforting belief that the Soviet Union is the sole source of our troubles. I ask the Senate to put it aside long enough to examine what it is we ourselves are doing to destroy the position this Nation has occupied in the world since the end of the second great conflict. Perhaps if we do this, we shall have a better understanding of why even now the trap is fast closing on us, and why we find ourselves being slowly snared between the prospect of a catastrophic war and a forced isolation from the rest of the world.

A principal factor involved in this process is that in the fear of the deviltry of communism, we have cast ourselves indiscriminately in the role of the defender of the status quo throughout the world. Look at the image of this country through the eyes of the rest of the world. Here we are, a Nation that for decades prided itself on its revolutionary tradition, on its willingness to experiment, to abandon the outworn traditions of a bygone age and move on to new horizons. We Americans conceived of our civilization as a movement not as a condition, as a voyage not as a harbor, as one noted historian put it. But today, this dynamic Nation is shrinking in the eyes of the world from the spectre of revolution. Here is this Nation appearing before the world as an obstacle to change at the very time when the world is in a ferment of cataclysmic change.

I do not ascribe this particular weakness in our position to the present administration. I suspect the roots of this fearful clinging to the status quo go back at least to the time of the collapse of Nationalist China. There is a popular concept in this country, Mr. President, that the chief trouble with our policies with respect to China was that we failed to give sufficient military and other aid in sufficient time; in effect, that we did not become sufficiently involved with the Nationalist Government to sustain it. I am afraid that the opposite may be the case, that in an urge to maintain the status quo in China we gave too much and became too deeply involved with a government which had failed to meet the demands of its people for change. Those tragic events in China seem to have set a rigid pattern which has been followed almost unbrokenly ever since. Too often when peoples elsewhere have sought to assert their god-given rights against an intolerable status quo, we have appeared to be on the side of those who opposed the assertion of these rights. Too often, we have found ourselves alined against those who would strike at tyranny or corruption. We have found ourselves alined with landlords who have exploited tillers of the soil and with militarists who have kept the people in line.

Look through the sorry record of the past 10 years. What does it show? It shows aid extended indiscriminately to governments which serve the needs of their peoples and alike to those which do not. It shows aid eagerly and lavishly given to governments which profess their anticommunism even though their peoples with valid reason might have been disenchanted with those governments. At the same time it shows aid, reluctantly given, if at all, to governments which refuse to parrot anti-Communist lines but which, nevertheless, have deep roots in their own peoples.

Nor is that all, Mr. President. When it has been a question of spending on anti-Communist propaganda through the blatant information program, the tens of millions of dollars have poured out, willingly and without much critical judgment. But when it has been a question of exchanging students, of interchanging the best of cultural achievements between nations, there has been much rending of hair over economy and a parsimonious doling out of the shekels. For this particular policy, the Congress must bear a large part of the responsibility.

Ever since the end of the Marshall plan, when it has been a question of meeting the desperate needs of people elsewhere for economic and social progress, we have been pinchpenny in our approach. But when it has been a question of aid for the military establishments of other countries, the hand has gone deep and unhesitatingly into the pocket of the American people. We have on a grandiose scale provided peoples of the underdeveloped nations with the weapons of destructive warfare, and have been miserly in providing them weapons to wage war on their own poverty, economic ills, and internal weaknesses. Military aid has been on the most lavish scale. Look at what has now happened in Iraq. The Iraqi Army, which was the recipient of our arms, has thrown out the Government which we regarded as the most friendly and most reliable of the Arab States in its adherence to the West. It is not at all impossible that the weapon with which the unfortunate young king was assassinated was provided with the best intentions, but with the utmost shortsightedness, under the military aid program.

How many similar plots are being hatched in other armies which we are aiding, Mr. President? There are billions of dollars worth of arms and military supplies loose in the world as a result of this aid. Before this equipment rusts, before these supplies are exhausted, I am afraid that we are in for many other unpleasant shocks on the model of Iraq, from one end of the globe to the other. Nor is this sudden unexpected use of military aid in Iraq the first time that has happened. How much of the equipment furnished to the Nationalist Government of China was subsequently used by the Communists to kill Americans in Korea? Will we never learn, Mr. President? How many more Americans must be killed by our own foolish gifts of weapons to shaky governments before we learn?

Mr. President, I know that this administration is not solely responsible for the corner into which we are being inexorably driven in our own relations with other nations. While foreign policy in this country is basically a function of the executive branch of the Government, Congress also has a share of the responsibility.

While we are asking questions about how the United States got in the world predicament in which it now finds itself, it behooves us in Congress, Mr. President, to take a look at our own part in the process. It is putting it mildly to say that Congress has not always been wise in its foreign policy actions. This is particularly true in regard to appropriations. We have, I think, been too generous with regard to military assistance and too niggardly with regard to economic and cultural matters. This is a reflection, first, of the parochial attitude Congress frequently takes in regard to money matters; and second, of the lack of strong political leadership in the administration. I do not think much can be done about the first factor. It is a natural result of the fact that one branch of Congress must answer every 2 years to local constituencies far removed from foreign contacts. But the effect could largely be overcome by strong, astute, political leadership from the White House, which is in a position—if it has the will and the know-how—to create a more informed public opinion, to help its political friends, and to hurt its political enemies.

It is easy, Mr. President, to prescribe a strong, farsighted, and wise executive as the cure for our affliction. To fill that prescription is another matter. There is no corner drugstore to which this prescription can be taken. And I might add that if the prescription for our trouble involves any substantial change in the traditional constitutional Congressional system, the patient will not swallow it.

I do not know, Mr. President, where we are heading under the present leadership of this country which, when it is not weak and desultory, trends to be impetuous and arbitrary. I doubt that the leadership itself knows. I do know that unless there is a drastic, sweeping revision of our foreign policy and in the execution of that policy, we are heading for far greater troubles than those in which we now find ourselves. Frankly, I do not see anywhere on the horizon the will, the understanding, the initiative, or the imagination to bring about the revision which is so desperately needed in order to stop the drift to disaster. I do not see these characteristics; yet they are essential to a peaceful solution of the Middle East situation. They are essential to the maintenance of the close alliance among the western nations. They are essential to a restoration of the sound, neighborly relations which we once enjoyed with Latin America. They are essential for stability and the growth of friendly relations with the nations of Asia and Africa and to a solution of the complex problems of the Far East.

If we are going to solve these problems, Mr. President, we must stop thinking about them in terms of a stereotyped view of the world. We must abandon the clichés and reconsider all our assumptions. One of the key questions we must ask ourselves is, What do we want the world to look like 5, 10, 25 years from now? And, in answering that question, we must hardheadedly distinguish between what are really vital national interests and what would be nice if we could have it.

For example, what, really, is our policy in the Middle East? Can we live with Arab unity, or can we not? In this connection, we should determine to our own satisfaction the real relationship between pan-Arabism and communism. The assumption made by the administration that Nasser is merely a tool of the Kremlin should be tested as to its validity.

Would it not be wise for us to revive the proposal, which has been tentatively advanced on several occasions, to create a regional development authority under the direction of Arab leaders primarily and drawing at least some of its funds from regional sources, that is, production or transportation of oil?

Should we not give careful and thorough consideration to a policy of neutralization of the area, with guaranties from all interested parties? And, as a corollary of this, would it not be wise to embargo the shipment of arms into the area?

The administration might well review the validity of the concept of the Baghdad Pact and of the Eisenhower doctrine. If these proposals are as worthless as I believe them to be, it is high time they be reconsidered and abandoned. A fresh, new, uncommitted look should be taken at the mistaken policies we have been following, and which have led us into our present impasse.

Where are we going in the Far East? That great area is temporarily quiescent, but by no means peaceful. What is our policy? We cannot forever ignore 600 million people on the mainland of China, but what are we doing to make it possible to deal with them on the best terms possible?

If anybody in the administration is giving serious, imaginative, uninhibited thought on a full-time basis to these and many other similar questions which I could cite, I have so far been unable to discover it. Yet there are competent people in private life throughout the country who are thinking about these questions, and who, I hope, are beginning to formulate some answers.

I wish the administration would make more use of these people. In any event, I hope the Senate can take advantage of this special competence.

This is one reason, Mr. President, why I attach so much importance to the forthcoming foreign-policy study by the Committee on Foreign Relations. I refuse to believe that the American people have lost all knack for creative, original thinking.

I do not pretend that there are answers to all our problems. Some difficulties in human affairs are insoluble. If this proves to be the case in regard to our present situation, we had then better begin to search for ways and means of accommodating ourselves to that fact.

But, at least, Mr. President, let us try to develop a set of coherent realistic, well-thought-out objects and feasible policies to attain them.

COMMENT

Instead of fresh ideas and creative thinking to advance the cause of peace, our approach to world affairs has remained sterile and timid. It has remained tied to old methods, old thinking, and old slogans. We are trying to meet new conditions and challenges with old methods and means. It won't work. It never does.

Adlai E. Stevenson, Democratic nominee for the presidency, at a political rally in Cincinnati, Ohio, October 19, 1956. *Vital Speeches*, xxiii (November 1, 1956), 37.

It is time to quit selling America short. We are not a second-rate country, with second-rate military strength and a second-rate economy. . . . No aggressor in the world today can knock out the deterrent striking power of the United States and its allies. . . . We know this, our political critics should know it and . . . Khrushchev knows it.

Vice President Richard Nixon in an address to Chicago Republicans. Chicago (Ill.) *Sun-Times*, January 28, 1960.

99. *JUNE 14, 1960*

Senator John F. Kennedy
Appraises U.S. Foreign Policy

By the late 1940's, containment of Russian military power had become the cornerstone of American foreign policy. Such a policy implied the permanent commitment of American resources around the perimeter of the Soviet empire. But by 1960, several fundamental changes had taken place in world affairs which created for the United States different problems from those which existed immediately after the Second World War and which had persisted for approximately a decade. First of all, the United States and the Soviet Union possessed the capability of destroying each other in an all out nuclear war. The second transformation was the restoration of the economic and political health of most of the nations of western Europe. Third, the foreign policy of Russia had changed. Khrushchev's policies were aimed not so much at the conquest of territories by diplomatic pressure or military threats as at the subversion of the entire noncommunist world through the impact which the technology and economic accomplishments of the Soviet Union could make upon the world. Fourth, there had been the rise of the former colonial nations in Africa and Asia, which had rapidly become the great prize in the struggle between the East and the West.

While campaigning for the Democratic nomination for the presidency, Senator John F. Kennedy made the following address to the Senate, during which he pointed out that the crisis of

Vital Speeches, xxvi (July 15, 1960), 580–83.

American foreign policy lay in the inadequacy of the nation's responses to these great transformations. Less than five months later, the American people elected the Massachusetts senator as their next president. His speech is significant in that it was the clearest statement which he had made on foreign policy prior to his inauguration as president.

Mr. President, May 17, 1960, marked the end of an era—an era of illusion, the illusion that personal good will is a substitute for hard, carefully prepared bargaining on concrete issues, the illusion that good intentions and pious principles are a substitute for strong creative leadership.

For on May 17, 1960, the long-awaited, highly publicized summit conference collapsed. That collapse was the direct result of Soviet determination to destroy the talks. The insults and distortions of Mr. Khrushchev and the violence of his attacks shocked all Americans, and united the country in admiration for the dignity and self-control of President Eisenhower. Regardless of party, all of us deeply resented Russian abuse of this Nation and its President, and all of us shared a common disappointment at the failure of the conference. Nevertheless, it is imperative that we, as a nation, rise above our resentment and frustration to a critical reexamination of the events at Paris and their meaning for America.

I do not now intend to rehash the sorry story of the U-2 incident. The Senate Foreign Relations Committee has raised, in a constructive manner, the questions which must be raised, if we are to profit from the unfortunate experience. Nor do I wish to exaggerate the long-range importance of the U-2 incident or the Khrushchev attacks in Paris.

For the harsh facts of the matter are that the effort to eliminate world tensions and end the cold war through a summit meeting—necessary as such an effort was to demonstrate America's willingness to seek peaceful solutions—was doomed to failure long before the U-2 ever fell on Soviet soil. This effort was doomed to failure because we have failed for the past 8 years to build the positions of long-term strength essential to successful negotiation. It was doomed because we were unprepared with new policies or new programs for the settlement of outstanding substantive issues. It was doomed because the Soviet Union knew it had more to gain from the increasing deterioration of America's world position than from any concessions that might be made in Paris. Only Mr. Khrushchev's intransigence and violent temper saved the United States from an embarrassing exposure of our inability to make the summit meaningful.

Trunkloads of papers, I am told, were sent to Paris, but no new plans or positions were included. Our unwillingness to go to the summit had changed, but the steady decrease in our relative strength had not changed. Our allies and our own people had been misled into believing that there was some point to holding a summit conference, that we were prepared to say more than what changes in the status quo we would not accept, that by a miracle of personal charm and public relations the Russians could be cajoled into yielding some of their hardwon positions of strength, that we had some conception of alternative settlements that were both acceptable to us and possibly acceptable to the Soviets.

But the truth of the matter is that we were not prepared for any such negotia-tions and that there was no real success which the summit could have achieved, for words and discussions are not a substitute for strength—they are an instrument for the translation of strength into survival and peace.

We are, in short, in a way, fortunate that the violent manner in which the Soviets carried out their determination to wreck the summit made it clear to the world that the blame for the collapse of the conference rests on Mr. Krushchev. And we shall also be fortunate if the violence of the Paris encounters shocks American leaders and the American people into a renewed awareness of the perils we face, the sacrifices we must make and the urgency of our need for leadership.

This is the real issue of American foreign policy today, not the ill-considered timing of the U-2 or the inconsistent statements of our Government. The real issue—and the real lesson of Paris—is the lack of long-range preparation, the lack of policy planning, the lack of a coherent and purposeful national strategy backed by strength.

This is an issue worthy of a great debate, a debate by the American people through the media of their political parties—and that debate must not be stifled or degraded by empty appeals to national unity, false cries of appeasement, or deceptive slogans about "standing up to Khrushchev." For the issue is not who can best "stand up to Khrushchev" or who can best swap threats and insults. The real issue is who can stand up and summon America's vast resources to the defense of freedom against the most dangerous enemy it has ever faced.

If the 1960 campaign should degenerate into a contest of who can talk toughest to Khrushchev, or which party is the "party of war" or the "party of appeasement," or which candidate can tell the American voters what they want to hear, rather than what they need to hear, or who is soft on communism, or who can be hardest on foreign aid, then, in my opinion, it makes very little difference who the winners are in July and in November, the American people and the whole free world will be the losers.

For the next President of the United States, whoever he may be, will find he has considerably more to do than "stand up to Krushchev," balance the budget, and mouth popular slogans, if he is to restore our Nation's relative strength and leadership. For he will find himself with far-flung commitments without the strength to meet them or to back them up. He will inherit policies formed largely as reactions to Soviet action, their limits set by budgeteers without regard to world conditions or America's needs, their effectiveness often undercut by overlapping or competing agencies. He will inherit membership in alliances of uncertain stability and in international organizations of obsolete structure. He will inherit programs which have been frequently administered by shortsighted, unsympathetic men opposed to the very programs they are administering, awaiting their own return to private industry, and so lacking in compassion for our domestic needs as to be incapable of compassion for the desperate needs of the world's peoples. He will face a world of revolution and turmoil armed with policies which seek only to freeze the status quo and turn back the inevitable tides of change.

To be sure, we have, in 1960, most of the formal tools of foreign policy: We have a Defense Establishment, a foreign-aid program, a Western alliance, a Disarmament Committee, an information service, an intelligence operation, and a National Security Council. But, except for the brilliant legislative inquiry being conducted by the subcommittee of the Senator from Washington (Mr. Jackson) we have failed to appraise and reevaluate these tools in the light of our changing world position. We have failed to adapt these tools to the formulation of a long-range, coordinated strategy to meet the determined Soviet program for world domination—a program which skillfully blends the weapons of military might, political subversion, economic penetration, and ideological conquest. We are forced to rely upon piecemeal programs, obsolete policies, and meaningless slogans. We have no fresh ideas with which to break the stalemate in Germany, the stalemate over arms control, the stalemate in Berlin, and all the rest. We have as our grand strategy only the arms race and the cold war.

Our conferees have consistently gone to the international bargaining table ill staffed, ill prepared, and ill advised. Coordinated efforts—with all agencies and all allies—have faltered without strong direction from the top; and strong direction from the top has faltered because the President was not kept fully informed. The fact of the matter is that long-range problems in foreign affairs cannot be faced effectively by a party which is unwilling to face long-range problems at home. The destinies of a fast-changing world cannot be shaped effectively by a party traditionally opposed to change and progress. Coherent direction and purpose for the free world cannot be provided effectively by a party which does not provide them for our own people.

As a substitute for policy, President Eisenhower has tried smiling at the Russians; our State Department has tried frowning at them; and Mr. Nixon has tried both. None have succeeded. For we cannot conceal or overcome our lack of purpose and our failure of planning, by talking tough; nor can we compensate for our weaknesses by talking smoothly and by assuming that the righteousness of our principles will ensure their victory. For just as we know that might never makes right, we must also remember that right, unfortunately, never makes might.

Thus, neither our smiles nor our frowns have ever altered Mr. Krushchev's course, however, he may alter his expression. His real goals have remained unmoved, his interests unchanged, his determination unending. And so long as Mr. Khrushchev is convinced that the balance of world power is shifting his way, no amount of either smiles or toughness, neither Camp David talks nor kitchen debates, can compel him to enter fruitful negotiations.

So let us abandon the useless discussion of who can best "stand up to Krushchev," or whether a hard or soft line is preferable. Our task is to rebuild our strength and the strength of the free world—to prove to the Soviets that time and the course of history are not on their side, that the balance of world power is not shifting their way—and that, therefore, peaceful settlement is essential to mutual survival. Our task is to devise a national strategy—based not on the 11th-hour responses to Soviet created crisis—but a comprehensive set of carefully prepared, long-term policies to increase the strength of the non-Communist world. Until this task is accomplished, there is no point in returning to the summit—for no President of the United States must ever again be put in the position of traveling across the seas, armed only with vague, speculative hopes, in order to provide an occasion for public humiliation. And unless this task is accomplished as we move into the most critical period since the founding of our Nation, our national security and our survival itself will be in peril.

The hour is late, but the agenda is long.

First. We must make invulnerable a nuclear retaliatory power second to none—by making possible now a stop-gap air alert and base-dispersal program—and by stepping up our development and production of the ultimate missiles that can close the gap and will not be wiped out in a surprise attack—Polaris, Minuteman, and long-range air-to-ground missiles—meanwhile increasing our production of Atlas missiles, hardening our bases and improving our continental defense and warning systems. As a power which will never strike first, we require a retaliatory capacity based on hidden, moving, or invulnerable weapons in such force as to deter any aggressor from threatening an attack which he knows could not destroy enough of our force to prevent his own destruction. And we must also critically reexamine the far-flung oversea base structure on which much of our present retaliatory strength is based. We must contribute to the political and economic stability of the nations in which our vital bases are located—and develop alternative plans for positions which may become untenable.

Second. We must regain the ability to intervene effectively and swiftly in any limited war anywhere in the world, augmenting, modernizing, and providing increased mobility and versatility for the conventional forces and weapons of our Army and Marine Corps. So long as those forces lack the necessary airlift and sea-lift capacity and versatility of firepower, we cannot protect our commitments around the globe—resist non-nuclear aggressions or be certain of having enough time to decide on the use of our nuclear power.

Third. We must rebuild NATO into a viable and consolidated military force capable of deterring any kind of attack, unified in weaponry and responsibility. Aiming beyond a narrow military alliance united only by mutual fears, a return to mutual consultation and respect and a determined American effort to create a free world economy—can help overcome schismatic economic rivalries between the Continent and Britain, and the Common Market and the Outer Seven, as well as other Western differences in military and political policy. We need a common effort to protect vital international reserves, to adopt more consistent policies on both sides of the Atlantic, and—perhaps most important—to merge Western contributions to the underdeveloped areas.

Fourth. We must, in collaboration with Western Europe and Japan, greatly increase the flow of capital to the under-developed areas of Asia, Africa, the Middle East, and Latin America—frustrating the Communist hopes for chaos in those nations—enabling emerging nations to achieve economic as well as political independence and closing the dangerous gap that is now widening between our living standards and theirs. Above all, it is vital that we aid India to make a success of her new 5-year program—a success that will enable her to compete with Red China for economic leadership of all Asia. And we must undertake this effort in a spirit of generosity motivated by a desire to help our fellow citizens of the world, not as narrow bankers or self-seeking politicians. Our present foreign aid programs have neglected the great, visionary, partnership principles of the Marshall plan and Point 4—they have been subordinated to narrow, expedient, and temporary ends. Money has been poured into military assistance programs, and in many cases has been wasted, at the expense of vitally necessary economic development. The next President will have to devise an entirely revamped foreign aid program which will make the long-term commitments essential to successful planning—a program whose administration will not be hampered by waste and mismanagement or by unsympathetic and unqualified administrators. And part of this program must be a new and expanded effort to use our food surpluses to feed the world's hungry, storing these surpluses in "food banks" abroad.

Fifth. We must reconstruct our relations with the Latin American democracies, bringing them into full Western partnership; working through a strengthened Organization of American States, increasing the flow of technical assistance, development capital, private investment, exchange students, and agricultural surpluses, perhaps through the large-scale "operation Pan-America," which has been proposed by the President of Brazil, and pursuing practical agreements for stabilizing commodity prices, trade routes, and currency convertibility. A return to the good neighbor policy is not enough. Dollar diplomacy is not enough. A patronizing attitude, taking for granted their dedication to an anti-Communist crusade, is not enough. We will need a whole new set of attitudes and emphasis to make the nations of Latin America full partners in the rapid development of the Western Hemisphere.

Sixth. We must formulate, with both imagination and restraint, a new approach to the Middle East—not pressing our case so hard that the Arabs feel their neutrality and nationalism are threatened, but accepting those forces and seeking to help channel them along constructive lines, while at the same time trying to hasten the inevitable Arab acceptance of the permanence of Israel. We must give our support to programs to help people instead of regimes—to work in terms of their problems, as well as ours, and seek a permanent settlement among Arabs and Israelis based not on an armed truce but on mutual self-interest. Guns and anti-Communist pacts and propaganda and the traditional piecemeal approach to the Middle East are not enough—refugee resettlement and a regional resources development fund in full partnership with the Middle Eastern nations, are all parts of a long-range strategy which is both practical and in the best interests of all concerned.

Seventh. We must greatly increase our efforts to encourage the newly emerging nations of the vast continent of Africa.

And, as chairman of the Subcommittee on African Affairs of the Committee on Foreign Relations, let me remind the Senate that in a few years, the countries of Africa will control one-quarter of all the votes in the General Assembly of the United Nations. We must greatly increase our efforts to persuade them that they do not have to turn to Moscow for the guidance and friendship they so desperately need—to help them achieve the economic progress on which the welfare of their people and their ability to resist Communist subversion depends. We can no longer afford policies which refuse to accept the inevitable triumph of nationalism in Africa, the inevitable end of colonialism, and, fortunately, colonialism will end, not only in Africa, but, in the long run resistance to colonialism and the rise of nationalism will be the basic influence which will undermine the great Communist colonial empire. Nor can we afford policies which refuse to accept the unyielding determination of the new African states to lift their people from their age-old poverty and hunger and ignorance. The case history of the newly formed country of Guinea is a warning of what can happen to other countries of Africa if the United States remains indifferent to their pressing needs. We must answer the critical African needs for educated men to build the factories, run the schools, and staff the governments, by sending a growing stream of technical experts and educators to Africa—and by bringing far greater numbers of African students—future African leaders—to our own universities for training.

Agricultural experts must be sent into areas where the land is unproductive and where modern methods of agriculture are unknown in order to raise subsistence levels of farming and insure adequate supplies of food—and while this is being done we must use our own food surpluses to prevent hunger. We must establish a multination economic development loan fund—a full working partnership between the nations of the West and the nations of Africa—to provide the capital necessary to start African economic growth on its way.

And finally, if our policies toward Africa are to be effective, we must extend this aid in terms of America's desire to bring freedom and prosperity to Africa —not in terms of a narrow self-interest which seeks only to use African nations as pawns in the cold war.

Eighth. We must plan a long-range solution to the problems of Berlin. We must show no uncertainty over our determination to defend Berlin and meet our commitments—but we must realize that a solution to the problems of that beleaguered city is only possible in the long run, in the context of a solution of the problems of Germany and, indeed, the problems of all Europe. We must look forward to a free Berlin, in a united Germany in a Europe where tensions and armaments have been reduced—where perhaps the suggestions of General de Gaulle and Premier Adenauer requiring Soviet withdrawal behind the Urals can be accepted. Such a solution is far from a reality today—but both our good faith and our will to resist are dependent on our willingness to face the total problem of tension and conflict in this section of Europe. We must remain precise in our determination to meet our commitments until a change in Soviet policy permits a constructive solution. In the meantime, we should explore how the moral authority of the U.N. could be used to strengthen the security presently provided to the people of West Berlin.

Ninth. We must prepare and hold in readiness more flexible and realistic tools for use in Eastern Europe.

Tools such as those contained in the legislation sponsored by the Senator from Vermont and myself which the Senate passed last summer, and which would provide the President with discretion to give economic aid to disaffected Iron Curtain countries. The policy of liberation, proudly proclaimed 8 years ago, has proved to be a snare and a delusion. The tragic uprising in East Germany, in Poland, and in Hungary demonstrated clearly that we had neither the intention or the capacity to liberate Eastern Europe —and the false hopes raised by our promises were cruelly crushed. We must now begin to work slowly and carefully toward programs designed to encourage discontented Iron Curtain countries to permit the spread of what Thomas Jefferson called the disease of liberty—to nourish the seeds of liberty in any cracks appearing in the Iron Curtain by reducing economic and ideological dependence on Russia.

There are already opportunities in Poland for greater American initiative, aid, trade, tourism, information services, student and teacher exchanges, and the use of our capital and technology to advance the standard of living of the Polish people. Closer relationships can in time be offered in other so-called captive nations as well—showing a creative interest, not a closed mind, by the nation that represents their one great home for freedom.

Why should we permit the Soviet Union to work, night and day, to subvert the determination of the people of Africa to remain free, while at the same time our policies make it impossible for us to carry out any effective relationships with the countries of Eastern Europe—the most vulnerable part of the Soviet Empire? To give Soviet Russia a free hand in her vulnerable areas, while Russia is permitted to move unhampered in Africa, Asia, and South America, both is shortsighted and unwise.

Tenth. We must reassess a China policy which has failed dismally to move toward its principal objective of weakening Communist rule in the mainland— a policy which has failed to prevent a steady growth in Communist strength— and a policy which offers no real solution to the problems of a militant China. We need to formulate proposals for a reduction of tension in the Formosa Straits—at the same time making clear our determination to defend that island and to meet our treaty commitment. We must act through an Asian regional development organization to stabilize the nations of non-Communist Asia both politically and economically, so as to strengthen their resistance to Communist pressures. And, although we should not now recognize Red China or agree to its admission to the United Nations without a genuine change in her belligerent attitude toward her Asian neighbors and the world—and regrettably there is evidence that her belligerence is rising rather than receding—we must nevertheless work to improve at least our communications with mainland China. Perhaps a way could be found to bring the Chinese into the nuclear test ban talks at Geneva, for if we reached an agreement which did not bind Red China, then atomic tests could be continued on the mainland of China without inspection— and Red Chinese possession of atomic weapons could drastically alter the balance of power. If that contact proves fruitful, further cultural and economic contact could be tried. For only in this way can we inform ourselves of Communist activities, attempt to restore our historic friendship with the Chinese people, and—perhaps most important— make sure that we are not plunged into war by a Chinese miscalculation of our determination to defend all of free Asia. Today we have no affirmative policies— only an attitude of negative resistance in the face of a growing danger of hostile action resulting from mutual miscalculation. This cannot last in a world where the Red Chinese are increasingly important, increasingly menacing, and increasingly impossible to omit from effective international agreements on subjects such as arms control.

Eleventh. We must begin to develop new, workable programs for peace and the control of arms. We have been unwilling to plan for disarmament.

We have had less than 100 people working in the entire administration on the subject of disarmament, and we have always left the initiative in the hands of the Russians. An Arms Control Research Institute—or a Peace Institute, as suggested by the Senator from Minnesota (Mr. Humphrey) could undertake the technical studies needed before we can detect and monitor the vast and complex weapons systems of modern warfare. The entire world hopes that the collapse at the summit has not destroyed man's hope for a nuclear test ban. But if such a ban is achieved, it must only be the first step toward halting the spiraling arms race which burdens the entire world with a fantastic financial drain, excessive military establishments, and the chance of an accidental or irrational triggering of a worldwide holocaust. At the same time, we must move toward the eventual rule of international law by working to strengthen the United Nations and to increase its role in resolving international conflicts and planning for international scientific and economic development.

Twelfth, and finally, we must work to build the stronger America on which our ultimate ability to defend ourselves and the free world depends. We must increase our own scientific effort—not only by strengthening and revamping existing research programs in all fields, including the exploration of space—but by building an edcuational system which can produce the talent and skill on which our future strength and progress depends. We must work to create an America with an expanding economy, where growth is not dissipated in inflation, and consumer luxuries are not confused with national strength—an economy capable of supporting our massive needs and our new programs. And we must also work to create an America of equal opportunity and economic justice for all men of all ages, races, and creeds—an America which will be, as this country was intended by the Founding Fathers to be, a living example of freedom to the world.

This is a large agenda—a challenging agenda—and yet I do not pretend that it is, in any sense, complete. For if there is one certain thing in a world of change, it is that the coming years will bring new problems, undreamed-of challenges, unanticipated opportunities.

The next President will confront a task of unparalleled dimensions. But this task will not be his alone. For just as he must offer leadership and demand sacrifices, the American people must be willing to respond to these demands.

I realize also that the length of this agenda is in sharp contrast with the rosy reassurances of the administration. "America is today," the Vice President told his national committee Saturday, summarizing our position in the world, "the strongest country militarily, the strongest country economically, with the best educational system and the finest scientists in the world, over all." To feed that kind of diet to the American people during the coming months—to confine our national posture to one of talking louder and louder while carrying a smaller and smaller stick—is to trade the long-range needs of the Nation and the free world for the short-term appearance of security.

For all America—its President, and its people—the coming years will be a time of decision. We must decide whether we have reached our limit—whether our greatness is past—whether we can go no further—or whether, in the words of Thomas Wolfe, "the true discovery of America is before us—the true fulfillment of our mighty and immortal land is yet to come."

COMMENT

Senator John F. Kennedy is already working on his strategy for beating Vice President Nixon in November. . . . This was what he was doing in the Senate today. . . . He was addressing himself to the main issue of the campaign—the peace issue—and trying to knock down Mr. Nixon's principal argument, which is that the Vice President has more experience in the field of foreign policy and knows how to deal with Khrushchev.

> Columnist James Reston in the New York *Times*, June 15, 1960.

Senator Kennedy condemned or ignored all of the Eisenhower administration's programs, but in the next breath he indorsed the Administration's policies but said that they should be carried out with brighter, nicer people.

> Senator Thruston B. Morton, Republican national chairman, on June 14, 1960. New York *Herald Tribune*, June 15, 1960.

Senator Kennedy made it clear . . . that he intends to continue his criticism of the alleged weaknesses of the United States. . . . we have responsibility in avoiding . . . statements which . . . can encourage Krushchev . . . to believe that this nation, the leader of the free world, is weak of will, . . . is unsure of and hesitant to use its vast power, is poorly defended.

> Vice President Richard M. Nixon in *Life*, XLI (October 3, 1960), 25.

100. *SEPTEMBER 22, 1960*

President Eisenhower Addresses the United Nations General Assembly

In September, 1960, the world focused its attention on the United Nations as heads of state from many nations arrived for a meeting of the General Assembly. During this session, President Eisenhower made his last address to the General Assembly. His speech marked a significant shift from his Administration's previous cool attitude toward the United Nations and neutral countries. During Eisenhower's early years of office, Secretary of State Dulles frequently hectored neutral nations by questioning their morality and assuming that any country not for the United States was automatically against it. In contrast to Khrushchev's recent criticisms of the United Nations and neutral countries, Eisenhower now committed the United States to full support of

Department of State Bulletin, XLIII (October 10, 1960), 551–57.

the United Nations in all future crises. He made it evident that his Administration viewed the United Nations as an immensely valuable instrument of peace. Moreover, he made it unmistakably clear that the neutral members of the United Nations, though determined to avoid entangling alliances in the cold war, had an ambition comparable to the United States' foreign policy goals of a world of peaceable, independent nations, free to develop politically and economically within a system which attempts to preserve law and order.

The people of the United States join me in saluting those countries which, at this session of the General Assembly, are represented here for the first time. With the admission of new members, mainly from the giant continent of Africa, almost 100 nations will be joined in a common effort to construct permanent peace, with justice, in a sorely troubled world.

The drive of self-determination and of rising human aspirations is creating a new world of independent nations in Africa, even as it is producing a new world of both ferment and of promise in all developing areas. An awakening humanity in these regions demands as never before that we make a renewed attack on poverty, illiteracy, and disease.

Side by side with these startling changes, technology is also in revolution. It has brought forth terrifying weapons of destruction which, for the future of civilization, must be brought under control through a workable system of disarmament. And it has also opened up a new world of outer space—a celestial world filled with both bewildering problems and dazzling promise.

This is, indeed, a moment for honest appraisal and historic decision.

We can strive to master these problems for narrow national advantage, or we can begin at once to undertake a period of constructive action which will subordinate selfish interest to the general well-being of the international community. The choice is truly a momentous one.

Today I come before you because our human commonwealth is once again in a state of anxiety and turmoil. Urgent issues confront us.

The first proposition I place before you is that only through the United Nations Organization and its truly democratic processes can humanity make real and universal progress toward the goal of peace with justice. Therefore I believe that to support the United Nations organization and its properly constituted mechanisms and its selected officers is the road of greatest promise in peaceful progress. To attempt to hinder or stultify the United Nations or to deprecate its importance is to contribute to world unrest and, indeed, to incite the crises that from time to time so disturb all men. The United States stands squarely and unequivocally in support of the United Nations and those acting under its mandate in the interest of peace.

Nowhere is the challenge to the international community and to peace and orderly progress more evident than in Africa, rich in human and natural resources and bright with promise. Recent events there have brought into being what is, in effect, a vast continent of newly independent nations.

Outside interference with these newly emerging nations, all eager to undertake the tasks of modernization, has created a serious challenge to the authority of the United Nations.

That authority has grown steadily during the 15 years since the United Nations pledged, in the words of its own charter, "to bring about by peaceful means, and in conformity with the principles of justice and international law, adjustment or settlement of international disputes or situations which might lead to a breach of the peace." And during those years the United Nations successfully supported Iran's efforts to obtain the withdrawal of foreign military forces; played a significant role in preserving the independence of Greece; rallied world resistance to aggression against the Republic of Korea; helped to settle the Suez crisis; countered the threat to Lebanon's integrity; and, most recently, has taken on an even more important task.

In response to the call of the Republic of the Congo, the United Nations, under its outstanding Secretary-General, has recently mounted a large-scale effort to provide that new republic with help. That effort has been flagrantly attacked by a few nations which wish to prolong strife in the Congo for their own purposes. The criticism directed by these nations against the Secretary-General, who has honorably and effectively fulfilled the mandate which he received from the

United Nations, is nothing less than a direct attack upon the United Nations itself. In my opinion, he, the Secretary-General, has earned the support and gratitude of every peace-loving nation.

The people of the Congo are entitled to build up their country in peace and freedom. Intervention by other nations in their internal affairs would deny them that right and create a focus of conflict in the heart of Africa.

The issue thus posed in the Congo could well arise elsewhere in Africa. The resolution of this issue will determine whether the United Nations is able to protect not only the new nations of Africa but also other countries against outside pressures.

It is the smaller nations that have the greatest stake in the effective functioning of the United Nations. If the United Nations system is successfully subverted in Africa, the world will be on its way back to the traditional exercise of power politics, in which small countries will be used as pawns by aggressive major powers. Any nation, seduced by glittering promises into becoming a cat's paw for an imperialistic power, thereby undermines the United Nations and places in jeopardy the independence of itself and all others. It is imperative that the international community protect the newly emerging nations of Africa from outside pressures that threaten their independence and their sovereign rights.

To this end I propose a program which contains five major elements:

First. A pledge by all countries represented at this Assembly to respect the African peoples' right to choose their own way of life and to determine for themselves the course they choose to follow. And this pledge would involve three specific commitments:

To refrain from intervening in these new nations' internal affairs—by subversion, force, propaganda, or any other means;

To refrain from generating disputes between the states of this area or from encouraging them to wasteful and dangerous competition in armaments;

And to refrain from any action to intensify or exploit present unsettled conditions in the Congo—by sending arms or forces into that troubled area, or by inciting its leaders and peoples to violence against each other.

These actions my country—and many others—are now avoiding. I hope this Assembly will call upon all its members to do likewise and that each speaker who follows me to this platform will solemnly pledge his country to honor this call.

Second. The United Nations should be prepared to help the African countries maintain their security without wasteful and dangerous competition in armaments.

United Nations experts are being asked to train the Congo's security forces. If the Secretary-General should find it useful to undertake increased activity in order to meet requests of this nature elsewhere, my country would be glad to join other member states in making essential contributions to such United Nations activity.

More importantly, I hope that the African states will use existing or establish new regional machinery in order to avert an arms race in this area. In so doing they would help to spare their continent the ravages which the excesses of chauvinism have elsewhere inflicted in the past. If, through concerted effort, these nations can choke off competition in armaments, they can give the whole world a welcome lesson in international relations.

The speed and success of the United Nations in dispatching substantial forces to the Congo should give these states assurance that they can rely on the United Nations to organize an effective response if their security is threatened. This should reduce any pressures on them to raise larger forces than are required to maintain internal security. Thus they would help to free their resources for more constructive purposes.

Third. We should all support the United Nations response to emergency needs in the Republic of the Congo which the Secretary-General has shown such skill in organizing. I hope that states represented here will pledge substantial resources to this international program and agree that it should be the preferred means of meeting the Congo's emergency needs. The United States supports the establishment of a United Nations fund for the Congo. We are prepared to join other countries by contributing substantially for immediate emergency needs to the $100-million program that the Secretary-General is proposing.

Fourth. The United Nations should help newly developing African countries shape their long-term modernization programs. To this end:

The United Nations Special Fund and Expanded Technical Assistance Program should be increased so that in combination they can reach their annual $100-million goal in 1961. The Special Fund's function should be expanded so that it can assist countries in planning economic development.

The United Nations operational and executive personnel program for making available trained administrators to newly developing countries should be expanded and placed on a permanent basis. The United States is prepared to join other countries in contributing increased funds for this program, and for the Special Fund, and for the United Nations Technical Assistance Program.

The World Bank and International Monetary Fund should be encouraged increasingly to provide counsel to the developing countries of Africa through missions and resident advisers. We should also look forward to appropriate and timely financial assistance from these two multilateral financial sources as the emerging countries qualify for their aid.

Of course, many forms of aid will be needed: both public and private, and on a bilateral and multilateral basis. For this assistance to be most effective it must be related to the basic problems and changing needs of the African countries themselves.

Fifth. As the final element of this program I propose an all-out United Nations effort to help African countries launch such educational activities as they may wish to undertake.

It is not enough that loudspeakers in the public square exhort people to freedom. It is also essential that the people should be furnished with the mental tools to preserve and develop their freedom.

The Union States is ready to contribute to an expanded program of educational assistance to Africa by the family of United Nations organizations, carried out as the Secretary-General may deem appropriate and according to the ideas of the African nations themselves.

One of the first purposes of this assistance, after consultation and approval by the governments involved, might be to establish, staff, and maintain—until these governments or private agencies could take over—institutes for health education, for vocational training, for public administration and statistics, and perhaps other purposes. Each institute could be appropriately located and specifically dedicated to training the young men and women of that vast region, who are now called upon to assume the incredibly complex and important responsibilities inherent in an explosive emergence into nationhood.

If the African states should wish to send large numbers of their citizens for training abroad under this program, my country would be glad to set up a special commission to cooperate with the United Nations in arranging to accommodate many more of these students in our institutions of learning.

These then are the five ingredients of the program I propose for Africa:

Noninterference in the African countries' internal affairs;

Help in assuring their security without wasteful and dangerous competition in armaments;

Emergency aid to the Congo;

International assistance in shaping long-term African development programs;

United Nations aid for education.

Such a program could go far to assure the African countries the clear chance at the freedom, domestic tranquillity, and progress they deserve.

The changes which are occurring in Africa are also evident elsewhere. Indeed, Africa is but one part of the new world of change and progress which is emerging in all the developing areas.

We must carry forward and intensify our programs of assistance for the economic and social development in freedom of other areas, particularly in Latin America, Asia, and the Middle East.

Beyond this, we must never forget that there are hundreds of millions of people, particularly in the less developed parts of the world, suffering from hunger and malnutrition, even though a number of countries, my own included, are producing food in surplus. This paradox should not be allowed to continue.

The United States is already carrying out substantial programs to make its surpluses available to countries of greatest need. My country is also ready to join with other members of the United Nations in devising a workable scheme to provide food to member states through the United Nations system, relying on the advice and assistance of the Food and Agriculture Organization.

I hope this Assembly will seriously consider a specific program for carrying forward the promising food-for-peace program.

In the developing areas we must seek to promote peaceful change, as well as to assist economic and social progress. To do this—to assist peaceful change—the international community must be able to manifest its presence in emergencies through United Nations observers or forces.

I should like to see member countries take positive action on the suggestions in the Secretary-General's report looking to the creation of a qualified staff within the Secretariat to assist him in meeting future needs for United Nations forces.

To regularize the United Nations emergency force potential, I proposed in 1958 creation of standby arrangements for United Nations forces. Some progress has been made since that time. Much remains to be done.

The Secretary-General has now suggested that members should maintain a readiness to meet possible future requests from the United Nations for contributions to such forces. All countries represented here should respond to this need by earmarking national contingents which could take part in United Nations forces in case of need.

The time to do it is now—at this Assembly.

I assure countries which now receive assistance from the United States that we favor use of that assistance to help them maintain such contingents in the state of readiness suggested by the Secretary-General. To assist the Secretary-General's efforts, the United States is prepared to earmark also substantial air and sea transport facilities on a standby basis to help move contingents requested by the United Nations in any future emergency.

Over the long run, further progress toward increasing the United Nations' ability to respond to future needs is surely possible. The prospects for such progress, however, will remain just that—prospects —unless we move now to exploit the immediate possibilities for practical action suggested by the Secretary-General.

Another problem confronting us involves outer space.

The emergence of this new world poses a vital issue: Will outer space be preserved for peaceful use and developed for the benefit of all mankind? Or will it become another focus for the arms race—and thus an area of dangerous and sterile competition?

The choice is urgent. And it is ours to make.

The nations of the world have recently united in declaring the continent of Antarctica "off limits" to military preparations. We could extend this principle to an even more important sphere. National vested interests have not yet been developed in space or in celestial bodies. Barriers to agreement are now lower than they will ever be again.

The opportunity may be fleeting. Before many years have passed, the point of no return may have passed.

Let us remind ourselves that we had a chance in 1946 to insure that atomic energy be devoted exclusively to peaceful purposes. That chance was missed when the Soviet Union turned down the comprehensive plan submitted by the United States for placing atomic energy under international control.

We must not lose the chance we still have to control the future of outer space.

I propose that:

1. We agree that celestial bodies are not subject to national appropriation by any claims of sovereignty.

2. We agree that the nations of the world shall not engage in warlike activities on these bodies.

3. We agree, subject to appropriate verification, that no nation will put into orbit or station in outer space weapons of mass destruction. All launchings of space craft should be verified in advance by the United Nations.

4. We press forward with a program of international cooperation for constructive peaceful uses of outer space under the United Nations. Better weather forecasting, improved worldwide communications, and more effective exploration not only of outer space but of our own

earth—these are but a few of the benefits of such cooperation.

Agreement on these proposals would enable future generations to find peaceful and scientific progress, not another fearful dimension to the arms race, as they explore the universe.

But armaments must also be controlled here on earth if civilization is to be assured of survival. These efforts must extend both to conventional and nonconventional armaments.

My country has made specific proposals to this end during the past year. New United States proposals were put forward on June 27, with the hope that they could serve as the basis for negotiations to achieve general disarmament. The United States still supports these proposals.

The Communist nations' walkout at Geneva, when they learned that we were about to submit these proposals, brought negotiations to an abrupt halt. Their unexplained action does not, however, reduce the urgent need for arms control.

My country believes that negotiations can—and should—soon be resumed. Our aim is to reach agreement on all the various measures that will bring general and complete disarmament. Any honest appraisal, however, must recognize that this is an immense task. It will take time.

We should not have to wait until we have agreed on all the detailed measures to reach this goal before we begin to move toward disarmament. Specific and promising steps to this end were suggested in our June 27 proposals.

If negotiations can be resumed, it may be possible to deal particularly with two pressing dangers—that of war by miscalculation and that of mounting nuclear weapons stockpiles.

The advent of missiles, with ever shorter reaction times, makes measures to curtail the danger of war by miscalculation increasingly necessary. States must be able quickly to assure each other that they are not preparing aggressive moves

—particularly in international crises, when each side takes steps to improve its own defenses, which actions might be misinterpreted by the other. Such misinterpretation, in the absence of machinery to verify that neither was preparing to attack the other, could lead to a war which no one had intended or wanted.

Today the danger of war by miscalculation could be reduced in times of crisis, by the intervention, when requested by any nation seeking to prove its own peaceful intention, of an appropriate United Nations surveillance body. The question of methods can be left to the experts.

Thus the vital issue is not a matter of technical feasibility but the political willingness of individual countries to submit to inspection. The United States has taken the lead in this field.

Today I solemnly declare, on behalf of the United States, that we are prepared to submit to any international inspection provided only that it is effective and truly reciprocal. This step we will take willingly as an earnest of our determination to uphold the preamble of the United Nations Charter, which says its purpose is "to save succeeding generations from the scourge of war, which twice in our lifetime has brought untold sorrow to mankind. . . . "

The United States wants the Soviet Union and all the nations of the world to know enough about United States defense preparations to be assured that United States forces exist only for deterrence and defense—not for surprise attack. I hope the Soviet Union will similarly wish to assure the United States and other nations of the nonaggressive character of its security preparations.

There is a more basic point: In an age of rapidly developing technology, secrecy is not only an anachronism—it is downright dangerous. To seek to maintain a society in which a military move can be taken in complete secrecy, while

professing a desire to reduce the risk of war through arms control is a contradiction.

A second danger which ought to be dealt with in early negotiations is posed by the growth and prospective spread of nuclear weapons stockpiles.

To reverse this trend I propose that the nations producing nuclear weapons immediately convene experts to design a system for terminating, under verification procedures, all production of fissionable materials for weapons purposes. That termination would take effect as soon as the agreed inspection system has been installed and is operating effectively, while progress in other disarmament fields is also being sought.

The United States is prepared, in the event of a termination of production, to join the U.S.S.R. in transferring substantial quantities of fissionable materials to international stockpiles. The United States Disarmament Commission has already heard the proposal of Ambassador Lodge to set aside not pounds, as was proposed by the United States in 1954, but tons of fissionable materials for peaceful purposes. Additional transfers would be made as progress in other aspects of disarmament is accomplished.

If the U.S.S.R. will agree to a cessation of production of fissionable materials for weapons purposes, some production facilities could be closed without delay. The United States would be willing to match the U.S.S.R. in shutting down major plants producing fissionable materials, one by one, under international inspection and verification.

The proposed working group of experts could also consider how to verify the complete elimination of nuclear weapons, which is part of the third stage of our proposed disarmament program of June 27. There is as yet no known means of demonstrably accomplishing this; we would hope that the experts could develop such a system.

United States officials are willing to

meet immediately with representatives of other countries for a preliminary exchange of views on these proposals.

Some who have followed closely the many fruitless disarmament talks since the war tend to become cynical—to assume that the task is hopeless. This is not the position of the United States.

Men everywhere want to disarm. They want their wealth and labor to be spent not for war but for food, for clothing, for shelter, for medicines, for schools.

Time and again the American people have voiced this yearning—to join with men of good will everywhere in building a better world. We always stand ready to consider any feasible proposal to this end. And as I have said so many times, the United States is always ready to negotiate with any country which in integrity and sincerity shows itself ready to talk about any of these problems. We ask only this—that such a program not give military advantage to any nation and that it permit men to inspect the disarmament of other nations.

A disarmament program which was not inspected and guaranteed would increase, not reduce, the risk of war.

The international control of atomic energy and general and complete disarmament can no more be accomplished by rhetoric than can the economic development of newly independent countries. Both of these immense tasks facing mankind call for serious, painstaking, costly, laborious, and nonpropaganda approaches.

I have specifically avoided in this address mention of several immediate problems that are troubling the United States and other nations. My failure to do so does not mean in any sense that they are not of great concern both to the United States and to the entire international community.

For example, accumulating evidence of threatening encroachments to the freedom of the people of West Berlin continues to disturb us deeply.

Another instance, though, of especial concern to the United States, the shooting down of an American aircraft last July 1st over international waters, the apparent killing of four of its crew members, and the imprisonment of two others on trumped-up spy charges, is a shocking affront to the right of all nations to peaceful passage on and over the high seas. By its veto in the Security Council the Soviet Union prevented a full investigation of the facts of the case. But these facts still demand to be heard as a proper matter for the consideration of an impartial tribunal.

The particular problems I have just mentioned are not merely isolated instances of disagreements among a few nations. They are central to the issue of peace itself and illustrative of the continuous and interdependent nature of our respective national concerns. They must be confronted with the earnestness and seriousness which their settlement demands.

The basic fact today of all change in the domain of international affairs is the need to forge the bonds and build the structure of a true world community.

The United Nations is available to mankind to help it create just such a community. It has accomplished what no nation singly, or any limited group of nations, could have accomplished. It has become the forum of all peoples and the structure about which they can center their joint endeavors to create a better future for our world.

We must guard jealously against those who in alternating moods look upon the United Nations as an instrument for use or abuse. The United Nations was not conceived as an Olympian organ to amplify the propaganda tunes of individual nations.

The generating force behind a successful United Nations must be the noble idea that a true international community can build a peace with justice if only people will work together patiently in an atmosphere of open trust.

In urging progress toward a world community, I cite the American concept of the destiny of a progressive society. Here in this land, in what was once a wilderness, we have generated a society and a civilization drawn from many sources. Yet out of the mixture of many peoples and faiths we have developed unity in freedom—a unity designed to protect the rights of each individual while enhancing the freedom and well-being of all.

This concept of unity in freedom, drawn from the diversity of many racial strains and cultures, we would like to see made a reality for all mankind. This concept should apply within every nation as it does among nations. We believe that the right of every man to participate through his or her vote in self-government is as precious as the right of each nation here represented to vote its own convictions in this Assembly. I should like to see a universal plebiscite in which every individual in the world would be given the opportunity freely and secretly to answer this question: Do you want this right? Opposed to the idea of two hostile, embittered worlds in perpetual conflict, we envisage a single world community, as yet unrealized but advancing steadily toward fulfillment through our plans, our efforts, and our collective ideas.

Thus we see as our goal, not a super-state above nations, but a world community embracing them all, rooted in law and justice and enhancing the potentialities and common purposes of all peoples.

As we enter the decade of the 1960's, let us launch a renewed effort to strengthen this international community, to forge new bonds between its members in undertaking new ventures on behalf of all mankind.

As we take up this task, let us not delude ourselves that the absence of war alone is a sufficient basis for a peaceful world. I repeat, we must also build a world of justice under law, and we must overcome poverty, illiteracy, and disease.

We of the United States will join with you in making a mounting effort to build the structure of true peace—a peace in which all peoples may progress constantly to higher levels of human achievement. The means are at hand. We have but to use them with a wisdom and energy worthy of our cause.

I commend this great task to your hearts, to your minds, and to your willing hands. Let us go forward together, leaving none behind.

Thank you, and God bless you.

COMMENT

. . . the outlook is that the United States is gaining standing and influence and prestige because of the President's concrete and constructive proposals which seek a stronger, not a weaker, U.N., and which Mr. Eisenhower pledged to push financially, diplomatically, and morally.

Columnist Roscoe Drummond in the Chicago (Ill.) *Sun-Times*, September 24, 1960.

If implemented, the President's proposals would make the U.N. the most powerful body on earth. Its Secretary General would become a sort of global Chief Executive. . . . in offering to place American forces under U.N. inspection, the President was relegating to the scrapbook the concept of "total sovereignty" that still is demanded in impassioned speeches in the halls of Congress. His proposals foreshadowed some massive shifts in U.S. foreign policy.

Newsweek, LVI (October 3, 1960), 22.

The most striking feature of the President's speech was the thorough-going way in which he backed the U.N. . . . This was a response to the need and mood of the hour. The world has grown too large, in numbers of independent states, too small, in speed of communication, too complex, in almost every way, for great issues to be decided purely on the basis of competition between two major powers.

New York *Herald Tribune*, September 23, 1960.

---

101. JANUARY 20, 1961

President John F. Kennedy's Inaugural Address

The presidential election of 1960 was one of the closest and least predictable in American history. The amount of ticket-splitting in the election was notable. In state after state, heavy majorities for one presidential candidate or the other bore no necessary relationship to the outcome of contests further down the ticket. The election demonstrated that some of the most persistent geographic clichés of American politics were becoming obsolescent. Moreover, the drop in Vice President Nixon's strength from that shown by President Eisenhower in 1952 and 1956 demonstrated how greatly the Republicans had depended in the two previous elections on the personality of Eisenhower.

As Eisenhower left the presidency, he was widely praised for having upheld the dignity and honor of his office and for avoiding war and depression. He also received much credit for breaking the isolationist tradition of his party and for consolidating the New and Fair Deal policies which his party had fought against for a whole generation. Nevertheless, there were many forces to which the nation had not adjusted and about

New York *Times*, January 21, 1961.

which President Kennedy had to make urgent decisions. As Kennedy entered the White House, the United States was confronted with the prospect of seeing the NATO alliance move forward to a much more radical form of interdependence or move backward toward national protectionist or even isolationist policies. Meanwhile, the outflow of gold from the United States was causing serious economic problems. American industry, seeking cheaper labor markets, was investing heavily in the Common Market countries of western Europe, at a time when there were already more than 5,000,000 Americans unemployed. France was removing its Mediterranean fleet and some of its air force from the North Atlantic Treaty command. Britain had ended its compulsory military draft, and the Liberal party in Canada was threatening to take that country out of the joint air defenses of the North American continent. Because of these and many other pressing problems, as Kennedy began his administration there was a new atmosphere of conversation in Washington, more venturesome and experimental than anything heard in the Capitol for years.

We observe today not a victory of party but a celebration of freedom—symbolizing an end as well as a beginning—signifying renewal as well as change. For I have sworn before you and Almighty God the same solemn oath our forebears prescribed nearly a century and three-quarters ago.

The world is very different now. For man holds in his mortal hands the power to abolish all forms of human poverty and all forms of human life. And yet the same revolutionary beliefs for which our forebears fought are still at issue around the globe—the belief that the rights of man come not from the generosity of the state but from the hand of God.

We dare not forget today that we are the heirs of that first revolution. Let the word go forth from this time and place, to friend and foe alike, that the torch has been passed to a new generation of Americans—born in this century, tempered by war, disciplined by a hard and bitter peace, proud of our ancient heritage—and unwilling to witness or permit the slow undoing of those human rights to which this nation has always been committed, and to which we are committed today at home and around the world.

Let every nation know, whether it wishes us well or ill, that we shall pay any price, bear any burden, meet any hardship, support any friend, oppose any foe to assure the survival and the success of liberty.

This much we pledge—and more.

To those old allies whose cultural and spiritual origins we share, we pledge the loyalty of faithful friends. United, there is little we cannot do in a host of new cooperative ventures. Divided, there is little we can do—for we dare not meet a powerful challenge at odds and split asunder.

To those new states whom we welcome to the ranks of the free, we pledge our word that one form of colonial control shall not have passed away merely to be replaced by a far more iron tyranny. We shall not always expect to find them supporting our view. But we shall always hope to find them strongly supporting their own freedom—and to remember that, in the past, those who foolishly sought power by riding the back of the tiger ended up inside.

To those peoples in the huts and villages of half the globe struggling to break the bonds of mass misery, we pledge our best efforts to help them help themselves, for whatever period is required—not because the Communists may be doing it, not because we seek their votes, but because it is right. If a free society cannot help the many who are poor, it cannot save the few who are rich.

To our sister republics south of our border, we offer a special pledge—to convert our good words into good deeds—in a new alliance for progress—to assist free men and free governments in casting off the chains of poverty. But this peaceful revolution of hope cannot become the prey of hostile powers. Let all our neighbors know that we shall join with them to oppose aggression or subversion anywhere in the Americas. And let every other power know that this hemisphere intends to remain the master of its own house.

To that world assembly of sovereign states, the United Nations, our last best hope in an age where the instruments of war have far outpaced the instruments of peace, we renew our pledge of support—to prevent it from becoming merely a forum for invective—to strengthen its shield of the new and the weak—and to enlarge the area in which its writ may run.

Finally, to those nations who would make themselves our adversary, we offer not a pledge but a request: that both sides begin anew the quest for peace, before the dark powers of destruction unleashed by science engulf all humanity in planned or accidental self-destruction.

We dare not tempt them with weakness. For only when our arms are sufficient beyond doubt can we be certain beyond doubt that they will never be employed.

But neither can two great and powerful groups of nations take comfort from our present course—both sides overburdened by the cost of modern weapons, both rightly alarmed by the steady spread of the deadly atom, yet both racing to alter that uncertain balance of terror that stays the hand of mankind's final war.

So let us begin anew—remembering on both sides that civility is not a sign of weakness, and sincerity is always subject to proof. Let us never negotiate out of fear. But let us never fear to negotiate.

Let both sides explore what problems unite us instead of belaboring those problems which divide us.

Let both sides, for the first time, formulate serious and precise proposals for the inspection and control of arms—and bring the absolute power to destroy other nations under the absolute control of all nations.

Let both sides seek to invoke the wonders of science instead of its terrors. Together let us explore the stars, conquer the deserts, eradicate disease, tap the ocean depths and encourage the arts and commerce.

Let both sides unite to heed in all corners of the earth the command of Isaiah—to "undo the heavy burdens . . . [and] let the oppressed go free."

And if a beach-head of cooperation may push back the jungles of suspicion, let both sides join in creating a new endeavor, not a new balance of power, but a new world of law, where the strong are just and the weak secure and the peace preserved.

All this will not be finished in the first 100 days. Nor will it be finished in the first 1,000 days, nor in the life of this Administration, nor even perhaps in our lifetime on this planet. But let us begin.

In your hands, my fellow citizens, more than mine, will rest the final success or failure of our course. Since this country was founded, each generation of Americans has been summoned to give testimony to its national loyalty. The graves of young Americans who answered the call to service surround the globe.

Now the trumpet summons us again —not as a call to bear arms, though arms we need—not as a call to battle, though embattled we are—but a call to bear the burden of a long twilight struggle year in and year out, "rejoicing in hope, patient in tribulation"—a struggle against the common enemies of man: tyranny, poverty, disease and war itself.

Can we forge against these enemies a grand and global alliance, north and south, east and west, that can assure a more fruitful life for all mankind? Will you join in that historic effort?

In the long history of the world, only a few generations have been granted the role of defending freedom in its hour of maximum danger. I do not shrink from this responsibility—I welcome it. I do not believe that any of us would exchange places with any other people or any other generation. The energy, the faith, the devotion which we bring to this endeavor will light our country and all who serve it—and the glow from that fire can truly light the world.

And so, my fellow Americans: ask not what your country can do for you— ask what you can do for your country.

My fellow citizens of the world: ask not what America will do for you, but what together we can do for the freedom of man.

Finally, whether you are citizens of America or citizens of the world, ask of us here the same high standards of strength and sacrifice which we ask of you. With a good conscience our only sure reward, with history the final judge of our deeds, let us go forth to lead the land we love, asking His blessing and His help, but knowing that here on earth God's work must truly be our own.

COMMENT

President Kennedy . . . and all America are facing a new world, as different from that of Franklin Roosevelt's day as Roosevelt's of 1933 was from Wilson's before the First World War.

Editorial in the New York *Times*, January 21, 1961.

The new President issued a ringing challenge to the Communist world, without belligerence, but with determination and firmness. He expressed the purpose of his country and of the free world as ably as they have been expressed by any statesman.

Editorial in the Des Moines (Ia.) *Register*, January 21, 1961.

Not promising to end all wrong, but pledging to begin, Mr. Kennedy showed a commanding reach and grasp of essentials in this speech.

Editorial in the Atlanta (Ga.) *Constitution*, January 21, 1961.

102. *SEPTEMBER 17, 1961*

Senator Barry Goldwater on Winning the Cold War

During the presidential campaign of 1960, John F. Kennedy convinced much of the nation that he had new answers to the old problems of allied disunity and communist aggression abroad and of inflation, unemployment, and education at home. But after many months in the White House, Kennedy failed to mark a sharp break with the past. Instead, his policies were little more than modifications of the policies pursued by the Eisenhower Administration.

As it became evident that the words and style of Kennedy were not sufficient to solve political and economic problems, many Americans became disillusioned. With tension over Berlin, Laos, and Cuba mounting, the nation's conservatives in

New York Times Magazine, September 17, 1961. Reprinted with permission of *New York Times Magazine* and Senator Barry Goldwater.

particular became increasingly vocal concerning the failure of the United States to win the cold war. Because President Eisenhower had an uncanny ability to communicate with the American people, he had been able to divide the loyalties of the conservatives and frustrate their aims. But his retirement from public office swelled the numbers and vociferousness of those who were convinced that the nation's foreign policy was not geared to victory.

Riding the wave of this national discontent was the junior senator from Arizona, Barry Goldwater, who quickly became one of the most publicized political figures in the nation. As chairman of the Senate Republican Campaign Committee, Goldwater was in frequent contact with party leaders and was flooded with requests to address political gatherings.

Convinced that there could be no stalemate in the cold war, Goldwater, in the selection below, presented his plans for a successful foreign policy.

That we are losing the cold war is tragically apparent. Over the past decade and a half, international communism has gained millions of square miles, enslaved hundreds of millions of people and moved its threat to within 90 miles of our shores. Country after country has slipped behind the Iron Curtain during the course of the cold war. Communist inroads have been made in the Far East, in the Middle East, in Africa and in the Western Hemisphere.

On the military front, the nuclear superiority which we held at the end of World War II has slipped away from us. On the economic front, the Soviets are claiming big gains. On the psychological front, even the upstart Castro has been able to humiliate and demean us. On the diplomatic front, we have lost the initiative and subordinated our national interests to the concerns of other nations to whom timidity and appeasement have become ingrained aspects of policy.

On a tactical plane, the Communists have dwarfed our concept of the world struggle with a long-range strategy of total war, flexible enough to permit the interchangeable use of both military and political weapons. Theirs is an integrated plan, aimed at world conquest, which never changes and which makes the maximum use of territorial attrition and turns the passage of time into their stanchest ally.

While the Communists have been waging a new kind of total war with every means at their command—economic, psychological, military and subversive—we have been treating the whole thing as a part-time project, turning our attention from one brush-fire zone to another in direct response to Russian maneuvers. They call the tune while we dance. They select the areas of conflict, and we hurry to them with weakness rather than with our effective weapons.

It is certainly time for a change here. If we are to have victory in the cold war, our officials must grasp the true dimensions of the all-out struggle we are engaged in and map policy to conform to a total concept. The need is for a policy grounded in strength which is willing to run any risk in the cause of freedom. It is long past time for us to think in terms of containment and peaceful coexistence. This is playing the enemy's game. International communism cannot be contained with talk and treaty and this has been proved to our dismay over and over again in almost every part of the world.

Nor is there such a thing as peaceful coexistence. What we were fooled into thinking were brief periods of cold-war peace in the past—periods when the rantings of Krushchev were muted and Russia was throwing us a few diplomatic bones—were actually periods of Soviet aggression under a different guise.

We cannot allow ourselves to forget for a single minute that the never-changing aim of the Soviet Union is world domination and to that end the Communists are bending all the efforts of a regimented society. The Communists are not interested in containing freedom; they want to destroy it. The Communists do not want peaceful coexistence with the forces of freedom. Their aim is consistent, while ours is just the reverse. We meet the menace of international communism with all conceivable types of reaction—none of which bears any apparent relationship to the others.

At times, we resist vigorously, in full keeping with an attitude and a policy worthy of freedom's leader in the world. But we have not been consistent in acting from strength. Too often our policy and our attitude have disclosed an underlying element of softness. Too often we have wasted our determination, our energy and our substance by becoming bemused with peaceful coexistence and by exploring the paths of least resistance—and always to be brought up short and frightened with a new display of Communist duplicity and aggression.

The great need today is for leadership and direction to bring the great might of this nation to bear on the No. 1 objective—the *winning* of the cold war. A stalemate will not suffice for there is no such thing as maintaining the "status quo" in a conflict where the other side never rests. This nation desperately needs an official statement that our objective is victory and a priority list of what is required to meet that objective.

In other words, the first essential of a formula for victory is a declaration of intent on the part of the President which will end once and for all every bit of public doubt as to the purpose behind our various policies.

The second essential is an estimate of what the winning of the cold war is likely to cost in terms of taxpayers' dollars.

The third is for a list of what items in the estimate are most important and which are least important. Only thus can the American people know where they stand and what is required of them right now and what might be required of them in the future.

It is impossible to obtain any idea of our true position when the Administration is busy telling the people that a housing bill is important to the national defense, when it argues as heatedly for Federal aid to education and for a disarmament agency as it does for additional military funds. Our people want to know, and need to know, what the job is so that they can get ahead with it. At the present time all they know is that everything the New Frontier asks for is an "emergency" which in some nebulous fashion gets related to the international crisis.

Nor has it lessened public confusion to have the Chairman of the Senate Foreign Relations Committee, who reflects the Administration's viewpoint on many matters, claim that our objective in the cold war is a "process of civilizing international relations and of bringing them gradually under a world-wide regime of law and order and peaceful procedures for the redress of legitimate grievances."

I believe the American people are well aware of our nebulous chances of civilizing international relations with Castro or Mao Tse-tung. And I believe further that they have little sympathy with an objective which has no application to the realities of our peril and which will take centuries to bring about.

Now, what do we do after we have our official sights firmly fixed on victory in the cold war and have developed the determination, as a people, to pay the price of that victory? First and foremost our job becomes one of convincing the enemy that we would rather follow the world to Kingdom Come than consign it to hell under communism. Having made that clear, we must seize opportunities as they arise to protect freedom and demonstrate our strength. Many such opportunities have arisen in the past, some of which we have used to good advantage.

For example, we were told by the weak of heart and the peddlers of despair that unless we yielded Quemoy and Matsu to the Communists, a terrible war would be the result. The Eisenhower Administration said, in effect, very well, if the Communist world chooses to go to war to occupy these islands, then that's the way it will have to be. But the Communist world did not choose to go to war over Quemoy and Matsu and those islands are free today. And they will be free tomorrow and just as long as our determination to face the threat of force with a threat of force remains strong.

The same story was repeated in Lebanon. We sent Marines there against the advice, and despite the quaking, of those who fear a display of determination and strength. And Lebanon is free today. We acted from strength, too, when Berlin was threatened in 1948—and Berlin remains free. In Korea, our trouble was that Stalin didn't know that we meant business, and the result was a costly, unnecessary war which we would not have had to fight if the Russians had been assured in advance of our determination.

On the other hand, our resolve was not strong enough in Cuba to back our intent with the strength that was required and which we possessed. The result is that Cuba languishes in chains while a bearded Communist dictator thumbs his nose at the United States and the Communists rush to build a military and ideological bastion on our own doorstep.

And, in using our strength, we must disabuse ourselves of the feeling that every time we stand up to the Communists we are risking nuclear war. The Russians don't want a nuclear war any more than we do. But this doesn't stop them from moving boldly ahead with their design for world conquest. Unfortunately, there are many in positions of influence today who would paralyze our foreign policy by advancing the alternatives that either we accommodate the Soviet Union—or we fight a nuclear war. We find these alternatives being advanced every time the Russians seek to advance their position.

Now what is the essential weakness of this reasoning? It lies in accepting the enemy's terms—in believing that the only alternative to self-destruction is to yield. First, we find ourselves yielding on one issue—completely unimportant, it appears, in the context of such a horrible alternative as nuclear war. Then, we yield on a second and a third and a fourth, ad infinitum. So what is finally left to us except the terrible dilemma we are confronted with on that first day when the enemy said, "yield or die"?

If we could finally satisfy the enemy's appetite by giving him one city or one country or one territory, who among us, Democrat or Republican, liberal or conservative, would not be tempted to say: Let them, in the name of peace and freedom for the rest of us—let them, once and for all—have their way and be done with it. But this is not possible. We are dealing with an enemy whose appetite is insatiable, whose creed demands slavery for everyone, Americans included. The more we give in to that enemy, the more he wants; the more we give in to him, the more he is encouraged to demand.

No matter how you reason, there is no escaping the conclusion that we cannot assure the enemy that, under no circumstances, will we ever consider war. If we are not prepared, under any circumstances, ever to fight a nuclear war, we might just as well do as the pacifists and the collaborationists propose—dump our nuclear arsenal in the ocean.

But those who propose accommodation of Communist demands do not suggest any such exercise in national suicide. They want us to save our bombs. Only they want us to act as though we did not have them—because the mere thought of having them terrifies those who are dedicated to the principle of coexistence. Thus, we are supposed to eliminate our possession of nuclear weapons from our consciousness in discussing the formulation of American foreign policy.

But can we be sure that, if we completely eliminate the possible use of nuclear weapons, the Russians will follow suit? Can we risk our future and the future of mankind on exclusive emphasis on conventional rather than nuclear weapons? Can we make any assumptions that would diminish our strength—in any field—when dealing with the Communists? Merely to ask the questions is to answer them. We can assume *nothing* where the Communists are concerned. We can trust *nothing* that the Communists say. We can accept *nothing* that the Communists sign as a conclusive guarantee.

Those who argue against any use of strength, against any military risk, against any unilateral action, fail to understand that political victory in the cold war is the only way to avoid a strictly military solution of the East-West crisis.

It involves some risk, but our experience shows that that risk is greatly exaggerated. Every time we have stood up to the Russians, they have backed down. Our trouble is we haven't stood up to them enough.

In the final analysis the choice is not: yield, or fight a nuclear war. It is: win, or fight a nuclear war. For a nuclear war we shall certainly have to fight, from whatever beleaguered outpost we are reduced to occupying, if we continue to yield, piece by piece, all over the world. And finally, in desperation, we would see the horrible alternatives clearly in view—a violent act of nuclear aggression or surrender.

Our only hope today is to proclaim victory as our aim, accept the cost, rid ourselves of fear and then press boldly forward on all fronts—always *prepared* to fight and always making sure the Communists know we are prepared to fight. And in developing a *formula for victory*, there are a number of immediate steps we should take to reorient our policy for maximum United States effectiveness in the cold war. They include the following:

(1) We must stop believing that our primary objective must be to humor the public opinion of neutral or uncommitted nations rather than to defend our strategic interests, cooperate closely with our allies, and to advance our positions of strength. This we must do the more readily because much of this so-called opinion, which entrances our coexistence proponents, is fabricated by the Communists to our detriment; and since we have no proper method by which we can judge what public opinion really believes throughout the world.

(2) We must stop lying to ourselves and our friends about disarmament. We must stop advancing the cause of the Soviet Union by playing along with this great Communist-inspired deception. We must abandon the illusion that the Soviets, in their disarmament policies, are interested in furthering peace rather than baiting a trap for us. Their objective is to contrive our unilateral disarmament while they continue to arm themselves secretly as fast as they can.

It is not "dialectics" but schizophrenia when we increase our military budget by 15 per cent and the Soviets theirs by 33 per cent, at the same time that we proclaim disarmament to be our highest goal and a practical method of composing the present conflict. The American people can stand the truth, but they cannot prosper under an official policy of self-deception.

(3) We must stop negotiating about things that are non-negotiable such as the rights of our allies and compromises of our security. We must not deceive ourselves and our friends into believing that nuclear weapons and modern technology can be negotiated out of existence.

(4) We must stop helping communism, whether by trade, political concessions, technical disclosures, soft talk in the United Nations, recognition of Outer Mongolia, pilgrimages to Moscow or support for revolutionaries of the Castro type.

(5) We must avoid economic collapse by scaling down extravagant and useless domestic programs and halt the squandering of our money on unrealistic world-wide aid programs.

COMMENT

It seems to me that it is these [right-wing] extremists who are advocating a "soft" approach. Their oversimplifications and their baseless generalizations reflect the "softness" of those who cannot bear to face the burden of a continuing struggle against a powerful and resourceful enemy. A truly "tough" approach . . . is one which accepts the challenge of communism with the courage and determination to meet it with every instrumentality of foreign policy . . . and with willingness to see the struggle through as far into the future as may be necessary.

> Senator J. W. Fulbright of Arkansas speaking at the National War College on August 21, 1961. New York *Times,* October 1, 1961.

I think what would be most helpful to the nation today would be constructive suggestions for alternative courses of actions and not merely generalized statements which show very little light on very complicated and dangerous matters.

> President John F. Kennedy during his press conference, October 11, 1961. New York *Times,* October 12, 1961.

So terribly much has happened, so terribly much is happening, and all with such terrible speed, that it is difficult to foresee where we are headed. The men who fancy themselves in control of events are no longer really in control. . . . Everyone wants peace and no one knows either just what it is or precisely how to find it.

> Columnist C. L. Sulzberger in the New York *Times,* September 20, 1961.

Why isn't anything negotiable rather than thermonuclear war? Are we going to wipe out two-and-a-half billion years of slow biological improvement? . . . To go to war under any circumstances for anything at all in our world in our time is utter absurdity.

> Columnist John Crosby of the New York *Herald Tribune.* Quoted in *Time,* LXXVIII (September 29, 1961), 57.

Index

Minority groups, see Immigration

Mississippi, Black Code Laws of, 6–12; limitation of Negro suffrage in 1890 Constitution, 81–82

Mobile (Ala.) *Register*, editorial on Cleveland's tariff reform plan, 80

Molotov, V., 368, 369

Money, Bryan's Cross of Gold speech, 106–11

Monopolies, Sherman Anti-trust Act and, 82–84; Standard Oil Co. of N. J. case, 157–61; see also Trusts

Monroe Doctrine, Clark, J. Reuben, on, 135; Hughes, Charles Evans, on, 135; Kellogg Peace Pact and, 233; Roosevelt Corollary to the, 133–35

Morgenthau, Hans J., on United Nations, 390

Morton, Thruston B., on John F. Kennedy, 475–76

Muckrakers, 142; Lippmann, Walter, on, 147; Roosevelt, Theodore, on, 147–48

Munn v. Illinois, 58–60

Murphy, Frank, Korematsu v. United States, 356, 359–62

NATO, see North Atlantic Treaty Organization

Natchez (Miss.) *Democrat*, editorial on World War I, 198

National Association of Manufacturers, 286

National Industrial Recovery Act, 273

National Labor Relations Act, 406, 407, 409; constitutionality of the, 308–17

National Labor Relations Board, 405, 406–15

National Labor Relations Board v. Jones and Laughlin, 308–17

National Recovery Administration, 273–75, 283

National Recovery Review Board, report of the, 273–75

Nativism, 84, 229

Negroes, Black Code Laws, 6–12; Civil Rights Act (1866), 21–24; Civil Rights Act (1875), 53–55, 62–68; Civil Rights Cases, 62–68; Freedmen's Bureau Act, 25–29; Hampton's speech to, 56–57; limitation of suffrage in Miss. Constitution (1890), 81–82; Plessy v. Ferguson, 101–6; segregation, see Segregation

Neutrality, Acts (1930's), 282, 295, 317–23; Hearst, William R., on, 175; Lamont, Thomas W., on, 175; Wilson's appeal for, 173–75

New Deal, 253, 421; farm policies, 289–94; Hacker, Louis M., on, 265; social security and the, 286–88; Stolberg, Benjamin, on, 275; Thompson, Dorothy, on, 265–66; see also Roosevelt, Franklin D.

New Freedom, 161–70, 175, 329

New Nationalism, 150–57, 162

New Republic, editorial on immigration, 90; on Versailles Treaty and League of Nations, 221

New York *American*, editorial on the Stimson Doctrine, 252

New York *Daily News*, editorial about Stimson Doctrine, 253

New York *Herald Tribune*, on Eisenhower's UN speech, 485

New York *Press*, editorial on Cleveland's tariff reform plan, 80

New York *Sun*, editorial on Roosevelt's Quarantine the Aggressors speech, 327; on McKinley's War Message, 123

New York *Times*, editorial on Cleveland's tariff reform plan, 80; editorial on John F. Kennedy, 488; editorial on the Truman Doctrine, 405; on depression of 1929, 251; on Hull's foreign policy speech, 300; on Johnson's First Annual Message to Congress, 18; on Wendell Willkie, 332

New York *Tribune*, editorial on Freedmen's Bureau Act, 28–29

Newsweek, on Eisenhower's UN speech, 484

Nicolson, Harold, on Wilson at Paris Peace Conference, 214

Nixon, Richard M., 475–76; election of 1960 and, 485; on John F. Kennedy, 475–76; on U.S. foreign policy, 467

Norris, George W., on TVA, 270; opposition to U.S. entry into World War I, 198–200

Norris-La Guardia Act, 180, 406

North Atlantic Treaty Organization, 427–34

Nuclear weapons, 452, 468

Nye, Gerald P., 276, 308

Nye Committee's Report, 275–77

Oil, see Petroleum industry

Open Door policy, 127–29, 148, 252

Outer space accomplishments, 460

Outlook, on Wilson's First Inaugural Address, 173

Panola (Miss.) *Star*, on the Freedmen's Bureau, 29

Patriotism, McCarthy on, 458–60

Pearl Harbor attack, Roosevelt, F. D., on, 341–46

Pelley, William Dudley, 335

Perkins, Frances, on the Social Security Act, 286–88

Petroleum industry, Standard Oil Co. of N. J. v. U.S., 157–61; U.S. v. Midwest Oil Co., 183–91

Philadelphia (Pa.) *Record*, editorial about Stimson Doctrine, 253

Philippines, annexation of, 126–27

Phillips, David Graham, 142

Pierson, George Wilson, on Turner's analysis of the frontier, 101

Plunkitt, George Washington, on political graft, 148